Microsoft SQL Server
2012 Reporting Services

Stacia Misner

Published with the authorization of Microsoft Corporation by:
O'Reilly Media, Inc.
1005 Gravenstein Highway North
Sebastopol, California 95472

ISBN: 978-0-735-65820-2

1 2 3 4 5 6 7 8 9 LSI 8 7 6 5 4 3

Printed and bound in the United States of America.

Microsoft Press books are available through booksellers and distributors worldwide. If you need support related to this book, email Microsoft Press Book Support at *mspinput@microsoft.com*. Please tell us what you think of this book at *http://www.microsoft.com/learning/booksurvey*.

Microsoft and the trademarks listed at *http://www.microsoft.com/about/legal/en/us/IntellectualProperty/ Trademarks/EN-US.aspx* are trademarks of the Microsoft group of companies. All other marks are property of their respective owners.

The example companies, organizations, products, domain names, email addresses, logos, people, places, and events depicted herein are fictitious. No association with any real company, organization, product, domain name, email address, logo, person, place, or event is intended or should be inferred.

The book expresses the author's views and opinions. The information contained in this book is provided without any express, statutory, or implied warranties. Neither the authors, O'Reilly Media, Inc., Microsoft Corporation, nor its resellers, or distributors will be held liable for any damages caused or alleged to be caused either directly or indirectly by this book.

Acquisitions and Developmental Editor: Michael Bolinger

Production Editor: Holly Bauer

Technical Reviewer: Jeff Rush

Copyeditor: Richard Carey

Indexer: Ellen Troutman Zaig

Cover Design: Twist Creative • Seattle

Cover Composition: Karen Montgomery

Illustrator: Rebecca Demarest

To Gerry, best of friends forever.

—Stacia Misner

To my loving mother, who got me into this mess, in every sense of the phrase.

—Erika Bakse

Contents at a Glance

Introduction   *xxvii*

PART I   GETTING STARTED WITH REPORTING SERVICES

CHAPTER 1   What's new in Microsoft SQL Server 2012 Reporting Services   3
CHAPTER 2   Introducing the Reporting Services environment   25
CHAPTER 3   Understanding deployment scenarios   45
CHAPTER 4   Installing Reporting Services   55
CHAPTER 5   Exploring Reporting Services fundamentals   99

PART II   DEVELOPING REPORTS

CHAPTER 6   Planning your report design   139
CHAPTER 7   Working with report server projects   151
CHAPTER 8   Retrieving data for a report   173
CHAPTER 9   Designing the report layout   209
CHAPTER 10   Working with the tablix   249
CHAPTER 11   Developing expressions   273
CHAPTER 12   Using functions   307
CHAPTER 13   Adding interactivity   345
CHAPTER 14   Creating dynamic reports with parameters   367
CHAPTER 15   Managing the page layout   395
CHAPTER 16   Using Analysis Services as a data source   425

PART III   ADDING DATA VISUALIZATIONS

CHAPTER 17   Creating charts   453
CHAPTER 18   Working with chart elements   485
CHAPTER 19   Comparing values to goals with gauges   517
CHAPTER 20   Displaying performance with indicators   539
CHAPTER 21   Mapping data   555
CHAPTER 22   Working with map elements   579

PART IV   MANAGING THE REPORT SERVER

CHAPTER 23	Deploying reports to a server	607
CHAPTER 24	Securing report server content	643
CHAPTER 25	Performing administrative tasks	669

PART V   VIEWING REPORTS

CHAPTER 26	Accessing reports online	707
CHAPTER 27	Working with subscriptions	739
CHAPTER 28	Data alerting	759

PART VI   AD HOC REPORTING

CHAPTER 29	Reusing report parts	781
CHAPTER 30	Preparing to use Power View	797
CHAPTER 31	Using Power View	823

PART VII   USING REPORTING SERVICES AS A DEVELOPMENT PLATFORM

CHAPTER 32	Understanding Report Definition Language	859
CHAPTER 33	Programming report design components	877
CHAPTER 34	Programming report server management	905
CHAPTER 35	Programming report access	927

| | *Index* | *949* |

Contents

Introduction . . . .*xxvii*

PART I   GETTING STARTED WITH REPORTING SERVICES

**Chapter 1   What's new in Microsoft SQL Server 2012
             Reporting Services   3**

Introducing new features. 3

   Power View 3

   SharePoint integration 13

   Data alerts. 13

Reviewing other changes. 16

   SQL Server Data Tools 16

   New rendering extensions 16

Parting with Report Builder 1.0 17

Upgrading from prior versions. 18

   Preparation 18

   In-place upgrade 20

   Migration. 22

Chapter 2   Introducing the Reporting Services environment   25

A reporting platform 25

Reporting life cycle. 27

   Report development 28

   Report administration 28

   Report access 29

What do you think of this book? We want to hear from you!

Microsoft is interested in hearing your feedback so we can continually improve our
books and learning resources for you. To participate in a brief online survey, please visit:

microsoft.com/learning/booksurvey

Reporting Services architecture 30

    Native mode 30

    SharePoint integrated mode 38

Chapter 3 Understanding deployment scenarios 45

Single-server deployment 45

    Memory 46

    Disk space 46

    Disk activity 47

Distributed deployment 47

    Native-mode distribution 47

    SharePoint integrated-mode distribution 48

    Other components 50

Scale-out deployment 50

    Load balancing 51

    Failover cluster 51

    Distributed workload 52

Internet deployment 52

Chapter 4 Installing Reporting Services 55

Reviewing hardware and software requirements .55

    Selecting an operating system 55

    Choosing a Database Engine edition 58

    Reviewing SharePoint integrated-mode requirements 59

Planning accounts for reporting services 60

Performing the installation 61

    Installing prerequisites 61

    Installing SQL Server 2012 63

Configuring native-mode Reporting Services 72

Configuring partial integration with SharePoint .83

Configuring SharePoint for local mode reporting 84

Configuring SharePoint integrated mode 84

    Installing the Reporting Services Add-in for SharePoint 86

Creating a SharePoint web application 87

Creating a business intelligence center site. 89

Configuring SharePoint for Reporting Services integration. 91

Installing Report Builder 96

Installing sample databases 97

Chapter 5   Exploring Reporting Services fundamentals   99

Understanding design environments 99

Comparing design environments 99

Choosing a report designer 103

Developing a report with Report Builder. 105

Launching Report Builder. 105

Getting Started Wizard. 106

Using the dataset designer. 108

Getting familiar with the Report Builder interface. 111

Adding a data source 114

Adding a dataset 117

Adding a report title 117

Using data region wizards 118

Adding a data region manually. 122

Adding fields to a table. 123

Adding a total. 125

Grouping data 125

Inserting page breaks 127

Formatting a report. 127

Previewing a report. 129

Saving a report. 130

Managing a report. 130

Publishing a report 131

Adding a description. 131

Reviewing processing options. 132

Viewing a report. 134

Opening a report. 135

Using the HTML Viewer 136

PART II   DEVELOPING REPORTS

Chapter 6   Planning your report design   139

Knowing your audience 139

Reviewing report options 143

    Layout decisions 143

    Data considerations 145

    Parameters 145

    Mobile devices 146

    Printed reports 147

Developing standards 148

Chapter 7   Working with report server projects   151

Getting started with report server projects 151

    Creating a Reporting Services project 151

    Selecting a project type 154

    Getting familiar with the Visual Studio interface 155

    Removing a project from a solution 157

Working with report project files 157

    Reviewing report project file types 157

    Using the Report Wizard 158

    Adding a new item to a project 165

    Adding an existing item to a project 165

    Removing an item from a project 166

Using report project commands 166

    Project menu 166

    Build menu 167

Configuring report project properties 167

    Working with project configurations 168

    Setting project properties 169

Chapter 8   Retrieving data for a report   173

Understanding data source types 173

    Relational data sources 174

Multidimensional data sources 177

Miscellaneous data sources 178

Connecting to data with data sources 179

Comparing embedded and shared data sources. 179

Working with an embedded data source .181

Working with a shared data source 185

Setting data source credentials. 188

Retrieving data with datasets. 190

Comparing embedded and shared datasets. 190

Working with an embedded dataset 191

Working with a shared dataset 195

Exploring query designers 198

Understanding dataset properties 206

Chapter 9 Designing the report layout 209

Reviewing report items 209

General report items. 210

Tablix data regions. 211

Graphical data regions 212

Adding general report items to a report 213

Adding a text box. 214

Adding a line. 215

Adding a rectangle 216

Adding an image 217

Adding a subreport 221

Working with data regions 224

Adding a table 224

Binding data to a data region 225

Grouping data 226

Adding a total to a table. 230

Adding a matrix 231

Sorting groups 232

Adding a list 234

Using properties to control appearance and behavior 237

    Configuring the placement and size of a report item 237

    Changing the appearance of a report item 240

Chapter 10 Working with the tablix   249

Exploring the tablix 249

    What is a tablix? 249

    Tablix data regions 250

    Tablix cells 256

Transforming a tablix 259

    Table to matrix 259

    Matrix to table 260

    Detail list to grouped list 261

Configuring tablix properties 261

    No data rows 262

    Groups before row header 262

    Sort 262

Working with tablix groups 263

    Row groups 263

    Static columns 265

    Adjacent groups 267

    Group properties 268

Chapter 11 Developing expressions   273

Introducing expressions 273

    Simple expressions 273

    Complex expressions 277

Using the Expression dialog box 278

    Opening the Expression dialog box 278

    Exploring the Category tree 280

    Using IntelliSense 284

Using built-in collections 287

    DataSets collection 288

    DataSources collection 288

Fields collection 289

Globals collection. 289

Parameters collection 290

ReportItems collection. 291

User collection 291

Variables collection 292

Working with expressions 292

Adding calculations to a report. 292

Applying conditional formatting. 299

Working with variables 300

Using expressions for dynamic connections and datasets 304

Chapter 12 Using functions   **307**

Getting help for functions. 307

Function description and syntax 307

Function tooltip 308

Using text functions 308

The character functions 308

The search functions 309

The formatting functions 312

The array functions 313

The conversion functions 315

The string manipulation functions 316

The string evaluation functions. 317

The cleanup functions. 318

Using date and time functions 319

The date calculation functions. 319

The date manipulation functions 321

The date conversion functions. 322

The current date and time functions 323

Using math functions. 323

The trigonometry functions. 323

The sign functions 324

The exponent functions 325

The rounding functions. 325

Other math functions 326

Using inspection functions 326

Using program flow functions 327

The *Choose* function 327

The *Iif* function 327

The *Switch* function 327

Using aggregate functions 328

The aggregate functions. 328

The *Scope* argument 329

The *RunningValue* function 330

Using financial functions 332

Using conversion functions. 333

Using miscellaneous functions 334

The *InScope* function. 335

The lookup functions. 335

The row functions 339

Working with hierarchical data. 340

The *Level* function 341

The *Recursive* keyword 342

Chapter 13 Adding interactivity   345

Interacting with the report layout 345

Interactive sorting 345

Using fixed headers. 351

Configuring visibility 352

Adding tooltips. 355

Adding navigation features. 356

Defining a document map 356

Using embedded HTML tags. 359

Working with report actions 361

Chapter 14 Creating dynamic reports with parameters   367

    Working with report parameters 367

        Creating a report parameter 367

        Setting report parameter properties 368

        Deleting a report parameter 379

        Displaying parameter selections in a report 379

    Using filters 379

        Creating a filter. 380

        Using a report parameter as a filter 382

        Understanding filter operators 383

        Applying OR logic to multiple filters 386

    Using parameters with subreports and drillthrough 387

        Passing a parameter to a subreport 387

        Passing a parameter to a drillthrough report 388

    Working with query parameters 389

        Creating a query parameter. 389

        Linking report and query parameters 390

        Deleting a query parameter. 391

    Cascading parameters 392

        Creating a child report parameter dataset 392

        Linking a parent report parameter to a query parameter 392

        Changing parameter order. 393

Chapter 15 Managing the page layout   395

    Understanding rendering 395

        Reviewing rendering formats by pagination type 395

        Using the *RenderFormat* global variable .397

    Adjusting the report size 400

        Understanding the page structure properties 400

        Using device information to change page properties. 406

    Working with the page header and footer. 409

        Adding a page header or footer 409

        Configuring page header or footer properties. 409

Using expressions in a page header or footer 411

Removing a page header or footer. 414

Configuring page breaks. 414

Creating page breaks 415

Using the *KeepTogether* property 416

Adding page breaks by group. 417

Repeating headers. 418

Numbering pages 420

Naming pages. 421

Chapter 16 Using Analysis Services as a data source   425

Creating an Analysis Services dataset 425

Analysis Services data source. 426

MDX graphical query designer 426

Building a report. 435

Analysis Services dataset fields 435

Extended field properties. 436

Aggregate function 437

Aggregate values in detail rows 438

Show Aggregations button 440

Designing parameters 442

Auto-generated query and report parameters 442

Custom query parameter 447

PART III   ADDING DATA VISUALIZATIONS

Chapter 17 Creating charts   453

Adding a chart to a report 453

Selecting a chart type 453

Understanding chart types. 454

Using the chart data pane. 456

Values. 457

Category groups 461

Series groups. 464

Formatting chart elements 466

Working with data bars 476

    Adding a data bar 476

    Configuring data bar properties 478

Working with sparklines. 480

    Adding a sparkline 480

    Configuring sparkline properties 481

Chapter 18 Working with chart elements   **485**

Changing color palettes. 485

    Built-in color palettes 485

    Custom color palette. 486

Working with vertical axis properties 487

    Scale break 488

    Logarithmic scale 491

Working with horizontal axis properties. 493

    Axis type 493

    Intervals 495

Working with series properties. 500

    Empty points. 500

    Bubble charts 503

    Calculated series. 505

    Secondary axis 508

    Multiple chart types. 510

    Multiple chart areas. 510

Working with pie charts. 513

    Slice consolidation 514

    Secondary pie chart. 515

Chapter 19 Comparing values to goals with gauges   **517**

Adding a gauge to a report 517

    Understanding gauge types. 517

    Creating a gauge 518

Working with gauge elements 520

    Understanding gauge elements 521

    Pointer 522

    Scale 526

    Range 530

    Gauge. 531

    Gauge label. 534

    Gauge panel 535

Grouping gauges 536

    Multiple gauges in a gauge panel. 536

    Repeating gauges 537

Chapter 20   Displaying performance with indicators   539

Adding an indicator to a report 539

    Understanding indicator types 539

    Creating an indicator. 540

Configuring an indicator 540

    Assigning an indicator value 541

    Defining indicator properties. 541

    Grouping indicators. 548

Customizing indicators 550

    Using customized images. 550

    Adding labels 551

    Adjusting location and size 553

    Dynamic sizing 553

Chapter 21   Mapping data   555

Understanding spatial data 555

    Types of spatial data 555

    SQL Server spatial data types. 558

Using the Map Wizard 558

    Selecting a spatial data source 559

    Choosing spatial data and map view options. 562

    Choosing map visualization 566

        Adding an analytical data set. 571

        Setting theme and data visualization options 572

    Finalizing the map. 576

        Map preview 576

        Simple adjustments 577

Chapter 22   Working with map elements   579

    Configuring map elements 579

        Map. 582

        Viewport 582

        Map title. 589

        Legend 589

        Scales 590

    Working with map layers. 591

        Map Layers pane 591

        Map layer properties. 593

        Common spatial element properties 594

        Color rules 595

        Point maps. 599

        Line maps. 601

        Polygon maps. 602

        Tile layer maps 603

    Inserting custom points. 603

    Understanding order of precedence. 604

PART IV   MANAGING THE REPORT SERVER

Chapter 23   Deploying reports to a server   607

    Deploying content 607

        Deploying a report project. 608

        Saving a report from Report Builder 610

        Uploading a report 611

        Using the rs utility 614

        Deploying a report model 615

Managing content 616

    Using folders to organize content. 616

    Moving content 617

    Creating a linked report 619

    Copying a report 620

    Configuring report parameters 621

Configuring data source properties. 624

    Selecting a data source for a report. 625

    Sending credentials to a data source 627

Configuring report processing options. 630

    Executing a report on demand 630

    Caching reports 632

    Configuring report time-out 634

    Refreshing the cache 634

Working with snapshots 636

    Creating report snapshots 636

    Saving report snapshots in report history. .638

Chapter 24 Securing report server content   643

Configuring report server security policies 643

    Understanding authentication types 644

    Reviewing default authorization policies. 644

Assigning user permissions. 650

    Native-mode role assignments 650

    SharePoint permission-level assignments .652

Configuring item-level security 653

    Securing folders and document libraries. .653

    Approving data sources in SharePoint integrated mode 658

    Securing an item 659

    Assigning a system role. 660

    Securing a report model. 662

Implementing data security 664

    Using a query parameter and a role to secure data 664

Using a permissions table to secure data .665

Using a dataset filter to secure data. 667

Chapter 25 Performing administrative tasks   669

Configuring the report server. 669

Updating report server properties 670

Managing encrypted information. 678

Configuring authentication 681

Managing memory 683

Disabling report server features 684

Disabling an extension 685

Managing the report server 685

Canceling jobs 685

Suspending report execution. 686

Performing backup and recovery 687

Monitoring the report server 690

Checking the application database size. 691

Monitoring the Windows application event log. 691

Using the trace logs. 691

Adding the HTTP log. 693

SharePoint diagnostic logging. 694

Execution logging 696

Using the ExecutionLog3 view. 698

Using performance counters 699

PART V   VIEWING REPORTS

Chapter 26 Accessing reports online   707

Using Report Manager. 707

Searching for a report. 707

Using the HTML Viewer 709

Using the document map. 711

Printing a report. 712

Using the My Reports folder 712

Accessing reports in SharePoint. 714
    Searching for a report. 714
    Using the SharePoint Report Viewer 716
    Creating a dashboard 718

Exporting reports 725
    Using soft page-break renderers 725
    Using hard page-break renderers. 730
    Exporting a report for data exchange 733

Chapter 27   Working with subscriptions   739

Creating a shared schedule. 739
    Schedules list. 739
    New schedule 741

Creating standard subscriptions. 742
    New subscription 742
    Delivery providers 743
    Report parameter values 749
    Subscription processing options 750

Creating data-driven subscriptions 750
    Creating a subscription delivery table 751
    Configuring data-driven subscription settings. 751

Managing subscriptions. 757
    Using the My Subscriptions page 757
    Deleting a subscription 758

Chapter 28   Data alerting   759

Understanding the data alerting architecture. 759
    Data alert workflow. 759
    Alerting service. 760

Creating data alerts 761
    SharePoint Report Viewer. 761
    Data feeds 762
    Data alert rules. 763

　　　　Schedule settings 766

　　　　Email settings 767

　　Receiving data alerts 768

　　　　Successful alert 768

　　　　Alert failure 770

　　Managing alerts 770

　　　　Alert status 770

　　　　Edit command. 772

　　　　Delete command 772

　　　　Run command. 772

　　Configuring data alerting 772

　　　　RsReportServer.Config file settings. 773

　　　　SharePoint configuration database settings 774

　　Monitoring the alerting process. 775

　　　　Execution log 776

　　　　Alerting stored procedures 776

　　　　Performance counters. 777

PART VI　　AD HOC REPORTING

Chapter 29　Reusing report parts　　　　　　　　　　　　　781

　　Introducing report parts 781

　　　　Report part 782

　　　　Report part benefits 782

　　Deploying report parts 783

　　　　Deployment from SSDT. 783

　　　　Deployment from Report Builder 785

　　　　Redeployment of a report part 788

　　　　Report part management on the report server 789

　　Using report parts. 790

　　　　Report Part Gallery 790

　　　　Update notification 792

　　Choosing report parts vs. subreports 795

Chapter 30 Preparing to use Power View   **797**

Using tabular models with Power View 797

    Introducing tabular models 797

    Creating a BI Semantic Model connection 798

Enhancing tabular models for Power View 803

    Summarizing values. 803

    Formatting values 806

    Setting the default sort. 807

    Marking the date table 810

    Managing grouping behavior 811

    Adding images 816

    Improving the appearance of identifying information 818

    Simplifying the creation of a new table. 821

Chapter 31 Using Power View   **823**

Getting started with Power View. 823

    Verifying browser requirements 823

    Connecting to a data source 824

    Getting familiar with the design environment 825

Visualizing data 832

    Table. 833

    Matrix. 835

    Charts. 836

    Cards. 843

Filtering data 843

    Highlighted values. 844

    Slicer. 844

    Tiles. 845

    View filter. 848

Selecting a display mode. 852

Saving a Power View report 854

    File save options. 855

    PowerPoint export. 855

**PART VII   USING REPORTING SERVICES AS A
              DEVELOPMENT PLATFORM**

Chapter 32 Understanding Report Definition Language   859

    Introducing Report Definition Language 859

        RDL schema definition 859

        RDL usage 860

    Exploring key elements 860

        Report element. 861

        DataSources and *DataSource* elements 862

        DataSets and *DataSet* elements 864

        Tablix element. 865

    Working with RDL. 867

        Manual RDL edits. 867

        Programmatic RDL edits 868

        RDL generation. 868

Chapter 33 Programming report design components   877

    Embedding code in a report. 877

        Code property. 878

        Custom function call 880

    Using assemblies to share custom code 881

        Class library 881

        Custom assembly call 885

    Creating a custom data processing extension. 887

        Data processing extension overview 888

        Data processing extension development .889

        Data processing extension deployment. .900

Chapter 34 Programming report server management   905

    Scripting administrative tasks. 905

        Deploying reports 906

        Creating a linked report 911

Working with configuration settings. 914

    Using the WMI provider 914

    Using Windows PowerShell cmdlets. 917

Using the web service 918

    Web.config 918

    References. 918

    Initial variable declarations. 920

    Page load. 920

    Recipient list 920

    Schedule list 921

    Report list 921

    Subscription creation. 922

    Web application execution. 924

Chapter 35 Programming report access   **927**

Linking to reports with URL access 927

    Viewing a report. 927

    Using URL access parameters. 931

Using the *ReportViewer* control 938

    Reports Application project 939

    Report Wizard. 939

    ReportViewer control. 940

    ReportViewer properties. 942

    ReportViewer application 943

Accessing a report with the web service. 944

    References. 944

    Load method. 945

    Render method. 945

    Solution deployment. 947

Index   *949*

Introduction

Microsoft Reporting Services is the component of Microsoft SQL Server 2012 that provides an enterprise-ready and extensible presentation layer for the Microsoft business intelligence platform. In its fifth release, Reporting Services continues its support for the three stages of the reporting life cycle, adds a new option for self-service reporting, and provides tighter integration with Microsoft SharePoint 2010 technologies. This book provides in-depth explanations of these new features and also includes comprehensive coverage of all other features that have made Reporting Services a popular choice for implementing a reporting platform in organizations of all sizes since its initial release in 2004.

We have written previously about Reporting Services as part of the Step by Step series published by Microsoft Press. Although we have borrowed many of our explanations for performing tasks from our previous work, the format of the current book allows us to expand on these explanations, explore a variety of techniques, and describe aspects of Reporting Services that are not fully documented elsewhere. We want this book to be useful to anyone new to Reporting Services as well as to seasoned professionals who need a good reference for properties that are not used often but come in handy when the need arises.

> **Note** A few months after the manuscript for this book was completed, the release of Microsoft SQL Server 2012 Service Pack 1 (SP1) and Microsoft SharePoint 2013 introduced some new features that modify or replace some of the topics we cover in this book related to installation and to Power View. If you are running Reporting Services in native mode, these new features do not affect you. If you are running Reporting Services in SharePoint integrated mode with Microsoft SharePoint Server 2010, the installation of SP1 adds pie charts, maps, and a variety of other features about which you can learn more at *http://officepreview.microsoft.com/en-us/excel-help/whats-new-in-power-view-in-excel-2013-and-in-sharepoint-2013-HA102901475.aspx* to enhance the coverage in Chapter 30, "Preparing to use Power View," and Chapter 31, "Using Power View." If you prefer to use Microsoft SharePoint Server 2013 to run Reporting Services in integrated mode, replace the instructions we provide in Chapter 4, "Installing Reporting Services," with the instructions available at *http://msdn.microsoft.com/en-us/library/jj219068.aspx*.

Who should read this book

Because Reporting Services is a platform of technologies rather than a single application, a variety of people serving in different roles and having different skill sets all need to learn how to work with some aspect of Reporting Services. Whether you're a report developer, IT administrator, or business user, you can use this book to learn how to perform the tasks for which you are responsible. If you're completely new to Reporting Services, this book teaches you the fundamental concepts required to build, manage, and access reports. You need no prior experience with Reporting Services to use this book successfully. If you're already familiar with an earlier version of Reporting Services, this book highlights new features in SQL Server 2012 and provides information about many seemingly mysterious properties and functions that have long been part of Reporting Services.

Assumptions

Throughout most of the book, we assume you currently know nothing about Reporting Services. We make an exception in Chapter 1, "What's new in SQL Server 2012 Reporting Services," to provide you with a jump-start into the new features if you're already using an earlier version of the product. We also assume that you know something about relational databases, but we don't require you to know how to write a query. We have samples that you can use to explore the features of Reporting Services without writing queries. There are some chapters that application developers can use to extend the functionality of Reporting Services, and we expect that you are familiar with Visual Basic or Visual C# before you read those chapters.

Organization of this book

Even if your primary responsibility with Reporting Services requires you to focus on only one component, you benefit from an understanding of all the capabilities that Reporting Services supports. For this reason, if you have time, you should read through the book from beginning to end for the best experience.

Because this book can be used by readers with different needs, you can also choose to read through only the chapters that focus on your area of responsibility. Each part of the book contains chapters related to a different part of the reporting life cycle. However, unlike our previous Step by Step books, in which we used procedures to build up your skills progressively, we have written each chapter without interdependencies. By using this approach, we were able to fully explore options available for performing a task or configuring a feature without the constraints of developing a linear, task-based sequence of steps to follow.

In Part I, we introduce Reporting Services, starting with the new features in SQL Server 2012 in Chapter 1, and continuing with an explanation of its usage and architecture in Chapters 2 and 3. We also explain how to install Reporting Services in either native mode or SharePoint integrated mode in Chapter 4. We conclude this part of the book with Chapter 5, which provides an overview of Report Builder as a user-friendly report development tool and introduces the deployment and report access stages of the report life cycle.

Part II focuses on report development. We start first by providing some guidelines for preparing to develop reports in Chapter 6 and then explain how to work with report projects in SQL Server Data Tools in Chapter 7. Chapter 8 covers all the different ways that you can retrieve data for your reports. Finally, in Chapter 9, you learn how to create the report itself by using different report items. In Chapter 10, we describe the nuances of the tablix in detail so that you can better take advantage of its flexibility. Then in Chapters 11 and 12 we explore the many different ways that you can create expressions and work with functions to change the behavior and appearance of reports at runtime. Chapter 13 describes the interactive features you can add to reports, while Chapter 14 describes another type of interactivity possible through the use of parameters and filters. In Chapter 15, we discuss many of the options you have for controlling pagination in reports. Then we wrap up report development in Chapter 16, where we explain how to use Analysis Services as a data source for your reports.

In Part III, we continue our focus on report development but with an emphasis on data visualizations. Chapters 17 and 18 explain everything you need to know to successfully develop charts. Chapters 19 and 20 show you how to display key performance data as gauges and indicators. Then Chapters 21 and 22 detail spatial data visualization techniques with the map feature.

Part IV moves on to the management stage of the reporting life cycle. In Chapter 23, you learn the different ways to make reports available to users on the report server. After reports are deployed, you can secure access to reports by using the techniques described in Chapter 24. Chapter 25 addresses all the remaining administrative tasks, such as configuration of the report server, backup and recovery procedures, and report server monitoring.

Part V includes chapters describing the user-focused stage of the reporting life cycle, report access. In Chapter 26, you learn the basics of working with Report Manager or SharePoint to view reports online. You can also set up subscriptions to receive reports in other ways, as you learn in Chapter 27. You can also receive notifications about changes to report data, as described in Chapter 28.

For a more interactive reporting experience, Part VI covers ad hoc reporting. Chapter 29 explains a simple approach to ad hoc reporting through the use of report parts. Then Chapters 30 and 31 introduce the newest ad hoc reporting tool in Reporting Services, Power View.

If you need Reporting Services to provide additional functionality, you can customize it through simple scripts or complex applications. The chapters of Part VII describe the various options you have for each stage of the reporting life cycle. Chapter 32 begins with an explanation of Report Definition Language, and then Chapter 33 shows you how to use code in reports, either as custom functions or as custom assemblies, to expand the capabilities of Reporting Services, such as retrieving data from an unsupported source. Chapter 34 shows you examples of how to use scripts or applications to manage the report server, and Chapter 35 caps off the book with techniques for retrieving reports programmatically.

Conventions and features in this book

This book presents information using conventions designed to make the information readable and easy to follow:

- Boxed elements with labels such as "Note" provide additional information or alternative methods for completing a step successfully.

- Text that you type (apart from code blocks) appears in bold.

- A plus sign (+) between two key names means that you must press those keys at the same time. For example, "Press Alt+Tab" means that you hold down the Alt key while you press the Tab key.

- A vertical bar between two or more menu items (for example, File | Close) means that you should select the first menu or menu item, then the next, and so on.

System requirements

You will need the following hardware and software to install the code samples and sample database used in this book:

- Windows Vista SP2, Windows 7, Windows Server 2008 SP2 or greater, 32-bit or 64-bit editions.

- At least 6 GB of free space on disk.

- At least 1 GB of RAM.

- A 1.0GHz x86 or 1.4GHz x64 processor or better.

- At minimum, an instance of SQL Server 2012 Database Engine and Reporting Services plus client components. Optionally, you can also install SQL Server 2012 Analysis Services in multidimensional mode and another instance in tabular mode. Reporting Services can be a native-mode or SharePoint integrated-mode installation. Full instructions about how to install the required components are provided in Chapter 4, "Installing Reporting Services."

Code samples

The database used for examples in this book is based primarily on Microsoft's Adventure Works DW 2012 sample database and, in a few cases, on some sample databases we provide. We recommend that you download the database from the link below rather than use your own copy of Adventure Works to reproduce the examples in this book.

All sample projects and the sample databases can be downloaded from the following page:

http://aka.ms/SQL2012RS/files

Follow the instructions to download the SSRS2012Samples.zip file and the sample database.

Installing the code samples

Follow these steps to install the code samples on your computer so that you can follow the examples in this book:

1. Unzip the samples file onto your hard drive.

2. Each chapter has its own directory containing code samples. In many cases, this takes the form of a report server project that must be opened in SQL Server Data Tools. You can find installation instructions for SQL Server Data Tools in Chapter 4.

3. Each chapter relies on the Adventure Works DW 2012 database. In most cases, you use the relational database, but Chapter 16 requires the multidimensional database and Chapters 30 and 31 require the tabular database. You can find instructions for obtaining and installing these databases in Chapter 4.

4. The code samples in Chapter 21 and Chapter 22 require you to use the Spatial-Data database. You can restore it from the BAK file in the Chapter 21 directory. Similarly, the code samples in Chapter 32 and Chapter 35 require the Custom-Reports database, which you can restore from the BAK file in the Chapter 32 or Chapter 35 directory. Refer to *http://msdn.microsoft.com/en-us/library/ms177429.aspx* to learn how to restore a database backup.

Acknowledgments

We'd like to thank the following people for their help, advice, and the insights they have provided over the years that we have worked with Reporting Services: Robert Bruckner, Carolyn Chau, Thierry D'Hers, Dan English, Teo Lachev, Peter Myers, Grant Paisley, Lukasz Pawlowski, Carl Rabeler, Simon Sabin, and Paul Turley.

We'd also like to thank Aaron Nelson for his help with PowerShell and Jeff Rush for technical editing. In addition, there is a whole team of people to thank for helping this book transition from idea to print, including Ken Jones, Michael Bolinger, Holly Bauer, Richard Carey, and the production team at O'Reilly Media. Thanks, everyone!

Errata & book support

We've made every effort to ensure the accuracy of this book and its companion content. Any errors that have been reported since this book was published are listed on our Microsoft Press site at *oreilly.com*:

> *http://aka.ms/SQL2012RS/errata*

If you find an error that is not already listed, you can report it to us through the same page.

If you need additional support, email Microsoft Press Book Support at *mspinput@ microsoft.com*.

Please note that product support for Microsoft software is not offered through the addresses above.

We want to hear from you

At Microsoft Press, your satisfaction is our top priority and your feedback our most valuable asset. Please tell us what you think of this book at:

> *http://www.microsoft.com/learning/booksurvey*

The survey is short, and we read every one of your comments and ideas. Thanks in advance for your input!

Stay in touch

Let's keep the conversation going! We're on Twitter: *http://twitter.com/MicrosoftPress*.

PART I

Getting started with Reporting Services

The chapters in Part I provide you with a foundation for Microsoft SQL Server 2012 Reporting Services in preparation for learning about its features in detail throughout the remainder of this book. In Chapter 1, "What's new in Microsoft SQL Server 2012 Reporting Services," you learn how to use the new features in Reporting Services and how to upgrade reports if you already have an earlier version of Reporting Services in place. In Chapter 2, "Introducing the Reporting Services environment," you learn about the features and architecture of Reporting Services, which we expand upon in Chapter 3, "Understanding deployment scenarios," by describing the different deployment topologies so that you can decide which is best for you. In Chapter 4, "Installing Reporting Services," you learn how to plan for and complete an installation. Chapter 5, "Exploring Reporting Services fundamentals," provides an overview of report development with Report Builder and introduces the deployment process and report access with Report Manager.

CHAPTER 1

What's new in Microsoft SQL Server 2012 Reporting Services

Of all the business intelligence components in Microsoft SQL Server, Reporting Services has consistently expanded its feature base in each release since it first appeared as an update to SQL Server 2000. If you have used earlier versions of Reporting Services, you can use this chapter to familiarize yourself with these major new features and other miscellaneous changes. We also let you know about features that have been deprecated in this release and how to upgrade Reporting Services from prior versions.

Introducing new features

The most significant new feature in the latest version of Reporting Services is the introduction of Power View, an ad hoc reporting tool that combines data visualization and self-service reporting in a SharePoint integrated-mode deployment. Another change in this release is the new architecture of Reporting Services as a SharePoint service application, which improves the administration and scalability of your reporting environment in this mode. You can also take advantage of the new data alerts feature in SharePoint integrated mode when you want to receive an email notification when a report contains data that matches rules you have defined.

Power View

As an ad hoc tool, the target audience for Power View is a business user rather than a professional report developer. It's simpler to use than Report Builder or Report Designer in many ways and yet provides some more advanced data visualization capabilities. To use Power View, you must have access to a server running SharePoint Server 2010 Enterprise Edition and a supported data source. In this section, we provide an introduction to Power View to highlight its main features. You can learn much more about it in Chapter 31, "Using Power View."

Data sources

To get started, you select a data source and then launch Power View to explore its data. You can choose from one of the following data source types:

- **PowerPivot workbook**   Locate a PowerPivot workbook in the PowerPivot Gallery or in a SharePoint document library, and then click the Create Power View Report icon in the upper-right corner of the PowerPivot workbook tile.

- **Shared data source**   A Reporting Services Shared Data Source (RSDS) file can have its *Data Source Type* property set to Microsoft BI Semantic Model For Power View. For this type of data source, the connection string references a PowerPivot workbook (such as *http://SharePointServer/ PowerPivot Gallery/myWorkbook.xlsx*) or an Analysis Services tabular model (such as *Data Source=MyAnalysisServer; Initial Catalog=MyTabularModel*). To use this type of shared data source for a Power View report, point to the shared data source name in the document library, click the down arrow, and then click Create Power View Report.

- **Business Intelligence Semantic Model (BISM) connection file**   Like a shared data source, a BISM file can connect either to a PowerPivot workbook or to an Analysis Services tabular model. However, you can use a BISM file not only as a data source for Power View reports but also for Microsoft Excel workbooks. To create a new Power View report using a BISM file as a data source, point to the file name in a SharePoint document library, click the down arrow, and then click Create Power View Report.

Data visualization

Power View is unique because it allows you to interact directly with the data, starting with a table layout to select and group fields, switching to alternate data visualizations such as a column or line chart, combining multiple data visualizations on a page, as shown in Figure 1-1, and highlighting values or applying filters to one or data visualizations on the page. You can even create multiple pages, known as views, in the same report.

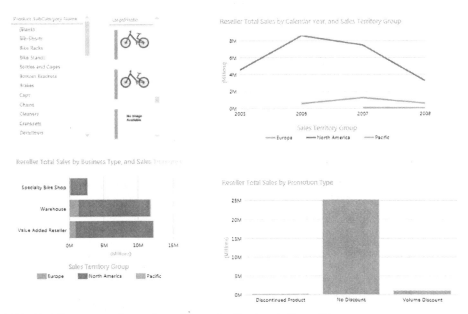

FIGURE 1-1 You can create a variety of data visualizations in Power View.

You start with a blank view workspace, as shown in Figure 1-2. As you develop the report, you add tables and data visualizations to the view workspace. The view size is a fixed height and width, just like the slide size in PowerPoint. If you need more space to display data, you can add more views to the report and then navigate between views by using the Views pane.

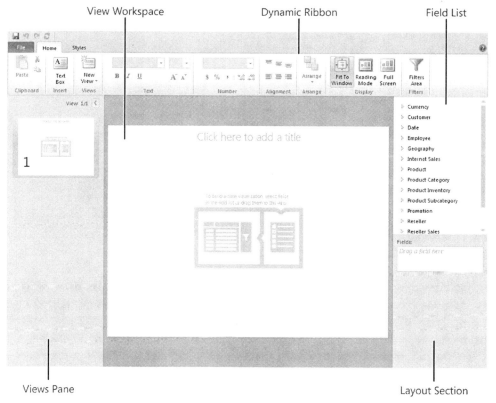

View Workspace   Dynamic Ribbon   Field List

Views Pane   Layout Section

FIGURE 1-2 You use the Power View design environment to explore the data source and develop data visualizations.

To begin your exploration of the data, you select fields from the field list on the right. Fields are organized by table name. You can double-click a table to create a tabular arrangement of default fields defined in the data source, or you can expand the table to select individual fields. As you add fields to the view workspace or select an item in the view workspace, the dynamic ribbon at the top of the screen changes to show the buttons and menus applicable to your current selection. For example, you can select the table of fields in the view and use the Column button on the Chart Tools Design tab of the ribbon to change the visualization type.

Power View displays only as much data as it can fit in the space allotted to the current visualization. If more data is available, scroll bars display to allow you to access the remaining data incrementally. By limiting the amount of data you can see at one time, Power View can optimize the query performance of very large data sources.

As you add fields to a data visualization, your selections display in the layout section in the bottom right of your screen. The structure of the layout section depends on the current visualization. For example, the layout section for a column, bar, or line chart, shown in Figure 1-3, allows you to define which fields to display as values, the horizontal axis category, and the series grouping. You can rearrange the sequence of fields in the layout section by using drag-and-drop, or you can click the arrow next to the field name to change the behavior of a field, such as changing which aggregation function to use or whether to display rows with no data.

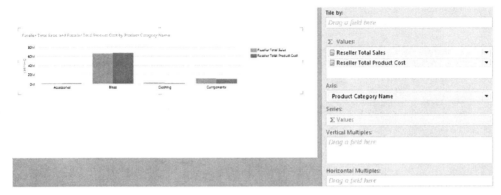

FIGURE 1-3 You use the layout section to arrange fields in a data visualization.

You can move or resize a data visualization at any time. You can move it by pointing to its border and then dragging it to another location in the same view when the cursor changes to a hand. Another option is to use the data visualization as the starting point for a new data visualization. When you see the cursor change to a hand, click the Copy button on the Home tab of the ribbon, and then click the Paste button to add the copy to the same view. You can also click the New View button on the ribbon if you want to add another page to your report. Either way, you can then move the copy to a new position. Also, when you point to the border and see the cursor change to a double-headed arrow, you can drag the border to make the data visualization larger or smaller.

Of course, Power View contains standard chart types, such as column, bar, and line charts, but it does not support other chart types that you can create in Report Builder or Report Designer. However, some unique data visualizations are available, such as the cards visualization shown in Figure 1-4, which is a scrollable list of grouped fields. You can use the cards visualization simply to display information about an entity, or you can use it as a type of filter for other data visualizations on the same view.

FIGURE 1-4 You can arrange a set of fields as a cards visualization.

Interactive scatter chart

Another feature of Power View is the ability to create an interactive scatter chart. This type of chart requires two numeric values. You place one value on the X axis and another value on the Y axis and then add a Details field that Power View uses to calculate corresponding X and Y coordinates. You can also add a third value to display points as bubbles for which the size increases as that value increases. A scatter chart can also include a field in the Color section to use for grouping. The interactive feature of the scatter chart applies when you add a field to the Play Axis, as shown in Figure 1-5.

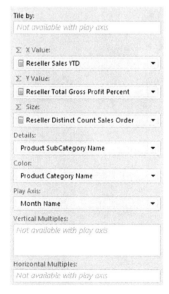

FIGURE 1-5 An interactive scatter chart includes X Value, Y Value, Details, and Play Axis fields, and optionally includes Size and Color fields.

The addition of a Play Axis field displays a play button below the scatter chart in the view. When you click the play button, the scatter chart cycles through each distinct value specified as the Play Axis field (which is typically a time period). You can also use the slider to select a specific value on the Play Axis. Whether you use the play button or the slider, you can see a watermark in the background of the chart for the current item in the Play Axis. You can filter the scatter chart to focus on a single Details value and see the path that it travels for each Play Axis value, as shown in Figure 1-6. Like other data visualizations, you can point to an area of the scatter chart to display a tooltip for more information.

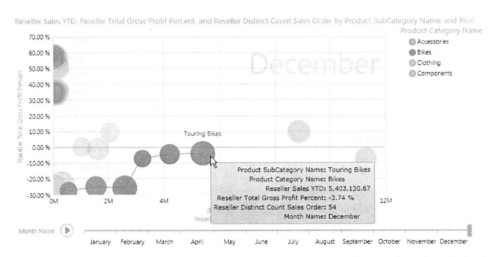

FIGURE 1-6 You can click a point or bubble in a scatter chart to see its path up to the selected value in the play axis.

Multiples

You can compare trends in data by creating multiple copies of the same chart. To do this, add a field to the Vertical Multiples or Horizontal Multiples area of the layout section, as shown in Figure 1-7. You can fine-tune the arrangement of tiles by using the Grid button on the Layout tab of the ribbon.

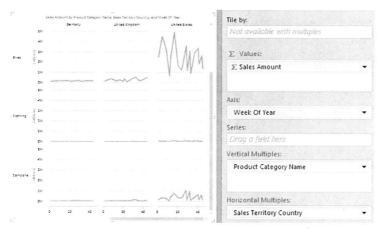

FIGURE 1-7 You can break out a chart by groupings called multiples

Highlighted values

When you have multiple visualizations in the same view, you can select a value, such as a column or a legend item, to see relationships across all visualizations. Power View highlights related values in all visualizations and dims the other values to help you see the proportional relationships. For example, in Figure 1-8, the selection of Europe in the bar chart's legend highlights the proportion of sales in Europe compared to all other sales in each chart. Furthermore, the table displays only sales data for Europe. To clear the highlighting, click elsewhere in the chart without clicking another value.

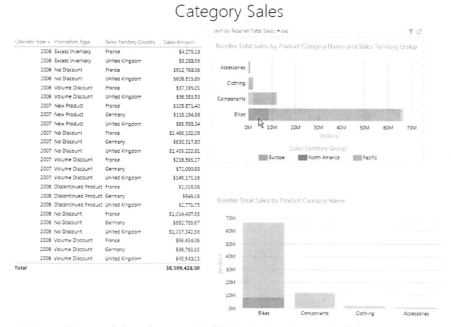

FIGURE 1-8 You can click a value to see highlighted values that are in all charts in a view and filter other visualizations, such as a table or matrix.

Slicer

A slicer is a single-column table that you add to the view for use as a filter. The table can contain labels or images. When you select one or more items in the slicer, Power View filters everything else in the same view, including other slicers, as shown in Figure 1-9. You can restore the unfiltered view by clicking the Clear Filter icon in the upper-right corner of the slicer.

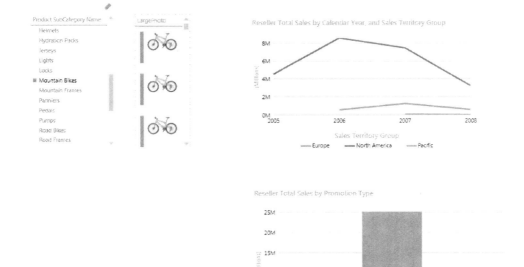

FIGURE 1-9 You can use a slicer to filter all content in a view.

Tiles

Rather than filter everything in a view, you can use a tile container to filter only visualizations inside the container, as shown in Figure 1-10. You can convert an existing table or matrix to a tile container by clicking the Tiles button on the Design tab of the ribbon. You then transform the table or matrix to another visualization type, if you like, and define the Tiles By field in the layout section to create a tile strip. To filter the tile container, you select one of the items in the tile strip. You can resize the tile container and add more visualizations to it if you want the filter to have broader scope without filtering the entire view.

FIGURE 1-10 You can use a tile container to filter only the visualization it contains.

View filter

To use yet another type of filtering, you can set up filter criteria for the current view. Click the Filters Area button on the Home tab of the ribbon to toggle the visibility of the Filters area, which is not visible initially in a new report. Then drag a field to the Filters area and configure the criteria for basic filters, as shown in Figure 1-11.

FIGURE 1-11 You can add basic filters to a view by selecting specific items, dates, or numeric value ranges.

The first icon in the toolbar to the right of the field name in the Filters area opens the advanced filter mode for that field. When a field has a string data type, you can create filter criteria based on partial words by using operators such as Contains, Starts With, and so on. A filter for a numeric field allows you to use a comparison operator like Greater Than Or Equal To, while a filter for a date data type allows you to use a calendar control in combination with a comparison operator like Is On Or After. You can also create compound filters consisting of two conditions by using a logical AND or logical OR operator, as shown in Figure 1-12.

FIGURE 1-12 You can create a compound filter by using the logical AND or logical OR operator.

Visualization filter

To use the basic or advanced filter modes for a single visualization, click the Filter icon in the top-right corner of the visualization. The Filters area then displays a tab for the selected visualization where you can add fields and define filter criteria, as shown in Figure 1-13.

FIGURE 1-13 You can create basic or advanced filters to apply only to a selected visualization.

Report sharing

When you want to save your report to review later or to share with others, you can save it by using the File menu, as long as you have the Add Items permission on the target document library. If you save it to a PowerPivot Gallery, you can use the Save Preview Images With Report option to include thumbnail images for display in the gallery views. Otherwise, save the file without images. Either way, your report saves as an RDLX file, which you can open only from SharePoint in Power View. This file type does not work with Report Builder or Report Designer.

You can also print the current view when you use Fit To Window or Reading mode only. You can switch to these viewing modes by using the applicable button on the Home tab of the ribbon. Then open the File menu and then click Print to print the current view in landscape orientation.

You can also share your report with other users by saving the report as an RDLX file to a Share-Point document library. If you prefer, you can export the report as a Microsoft PowerPoint file. In the latter case, other users can interact with the data within PowerPoint as long as they have an active connection to SharePoint and have the necessary permissions to view the tabular model. When a user displays a slide in Reading View or Slideshow modes, a Click To Interact link displays in the lower-right corner of the slide. Clicking this link loads the view from Power View and allows the user to change filter values in the Filters area, in slicers, in tile containers, and to highlight values.

SharePoint integration

The integration of Reporting Services into a SharePoint technology was first possible in SQL Server 2005. Since that introduction, incremental improvements to Reporting Services integration with SharePoint have been made in subsequent releases of SQL Server. However, the architecture received a complete overhaul in SQL Server 2012. Reporting Services is now a shared service application, which simplifies configuration. Chapter 4, "Installing Reporting Services," provides detailed instructions on installation and configuration.

The shared service application architecture means that you can now scale Reporting Services across web applications and SharePoint Server 2010 farms more easily. This architecture allows Reporting Services to take advantage of built-in network load balancing and use fewer resources. Consequently, Reporting Services delivers better performance overall as compared to previous versions. You can learn more about scalability in Chapter 3, "Understanding deployment scenarios."

Furthermore, deeper integration with SharePoint technology also simplifies administration. If you're using claims-based authentication in your SharePoint farm, you can extend it for use with Reporting Services. Another integration point is the backup and recovery process built into SharePoint backup that you can now use for Reporting Services content. We describe backup and recovery in Chapter 25, "Performing administrative tasks."

> **Note** For more information about claims-based authentication, see *http://msdn.microsoft .com/en-us/library/hh231678.aspx*.

Data alerts

Ever since the first release of Reporting Services, you have had the option to configure standard and data-driven subscriptions. A data-driven subscription is one in which you use a query to provide values for a subscription definition, such as recipient names or parameters to set. However, nothing in Reporting Services has been available to monitor the report content. That is, the data in the reports could not be evaluated against a set of predefined criteria. In SQL Server 2012, you can create a data alert to send an email when conditions in the predefined criteria are satisfied, but only if you are running Reporting Services in integrated mode on a SharePoint Server 2010 Enterprise Edition server. In this section, you learn the basic operations of data alerts; you can learn more by referring to Chapter 28, "Data alerting."

Data Alert Designer

If the report returns data when you open it, contains at least one data region, and all data sources use stored credentials or no credentials, you can create a new data alert. In fact, you can create one or more data alerts for any report that you can access, as long as the prerequisites are met. To do this, open a report in a SharePoint document library and select New Data Alert from the report's Action menu. You use the Data Alert Designer, shown in Figure 1-14, to define rules for each data region in the report, assign a schedule for checking the rules, configure email settings for recipients of the alerts, and provide a static subject and description.

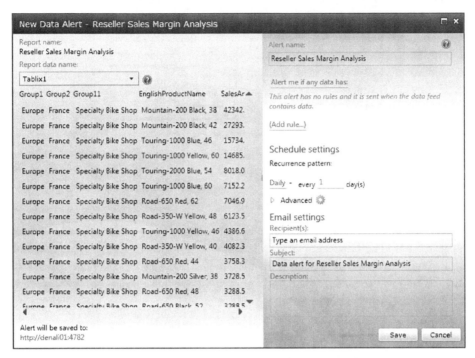

FIGURE 1-14 You can define criteria and a schedule for each data region in a report.

If the report runs successfully at the scheduled time and the report data satisfies the rules you specify, the alerting service sends an email message to each recipient. The email includes the description that you define when creating the alert and lists the raw data values that satisfied the alert criteria, similar to the one shown in Figure 1-15. If the report uses report parameters, the report parameter values also display in the rendered report. However, if the report execution fails, each recipient specified in the Data Alert Designer receives an email describing the error.

FIGURE 1-15 An email notification is sent to you with raw data values satisfying the alert rules and the description that you specify for the data alert.

Data Alert Manager

The Data Alert Manager keeps track of all your data alerts. To open the Data Alert Manager, open the document library containing your report, click the down arrow to the right of the report name, and then select Manage Data Alerts. The Data Alert Manager shows you the number of alerts sent by data alert, the last time it was run, the last time it was modified, and the status of its last execution. A portion of the Data Alert Manager page is shown in Figure 1-16.

FIGURE 1-16 You use the Manage Data Alerts page to keep track of alert execution and to change, delete, or execute a data alert.

You can right-click a data alert here to edit, delete, or run it on demand. A site administrator can view and delete your data alerts, but no one other than you can edit and run your data alerts on demand.

Reviewing other changes

Although the majority of changes to Reporting Services in SQL Server 2012 are new to the product, two others don't change your usage of Reporting Services as significantly but are important to know about. First, the design environment moves to a Microsoft Visual Studio 2010 Shell called SQL Server Data Tools (SSDT). Second, two new rendering extensions are available.

SQL Server Data Tools

Business Intelligence Development Studio (BIDS) has been the host of the design environment for Reporting Services since SQL Server 2005. The only place you see this name for the tool is in the program group for SQL Server on the Start menu. After you launch it, you never see the name again. That's because it's really just a shell for the version of Visual Studio for which it was made. The release cycles of SQL Server and Visual Studio have never been aligned, so a newer version of Visual Studio has always been available long before SQL Server business intelligence components begin using that version.

SQL Server 2012 is no exception. The difference this time is that the BIDS is gone from the Start menu, replaced by SSDT. Otherwise, the experience is the same. The same business intelligence project types, Report Server Project Wizard and Report Server Project, are available. You use the same user interface for developing reports as you did in BIDS, although the color scheme of Visual Studio is different. The advantage of having SSDT is the ability to add related projects to the solution containing your report project and use the Visual Studio 2010 integrated development environment for developing a class library or custom application.

New rendering extensions

This version of Reporting Services adds support for the most current versions of Microsoft Excel and Microsoft Word as output formats. Previously, you could export a report only as an XLS file in all versions of Reporting Services or as a .doc file in SQL Server 2008 and SQL Server 2008 R2. These file formats provide compatibility with Excel 2003 and Word 2003, respectively. Although users of Excel 2010 and Word 2010 can also open these file formats, there were some limitations that affected the size of the report that you could export to Excel and the size of the output file for both Excel and Word documents. These limitations are removed in SQL Server 2012.

Excel 2010 renderer

When you select Excel as the export option in SSDT, Report Manager, or the SharePoint Report Viewer, you now save the report as an XLSX file in Open Office XML format. That means you can open the file in either Excel 2007 or Excel 2010, as long as you have the client installed on your computer. It also means you can export a larger report to Excel, which supports 1,048,576 rows and 16,384 columns. In addition, the XLSX format supports 16 million colors in the 24-bit color spectrum. Another benefit of the new renderer is the smaller file size for the exported report, made possible by better compression.

Tip You can download the Microsoft Office Compatibility Pack for Word, Excel, and PowerPoint at *http://office.microsoft.com/en-us/products/microsoft-office-compatibility-pack-for-word-excel-and-powerpoint-HA010168676.aspx* if you prefer to produce XLS files for Excel 2003. If you need to support both formats, you can enable the Excel 2003 renderer in the RSReportServer.config and RSReportDesigner.config files by following the instructions at *http://msdn.microsoft.com/en-us/library/dd255234(SQL.110).aspx#AvailabilityExcel*.

Word 2010 renderer

Exporting a report as a Word document in prior versions of Reporting Services did not have the same limitations as exporting an Excel workbook. However, the benefit of having a Word 2010 renderer is in maintaining consistency across the Office products as well as producing a smaller file than the Word 2003 renderer. The new renderer compresses the report to generate a .docx file in Open Office XML format.

Tip If you want to open the exported document in Word 2003, you can install the Microsoft Office Compatibility Pack for Word, Excel, and PowerPoint, available for download at *http://office.microsoft.com/cn us/products/microsoft-office-compatibility-pack-for-word-excel-and-powerpoint-HA010168676.aspx*. Another option is to enable the Word 2003 renderer in the RSReportServer.config and RSReportDesigner.config files by following the instructions at *http://msdn.microsoft.com/en-us/library/dd283105(SQL.110).aspx#AvailabilityWord*.

Parting with Report Builder 1.0

Report Builder 1.0 was known simply as Report Builder when it was first released in SQL Server 2005 as a simple ad hoc reporting tool. Then SQL Server 2008 released Report Builder 2.0, and the first Report Builder was known thereafter as Report Builder 1.0. Although both versions of Report Builder are intended for self-service reporting, the user interface and report development process in each version are completely different. Report Builder 1.0 requires you to create a semantic model describing the tables and fields available for reporting, whereas Report Builder 2.0 allows you to create data sources and data sets much like you do in SSDT. In fact, Report Builder 2.0 is the predecessor to Report Builder in SQL Server 2012. Likewise, the current version of Report Builder (described in Chapter 5, "Exploring Reporting Services fundamentals") is nothing like the original Report Builder in SQL Server 2005.

In SQL Server 2008 and SQL Server 2008 R2, Report Builder 1.0 coexists with Report Builder 2.0 and Report Builder 3.0, respectively. In those versions, BIDS also includes a Report Model Project that you use to develop the semantic model required to use Report Builder 1.0. This project type is no longer available in SQL Server 2012, nor is Report Builder 1.0. Nonetheless, if you have an existing report model, you can continue to use it as a data source in the SQL Server 2012 Report Builder or SSDT, as described in Chapter 8, "Retrieving data for a report."

Upgrading from prior versions

You can transition your reports from a prior version of Reporting Services to SQL Server 2012 in two ways. One way is to perform an in-place upgrade to update your existing environment and keep everything in its current location. Another way is to migrate by creating a new environment and copying your reports to that new environment. You can use SQL Server Setup or a command-line utility to upgrade your existing report server database to the schema required for SQL Server 2012. When you run the setup wizard on a computer containing an earlier version of SQL Server, you can choose to upgrade or to install a new instance of SQL Server for a side-by-side installation. Regardless of which option you choose, the System Configuration Checker runs during setup to ensure that your computer meets the requirements for a successful installation.

> **Important** This section provides an overview of the process to upgrade or to migrate a standard Reporting Services environment. If you have customized your environment by adding custom applications, custom assemblies, or modifying configuration files, you should refer to *http://msdn.microsoft.com/en-us/library/ms143747.aspx* for more detailed information.

Preparation

Although SQL Server Setup proceeds with an upgrade only when your computer meets the requirements, you should also prepare for the upgrade by running the Upgrade Advisor to analyze your environment to uncover any potential problems in advance. Even if you are performing a migration, you should run the Upgrade Advisor to identify potential issues and to show custom settings of which you might not be aware if you did not configure the existing report server.

> **Tip** You can download the Upgrade Advisor from *http://www.microsoft.com/en-us/download/details.aspx?id=29065&ocid=aff-n-in-loc--pd* or install it from the Servers\redist\Upgrade Advisor folder of your SQL Server 2012 installation media.

It's also a good idea to back up important files and databases before you perform an upgrade or migration. That way, if the process fails before completing, you can restore everything and resume normal operations in the prior version until you can resolve the problem. You should back up the following items:

- **Symmetric key**   Use Reporting Services Configuration Manager or the Rskeymgmt command-line utility to back up the symmetric key. The procedure to do this in earlier versions is the same as we describe for SQL Server 2012 in Chapter 25. In SQL Server 2012, you use Report Configuration Manager only for a native-mode report server, but you can use it for both types of report servers in all previous versions.

- **Report server database**   Back up the ReportServer database (and optionally the Report-ServerTempDB database) by using the same process you use to back up other databases in SQL Server. It's possible that the report server database has a different name, so be sure to correctly identify the database. This database exists for both a native-mode and SharePoint integrated-mode report server.

- **Rsreportserver.config**   Save a copy of this file, which contains important settings for your report server. You can find it in the folder for the Reporting Services instance, which is in the Program Files\Microsoft SQL Server folder. The instance might be in a folder like MSSQL.3 or MSRS10.MSSQLServer. Within that folder, you can navigate through the folder hierarchy to locate the ReportServer folder, which contains this configuration file.

- **Rssvrpolicy.config**   Save a copy of this file, which contains the security policies for the report server. You can find it in the ReportServer folder.

- **Reportservicesservice.exe.config**   If you are running a native-mode report, this file is located in the bin folder that you find in the ReportServer folder.

- **Rswebapplication.config**   Save a copy of this file, which contains settings for Report Manager and is used only for a native-mode report server. It's found in the ReportManager folder, which is a sibling to the ReportServer folder.

- **Rsmgrpolicy.config**   If you are running a native-mode report server, save a copy of this file, which contains security policies for Report Manager. You can find it in the ReportManager folder.

- **Web.config**   Locate and save each Web.config file for your report server. Both types of report servers have a Web.config file in the ReportServer folder, and a native-mode report server has one in the ReportManager folder.

- **Machine.config**   If you have modified the Machine.config file for use with Reporting Services (which is not a common occurrence), you should save a copy of this file as well. You can locate this file in the applicable Windows folder for your operating system in the Microsoft .NET\Framework\v.1.1.4322\CONFIG folder for SQL Server 2005 and in the Microsoft.NET\Framework\v2.0.50727\CONFIG folder for SQL Server 2008 and SQL Server 2008 R2.

- **Virtual directories**   If you are upgrading from SQL Server 2005 and have added files to the virtual directories used by the report server, back up those files. Reporting Services no longer uses Internet Information Services (IIS).

Important If you have invalid or expired SSL certificates on the report server, you must remove them first. Otherwise, the upgrade will fail.

In-place upgrade

If your computer passes the System Configuration Checker in SQL Server 2012 Setup, you can proceed with an in-place upgrade of a native-mode or SharePoint integrated-mode report server. Depending on the version of Reporting Services that you are upgrading, you might need to manually complete some steps before or after the upgrade process.

Note If you prefer to use the Setup.exe command-line utility to perform the upgrade, refer to *http://msdn.microsoft.com/en-us/library/ms144259.aspx* for instructions.

Native-mode report server upgrade

You can perform an in-place upgrade for the following versions of Reporting Services running in native mode:

- SQL Server 2005 Reporting Services Service Pack 4

- SQL Server 2008 Reporting Services Service Pack 2

- SQL Server 2008 R2 Reporting Services Service Pack 1

SQL Server Setup creates folders for a new Reporting Services instance in the Program Files\ Microsoft SQL Server folder. The root folder for this collection of folders is named MSRS11.MSSQLServer for a default instance or MSRS11.<*instance*> for a named instance. SQL Server Setup also adds all the files necessary to support the report server, configuration tools, and utilities and upgrades the schema of the report server databases.

Setup does not upgrade existing installations of client tools like BIDS or SQL Server Management Studio. Instead, it adds new versions as a side-by-side installation. You can delete these tools following the upgrade if you have no further need for these tools for working with other Reporting Services instances.

Important If the report server database is on a separate computer from the report server, your Windows login must have sysadmin or database update permissions. Otherwise, SQL Server Setup prompts you for credentials with the required permissions.

Each version of Reporting Services relies on a set of configuration files. Depending on the version you are upgrading, Setup creates new configuration files by merging settings from the existing files and leaves the existing files in place. You can manually remove the folders for the previous Reporting Services instance after you confirm that the upgrade is successful. Reporting Services will use only files in the folder with the MSRS11 prefix.

If you are upgrading from SQL Server 2005, Setup uses the virtual directory settings for Reporting Services to reserve corresponding URLs. It might be necessary to manually remove the virtual directories when the upgrade is complete. Also, if your version of SQL Server 2005 is prior to Service Pack 1, Setup adds Database Owner permissions to the RSExecRole.

SharePoint integrated-mode report server upgrade

You can perform an in-place upgrade for the following versions of Reporting Services as long as you have already upgraded the SharePoint farm to SharePoint Server 2010:

- SQL Server 2005 Service Pack 2

- SQL Server 2008 Reporting Services Service Pack 2

- SQL Server 2008 R2

Regardless of the version you are upgrading from, you start the upgrade process on your SharePoint farm by installing the Reporting Services add-in on all web front-end servers. Then start the SQL Server 2012 upgrade process by running Setup on the report server. During the upgrade process, you might see a prompt asking you to provide credentials for SQL Server Reporting Services SharePoint Mode Authentication. The upgrade process uses these credentials to create a new SharePoint application pool.

> **Important** The SharePoint Server 2010 prerequisite installer installs the SQL Server 2008 R2 add-in for Reporting Services. You must download and install the SQL Server 2012 version of this add-in from *http://www.microsoft.com/en-us/download/details.aspx?id=29068*.

Reports upgrade

Reports are stored in the ReportServer database. Setup upgrades only the schema of this database, without modifying the reports it contains. When a user or a background process executes a report, the report server upgrades the report and replaces the compiled version of the report in the ReportServer database. Any RDL files found on the same computer are not upgraded. You must open these files in SSDT to upgrade them to the current RDL schema.

Migration

If you are unable to perform an upgrade in place, you can perform a migration instead. You might also opt to perform a migration to minimize downtime. Your report server is unavailable to users during an upgrade but remains available during a migration.

Native-mode report server migration

You can perform a migration of a native-mode report server running SQL Server 2005 or later by installing SQL Server 2012, as described in Chapter 4, on the same computer as a side-by-side installation. If you prefer, you can install SQL Server 2012 on a separate computer. Either way, choose the Install Only option on the Reporting Services Configuration page of Setup so that you can configure Reporting Services to use your existing report server database after installation completes.

> **Important** If you want to use a new Database Engine instance to host your report server databases, move the databases before configuring the new report server. To preserve all security settings, it's important that you move the databases by performing detach and attach operations rather than copying these databases. If the Database Engine instance has never hosted report server databases, you must create the RSExecRole in the *master* and *msdb* databases as described at *http://msdn.microsoft.com/en-us/library/cc281308*. Then use the Reporting Services Configuration Manager to restore the encryption key that you saved as part of the preparation process.

For a scale-out deployment, you must take each report server node offline and perform a migration on each one individually. You must also manually delete records from the Keys table in the ReportServer database before you configure Reporting Services.

Use Reporting Services Configuration Manager to configure the Report Manager and web service URLs and connect to the report server databases. When you connect the first report server to the report server database, an upgrade is performed on the database to make it compatible with SQL Server 2012 Reporting Services. You also use the Reporting Services Configuration Manager to restore the symmetric key that you saved during the preparation process. Last, you can add the other report servers if you have a scale-out deployment.

Make sure port 80 is open if you have a firewall running on the report server. You can use the Reporting Services Configuration Manager to use a different port if you prefer, but you must open that port manually in your firewall to enable remote access to the report server.

Open Report Manager and run several reports to ensure that the new installation works correctly. If so, you can uninstall the previous version of Reporting Services. You might also need to manually remove the following items:

- RSExecRole (in *master* and *msdb* databases of original Database Engine), if you moved the report server databases to a new Database Engine instance

- Service account running Reporting Services

- Reporting Services log files

If you migrated from SQL Server 2005, you should remove the following items:

- Application pool for the Report Server web service

- Virtual directories for Report Manager and web service

- IIS server, if not used for other purposes

SharePoint integrated-mode report server migration

You must perform the report server migration within the same SharePoint farm due to the use of unique identifiers within the farm. An exception to this requirement is a migration of all SharePoint content to a new farm. If you plan to host SharePoint configuration and content databases, including those used for Reporting Services in a SQL Server 2012 Database Engine instance, you must upgrade the farm to SharePoint 2010 and apply Service Pack 1.

In addition to performing a backup of the items listed in the "Preparation" section of this chapter, you should back up the SharePoint content databases and detach them. Also, back up the following files in Program Files\Common Files\Microsoft Shared\Web Server Extensions\14\Web Services\Reporting:

- Rsreportserver.config

- Rssvrpolicy.config

- Web.config

Next, to perform a complete migration of a farm, create the new SharePoint 2010 farm and install Reporting Services in SharePoint mode, as described in Chapter 4, but don't create the Reporting Services service application yet. Restore the SharePoint content database on the new server, and attach it to a web application. You can also restore the report server databases at this time.

 Important You can attach a SharePoint content database to a web application by using Windows PowerShell or the stsadm utility. SharePoint Central Administration does not include a page to perform this task. For more information, see *http://technet.microsoft.com/en-us/library/cc263299.aspx#AddDB*.

Copy the Rsreportserver.config file to the new server. You need to place it in the folder that has the same name as the one from which you originally backed it up, Program Files\Common Files\Microsoft Shared\Web Server Extensions\14\Web Services\Reporting.

Next, create the Reporting Services service application by following the instructions in Chapter 4, with one exception. On the page you use to create the new service application, change the Database Server and the Database Name to the correct values for the restored report server database.

The last step is to restore the Reporting Services encryption key. To do this, click the Manage Service Applications link in SharePoint Central Administration and click the Reporting Services service application link, the Key Management link, and the Restore Encryption Key link. Click the Browse button, navigate to the location where you stored the symmetric key that you saved in the "Preparation" section, and then provide the password.

CHAPTER 2

Introducing the Reporting Services environment

To use Reporting Services effectively, you need to know what it can do. In this chapter, you learn the different ways that people use it as a reporting platform and how its features support each stage of the reporting life cycle. You also learn how each component of the platform fits together architecturally to deliver these capabilities.

A reporting platform

Put simply, a *report* is a structured arrangement of information. Typically, the information in a business report comes from data in a business application, although report information can be derived from a variety of sources. A *reporting platform* is an integrated set of applications that supports all required activities in a managed report environment, including report development, management, and viewing.

Historically, reports were available only as part of the business applications used in an organization and were not managed separately from these applications. However, preprogrammed reports like these rarely answered all the questions that business users needed answered. Increasing demand for access to the underlying data in these business applications prompted software vendors to include report-generation tools in their applications and eventually to allow direct access to the database with third-party client-side reporting tools. When only a limited number of people required access to reports, these reporting solutions were adequate. However, when the need to deliver reports to a larger audience arose, organizations found that reporting tools with a server component capable of scaling to a large number of users were expensive, complex to implement and manage, and difficult to integrate into custom applications and technical infrastructures.

The Reporting Services reporting platform was introduced in 2004 as an additional component of Microsoft SQL Server 2000 to address these problems. Since then, organizations small and large have migrated to Reporting Services to take advantage of the many benefits it has to offer. Each subsequent version of Reporting Services has made it even easier for report developers, administrators, and business users to use this reporting platform to accomplish their respective objectives. In particular, most of the features in the Microsoft SQL Server 2008 R2 and Microsoft SQL Server 2012 versions of Reporting Services were developed with the self-service needs of business users in mind.

One of the primary reasons that organizations implement Reporting Services is to provide *managed reports* to a large number of internal users. This type of report is typically characterized by detailed operational data or summarized management information that is gathered from a variety of data sources and formally organized into a central repository. Often, managed reports must conform to specific formatting standards. Reports intended for print also require precise page layout and pagination. Consequently, a limited group of report developers is usually responsible for creating managed reports. Users can access these reports online by navigating through a report catalog when they need information, or they can receive reports as email attachments on a scheduled basis. Some organizations also distribute information externally, making reports available to customers or partners by incorporating Reporting Services into an extranet environment.

Another important feature of the Reporting Services platform is its ability to reproduce a report in a variety of formats. This process of converting the report layout and report data into a specific file format is called *rendering*. Often, a business user's question might be answered by simply locating and viewing a report rendered online in Hypertext Markup Language (HTML) format. At other times, the business user might want to analyze the data further by rendering the data as a Microsoft Office Excel workbook and adding calculations to the data, or the business user might want to share information with someone else by rendering the report as a Portable Document Format (PDF) file.

As data proliferates throughout an organization, IT departments are challenged to keep up with the requests to develop new reports. To help solve this problem, Reporting Services includes two tools to develop ad hoc reports: Power View and Report Builder. Power View is accessible only from a Reporting Services implementation that integrates with SharePoint, whereas Report Builder is an option for both native-mode and SharePoint-integrated implementations of Reporting Services. We explain the architectural differences between these implementation modes in the "Reporting Services architecture" section of this chapter.

With access to ad hoc reporting capabilities, users with limited technical skills can produce new, simple reports on their own, and they can choose whether to save them privately or to share them with others by publishing to the Reporting Services centralized store. Because ad hoc reports usually don't have the same layout requirements as managed reports and because the ad hoc tools are easier to use than the managed report designer, typically anyone with permission to see data used for reporting is allowed to create ad hoc reports. Power View is the better choice when users want to explore and interact with data online, while Report Builder is better when users want to control layout more precisely or work with a broader array of data sources.

Before business users can begin creating ad hoc reports by using Power View, an IT professional or a more technical business user can develop a *tabular model* that organizes fields from a data source into a user-friendly collection of related tables. The user then accesses the tabular model to construct an ad hoc report and to automatically generate the query language required to retrieve the requested data. Reports built using a tabular model can be a springboard for data exploration because the user can easily filter and sort the data and add alternate views of the data for deeper insights.

Note You can develop a tabular model by creating a workbook using the Microsoft Power-Pivot Add-in for Excel (available for download at *http://www.microsoft.com/en-us/bi/powerpivot.aspx*) and publishing the workbook to a PowerPivot-enabled SharePoint Server 2010 site. Another option is to develop a tabular model by using SQL Server Data Tools and deploying the model to an Analysis Services server running in tabular mode. You can learn more about tabular modeling at *http://msdn.microsoft.com/en-us/library/hh212945(v=SQL.110).aspx*.

Similarly, users of Report Builder rely on advanced business users and IT professionals to publish components that are available for ad hoc report development. These components include pre-packaged queries called *shared datasets* and individual report items called *report parts*. Shared datasets insulate the Report Builder user from the technical details of the query but allow the business user to freely arrange the data returned by the query in any type of layout supported by Reporting Services. Report parts are report items that are associated with a shared dataset and preconfigured to display data in a structured format. The business user can construct a new report by focusing only on the arrangement of one or more report parts on the page rather than selecting data first and designing a layout for that data.

 Note Although Report Builder provides a user-friendly interface for ad hoc reporting, it also includes all the features necessary to develop managed reports.

In addition to managed and ad hoc reports, you can use Reporting Services to develop and manage *embedded reports* for an organization's portals or custom applications. This capability means that Reporting Services is more than a reporting application. As a fully extensible system, it's also a development platform that can be used by in-house developers or third-party independent software vendors to create either Microsoft Windows or web reporting applications.

Finally, system administrators need the right tools to manage a reporting platform. Reporting Services provides configuration and management tools with a graphical user interface (GUI) to manage server resources, organize content, and implement security. For repetitive tasks, a utility to execute scripts is available. Alternatively, developers can create custom applications or Windows PowerShell scripts to perform administrative tasks.

Reporting life cycle

The *reporting life cycle* is the sequence of activities associated with a report from creation to delivery. Reporting Services fully supports the three phases of the reporting life cycle, which include report development, management of the report server, and report access by users.

> **Note** In this section, we review the reporting life cycle of managed reports, which is also applicable to reports that you develop by using Report Builder if you publish the reports to a report server or to a SharePoint site. However, the reporting life cycle for Power View reports is much different and is explained in Chapter 31, "Using Power View."

Report development

Regardless of which tool you use to develop reports, the process is very similar. You develop reports on your own computer by selecting data for the report, organizing the report layout, and enhancing the report with formatting and, optionally, interactive features. At any time during report development, you can preview the report to test its appearance and any interactive features that you added. If you're building a managed report, you can deploy the report from the authoring tool to the report server or to a Microsoft SharePoint Server 2010 website. If you're building an ad hoc report, your options depend on the tool you use to create the report. With Report Builder, you can choose to store your report on your computer, but you also have the option to save it to the report server or a SharePoint site.

When you select data for your report, you can choose from a wide variety of data sources, typically relational or multidimensional databases or hierarchical data files. If Reporting Services doesn't provide a data source that you need for a report, you can develop or purchase custom data processing extensions, which are discussed further in the section "Server Tier" later in this chapter.

After defining the data query for your report, you organize the data fields into a table, cross-tab, or chart layout. Alternatively, you can use free-form text boxes to present the data in a less-structured format. You might add grouping to the data layout to display subtotals. You can also add calculations to display information such as averages or record counts or to concatenate strings into a single result, such as a first name and last name. In addition to standard chart formats, you can also choose from several different types of data visualizations to display key performance indicators, maps, and charts embedded within a table or cross-tab layout.

Today's business users have become increasingly sophisticated and expect reports to be designed with flexibility and interactivity in mind. With Reporting Services, you can build flexible reports by using parameters to filter content or change the appearance of the report. You can also add interactive features to allow the user to sort data or to hide or show details. Interactive features in Reporting Services also include the ability to add a document map for easy navigation within a large report and to add links to allow the user to jump to a related report or web location.

Report administration

Administrators manage the technical environment for the reporting platform. The administrative responsibilities might be performed by one individual or might be distributed among several people. Before reports can be deployed to the report server and accessed by users, an administrator must configure the report server and optionally integrate the report server with SharePoint. Occasionally, an administrator might reconfigure the report server to fine-tune its performance.

Administrators also manage the location, security, and execution properties of reports, although you might delegate these responsibilities to some power users. Report developers can deploy reports directly to the report server if given permission to do so, or they can provide reports to an administrator to upload directly to the report server or to deploy in a batch by using a script utility. After a report is deployed to the report server, as an administrator, you can place the report in a folder with other related reports. You can then apply security to the report or the folder containing the report to control who can view the report and who can modify report properties.

In addition to security, a report has many properties that you can configure to control what happens when a user views the report. For example, you can change the data source connection information to have the report's queries access a production database server instead of a test server.

By default, a report executes on demand, which means that the report queries execute to retrieve data from the applicable data sources at the time the user opens the report for viewing. Configuring a report's execution properties allows you to balance when the report queries execute against the acceptable level of data latency. For example, you can cache the report for faster viewing of a frequently requested report if the underlying data isn't volatile, or you can create a snapshot report to execute a report at a time when most users are offline if the queries take a long time to complete. Another option is to save multiple snapshots of a report in history to preserve the report data at specific points in time.

Report access

The most common way for users to access reports is to use a browser and navigate to a central report repository. As another alternative, you can create your own portal application with links to guide users to reports in Reporting Services. A user can also optionally store a selection of reports in a personal folder for easy access or can create a subscription to a report to receive it on a scheduled basis in an email inbox, a network file share, or a SharePoint document library.

When you set up a subscription to receive a report, you must scan the report to see whether data has changed since the last time that it was sent to you. Now you can set up data alerting for any report that you can access in a SharePoint document library. A *data alert* is an email notification that data in the report has changed according to one or more conditions that you specify in the data alert definition. The data alert includes a list of the data to which the conditions apply and a link to the report.

By default, you view a report rendered in HTML format, but you can instead render it to a PDF or Tagged Image File Format (TIFF) format to share your report in printed form or to Comma Separated Values (CSV) or Extensible Markup Language (XML) format to import the report data into other applications. Other rendering formats include Microsoft Excel 2010 or Microsoft Word 2010. You can also request a specific format for subscription delivery of reports.

Another way that you might access Reporting Services reports is through corporate applications. Reports might be embedded into applications developed by your organization or by third-party vendors. Reports can also be used to provide supplemental information for scorecard and dashboard applications in PerformancePoint Services, a shared service in SharePoint.

Reporting Services architecture

To deliver the functionality required by a reporting platform, Reporting Services uses a variety of components, extensions, and application programming interfaces (APIs) in a multitier architecture with data, application, and server tiers. For most reporting scenarios, implementation of the standard architecture suffices, but the modular nature of the architecture allows you flexibility when you plan to use only some features or when you need to distribute components across multiple servers for scalability.

Reporting Services can run in native mode (the default configuration), in which it runs as a stand-alone application server, or in integrated mode, which requires the report server to run in a Share-Point farm. You can find more information about integrated mode later in this chapter in the section "SharePoint integrated mode."

Native mode

Figure 2-1 illustrates the relationship between components across three tiers in native mode.

Data tier

The data tier in the Reporting Services architecture consists of the following databases:

- **ReportServer**   This is the primary database for permanent storage of reports and other data related to the management of the report server.

- **ReportServerTempDB**   This database stores session cache information and cached instances of reports for improved report delivery performance. In a scale-out deployment of Reporting Services across multiple report servers, these two databases in the data tier are the only requirements. These databases do not need to be on the same server as the report server.

> **Note** The *ReportServer* and *ReportServerTempDB* databases do not need to be on the same server as the report server.

The data presented in the reports comes from many possible sources and relational and non-relational formats. These data sources are typically located on separate servers from the report server. A connection string embedded in a data source that is defined for the report provides the information required by the report server to connect and authenticate to the server hosting the data.

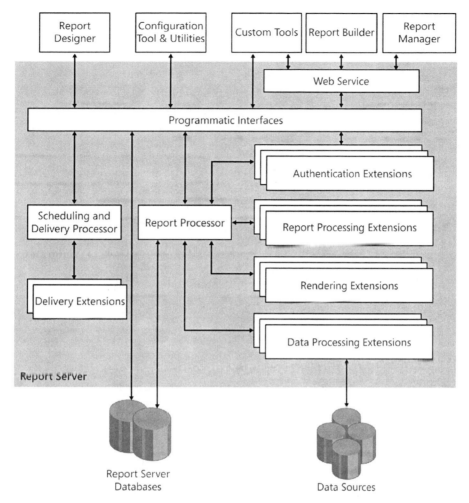

FIGURE 2-1 Native-mode component architecture.

Application tier

The application tier in the Reporting Services architecture is the collection of tools that you use to develop reports and manage the reporting platform: report development tools, report viewers, and management tools.

Each of the following report development tools produces a Report Definition Language (RDL) file:

- **Report Designer** For the full range of report development features, you use Report Designer, a project template available in SQL Server Data Tools (SSDT), one of the management tools you install with Reporting Services. SSDT might look familiar if you've ever used Microsoft Visual Studio. That's because SSDT is a Visual Studio 2010 shell that enables you to use the same integrated development environment that developers use to build applications but that does not require installation of Visual Studio 2010. You start learning how to use Report Designer in Chapter 7, "Working with report server projects."

- **Report Builder**   For both ad hoc and managed reporting, you can use Report Builder. It's simple enough for business users who need access to information but lack the skills to write a Structured Query Language (SQL) query. Despite this simplicity, Report Builder also provides many of the same features you use in Report Designer. Instead of using the Visual Studio 2010 interface, you use an interface much like the Office 2010 family of products. In Chapter 5, "Exploring Reporting Services fundamentals," you learn how to use Report Builder.

- **Programmatic Interface for Report Development**   Reporting Services includes APIs that allow you to build a custom report development tool. You can also build a program to produce a .rdl file, which is the same output generated by the Report Designer and Report Builder tools.

Note Power View is also a report development tool, but applicable only to a SharePoint integrated mode report server. We provide an introduction to Power View in the "SharePoint integrated mode" section later in this chapter.

Tabular models replace semantic models

In previous versions of Reporting Services, you could use a tool known as Model Designer to create a semantic model for data exploration and then use Report Builder 1.0 to explore that semantic model. Beginning with the current release, these two components are no longer available in Reporting Services. Instead, you use SSDT or PowerPivot for Excel to create tabular models and then use Power View to explore model data. These two new ad hoc reporting tools accomplish similar objectives as the former tools but provide a much richer set of capabilities, as you learn in Chapter 31. However, the service architecture continues to include a model processing component so that you can continue to develop reports that use a semantic model as a data source, as long as that data source is deployed to a SQL Server 2005, SQL Server 2008, or SQL Server 2008 R2 instance of Reporting Services.

Reporting Services provides three ways to view reports on a native-mode server:

- **Report Manager**   To view a report on a server running in native mode, you use a web application called Report Manager to locate and render the desired report for online viewing. You can page through a large report, search for text within a report, zoom in or out to resize a report, render a report to a new format, print the report, and change report parameters by using a special toolbar provided in the report viewer. You learn how to use Report Manager for report viewing in Chapter 26, "Accessing reports online."

- **SharePoint**   Even if you choose not to run Reporting Services in SharePoint integrated mode, you can install Web Parts to support user access to reports hosted on a native-mode report server. Chapter 4, "Installing Reporting Services," includes information about installing these Web Parts.

- **Programmatic interface for viewing or delivering reports**   You can integrate report viewer functionality into a custom application by using the Reporting Services API or by accessing reports using Uniform Resource Locator (URL) endpoints. You can also extend standard functionality by customizing security, data processing, rendering, or delivery options. You can find examples for customizing user access to reports in Chapter 35, "Programming report access."

Use the following tools to manage your report server:

- **Reporting Services Configuration Manager**   You use the Reporting Services Configuration Manager to configure a local or remote native-mode Reporting Services installation. Using this tool, you can assign service accounts for running the service and for processing reports for scheduled operations. You also use this tool to configure the URLs to be used by the Reporting Service application or to create the report server databases to host the application data. If you plan to use email delivery of reports, you use this tool to identify the Simple Mail Transfer Protocol (SMTP) server in your network. Finally, you use this tool to connect a report server to a scale-out deployment if you require multiple servers to support your reporting environment. You learn how to use the Reporting Services Configuration Manager to complete an installation in Chapter 4.

- **SQL Server Management Studio**   This tool is the management interface for many of the server components in SQL Server. You can connect to a local or remote native mode report server by using this tool. In Chapter 24, "Securing report server content," you learn how to use SQL Server Management Studio for role-based security management, and then in Chapter 25, "Performing administrative tasks," you learn how to use it to configure report server properties and to manage jobs and shared schedules.

- **SQL Server Configuration Manager**   You use SQL Server Configuration Manager when you need to start or stop the report server Windows service.

- **Report Manager**   You use Report Manager in a native-mode report server environment to organize and configure reports, which you learn about in Chapter 23, "Deploying reports to a server." You also use Report Manager to secure reports, which you learn how to do in Chapter 24, and to manage subscriptions, as we describe in Chapter 27, "Working with subscriptions."

> **Note** For a report server in SharePoint integrated mode, you perform these same tasks, but you use a SharePoint interface. More information about how to perform a particular task in SharePoint is provided in each chapter describing management tasks using Report Manager.

- **Command-Line utilities**   For performing repetitive tasks in bulk, whether on a local or remote report server, you can use the Reporting Services command-line utilities. For example, you can publish reports to a server and configure report properties or security in bulk by creating a Microsoft Visual Basic .NET script, which you can execute with a command-line utility called Rs.exe (described in Chapter 34, "Programming Report Server management"). Other command-line utilities let you manage encryption keys used to provide access to report server databases after moving to a new server or restoring from a backup. You learn more about these utilities in Chapter 25.

- **Programmatic interface for management**   All the management tasks that you can perform using Report Manager can be built into a custom application by using the Reporting Services API. However, some capabilities supported in a native-mode environment are not supported in SharePoint integrated mode, such as custom security extensions, linked reports, and batch operations.

Server tier

The server tier is the central layer of the Reporting Services architecture. It contains processor components and server extensions. The processor components respond to and process requests to the report server and delegate certain functions to subcomponents called *server extensions*, which are simply processors that perform very specific functions. The server tier is implemented as a Windows service.

Activity on the report server is managed by the following processor components:

- **Report Processor**   The Report Processor receives all requests that require execution and rendering of reports. The tasks performed by the Report Processor depend on whether the user requests an on-demand report, a cached report, or a report snapshot. For a request for an on-demand report, the Report Processor calls a data processing extension to execute the report queries and then merges the query results into a temporary format that organizes the data according to the defined layout, but that is not yet the finished report. A cached report is stored in the *ReportServerTempDB* database in this temporary format while a report snapshot is stored in the *ReportServer* database in the temporary format. After generating the report in temporary format or retrieving it from the applicable database, the Report Processor calls a rendering extension to finalize the report for the user. You learn about all the report processing options in Chapter 23.

- **Scheduling and Delivery Processor**   The Scheduling and Delivery Processor receives all requests for scheduled events such as snapshots and subscriptions. When a user creates a snapshot or subscription schedule for a report, the Scheduling and Delivery Processor in turn creates a SQL Server Agent job. Later, when the job executes, SQL Server Agent sends a request to the Scheduling and Delivery Processor, which in turn forwards the request to the Report Processor to execute and render the report. The Report Processor returns the finished report to the Scheduling and Delivery Processor, which calls a delivery extension to email the report or store it on a network share as applicable.

You can disable an out-of-the-box server extension or add your own extension, whether developed in-house or purchased from a third party. Reporting Services includes the following types of server extensions:

- **Authentication extension**   By default, Reporting Services uses Windows authentication to allow users to access the server and to authorize the content that users can see and the tasks that users can perform. Unlike other server extensions, there can be only one active authentication extension per report server instance. If you want to use a custom security extension, you must remove the default security extension provided by Reporting Services.

- **Data processing extension**   The Report Processor sends query requests to the applicable data processing extension, which in turn connects to a data source, executes a query (with query parameters if applicable), and returns the query results as a flattened rowset to the Report Processor. Reporting Services includes data processing extensions for the following data sources: SQL Server, SQL Azure, SQL Server Parallel Data Warehouse, Analysis Services, SharePoint list, Hyperion Essbase, Oracle, SAP Netweaver Business Intelligence, Teradata, XML, Object Linking and Embedding Database (OLE DB), and Open Database Connectivity (ODBC).

  In general, the data processing extension performs the following steps to retrieve data:

  1. Opens a connection to the designated data source.

  2. Analyzes the query to produce a list of field names that the report developer will reference in the layout during the report development process.

  3. Executes the query to obtain a rowset.

  4. Passes query parameters to the query when applicable.

  5. Iterates through the rowset to retrieve the data for use in the report.

- **Report processing extension**   The report processing extension is an optional component used to process custom report items from third-party vendors. For example, you can obtain charting or mapping add-ins to enhance your reports. To merge the data into the format required by these add-ins, the Report Processor calls a report processing extension to produce the temporary format of the report. You can, of course, develop both your own report items and the report processing extension required for the server to include these custom report items in a report.

- **Rendering extension**   The Report Processor calls a rendering extension to convert a report in temporary format into a finished format for the user. The rendering extensions included with Reporting Services are HTML, Microsoft Office Excel, CSV, XML, TIFF, PDF, and Microsoft Office Word. If you need a different output format, you can develop your own rendering extension. You learn more about rendering in Chapter 26.

- **Delivery extension**   The Scheduling and Delivery Processor uses delivery extensions (described in Chapter 27) to handle scheduled report requests, as follows:

  - The email delivery extension sends an email message to one or more recipients with the report embedded in the report body, attached as a file or referenced as a URL link to the report on a report server.

- The file share delivery extension saves a report in a specified format to a network share that is independent of the reporting platform for archiving or providing a more scalable storage and access mechanism for large reports.

To meet other requirements for report delivery, you can develop a custom delivery extension for sending reports to other destinations, such as a fax device or printer, or to another application.

Service architecture

Reporting Services includes several applications running as a single Windows service process that supports the functioning of the server tier. Figure 2-2 illustrates the relationship between these features.

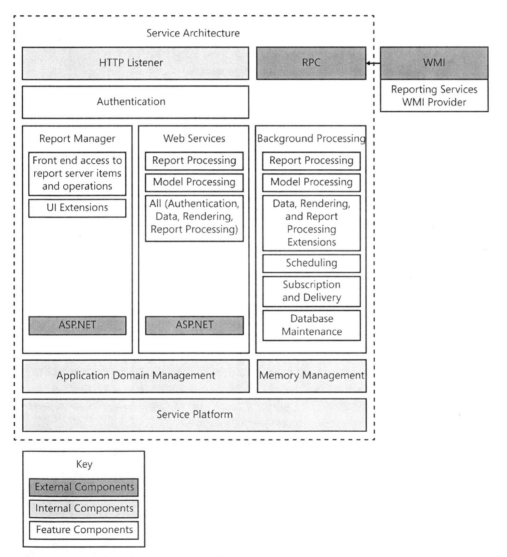

FIGURE 2-2 Reporting Services service architecture.

The service architecture consists of the following components:

- **HTTP Listener**   Beginning with the Reporting Services 2008 version, Reporting Services no longer requires an installation of Internet Information Services (IIS). Instead, Reporting Services uses Http.sys directly from the server's operating system to accept requests directed to URLs and ports configured for Reporting Services. This architectural change allows Reporting Services to exist without IIS and still provide the same functionality. You use the Reporting Services Configuration Manager (described in Chapter 4) to register the protocol, path, port, and virtual directory with Http.sys, which uses this information to identify incoming Reporting Services requests. Even if IIS is installed on the same server with Reporting Services, the HTTP listener forwards those requests to the authentication layer for Reporting Services.

- **Authentication**   The authentication layer supports both Windows-based and custom authentication to confirm the identity of the user or application making the request. Reporting Services uses Windows integrated security by default, using either NT LAN Manager (NTLM) or Kerberos authentication, but it also supports basic and anonymous access authentication. You can use anonymous authentication only if you implement custom ASP.NET Forms authentication. Despite this range of options, you can use only one authentication type on a report server instance and within a scale-out deployment. In Chapter 24, you learn about configuring authentication. The authentication layer calls the Report Server web service after the incoming request is authenticated.

- **Application Domains**   The application domain layer contains the following separate feature areas of Reporting Services, which you can enable or disable independently (as described in Chapter 25): Report Manager, Report Server web service, and background processing. Combining the application domains as a single Windows service makes it easier to configure and maintain Reporting Services. The application domain layer also hosts the ASP.NET and Microsoft .NET Framework technologies that are part of SQL Server common language runtime (CLR) integration.

- **Report Manager**   Report Manager is a front-end component for a native-mode report server and an ASP.NET application domain. Both users and server administrators use this component to interact with the Report Server web service when viewing reports (as described in Chapter 26), managing content (as described in Chapter 23), or managing server operations (as described in Chapter 25).

- **Report Server Web Service**   The Report Server web service is another ASP.NET application domain on the report server. It serves as the report processing engine for on-demand requests, authenticates and authorizes user requests, and also provides the programmatic interfaces for custom applications if you choose not to use Report Manager for interactions with the report server.

- **Background Processing**   The background processing component manages scheduling, subscriptions, and delivery as well as data, rendering, and database maintenance. It also performs all report processing that is not explicitly handled by the Report Server web service. Because these report processing tasks occur on a scheduled basis without the security context of a user, background processing uses Authz.dll to confirm that the user who created the request is still a valid domain user who continues to have the correct permissions to execute the request. In addition to using a separate security mechanism, background processing also uses a separate memory management process. Memory for background processing is given a lower priority on the report server than on-demand processing.

- **Application Domain Management**   The application domain management layer replaces the functionality of IIS.

- **Memory Management**   The memory management layer extends SQL Server memory management features to the Reporting Services Windows service and is responsible for monitoring thread processing. When the report server starts, each application domain requests a minimum amount of memory and then continually interacts with the memory manager to report current usage and to respond to directions to acquire or release memory. You learn about managing memory thresholds in Chapter 25.

- **Service Platform**   The service platform allows Reporting Services to take advantage of the following SQL Server services: SQL OS, SQL CLR, and SQLNetworkInterface. Because these services install with the report server, there is no requirement to install a SQL Server database engine instance on the same computer.

- **Remote Procedure Call (RPC)**   RPC supports execution of procedures on a remote server and is used by the Reporting Services Windows Management Instrumentation (WMI) provider.

SharePoint integrated mode

The architecture of a report server running in integrated mode has changed in the current release. It now runs as a shared service application on SharePoint Foundation 2010 or a SharePoint Server 2010 farm. Integration of Reporting Services with SharePoint offers the following benefits:

- Users view reports and administrators manage content by accessing a SharePoint site that you use to centralize storage of reports and other types of useful content. Users have only one place to look for information that they need, by using a single, familiar graphical user interface in SharePoint.

- Users can send reports to other document libraries on a scheduled basis by using subscriptions.

- SharePoint provides a single security model for user access to reports and other enterprise content. You can optionally use claims-based authentication to control access to reports rather than use Kerberos to access back-end servers.

- Many SharePoint features are available for your reports that are not available in native-mode Reporting Services, such as alternate access mapping, versioning, workflows, and dashboard integration. Dashboards can now display reports both from the current farm and from a trusted farm.

- Reporting Services scales across web applications and SharePoint Server 2010 farms with fewer resources than possible in previous versions because it is now instantiated as a shared service application. Round robin load balancing for the Reporting Services shared service is built into SharePoint.

- Administrators can more easily configure, manage, and monitor an integrated-mode Reporting Services implementation by accessing the SharePoint Central Administration portal or by using PowerShell cmdlets. Also, they can use SharePoint backup and recovery processes for Reporting Services content.

To support Reporting Services integration, you must either execute the SharePoint prerequisite installer or separately install the Microsoft SQL Server 2012 Reporting Services Add-in for Microsoft SharePoint Technologies on a SharePoint server. The add-in installs a proxy endpoint for Reporting Services, adds a Report Viewer Web Part to the SharePoint gallery, adds the Data Alert Designer and Power View applications, and adds application pages to SharePoint for viewing and managing report server content on a SharePoint site. You learn how to configure an environment for SharePoint integration in Chapter 4.

Note You can install and register SharePoint Web Parts for Reporting Services to enable users to locate and view reports stored on a report server in native mode from a SharePoint site. This approach is much simpler to deploy, but it prevents you from using the collaboration and document management features of SharePoint that are available if you configure the report server to run in integrated mode.

Figure 2-3 illustrates the architecture of Reporting Services in SharePoint in integrated mode.

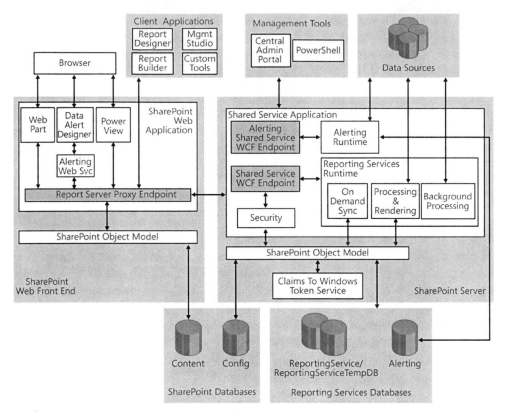

FIGURE 2-3 Integrated mode report server architecture.

Data tier

In the SharePoint integrated-mode architecture, the following types of databases support the reporting platform:

- **SharePoint Content Database**   Reports, data sources, and security permissions are stored in the SharePoint content database.

- **SharePoint Configuration Database**   The configuration database stores information about the report server, including the report server database names, enabled extensions, and the application pool identity for each shared service application.

- **Reporting Services Databases**   The *ReportServer* and *ReportServerTempDB* databases are now set up as shared service application databases. That means you will see this pair of databases (plus the *Alerting* database) for each Reporting Services service application that you create. These two databases have new names, *ReportingService_<GUID>* and *Reporting-Service_<GUID>TempDB* respectively, and take the place of the report server databases for all content not managed in the SharePoint content database: snapshots, subscriptions, schedules, server settings, and cached reports. The *ReportingService_<GUID>* database also keeps a copy of the reports stored in the SharePoint content database to facilitate faster processing.

- **Reporting Services *Alerting* Database** The *ReportingService_<GUID>_Alerting* database is one of three databases that is created when you set up a new shared service application for Reporting Services. It contains alert definitions, alert instances, alert schedules, and execution log details.

> **Note** The three Reporting Services databases must be on the same database server but do not need to be on the same server as the SharePoint content and configuration databases.

Application tier

The SharePoint integrated-mode architecture includes several tools in the application tier that are not available in the native-mode architecture. Report development tools such as Report Designer and Report Builder work with either architecture, but Power View is available only in SharePoint integrated-mode. The following tools are specific to integrated mode:

- **Power View** Power View is a Silverlight application that supports ad hoc report development within a browser. The only data source that it supports is a tabular data model. The report design process in Power View is highly interactive and visual, which makes it less of a traditional report development tool and more of a data exploration tool. You can save your findings as a report to a SharePoint document library, or you can export the report to a PowerPoint file. You learn how to design and export Power View reports in Chapter 31, "Using Power View."

> **Note** There are two options for developing a tabular data model. One option is to use Microsoft PowerPivot for Excel to design the tabular model and then publish a workbook containing the tabular model to a SharePoint farm that supports PowerPivot for SharePoint. Another option is to create a tabular model project in SSDT and deploy it to an Analysis Services instance running in tabular mode.

- **Report Viewer Web Part** In SharePoint integrated-mode, you can navigate to a SharePoint document library to locate and render a report much as you can when using Report Manager. A Web Part is also available for embedding a report into a SharePoint webpage, such as a dashboard. Whether you open the report in a document library or in a Web Part, the same capabilities to page, search, zoom, render, print, and select parameters available in Report Manager are available in SharePoint. You learn how to work with reports in SharePoint in Chapter 26.

- **Data Alert Designer** You use the Data Alert Designer to define the conditions that will generate a data alert, the schedule for checking the conditions, and the recipients of the data alert that is sent when the conditions are met. Chapter 28, "Data alerting," shows you how to configure and manage alerts.

- **SharePoint Central Administration**   The SharePoint Central Administration portal contains links to pages that you use to create, manage, and monitor your Reporting Services shared service application. You learn how to perform these tasks in Chapter 4 and Chapter 25.

- **Windows PowerShell Cmdlets**   As an alternative to using SharePoint Central Administration, you can use Windows PowerShell cmdlets to create and configure the shared service application. More information about using Windows PowerShell cmdlets is available in Chapter 4 and Chapter 25.

- **SQL Server Management Studio**   You can connect to a SharePoint site enabled for Reporting Services integration to configure properties such as time-out values or to configure security. In Chapter 25, you learn more about using SQL Server Management Studio for configuring a SharePoint site.

Server tier

The architecture of the server tier is much different in this release from the previous version. Now Reporting Services runs as a shared service application, which greatly simplifies the management process and allows you take advantage of existing SharePoint administration skillsets within your organization. The SharePoint integrated-mode server tier uses the following components:

- **Service Machine Instance**   The service machine instance is the server that hosts one or more Reporting Services shared service applications. You can start or stop the shared service on this server. SharePoint automatically manages the load balancing when you have multiple service machine instances in your farm.

- **Report Server Proxy Endpoint**   Client applications, such as Report Viewer or any application using the SOAP API, connect to Reporting Services by using the report server proxy endpoint on the SharePoint Web Front End. This endpoint associated a SharePoint web application with the Reporting Services web service by using a URL such as http://<SharePoint web application>/_vti_bin/ReportServer. In a scale-out scenario, this endpoint communicates with the load balancer to access the available service machine instances.

- **Shared Service Application**   A shared service application is analogous to a native-mode report server instance. It contains everything necessary to manage report processing and has its own set of databases. One way to scale Reporting Services in SharePoint integrated mode is to create multiple shared service applications.

- **Shared Service Windows Communication Foundation (WCF) Endpoints**   There are two WCF endpoints on the service machine instance. The report server proxy endpoint communicates with the Reporting Services and Alerting services by using a separate endpoint for each shared service.

- **Reporting Services Runtime Engine**   This engine functions like a native-mode report server, with the exception of managing security, which is handled by SharePoint instead. In addition, it contains an On Demand Sync component that it uses whenever you add, replace, or open a report to determine whether a report in the Reporting Service content database is as current as its counterpart in the SharePoint content database, and it copies the newer version to the Reporting Services content database when necessary. The integrated-mode engine also contains a SharePoint delivery extension to support delivery of reports to a SharePoint document library. Otherwise, just like the native-mode engine, the integrated-mode engine has a report processor to manage report requests and uses data processing, report processing, and rendering extensions as needed. It also has a background processing component to manage schedules, snapshots, and subscriptions.

- **Claims to Windows Token Service** The Reporting Services runtime engine relies on the Claims to Windows Token Service when a request to execute a report using Windows integrated security comes from a web application that uses claims-based authentication. The Claims to Windows Token Service provides the report processor with a token that it uses to impersonate the user when querying a data source for the report.

- **Alerting Service Runtime Engine** The alerting service runtime engine refreshes the data feeds associated with alert definitions, assesses whether the alert conditions are met, and adds an alerting instance to the alerting database to document the results. If alert conditions are met, the alerting service runtime engine sends an email containing the alert results to each recipient listed in the alert definition, as explained in Chapter 29.

After reading this introduction to the features of Reporting Services, the activities performed during the reporting life cycle, and learning about its architecture, you are probably ready to roll up your sleeves and put together your own reporting platform. In the next chapter, you learn how to prepare the environment and perform an installation in preparation for building, managing, and viewing reports.

CHAPTER 3

Understanding deployment scenarios

Because SQL Server 2012, including Reporting Services, is not a single application but consists of multiple components, there are multiple ways to implement it in your organization. In this chapter, we review the most common deployment scenarios for "out-of-the-box" Reporting Services. For each scenario, there are several key considerations to help you decide which deployment is best suited for your environment.

Single-server deployment

In the simplest deployment scenario, all SQL Server components coexist on the same computer, as shown in Figure 3-1. This is a suitable approach to use whether you need to set up a developer's laptop as an isolated environment for experimenting with design strategies or a shared development server for all report developers to access. For small organizations with a limited number of concurrent users and relatively simple reports that execute on demand, this configuration can also work well.

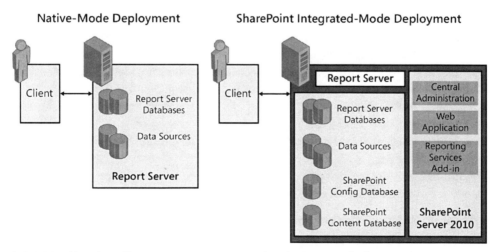

FIGURE 3-1 You place all components on one server in a single-server deployment.

In a single-server deployment, the report server components and the report server databases are on the same server with other SQL Server components, such as the relational and Analysis Services data sources accessed by reports. The primary challenge for this environment is that each of these components requires a lot of memory and CPU. In particular, Reporting Services places heavy demands on memory when rendering large reports as Excel or PDF files.

If your server hardware can adequately support all the required components and deliver acceptable performance, a single-server deployment is the easiest to install, configure, and maintain. However, it does introduce a risk as a single point of failure. If the amount of time required to restore a database, including but not limited to the report server database, or to reinstall a component adversely impacts your organization, you should consider a distributed or scale-out deployment. However, there are additional licensing requirements for these alternate deployment scenarios, so a scale-up approach that adds more memory, more processing power, or faster disk on a single server might be a more cost-effective solution.

Memory

You might not be able to put as much memory as you would like on a developer's laptop due to hardware constraints, but you typically are working as a single user with a subset of data in this environment. Also, your computer doesn't need to support multiple users and large data volumes, so it doesn't require as much memory as a production server. On a shared development server, you should have at least 8 gigabytes (GB) of memory, but add more if you can. Similarly, on a production server, all components will perform better if you provide as much memory as possible, but you should plan no less than 4 GB per processor.

Disk space

You must also plan for adequate disk space after accounting for source databases. Initially, the Reporting Services databases are small. Even when you deploy a lot of reports to the server, the report definition files stored in the Reporting Services catalog do not consume a lot of space. These files are measured in kilobytes (KB), not megabytes (MB) or GB. However, if you enable report caching or snapshots, the report server databases store data as binary large objects (BLOBs), that consume much more space. Another consideration is that any increase in concurrent users on the report server means there are more session caches adding to the disk space consumption of the *ReportServer-TempDB* database. The size of cached reports and snapshots depends on the amount of data returned for the report's dataset queries. Furthermore, if a cached report has parameters, the report server temporary database storing the cached instance increases to hold another copy of the report when a user requests a new combination of parameter values.

To estimate disk space requirements for the *ReportServer* database, factor 100–200 KB of disk space for each report definition file of average size. You can estimate snapshot sizes by assuming a 5:1 compression ratio, which requires 1 MB of disk space to store a snapshot of a report containing 5

MB of data. The *ReportServerTempDB* database fluctuates as the number of concurrent users and the number of reports they view change throughout the day. To accommodate this variability, you should assume that 10%–20% of your user base represents the maximum number of concurrent users on the report server at any given point in time. If your estimation is that a maximum of 100 concurrent users require access to a 5-MB report, you can calculate the disk space requirement by multiplying the number of users by the report size and applying to the compression factor to arrive at 100 MB of temporary storage for this one report.

Disk activity

Every request for a report, whether executed on demand or from a cache or snapshot, impacts the report server databases. In addition, activity on the report server as the users page through reports generates transactions that store current state to ensure consistency. As the number of concurrent users increases, the number of writes to the *ReportServerTempDB* database increases as well. This high volume of disk activity can create a bottleneck in the Database Engine.

> **Tip** For more information about managing the report server database with a high number of users or heavy reporting workload, see Report Server Catalog Best Practices at *http://sqlcat .com/sqlcat/b/technicalnotes/archive/2008/06/26/report-server-catalog-best-practices.aspx*. Although the article was written for an earlier version of Reporting Services, the principles still apply.

Distributed deployment

If the Database Engine is already using most of the memory on a server, you should not put Reporting Services on the same server. Instead, you can implement a distributed deployment. In this type of deployment, you spread components of a single instance across two or more servers.

Native-mode distribution

For a native-mode distributed deployment, shown in Figure 3-2, you can put the report server on one computer and the report server database on another computer. This approach alleviates some of the resource contention problems between Reporting Services and the Database Engine by giving each component access to the majority of memory on its own server.

> **Important** Each server that you use in a distributed deployment must have its own SQL Server 2012 license.

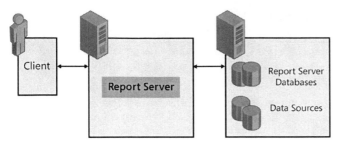

FIGURE 3-2 In a distributed native-mode environment, you place the report server and report server database on separate computers.

If you place the report server databases on the same server as your SQL Server data sources, you run the risk of creating a resource contention problem within the Database Engine. As we mentioned in the "Single-server deployment" section, user requests for reports generate considerable activity in the report server databases. If the same Database Engine must also return high volumes of data for dataset queries, a bottleneck in SQL Server resources might occur. In this situation, you should use a dedicated server for the report server databases, as shown in Figure 3-3.

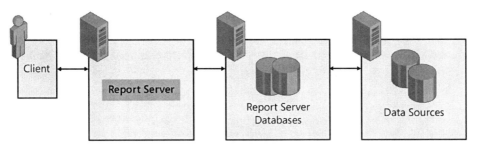

FIGURE 3-3 You can place the report server databases on a dedicated server to alleviate resource contention with data sources.

SharePoint integrated-mode distribution

Similarly, for a SharePoint integrated-mode report server, you can distribute the components in multiple ways. One option is to put the SharePoint server components on one computer and put the Database Engine and Reporting Services on a second computer, as shown in Figure 3-4. In this case, you must install the Reporting Services Add-in on both SharePoint servers, install SharePoint on the second server with the report server, and then connect that second SharePoint server to the Share-Point farm.

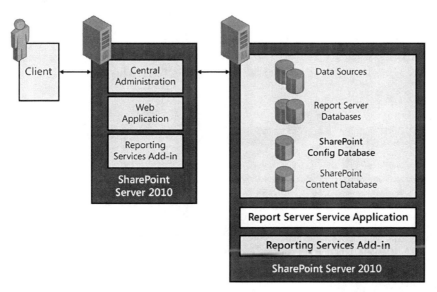

FIGURE 3-4 You can combine the report server, database server, and a SharePoint server in a distributed deployment.

This scenario has the advantage of requiring only one SQL Server license, but you require two SharePoint licenses. Furthermore, this two-server deployment has the same disadvantages that we described for a single-server deployment. In fact, these disadvantages are further aggravated by the addition of the SharePoint databases to the second server.

A variation of this theme is to use only a single SharePoint server and place the report server on the SharePoint server, as shown in Figure 3-5. Then you use a second server to host the SharePoint databases, the report server databases, and the report data sources. In this case, you need only one SharePoint license, but two SQL Server licenses.

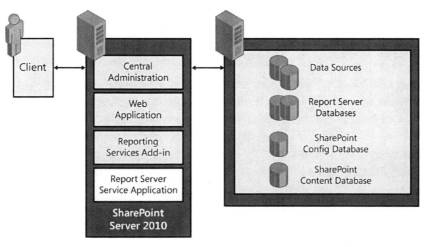

FIGURE 3-5 You can place the report server with SharePoint and place all databases on a dedicated server.

Another option is to take the distribution one step further and maintain SharePoint on a dedicated server, as shown in Figure 3-6. SharePoint performs best in this deployment scenario. You can then add another SharePoint server to the farm with Reporting Services and use a third computer to host all the databases. Here you need two SharePoint licenses and two SQL Server licenses.

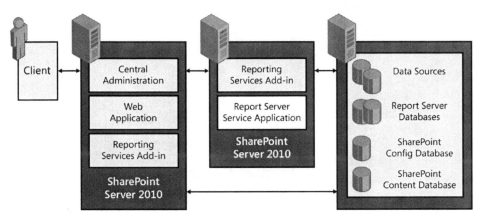

FIGURE 3-6 You can maintain the report server and databases on dedicated servers separate from the SharePoint server.

Other components

If you are using Analysis Services as a data source, you can keep it on the same server as the Database Engine. However, keep in mind that Analysis Services requires a lot of memory itself, whether responding to queries or processing data to store in cubes. Similarly, extract, transform, and load processes for a data warehouse using Integration Services can impact the Database Engine and consume memory and CPU. You should consider whether these components can perform more optimally if you place them on dedicated servers.

Scale-out deployment

If you have SQL Server 2012 Enterprise Edition and must support a thousand users or more who regularly execute reports on demand, you can implement a scale-out deployment with a web farm of report servers, as shown in Figure 3-7. In this deployment scenario, you can add another report server to the web farm as needed. All report servers in the web farm connect to the same report server database, which can be on a server with one of the report server instances or on a separate server. To support high availability for the report server database, you can install it on database server cluster.

Note You can use Developer Edition and Evaluation Edition in a test scale-out deployment, but you must use Enterprise Edition for a production deployment. Furthermore, you must have an Enterprise Edition license for each report server in the web farm.

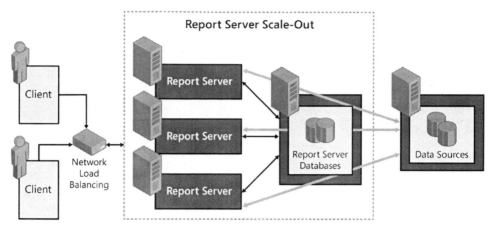

FIGURE 3-7 You can support more users by implementing a report server scale-out deployment with network load balancing and a separate server for data sources.

Load balancing

A native-mode Reporting Services deployment includes no support for high availability or web farm management. You must use network load balancing (NLB) software or hardware to establish a virtual server name as a single point of entry. The NLB technology is solely responsible for distributing the workload across the report servers, usually in a round-robin sequence. The state of a report is kept in a shared report server database so that subsequent requests from a user remain consistent regardless of which report server processes those requests.

> **Note** Because Reporting Services runs as a service application in SharePoint integrated-mode, you can use the built-in load balancing features of SharePoint Server 2010, with no additional hardware required.

In a high-traffic reporting environment, you might find that the network becomes a bottleneck. You might consider placing two network interface cards (NICs) in each report server. You can use one NIC for client connections and the second one for traffic between the report server and the database server.

Failover cluster

You can install the report server database on a SQL Server failover cluster that already exists. The other Reporting Services components do not participate in a failover cluster, even if they are installed on a computer that is part of a cluster.

Distributed workload

If your reporting environment must support both a large number of concurrent users and a high volume of scheduled reports, you can separate Reporting Services components by configuring report servers to perform only one of these tasks, as shown in Figure 3-8. That way, you can mitigate any resource contention problems that one type of workload might have on the other. We describe how to disable report server features in Chapter 25, "Performing administrative tasks."

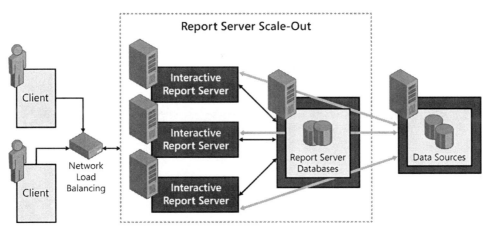

FIGURE 3-8 You can configure report servers to perform specific tasks, such as interactive report processing or background processing only.

Internet deployment

Regardless of the number of servers used to deploy Reporting Services, a typical environment restricts access to an internal network. However, because Reporting Services uses the Hypertext Transfer Protocol (HTTP) protocol to respond to client requests, you can configure an environment to enable Internet access to Reporting Services. Your primary concern with this type of deployment is maintaining a secure environment for the report server, your data, and your corporate network.

If the data for reports is public data, you can create a single-server environment to store the data in SQL Server, as shown in Figure 3-9, and enable access to reports for everyone. To further insulate the data on the report server, you might consider setting up reports as snapshots so that users cannot execute reports and the corresponding queries directly. In this deployment scenario, you should not connect the report server to your corporate network.

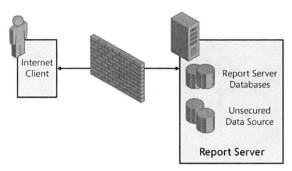

FIGURE 3-9 You can set up an isolated, dedicated report server for Internet access.

More often, you want to control who can access the report server. In that case, you can set up each external user with a Windows account in Active Directory and then use Windows integrated security or basic authentication to manage access to the report server, as shown in Figure 3-10. You should implement Secure Socket Layer (SSL) to protect data in transit between the client and report server. The benefit of this approach is that you can use role-based security in Reporting Services to control access to reports. You should assign these users to low privilege roles, such as Browser and System User, as described in Chapter 24, "Securing report server content."

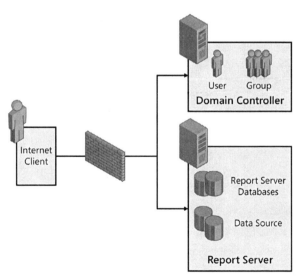

FIGURE 3-10 You can set up Internet access to your report server for users authenticated by your network domain's Active Directory.

When it's not practical to create a Windows account for external users, you can build a web application to present a login form and authenticate users. You can then implement a custom security extension to use your authentication application with Reporting Services. Yet another alternative is to use a custom application to bypass Report Manager and provide your own methods for opening and viewing reports, as shown in Figure 3-11. In that case, you should disable Report Manager to reduce the surface area exposure on the Internet.

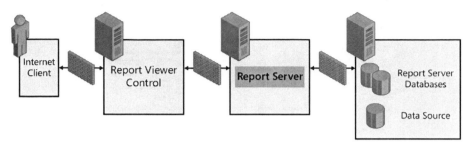

FIGURE 3-11 You can bypass Report Manager by using a custom application that implements the ReportViewer control.

With any of these Internet-facing deployment options for which Report Manager is the primary interface for interacting with reports, you can put the Report Manager component on its own server, as shown in Figure 3-12, and then disable all other Reporting Services features as described in Chapter 25. Then you can add a second report server (as described in the "Scale-out deployment" section of this chapter) to manage report processing and rendering. You must update the Rsreportserver. config file to redirect processing and rendering to this second server by updating the *ReportServerUrl* element on the first server with the virtual directory of the report server on the second server.

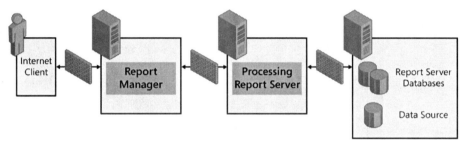

FIGURE 3-12 You can dedicate one server as a front-end with Report Manager and another server for processing and rendering.

Note You can learn more about correctly configuring a stand-alone Report Manager at *http://msdn.microsoft.com/en-us/library/cc281384.aspx.*

CHAPTER 4

Installing Reporting Services

I n Chapter 1, "What's new in SQL Server 2012 Reporting Services," you learned how Reporting Services components create a reporting platform. Making sure you have all the right combinations of hardware and software for the SQL Server edition you want to use and then getting SQL Server installed and configured can be challenging because the product documentation spreads this information out across multiple subject areas. In this chapter, we consolidate this information so that you can see at a glance the requirements to meet before installing Reporting Services, how to proceed through the installation process, and what steps to perform to configure Reporting Services correctly.

Reviewing hardware and software requirements

Before you proceed with the installation of Reporting Services as a feature of SQL Server 2012, you should make sure your computer has the right operating system, ample memory, and plenty of hard disk space. It is also important that you install all operating system service packs before beginning the installation of SQL Server 2012. In most cases, the minimum memory requirement is 1 gigabyte (GB), but the recommended memory is 4 GB or more. If you're installing SQL Server 2012 Express with Advanced Services, the only Express edition that includes Reporting Services, the minimum memory is 512 megabytes (MB), with 1 GB recommended. You should have as much available memory as possible to get the best performance from Reporting Services. As for disk space, you should plan to have at least 6 GB available before beginning the installation. The actual amount of space required depends on the combination of components that you choose to install.

Selecting an operating system

You can install SQL Server 2012 on most 32-bit or 64-bit operating systems: Microsoft Windows Vista, Microsoft Windows 7, Microsoft Windows Server 2008, and Microsoft Windows Server 2008 R2 SP1. You can install the 64-bit editions, shown in Table 4-1 by supported operating system, only on 64-bit computers. Although the management tools run in 32-bit mode, they are supported by Windows on Windows 64-bit (WOW64), which allows you to install these tools on a 64-bit system.

TABLE 4-1 Operating system support for SQL Server 2012 64-bit editions.

Operating System	Enterprise	Business Intelligence	Standard	Web	Developer	Express
Windows Server 2008 R2 SP1 64-bit						
Datacenter	✓	✓	✓	✓	✓	✓
Enterprise	✓	✓	✓	✓	✓	✓
Standard	✓	✓	✓	✓	✓	✓
Foundation			✓			✓
Web	✓	✓	✓	✓	✓	✓
Windows Server 2008 SP2 64-bit						
Datacenter	✓	✓	✓	✓	✓	✓
Enterprise	✓	✓	✓	✓	✓	✓
Standard	✓	✓	✓	✓	✓	✓
Foundation			✓			✓
Web	✓	✓	✓	✓	✓	✓
Windows 7 SP1 64-bit						
Ultimate			✓		✓	✓
Enterprise			✓		✓	✓
Professional			✓		✓	✓
Home Premium					✓	✓
Home Basic					✓	✓
Windows Vista SP2 64-bit						
Ultimate			✓		✓	✓
Enterprise			✓		✓	✓
Business			✓		✓	✓
Home Premium					✓	✓
Home Basic					✓	✓

You can install the SQL Server 2012 32-bit editions on either 64-bit or 32-bit computers, as shown in Table 4-2.

TABLE 4-2 Operating system support for SQL Server 2012 32-bit editions.

Operating System	Enterprise	Business Intelligence	Standard	Web	Developer	Express
Windows Server 2008 R2 SP1 64-bit						
Datacenter	✓	✓	✓	✓	✓	✓
Enterprise	✓	✓	✓	✓	✓	✓
Standard	✓	✓	✓	✓	✓	✓
Foundation			✓			✓
Web	✓	✓	✓	✓	✓	✓
Windows Server 2008 SP2 64-bit						
Datacenter	✓	✓	✓	✓	✓	✓
Enterprise	✓	✓	✓	✓	✓	✓
Standard	✓	✓	✓	✓	✓	✓
Foundation			✓			✓
Web	✓	✓	✓	✓	✓	✓
Windows Server 2008 SP2 32-bit						
Datacenter	✓	✓	✓	✓	✓	✓
Enterprise	✓	✓	✓	✓	✓	✓
Standard	✓	✓	✓	✓	✓	✓
Web	✓	✓	✓	✓	✓	✓
Windows 7 SP1 64-bit						
Ultimate			✓		✓	✓
Enterprise			✓		✓	✓
Professional			✓		✓	✓
Home Premium					✓	✓
Home Basic					✓	✓

Operating System	Enterprise	Business Intelligence	Standard	Web	Developer	Express
Windows 7 SP1 32-bit						
Ultimate			✓		✓	✓
Enterprise			✓		✓	✓
Professional			✓		✓	✓
Home Premium					✓	✓
Home Basic					✓	✓
Windows Vista SP2 64-bit						
Ultimate			✓		✓	✓
Enterprise			✓		✓	✓
Business			✓		✓	✓
Home Premium					✓	✓
Home Basic					✓	✓
Windows Vista SP2 32-bit						
Ultimate			✓		✓	✓
Enterprise			✓		✓	✓
Business			✓		✓	✓
Home Premium					✓	✓
Home Basic					✓	✓

Note For a complete review of requirements and a full list of supported operating systems, refer to "Hardware and Software Requirements for Installing SQL Server 2012," at *http://msdn.microsoft.com/en-us/library/ms143506(v=sql.110).aspx*.

Choosing a Database Engine edition

Most of the time, you install the Database Engine and Reporting Services using the same edition, but it's possible to install Reporting Services separately and then host the Reporting Services databases using a Database Engine from a different edition, as shown in Table 4-3.

TABLE 4-3 Database Engine support for hosting Reporting Services databases.

Reporting Services Edition	Enterprise	Business Intelligence	Standard	Web	Express	Evaluation
Enterprise	✓	✓	✓			
Business Intelligence	✓	✓	✓			
Standard	✓		✓			
Web				✓		
Express with Advanced Services					✓	
Evaluation						✓

Reviewing SharePoint integrated-mode requirements

If you plan to deploy Reporting Services in SharePoint integrated mode, the order in which you install Reporting Services and SharePoint on the same server does not matter. However, there are additional requirements that you must consider. For example, you are restricted to specific editions of SQL Server 2012 and SharePoint. Furthermore, you must follow certain guidelines when selecting a SharePoint edition.

> **Note** You can find more information about hardware and software requirements for Reporting Services in SharePoint integrated mode at *http://msdn.microsoft.com/en-us/library/bb283190(v=sql.110).aspx*. Another useful resource is "Guidance for Using SQL Server BI Features in a SharePoint Farm," available at *http://msdn.microsoft.com/en-us/library/hh231680(v=sql.110).aspx*.

Most SQL Server 2012 editions support the standard features in Reporting Services in SharePoint integrated mode (with some limitations that we explain, where relevant, in Part IV, "Managing the report server," and Part V, "Viewing reports"). Table 4-4 shows these editions as well as the two that include support for Power View and Data Alerts.

TABLE 4-4 Feature support by SQL Server 2012 edition.

SQL Server 2012 Edition	Standard Reporting Services	Power View	Data Alerts
Enterprise	✓	✓	✓
Business Intelligence	✓	✓	✓
Standard	✓		
Developer	✓		
Evaluation	✓		

All standard reporting services (except as we noted above) are supported in the following editions of SharePoint:

- SharePoint Foundation 2010

- SharePoint Server 2010 Standard

- SharePoint Server 2010 Enterprise

Power View and Data Alerts require you to use SharePoint Server 2010 Enterprise. In addition, you must choose the Server Farm installation of SharePoint, rather than the Standalone installation.

SharePoint has a dependency on the SQL Server Database Engine for storage of configuration and catalog databases. The basic installation of SharePoint creates a database using the SQL Server Express edition, which is incompatible for hosting the Reporting Services database. You can install another instance of the Database Engine using an appropriate SQL Server edition for use exclusively by Reporting Services, or you can use SharePoint's Advanced installation option to allow SharePoint to share that Database Engine instance with Reporting Services.

Note If you plan to use SQL Server 2012 to host the SharePoint content or catalog databases, you must install SharePoint 2010 Service Pack 1 (SP1).

An additional software component, Microsoft Reporting Services Add-in for SharePoint Technologies, must be installed on a stand-alone SharePoint server or, if you have a SharePoint farm, on each web front-end server that hosts reporting.

Planning accounts for reporting services

Before you install Reporting Services, you must decide whether to run the report server service under a built-in service account or a Windows account on your computer or on your network domain. If you use a Windows account, the account you use should be a least-privilege account with permission to connect to the network and the Allow Log On Locally permission on the report server and the computer hosting the report server database, if they are different. Ideally, you should dedicate this account to only the report server service.

Important If you plan to use a Windows account, be sure to create the account before starting the installation of Reporting Services.

By default, the native-mode report server service account is also used for connecting to the report server database, although you can change this to a domain account or a SQL Server login by using the Reporting Services Configuration Tool (as explained later in this chapter). If you're deploying Reporting Services in SharePoint integrated mode, you configure this account when you create the

Reporting Services service application (also explained later in this chapter). This connection account is used when the report server needs to store and retrieve reports, metadata, and server state information and is the only account requiring access to the report server database.

Performing the installation

You can install Reporting Services by using a setup wizard or by using a command-line executable. The installation process includes installation of prerequisites, installation of setup support files, and feature selection and configuration. You can install Reporting Services on the same server as other SQL Server components, as described in this chapter, or you can install it alone. If you install Reporting Services alone, the report server requires access to a SQL Server for hosting the report server database.

Important To run Setup on your computer, you must be logged in to the computer with an account that is a member of the local administrator group.

Note If you prefer to install Reporting Services from the command-line, refer to *http://msdn.microsoft.com/en-us/library/ms144259(v=sql.110).aspx*.

Installing prerequisites

Before you start the installation process, you might need to install some prerequisites manually. For example, if the computer already has Visual Studio installed, you must download and install Visual Studio 2010 SP1 before running SQL Server Setup. Another prerequisite of SQL Server 2012 is .NET 4.0, but the setup process installs it automatically unless you are installing SQL Server Express edition on a computer with Windows 2008 R2 SP1. In that case, you must manually download and install .NET 4.0 prior to beginning the SQL Server Express installation.

All other prerequisites will be identified for you during setup, which you start on the server where you want to install Reporting Services. Simply run Setup from your SQL Server 2012 installation CD or from a network share containing the contents of the installation CD. In the left pane of the SQL Server Installation Center, click Installation. You can then click the New SQL Server Stand-Alone Installation Or Add Features To An Existing Installation link to start the installation process.

The installation process then continues to the Setup Support Rules page of the wizard, where you can click Show Details to view the requirements and the status of each of the following requirements:

- Your computer must use a supported operating system.

- You must be an administrator.

- Your account specifically must have the right to back up files and directories, to manage auditing and the security log, and to debug programs. If you are set up as a local administrator, you will have these privileges.

- The Windows Management Instrumentation (WMI) service must be running.

- The computer must not require a restart.

- SQL Server registry keys must be consistent and can support SQL Server installation or upgrade.

- SQL Server installation media path names must not be too long.

- Setup must not detect any product incompatibilities.

- .NET 2.0 and .NET 3.5 Service Pack 1 update for the operating system must be installed.

If problems are detected, you must correct them before continuing with the installation. You can leave the SQL Server 2012 Setup wizard open, fix a problem, return to the wizard, and click Re-Run to run the requirement tests again. Continue with this process until your computer passes, and then you can continue with the wizard.

After installing the setup support files, which could take several minutes, the wizard displays a new Setup Support Rules page with the status of additional setup requirements. You can click the View Detailed Report link to review the status of the following requirements:

- The computer must not require a restart due to a broken Fusion Active Template Library (ATL) assembly.

- The setup checks whether SQL Server 2008 Business Intelligence Development Studio exists on the computer.

- There is no side-by-side install with SQL Server 2012 Community Technology Preview 0.

- The SQL Server registry keys pass a consistency validation.

- The computer should not be a domain controller. Setup displays a warning if it is.

- The computer is connected to the Internet and can complete .NET security checks.

- For a 64-bit operating system, the SQL Server edition supports the operating system and can use the WOW64 platform for SQL Server Setup.

- The setup checks whether the Windows Firewall is enabled.

 Note If you see a warning in the Status column for Windows Firewall, refer to *http://msdn.microsoft.com/en-us/library/cc646023(v=sql.110).aspx* for instructions about how to allow SQL Server access through a firewall.

Again, you must resolve any outstanding issues before continuing to the next step of the wizard. At this point, all requirements must be met before installation can begin.

Installing SQL Server 2012

After installing the prerequisites, the wizard walks you through several pages to acquire the information necessary to complete the installation. The specific pages you see depend on the feature selections you make.

Product key

After the setup support files are installed, you proceed to the Product Key page of the wizard. Here you can choose whether to install a free or purchased edition. If you select Specify A Free Edition, you can select either Evaluation or Express from the drop-down list. If you have already purchased a SQL Server 2008 license for installation on your computer, you should instead select Enter The Product Key and then type the product key into the box.

License terms

On the License Terms page of the wizard, you can scroll through the Microsoft License Terms. To continue the wizard, you must select the I Accept The License Terms check box. Optionally, you can select the check box to send usage data to Microsoft.

Setup role

The Setup Role page is the next step of the wizard. Here you have the following options:

- **SQL Server Feature Installation**   You use this option when you want to install a subset of the available features.

- **SQL Server PowerPivot for SharePoint**   You use this option to install another type of Analysis Services server mode that integrates with SharePoint. You can use PowerPivot for SharePoint workbooks as a data source for reports, as we explain in Chapter 8, "Retrieving data for a report," and in Chapter 30, "Preparing to use Power View."

- **All Features With Defaults**   When you use this option, the wizard installs all available features and configures those features to use default values.

Feature selection

When you choose the SQL Server Feature Installation option, you continue to the Feature Selection page of the SQL Server 2012 Setup wizard. In the Features list, you select all the components that you want to install along with Reporting Services, as shown in Figure 4-1.

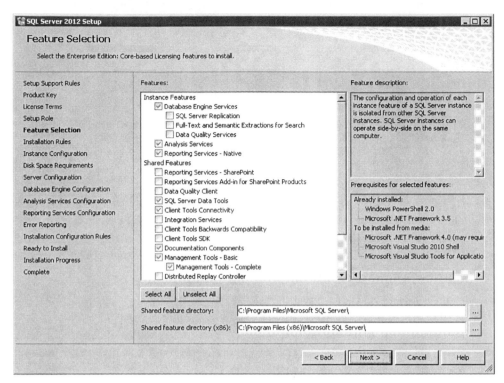

FIGURE 4-1 Feature selection in SQL Server 2012 Setup.

In a production environment, you should install only the features necessary to run the report server, such as the Database Engine, Reporting Services – Native, and Client Tools Connectivity. As a security measure to reduce the surface attack area, you should not include shared features, such as SQL Server Data Tools or Management Tools. However, a development environment typically includes most, if not all, of the following features:

- **Database Engine Services** The Database Engine Services feature is required to host the Reporting Services databases. If you plan to host Reporting Services by using a separate instance of SQL Server on your computer or a remote server, you can ignore this selection.

- **Analysis Services** The Analysis Services feature is not required for Reporting Services, but you must install it if you plan to use it as a data source for reports. However, Analysis Services is not required to be on the same server as the report server. For example, in production, you might want to place Analysis Service on its own server for better performance. The examples we show in Chapter 16, "Using Analysis Services as a data source," assume that Analysis Services is on the same server as Reporting Services.

- **Reporting Services - Native** This feature is the primary focus of this book, of course, and is a required selection on this page unless you plan to install the report server in SharePoint integrated mode. In that case, you do not select this check box.

- **Reporting Services - SharePoint**   You select this check box when you intend to use Reporting Services in SharePoint integrated mode, but leave it clear when you want to use a native-mode report server only. You can run a side-by-side installation of Reporting Services for each mode, but the server should have plenty of memory in that case.

- **Reporting Services Add-in For SharePoint Products**   Normally, you select this feature when you choose the Reporting Services – SharePoint feature. If you have a SharePoint farm, you can select this feature only to install the add-in on a Web Front End server. As an alternative, you can download and install this add-in separately, as we explain in the "Installing the Reporting Services Add-in for SharePoint" section later in this chapter. Another option is to install this add-in when you want to render reports in local mode without integrating SharePoint with a report server, as we explain in the "Configuring SharePoint for local mode reporting" section of this chapter.

- **SQL Server Data Tools**   Because you use SQL Server Data Tools (SSDT) to build reports, as described in the chapters of Part II, "Developing reports," and to build report parts as described in Chapter 29, "Reusing report parts," it is typically a required selection for a development environment. However, you might choose to install SSDT only on a developer's computer and install the server features on a separate computer. You are not required to install this feature in a production environment.

- **Client Tools Connectivity**   This feature includes the components and network libraries that Reporting Services uses for Open Database Connectivity (ODBC) and Object Linking and Embedding Database (OLE DB) connectivity when executing report queries. Therefore, it is also a required selection.

- **Documentation Components**   Documentation is not required, but it is useful to install on your computer as a reference tool. Alternatively, you can refer to Books Online for SQL Server 2012 at *http://msdn.microsoft.com/en-us/library/ms159106(v=sql.110).aspx*.

- **Management Tools - Complete**   The Management Tools - Complete feature includes SQL Server Management Studio with the necessary tools for managing the report server. This feature is required when you manage the report server, as we describe in Chapter 24, "Securing report server content," and Chapter 25, "Performing administrative tasks."

At the bottom of the Feature Selection page, you can see the default location for installation of the SQL Server 2012 features is C:\Program Files\Microsoft SQL Server, but you can choose a different location if you prefer. If you are installing SQL Server 2012 on a 64-bit computer, you can also change the default location for the 32-bit features from C:\Program Files (x86)\Microsoft SQL Server to an alternate location.

Installation rules

The next step of the wizard is the Installation Rules page where setup tests your computer for the following rules:

- If your computer has Microsoft Visual Studio 2010 installed, Visual Studio 2010 SP1 must also be installed.

- Microsoft .NET Framework SP1 must be installed.

If a rule fails, you can leave setup running and resolve the issue. Then return, and click the Re-Run button to re-execute the test. When the rules pass, you can continue to the next step of the wizard.

Instance configuration

On the Instance Configuration page, as shown in Figure 4-2, you can keep the default selection of Default Instance or you can select Named Instance and type a unique name for the instance. By using named instances, you can install multiple copies of SQL Server components on your computer, which you can allocate to different purposes and configure with different properties. For example, you might install one instance of Analysis Services to run in Multidimensional And Data Mining mode and then install another instance of Analysis Services on the same computer to run in Tabular mode. Of course, your computer should have plenty of memory to accommodate multiple instances. Whichever option you choose here, you can change the default directory of the instance from the default of C:\ Program Files\Microsoft SQL Server.

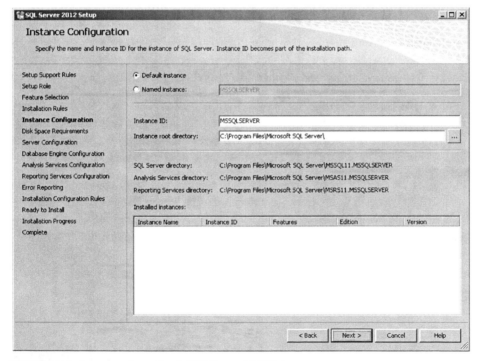

FIGURE 4-2 Instance configuration in SQL Server 2012 Setup.

Important Notice that the directory for a default instance of Reporting Services is C:\ Program Files\Microsoft SQL Server\MSRS11.MSSQLServer. If you set up a named instance, the directory name incorporates the instance name, such as C:\Program Files\Microsoft SQL Server\MSRS11.DENALI when the instance name is DENALI. This naming convention makes it much easier to identify where Reporting Services files are found in the SQL Server root directory. You need to know this location if you want to change configuration files later or to review logs, which are covered in Chapter 25.

Disk space requirements

On the Disk Space Requirements page, confirm that you have enough disk space on your computer to install the selected features. Here you will see a breakdown of requirements by directory. Some files will be placed on the system drive, which you cannot change. Files for shared features will be placed in the shared install directory that you specified on the Feature Selection page of the wizard (Figure 4-1). Instance files will be placed in the respective directories that you specified on the Instance Configuration page (Figure 4-2). If necessary, you can step backwards through the wizard to modify the target directories.

Server configuration

On the Server Configuration page, as shown in Figure 4-3, you can see a default Account Name for each service required for the features you are installing. For example, if your computer has a Windows 7 or Windows Server 2008 R2 operating system, the Account Name for Reporting Services is the virtual account NT Service\ReportServer (or NT Service\ReportServer$DENALI for a named instance called DENALI). You can type a domain user in the Account Name box or use its drop-down list to browse the Active Directory for a user. You must also specify a password if you set up a domain user as the Account Name.

Note Microsoft recommends that you establish separate low-privilege service accounts for each service.

You also use this page to specify a Startup Type for each service. The default is Automatic, but you can choose Manual if you prefer not to start a service when the server starts or Disabled if you prefer to prevent the service from starting. Unless you have a specific reason not to start a service, it's a good idea to keep the default Startup Type settings on this page. However, you should consider changing the Startup Type to Automatic for SQL Server Agent if you plan to configure caching or snapshots for reports (as explained in Chapter 23, "Deploying reports to a server"), support report subscriptions (as explained in Chapter 27, "Working with subscriptions"), or assign stored credentials to data sources (as explained in Chapter 23). If SQL Server Agent is not running, you cannot implement these features.

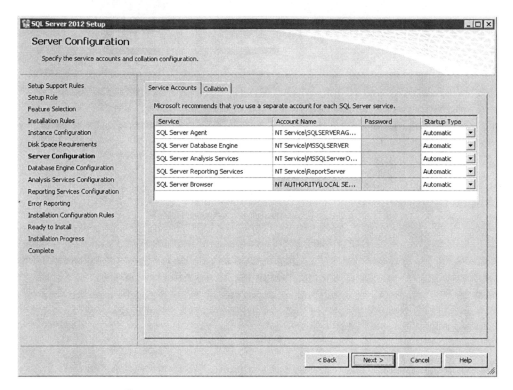

FIGURE 4-3 Server configuration in SQL Server 2012 Setup.

Tip If you plan to set up multiple instances for SQL Server features, you should consider changing the Startup Type of SQL Browser to Automatic. That way, you can easily browse for available instances when connecting to a server in SQL Server Management Studio.

On the Collation tab, you can set collation for the Database Engine and for Analysis Services. In general, collation determines how the respective engines evaluate character data for sorting and for comparison expressions. By default, both Database Engine and Analysis Services use Latin1_General collation, which works well with western European languages. In addition, the default collation behavior for these two engines is case-insensitive, accent-sensitive, kanatype-insensitive, and width-insensitive. The Database Engine also uses SQL Server Sort Order 52 on Code Page 1252 for non-Unicode data. You have the option to customize the collation for each engine if you require different collation behavior.

Database Engine configuration

If you are installing the Database Engine feature, the next step of the wizard is Database Engine Configuration, as shown in Figure 4-4. On this page, you specify the Authentication Mode, which defaults to Windows authentication mode. If necessary, you can change to Mixed Mode. If you change to Mixed Mode, you must supply a password for the SQL Server system administrator account.

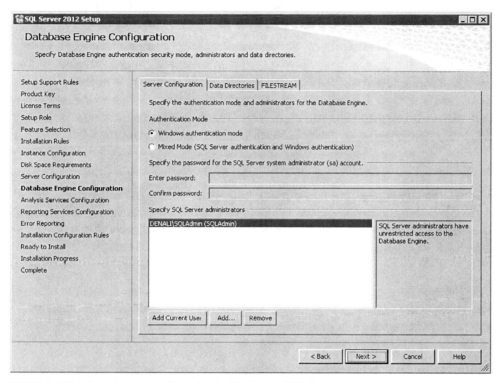

FIGURE 4-4 Database Engine configuration in SQL Server 2012 Setup.

You must also add at least one user as the SQL Server administrator. You can click the Add Current User button to add your user account, or you can click the Add button to select other users from Active Directory. Best practice dictates that you should keep the number of SQL Server administrators to a minimum.

You use the Data Directories tab on this page to specify an alternate location for storing database and related data files. The default location will be the directory that you specified for the SQL Server instance on the Instance Configuration page of the wizard. You can override locations for user databases, user database logs, Temp DB, Temp DB log, and backup.

A third tab on this page allows you to enable FILESTREAM for Transact-SQL access and, optionally, for file input/output (I/O) access. You can also specify whether to allow remote clients to access FILESTREAM. FILESTREAM is a SQL Server feature that allows you to store text documents, images, and video in a database.

Analysis Services configuration

If you are installing the Analysis Services feature, you must complete the Analysis Services Configuration page next. Here you must select a server mode for Analysis Services. The default selection of Multidimensional And Data Mining Mode uses the same Analysis Services engine available in SQL Server 2005 and later versions. The other option, Tabular Mode, uses the xVelocity in-memory analytics engine introduced as VertiPaq in SQL Server 2008 R2 as part of PowerPivot for SharePoint. Like PowerPivot for SharePoint, Tabular Mode compresses data for storage at runtime.

Important After you assign a server mode to an instance, you cannot change it. Instead, you must install a new instance, which can coexist on the same server as the original instance. However, there is no direct migration path for moving data from one mode to another. You must manually re-create the business intelligence semantic model by using the tools applicable to the server mode to which you plan to deploy the model.

Note We provide examples of working with both server modes in this book. In Chapter 16, we show you how to develop reports working with an Analysis Services instance in multi-dimensional and data mining mode. The examples in Chapter 30 and Chapter 31, "Using Power View," require a second Analysis Services instance in tabular mode.

On the Analysis Services Configuration page, you must add at least one user as the Analysis Services administrator. You can click the Add Current User button to add your user account, or you can click the Add button to select other users from Active Directory. For security reasons, you should restrict the number of Analysis Services administrators.

The Analysis Services Configuration page also includes a Data Directories tab that you use to specify an alternate location for storing database and related data files. The base path for the Analysis Services files is the directory that you specified for the Analysis Services instance on the Instance Configuration page of the wizard. On the Data Directories tab, you can override locations for data, the log file, temporary files, and backup files.

Reporting Services configuration

On the Reporting Services Configuration page, you choose the method to use for installing Reporting Services. As shown in Figure 4-5, you choose from the following options:

- **Reporting Services Native Mode: Install And Configure** This option is available only when you select the native-mode Reporting Services feature for an instance that also hosts the Database Engine and when the account running Setup has permissions to access and create databases on that instance. Setup creates the databases and configures the report server by using default values, allowing you to begin using the report server immediately following installation.

- **Reporting Services Native Mode: Install Only**   This option is always available when you select the native-mode Reporting Services for installation. You must manually create the Reporting Services databases and configure server properties by using the Reporting Services Configuration Manager before you begin using the server. (See the "Configuring native-mode Reporting Services" section of this chapter for more information.)

- **Reporting Services SharePoint Integrated Mode: Install Only**   This option is available only when you select the SharePoint integrated-mode feature for installation. This option does not require you to have SharePoint installed on your computer, but the report server is not available until you install SharePoint and finish configuring the report server in SharePoint Central Administration (as explained later in this chapter in the "Configuring SharePoint integrated mode" section).

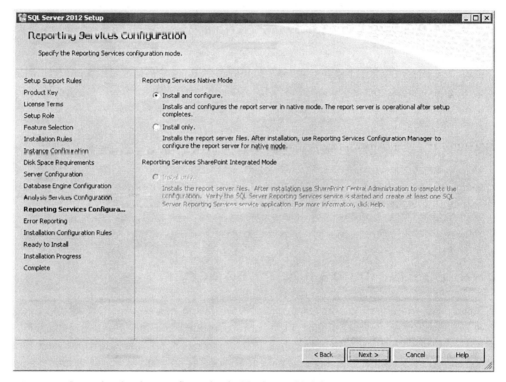

FIGURE 4-5 Reporting Services configuration in SQL Server 2012 Setup.

Installation configuration rules

On the Installation Configuration Rules page, another series of tests is run to confirm your computer is ready for installation. This time, setup checks the status of the following conditions (assuming that you are installing the features illustrated in Figure 4-1):

- The target drive for installation must not be a FAT32 file system.

- There must not be an existing cluster or cluster-prepared instance with the same instance name that you specified on the Instance Configuration page.

- If SQL Server features are already installed on your computer, the language used by Setup is the same language used by the existing SQL Server features. That is, you are not performing a cross-language installation.

- The CPU architecture of the features you are installing matches the architecture of the instance.

- The Reporting Services Catalog Database does not already exist.

- The Reporting Services Catalog Temporary Database does not already exist.

- The SQL Server edition you are installing supports the selected server mode for Analysis Services.

When you successfully pass the installation configuration rules, you proceed at last to the Ready To Install page where you begin the installation. The installation might take up to an hour, especially if you install other SQL Server features in addition to the features required solely for Reporting Services.

Important If you plan to work with Power View, you must run SQL Server Setup again to install Tabular mode or to install PowerPivot for SharePoint unless you have these features available on an existing server elsewhere. You can find instructions for installing PowerPivot for SharePoint at *http://msdn.microsoft.com/en-us/library/ee210708(v=sql.110).aspx*.

Configuring native-mode Reporting Services

When you choose the option to install and configure Reporting Services in native mode, Reporting Services is ready to use. However, you might need to complete more configuration steps if you intend to use email subscriptions or use remote data sources. In addition, you should use the Reporting Services Configuration Manager to back up the encryption key so that you can later access encrypted data in the database if you have to restore the Reporting Services database at some point in the future. Finally, if you have implemented a scale-out deployment, you use the Reporting Services Configuration Manager to add servers to the scale-out.

The Reporting Services Configuration Manager is available in the Configuration Tools folder of the Microsoft SQL Server 2012 program group. After opening this tool, you must connect to a Reporting Services instance by selecting the applicable Server Name and Report Server Instance in the Reporting Services Configuration Connection dialog box. The Report Server Status page of the Reporting Services Configuration Manager displays after you successfully connect to the report server, as shown in Figure 4-6.

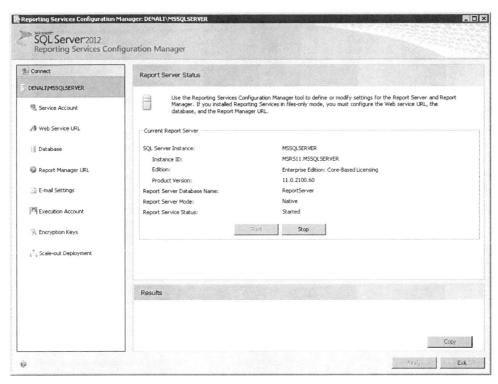

FIGURE 4-6 You can view the Report Server status in the Reporting Services Configuration Manager.

Service account

On the Service Account page, you configure the account that you will use to run the report server Windows service. If you selected the Install and Configure option during Setup, the service account displays here. You can change the service account to a different built-in account or to a domain account at any time. After you specify a new service account, click Apply to implement the change.

> **Important** Because it's a Windows service, you see Reporting Services listed in the Services management console. You might be tempted to change the service account in that interface. However, it's recommended that you always use the Reporting Services Configuration Manager to make service account changes.

Web service URL

You use the Web Service URL page of the Reporting Services Configuration Manager (shown in Figure 4-7) to configure the virtual directory for the web service as well as the *URL reservation*, which describes one or more URLs that can be used to access the report server web service. By using the web service URL, you can bypass the Report Manager and access a report directly (as described in Chapter 35, "Programming report access").

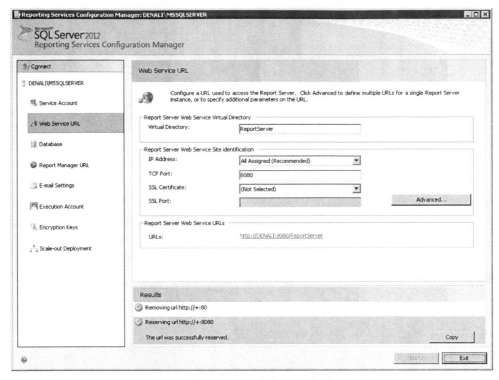

FIGURE 4-7 You must configure the web service URL before deploying reports.

> **Note** If you selected the Install option (rather than Install And Configure) for Reporting Services during Setup, you must configure the web service URL before you can deploy reports to the report server.

When you define the URLs for the web service (and for Report Manager, as we explain later in this section) by using the Reporting Services Configuration Manager, you create a URL reservation that defines a URL endpoint. That endpoint is registered on the server when the Report Server service starts, if the service is enabled in SQL Server Surface Area Configuration. A request queue is created at that time, and HTTP.SYS can route requests to the report server's request queue when registration completes.

The URL reservation consists of the following elements:

- **Scheme** Identifies the protocol used to send a request to Reporting Services, such as HTTP or Hypertext Transfer Protocol Secure (HTTPS).

- **Host name** Defines the server hosting Reporting Services, such as adventureworks.com.

- **Port** Specifies the port configured to listen for HTTP requests, which is port 80 by default.

- **Virtual directory**   Refers to the name that identifies the URL reservation, similar to an Internet Information Services (IIS) virtual directory, such as ReportServer for the report server web service.

Tip You can have multiple URLs configured for the report server web service (or the Report Manager), but you must keep the same virtual directory for all those URLs. For example, you might require multiple URLs when supporting both intranet and extranet deployment scenarios by the same report server.

HTTP.SYS uses the following hierarchical system of URL reservation types to determine how to route requests:

- **All Assigned**   All requests on the specified port for the specified virtual directory are routed to Reporting Services. This type of URL reservation (for example, *http://+:80/ReportServer*) uses the plus (+) sign as a strong wildcard and is the default for Reporting Services.

- **Specific**   Only requests matching the host, port, and virtual directory are sent to Reporting Services, such as *http://adventureworks.com:80/ReportServer*.

- **All Unassigned**   Any request not already handled by another reservation is sent to Reporting Services, such as *http://*:80/ReportServer*. In this case, the asterisk (*) symbol is used as a weak wildcard.

To configure the URL reservation, you select a value for the IP Address, which by default is All Assigned (Recommended). You can choose an alternative value in the drop-down list to create a specific or All Unassigned reservation type. In addition, you specify a port number in the TCP Port box.

If you have a Secure Sockets Layer (SSL) certificate installed on the report server, it appears in the SSL Certificate drop-down list. After you select the certificate, you can specify a port to use for SSL communications.

Important If you install Reporting Services 2012 on a computer that already has Reporting Services 2005 or any version of SharePoint installed, you must change the URL reservation. Reporting Services 2005 uses *http://<servername>:80/ReportServer* (or *http://<servername>:8080/ReportServer* on a Windows XP 32-bit system), and SharePoint uses port 80 (*http://<servername>:80*). For Reporting Services 2012, use a different port number or a different virtual directory name in the URL reservation to avoid a conflict.

Click the Advance button to open the Advanced Multiple Web Site Configuration dialog box, which you use to configure multiple identities for the same report server's web service. Here you can add, edit, or delete a URL reservation, as shown in Figure 4-8.

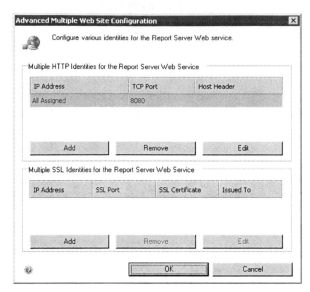

FIGURE 4-8 You can configure multiple HTTP identities for the same report server.

Under Multiple HTTP Identities For The Report Server Web Service, click Add to display the Add A Report Server HTTP URL dialog box, as shown in Figure 4-9. Here you can specify the reservation type All Assigned, All Unassigned, or a specific Internet Protocol (IP) address as well as the port number for a URL reservation. The full URL displays in the dialog box to allow you to confirm the configuration.

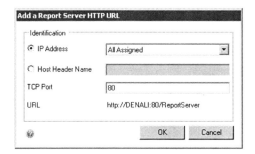

FIGURE 4-9 You can create a new HTTP identity by specifying an IP address or Host Header Name, in addition to specifying the TCP Port and URL.

To ensure that the web service is configured correctly, you should click the Report Server web service URL in Reporting Services Configuration Manager. A browser window opens and displays the version information for Reporting Services, as shown in Figure 4-10. You might be prompted for credentials before you can view the web service page.

FIGURE 4-10 Test the web service URL to ensure that the report server is running correctly.

Note If you get an error that "The permissions granted to user 'domain\user' are insufficient for performing this operation," even though you are an administrator, the problem is likely due to User Account Control (UAC). If you are the only person who logs on to the server locally, you can change the local security policy and disable the "User Account Control: Run All Administrators in Admin Approval mode" to disable UAC. You must restart your computer to complete the change.

If you are prompted for credentials, you might need to add the site to the local Intranet zones in the Internet Options in Internet Explorer. The problem could be related to enhanced security configuration, which you can learn more about at *http://technet.microsoft.com/en-us/library/dd883248(v=ws.10).aspx*.

Database

If you selected the Install option for Reporting Services, you need to configure the report server database in the Reporting Services Configuration Manager. The Install And Configure option creates and configures the database for you, as shown in Figure 4-11. On this page, you can see the server hosting the report server database and the database name, which defaults to *ReportServer*. You can also see the current server mode for the report server. Finally, you can see the account used to connect to the report server database.

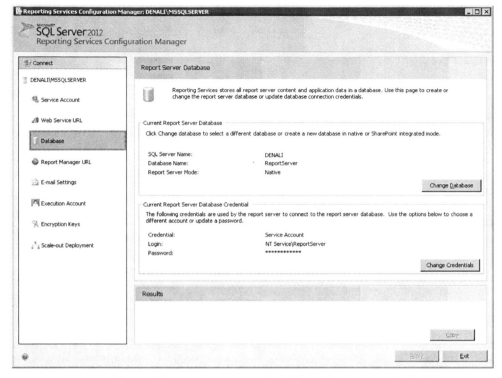

FIGURE 4-11 You use the Database page to create and configure the report server databases.

If you want to set up a new report server database, click the Change Database button. A wizard steps you through the process of identifying the database server, providing a name for the database, and specifying the credentials for the report server to use to connect to the database.

 Important If you configure Reporting Services to use a remote server running SQL Server, your account needs permission to create and access databases on that server.

To change the report service connection account, click the Change Credentials button. Your options are to use Windows Credentials, SQL Server Credentials, or Service Credentials. If you select Windows or SQL Server Credentials, you must provide a user name and password.

Report Manager URL

On the Report Manager URL page of Reporting Services Configuration Manager, you configure the virtual directory used to access Report Manager, as shown in Figure 4-12. As you learned in Chapter 2, "Introducing the Reporting Services environment," Report Manager is the web application that is the standard user interface for accessing reports and performing certain administrative tasks. As with the Report Server web service URL, you can click Advanced to configure multiple URL reservations. Each URL reservation listed in the URLs section is a link that you can use to confirm that Report Manager opens on request.

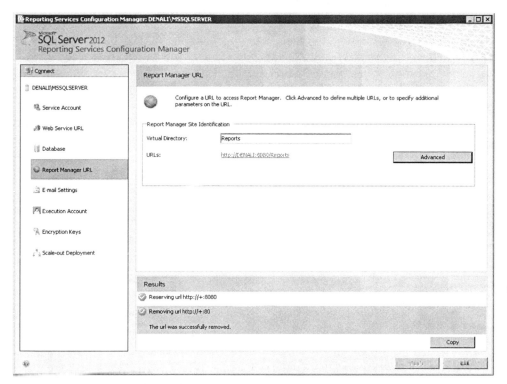

FIGURE 4-12 You must configure the Report Manager URL to provide a graphical interface for accessing and managing report server content.

You can test the configuration of the Report Manager URL by clicking the link on this page to display Report Manager in the browser, as shown in Figure 4-13. That way, you can confirm that Reporting Services is correctly installed and configured. You learn more about Report Manager in Chapter 26, "Accessing reports online."

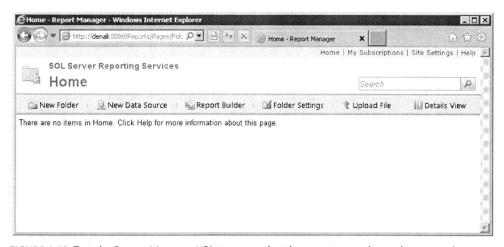

FIGURE 4-13 Test the Report Manager URL to ensure that the report server is running correctly.

Email settings

On the E-Mail Settings page, shown in Figure 4-14, you provide the settings that enable email subscriptions in Reporting Services. In the Sender Address box, type a valid email account in your computer's domain in the format *sendername@domain.com*. Reporting Services uses this account to specify the sender in an email subscription delivered to recipients. In the SMTP Server box, type the name of a Simple Mail Transfer Protocol (SMTP) server in your domain. If you are using a stand-alone server as a development environment, you can type **localhost**. Be sure to click Apply to save the settings.

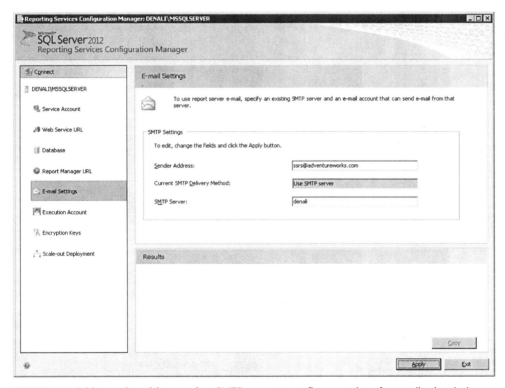

FIGURE 4-14 Add a sender address and an SMTP server to configure settings for email subscriptions.

Note To test email delivery, you must have SMTP installed on your computer or accessible on the network by your computer. If you are configuring a development or test server, you might consider evaluating a free resource, SMTP4DEV, at *http://smtp4dev.codeplex.com/* to use as a dummy SMTP server.

Execution account

If the reports that you manage on the report server require access to data on remote servers, you must configure a domain user account to enable access to the server by using the Execution Account page, as shown in Figure 4-15. Reporting Services uses this account for reports using database authentication, or to connect to servers hosting data for which access to the data itself does not require authentication. Reporting Services also uses the execution account for authenticating image files that are used in a report but that are stored in a separate location that does not allow Anonymous access.

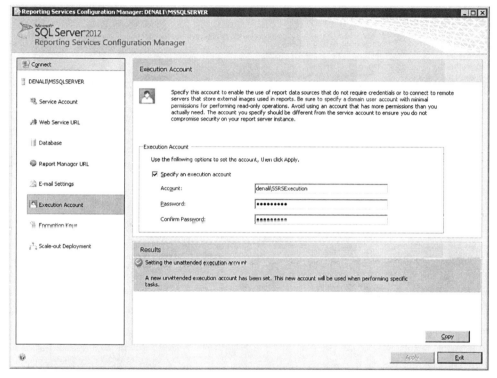

FIGURE 4-15 Configure an execution account to access data or images stored as files on remote servers.

Encryption keys

If you later need to restore the ReportServer database, you need a backup of the encryption key used to store data in that database. You learn more about working with the encryption key in Chapter 25. In the Backup Encryption Key dialog box, type a file location and file name, such as **C:\Backup\ RS.snk**, and provide a strong password.

Note You must create the folder for the file location before you attempt to save the file.

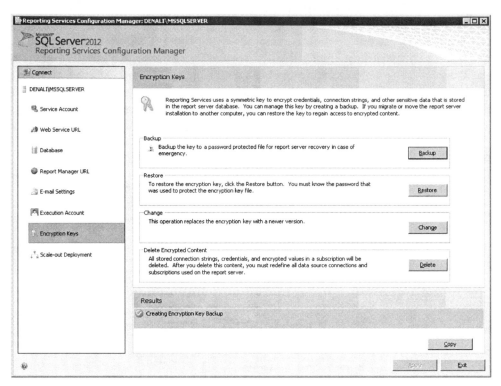

FIGURE 4-16 Back up the encryption key in preparation for an emergency restore of the report server databases.

Scale-out deployment

In a scale-out deployment, only one set of report server databases is used, as we explained in Chapter 3, "Understanding deployment scenarios." Using Reporting Services Configuration Manager, you connect to a report server that is already part of a scale-out deployment (or the first server in the scale-out deployment), and then use the Scale-Out Deployment page, shown in Figure 4-17, to add one or more report servers to the scale-out.

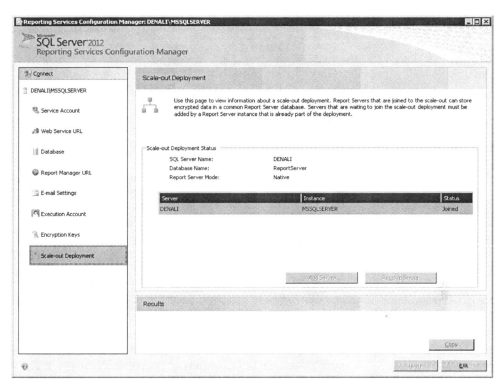

FIGURE 4-17 Add another report server to create a scale-out deployment.

Configuring partial integration with SharePoint

For partial integration of a native-mode report server with a SharePoint product, you can install SharePoint 2.0 Web Parts on your SharePoint server. These Web Parts are compatible with Windows SharePoint Services 2.0, Windows SharePoint Services 3.0, Microsoft SharePoint Portal Server, Microsoft Office SharePoint Server 2007, SharePoint Foundation 2010, and SharePoint Server 2010. When installed, you can select the Report Viewer or Report Explorer Web Parts from the Web Part Gallery to add to a SharePoint Dashboard, as we show you in Chapter 26, "Accessing reports online."

To install the Web Parts, you must copy the RSWebParts.cab file from C:\Program Files (x86)\Microsoft SQL Server\110\Tools\Reporting Services\SharePoint on the report server to a folder on your SharePoint server. You can then open a Command Prompt window and navigate to the folder containing the STSADM.EXE file. For example, if you are working with SharePoint Server 2010, navigate to C:\Program Files\Common Files\Microsoft Shared\web server extensions\14\BIN. In the Command Prompt window, execute the following command (replacing the path to the CAB file if necessary):

```
STSADM.EXE -o addwppack -filename "C:\RSWebParts.cab" -globalinstall
```

Configuring SharePoint for local mode reporting

You can add basic reporting capabilities to SharePoint Server 2010 by using the local mode feature of Reporting Services. This approach works only for reports that use a SharePoint list as a data source. You develop reports by using this data source type just as you would develop reports for a report server, but you must manually upload these reports to a document library. Users can then open the reports by using the same Report Viewer available for SharePoint integrated-mode reports, as we show you in Chapter 26. However, the document library does not support management of local mode reports. For example, you cannot configure execution properties nor can you set up a subscription.

 Note If you want to use another data source with local mode reporting, you must develop a custom data processing extension.

To set up your SharePoint server to support local mode reporting, you must install the SQL Server 2012 Reporting Services Add-In. We describe how to do this later in this chapter in the "Installing the Reporting Services Add-in for SharePoint" section. Your next step is to enable the ASP.NET session state. If you have implemented Access Services in your SharePoint farm, this step is complete. Otherwise, you must open the SharePoint 2010 Management Shell and execute the following Windows PowerShell command (replacing the database name *SPSessionState* with a name of your own choosing):

```
Enable-SPSessionStateService –DatabaseName "SPSessionState"
```

After this command completes successfully, you open a command prompt window to execute the IISreset command.

Configuring SharePoint integrated mode

As we discuss in Chapter 2, you can integrate the Reporting Services report server with SharePoint Server 2010 to deliver most (but not all) of the capabilities that the native-mode report server provides. To do this, you must install both the add-in component for SharePoint and the integrated-mode report server as described in the "Installing SQL Server 2012" section. In addition, you must configure SharePoint for integration with Reporting Services. The order in which you install Reporting Services and SharePoint on a server doesn't matter, but you must follow the configuration steps in sequence as described in this section.

Note If you install Reporting Services first, you will see an error after installation of the SharePoint prerequisites that the SQL Server 2008 R2 Reporting Services Add-in could not be installed. Installation of the SQL Server 2012 Reporting Services Add-in prevents the earlier version from installing. You can safely ignore this warning because the SQL Server 2012 Reporting Services Add-in is the only add-in required.

SharePoint installation

Exploring all the possible ways that you can set up a SharePoint environment is beyond the scope of this book. Here are some resources that you might find helpful:

- If you don't have access to an existing SharePoint server, you can download an evaluation edition of SharePoint Server 2010 at *http://www.microsoft.com/download/en/details .aspx?displaylang=en&id=16631*.

- Follow the instructions to install and configure SharePoint on a single development computer at *http://msdn.microsoft.com/en-us/library/ee554869.aspx*. However, if you plan to also use PowerPivot for SharePoint or Power View, you cannot follow "Step 3: Install SharePoint 2010" as written because you will need to select the Server Farm installation type instead

- If you plan to use Power View, you must install and configure PowerPivot for SharePoint as described at *http://msdn.microsoft.com/en-us/library/ee210708.aspx*.

- If you have a SharePoint farm, you can install Reporting Services on a Web Front End server rather than the SharePoint server. For more information, see *http://msdn .microsoft.com/en-us/library/aa905869(v=sql.110).aspx*.

- If you have an existing SharePoint farm integrated with either SQL Server 2008 or SQL Server 2008 R2 Reporting Services, you can find instructions for performing either an in-place upgrade or a migration at *http://msdn.microsoft.com/en-us/library/ hh231676(v=sql.110).aspx*.

Manual registration of Reporting Services into a SharePoint farm

If you uninstall SharePoint without removing the Reporting Services components and then later reinstall SharePoint, you will find that you cannot reinstall the Reporting Services components because they are still on the computer. However, you will not be able to proceed with configuring SharePoint for Reporting Services integration until you manually register Reporting Services into the SharePoint farm. To do this, run the SharePoint 2010 Management Shell as an administrator, and execute the following command:

```
Install-SPRSService
```

Next, install the service proxy by executing the following command:

```
Install-SPRSServiceProxy
```

Last, start the service by executing the following command:

```
get-spserviceinstance -all |where {$_.TypeName -like "SQL Server Reporting*"} | Start-
SPServiceInstance
```

On successful completion of this last command, the Reporting Services service will be started, which you can verify by opening the Manage Services On Server link in the System Setting section of Central Administration. You can now proceed with all SharePoint integrated-mode configuration tasks.

Important You must install SharePoint Server 2010 SP1 to create a SQL Server 2012 SharePoint integrated-mode report server. You can download the service pack from *http:// www.microsoft.com/download/en/details.aspx?displaylang=en&id=26623*.

Installing the Reporting Services Add-in for SharePoint

To use Reporting Services features in SharePoint, you must install the Microsoft SQL Server 2012 Reporting Services Add-in for Microsoft SharePoint Technologies 2010 on the SharePoint server. This component adds web application pages to SharePoint for managing content and adds a Report Viewer Web Part for viewing reports online and exporting reports to an alternate format. Furthermore, the component adds support for synchronization between the SharePoint content database and the report server database and for custom security to control access to reports and reporting tasks by using the SharePoint security model.

You can use one of the following methods to install this add-in:

- **SQL Server 2012 Setup**   You can use Feature Selection page of the SQL Server 2012 Setup wizard to install the add-in by itself or in conjunction with other features, as we explained in the "Installing SQL Server 2012" section earlier in this chapter. This add-in must be installed on all web front-end servers in a SharePoint farm.

- **Standalone Add-In**   You can download the RSSharePoint.MSI file from *http://www.microsoft .com/download/en/details.aspx?id=29068*. Be sure to select the language applicable to your environment. To install the stand-alone add-in, you must open a command prompt window by using administrator privileges and execute the RSSharePoint.MSI file.

Important   You must be both a SharePoint web farm administrator and a site collection administrator to install the Reporting Services Add-in.

Creating a SharePoint web application

Before you configure the Reporting Services service application in SharePoint, you need to have a SharePoint web application ready. The purpose of this web application is to host the document libraries in which you store reports and data sources. Essentially, the web application defines the URL and port used to connect to those document libraries and stores its content in a database associated with an application you create.

You can use an existing SharePoint web application with Reporting Services, or you can create a new one dedicated to reports. To create a new SharePoint web application, go to the Application Management page of Central Administration, and click the Manage Web Applications link in the Web Applications section. On the ribbon, click the New button. On the Create New Web Application page, shown in Figure 4-18, you can select the type of authentication you want to use, provide a name for the new website, and specify a port number for the application. If this is the first web application created for SharePoint, you can use the default port 80. SharePoint suggests an alternative port number if port 80 is not available, but you can provide a different available port number if you prefer.

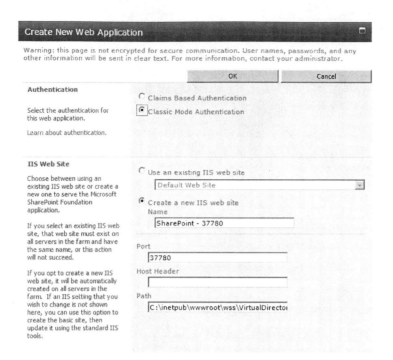

FIGURE 4-18 Create a new web application to host a site for Reporting Services content.

In the Security Configuration section, as shown in Figure 4-19, you can select an authentication provider. Many people find the default authentication provider NTLM to be the easier of the two options to implement. You can select Negotiate (Kerberos) if your network is already configured to use Kerberos security.

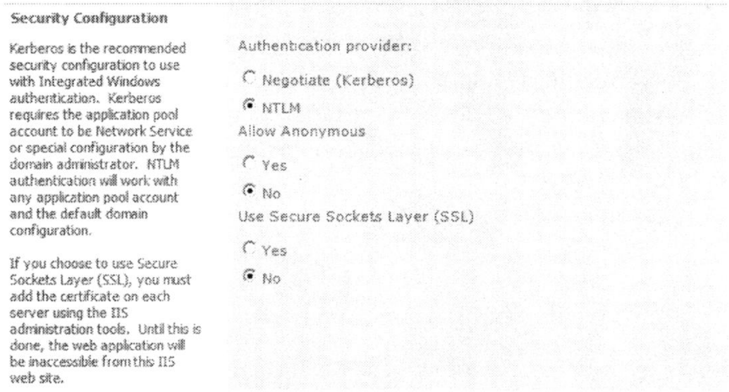

FIGURE 4-19 You must specify the security configuration when creating the web application.

In the Application Pool section, as shown in Figure 4-20, under Create New Application Pool, you can select a built-in service account in the Predefined drop-down list or provide a *managed account* for the application pool. A managed account is a domain user account that you manage within Share-Point rather than in Active Directory.

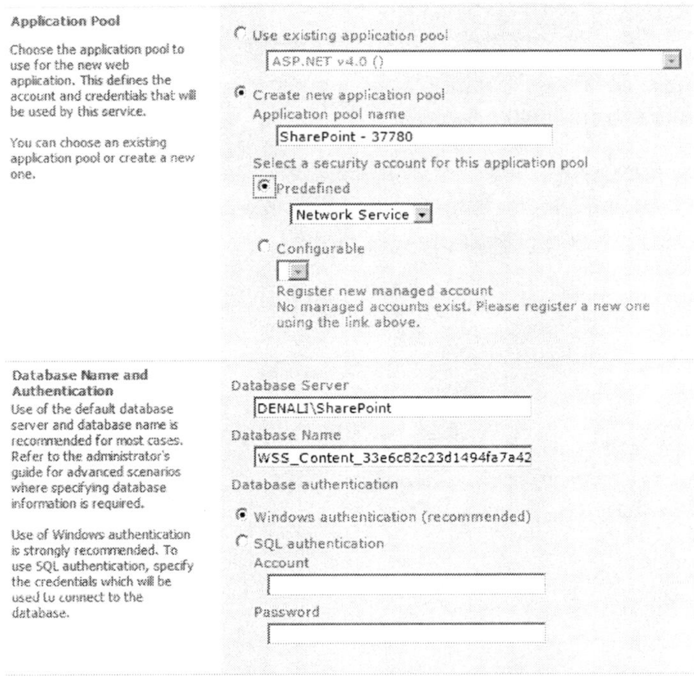

Application Pool

Choose the application pool to use for the new web application. This defines the account and credentials that will be used by this service.

You can choose an existing application pool or create a new one.

○ Use existing application pool
  ASP.NET v4.0 ()

● Create new application pool
  Application pool name
  SharePoint - 37780

  Select a security account for this application pool
  ● Predefined
    Network Service

  ○ Configurable

    Register new managed account
    No managed accounts exist. Please register a new one using the link above.

Database Name and Authentication

Use of the default database server and database name is recommended for most cases. Refer to the administrator's guide for advanced scenarios where specifying database information is required.

Use of Windows authentication is strongly recommended. To use SQL authentication, specify the credentials which will be used to connect to the database.

Database Server
DENAL1\SharePoint

Database Name
WSS_Content_33e6c82c23d1494fa7a42

Database authentication

● Windows authentication (recommended)
○ SQL authentication
  Account

  Password

FIGURE 4-20 You must configure the application pool and security account as well as the database server, database name, and database authentication requirements.

In the Database Name and Authentication section, in the Database Server box, type the name of a database instance to host the content database for the web application. You should keep the default database name to guarantee a unique database name, but you do have the ability change the name here if you prefer. Last, you can keep the default Windows Authentication or provide a user account and password if you prefer to use SQL Authentication when SharePoint connects to the web application's content database.

You can leave the default values for the remaining configuration options for the web application if you have a single-server SharePoint deployment. Otherwise, consult your SharePoint administrator to determine the appropriate settings for the failover server, the search server, and service application connections.

Creating a business intelligence center site

After creating a web application, you can create a SharePoint *site collection* and a *site* to complete preparations within SharePoint for Reporting Services integration. A site collection is a container for one or more sites. In turn, each site is a set of one or more webpages that organize content for a particular purpose, such as team collaboration or document management. To access and view reports, you can use any site that includes a SharePoint document library.

In SharePoint Central Administration, click the Create Site Collections link in the Application Management section. If the web application that you want to use does not display in the Web Application box, click the link in the box, and click Change Web Application. In the Select Web Application – Webpage dialog box, click the correct web application to select it.

On the Create Site Collection page, type a name for your site in the Title box, as shown in Figure 4-21. You can also prepare the Web Site Address for multiple sites by selecting /sites/ in the URL drop-down list, and then type a path for the current site collection.

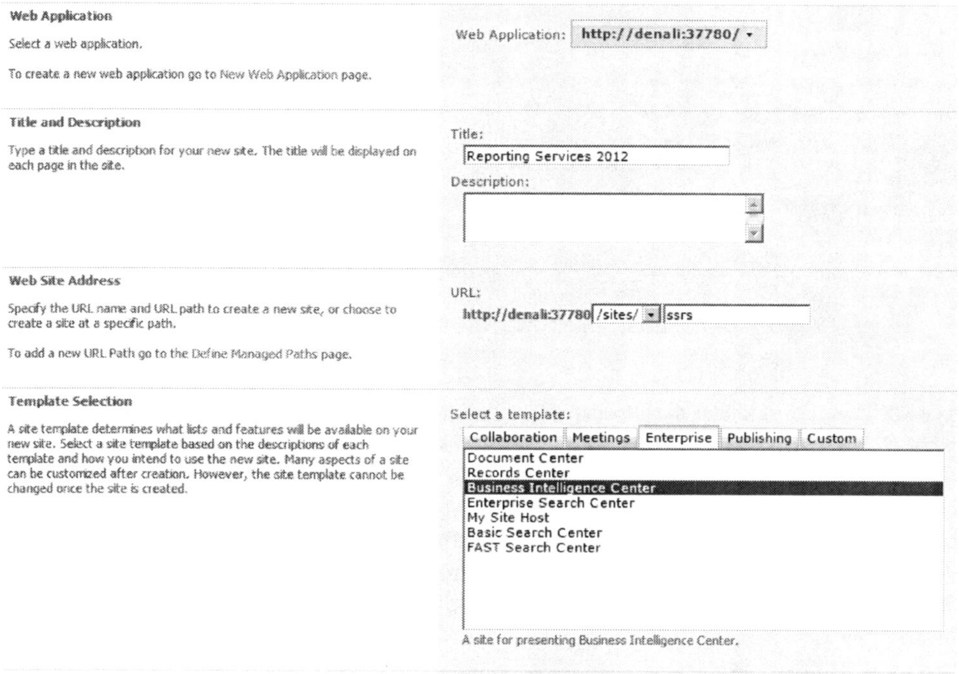

FIGURE 4-21 Use the Business Intelligence Center template to create a site collection for reports.

The Enterprise Edition of SharePoint Server 2010 has a Business Intelligence Center site, which contains document libraries and other business intelligence features that use Reporting Services reports. However, you're not required to use Enterprise Edition to implement Reporting Services in SharePoint integrated-mode. Using the Business Intelligence Center site enables you to integrate Reporting Services reports with other SharePoint content on dashboard pages more easily, which you learn how to do in Chapter 26.

The last required step on this page is to assign a user as the Primary Site Collection Administrator section. You can type a name in the User Name box, and then click the Check Names icon on the right to validate it. You are not required to supply a secondary site collection administrator or to assign a quota template.

Configuring SharePoint for Reporting Services integration

The Reporting Services Add-in modifies the SharePoint Central Administration application pages to add pages that you use to configure Reporting Services. Installation of the SharePoint integrated-mode report server adds the necessary files to the SharePoint server but does not register Reporting Services as a service application or start the service. Therefore, you must perform some additional steps before you can deploy reports to the report server. In this section, we explain how to set up a new service application, how to create a SharePoint web application and a Business Intelligence Center site for storing reports, and how to add the Reporting Services content types to document libraries.

Configuring the service application

After installing the Reporting Services components, you must create and then configure the service application. To do this, you can use the graphical interface in SharePoint Central Administration or use Windows PowerShell cmdlets.

> **Tip** Refer to *http://msdn.microsoft.com/en-us/library/gg492278(v=sql.110).aspx#bkmk_powershell_create_ssrs_serviceapp* for information about using Windows PowerShell cmdlets to configure the Reporting Services service application.

In SharePoint Central Administration, click the Manage Service Applications link in the Application Management section. On the SharePoint ribbon, click the New button and select SQL Server Reporting Services Service Application. In the Create SQL Server Reporting Services Service Application dialog box (shown in Figure 4-22), provide a name for the service, and specify the application pool under which Reporting Services runs. You can use an existing application pool or create a new one. If you create a new application pool, you can select or add a managed account as the application pool identity.

Next, you identify the SQL Server that will host the Reporting Services database. SharePoint assigns a default database name by appending a global unique identifier (GUID) to a base name of *ReportingService*. You can change this name if you like, but you must take care to ensure that the database name is unique for each Reporting Services service application that you create. You must also specify the authentication used to connect to the Reporting Services database. Typically, you use Windows Authentication, but you can supply an account and password as Stored Credentials if you need to use SQL Authentication instead.

Behind the scenes, the configuration process creates three report server databases rather than the two that are used in a native-mode implementation—one for storing server and catalog data; another for storing cached data sets, cached reports, and other temporary data; and a third for data-alert management. The database names share the same unique identifier that is assigned to the service application, which means that you can create multiple service applications for Reporting Services in the same SharePoint farm.

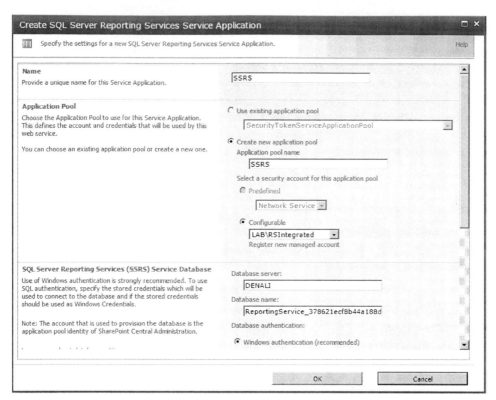

FIGURE 4-22 Configure the integrated server by creating a Reporting Services service application.

Important If SharePoint uses the Express Edition of SQL Server for storing the configuration and content databases, you cannot use the same database instance for storing the Reporting Services databases, as we explained in the "Choosing a Database Engine edition" section earlier in this chapter. You must specify another SQL Server database instance.

The last step is to associate the service application with one or more web applications. You can associate one Reporting Services service application only to a web application. When you click OK, SharePoint creates the service application and can take several minutes to finish.

After the service application has been successfully created, you can click the Provision Subscriptions And Alerts (which we describe in the next section) or you can click OK to return to the Manage Service Applications page. On that page, you can click the link for the service application that you just created to open the Manage Reporting Services Application page. Here you access many of the same configuration settings for the Reporting Services that you find in the Reporting Services Configuration Manager or in SQL Server Management Studio when working with a native-mode report server.

Note We provide more details about these settings in Chapter 25. In this chapter, we introduce you to the location of these settings and point out the configuration changes you must make to get your SharePoint integrated-mode report server up and running correctly.

The Manage Reporting Services Application page includes the following links:

- **System Settings** You use this page to configure various report server properties. For example, you can set time-out values for retrieving external images, report processing, and report sessions. You can also specify limits for storing snapshots and parameter storage. This page also includes various security settings and client settings.

- **Manage Jobs** This page lists running jobs and allows you to delete a job if necessary.

- **Key Management** You use this page to back up, restore, or change the Reporting Services encryption key or to delete encrypted content in a report server database. When you first configure your service application, you should make a backup of the encryption key.

- **Execution Account** You must specify a domain user and password here to provide the report server with a security context to use when connecting to data on remote servers in the same way that we describe for the same setting in the "Configuring native-mode Reporting Services" section.

- **E-Mail Settings** If you plan to support email subscriptions, you must select the Use SMTP Server check box on this page. Then you can specify the SMTP server to use for forwarding the emails from the report server and provide a valid email account in your computer's domain in the format *sendername@domain*.

- **Provision Subscriptions and Alerts** You use this page to complete the provisioning process for subscriptions and alerts as explained in the next section.

Provisioning subscriptions and alerts

Before you can use subscriptions or data alerts, you must configure SQL Server Agent permissions correctly. One way to do this is to open the Provision Subscriptions And Alerts page as described in the previous section. On that page, you must provide a user name and password for an account that has db_owner permissions on the Reporting Services databases. If you prefer, you can download a Transact-SQL script from the same page, which you can later execute in SQL Server Management Studio.

 Tip You can also use a Windows PowerShell cmdlet to generate the Transact-SQL script. For the syntax and an example, see *http://msdn.microsoft.com/en-us/library/hh231725(v=sql.110).aspx*.

The provisioning process creates the RSExec role if necessary, creates a login for the application pool identity, and assigns it to the RSExec role in each of the three report server databases. If any scheduled jobs, such as subscriptions or alerts, exist in the report server database, the script assigns the application pool identity as the owner of those jobs. In addition, the script assigns the login to the SQLAgentUserRole and grants it the necessary permissions for this login to interact with SQL Server Agent and to administer jobs.

Configuring a SharePoint site

The final step is to configure the SharePoint site to use Reporting Services. First, you might need to activate the Report Server Integration Feature. If you are implementing Power View in SharePoint, you must also activate the Power View Integration Feature and PowerPivot Feature Integration For Site Collections. Then you add SharePoint content types to the document libraries in the site in which you want to use reports, data sources, and report models. The Business Intelligence Center site template includes two document libraries to which you should add the Reporting Services content types, Documents and Data Connections. You can also add Reporting Services content types to any document library in a site collection in which the Report Server Integration Features has been activated.

To activate the Report Server Integration Feature or the Power View Integration Feature, open your browser and navigate to the top-level site of the site collection you want to activate. Click the Site Actions link in the upper-left corner, and select Site Settings from the Site Actions menu. In the Site Collection Administration section, click the Site Collection Features link, and then click the Activate button to the right of the feature you want to activate.

Note The Power View Integration Feature is available only if you are using SharePoint Server 2010 Enterprise.

To update the content types on the document libraries, you must configure the library settings. Start by clicking the Data Connections link in the Quick Launch panel on the left. Next, click the Library tab in the ribbon, and then click the Library Settings button in the ribbon. If Report Data Source does not appear in the Content Type list, click Add From Existing Site Content Types and then select Report Data Source in the Available Site Content Types list, click the Add button, as shown in Figure 4-23, to update the Data Connections library. If you plan to use Power View on this site, you can also add the BI Semantic Model Connection here.

Note If the BI Semantic Model Connection does not appear in the Available Site Content Types list, be sure to enable the PowerPivot Feature Integration For Site Collections in the site collection settings.

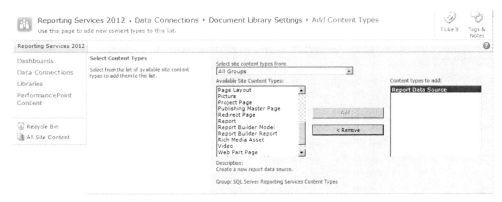

FIGURE 4-23 Add the Report Data Source and BI Semantic Model Connection content types to the Data Connections document library.

Now open the Libraries list by using the Quick Launch link, open the Documents document library, and then open its Document Library Settings page in the same way that you do for the Data Connections document library. This time you must click the Advanced Settings link in the General Setting section to change the library setting to allow management of content types. Then when you return to the Document Library Settings page, click Add From Existing Site Content Types, select both the Report and Report Builder Report content types, and click the Add button. We will explain the purpose of these content types in Chapter 26

Adding another report server

You can distribute the reporting workload across multiple report servers to accommodate high demand. SharePoint automatically manages load balancing when the SharePoint farm includes multiple report servers. To set up an additional application server in your farm, follow these steps:

1. Install SharePoint 2010 on the new server, using the Server Farm installation type and Complete server type. Before you run the SharePoint 2010 Products Configuration Wizard, install SharePoint 2010 SP1.

2. Run the SharePoint 2010 Products Configuration Wizard and select the Connect To An Existing Farm option. You must also specify the database server hosting the configuration database for the farm and the name of that database. In addition, you must provide the farm passphrase.

 Important The database server must be configured to accept remote connections.

3. Use SQL Server 2012 Setup to install the Reporting Services – SharePoint feature as described in the "Installing SQL Server 2012" section of this chapter. It is not necessary to install the Reporting Services Add-in for SharePoint Products.

Note For additional information about adding a report server to the SharePoint farm, see *http://msdn.microsoft.com/en-us/library/hh479774(v=sql.110).aspx*.

Adding another Reporting Services web front-end

Whereas an additional application server helps the SharePoint farm by distributing the processing workload, an additional Reporting Services web front-end (WFE) helps by reducing resource contention problems. You can dedicate server resources on the WFEs to serving pages and application server resources to the applications they support, like Reporting Services. To distribute the users across WFEs, you can implement Windows Network Load Balancing. You can set up a Reporting Services WFE by following these steps:

1. Install SharePoint 2010 on the new server, using the Server Farm installation type and Complete server type. Before you run the SharePoint 2010 Products Configuration Wizard, install SharePoint 2010 SP1.

2. Run the SharePoint 2010 Products Configuration Wizard, and select the Connect To An Existing Farm option. You must also specify the database server hosting the configuration database for the farm and the name of that database. In addition, you must provide the farm passphrase.

Important The database server must be configured to accept remote connections.

3. Use SQL Server 2012 Setup to install the Reporting Services Add-in for SharePoint Products. Do not install the server feature, Reporting Services – SharePoint.

4. Update your Network Load Balancing hardware or software to include the new WFE.

Note To learn more about adding a Reporting Services WFE to the SharePoint farm, see *http://msdn.microsoft.com/en-us/library/hh479775(v=sql.110).aspx*.

Installing Report Builder

The Report Builder component is an alternative client tool for building both managed and ad hoc reports. Power users will appreciate the familiar Office-like appearance. Users can launch Report Builder from Report Manager in a native-mode deployment or from a document library in a SharePoint integrated-mode deployment. We provide a guided tour of Report Builder in Chapter 5, "Exploring Reporting Services fundamentals."

When using Report Builder in this way, the users will always use a version of Report Builder that includes the latest software updates. However, the users must be connected to the network to use this tool. As an alternative, you can install a local copy of Report Builder on selected users' computers. Then these users can work with reports away from the network if the reports use local data sources.

You can download the ReportBuilder3.MSI file from *http://www.microsoft.com/download/en/details.aspx?id=29072*. When you execute the MSI file, a wizard steps you through the installation process. On the Default Target Server page of the wizard, you specify the name of the report server to which reports will be most often deployed. You can always deploy a report to another server, as we explain in Chapter 5. To deploy to a native-mode report server, you define the target server as http://<servername>/reportserver, but you use a URL like http://<servername>/sites/<sitename> for a SharePoint integrated mode report server.

Installing sample databases

Beginning with the release of SQL Server 2008, Microsoft no longer packages sample databases with the installation media. Instead, the sample databases are available for download from the CodePlex community website. The samples in this book use the *AdventureWorksDW2012* sample database for SQL Server 2012, which is a star schema database design typical in data warehouses and often used as a source for reporting. Of course, you can use other database design types in your reports, but a star schema design is easier to query and is useful for learning how to build reports in the report development chapters of this book.

> **Note** A star schema design denormalizes multiple tables in a transactional database into a set of fact tables and dimension tables. A fact table contains numeric columns for data, such as sales, quantities, and columns having foreign key relationships with dimension tables. The foreign key columns function as a compound primary key for the fact table. A dimension table contains a primary key and one or more columns to store attributes relating to a dimension record.

You can obtain the sample databases used for the examples in this book from *http://msftdbprodsamples.codeplex.com*. On that page, click the SQL Server 2012 OLTP and SQL Server 2012 DW item in the grid to see all the samples available for this product release. If you want to run our example reports, click the SQL Server 2012 DW item, and then download and install the following files:

- **AdventureWorksDW2012 Data File**   You use this file for working with the reports based on relational data throughout most of this book. Place the file in the Data folder for the SQL Server database instance, commonly C:\Program Files\Microsoft SQL Server\MSSQL11.MSSQL-SERVER\MSSQL\DATA. Then open SQL Server Management Studio, connect to the Database Engine, right-click the Database folder, and click Attach. In the Attach Databases dialog box, click the Add button, and select AdventureWorksDW2012_Data.mdf. When you return to the Attach Databases dialog box, select the bottom row containing the Log file type and click

Remove. Then click OK to add the database to your server. If you set up an Analysis Services tabular mode instance, you must grant read permission for this database to the service account running the Analysis Services tabular instance.

- **AdventureWorks Multidimensional Models SQL Server 2012**   You use this file for the reports in Chapter 16. Extract the ZIP file, and then open the Standard folder in the extracted files folder. Double-click the AdventureWorksDW2012Multidimensional-SE.sln file to open the project in SQL Server Data Tools. The project assumes the AdventureWorksDW2012 is in the local instance of SQL Server. If it is not, double-click the Adventure Works DW.ds file in the Solution Explorer window and edit the connection string. Then right-click the project name in Solution Explorer, AdventureWorksDW2012Multidimensional-SE, and click Deploy. If prompted, click Overwrite to update the project file.

- **AdventureWorks Tabular Model SQL Server 2012**   You use this file for the examples in Chapters 30 and 31. Extract the ZIP file, open the folder, right-click the AdventureWorks Tabular Model SQL 2012 folder, select Properties, and remove the Read-only attribute on the folder and its subfolders and files. Then double-click the AdventureWorks Tabular Model SQL 2012.sln file to open the project in SQL Server Data Tools. In the Workspace And Deployment Server Configuration dialog box, select a server in the Default Server drop-down list. If the AdventureWorksDW2012 database is not on localhost, double-click the Model.bim file in Solution Explorer. On the Model menu, select Existing Connections and edit the connection string for the SqlServer localhost connection. If the Analysis Services tabular mode instance is not localhost, right-click the project name in Solution Explorer, Adventure Works Tabular Model SQL 2012, and click Properties. Change the Server property, and click OK. Right-click the project name, and click Deploy.

CHAPTER 5

Exploring Reporting Services fundamentals

I n Chapter 2, "Introducing the Reporting Services environment," we describe the variety of features that Reporting Services provides in a complete reporting platform. Then, in Chapter 4, "Installing Reporting Services," we describe how to install and configure all these features. In this chapter, it's time to explore some of these features in each stage of the reporting life cycle. First, you learn about the design environments that you can use to develop reports, and then you learn how to work with a report using Report Builder. You continue your exploration through the life cycle by learning about publishing reports and performing common administrative tasks to manage content on the server. Last, you complete the life cycle by learning how to access your report online.

Understanding design environments

Reporting Services provides three separate design environments: Report Designer, Report Builder, and Power View. Although there is some overlap in the features that each tool provides, there are also distinct features that you find only in one. The mode in which the report server runs, the type of functionality that you want to support in a report, and the data sources that you want to use affect your options.

Comparing design environments

You can use Table 5-1 to compare the characteristics of the three tools and your options for sharing the reports that you produce with each tool.

TABLE 5-1 Comparison of report design environments

Characteristic	Report Designer	Report Builder	Power View
User Interface			
Visual Studio shell for professional report developers	✓		
Integration with custom programs and other BI solutions	✓		

Characteristic	Report Designer	Report Builder	Power View
Source control support	✓		
Update RDL directly	✓		
Business user-friendly environment		✓	✓
Data Sources			
Shared data source creation and use	✓	✓	
Report server shared data source access		✓	✓
Embedded data source creation and use	✓	✓	
Multiple data sources in single report	✓	✓	
Relational data source	✓	✓	
Multidimensional data source	✓	✓	
Data mining model data source	✓	✓	
Tabular model data source	✓	✓	✓
Report model data source	✓	✓	
SharePoint list data source	✓	✓	
XML data source	✓	✓	
Spatial data source	✓	✓	
Datasets			
Shared dataset creation and use	✓	✓	
Report server shared dataset access		✓	
Embedded dataset creation and use	✓	✓	
Graphical query designer	✓	✓	
Text-based query designer	✓	✓	
Run-time query generation based on field selection from model	✓	✓	✓
Query import from SQL files of reports	✓	✓	

Characteristic	Report Designer	Report Builder	Power View
Wizards			
New report wizard	✓	✓	
New data region wizard		✓	
New map wizard	✓	✓	
Report Parts			
Create and publish report parts	✓	✓	
Report part gallery access		✓	
Report Layout			
Multiple data regions in one report	✓	✓	✓
Nested data regions	✓	✓	✓
Grouping, filtering, and sorting	✓	✓	✓
Charts	✓	✓	✓
Advanced charts	✓	✓	
Playable chart (view over time)			✓
Gauges	✓	✓	
Indicators	✓	✓	
Pixel-perfect layout and pagination	✓	✓	
Report parameters	✓	✓	
Document maps	✓	✓	
Conditional visibility	✓	✓	
Interactive sorting	✓	✓	✓
Interactive links	✓	✓	
Interactive highlighted filtering			✓
Slicers and tile containers			✓

Characteristic	Report Designer	Report Builder	Power View
Rendering			
Standard export formats: HTML, CSV, Excel, PDF, TIFF, Word, XML	✓	✓	
ATOM data feed output	✓	✓	
Export to PowerPoint			✓
Print	✓	✓	
Subscriptions	✓	✓	
Report Server			
Native mode	✓	✓	
SharePoint integrated mode	✓	✓	✓
URL Access	✓	✓	

Report Builder versions

Report Builder as a client tool first appeared in SQL Server 2005 Reporting Services as an interface for creating ad hoc reports based exclusively on report models. In SQL Server 2008 Reporting Services, Report Builder 2.0 was introduced as another ad hoc reporting tool, but it supported most of the features available in Report Designer. This design environment was simplified to make it more appealing to business users by providing menus and a ribbon similar to Microsoft Office 2007 products. Despite this simplification, most report design capabilities of Report Designer were also available in Report Builder 2.0, and the report files generated by either tool were interchangeable. The initial Report Builder continued to be available and was renamed Report Builder 1.0 to distinguish the two tools.

SQL Server 2008 R2 Reporting Services included yet another tool, Report Builder 3.0, which was the successor to Report Builder 2.0. It included some additional features, such as easier report development with more wizards and access to report parts. Report Building 3.0 also added caching of data to improve performance when previewing reports during development.

In a SQL Server 2008 R2 Reporting Services deployment, it was possible to allow users to use any of these three tools. Now, in SQL Server 2012 Reporting Services, there is only one tool known as Report Builder, which you should not confuse with the tool available with SQL Server 2005 Reporting Services. You can think of it as Report Builder 4.0, but the version number has dropped, ostensibly to avoid confusion.

Choosing a report designer

Report development is the first phase of the reporting life cycle, but first you must choose the report designer tool to use during this phase. As you can see in Table 5-1, there is considerable overlap between Report Designer and Report Builder, and less overlap between those tools and Power View. One way to choose a report designer is to match the tool to the skill level of the user. Another way is to select the tool according to the type of output desired or the type of interactions the report must support.

Using Report Designer

Most report developers use Report Designer because it has the most complete feature set, and it has been part of the Reporting Services platform since the release of the initial version. Report Designer (which you access in SQL Server Data Tools [SSDT]) fully integrates with the Visual Studio 2010 integrated development environment (IDE). Report Builder provides a familiar interface for professional report developers and is best for large managed projects because it integrates with source control systems. If you often work with multiple reports, SSDT is the again the best choice because you can copy and paste elements from report to report. In addition, you can deploy reports as a group.

Another reason to use Report Designer is the ability to work within the same environment if you are calling an assembly to calculate a value or implementing a custom extension for rendering. The solution that contains your report-server project can include another project for the class library that you develop for the custom assembly. You must have a license for Visual Studio 2010 to support this capability.

Last, you can use this environment to author reports for Reporting Services 2008, Reporting Services 2008 R2, or Reporting Services 2012. You specify the target schema as a project property, and the deployment process validates the reports to alert you to potential problems when a design feature in a report is not supported by the target schema.

Because the primary audience for Report Designer is the professional report developer, the self-service features available in Report Builder are not available. Consequently, the report developer must manually create data sources or data sets or manually add existing files to the report project. There is no built-in mechanism for retrieving these items or published report parts from the report server.

Report Designer produces an RDL file that you publish to either a native-mode or SharePoint integrated-mode report server. Users can export the report to all the standard formats supported by Reporting Services or print the output. To produce the best possible layout using Report Designer, the report developer must understand how the users plan to export or print reports.

 Note The chapters in Part II, "Developing reports," and Part III, "Adding data visualizations," explain everything you need to know about working with Report Designer.

Using Report Builder

Report Builder is simple enough for a business user and yet includes enough features to satisfy a more technically skilled report developer. It is available as an application that users can launch from Report Manager or from a SharePoint integrated-mode document library. It is also available as a separate download to install on a user's computer.

Report Builder has a look-and-feel similar to an Office 2007 application. It uses a similar color scheme and includes a ribbon interface. Report Builder supports all the same report design features that you find in Report Designer but within an environment that business users find to be more user-friendly. It shares the same layout surface and dialog boxes as Report Designer. This application is a good option if you typically work with one report at a time and are producing reports for personal consumption.

Less technically skilled users can import queries from other reports, or they can use shared datasets and thereby avoid the need to write SQL. More advanced users have the ability to write their own queries by using any of the data sources supported by Report Designer. Also, Report Builder provides access to the Report Gallery, which allows users to search for reusable report parts that have been published to the report server so that users can focus on combining existing items rather than building a report from scratch. Report Builder supports multiple datasets, multiple data regions, and almost everything else that you can do in Report Designer. The primary limitation with this application is the requirement to work with only one report at a time.

Like Report Designer, Report Builder produces an RDL file that you publish to either a native-mode or SharePoint integrated-mode report server. Report Builder also gives you the same degree of control over the layout of the report so that you can design the report for multiple types of rendering formats or for print.

> **Note** The "Developing a report with Report Builder" section of this chapter introduces you to the fundamental concepts of report development by using Report Builder. You also learn how to use the unique wizards that it provides and about the features that it includes that are not available in Report Designer. Even if you plan to use Report Builder only, you should review the chapters in Parts II and III to learn about additional features that are applicable to both Report Designer and Report Builder.

Using Power View

Power View is tool that provides a completely different report development experience than Report Designer and Report Builder. It is a Silverlight application that runs in the user's browser and connects to a tabular data model as the sole data source. The tabular data model is either a workbook deployed to a PowerPivot for SharePoint service or a model deployed to a tabular-mode instance of Analysis Services. The benefit of the tabular model as a data source is that it insulates the user from the technical details of integrating multiple data sources, defining relationships between fields, and creating calculations.

Power View provides the user with a highly interactive and visual experience for exploring data. It does not require a significant investment of time to learn how to use it. The user can quickly and easily set up the report and then continually refine it and see the results of each change immediately on the design surface. Although Power View supports advanced filtering and multiple styles of data visualizations, it does not include as many features for fine-tuning the appearance and the layout as you find in the two other tools. Its primary purpose is to support ad hoc analysis rather than development of print-ready reports.

You can save the final report as an RDLX file that you save to a SharePoint document library, but you cannot print the report from within SharePoint. However, you can export the report as a PowerPoint file. As long as you have a live connection to SharePoint and the tabular model when viewing a PowerPoint slide containing a Power View report, you can interact with the report within PowerPoint. If you need a print version of the report, you can print the PowerPoint slide.

Note You learn about your options for ad hoc interactive reports in Chapter 31, "Using Power View."

Developing a report with Report Builder

You can use Report Builder to develop both ad hoc and managed reports. It has a ribbon interface to organize commonly used commands for adding items to a report, formatting report items, and setting display options. Report Builder is very similar in functionality to Report Designer, although the interface is different and you are limited to working on one report at a time.

Launching Report Builder

The steps you perform to launch Report Builder depend on whether you rely on the report server to provide the most current version of Report Builder or whether you maintain a local installation of Report Builder on your computer. The more common approach is to launch Report Builder from the report server to ensure that each user always has the most current version, as service packs are applied to the server over time.

Note Report Builder is available on the report server by default, unless you use role security to prevent a user or group from using the feature, as we explain in Chapter 24, "Securing report server content," or disable the feature at the server level, as we explain in Chapter 25, "Performing administrative tasks."

Native mode

The Report Builder button is available on the Report Manager toolbar from any folder that you can open on the report server. When you click the button, the report server uses ClickOnce technology to check whether the application already exists on your computer. If it does not, a security warning displays, requesting your permission to run the application. When you click the Run button, the application downloads, installs the program files, and then opens Report Builder. Each subsequent time that you click the Report Builder button from Report Manager, the report server downloads any updates as applicable and then opens Report Builder.

SharePoint integrated-mode

To launch Report Builder on a SharePoint integrated-mode report server, you must open a document library that has been configured to include the Report Builder Report content type. On the Documents tab of the ribbon, click the arrow to the right of the New Document icon, and then click Report Builder Report. Just as with a native-mode report server, the ClickOnce technology checks for the existence of the application and downloads it or any applicable update if necessary. You must authorize the download if the program does not already exist on your computer. Even if you have previously downloaded Report Builder from a native-mode report server, you must install another copy of Report Builder to use with a SharePoint integrated-mode report server.

> **Note** We describe how to add the Report Builder Report content type to a SharePoint document library in Chapter 4.

Stand-alone application

When you install Report Builder as a stand-alone application, as we describe in Chapter 4, you can start the application from the Microsoft SQL Server 2012 Report Builder program group on the Start menu. You then select Report Builder to open the application window. There is no functional difference between the version of Report Builder that you install from the report server or the one that you install as a stand-alone application. However, if Microsoft releases an update to Report Builder, you must download the new stand-alone version and reinstall the application.

Getting Started Wizard

The first time you open Report Builder, the Getting Started Wizard displays, as shown in Figure 5-1. If you prefer not to use this wizard, you can select the Don't Show This Dialog Box At Startup check box in the lower-left corner and then close the window. Otherwise, you use the wizard to help you start a new task, which is helpful when you are unfamiliar with the tool. You can choose from the following options:

- **New Report**   When you start a new report, you can use another wizard to guide you through the process of designing a table or matrix, a chart, or a map. These data region wizards are also available from the ribbon if you to prefer to start a different task first. For example, you can bypass the use of a wizard altogether and start a blank report.

> **Note** We describe how to use the wizards in the "Using data region wizards" section of this chapter. Whether you launch these wizards from the Getting Started Wizard or from the ribbon, the wizard steps are identical.

- **New Dataset**   Rather than start with the report layout, you can use the dataset designer to create a shared dataset that you can publish to the report server for reuse across multiple reports. A shared data source or report model must be available on the report server before you can use this option.

> **Note** A shared data source is a file that describes the location and format of data, whereas a shared dataset is a file that describes the query that retrieves data from the source. Chapter 8, "Retrieving data for a report," explains these concepts in greater detail.

- **Open**   When a report already exists on the report server, you can use this option to navigate to the folder containing the report and then open it for editing in Report Builder. When you have finished making changes, you can save the modified version to your local computer or to a network share, overwrite the report server version with the modified version, or save the report with a new name (or even to a location) on the report server.

- **Recent**   After you open a report, even if you don't make changes to it, a shortcut to that report appears in the Recent list. That way you can easily return to a report that you view often or to one that you changed recently.

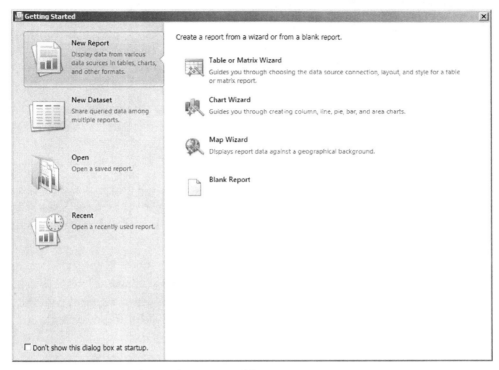

FIGURE 5-1 Getting Started Wizard in Report Builder.

Using the dataset designer

When you have a data source available, you can define a *dataset* to retrieve data for your report. A dataset is a container for the information used by the Report Processor to execute a query and return results, such as a pointer to the data source, the query string to execute, and a field list describing the data types of the query results. Using the New Dataset option in the Getting Started Wizard, you first select a shared data source from a list of recently viewed shared data sources or use the Browse Other Data Sources link to locate a shared data source in a folder on the report server. Then you click the Create button in the lower-right corner of the wizard to display the dataset designer, as shown in Figure 5-2.

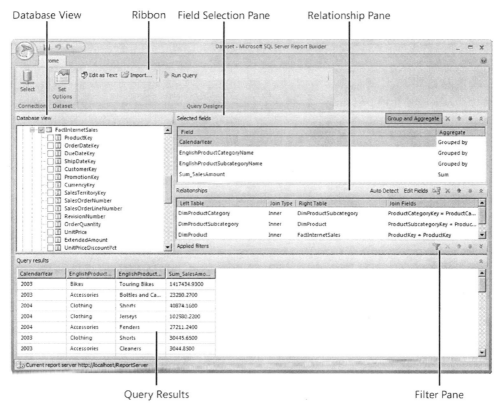

Database View   **Ribbon**   **Field Selection Pane**   **Relationship Pane**

Query Results   **Filter Pane**

FIGURE 5-2 Creating a dataset in the dataset designer.

The following groups are available on the ribbon at the top of the dataset designer:

- **Connection** You use the Select command to change the data source or create a new data source if you did not select one before opening the dataset designer. You can select only an existing shared data source from a report server. There is no option to create one here.

- **Dataset Options** The Set Options command allows you to set the dataset properties for fields, collation, filters, and parameters. Chapter 8 describes these properties in detail.

- **Query Designer** The Edit As Text command allows you to toggle to a text editor in which you type the query string rather than make selections in each pane of the graphical editor, which is the default view of the dataset designer. As an alternative, you can use the Import command to retrieve a query from a SQL file or from another report definition file. Regardless of how you construct the query, you use the Run Query command to execute the query and view the results at the bottom of the dataset designer.

On the left side of the dataset designer is the Database View pane, which shows you the fields available from the selected data source. If the data source is relational, like a SQL Server database, you see fields organized by tables, views, and stored procedures. To include a field in the dataset, select the check box in the Database View pane.

Each field that you choose appears in the Selected Fields pane on the right side of the dataset designer. If you want to aggregate the results rather than return each record from the data source, you can choose an aggregate function in the Aggregate drop-down list. A quick way to add groupings and aggregations is to focus first on one of the fields that you want to aggregate. For example, you can select Sum for a numeric field or Count for a non-numeric field. When you select an aggregate function for one field, the function for all other fields is set automatically to Grouped By. Then you can apply the correct aggregate function to other fields as needed.

The Relationships pane appears below the Selected Fields pane and is collapsed by default. If you use fields from one table only, no relationships exist. However, when you use fields from multiple tables, you must define relationships correctly to get the correct results. Sometimes the query will not execute until you correct the relationships. To work with the relationships, click the double arrows to expand the Relationships pane and then click the Auto Detect button to enable editing. Next, click the Add Relationship button (to the left of the double arrows). Click the Left Table box to open a panel from which you select one table, and then click the Right Table box to select the related table. If necessary, you can use the Join Type drop-down list to change from the default of Inner to Left Outer, Right Outer, or Full Outer.

Tip Take care not to click the Add Relationships button too many times. If you add a relationship but neglect to define tables for that relationship, the query will fail. You can select the empty row and click the Delete button (to the right of the Add Relationships button) to remove the relationship.

Click the Join Fields box to check the related fields and remove any extra relationships that will change your query. For example, when working with the sample database *AdventureWorksDW2012*, a query that uses DimDate and FactInternetSales requires a relationship between those two tables. When you add a relationship, the dataset designer uses three join fields because FactInternetSales has three columns that related to DimDate. However, most queries focus on using only one of those three dates. Therefore, you must remove the join fields that are not required for your query.

You can also filter a query if you want to reduce the number of rows to return from the data source. Usually it's better to apply a dataset filter because the Database Engine can perform filtering quickly and the resulting network traffic is less. To do this, click the Add Filter button in the Filter pane. Click the Field Name box to open a panel from which you select a field. Then choose an operator, such as Is or Is Not, and click the Value field to type a comparison value. You can select the Parameter check box to allow the user to change the filter when executing the report.

Tip Sometimes it's better to retrieve all data from the data source and then apply the filter in the report. We explain the advantages of filtering in the report in Chapter 14, "Creating dynamic reports with parameters."

When you click the Close button in the upper-right corner of the window, a message box displays to prompt you whether to save the changes to the dataset. If you choose Yes, you must save the dataset as an RSD file to your computer, the network, or the report server. After you provide a name and save the shared dataset, Report Builder closes. The shared dataset is now available for use by anyone having permission to access the file.

Getting familiar with the Report Builder interface

When you select the Blank Report option or disable the Getting Started Wizard, Report Builder displays in its own application window, as shown in Figure 5-3. Across the top of the application window is the ribbon that organizes commands into logical groups. On the left side of the application window is the Report Data pane, which organizes information used in the report, such as built-in fields, report parameters, images, data sources, and data sets. At the bottom of the application window is the Grouping pane, which displays groups that you create in the report layout. In the center of the application window is the report design surface, which you use to arrange and configure report items.

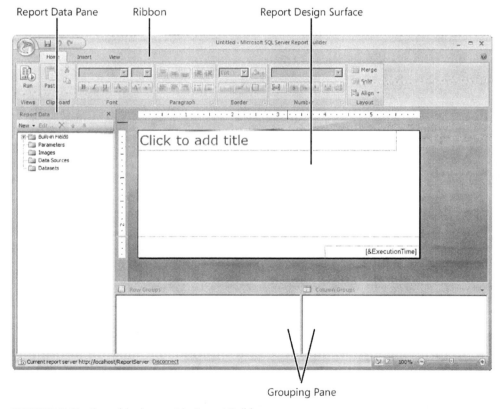

FIGURE 5-3 Starting a blank report in Report Builder.

The Home tab on the ribbon, shown in Figure 5-4, contains commands that you use to preview the report, to copy and paste objects, and to apply formatting to items that you add to the report. Whether you use a wizard to add a data region to the report or manually add one, the contents of each text box in the data region use an Arial 10pt font by default. You can set properties for each text box individually, but it's easier to select one or more text boxes and use the ribbon commands to improve the formatting.

FIGURE 5-4 The Home tab of the Report Builder ribbon.

On the Home tab, there are seven groups of commands:

- **Views**   When you are in the Design view, this group contains the Run command to preview the report. When you are in the Report preview, this group contains the Design command to return to the Design view.

- **Clipboard**   You can use the Clipboard to cut, copy, and paste report items.

- **Font**   To format text, you can select a font style, size, color, and other properties just as you do when you work with word processing software like Microsoft Word.

- **Paragraph**   You can choose a command to align text horizontally or vertically within a text box, to increase or decrease the indent level of a paragraph, or to start a bulleted or numbered list.

- **Border**   You can select a command to define properties for a text box border, including border width, line color, style, and fill color.

- **Number**   You can use these commands to format numerical values. The drop-down list includes standard formats such as Number, Currency, and Date, among others. The Placeholder Styles command allows you to toggle between the default display of a placeholder with a sample value, as shown below, after you change the standard format from General to one of the other available formats. This group also includes commands to quickly add or remove a comma as a thousands separator or to add or remove decimal places.

Calendar Year	Sales Amount
[CalendarYear]	[$12,345.00]

- **Layout**   You can merge or split cells in a data region or align the edges of multiple items that you select in the report design surface.

In the lower-right corner of the Font, Paragraph, Border, and Number groups, you can click an arrow to open the corresponding page of the Text Box Properties dialog box shown in Figure 5-5. In the dialog box, you can access many properties that you can change by using the ribbon commands. For example, click the arrow in the Number group to open the Number page where you can change properties to control the display of zero, the appearance of negative numbers, the applicable currency symbol, and more.

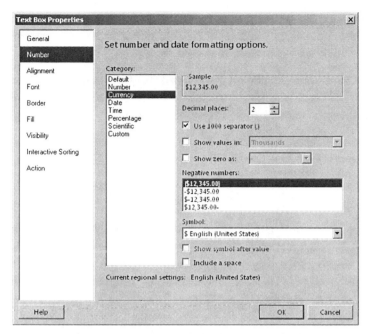

FIGURE 5-5 The Text Box Properties dialog box is accessible by using the arrows on the Home tab of the ribbon.

To add items to your report, you use the Insert tab, show in Figure 5-6. These same items appear in Report Designer, although the method to add them to your report layout differs. In Report Builder, you simply click an item to add it to your report. In some cases, you can choose whether to add the item directly to the report or use a wizard to step you through the process of associating data fields with the item.

FIGURE 5-6 The Insert tab of the Report Builder ribbon.

On the Insert tab, there are six groups of commands:

- **Parts** A *report part* is a reusable element in a report such as a table or a parameter. The Report Parts command opens the Report Part Gallery, from which you can select a report part to add to your report. Chapter 29, "Reusing report parts," provides more information about this feature.

- **Data Regions** A *data region* is a special type of report item that you add to the report layout and is bound to a data set, such as a table, matrix, or list. When using Report Builder, you can add one or more data regions to your report. You learn the basics about data regions in Chapter 9, "Designing the report layout."

- **Data Visualizations** Report Builder includes many different types of data regions known as *data visualizations*. You use data visualizations to summarize data in graphical form. Some data visualizations stand alone in a report, such as a chart, while others appear within other data regions, such as a data bar. Part III, "Adding data visualizations," includes several chapters to help you explore your options for communicating data visually.

- **Report Items** You use report items to add graphical elements, such as an image or line to a report. Using a text box, you can display static text, such as a report title, or text from a data set. Chapter 9 includes examples of using each of these report items.

- **Subreports** A *subreport* is a report item used to display another report inside the current report and is described in more detail in Chapter 9.

- **Header & Footer** The header and footer are optional sections of a report page that you can remove if you prefer not to use them.

On the View tab of the ribbon, shown in Figure 5-7, there is one group, Show/Hide. You use the check boxes in this group to toggle the display of the Report Data pane, the Grouping pane, the Properties pane, and the Ruler. The Properties pane is disabled by default when you first open Report Builder. It behaves like the Properties pane in Microsoft Visual Studio by listing the properties associated with a report item selected on the design surface. The ruler is useful for sizing and positioning report items on the design surface.

FIGURE 5-7 The View tab of the Report Builder ribbon.

Tip Sometimes you might find it easier to work on your report when you hide all the panes, thereby maximizing the design surface in the application window. Alternatively, you might keep the Properties pane open if you prefer to use it rather than the ribbon commands or the dialog box for a report item's properties.

Adding a data source

Before you can build a report, you must add a data source to the report definition to identify the source of the data that you'll display in the report. A data source provides the information necessary for executing queries to the report processor, such as a data source type, a connection string, and authentication information. You can use a shared data source that has been published to the report server, or you can add a new data source in Report Builder.

You can add a new data source as one of the steps that you perform when using one of the data region wizards, or you can add a new data source by clicking New in the Report Data pane and selecting Data Source. Either way, you use the Data Source Properties dialog box and provide a name for it.

Tip It's considered good practice to provide a more meaningful name than DataSource1, such as the name of a database, to make it easier for yourself and others to recognize the source of the data if it becomes necessary to modify the report later.

If you create a data source when using a data region wizard, your only option is to create an *embedded data source*, which means the data source is associated only with this report. Otherwise, you must choose whether to create a shared or embedded data source. In Chapter 8, we explain the pros and cons of this choice.

Report Builder allows you to connect to the same twelve types of data sources that Report Designer supports: Microsoft SQL Server, Microsoft SQL Azure, Microsoft SQL Server Parallel Data Warehouse, Object Linking and Embedding Database (OLE DB), Microsoft SQL Server Analysis Services, Oracle, Open Database Connectivity (ODBC), Extensible Markup Language (XML), Microsoft SharePoint List, SAP NetWeaver BI, Hyperion Essbase, and TERADATA. The type of data source that you select determines the structure of the connection string you must provide. For example, a SQL Server data source requires a connection string that contains, at minimum, values for Data Source and Initial Catalog, as shown in Figure 5-8.

Tip Rather than type the connection string, you can use the Build button to open the Connection Properties dialog box, which builds the connection string for you. However, this technique is not an option when you use the following data sources: Parallel Data Warehouse, XML, or SharePoint List.

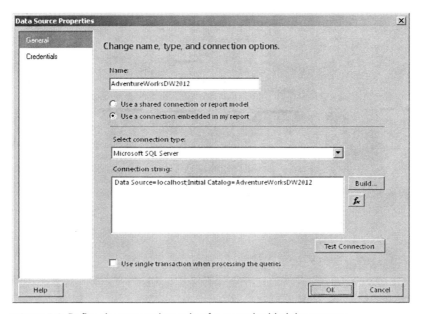

FIGURE 5-8 Define the connection string for an embedded data source.

The data source file must also include information required for authenticating the user at the data source. On the Credentials page of the Data Source Properties dialog box, shown in Figure 5-9, you can provide this information. The Use Current Windows User option is the default method for authenticating a data source. When a user runs the report, the user's Windows account must have permissions to read the data source. If you prefer, you can give a specific user account Read permissions on the database and then select the Use This User Name And Password option and provide the user name and password for that account. A less commonly used approach is the Prompt For Credentials option, which forces the user to type a user name and password before viewing the report. For reports requiring no security at all, you can use the Do Not Use Credentials option.

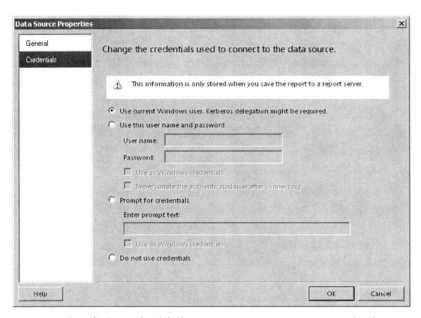

FIGURE 5-9 Specify the credentials the report server uses to connect to the data source.

After you add a data source, it appears in the Report Data pane. A shared data source has an arrow superimposed over the data source icon to distinguish it from an embedded data source, as shown in Figure 5-10.

FIGURE 5-10 Embedded and shared data sources display in the Data Sources folder of the Report Data pane.

Adding a dataset

When using a data region wizard, you have the option to create a new dataset by using a dataset designer similar to the one shown in Figure 5-2. (Refer to the "Using the dataset designer" section to learn more about working with this interface.) After you create the dataset, subsequent steps of the wizard lead you through the process of arranging the dataset fields in the data region layout.

Another option for creating a dataset is to click New in the Report Data pane and select Dataset. In this case, you can select a shared dataset available on the report server or create an embedded data source specific to your report. When you create an embedded data source, you must specify a data source and then provide a query. Your options are to type in the query text, import a query from a SQL file or from another report, use a query designer, or create an expression that evaluates as query text. Regardless of which option you choose, the query text must be compatible with the data source. That is, you cannot use a T-SQL query for an XML data source.

Note The Dataset Properties dialog box that you use in Report Builder for adding a new dataset from the Report Data pane is identical to the one that you use in Report Designer. You can learn how to work with the query designer or set up the query using other techniques, as well as learn about other dataset properties, in Chapter 9.

Each dataset that you add to the report displays in the Datasets folder in the Report Data pane. Just like a shared data source, a shared dataset has an arrow superimposed over its icon, whereas an embedded dataset has an unadorned icon. You can expand each dataset to view the fields that it contains, as shown in Figure 5-11.

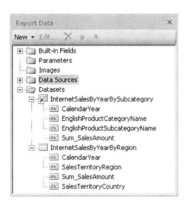

FIGURE 5-11 Embedded and shared datasets display in the Datasets folder of the Report Data pane.

Adding a report title

Report Builder includes a text box at the top of the report that you can use to hold static text for your report title. Click in the text box and type a title. If the title is too wide for the text box, you can drag the right edge of the text box to make it larger. However, if the title is still too wide, the report will render with no problem. By default, the text box will expand vertically and apply word wrap so that the full text of your title is always completely visible. Similarly, you can drag the right edge of the text box to make it smaller. As you move the cursor across the design surface, the current position of the cursor is marked on both the horizontal and vertical rulers, as shown in Figure 5-12, which makes it very easy to resize a report item or move it to a specific location.

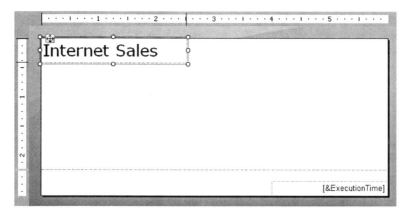

FIGURE 5-12 Resize the report title text box by dragging the right edge left or right as needed.

The format properties of the report title text box default to the Verdana font with a size of 20pt. To change the formatting, click anywhere in the report layout (to remove the selection of the text), and then click the edge of the text box to select it. Now you can use the commands on the Home tab of the ribbon to change the font properties and other formatting as you like.

Using data region wizards

The data region wizards provide an easy way to lay out data on a report when you're new to the report development process. There are three data region wizards available in Report Builder: Table Or Matrix Wizard, Chart Wizard, and Map Wizard. One way to launch a wizard is to select the wizard you want to use in the Getting Started Wizard. Another way is to click the Insert tab of the ribbon and then click the button for the type of data region that you want to add to the report. Regardless of which you choose, the wizards all start similarly by prompting you to select an existing dataset or leading you through the process of creating one. You use the subsequent steps of a wizard to arrange the dataset fields and apply simple formatting.

Table Or Matrix Wizard

The Table Or Matrix Wizard is unique to Report Builder. You begin by selecting the dataset in the Table Or Matrix Wizard, and then you arrange the fields in the dataset as groups. To produce a table, which has a fixed number of columns but a variable number of rows, you arrange text fields only in the Row Groups box and numeric fields in the Value box, as shown in Figure 5-13. When you add a field to the Column Groups box, the wizard produces a matrix, which has a variable number of rows and columns. You learn more about the differences and similarities between a table and a matrix in Chapter 9.

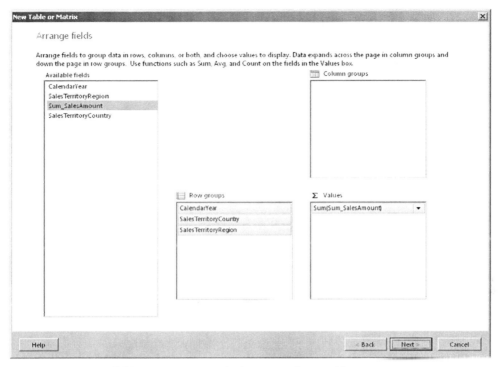

FIGURE 5-13 Arrange fields as row groups and values to produce a table.

The next page of the wizard asks you to choose the layout and includes a preview pane so that you can see how your selection changes the appearance of the data region. You can choose one of the following layout options:

- **Show Subtotals And Grand Totals Blocked, Subtotal Below** This layout option places each group in a separate column and places a subtotal value for each group in rows below the value to sum. The innermost group's subtotal appears as the first row of a *grouping instance* (the set of rows related to a single group value, such as *2001* for CalendarYear), while the outermost group's subtotal appears in the last row for that grouping instance. The last row of the table is the grand total.

- **Show Subtotals And Grand Totals Blocked, Subtotal Above** This layout option also places each group in a separate column but displays the subtotal values for each group in rows above the value to sum. The outermost group's subtotal appears in the top row of a grouping instance, while the innermost group's subtotal appears in the last row for that grouping instance. The last row of the table is the grand total.

- **Show Subtotals And Grand Totals Stepped, Subtotal Above**   This layout option places all groups in the same column but displays the subtotal values for each group in rows above the innermost group's value. The last row of the table is the grand total.

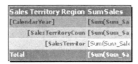

With each of the preceding options, you can also select an additional option, Expand/Collapse Groups. When you do not select this option, a row displays in the table for every row group field, as shown in Figure 5-14. In a matrix, you also see a column display for every column group field. You ignore this option when you want a detailed report without user interaction.

Internet Sales

Sales Territory Region	Sum Sales Amount
2001	3266373.6566
Australia	1309047.1978
Australia	1309047.1978
Canada	146829.8074
Canada	146829.8074
France	180571.6920
France	180571.6920
Germany	237784.9902
Germany	237784.9902
United Kingdom	291590.5194
United Kingdom	291590.5194
United States	1100549.4498
Northwest	415203.4930
Southwest	685345.9568

FIGURE 5-14 Clear the Expand/Collapse Groups option to display all rows and columns in a data region.

You select the Expand/Collapse Groups option when you want the user to drill from a summary value to a detail value, as shown in Figure 5-15. This drill to detail feature works on rows in a table and works on both rows and columns in a matrix. If you want more control over which rows or columns to expand and collapse, you can manually set the Visibility properties, as you learn to do in Chapter 13, "Adding interactivity." This feature works only when the user can interact with the report, such as when the user opens the report online to view it in HTML format or when exporting it to Excel format. If the user exports the report to PDF, the user sees rows or columns in their expanded or collapsed state at the time of export.

Internet Sales

Sales Territory Region1		Sum Sales Amount
⊟	2001	3266373.6566
⊞	Australia	1309047.1978
⊞	Canada	146829.8074
⊞	France	180571.6920
⊞	Germany	237784.9902
⊞	United Kingdom	291590.5194
⊟	United States	1100549.4498
	Northwest	415203.4930
	Southwest	685345.9568
⊞	2002	6530343.5264
⊞	2003	9791060.2977
⊞	2004	9770899.7400
Total		29358677.2207

FIGURE 5-15 Select the Expand/Collapse Groups option to enable drill to detail in a data region.

The final page of the wizard prompts you to choose a style: Corporate, Forest, Generic, Mahogany, Ocean, or Slate. Just like the layout selection, the wizard includes a preview for style selection so that you can see how your choice changes the appearance of the table or matrix. When you finish the wizard, the table or matrix displays on the report design surface.

To style or not to style?

In general, a style is a collection of fonts and color schemes that apply to the data region that a data region wizard produces. It provides a simple way to make a data region look more appealing in the fewest number of clicks possible. You can make changes to these fonts and colors later, but you make the changes to each data region element individually or as a group by using the ribbon or the Properties pane. There is no wizard to adjust the color scheme for the data region as a whole or to adjust the color scheme globally for all data regions in a report.

Chart Wizard

The Chart Wizard is also unique to Report Builder. It begins like the Table Or Matrix Wizard by requiring you to choose an existing dataset or to create one within the wizard. Then you select a chart type, such as a column chart or line chart. Next you arrange the chart fields into category groups, series groups, and values, as shown in Figure 5-16. In general, you can think of category groups as the labels across a horizontal axis and the series groups as the breakdown of categories that you see in a legend. However, the actual implementation of categories and series depends on the chart type, which we discuss in greater detail in Chapter 17, "Creating charts."

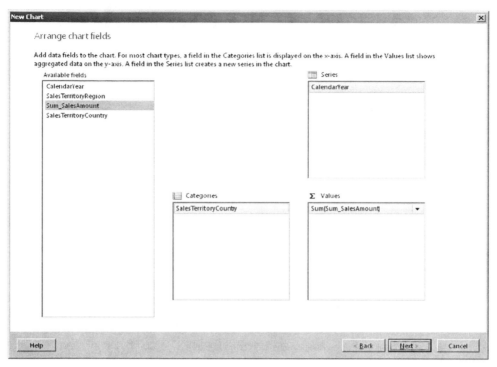

FIGURE 5-16 Arrange fields as category groups, series groups, and values to produce a chart.

On the last page of the wizard, you choose a style in the same way that you do for the table or matrix. Your choice of styles remains the same, and you can preview the style before making the final selection. When you finish the wizard, the chart appears in the report design surface.

Map Wizard

The Map Wizard is the only data region wizard that you can use in both Report Builder and Report Designer. To use it, you must at minimum have data that you can associate with a map of the United States, such as sales by state. You can also use it if you have spatial data in a SQL Server database or in an Environmental Systems Research Institute (ESRI) shapefile. To learn how to use the Map Wizard with any of these three types of spatial data, see Chapter 21, "Mapping data."

Adding a data region manually

The result of using a data region wizard is the placement of a data region on the report design surface with dataset fields assigned to text boxes in the data region and with expressions for subtotals and grand totals. The data region also has some font and color formatting, if you chose the option to apply a style. When you're more familiar with working with data regions and properties directly, you might find it just as easy to add a data region manually and configure its elements as needed.

Note You can use fields from only one dataset in a data region at a time. To display information from multiple datasets in the same report, you must use separate data regions for each dataset. An alternative approach is to use the *Lookup* function, introduced in SQL Server 2008. We explain the *Lookup* function in Chapter 12, 'Using functions."

The steps to add a data region manually in Report Builder are very similar to those you follow in Report Designer. Therefore, in this chapter, we provide only a brief introduction to working with a table. Everything we discuss in later chapters about working with Report Designer is usually applicable to Report Builder too. The most significant difference is that instead of using the toolbar as you do in Report Designer, you use the Insert tab of the ribbon in Report Builder.

As you now know, you can add a table to a new report by launching the Table Or Matrix Wizard. You can also add a table by selecting the Insert Table command on the Insert tab of the ribbon. When you do this, you click the report design surface at the point at which you want to position the top-left corner of the table. A three-column two-row table displays, as shown in Figure 5-17. You can use the crosshairs cursor to drag the table to a more suitable position if you like.

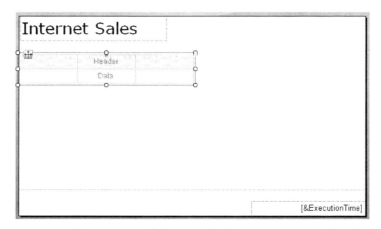

FIGURE 5-17 You can manually insert a table into your report and drag it to the desired position.

Adding fields to a table

A field is a placeholder for data that displays in a data region. In relational database terms, a field represents a column. In this section, you learn two ways to add a field to a table: by dragging fields from the dataset listed in the Report Data pane or by using the Field List icon to update the contents of a text box in place.

Dragging fields from the Report Data pane

One way to add a field to a table is to drag the field from the dataset tree that appears in the Report Data pane and then drop it into one of the cells in the data row. When you add a field to the data row, a column title also displays in the header row, as shown in Figure 5-18. The column title is derived from the field name. Report Builder uses the capitalized letters in the field name to identify separate words and inserts a space between each word. Similarly, if your field name uses an underscore symbol (_) between words, Report Builder replaces the underscore with a space to create a column title.

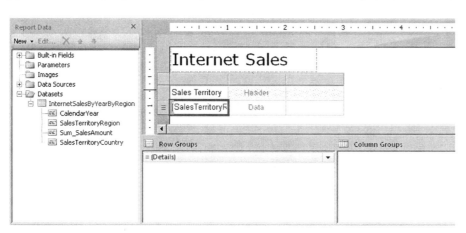

FIGURE 5-18 You drag a field from the Report Data pane to add it to a text box in a table.

Notice that a Details row group displays in the Row Groups section of the Grouping pane. You can access properties associated with the Details row group when you right-click the group in the Grouping pane and then choose Group Properties. You learn more about these properties in Chapter 10, "Working with the tablix."

Notice also that the field in the data row displays with brackets around the field name. This syntax is an expression placeholder for the expression *=Fields!SalesTerritoryRegion.Value,* which is stored in the report definition and evaluated by the Report Processor when executing the report. If you are familiar with earlier versions of Reporting Services, you know that it's sometimes difficult to see the name of a field in a narrow column because only the beginning of the expression is visible. The new expression placeholder display on the design surface allows you to see more easily which field is defined for the text box.

Using the Field List icon

Another way to add a field to a table is to point to a text box in a data row to display the Field List icon, as shown in Figure 5-19. You can then click the Field List icon to view the available fields. When you click a field, Report Builder adds it to the text box.

FIGURE 5-19 Point to a text box to display the Field List icon.

Tip Yet another option is to type a field expression, such as *=Fields!SalesAmount.Value,* directly into the text box, but it's best to use drag-and-drop or use the field list to make sure the spelling and capitalization are correct. Expressions in Reporting Services are case-sensitive, and failure to use the correct case is a common problem for report developers new to Reporting Services.

Adding a total

The table does not include a total row by default, but you can easily add one. Right-click a text box on the data row that contains a numeric value, and select Add Total. Report Builder adds a total row and inserts an expression placeholder into the text box below the one you right-clicked. In Figure 5-20, the expression placeholder holder for the Sum Sales Amount total is *[Sum(Sum_SalesAmount)]*. The full syntax for this expression is *=Sum(Fields!Sum_SalesAmount.Value)*. When you add a total row to the table, the *Sum* aggregate function is used automatically with the field you selected. You learn more about working with aggregate functions in Chapter 12.

Important You must right-click the text box without selecting its text. Otherwise, the shortcut menu will not include the Add Total command. Furthermore, the Add Total command is enabled only for a text box containing a numeric value.

FIGURE 5-20 You can use the Add Total command to add a total row and expression to the table.

Tip You can manually adjust the width of a column by positioning your cursor on the line between column handles and dragging the column to the right to increase the column width, or to the left to decrease the column width.

Grouping data

When you have several detail rows to display in your report, you can organize rows with a common field value into a *group*. For example, you can create a group by CalendarYear to display all sales by sales territory region with a CalendarYear value of *2001* as one group instance and all sales with a CalendarYear value of *2002* as another group instance. You can also display a total for each group instance.

To add a group, right-click a field that you want to place in the group, select Add Group, and select Parent Group in the Row Group section. In the Tablix Group dialog box, select the field to use for grouping in the Group By drop-down list, as shown in Figure 5-21. You can also use this dialog box to control whether the group has a header, a footer, or both.

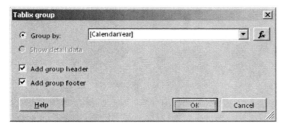

FIGURE 5-21 You use the Tablix Group dialog box to define the field or expression to use for grouping and whether to include a group header or footer in the data region.

Note You might be wondering why this dialog box refers to a Tablix group, when you are working with a table in your report. In the report definition, your table is actually represented as a special type of data region called a *tablix*, which is described in more detail in Chapter 10.

As you add each row group to your table, a new column appears in the table with the field name and a column title, as shown in Figure 5-22. In addition, a group header row appears above the data row and a group footer row appears between the data row and the table total row. Notice the icons in the row handles, which help you identify the details and group. The icon with three horizontal lines indicates the Details group, which currently contains only a single row. The icon spanning three row handles to the left of the Details icon identifies a group containing a group header row, the details row, and a group footer row.

FIGURE 5-22 A new column appears in the table when you add a parent row group to the data row.

You can click the Field List icon in the group footer row and select a numeric field, such as Sum_SalesAmount in this example, to update the table with a subtotal for each CalendarYear value. When you add a numeric field to a group header or footer, the *Sum* aggregate function is added automatically. The expressions in the group footer row and in the total row are identical but yield different results because the scope for each row is different. You learn more about scope and aggregate functions in Chapter 12.

Inserting page breaks

By default, the Report Processor fits as many rows as possible on a single page as determined by the vertical size defined for your report. As each page fills up, the Report Processor inserts a page break to begin a new page. You can override this behavior by configuring a page break for a row group. For example, you can force a page break in your report when the calendar year group instance value changes from *2001* to *2002*.

To add a page break by row group, right-click the applicable group in the Row Groups section of the Grouping pane. In the Group Properties dialog box, click Page Breaks, and then select the Between Each Instance Of A Group check box, as shown in Figure 5-23.

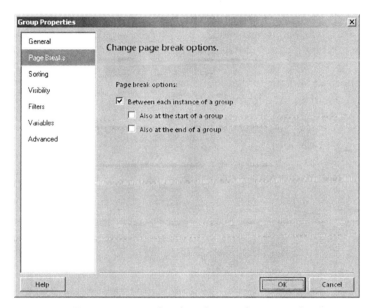

FIGURE 5-23 You can set page break options to place group instances on separate pages.

Formatting a report

You can use a number of properties to control the appearance of individual text boxes in a data region. Rather than set common property values for each text box one by one, you can also set properties for an entire row or column in a data region. After you select a text box or a group of text boxes, you can use several commands on the Home tab to set commonly used format properties, such as font color and style. You can also access many more format properties by opening the Properties pane.

To work with an entire row or column, you click the gray handles along the edge of the data region. If you don't see these handles, click anywhere in the data region to display the handles, and then click the handle. When you select an entire row or column in this way, the property you configure applies to the selected row or column.

For example, when you want to distinguish a table header from other rows in the table, you can select a table header row and set the font to Bold. You can also use the Shading command in the ribbon to set the *BackgroundColor* property for the entire row by choosing a dark shade from the color picker, as shown in Figure 5-24. If the color you want is not available in the color picker, you can click More Colors and choose from a broader assortment of colors.

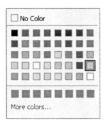

FIGURE 5-24 You use a color picker to set the properties for fonts and background colors.

Likewise, you can apply a consistent numeric formatting to all text boxes in a column by first selecting the column handle. You can then use the ribbon commands or open the Properties pane to provide a format string, as shown in Figure 5-25. You can use any Microsoft Visual Basic .NET format string in the *Format* property.

 Tip For a complete list of permissible format strings, refer to *http://msdn.microsoft.com/en-us/library/dwhawy9k.aspx*.

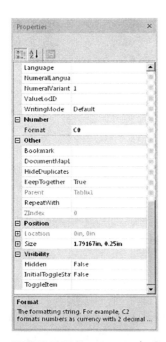

FIGURE 5-25 You can use the Properties pane to set the same property values for a group of text boxes.

Of course, there are many more ways to apply formatting to a report, but this introduction should give you a good understanding of the principles. We explain all the properties you can use to improve a report's appearance in Chapter 9.

Previewing a report

At any time during the report development process, you can preview your report to check your progress by clicking the Run button on the Home tab of the ribbon. You can then switch back to Design view to make changes to the report if necessary. The preview of your report shows you exactly what the report will look like when accessed from the report server. You can also preview the print layout and the export formats before you publish the report.

Another way to open the report preview is to click the Run button (to the right of the Design button) on the status bar, as shown in Figure 5-26. The status bar at the bottom of the application window allows you to toggle between Design view and the preview mode and also lets you use the slider to zoom in and out in either view.

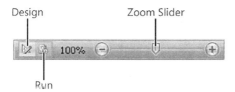

FIGURE 5-26 Use status bar buttons to toggle between design and run mode, and to zoom the view.

When you preview the report, you see only the first page, as shown in Figure 5-27. You can page through the report by clicking the Next button, represented by the blue arrow pointing right on the ribbon. The other commands on the ribbon correspond to the HTML viewer toolbar that we describe in detail in Chapter 26, "Accessing reports online."

The commands on the ribbon allow you to page through the report, skip to a new page, refresh the data by executing queries, print, and export the report to another file format. The Options group contains commands that toggle access to interactive features. Last, you can search a report by using the text box in the Find group.

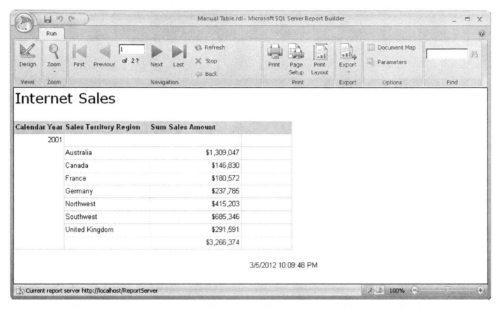

FIGURE 5-27 Preview the report to check the data and appearance before publishing it to the report server.

Saving a report

You can save a report that you created to a local folder for personal use without first publishing it to the report server. To do this, click the Report Builder button in the upper-left corner of the window, and click Save. In the Save As Report dialog box, you can navigate to a folder on your computer, type a name for your report in the File Name box, and click Save.

> **Note** The Save As Report dialog box does not allow you to create a folder. You can save your report to an existing folder only.

Managing a report

The second phase of the report life cycle includes all activities related to managing reports. After a report is published, you can then configure properties that control the report's appearance on the server, its query execution, and processing of the report—to name only a few of the tasks you can perform. In Part IV, "Managing the report server," you learn everything you need to know about report management, but in this section, you explore only a few of the features as a quick introduction to Reporting Services.

Publishing a report

Whether you're using a native mode or SharePoint integrated-mode server doesn't matter during the report development process. However, when you move into the management phase of the report life cycle, the procedures you follow differ, although you'll find that they are very similar. You can publish a report to a report server directly from the report development tool, although there are other publishing methods that you learn about in Chapter 23, "Deploying reports to a server."

Publishing to a native-mode report server

The process to publish a report to a report server is similar to saving a report to your local computer, except that you use a Uniform Resource Locator (URL) reference to find folders in the target report server. Start by clicking the Report Builder button in the upper-left corner of the window, and click Save As. If necessary, click the Recent Sites And Servers icon in the Look In list to open the folders in the default target server, type a name for the report, and click Save.

If you want to publish to a different server, you can type the URL in the Name text box. For example, type **http://<*servername*>/reportserver**, where <*servername*> is the name of your server, and press Enter. Replace Reportserver with the name of the virtual directory that you configured for the web service in Chapter 4 if you used a different virtual director name. When the URL opens, you can navigate to a target folder. When you click Save, Report Builder places the report on the report server.

Publishing to a SharePoint integrated-mode report server

The URL that you use to publish a report to a SharePoint integrated-mode report server depends on the SharePoint document library that you want to contain the report. Start by clicking the Report Builder button in the upper-left corner of the window, and click Save As. If necessary, click the Recent Sites And Servers icon in the Look In list to open the folders in the default target server, type a name for the report, and click Save.

If you have multiple sites and document libraries, the target server might not appear in the Recent Sites And Servers list. In that case, you can type the URL in the Name text box. For example, type **http://<*servername*>/<sitename>**, where <*servername*> is the name of your server and <sitename> is the name of your SharePoint site collection, and press Enter. When the URL opens, you can navigate to a target document library. When you click Save, Report Builder places the report on the report server.

Adding a description

You can add a report description to provide more details about a report, which can help a user decide whether the report contains the information needed. When a user wants to locate a report by using the Search feature in Report Manager, if a match is found in either the report name or its description, the report is included in the search results.

Tip As an alternative, you can add a report description in Report Builder or Report Designer by setting the *Description* property for the report. You can access this property by first selecting the report, by clicking any part of the area surrounding the report design surface, and then locating the *Description* property in the Properties pane.

Open the URL for Report Manager, such as *http://<servername>/Reports*, and navigate to the folder containing the report to which you want to add a description. Point to the arrow to the right of the report name to display the shortcut menu, and click Manage. On the Properties page, type a description in the Description text box, and click Apply. This report description displays on the Contents page in the Report Manager, as shown in Figure 5-28, and is visible only to users who have been granted permission to view the report.

FIGURE 5-28 You can add a report description that helps users understand the contents of a report.

Notice that the default view in Report Manager truncates a long description. When you click the Details View button on the right side of the toolbar, the view includes the entire description.

Note Report descriptions do not display in SharePoint integrated-mode.

Reviewing processing options

You can use a report's processing options to improve the user experience with Reporting Services when the report returns a large volume of data and requires a lot of processing time. By default, a report runs on demand, which means that the query is not executed until the user opens the report. To eliminate waiting time for the user, you can use processing options to implement caching or a report snapshot to execute a report in advance of the user's request for the report. You learn more about the impact of changing processing options in Chapter 23.

Reviewing processing options in Report Manager

Open the URL for Report Manager, such as *http://<servername>/Reports*, and navigate to the folder containing the report that you want to review. Point to the arrow to the right of the report name to display the shortcut menu, and click Manage. Click the Processing Options link in the left frame of the page to view the Processing Options page, shown in Figure 5-29.

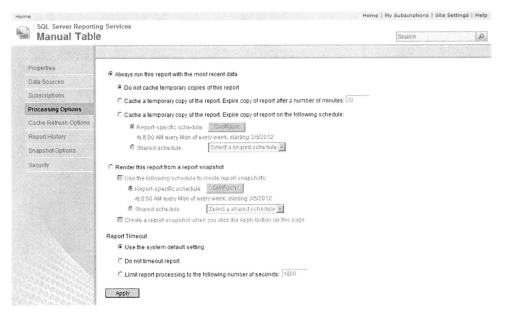

FIGURE 5-29 Use the Processing Options page to control on-demand, cached, or snapshot rendering.

As you can see, the default selection is Always Run This Report With The Most Recent Data. In addition, the option Do Not Cache Temporary Copies Of This Report is selected. As a result, each time a user opens this report, the report query executes and the Report Processor must render the report with the query results. When you select one of the caching options, the first user who opens the report must wait for the query execution and rendering of the report, but subsequent users opening the same report wait only for the report to render using the query results generated by the first report execution. Rendering a report usually processes much faster than executing a query. When you configure a report snapshot, the query execution occurs in advance of any user's request for the report, so all users will wait only for report rendering, which shortens their waiting time.

You can also use the Processing Options page to configure the report execution time-out. The system default setting limits report execution to 1800 seconds, but you can override this setting to prevent a time-out or to use a different time-out value for the selected report.

Reviewing processing options in a SharePoint document library

Open the SharePoint document library by using its URL, such as *http://<servername>/<sitename>/Documents*. Point to the arrow to the right of the report name to display the shortcut menu, and click Manage Processing Options to view the settings, as shown in Figure 5-30.

FIGURE 5-30 The Processing Options page in SharePoint integrated mode allows you to specify settings for on-demand, cached, or snapshot rendering.

Although the names of the processing options differ from the options accessible in Report Manager, their functions are the same. The Use Live Data option executes the report query and renders the report on demand. The Use Cached Data option executes the query on the first request of the report and renders the cached results each time a user requests the report. The Use Snapshot Data option produces a report snapshot that permanently stores the query results and renders the snapshot on demand. You can set processing time-out values on this page as well as set limits on the number of history snapshots that accumulate on the report server.

Viewing a report

The third phase of the report life cycle concerns user accessing of reports. For a native-mode report server, you use Report Manager to find and view reports. You use a SharePoint web application to find and view reports managed by a SharePoint integrated-mode report server. While the user interface depends on the report server mode, the same functionality is available in either mode, as you learn in this section.

Opening a report

You use a web interface both to manage report server content and to view reports. Regardless of the mode in which you're running the report server, it's common practice to organize reports into folders, which you navigate to find a list of reports. You then click the report link to view the report.

Opening a report in Report Manager

When you click a report link in Report Manager, the Report Processor executes the query, renders the report in Hypertext Markup Language (HTML) format, and displays the report, as shown in Figure 5-31. Notice that the display of the report by using Report Manager matches the way the preview of the report looked in Report Builder.

FIGURE 5-31 Viewing a report in Report Manager.

Opening a report in a SharePoint document library

You open a report in a SharePoint Document Library by clicking its link to execute the query, render the report in HTML format, and display the report, as shown in Figure 5-32. Although the rendering of the report matches what you see when the same report renders in Report Manager, notice that the toolbar is slightly different on each server type. In SharePoint, you use the Actions menu on the left side of the toolbar to open the report in Report Builder, print the report, or export it to another file format. Under certain conditions, you can also set up a data alert or subscribe to the report by using the Actions menu.

Actions ▾   ⊙ |◀ ◀ | 1   of 2 ? ▶ ▶| ✦ [   ] Find Next [100%   ▾] ▣

Internet Sales

Calendar Year	Sales Territory Region	Sum Sales Amount
2001		
	Australia	$1,309,047
	Canada	$146,830
	France	$180,572
	Germany	$237,785
	Northwest	$415,203
	Southwest	$685,346
	United Kingdom	$291,591
		$3,266,374

3/6/2012 12:01:23 AM

FIGURE 5-32 Viewing a report in SharePoint.

Using the HTML Viewer

The HTML Viewer is a special toolbar that displays when you view a report. You can use the HTML Viewer to navigate through the pages of your report, change the zoom factor of the page, search text in the report, export the report to another format, refresh the report, or print the report. You explore the HTML Viewer in more detail in Chapter 26.

136   PART I   Getting started with Reporting Services

PART II

Developing reports

The chapters in Part II teach you a variety of report development techniques that take advantage of the rich set of features available in Reporting Services. In Chapter 6, "Planning your report design," we explore various decisions you should make before deciding which features to implement in a report. Then in Chapter 7, "Working with report server projects," we show you to how work with report server projects in SQL Server Data Tools and how to manage report server project files and properties. Chapter 8, "Retrieving data for a report," describes all the data source types you can use to display data in your report, how to connect to these data source types by creating data sources, and how to design queries for these data source types to create datasets. Next in Chapter 9, "Designing the report layout," you learn how to work with each type of report item and how to configure properties to control appearance and behavior of each report item. In Chapter 10, "Working with the tablix," we delve into the details of the tablix report item by exploring its unique features, explaining properties specific to the tablix, and showing how to work with tablix groups.

Much of the flexibility that Reporting Services delivers is made possible by using expressions. In Chapter 11, "Developing expressions," you learn how to enhance reports by adding calculations and using expressions to change properties dynamically. Reporting Services includes many built-in functions that we describe in detail in Chapter 12, "Using functions."

Reporting Services also includes many features that provide interactivity for online reports. In Chapter 13, "Adding interactivity," you build more advanced reports to allow the user to modify the report layout and to navigate to other sections of the report, other reports, or even to a URL. Chapter 14, "Creating dynamic reports with parameters and filters," shows you how to add interactivity and control report content dynamically.

Next, you learn about features used in special cases. In Chapter 15, "Managing the page layout," you learn about working with printed reports, such as page sizing, page breaks, and page headers and footers. In Chapter 16, "Using Analysis Services as a data source," you learn how to use the MDX query designer to retrieve Analysis Services data for the reporting environment, how Analysis Services data behaves differently in a report, and how to work with parameters when using Analysis Services as a data source. After reading these chapters, you will be well prepared to develop your own reports to meet a variety of reporting requirements.

CHAPTER 6

Planning your report design

Before you read this chapter, you should have Reporting Services installed and have a general understanding of how to create a basic report. If you are still fairly new to Reporting Services report development, you might not fully understand how to implement some of the concepts that we discuss in this chapter, but that should not deter you from skimming through it. The purpose of this chapter is to help you think about how to prepare for the report development process. Knowing who will view reports and how they want or need to interact with reports has an impact on how you should design those reports.

Reporting Services provides a lot of flexibility in report design, which can be overwhelming at first. You can spend a lot of time trying out different approaches to report design before you discover that a feature that users need most conflicts with the features you've been implementing. With some advance planning, you can decide which features are most important for your current project and be more productive throughout the report development process. The suggestions we make in this chapter are not exhaustive, but they describe situations we commonly encounter in our consulting practice and strategies we have found useful.

Most importantly, we recommend that you involve users as much as possible during the development process. Prototype early in the development cycle with a subset of data (or even fake data if necessary) and solicit feedback. Make sure you ask questions to clarify your understanding of the requirements, and working with a prototype can help enormously with this process. A prototype is something tangible around which you can generate a discussion. With a prototype, uses can confirm that the design is right, wrong, or maybe close but not quite what it needs to be. Furthermore, users are better able to answer your questions about whether a particular design feature would be useful if they can see it in action.

Knowing your audience

Knowing your audience is important. An understanding of how users typically interact with information, their technical skill and interest level, and whether they plan to use the data in other ways will affect how you approach the design of reports. More likely, you will have a mixed audience and will need to create different styles of reports to accommodate a diverse audience.

One of the first things to know is how users will be viewing reports. The access method they use to view a report can give you more freedom for creativity in the report design or can impose certain restrictions. As you gather information about report access, consider the following scenarios:

- **Will users go online to find a report and view it there?** If users are viewing reports online, you can consider any interactive feature that Reporting Services supports. However, many of these features are useless if users will be referring to printed reports. For interactivity features that you can add to online reports, see Chapter 13, "Adding interactivity." If you must plan for printed reports, see the "Printed reports" section later in this chapter.

  When designing a report for online consumption, users typically don't want to scroll through pages and pages of a report to find needed information. The addition of report parameters, in conjunction with query parameters, can enable the user to focus on information of interest. You can learn more about parameters in Chapter 14, "Creating dynamic reports with parameters and filters."

- **Will users primarily receive reports via an email subscription?** If so, you need to find out whether the email should contain an embedded copy of the report, include an attachment to the report, or simply provide a link to the report online. In the latter case, you can design your report by using the same criteria for an online report.

  If the report must be embedded in the email, the report should be relatively small in size, containing a minimal number of records and using a layout that fits easily within the width of the user's monitor if they usually use a computer to view emails. If the users rely primarily on mobile devices for email, consider sending reports as an attachment instead. A report sent as a PDF attachment must be designed with pagination in mind, which we explain in Chapter 15, "Managing the page layout." However, if users need access to the data to combine with other sources or to perform computations, you can send the report as an Excel attachment, and you can focus more on the data structure and less on conforming the report appearance to a corporate standard.

- **Will users be using mobile devices to access reports?** A recent development is the increasing use of tablets and smartphones to access corporate information. Rather than try to fit everything into a one-size-fits-all dashboard-style of report, consider focusing on a few key subject areas and then provide access to additional information through links that open separate reports or jump to another section of the same report.

  When users are in the office, they're often accessing the BI system to check on the general status of operations. They'll be looking at the big picture to see whether things are going as expected or not, and they can then explore areas of interest to get into more specific information as needed. By contrast, the mobile audience is usually responding to a circumstance, either searching for something specific to answer a question or looking up the high-level status of some business process. They've either encountered a problem that needs to get resolved or anticipate that they're on the verge of a problem that they want to pre-empt. Mobile users might be under pressure standing in front of a client or in an otherwise distracting environment, so the reports must be designed to make it as easy as possible to get to specific information and to follow a train of thought by drilling from one type of information to another type of information, and to filter the data down to relevant details as needed. Parameters and actions are useful features to implement in mobile reports. See Chapters 13 and 14 to learn how to use these features.

The technical skills and interest level of your users also play a role in determining how best to make information available. Technical skills among users can vary widely in an organization or even within a department. You should be prepared to provide building blocks for users who are capable of some level of self-service reporting if interest exists. The following are some strategies to consider for different types of users:

- **Data-savvy advanced users** Some users spend their entire day focused on data. This group of users likely has the technical skills necessary to acquire and manipulate data from relational or multidimensional data sources. They want as much unfettered access to data as you're willing to give them. You can set this group up to work with Report Builder and allow them to build reports from scratch, or you can create a library of starter reports that they can modify as needed.

- **Motivated power users** This group of users knows their data very well. Perhaps they are capable of building reports but are unable to write their own queries. You can give this group permission to use Report Builder and publish shared datasets for them to use when creating their own reports. That way, they have the freedom to create the reports they want and you can control the data that they use. See Chapter 8, "Retrieving data for a report," for more information about shared datasets.

  Within this group, you might even have people who know what they want when they see it but are unable to put together their own queries and are intimidated by the thought of building a report from scratch. For this group, you can publish report parts that represent commonly accessed data in a variety of data structures—tables, charts, maps, and so on. Then this group can use the Report Part Gallery in Report Builder to browse published report parts and piece together multiple report parts to build a report just the way they like it. Chapter 29, "Reusing report parts," explains how to do this.

- **Basic users** Some users lack the time, the skills, or the interest to explore data and build their own reports. They just want access to information as quickly and flexibly as possible. When creating reports for this group, you might find a lot of similarities between reports. To save yourself from creating a maintenance nightmare and also save users the trouble of trying to determine which of the many possible reports has the answers they need, try to consolidate multiple reports into a single report as much as you can. Use parameters to modify the content of the reports, either by filtering the data or by hiding or showing elements dynamically. You can create linked reports, as we describe in Chapter 23, "Deploying reports to a server," to create the illusion of multiple reports if necessary and hide the parameters that you don't want users to change.

Yet another aspect to understand about your audience is how they plan to use the report. The intended use can make a difference in the direction you should focus your development effort. The following are some common ways that people use reports and related development considerations:

- **Standard reporting**   The most common reason to implement Reporting Services is to provide standard reporting at the department, division, or organizational level. This type of reporting typically requires the use of standard styling to produce a consistency of appearance across multiple reports.

    After the standards for your reporting environment are established, you can create one or more base reports to use as templates. For example, you might create a portrait version and a landscape version of a table layout and include common parameters in each version. You can store the report definition files in the Program Files (x86)\Microsoft Visual Studio 10.0\Common7\IDE\PrivateAssemblies\ProjectItems\ReportProject folder on your computer. When you use the Add A New Item command in SSDT to create a new report, you can select the template and continue report development by adding a dataset and assigning fields to a data region.

- **Raw data**   Reporting Services can export data to Excel, CSV, XML, and ATOM formats. Some people just want the raw data so that they can develop their own Excel workbooks or import it into PowerPivot for Excel or other applications. Creating a report to deliver data might be preferable to allowing direct access to data sources because you might need to enhance the data with calculations, you might want to schedule data retrieval to manage the impact on source systems or your network, or you might want to deliver the data by using subscriptions rather than require the user to go to the report server. If the report is simply a means to an end, you don't need to spend a lot of time conforming a report to a standard format with page heads and footers, and so on. You should keep these reports in a separate folder to emphasize their purpose as data structures.

- **Quick information retrieval**   Sometimes people need access to information without a lot of formality. This information might come in the form of an email to report the status of a process, or it might be a lookup to get customer contact information. Either way, this type of report is not typically something a user prints out to share with others or present at a meeting. Therefore, the layout can be simple, without the formatting that you would require for official corporate reports.

- **Operations monitoring**   This type of reporting can take the form of a dashboard or detailed reports that include conditional formatting to highlight trends and exceptions. When designing a dashboard, you should consider the standard size screen for the majority of users so that you can use the screen effectively. A dashboard should convey summarized information clearly at a glance, using data visualization techniques to provide comparisons, display trends, or highlight exceptions. Ideally, the user can see the entire dashboard without scrolling. Use the chapters in Part III, "Adding data visualizations," to learn about the variety of data visualizations at your disposal.

    You should also consider the questions that might result from viewing a dashboard and prepare supporting detailed reports. You can add actions to each data visualization to open a related report and pass the context of the user's click to that report. For example, in a chart that displays sales trends by week, a user can click a specific week to open a report that displays the daily detail for that week. See Chapter 13 for information about actions.

- **Management or external stakeholder reporting** The most formal type of reporting that you might have is the set of reports prepared for management or external stakeholders. Although these reports might be viewed online, you should anticipate that they might be printed or shared as PDF documents. You typically apply consistent styling and branding to this type of report and must take care to adjust the design so that the report produces a clean layout in print or PDF format. We provide suggestions for styling in the "Developing standards" section of this chapter.

- **Information as a service** You might produce a series of reports as a service to customers. This type of reporting often requires consistency in appearance. You might provide access to reports online, or you might deliver a set of reports as a single PDF document. To combine reports into one document, you create individual reports and then create one parent report that uses subreports to organize the individual reports in the correct sequence. When working with subreports in this way, to avoid introducing blank pages, you must take care to manage the page sizes of the individual reports as well as the parent report. See Chapter 14 for information about subreports, Chapter 15 for page size management, and Chapter 32, "Understanding Report Definition Language," for an alternative approach to combining reports.

Reviewing report options

Although many changes to a report can be made at any time during report development, the most important decision you need to make early in the process is the type of layout to use. However, there are other options to consider as well. You need to understand any limitations you might have when retrieving data, and you must give some thought to whether to implement parameters and how best to configure them. If your users intend to access reports by using mobile devices, you should also consider how best to design reports to accommodate the smaller form factor. Similarly, you need to consider how printing a report affects the layout.

Layout decisions

With some practice and a good understanding of how a tablix works, you can convert a table to a matrix or vice versa, but when you're new to Reporting Services, you might find the necessary steps to be unintuitive. Moreover, you cannot change a table into a chart or map nor turn a list with various nested data regions into a table. Therefore, deciding the layout to use is a critical decision to make.

You can use a table layout when you need to present a simple list of items with a relatively small number of fields per item. If there are a lot of fields, you need to consider whether it's acceptable for the user to scroll horizontally to view all the fields online. If the user is going to print the report, there are additional considerations we discuss in the "Printed reports" section of this chapter.

Generally, you should design the reports for online viewing to display a limited number of columns. It's much easier for users to scroll up and down to view information than to scroll left and right. For that matter, you should question whether users really need to see all available columns at once. It might make more sense to set up a parameter to allow users to choose the columns they want to see. Then you can hide or show columns on demand.

You can also use multiple detail rows and stack the fields vertically if necessary, as shown in Figure 6-1. That way, you can include a larger number of fields in the layout while keeping the width of the data region smaller than the user's screen width or the printed page.

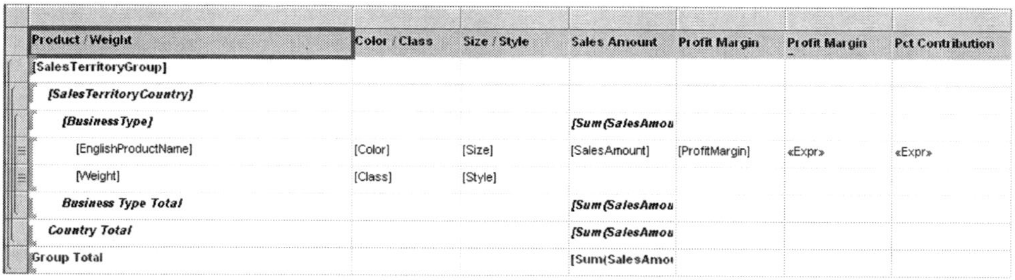

Product / Weight	Color / Class	Size / Style	Sales Amount	Profit Margin	Profit Margin	Pct Contribution
[SalesTerritoryGroup]						
[SalesTerritoryCountry]						
[BusinessType]			[Sum(SalesAmou			
[EnglishProductName]	[Color]	[Size]	[SalesAmount]	[ProfitMargin]	«Expr»	«Expr»
[Weight]	[Class]	[Style]				
Business Type Total			[Sum(SalesAmou			
Country Total			[Sum(SalesAmou			
Group Total			[Sum(SalesAmou			

FIGURE 6-1 You can use multiple detail rows to reduce the number of columns required to display all fields for a dataset row.

Another option for handling a large number detail fields is to create a grouped list. The advantage of a list is the ability to arrange text boxes in a freeform fashion. You can then accommodate text boxes of varying sizes on each "row" of the list, as shown in Figure 6-2.

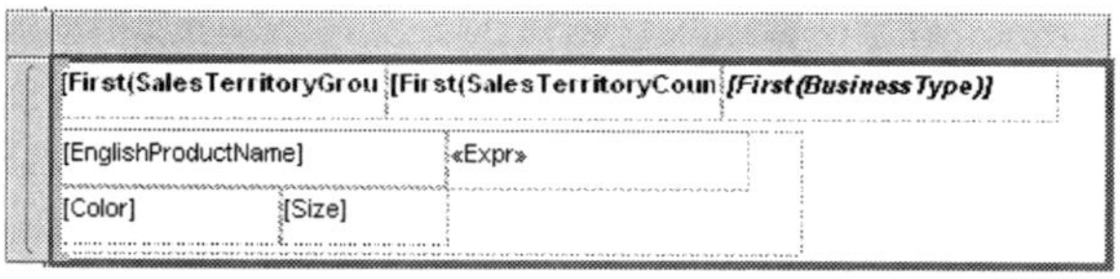

[First(SalesTerritoryGrou	[First(SalesTerritoryCoun	[First(BusinessType)]
[EnglishProductName]	«Expr»	
[Color]	[Size]	

FIGURE 6-2 You can arrange text boxes inside a grouped list to minimize the width of a report.

A matrix is useful when you need to provide a crosstab layout. However, you run the risk of having too many columns on the screen or printed page if you don't plan ahead. A table has a fixed number of columns that you define during report development, but a matrix can have a variable number of columns because the data determines the column groupings. Therefore, if your goal is to fit a matrix to a specific size, you should consider implementing a filter to reduce the number of possible column groupings.

On a more granular level, you need to consider how wide each text box should be to comfortably accommodate data. A text box will never grow wider than the size you define, but it has a CanGrow property that is set to True by default, which expands the text box vertically if the data is wider than the text box, as shown in Figure 6-3. This property might be acceptable for reports that you view online but can disrupt the alignment of printed reports by pushing report items from one page to another.

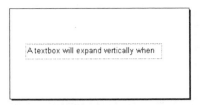

A textbox will expand vertically when
you keep the *CanGrow* property
default value of *True*

Design Mode   Preview Mode

FIGURE 6-3 When the *CanGrow* property is set to *True*, the text box expands vertically to display the entire text it contains.

Data considerations

Rather than create a large report that contains hundreds or thousands of pages, find out whether all that data is really necessary. Usually it's better to add a filter or create a query that aggregates data at the source. When users view reports online, they usually want to look up a piece of information and don't need to scan an entire report to find that one item of needed information.

Rather than create a report that includes pages of detail records with group totals, create a summary report to show only group totals. Have users start their review process from a summary report, and then include an action on the report to drill through to a detail report. The detail report displays only a subset of data related to the portion of the summary report that the user wants to investigate. In both cases, you have a report that retrieves a smaller number of records and generally runs faster than a report that retrieves thousands of records.

Another aspect of managing data in reports is the data definition itself. Some organizations have strict control over access to data sources, requiring report developers to use stored procedures or views maintained in the source database. This requirement simplifies maintenance of commonly used queries by centralizing the query.

Using stored procedures and views is not an option for data that comes from non-relational data sources. For those situations, you might consider using shared datasets to achieve a similar effect. The downside of shared datasets is that they are primarily intended for use in Report Builder. If you use SSDT to develop reports, you must either obtain the current version of a shared dataset from a source control system or download it from the report server. SSDT does not provide direct access to published shared datasets.

Parameters

Parameters are useful elements of a report. You can use them to filter data, set report item properties dynamically at run time, or provide input for calculations. Throughout this chapter, we suggest using parameters to address a variety of scenarios. As you plan your report, you must make several decisions about implementing each parameter, including the following:

- **User input**   You must decide whether a parameter accepts user input. In most cases, you should avoid this option due to the increased security risk of an injection attack and due to the limited validation available in Reporting Services. Usually it's better to give the user a list of values from which to make a selection, but you might prompt the user when you want to create a filter by using a user-defined string and wildcard or when the number of possible values is not practical to present in a list, such as a sales invoice number.

- **List of values**   The preferred method for prompting the user for a value is to provide a list of valid values. You can hard-code this list if necessary, but using a query gives you more flexibility in the long run and allows you to easily reproduce the same list of values when using the same parameter in multiple reports. You can create an independent query, or you can use a query that depends on the user's selection of a value for a separate parameter. This technique is known as cascading parameters and is described in Chapter 14. You must also decide whether the user can select only one value or multiple values.

- **Default value**   If you do not include a default value for a report parameter, the report cannot execute until the user provides a value. This might be a desired behavior when there is no reasonable default, such as a report that displays information about a specific sales invoice. Wherever possible, you should provide a default value. This default can be hard-coded in the report or produced as the result of a query.

Mobile devices

We pointed out earlier in this chapter that you should design reports to use screen space effectively and minimize scrolling when people are working on a desktop. However, with mobile devices, the same rules do not necessarily apply. Users are accustomed to not seeing all information on the screen at one time. A useful feature of tablet devices is the ability to use gestures on the screen to navigate, either by zooming in and out as necessary or scrolling. Therefore, you might not need to worry as much about fitting the contents of a report to the screen, but always check with your users to understand their expectations before establishing a policy one way or the other.

If you are reproducing a dashboard for mobile devices, you might consider limiting the number of perspectives or views of the data to no more than four. If you have four views laid out in a quadrant format, keep in mind that the most important information should be placed in the top-left quadrant. That's where our eyes naturally start, and on the tablet, that should be the information that's most likely to fit completely on the screen.

Another suggestion is to keep the report simple for mobile users. Having too much information on the screen makes it more difficult for users to focus on the information they're looking for, especially if they're in a hurry. Having legends or lots of parameters for filtering can create visual noise and interfere with their ability to locate the data. In particular, when you know your users will be viewing information on tablets, don't use tiny fonts. In addition, if there are actions in a report, associate the actions with report items big enough to handle comfortably on a touch screen.

Printed reports

When designing reports that are destined for printing at some point, you must factor in the page size as you position items in the report layout. You can set report properties to fix the orientation as portrait or landscape, which we explain in Chapter 15. Many of the same considerations that we describe in the "Layout decisions" section of this chapter also apply to printed reports, and perhaps more so. Preview your report, and switch to Print Layout mode so that you can see how the rendered report fits on each page. You should also export the report as a PDF file to check the rendering more carefully.

If a report spans multiple pages, you should configure repeating column headers in the tablix. That way, users don't have to flip back to the first page to determine what a particular column contains. Chapter 15 explains how to set properties in the tablix to repeat the column headers. The same principle applies to row headers for a matrix. You can repeat the row headers on the second page if a matrix is too wide to fit on a single page.

By default, Reporting Services tries to fit as much content as it can on a page and inserts logical page breaks for a report. For greater control over the location of page breaks, you can define explicit page breaks relative to report items or groups within a data region.

Regardless of whether you set explicit page breaks or rely on the default logical page breaks, each page of the report is assigned a page number. You can reset this page number to maintain a separate page numbering system within sections of a report, but there is also an overall page number that you can use. When you know a report will be printed, it's a good idea to include the current page number and the overall page number in the page header or page footer, which are the only locations in which the page number can display. That way, if a user inadvertently shuffles the pages of the report or misplaces ones, the presence of page numbers helps the user reorder the pages correctly or notice the missing page.

You should also include the report execution date and time in the page header or page footer. That way, the user can easily tell if the report is recent enough to remain useful. You might also consider including the report server name and report path to help the user locate the report online when it's time to execute a fresh report.

Sometimes you can design a report that looks good both online and in print, but that's not always possible. You might need to design two separate reports. Rather than have users open one report and then have to switch to another report, consider having a link visible in online mode only that users click to output the report as PDF or Excel. Reporting Services doesn't actually allow you to create links dynamically, but you can create an action and then underline the associated text to make it appear to be a link. In the action definition, you can use an expression to dynamically create the URL to produce the requested output. See Chapter 13 for information about actions and Chapter 35, "Programming report access," for information about URL access.

Developing standards

When your reports have a consistent look and feel, users know what to expect when they view a report and can focus on its important elements rather than spending time trying to figure out how to use the report. Similarly, during the report development cycle, standards provide clear guidelines that you can apply to your report quickly without resorting to trial and error to see what might look good. When you have a set of standards established, you can create a variety of templates with common elements in place to shortcut the development process, as we explain in the "Knowing your audience" section of this chapter.

If you don't already have reporting standards already established in your organization, consider defining standards for the following report elements:

- **Fonts**   Use a single font family. Be consistent with font sizes for different elements. For example, you might use a 10pt font for detail records and a 12pt font for column headers. Use 14pt or 16pt for titles. Use smaller fonts for text in page headers and page footers. Consider using a lighter shading for text in page headers and page footers, such as gray rather than black, to reduce the emphasis on the text. The user's eye should be drawn towards the primary information on the report through the use of larger fonts, darker colors, and bolding where appropriate.

- **Colors**   Use a consistent palette of colors for text and elements (other than data visualizations) that place color onto the report, such as lines, borders, or fill. Ideally, colors should be soft and neutral and should not distract from the information on the report.

- **Logo**   If your company has a logo to include on reports, upload it directly to the report server and then reference it as an external image in each report by using its URL access path (described in Chapter 35). That way, if the logo changes in the future, you can replace the file on the report server without the need to update each report individually.

- **Page Header**   Include a text box to display the report title and another text box to display the page number and total pages (such as Page 1 of 3). If you prefer, you can place the page number in the page footer. Suppress the page header on the first page if using a text box to display a title on the report body. Use a font smaller than the detail row fonts in the report.

- **Report Header**   The report does not include an explicit report header. We use this term to describe any report items, such as a free-standing text box, a rectangle, a line, or an image, that display at the top of the report in the body above a data region. The report header displays only once in the rendered report at the top of the first page. You can use this area to display a title and supplemental information as a subtitle, such as parameter selections and a date. Use a large font for the report title and a slightly smaller font for the subtitle.

- **Group Header or Footer**   Use a consistent styling for group headers and footers when you include them in a Tablix. Typically, you use a bold font to distinguish headers and footers from details. Consider using border or background color properties as another means to differentiate group headers and footers from details. Decide whether to include totals in the group header or footer. You should be consistent with the placement of totals in all reports.

- **Page Footer**   Include a text box to display the report execution date, report path, and the page numbering if you don't include it in the page header. Use a font smaller than the detail row fonts in the report.

- **Margins**   Set a minimum margin of 0.5in on each side of the page.

- **Parameters**   When defining a common set of parameters across multiple reports, use the same sequence in each report.

- **Calculations**   Decide how to handle a potential divide by zero error. You might use a conditional expression to test the calculation first and return a default string such as N/A or a dash (-).

- **Empty strings and NULL values**   You should use a consistent rule for handling empty strings or NULL values returned in the dataset. You might prefer to display nothing, convert numeric data types to a 0, or display a string. Whatever you decide to do, be consistent.

- **No rows**   If it is possible for a dataset query to return no rows, you can display a message to the user by setting the *NoRowsMessage* property of the data region. If you leave this property blank, the data region does not display. If it's the only element in the report, the user might not realize the problem is related to data and might think that the report server has failed to render the report correctly.

CHAPTER 7

Working with report server projects

The focus of the authoring phase of the reporting life cycle is the production of the report definition files that will later be centrally stored on the report server. As you learned in Chapter 5,
"Exploring Reporting Services fundamentals," you can choose to use either Report Builder or Report
Designer to author report definition files. However, Report Designer is the tool more commonly used
by professional report developers for a variety of reasons, including the ability to manage groups of
reports as projects. In this chapter, you learn about report server projects and the files that you manage within a report project. You also explore the Report Designer commands available to use with
report server projects and learn how to configure project properties.

Getting started with report server projects

When you author reports using Report Designer, you work with a version of Microsoft Visual Studio
2010 that is tailored for development of business intelligence solutions using Integration Services,
Analysis Services, or Reporting Services. This specialized version of Visual Studio installs on your computer when you select SQL Server Data Tools (SSDT) as part of the SQL Server 2012 setup. If you already have Visual Studio 2010 installed, the installation of SSDT simply adds the Business Intelligence
project types to your existing installation. In fact, whether you launch SSDT or launch Visual Studio
from their respective program groups, you are actually launching the same program.

 Note Installation of SSDT integrates only with Visual Studio 2010. If you have an earlier version of Visual Studio installed, the installation of SSDT will not add the Business Intelligence
project types to that version.

Creating a Reporting Services project

When you create a Reporting Services project, you also create a *solution*—a container for one or
more projects, each of which can be different project types. For example, in one solution, you might
have one project for reports, another project for an Analysis Services database, and a third project for
Integration Services packages. Alternatively, you might have three separate Report Server projects in

a single solution, with each project using different data sources for its group of reports. If you also use the full-blown Visual Studio 2010 version to develop custom applications, you might even have a solution that contains a Report Server project and a C# class library project for a custom assembly that you want to use for advanced calculation capabilities in your reports. The ability to work with multiple reports as part of a project is one of the key advantages of working with Report Designer rather than Report Builder, which limits you to working with one report at a time.

Creating a new project and solution

You start the process to create both a new project and a new solution by opening the SSDT application from the Microsoft SQL Server 2012 program group. On the File menu, point to New, and then click Project. In the New Project dialog box, shown in Figure 7-1, you select one of the Reporting Services project types (described in the "Selecting a project type" section of this chapter).

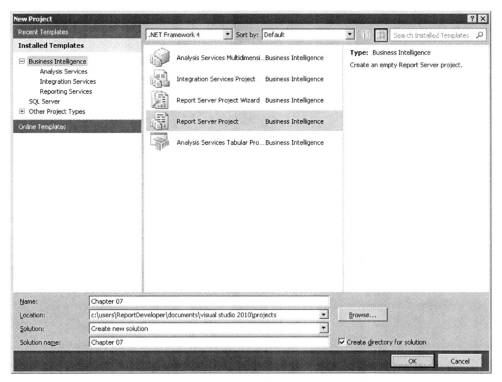

FIGURE 7-1 Use the New Project dialog box to create a new Reporting Services project in SSDT.

Regardless of which project type you choose, you must specify a value for each of the following fields:

- **Name** Provide a name for the project. SSDT uses this name to create a directory on the file system in which to store project files, so you must use the naming rules applicable to the target operating system. For example, you cannot use reserved characters, such as < (less than) or * (asterisk), or use reserved device names, such as CON or PRN.

> **Tip** You can review a complete list of naming rules at *http://msdn.microsoft.com/en-us/library/windows/desktop/aa365247(v=vs.85).aspx*.

- **Location**   Select a location on your local computer or a network file share for storing your solution and project.

- **Solution**   Specify whether to add the new project to a new solution or the currently open solution. If you are creating a new solution, you will not see this field in the New Project dialog box. It appears only when you currently have a solution open. The default selection is Create New Solution, which closes your current solution and creates a separate solution. The other option is to change the selection to Add To Solution if you want to add a new project to the open solution.

- **Solution Name**   Provide a name for the solution to which you want to add the project. This field does not display when you choose the Add To Solution option in the Solution drop-down list. SSDT creates a directory for the solution using this name, so the same naming rules used for the project name also apply to the solution name.

- **Create Directory For Solution**   Select the check box if you want SSDT to create a separate solution directory. As shown in Figure 7-2, you can maintain a separate directory for the solution file (with extension SLN) using the specified solution name and a subdirectory for the report project using the project name. As you add files to the project, those files are kept separate from the solution file. In contrast, when you don't set up a separate directory for the solution, a single directory contains the solution file and all project files.

FIGURE 7-2 Use the Create Directory For Solution check box to manage solution files separately from project files.

> **Note** There is no functional difference between the preceding options when working with multiple projects in a single solution, but you might find it easier to locate and open the solution file when it resides in its own directory.

Adding a new project to an existing solution

When you have an existing project open in SSDT, you can add another project to the same solution by pointing to Add on the File menu and clicking New Project. The Add New Project dialog box displays the same templates available in the New Project dialog box. After selecting a template, you specify a name for the project and its location. The default location is the solution directory, but you can save the project files in a separate location if you prefer. There is no option to associate the new project with a separate solution.

Adding an existing project to an existing solution

You can also add an existing project and its files to an existing solution by pointing to Add on the File menu and clicking Existing Project. The Add Existing Project dialog box allows you to navigate through the directories on your computer or a network file share to locate a report project file with an RPTPROJ file extension. When you add an existing project to the solution, all files associated with the project display in Solution Explorer. You can edit these files, remove a file from the project, or add new files to the project. Because the project continues to be associated with its original solution, all changes you make will be visible when you later open that solution.

Selecting a project type

In general, a project type is a design environment template that includes designers for developing project files and a predefined set of folders for organizing those project files. For example, for a report server project, you use Report Designer to create Report Definition Language (RDL) files and dialog boxes to create shared data source files and shared dataset files. By grouping these files together as a project, you can deploy them to the report server in one bulk operation rather than uploading them one by one. There are two types of project types available for Reporting Services: Report Server Project Wizard and Report Server Project.

Report Server Project Wizard

For quick development of a basic report, you can use the Report Server Project Wizard template. After you select this project type and name the project, the Report Wizard opens. It is the same wizard you can use when adding a new report to an existing project (described in more detail in the "Using the Report Wizard" section of this chapter) to step through the process of defining the data source, defining a query, and selecting a layout from a few options. Because you can make modifications to a report after using the wizard, it's an easy way to start a simple report. At the completion of the wizard, you have the same project structure as you do when creating a report server project. Your new project contains one report definition file and also a shared data source if you opt to make the data source shared when specifying the connection string.

Report Server project

The more frequently used project type for report development is the Report Server project. After you select this template, SSDT creates an empty project, which is visible in the Solution Explorer window of the Visual Studio design environment. After creating the project, you can add shared data sources, shared datasets, or reports to the file as we describe in the "Working with report project files" section of this chapter.

Getting familiar with the Visual Studio interface

After you create the project, the Visual Studio design environment is available for you to create report definition files and work with supporting objects. If you create the project using the Report Server project type, it is initially empty, as shown in Figure 7-3. You might see a different combination of open windows if you have previously used Visual Studio and changed the layout. Your default layout might also include windows that are not used with Reporting Services projects, such as the Server Explorer and Class View windows.

Solution Explorer

In the default layout, the Solution Explorer window displays in the upper-right corner. If you don't see the Solution Explorer window, press Ctrl+Alt+L or select Solution Explorer from the View menu. When a solution contains only one project, the solution name isn't visible in Solution Explorer, but there is a solution (*.sln) file added to your file system along with the report project (*.rptproj) file. The solution name appears only when you add more than one project to the same solution.

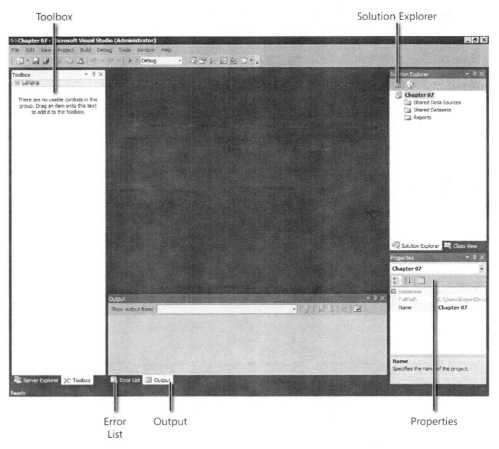

FIGURE 7-3 You use the Visual Studio integrated development environment to work with report projects.

A Reporting Services project in Solution Explorer always contains the following folders:

- **Shared Data Sources**   Use this folder as a container for files that store data source connection strings that you want to share with multiple reports, as we explain in Chapter 8, "Retrieving data for a report."

- **Shared Datasets**   Use this folder as a container for files that store datasets that you want to share with multiple reports. You learn about shared datasets in more detail in Chapter 8.

- **Reports**   Use this folder to store reports that you author.

You cannot create subfolders within these folders to further separate and organize the files. You must either add separate projects to the solution or move files into separate folders on the report server after you deploy them.

Properties window

Below the Solution Explorer window, the Properties window displays by default. If you don't see it, press F4 or select Properties Window from the View menu. When you select an item in the Solution Explorer window or in an active Report Designer window, you will see that item's properties display in the Properties window, where you can change any of the item's editable properties. You learn about report item properties in Chapter 9, "Designing the report layout."

Output window

On the bottom of the screen, there are two windows stacked together—the Output window and the Error List window. Typically, you see the Output window only when you preview a report or attempt to deploy a report to the report server. It contains one or more messages describing the status of the activity you just tried. To open the Output window at any other time, you can press Ctrl+Alt+O or select Output on the View menu.

Error List window

If errors occur, you can open the Error List window to see the error message. Likewise, you can view the Error List window by pressing Ctrl+ ` and then pressing E or by selecting Error List from the View menu.

Toolbox window

The Toolbox window appears on the upper-left side of the screen by default. This window is empty when no reports are open in the development environment. When you add a report to the project and open the Report Designer for that report, all the controls that you can add to a report appear in the Toolbox window for you to drag and drop into the report layout. We explain more about the Toolbox window in Chapter 9.

Report Data window

After you open a report to view its Report Designer, the Report Data window displays on the left side of the screen by default. It contains built-in fields for use in your report, such as expressions for page numbering or report execution time, which you learn about in Chapter 11, "Developing expressions." It also includes folders in which you organize information that you use to add data to the report, such as data sources and datasets, as we explain in Chapter 8. The Report Data window also includes a folder in which you store images embedded in the report (described in Chapter 9) and a folder for managing report parameters (described in Chapter 14, "Creating dynamic reports with parameters").

Removing a project from a solution

At some point, you might find that you no longer want to include a project in the same solution as other projects. In that case, you can right-click the project in Solution Explorer and click Remove. It is important to note that this action removes the project from the solution but does not remove it from the file system. Consequently, you will encounter an error if you remove a project from a solution and then later attempt to add a new project using the same name as the project you removed. You must delete the project and its files from the file system to permanently remove it.

Working with report project files

After you create a project, you add items to the project. Each item is s separate file type that you deploy to the report server. You can use a wizard to add a new report to the project or use a command to add any of the supported file types.

Reviewing report project file types

The report server project supports the following different types of items:

- **Report Data Source**   A Report Data Source, with an RDS file extension, is an XML file describing the data provider, such as Microsoft SQL Server or Hyperion Essbase, and the connection string that Reporting Services uses to connect to the data source.

- **Report Shared Dataset**   A Report Shared Dataset, with an RSD file extension, is an XML file containing the instructions that Reporting Services uses to retrieve data from the data source and properties affecting the usage of the retrieved data, such as data types and collation.

- **Report**   A report, with an RDL file extension, is an XML file that describes the layout, appearance, and behavior of data in a report. If you don't create a shared data source or shared dataset, you must embed the information that these file types store into the project's reports.

Resource files

You can also add other file types to your project as resources to deploy to the report server. For example, you can add image files to a project to reference as an external image rather than embed the image into the report. This technique is useful when you want to avoid updating reports individually when you need to update the image.

As another example, you can use Microsoft Word documents to provide documentation to users. In this case, users must have Word installed to open a Word document from the report server. This requirement applies to any file type you choose to deploy to the report server. Users can open the file only if the associated application is installed on their computer,

When you deploy file types other than RDS, RSD, or RDL files, the report server does not check the validity of the structure of these files. It simply serves as a central repository for multiple forms of information besides reports. You add other file types to a project in the same way described in the "Adding an existing item to a project" section of this chapter, changing the selection of Common Report Files (*.rdl, *.rds, *.rsd) in the file type drop-down list of the Add Existing Item dialog box to the alternate selection of All Files (*.*).

Using the Report Wizard

The Report Wizard launches automatically if you select the Report Server Project Wizard project type when creating a new project. You can also launch the wizard by right-clicking the Reports folder in Solution Explorer and selecting Add New Report.

Initial steps

After the welcome page displays, the first step of the wizard prompts you to select the data source for your report, as shown in Figure 7-4. After you select a data source provider type in the Type drop-down list, you can click the Edit button to open the Connection Properties if you want to use a graphical interface to construct the applicable connection string. Click the Credentials button to specify the authentication method to use when Reporting Services connects to the data source. (More information about configuring a data source is available in Chapter 8.) Select the Make This A Shared Data Source check box to create an RDS file for the project so that you can share the data source with other reports in the same project later.

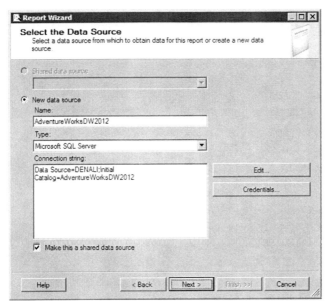

FIGURE 7-4 Add a data source provider type and connection on the first step of the Report Wizard.

On the next page of the wizard, shown in Figure 7-5, you can type a query string or click the Query Builder button to open the applicable query designer for your data source. We explain query designers in detail in Chapter 8.

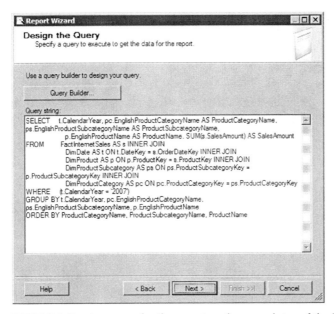

FIGURE 7-5 Create a query for the report on the second step of the Report Wizard.

Then you use the next page of the wizard, shown in Figure 7-6, to specify whether you want to show the data in tabular or matrix format. In a tabular format, the report displays data by using a fixed set of columns, with optional groupings that you define in a subsequent step of the wizard. A report with a matrix format displays data by using a variable number of rows and columns based on groupings that you define later.

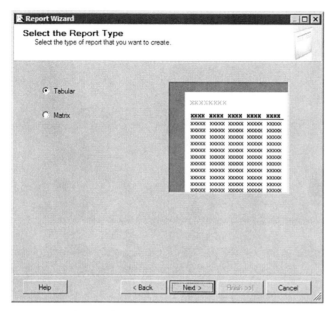

FIGURE 7-6 Choose whether to create a tabular or matrix report on the third step of the Report Wizard.

Tabular report

Your choice of report type determines which pages you can access next in the report wizard. When you choose to create a tabular report, you must then specify how to arrange the data fields from the query into page groups, row groups, or details (or ungrouped data), as shown in Figure 7-7.

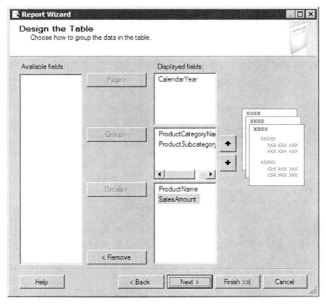

FIGURE 7-7 Define page groups, row groups, and detail fields on the fourth step of the Report Wizard.

Then you specify the table layout options on the next page of the wizard, as shown in Figure 7-8. Here you can choose between a stepped table or a block table, and whether to include subtotals or enable drilldown.

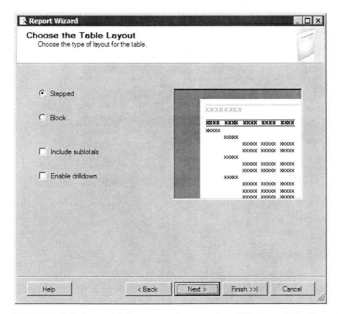

FIGURE 7-8 Select table layout options on the fifth step of the Report Wizard.

If you choose a stepped table, each row group and details field displays as a separate column and in separate rows, as shown in Figure 7-9. The block table, with the same row groups and details fields, also creates separate columns for the groupings but uses a more compact layout to include lower-level grouping values on the same row as the highest grouping.

Stepped

Product Category Name	Product Subcategory Name	Product Name	Sales Amount
Accessories			
	Bike Racks		
		Hitch Rack - 4-Bike	16440.0000
	Bike Stands		
		All-Purpose Bike Stand	18921.0000
	Bottles and Cages		
		Mountain Bottle Cage	8231.7600
		Road Bottle Cage	6355.9300
		Water Bottle - 30 oz.	8692.5800

Block

Product Category Name	Product Subcategory Name	Product Name	Sales Amount
Accessories	Bike Racks	Hitch Rack - 4-Bike	16440.0000
	Bike Stands	All-Purpose Bike Stand	18921.0000
	Bottles and Cages	Mountain Bottle Cage	8231.7600
		Road Bottle Cage	6355.9300
		Water Bottle - 30 oz.	8692.5800

FIGURE 7-9 A stepped table includes more rows than a block table.

With both the stepped and block tables, you can include subtotals, as shown in Figure 7-10. In the stepped table, the subtotal value displays on the row containing the grouping to which the subtotal applies. This row appears above the detail rows used to compute the subtotal. In contrast, a block table displays the subtotal row below the related grouping.

Stepped with Subtotals

Product Category Name	Product Subcategory Name	Product Name	Sales Amount
Accessories			293709.7100
	Bike Racks		16440.0000
		Hitch Rack - 4-Bike	16440.0000
	Bike Stands		18921.0000
		All-Purpose Bike Stand	18921.0000
	Bottles and Cages		23280.2700
		Mountain Bottle Cage	8231.7600
		Road Bottle Cage	6355.9300
		Water Bottle - 30 oz.	8692.5800

Block with Subtotals

Product Category Name	Product Subcategory Name	Product Name	Sales Amount
Accessories	Bike Racks	Hitch Rack - 4-Bike	16440.0000
	Total		16440.0000
	Bike Stands	All-Purpose Bike Stand	18921.0000
	Total		18921.0000
	Bottles and Cages	Mountain Bottle Cage	8231.7600
		Road Bottle Cage	6355.9300
		Water Bottle - 30 oz.	8692.5800
	Total		23280.2700

FIGURE 7-10 Stepped table and Block table with subtotals.

The Enable Drilldown option applies only to the stepped table, regardless of whether you choose to include subtotals. Figure 7-11 illustrates a stepped table with subtotals and drilldown. You must expand each grouping to view the lower grouping levels.

Product Category Name	Product Subcategory Name	Product Name	Sales Amount
⊟ Accessories			293709.7100
	⊞ Bike Racks		16440.0000
	⊞ Bike Stands		18921.0000
	⊟ Bottles and Cages		23280.2700
		Mountain Bottle Cage	8231.7600
		Road Bottle Cage	6355.9300
		Water Bottle - 30 oz.	8692.5800

FIGURE 7-11 Stepped table with subtotals and drilldown.

Matrix report

When you want to group data on both rows and columns, you choose the option to create a matrix report. You can also use page groupings when designing the matrix, as shown in Figure 7-12. However, you should avoid using non-numeric data in the Details group because the matrix will automatically apply aggregate functions to the fields you assign to Details. The *Sum* function applies to numeric fields, while the *First* function applies to non-numeric fields.

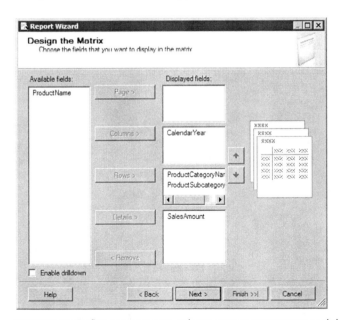

FIGURE 7-12 Define page groups, column groups, row groups, and detail fields for a matrix.

Figure 7-13 shows an example of a simple matrix report. If the dataset were to return data for multiple years, each year would appear as a separate column. The number of columns is determined only at rendering, based on the dataset's query results, unlike a table in which the number of columns is determined only by the report layout.

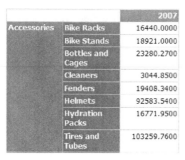

		2007
Accessories	Bike Racks	16440.0000
	Bike Stands	18921.0000
	Bottles and Cages	23280.2700
	Cleaners	3044.8500
	Fenders	19408.3400
	Helmets	92583.5400
	Hydration Packs	16771.9500
	Tires and Tubes	103259.7600

FIGURE 7-13 A matrix with two row groups and one column group.

Final steps

After completing the wizard steps to define the groupings and layout options, you select a style to apply to the table or matrix, as shown in Figure 7-14. A style is a collection of font and color properties that you can use to quickly produce an attractive report. However, none of the styles applies formatting to numeric values. You must add numeric formatting manually, as described in Chapter 9.

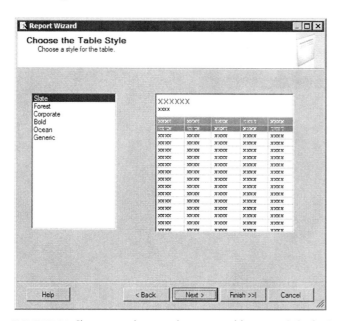

FIGURE 7-14 Choose a style to apply to your table or matrix in the Report Wizard.

On the final page of the wizard, you type a name for the report. You can close the wizard and view the report layout in the Report Designer, or select the Preview Report check box to execute the query, render the report, and display the result in the preview mode of the Report Designer. If you need to make further changes to the report, such as adjusting the formatting of a numeric value, you work with the design layout as described in Chapter 9. There is no way to restart the wizard for the current report.

Adding a new item to a project

Whether you want to add a shared data source, shared data set, report, or some other resource to your project, the steps to begin the process are the same. In Solution Explorer, right-click the project or any folder, point to Add, and click New Item. In the Add New Item dialog box, select the applicable template: Report Wizard (as yet another way to launch the wizard), Report, Data Source, or Dataset. Type a name for the new item, taking care to use the correct file extension for the type of item you're adding.

> **Tip** If your goal is to add a new report, you might be tempted to choose Add New Report instead of using the Add command with the New Item option. The Add New Report command launches the Report Wizard, which is useful when you want to quickly produce a report, but most report developers choose to start by creating a new item to add an empty report to the project.

Your next step depends on the template selection. If you chose Data Source or Dataset, you see the Shared Data Source Properties dialog box or the Shared Dataset Properties dialog box, respectively. You provide the required information in these dialog boxes, as we describe in Chapter 8, and the file appears in Solution Explorer. If you chose Report, a new RDL file appears in Solution Explorer, and the Report Designer displays the new, but blank, report.

Custom templates

SSDT creates the list of available templates you see in the Add New Item dialog box from the files available in the \Program Files\Microsoft Visual Studio 10.0\Common7\IDE\PrivateAssemblies\ ProjectItems\ReportProject folder. The file path starts from \Program Files (x86) if you're working on a computer with a 64-bit operating system. To make it easier to set up reports with common properties and report items, you can save your own report definition file to this folder and thus make it available as a custom template whenever you add a new report to a project.

Adding an existing item to a project

When you have an RDS, RSD, or RDL file available on the file system (or any file that you want to add to your project for deployment to the report server, as described in the "Resource files" sidebar in the "Reviewing report project file types" section), you can copy that file into your current project. In Solution Explorer, right-click the project or any folder, point to Add, and click Existing Item. In the Add Existing Item dialog box, navigate to the file location, and double-click the file that you want to add. Regardless of which folder you right-clicked to add the existing item, Solution Explorer displays an RDS file in the Shared Data Sources folder, an RSD file in the Shared Datasets folder, and all other files in the Reports folder.

Removing an item from a project

If you no longer want to include a shared data source, shared dataset, or report in your project, you can remove it from both your project and the file system by right-clicking the item in Solution Explorer and clicking Delete. If you multi-select several files, you can right-click one of the files and click Delete once to delete in bulk. You must confirm deletion before the action completes, because you cannot undo the deletion.

> **Tip** Rather than permanently delete a file from a project, you can temporarily exclude it. You might choose to do this if you want to deploy all but one of your reports. You can right-click a file in Solution Explorer and then click Exclude From Project. The file no longer displays in Solution Explorer, and you can deploy all remaining files in the project by using a single Deploy command. The excluded file remains in the file system in the project folder. To add it back, use the steps described in the "Adding an existing item to a project" section.

Using report project commands

The process of designing data sources, datasets, and reports is very similar whether you use Report Builder or Report Designer, notwithstanding some slight user interface differences between the two design environments. However, you work with these file types exclusively in Report Designer either individually or as a group within a project. Report Designer includes several commands and tools that you use to manage files and projects. These commands and tools are accessible on the Project and Build menus in SSDT or on the context menu when you right-click a project in Solution Explorer.

Project menu

First, let's look at the Project menu. It includes the following commands:

- **Add New Item**   Use this command to add a new data source, dataset, or report to your project as described in the "Adding a new item to a project" section.

- **Add Existing Item**   Use this command when you have a file to add to your current project. When you add it to the project, the existing item remains in its original location and Report Designer creates a new copy of that item to add to your project.

- **Import Reports**   Use this command as another way to add a report to your project by converting existing Microsoft Access reports. This import feature works only with Microsoft Access 2002 or later and requires Access to be installed on the same computer as BIDS. In fact, you won't see this command if Access is not installed. You select an Access database, and the import process converts the reports it contains. You cannot selectively import reports. Expect to spend some time editing the imported reports due to the differences in page layout between Access and Reporting Services. Some people prefer to re-create the report in Reporting Services rather than use the import feature.

Tip The import process can easily convert simple reports from Access, but some Access report features are not supported in the Reporting Services report definition language. For a complete list of supported features, see *http://msdn.microsoft.com/ en-us/library/ms157205.aspx*.

- **Exclude From Project** Use this command to temporarily remove a file from a project without deleting the file from the file system.

- **Project Properties** Use this command to open the project's Property Pages dialog box. We explain how to work with project configurations and project properties in this dialog box in the "Configuring report project properties" section of this chapter.

Build menu

Report Designer also includes a Build menu, which includes the following commands:

- **Build Reports** If you use Visual Studio for application development, you are already familiar with using the Build command to compile your code. However, the build process for reports is completely different. Because a report is an XML document, there is nothing to compile. Instead, the build process ensures that the report is free of errors that would prevent you from previewing the report in SSDT or deploying the report to the report server. You can review the errors that SSDT finds in the Error List.

- **Deploy Reports** When you're ready to publish your reports to the report server, you use the Deploy Reports command. You can select a single report, all reports in a project, or all reports in a solution when your solution contains multiple projects, and then select this command to start the deployment. Before deployment begins, SSDT automatically runs the build process to validate the reports first. If the reports are error-free, they deploy to a folder on the report server that you specify in the project properties (described in the next section in this chapter). Each project in a solution can have a different target folder, which is a consideration for deciding how to organize reports into projects.

Configuring report project properties

You don't need to worry about configuring project properties until you're ready to deploy your reports to the report server. SSDT uses these properties only when you use the Deploy command to identify the target locations for your various project files on the report server. Many of the project properties have default values. Valid values for some properties will depend on whether you deploy to a native-mode report server or a SharePoint integrated-mode report server.

Working with project configurations

If you maintain separate report servers for development, testing, and production, you can save project properties specific to each target server by creating project configurations. The three default project configurations available to you in SSDT are Debug, DebugLocal, and Release. You can access a project configuration by selecting it in the Configuration drop-down list, and then you can change the properties as needed. For example, you can use the Debug project properties to define the target folders and URL for your development report server, and you can use the Release project properties to define the respective properties for your production report server.

To create a new configuration, click the Configuration Manager button in the Property dialog box to open the Configuration Manager. In the Active Solution Configuration drop-down list, select <New...>. Then in the New Solution Configuration dialog box, type a name for the configuration, such as Test. You can select an existing configuration in the Copy Settings From drop-down list to copy its settings to the new configuration. If you have multiple projects in the same solution, you can keep the Create New Project Configurations check box selected to add the new configuration to each project.

You should also take the time to review the Project Context settings for each default configuration and any new configurations you added. For example, change the Active Solution Configuration to DebugLocal, as shown in Figure 7-15. For this configuration, only the Build setting is selected. The project context settings control the actions that occur when you debug the project by pressing F5 or select Start Debugging from the Debug menu. In this example, the Start Debugging command performs a build of the report files but does not attempt to deploy the reports and project files. You can select the Deploy check box if you want SSDT to both build and deploy the project when you debug, which is the default setting for the Release configuration. Of course, you can always run the Build or Deploy command without using the Debug feature.

Close the Configuration Manager after reviewing each configuration. Be sure to set the correct active configuration in the Solution Configurations drop-down list in the SSDT standard toolbar before using the debug feature.

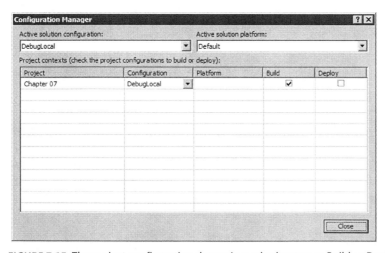

FIGURE 7-15 The project configuration determines whether to run Build or Deploy when you debug the project.

Setting project properties

Before you can use the Deploy command, you must update the project properties by identifying target locations for your project files on the report server. Many of the project properties have default values, but you must specify the URL for the report server before you can deploy reports. If you plan to deploy to a SharePoint integrated-mode server, the default values for all target folders are invalid. If a target folder does not yet exist on the report server, the deployment process creates the folders.

In Solution Explorer, right-click the project and click Properties as another option for opening the project's Property Pages dialog box, shown in Figure 7-16. If you are deploying the project to a native-mode report server, you need only add a value for the *TargetServerURL* property. Deployment will fail if this value is missing.

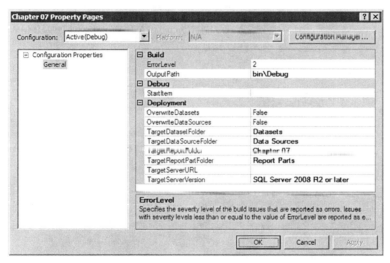

FIGURE 7-16 At minimum, update the *TargetServerURL* property before deploying to a native-mode report server.

Table 7-1 describes each project property and provides an example of a valid value for both a native-mode report server and a SharePoint integrated-mode report server when a difference exists.

TABLE 7-1 Report server project properties

Property	Description	Valid Value
ErrorLevel	Severity level of build violations to report as an error. Violations below this level appear as a warning. An error causes the build to fail. See Table 7-2 for more information.	2
OutputPath	Path within project in which to store report definition files during build, deploy, or preview tasks.	bin\Debug
StartItem	Report to execute when using the Start Debugging command.	Empty

Property	Description	Valid Value
OverwriteDatasets	Option to control whether report server datasets are overwritten by project datasets having the same name. Set by default to False to prevent changes resulting from use of the same dataset across multiple projects.	False
OverwriteDataSources	Option to control whether report server data sources are overwritten by project data sources having the same name. Set by default to False to prevent changes resulting from use of the same data source across multiple projects.	False
TargetDatasetFolder	Location on report server for storing datasets from the current project. Typically a shared location for storing datasets from multiple projects.	Native mode: Datasets Integrated mode: *http://server/site/Datasets*
TargetDataSourceFolder	Location on report server for storing data sources from the current project. Typically a shared location for storing data sources from multiple projects.	Native mode: Data Sources Integrated mode: *http://server/site/Data Connections*
TargetReportFolder	Location on report server for storing reports from the current project. No warning displays if this folder contains reports having the same name as reports in the current project. These reports are overwritten during deployment.	Native mode: <Project Name> Integrated mode: *http://server/site/Documents*
TargetServerURL	Endpoint for report server.	Native mode: *http://server/ReportServer* Integrated mode: *http://server/site*
TargetServerVersion	Format to use for RDL files for deployment to report server in *TargetServerURL*. Choose SQL Server 2008 for backward compatibility to support deployment to a SQL Server 2008 report server, or choose Detect Version to determine the *TargetServerURL* version and modify the RDL to a suitable version.	SQL Server 2008 R2 or later

Table 7-2 explains the error levels that you use to set the project's *ErrorLevel* property. During the build process, SSDT assigns an error level to each issue that it encounters. If the issue has an error level that is less than or equal to the value in the *ErrorLevel* property, the issue is reported in the Error List window as an error and the report cannot be previewed or deployed. If the issue has an error level higher than the *ErrorLevel* property, the issue is reported as a warning and the request to preview or deploy continues.

TABLE 7-2 Report server project error levels

Error Level	Description
0	Most severe issue preventing preview or deployment of report
1	Severe issue having high impact on report layout
2	Moderate issue having significant impact on report layout
3	Minor issue changing report layout slightly and perhaps unnoticeably
4	Minor issue qualifying as a warning only

Note For backward compatibility, you have the option to deploy reports to a SQL Server 2008 report server. That way, you can design your reports by using the SQL Server 2012 Report Designer but deploy to a SQL Server 2008 instance of the report server. If you design a report with a SQL Server 2012 feature, such as a map or a sparkline, and then set the *ErrorLevel* property to 0 and the version to SQL Server 2008, the SQL Server 2012 feature is removed from the report.

CHAPTER 8

Retrieving data for a report

Reports are powerful tools that help you visualize and share data in various ways. Therefore, the first step in creating a report is getting data! Reporting Services supports a number of different data sources you can use to easily create reports on your data, no matter how and where it's stored. After you identify where the data is stored, you provide Reporting Services with the query to use to retrieve data from each source.

Understanding data source types

The first step to accessing your data for a report is to create a *data source*. A data source is fundamentally a connection string. The content of this connection string depends on the data provider that you use. For example, a connection string for a SQL Server database looks different from a connection string used to connect to a SharePoint list. The purpose of the connection string is to describe where to find the data, what format it's in, and, depending on the data provider that you're using, the connection string might also include the credentials to use for authentication.

In Reporting Services, the data source also specifies the authentication method to use when establishing the connection. When creating your data source, you need to specify whether the report uses Windows authentication to pass through the current user's credentials or whether to use a hard-coded value for user name and password so that you don't have to include it in the connection string. You can also configure the data source to prompt the user to first enter credentials before executing the report, or you can specify that no credentials at all are required. Unless the data source has no security defined, which is highly unusual, the credentials are used by the data source to authenticate the user before the query executes. Because of this, the user account must have at least reader permissions on the data source.

Reporting Services supports many different types of data sources. When you create a new data source, you start by specifying the data provider to use. That is, you tell Reporting Services what type of data that it needs to retrieve. The following is a complete list of the data providers that you can use to define a data source:

- Microsoft SQL Server
- Microsoft SQL Azure
- Microsoft SQL Server Parallel Data Warehouse

- Oracle

- Teradata

- Object Linking and Embedding Database (OLE DB)

- Open Database Connectivity (ODBC)

- Microsoft SQL Server Analysis Services

- SAP NetWeaver BI

- Hyperion Essbase

- Extensible Markup Language (XML)

- Microsoft SharePoint List

- Report Server Model

After you define the data provider, you specify the connection string. In the following sections, we show you examples of the connection strings for each of the supported data providers by category: relational data sources, multidimensional data sources, and other data sources. You can always type the connection string directly into the data source definition, but in most cases, you also have the option of using Connection Properties dialog box to help build the data connection string, which we show you how to do in the "Connecting to data with data sources" section of this chapter.

Relational data sources

Probably the most common type of data that you'll use in reports is relational data. Reporting Services supports a wide range of relational data sources. If your relational database isn't listed here explicitly, you can probably access it by using the OLE DB or ODBC data providers.

SQL Server

In addition to using SQL Server for hosting the Reporting Services databases, you'll likely use it to store application and operational data that you want to display in a report. You can connect to the following versions of SQL Server using Reporting Services:

- SQL Server 2008 R2

- SQL Server 2008

- SQL Server 2005

The basic syntax for a SQL Server connection string looks like this:

```
Data Source=<servername>;Initial Catalog=<databasename>
```

For example, when you want to connect to the *AdventureWorksDW2012* database on a local server, the connection string looks like this:

```
Data Source=localhost;Initial Catalog=AdventureWorksDW2012
```

For a connection to a SQL Server named instance called Denali, the connection string looks this this:

```
Data Source=localhost\Denali;Initial Catalog=AdventureWorksDW2012
```

SQL Azure

From a report development perspective, there is not much difference between using an on-premises database engine like SQL Server and a cloud-based database engine like SQL Azure. The connection string for the SQL Azure data provider is similar to that of the SQL Server data provider, but you must provide the fully qualified name of the server like this (where MYSERVER is the server name associated your SQL Azure subscription):

```
Data Source=MYSERVER.database.windows.net;Initial Catalog=AdventureWorksDW2012;Encrypt=True
```

Important It's important to use the Encrypt property in the SQL Azure connection string to enable a Secure Sockets Layer (SSL) connection between Reporting Services and the SQL Azure server and thereby protect the data while it's in transit. This property also ensures that the SSL certificate from SQL Azure is truly generated by Microsoft.

SQL Server Parallel Data Warehouse

SQL Server Parallel Data Warehouse (PDW) is a massively parallel processing database engine that you use to manage very large data volumes. This data provider is one of the few for which you cannot use the Connection Properties dialog box to help build the connection string. The connection string for a PDW looks like this:

```
HOST=<IP address>;database=AdventureWorksDW2012; port=1234
```

Tip It is not required to include the database property in the connection string. If you omit it, Reporting Services connects to the default database assigned by the database administrator to the login it uses to make the connection.

You connect to a PDW by using SQL Authentication. However, you do not include the user name and password in the connection string. Instead, you provide the user name and password on the Credentials page of the Data Source Properties dialog box. When Reporting Services connects to a PDW during report processing, it appends the user name and password to the connection string.

Oracle

To use Oracle as a data source, you must install the Oracle client tools on the report development computer as well as on the report server. Reporting Services supports the following Oracle versions:

- Oracle 10g

- Oracle 9i

- Oracle 8i

For an Oracle 9i server named MyOracleServer (as found in the Tnsnames.ora configuration file) with support for the UTF16 character set, the connection string for Oracle looks like this:

```
Data Source="MyOracleServer"; Unicode="True"
```

> **Tip** Although the preceding example is typical, there are other properties that you can add to an Oracle connection string. To learn more, see *http://msdn.microsoft.com/en-us/library/system.data.oracleclient.oracleconnection.connectionstring(v=vs.71).aspx*.

Teradata

You must install the .NET Data Provider for Teradata on both the report development computer and on the report server. You can create a data source for any of the following versions of Teradata:

- Teradata v13

- Teradata v12

- Teradata v6.20

There is no connection builder to guide you when using this provider type. However, the connection string for Teradata uses only the Internet Protocol (IP) address of the Teradata server and looks like this:

```
data source=10.10.0.1;
```

OLE DB

Because the OLE DB provider type supports a variety of data providers, you must specify which OLE DB provider to use in the connection string. For example, to create a connection that uses the SQL Server Native Client 10 provider, the connection string looks like this:

```
Provider=SQLNCLI10.1;Data Source=localhost; Initial Catalog=AdventureWorksDW2012
```

ODBC

Similar to the OLE DB data source connection, an ODBC data source connection depends on the driver you want to use. For a connection using the SQL Server Native Client 10 ODBC driver, the connection string looks like this:

```
Driver={SQL Server Native Client 10.0}; Server=localhost; Database=AdventureWorksDW2012;
Trusted_Connection=yes;
```

Multidimensional data sources

You can also use multidimensional data in your reports. Multidimensional databases allow you to query high volumes of data more efficiently than relational databases.

SQL Server Analysis Services

You can connect to the following versions of Analysis Services using Reporting Services:

- SQL Server 2008 R2

- SQL Server 2008

- SQL Server 2005

When you want to query a database stored on an Analysis Services, the connection string looks like this:

```
Data Source=localhost;Initial Catalog=AdventureWorksDW2012Multidimensional-SE
```

Note The connection string syntax is the same for both a multidimensional and data mining mode instance and a tabular-mode instance of Analysis Services.

You can also connect to a PowerPivot for SharePoint workbook using the Analysis Services data provider. In that case, you use a connection string that represents the URL for the workbook. For example, if you have a workbook named Sales.xlsx in a PowerPivot document library on a SharePoint site at *http://denali*, you use a connection string that looks like this:

```
Data Source=http://denali/Sales.xlsx
```

SAP NetWeaver BI

Reporting Services supports a Simple Object Access Protocol (SOAP) connection to the SAP NetWeaver BI 3.5 version. To connect to a server named mySAPNetWeaverBIServer using port 8000, your connection string looks like this:

```
DataSource=http://mySAPNetWeaverBIServer:8000/sap/bw/xml/soap/xmla
```

Hyperion Essbase

You also use SOAP to connect to Hyperion Essbase 9.3.1. For example, if the database is named *Sample* and the server is a local instance using port 13080, the connection string for this type of data source looks like this:

```
Data Source=http://localhost:13080/aps/XMLA; Initial Catalog=Sample
```

Miscellaneous data sources

Reporting Services also allows you to retrieve data from non-traditional sources, such as XML documents, SharePoint lists, and report server models.

XML

An XML data source type allows you to connect to the following data sources:

- **XML Web service**   You can connect to a web service by using a Web Services Definition Language (WSDL) reference like this:

  ```
  Data Source=http://adventure-works.com/products.aspx
  ```

- **Online XML document**   You can connect to an XML document that has an XML file extension and is accessible using Hypertext Transfer Protocol (HTTP) by using a connection string like this:

  ```
  http://localhost/XML/Products.xml
  ```

- **Embedded XML document**   You can embed an XML document in the report definition by enclosing the XML text inside <XmlData> tags in the dataset. In this case, you leave the connection string empty.

SharePoint list

You can connect to the following versions of SharePoint using Reporting Services:

- SharePoint 2010 Products

- Office SharePoint Server 2007

- Windows SharePoint Services 3.0

To connect to a SharePoint list, the connection string is simply the URL of the site or subsite where the list you want exists. For example, if you have a list on the SharePoint site *http://denali:37780/sites/ssrs*, you use the site as the connection string like this:

```
http://denali:37780/sites/ssrs
```

When you create a dataset based on this data source, the query designer automatically displays all SharePoint lists for which you have read permissions on this site.

Report server model

Report server models (also known as report models) are objects that you can create by using SQL Server 2005, SQL Server 2008, or SQL Server 2008 R2 development tools. Although you can no longer develop report models in SQL Server 2012, you can deploy existing models to a native-mode or SharePoint integrated-mode report server. Professional report developers and business users alike can easily build reports by using a report model as a data source by using a drag-and-drop interface, without the need to know the query syntax for the underlying data source. You can connect to report models that use the following data sources:

- SQL Server 2008 R2
- SQL Server 2008
- SQL Server 2005
- SQL Server 2005 Analysis Services
- Oracle 9.2.0.3 or later
- Teradata v13, v12, and v6.2

If the report model called AdventureWorks is on a native report server in the Models folder, you use a connection string that looks like this:

```
Server=http://localhost/reportserver; Datasource=/Models/AdventureWorks
```

If you deploy the AdventureWorks report model to the Models folder in the Documents document library on a SharePoint site at *http://denali/sites/ssrs*, you use a connection string like this:

```
Server=http://denali; Datasource=http://denali/sites/ssrs/Documents/Models/AdventureWorks.smdl
```

Connecting to data with data sources

Regardless of the type of data source you are using in a report, the process to set up and manage the data source is similar. First, you must decide whether to use an embedded data source or a shared data source. Although both types of data sources provide a connection from your report to a data source, there are differences in behavior and usage that will impact your report development process.

Comparing embedded and shared data sources

There are two different types of data sources that you can use in a report. One option is to create an embedded data source, which exists solely within the context of a single report definition. The other option is a shared data source, which is reusable across many reports.

When you create an embedded data source, you add the data source explicitly to each report definition. The advantage of using an embedded data source is the ability to use dynamic connection strings (as we explain in Chapter 11, "Developing expressions"), but the disadvantage is that you must open every report and edit the embedded data source's connection string if you need to make a change to the connection string. That can be a very tedious process if you have a lot of reports.

Typically, you create a shared data source to define the connection information once for use with many reports. That is, the shared data source is defined once in the project and then referenced by multiple reports. If connection information changes later, such as when you move a source database to a different server, an administrator updates the data source definition once to update all associated reports. These reports will subsequently retrieve their data from the new source without any further change.

A shared data source added to a project is stored as an RDS file. Its contents are composed of XML data, as shown here:

```xml
<?xml version="1.0" encoding="utf-8"?>

<RptDataSource xmlns:xsi="http://www.w3.org/2001/XMLSchema-instance" xmlns:xsd="http://www.w3.org/2001/XMLSchema" Name="AdventureWorksDW2012Shared">

  <ConnectionProperties>

    <Extension>SQL</Extension>

    <ConnectString>Data Source=localhost;Initial Catalog=AdventureWorksDW2012</ConnectString>

    <IntegratedSecurity>true</IntegratedSecurity>

  </ConnectionProperties>

  <DataSourceID>8ae72df3-f1eb-4f3a-a1ed-8e34140bc2fe</DataSourceID>

</RptDataSource>
```

The key elements to note in this shared data source file are *Extension*, *ConnectString*, and *DataSourceID*. These elements contain the data provider and connection string information that the report server uses to retrieve data during report processing and a GUID for the DataSourceID to uniquely identify the data source. You can produce this file automatically by using the data source dialog box, or you can produce it manually or programmatically. It doesn't really matter how you create it, as long as it has the right structure.

An embedded data source has a similar structure, but it is part of the XML representing the report definition rather than a separate file. Its elements are enclosed within the *DataSources* element, as shown here:

```xml
<DataSources>

  <DataSource Name="AdventureWorksDW2012Embedded">

    <ConnectionProperties>

      <DataProvider>SQL</DataProvider>

      <ConnectString>Data Source=localhost;Initial Catalog=AdventureWorksDW2012</ConnectString>

      <IntegratedSecurity>true</IntegratedSecurity>

    </ConnectionProperties>
```

```
<rd:SecurityType>Integrated</rd:SecurityType>

<rd:DataSourceID>17c4931a-a5cb-451e-a979-7912c0fc8901</rd:DataSourceID>

</DataSource>

</DataSources>
```

Working with an embedded data source

You use the Report Data pane to manage embedded data sources for each report. It includes commands for you to add, edit, or delete data sources.

Creating an embedded data source

The Report Data pane provides two ways to add an embedded data source to a report. Both methods require you to open the Report Data pane. If it's not visible, you can open the View menu and select Report Data or press Ctrl+Alt+D.

After opening the Report Data pane, you can add a data source to your report by clicking New in the Report Data pane, as shown in Figure 8-1, and then selecting Data Source.

FIGURE 8-1 Add a data source by using the New button in the Report Data pane.

As an alternative, you can right-click the Data Sources folder in the Report Data pane, and then select Add Data Source, as shown in Figure 8-2.

FIGURE 8-2 Add a data source by right-clicking the Data Sources folder in the Report Data pane.

Either way, the Data Sources Properties dialog box opens, as shown in Figure 8-3. You should replace the default data source name with something more meaningful so that you can easily identify a report's data source by its name. The name must start with a letter and can include numbers or an underscore. However, it cannot contain spaces nor can it include the following characters:

\ ; ? : @ & = + , $ / * < > | " / -

When you create a new data source, Embedded Connection is selected by default. If you have already added a shared data source to the project, as we explain later in this chapter, you can choose the Use Shared Data Source Reference option here instead.

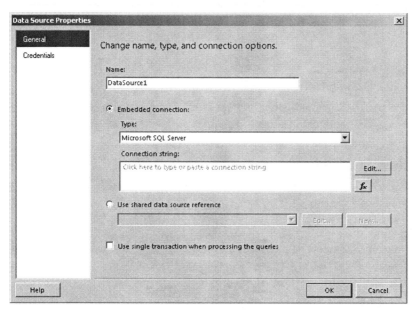

FIGURE 8-3 The Data Source Properties dialog box defaults to an embedded connection type.

For an embedded connection, you must select a data provider in the Type drop-down list. In the Connection String box, you can either manually type a connection string or click the Edit button to open the Connection Properties dialog box, shown in Figure 8-4, where you can use a graphical interface to specify properties that the report designer uses to generate a connection string. The appearance of the Connection Properties dialog box depends on the data source type that you select in the Data Source Properties dialog box. Figure 8-4 illustrates the properties for the SQL Server data provider.

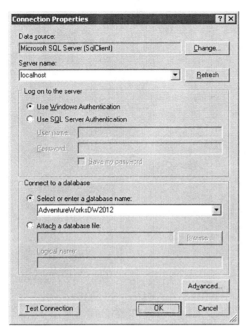

FIGURE 8-4 The Connection Properties dialog box prompts for the data source provider and other details necessary to construct the connection string.

> **Tip** Click the Advanced button to access a dialog box that lists all properties available for the selected data provider. You can enter values for these properties to extend the connection string when you have specific requirements for the connection.

When you click OK to close the Connection Properties dialog box, the report designer updates the Connection String box with the applicable connection string, as shown in Figure 8-5. You can make changes to the connection string here if you need to add more properties to the basic syntax generated by the Connection Properties dialog box. Your final step is to go to the Credentials page if you don't want to use Windows integrated security for data source authentication. We explain your options here in the "Setting data source credentials" section of this chapter.

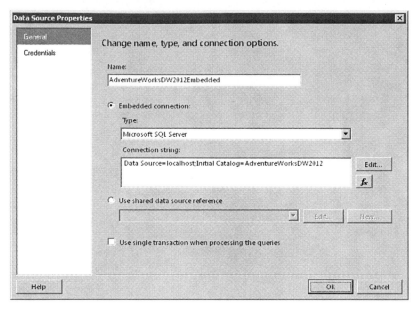

FIGURE 8-5 Update the Data Source Properties dialog box with a recognizable name and connection string.

Processing queries as a single transaction

At the bottom of the Data Source Properties dialog box is the Use Single Transaction When Process-ing The Queries check box. If this check box is clear, all queries using this data source execute in parallel. When you select this option, all queries dependent on this data source fail if any single query to the data source fails. You should select this check box when your report contains multiple datasets that reference the same data source and that data source cannot handle several parallel connections. Another reason to select this option is to force queries to execute as a single transaction.

Editing an embedded data source

After you create an embedded data source, it appears in the Report Data pane, as shown in Figure 8-6. To change its properties, you can double-click the embedded data source to open the Data Source Properties dialog box. Another option is to select the embedded data source and then click the Edit command in the Report Data pane toolbar.

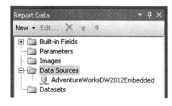

FIGURE 8-6 An embedded data source displays in the Data Sources folder of the Report Data pane.

Converting an embedded data source to a shared data source

You can easily convert an embedded data source to a shared data source if you change your mind later. Simply right-click the embedded data source in the Report Data pane, and select the Convert To Shared Data Source command. The icon for the data source changes to indicate its new status as a shared data source, and an RDS file containing the shared data source definition appears in the Solution Explorer.

Deleting an embedded data source

If you need to delete the embedded data source, you can right-click it in the Report Data pane and select the Delete command. As an alternative, you can select it and then click the Delete button in the Report Data pane's toolbar. If the data source is used with a dataset, a warning prompt will display to prevent you from invalidating the report. You can use the Undo button if you accidentally delete the wrong data source.

Working with a shared data source

You use the Solution Explorer to create a new shared data source and to edit the properties of an existing shared data source. Any change you make to the shared data source is inherited by reports that reference that data source. You add the shared data source to the Report Data pane of each report to create the reference.

Creating a shared data source

To make a single data source definition available to multiple reports, you can create a shared data source. In the Solution Explorer pane, right-click the Shared Data Sources folder, and then select Add New Data Source. The Shared Data Source Properties dialog box displays, as shown in Figure 8-7. Notice the similarity to the Data Source Properties dialog box that you use to configure embedded data sources.

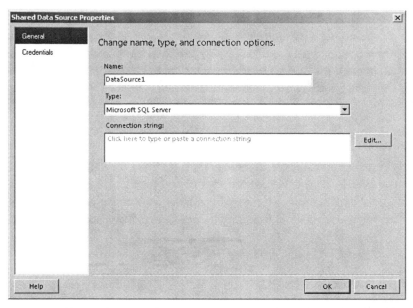

FIGURE 8-7 You set the name, data source type, connection string, and credentials in the Shared Data Source Properties dialog box.

Just as when you created the embedded data source, you should change the name to something more meaningful. In addition, you can type a connection string directly into the Connection String box or you can click the Edit button to generate the string. You can also change from Windows integrated security for the data source authentication to another option, as we explain in the "Setting data source credentials" section of this chapter. When you finish, your shared data source becomes a new file in the project and displays in the Solution Explorer, as shown in Figure 8-8.

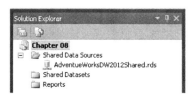

FIGURE 8-8 You can view shared data source files in the Solution Explorer.

Referencing a shared data source in a report

After you create a shared data source for the current report server project, you must manually associate each report with the shared data source. To do this, you use the Report Data Pane to add a data source to each report, as we describe in the "Creating an embedded data source" section earlier in this chapter, but you select the Use Shared Data Source Reference option when configuring the host database. You can then select one of your project's shared data sources in the drop-down list, as shown in Figure 8-9. If you don't have a shared data source in the project yet, you can click the New button to open the Shared Data Source Properties dialog box and create one.

Tip To eliminate confusion, it's a good idea to assign the name of the shared data source to the data source object that you add to the report. If you later have a need to update a data source and you have multiple data sources in a report with names like DataSource1, DataSource2, and so on, you must open each data source to find the one you want to change.

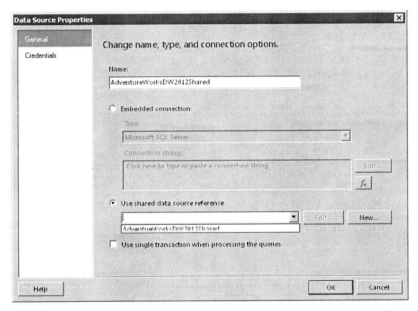

FIGURE 8-9 You can select a shared data source in the Data Source Properties dialog box.

Note Notice the Use Single Transaction When Processing The Queries check box that displays at the bottom of the Data Source Properties dialog box. This setting is applicable only at the report level when you add the shared data source reference to a report. See the "Processing queries as a single transaction" section to learn the purpose of this check box.

You can distinguish a shared data source from an embedded data source in the Report Data pane by the arrow icon, superimposed on the data source icon, as shown in Figure 8-10. However, you cannot convert it to an embedded data source. If you need to change it, you must delete the shared data source from the report by right-clicking it in the Report Data pane and selecting Delete, and then create a new embedded data source.

Note Deleting a shared data source from a report does not delete the shared data source from the project. If you want to delete the shared data source from the project, you must right-click it in the Solution Explorer and then select Delete.

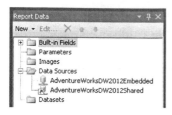

FIGURE 8-10 A shared data source reference appears with an arrow icon in the Report Data pane.

Editing a shared data source

If you need to change a connection string or the credentials assigned to a data source, you must open the file from Solution Explorer. To do this, double-click the file. The Shared Data Source Properties dialog box opens, and you can change properties as needed. Each report referencing the shared data source uses the new properties the next time you preview the report.

Deleting a shared data source

Right-click the shared data source file in the Solution Explorer, and select the Delete command. If a dataset uses the shared data source, a warning displays. Be aware that deleting the file from the project does not remove corresponding shared data source references in each report. You must manually delete the shared data source from the Report Data pane for each report individually. If you delete the wrong data source, you can use the Undo button to put it back.

Setting data source credentials

In most cases, you must provide a security context for a data source connection, whether it is an embedded data source or a shared data source. That is, you must tell Reporting Services which user account to use when connecting to that data source. Of course, that user account must be authorized to access data from the data source.

When you create a data source, you can choose from among four different options for configuring the credentials used to connect to that data source: Integrated Security, User Name and Password, Prompted, or simply no credentials at all. To change these credentials, open the Data Source Properties dialog box and select Credentials in the left pane, as shown in Figure 8-11.

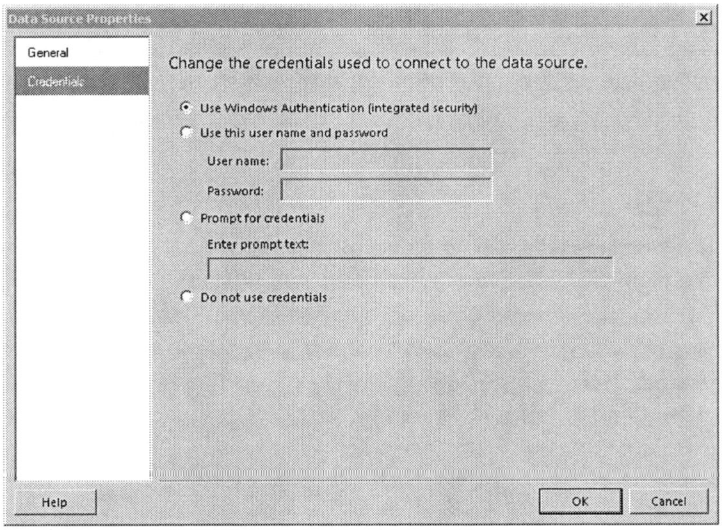

FIGURE 8-11 You can choose the method used to authenticate the request for data at the data source.

Integrated security

The Windows Authentication (Integrated Security) option is the default option for authenticating a user in the data source. When a user runs the report, Reporting Services sends the user's security token to the data source server and does not require the user to provide login credentials for the connection. This option works well when the data source server and the report server are located on the same computer or when network security supports impersonation and delegation. The user's Windows account must have permissions to read the data source.

User name and password

Rather than use the current user's credentials to connect to a data source, you can assign a specific user account as *stored credentials*. Reporting Services encrypts and stores these credentials in the report server database when you deploy the report to the report server. This option is required when you want to give users the ability to subscribe to the report or to schedule report execution for snapshots or caching.

In the Data Source Properties dialog box, select the Use This User Name And Password option, and then type the user's name and password for an account that has Read permissions on the database at minimum. You can use a Windows login or a database login as stored credentials. When you use a Windows login, Reporting Services uses these credentials for both the network connection and, when applicable, the database connection. For a database login, Reporting Services uses the Unattended Execution Account (explained in Chapter 4, "Installing Reporting Services") if one is defined or, otherwise, the Reporting Services service account to make the network connection to a remote server. It then appends the credentials to the data source connection string for database authentication.

Note A database login using stored credentials is required for connections to SQL Azure or PDW data sources. You cannot use database credentials to connect to an XML data source.

Prompt for credentials

The Prompt For Credentials option requires the user to type a user name and password before viewing the report. This option is less commonly used in reports. When you select this option, you must also provide the prompt text to display to the user when opening the report. The report will not execute until the data source successfully authenticates the user. For this reason, you can use this option only for reports that run on demand. That is, you cannot use a data source that prompts for credentials in a report used for snapshots or subscriptions or for which you configure cached execution.

No credentials

For reports requiring no security at all, you can select the Do Not Use Credentials option. This option is applicable when the remote data source does not require authentication for access or when you use a report only as a subreport embedded in another report. In the latter case, the subreport's data sources use the credentials specified in the parent report. If the data source is on another computer, Reporting Services uses the Unattended Execution Account (which we explain in Chapter 4) to connect to the remote computer.

Retrieving data with datasets

After creating a data source, you define a *dataset* to retrieve data for your report. A dataset is a container for the information used by the Report Processor to execute a query and return results. It includes a pointer to the data source, the query string to execute, and a list of fields corresponding to columns in the query results. During report development, you use these fields to define the report layout.

Comparing embedded and shared datasets

You can create a dataset to embed it directly into the report definition, or you can create a shared dataset that appears as an RSD file in your report project. If you need to use the same query repeatedly with many reports, a shared dataset is the preferred option, similar to how you can use a shared data source with many reports. If your goal is to facilitate self-service reporting for users of Report Builder, you can create multiple shared datasets for data that users commonly want to view in reports. When you use a shared dataset in a report, you can configure a caching schedule for the dataset on the report server to improve report execution performance. However, when you use an embedded dataset in a report, you can use a dynamic query string to produce a different query for each report execution by changing parameter values (as we explain in Chapter 11). A shared dataset must use a shared data source, whereas an embedded dataset can use either a shared data source or an embedded data source.

Working with an embedded dataset

The Report Data pane includes commands for you to add, edit, or delete embedded datasets. When editing the embedded dataset, you have the option to access all dataset properties or to go directly to the dataset query.

Creating an embedded dataset

Just as with data sources, there are multiple ways to add a dataset to a report. In the Report Data pane, you can click New and then select Dataset to open the Dataset Properties dialog box. You can also right-click the Datasets folder in the Report Data pane and then select Add Dataset to open the dialog box. Here you must select the Use A Dataset Embedded In My Report option to switch from the default option and to display the dataset properties, as shown in Figure 8-12. You can name the dataset by using the same rules applicable to data sources—no spaces and no special characters.

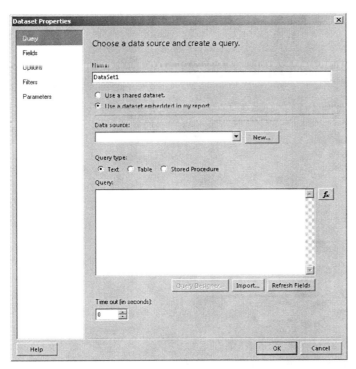

FIGURE 8-12 Use the radio button to switch the dataset type to embedded in the Dataset Properties dialog box.

Before you can create the query, you must specify the data source that you want to use. That way, the report designer knows whether to display a graphical query designer or a text-based query designer. You can select an existing data source in the Data Source drop-down list, or you can click the New button to set up a new embedded or shared data source if you missed that step earlier.

Additionally, you must choose one of the following query types:

- **Text** The default query type is Text, which means that you'll supply a query to select data from the source. For many data source types, you can click the Query Designer button to use a graphical query designer or text query designer to build the query. If you prefer, or when the Query Designer button is not enabled, you can type the query string in the Query box, as shown in Figure 8-13. Rather than type a query, you can click the Import button to copy a query string from a SQL file or from another report's RDL file.

- **Table** For some relational data sources, you can use the Table query type option to get all fields from a target table.

- **Stored Procedure** With this query type, you can select from a list of available stored procedures in the specific data source. If the stored procedure you choose returns multiple datasets, Reporting Services uses only the first one.

Another important property that you have in the dataset is the time-out property. By default, this property is set to 0, which means the query will wait indefinitely for the data source to return data. If you want to put a time limit on the query and fail the report if the data source is taking too long to respond with results, you can specify the maximum number of seconds to wait as the time-out value.

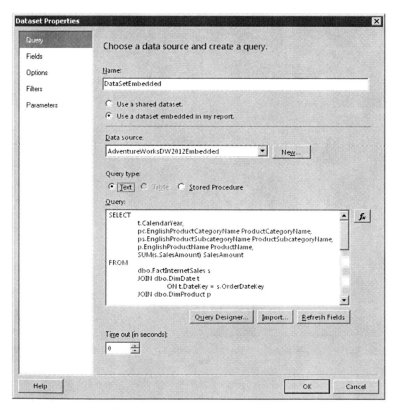

FIGURE 8-13 You update the properties on the Query page of the Dataset Properties dialog box to create an embedded dataset.

Editing an embedded dataset

Each embedded dataset appears only in the Report Data pane in the Datasets folder, as shown in Figure 8-14. Furthermore, you can see that every column returned by the dataset query appears in a list below the dataset. These are fields that you can use in your report design. You can open the Data Source Properties dialog box to make changes to the dataset by double-clicking the dataset in the Report Data pane or by clicking the Edit command in the Report Data pane toolbar. If you want to edit the query only, you can right-click the dataset and select the Query command to open the Query Designer.

FIGURE 8-14 An embedded dataset displays in the Datasets folder of the Report Data pane.

The dataset field names inherit from the column names returned by the dataset query. If you prefer to rename a field, you can right-click any field in the Report Data pane and select Field Properties to open the Fields page of the Dataset Properties dialog box, as shown in Figure 8-15. Here you can type a new name for the field in the Field Name column. You can also eliminate a field from the dataset by selecting it on this page and clicking the Delete button.

By default, the fields display in the sequence specified in the query. If there are a lot of fields for the dataset, you might prefer to rearrange the field order to make it easier to locate fields as you develop your report. When you cannot change the structure of the dataset query, as might be the case when working with a stored procedure, you can click on a field and then use the up or down arrow to move the field to a new location in the list.

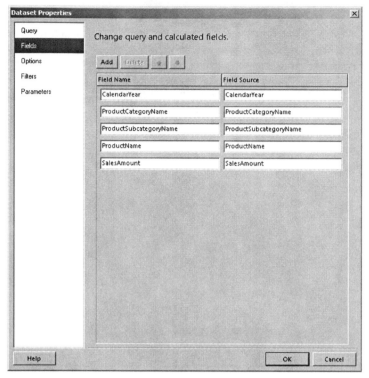

FIGURE 8-15 You can rename, delete, or rearrange fields on the Fields page of the Dataset Properties dialog box.

Converting an embedded dataset to a shared dataset

After you create an embedded dataset, you might decide later that it should be a shared dataset instead. You can right-click the embedded dataset in the Report Data pane, and select the Convert To Shared Dataset command. The shared dataset is distinguishable from the embedded dataset by its different icon. In addition, an RSD file containing the shared dataset definition appears in the Solution Explorer.

Deleting an embedded dataset

Right-click the embedded dataset in the Report Data pane, and select the Delete command to delete it from the report. Another way to do the same thing is to select the dataset and then click the Delete button in the Report Data pane's toolbar. If you accidentally delete the wrong dataset, you can use the Undo button to restore the deleted dataset.

Working with a shared dataset

When you create a shared dataset, you create an RSD file that has an XML structure like you see below, except that we eliminated the field elements to focus on the key dataset elements. The *DataSourceReference* element holds the identifier for the data source, and the *CommandText* element contains the query string. If the dataset has parameters or filters, they appear as additional elements, much like the fields. When you override an option, the setting you choose also appears in the XML structure, but default values are omitted.

```xml
<?xml version="1.0" encoding="utf-8"?>

<SharedDataSet xmlns:rd="http://schemas.microsoft.com/SQLServer/reporting/reportdesigner"
xmlns="http://schemas.microsoft.com/sqlserver/reporting/2010/01/shareddatasetdefinition">
  <DataSet Name="">
    <Query>
      <DataSourceReference>AdventureWorksDW2012Shared</DataSourceReference>
      <CommandText>SELECT        t.CalendarYear, pc.EnglishProductCategoryName AS
ProductCategoryName, ps.EnglishProductSubcategoryName AS ProductSubcategoryName,
                    p.EnglishProductName AS ProductName, SUM(s.SalesAmount) AS SalesAmount
FROM         FactInternetSales AS s INNER JOIN
                    DimDate AS t ON t.DateKey = s.OrderDateKey INNER JOIN
                    DimProduct AS p ON p.ProductKey = s.ProductKey INNER JOIN
                    DimProductSubcategory AS ps ON ps.ProductSubcategoryKey =
p.ProductSubcategoryKey INNER JOIN
                    DimProductCategory AS pc ON pc.ProductCategoryKey = ps.ProductCategoryKey
INNER JOIN
                    DimCustomer AS c ON c.CustomerKey = s.CustomerKey
WHERE       (t.CalendarYear = '2006')
GROUP BY t.CalendarYear, pc.EnglishProductCategoryName, ps.EnglishProductSubcategoryName,
p.EnglishProductName
ORDER BY ProductCategoryName, ProductSubcategoryName, ProductName</CommandText>
    </Query>
    <Fields>…</Fields>
  </DataSet>
</SharedDataSet>
```

Creating a shared dataset

To create a shared dataset, right-click the Shared Datasets folder in the Solution Explorer and click Add New Dataset. The Shared Dataset Properties dialog box displays, as shown in Figure 8-16, and looks almost the same as the Dataset Properties dialog box that you use to create an embedded dataset.

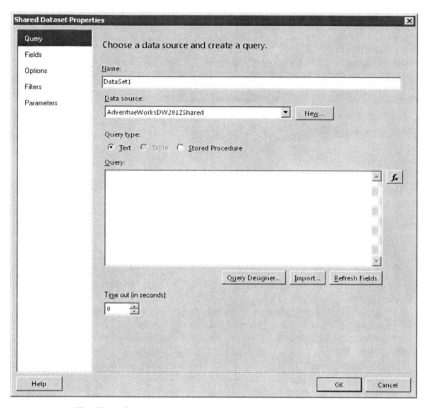

FIGURE 8-16 The Shared Dataset Properties dialog box is similar to the one you use to create an embedded dataset.

The data source defaults to one of the shared data sources if one exists, which you can change by selecting a different one in the Data Source drop-down list. However, you can use the New button to create a shared data source if none exists yet. You can use only shared data sources with shared datasets.

Just as you do with an embedded dataset, you must choose a query type (explained in more detail in the "Creating an embedded dataset" section of this chapter). You can type in the query text, open the Query Designer, or import a query string from a SQL file or from another report. Optionally, you can set the time-out property if you want the report to stop executing if the data source fails to respond in a timely manner. Your new shared data source becomes a new file in the project and displays in the Solution Explorer in the Shared Datasets folder, as shown in Figure 8-17.

FIGURE 8-17 The shared dataset appears in the Shared Datasets folder of the Solution Explorer pane.

Referencing a shared dataset in a report

If you plan to use the shared dataset in a report, you must add it to the Report Data pane. Right-click the Datasets folder, and click Add Dataset. In the Dataset Properties dialog box, leave the Use A Shared Dataset option selected, as shown in Figure 8-18. Unlike Shared Data Sources, there is no way to create a Shared Dataset inside a particular report. It must be created first in Solution Explorer.

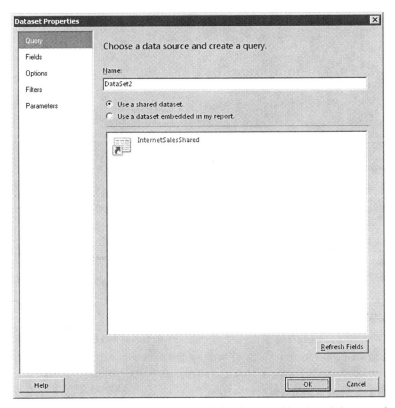

FIGURE 8-18 Use the Dataset Properties dialog box to add a shared dataset reference to a report.

A shared dataset has an arrow icon superimposed on the dataset icon, as shown in Figure 8-19. There is no way to convert it to an embedded data source if you change your mind about how to implement it. In that case, you must delete the shared data source from the report in the Report Data pane and then create a new embedded dataset.

> **Note** Shared datasets behave like shared data sources. Deleting a shared dataset from a report does not delete it from the project. You must manually delete it from Solution Explorer to completely remove it.

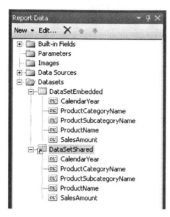

FIGURE 8-19 You can identify a shared dataset by its arrow icon in the Report Data pane.

Editing a shared dataset

You must open the shared dataset file by double-clicking it in Solution Explorer when you need to make changes to the query or the other dataset properties. If you add or remove fields from the dataset by modifying the query or editing the list of fields (as described in the "Editing an embedded dataset" section of this chapter), you must open each report referencing the shared dataset and open the corresponding Dataset Properties dialog box from the Report Data pane. Click the Refresh Fields button to update the list of fields available to the report.

Deleting a shared dataset

To permanently remove a shared dataset from a project, right-click it in the Solution Explorer and select the Delete command. There is no warning if you choose to delete a shared dataset that a report references. After you delete the shared dataset, a report is invalid until you remove the corresponding shared dataset reference in the Report Data pane.

Exploring query designers

When you create an embedded or shared dataset, you can click the Query Designer button to access an interface in which you can build the query and preview query results. For queries to SQL Server and related databases, you can use a graphical interface to explore table diagrams and use tools to help you generate the query. Other graphical interfaces are available to help you design queries for report models and multidimensional and data mining sources. For everything else, you can use a text-based query designer.

Graphical query designer

You can use the relational query designer, shown in Figure 8-20, when your dataset references a SQL Server, SQL Azure, or PDW data source and the query type is Text. This designer provides an interactive environment in which you can explore the available tables and views and set options that dynamically generate the query text. If you prefer to work with the text-based query designer, click the Edit As Text button in the Query Designer toolbar. You can also use the Import button to import an existing query from a SQL file or from another report, and then use the query designer to modify the query text.

> **Note** If the query type is Stored Procedure, you can open the Query Designer but it contains only a results pane. You can click the Run button to execute the stored procedure to see the data it returns.

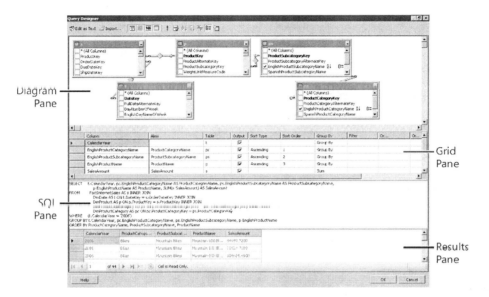

FIGURE 8-20 You use the graphical Query Designer to explore data and relationships as you build the query.

The graphical query designer consists of the following panes:

- **Diagram Pane** You can see the tables and views from the data source and select columns to use in your query. You can use the Add Table button in the toolbar or modify the query to include another table to add more tables or views to this pane. Select the * (All Columns) check box to add all columns from the table to your query, or select the check box for individual columns. You can drag a column in one table to a related column in a second table to create an inner join. If you need a different join type, you can modify the query in the SQL pane or right-click the join in the Diagram pane to select another option. You can select a column in a table and then select the Sort Ascending or Sort Descending buttons in the toolbar to include the column in an ORDER BY clause in the query. Similarly, you can use the Use Group By button to add a field to the GROUP BY clause when you want to produce a query that aggregates results. If you have defined a filter using a column, you can select the column here and use the Remove Filter button to clear it from the WHERE clause of the query.

- **Grid Pane**   Each column added to the query appears in this pane where you can assign an alias and specify the table containing the column. You use the Output check box to indicate whether the query should return the column in the results or use it for filtering. You can specify the sort order and direction for each column, apply an aggregate function, and define a filter condition. The changes you make in this pane update the query in the SQL pane.

- **SQL Pane**   This pane contains the SELECT statement for the query. Changes that you make to the Diagram and Grid panes update the query here. Likewise, the changes you make in the SQL pane create corresponding changes in the Diagram and Grid panes.

- **Results Pane**   To test the query, click the Run button in the toolbar. You can scroll through the rows returned by the query, jump to a specific row, or jump to the beginning or end of the result set. If the query takes too long to execute, you can click the Cancel button in the Results pane toolbar.

The Query Designer toolbar contains four buttons corresponding to each of these panes. You can click the button to toggle the visibility of each pane individually. For example, if you prefer not to use the Grid pane but find it helpful to see the Diagram pane while you create your query in the SQL pane, click the Show/Hide Grid Pane button to hide it.

Report model query designer

Although you can no longer develop a report model in SQL Server 2012 Reporting Services, you can deploy a report model developed in an earlier version to the report server and use it as a data source in a report you develop in the current version. The purpose of a report model is to provide access to a single data source to users who lack the technical skills to write a relational or multidimensional query. The report model is a semantic layer that allows you to select objects for a report and instructs the report server how to dynamically generate the query.

> **Note** If you have access to a report model's SMDL file, its data source view (DSV), and data source file, you can upload the files manually to a SQL Server 2012 Reporting Services report server. We explain how to upload and manage report models in Chapter 23, "Deploying reports to a server."

If the report model has *perspectives*, or collections of objects representing a subset of the entire model, you must specify whether you want the query designer to open the entire model or one of the perspectives. When the query design opens, you see the entities available in the selected model or perspective, as shown in Figure 8-21.

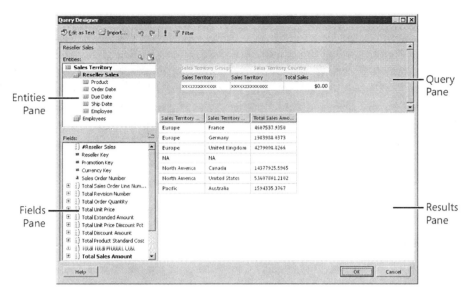

FIGURE 8-21 You use the report model Query Designer to arrange entity fields as a query.

The report model query designer consists of the following panes:

- **Entities Pane**   In general, entities are analogous to tables. As you select an entity in this pane, the fields associated with the selected entity display in the Fields pane. You can double-click an entity to add its default detail fields to the Query pane as defined by the report model developer. After you add a field to the Query pane, the Entities pane displays only entities related to the table containing that field. When you click an entity, you might see additional entities related to your current entity selection.

- **Fields Pane**   As you select an entity in the Entities pane, the entity's fields display in this pane. A field corresponds to a column in a table or an expression based on one or more table columns. To the left of each field name is an icon that identifies the field's data type. For example, the three yellow blocks next to a field tells you that the field is an aggregate numeric value, a pound (#) symbol indicates that the field is a scalar numeric value, and the letter *a* identifies the field as a string. You can double-click a field to add it to the query pane, or you can drag it into position on the design surface. To add more than one field at once, you can select the fields while pressing the Ctrl key, or the Shift key for a contiguous set of fields, and drag the group to the table.

Note You can click the New Field button at the top right of the Fields pane to open the Define Formula dialog box when you need to create a calculated field in the dataset. Calculated fields for relational data source types are described in more detail in Chapter 11, "Developing expressions." Calculated fields for most data sources use the same expression language that you use to create expressions in a report. However, when your data source is a report model, you use a different expression language, which you can learn more about at *http://msdn.microsoft.com/en-us/library/ee210538.aspx*.

- **Query Pane** This pane contains a design surface to which you add fields from the report model. You can rearrange fields by dragging the column header to a new location. You can also delete a field by right-clicking it and selecting Delete.

- **Results Pane** Click the Run button in the Query Designer toolbar to view the results of the query that Reporting Services generates based on your field selections. You might be prompted to add a filter.

You can use the Filter button in the Query Designer toolbar to apply a condition to all detail rows in the query results and display only rows or the aggregate of rows satisfying the condition. Just as you do in in the query designer, you can click an entity to locate a field to use in the filter. The configuration of the field in the report model determines how you set up the filter. For example, if the field is configured to use a drop-down list, you can select a value for the filter comparison. If it's a text box, you must type in a valid value.

The default condition operator for the filter is Equals, which allows you to type or select one value only. However, you can change the condition operator to allow multiple selections by clicking the Equals link and then clicking In A List. If the field has a drop-down list, you can now select a check box for each value that you want to include in the filter.

You can convert a filter to a parameter to prompt the user to make a selection before executing the report. To do this, right-click the field name and click Prompt. The green question mark next to the condition, shown in Figure 8-22, flags it as a parameter. As you add additional fields to the filter, the default behavior is to create a compound expression using AND logic, but you can click *and* to switch to OR logic.

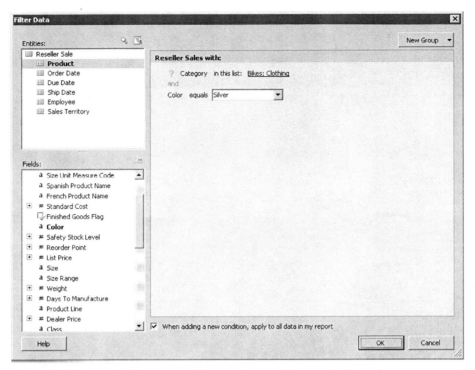

FIGURE 8-22 You can build compound filters and prompt the user for filter values as a parameter.

SharePoint list query designer

The SharePoint list query designer, shown in Figure 8-23, allows you to view all lists on a SharePoint site for which you have at least Read permission. Although you can view all lists here, you can select columns from only one list for your query. If you select columns from one list and then select columns from another list, a message displays to warn you that your new selection will replace your previous selections. You can click the Run Query button to see the data from the SharePoint list.

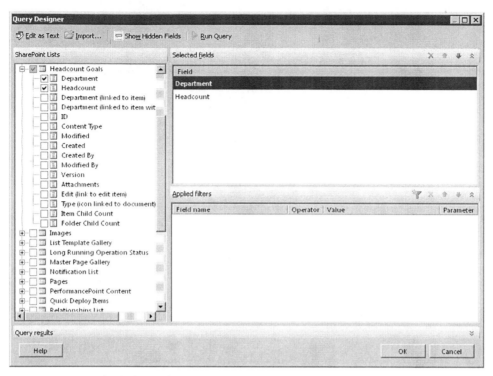

FIGURE 8-23 You select columns from a SharePoint list and apply filters using the SharePoint List Query Designer.

To limit the rows in the result set, click the Add Filter button in the Applied Filters pane. You can then select a field name to use in the filter, set an operator (such as *contains* or *is not*), and specify a comparison value. You can select the Parameter check box to create a report parameter for the filter. That way, a user can change the filter value when viewing the report as we explain in Chapter 14, "Creating dynamic reports with parameters."

MDX query designer

The MDX query designer, shown in Figure 8-24, appears when you associate the dataset with an Analysis Services data source. The SAP NetWeaver BI query designer and the Hyperion Essbase query designer are very similar to the MDX query designer. We discuss this query designer in greater detail in Chapter 16, "Using Analysis Services as a data source."

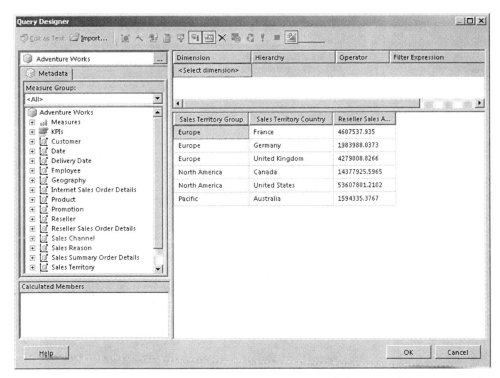

FIGURE 8-24 The MDX Query Designer displays when you use a multidimensional data source such as Analysis Services.

Text-based query designer

You use the text-based query designer, shown in Figure 8-25, for all other data sources, including Oracle, Teradata, XML, OLE DB, and ODBC. If you like, you can use it with a SQL Server data source too. If a graphical query designer is available for the data source selected, you can toggle between the graphical designer and the text-based designer using the Edit As Text button on the toolbar.

Note For relational queries, you use the syntax applicable to the underlying database. For XML queries, you can leave the query blank to retrieve all records from a document. Refer to "Queries for Databases with XML Sources" at *http://msdn.microsoft.com/en-us/library/ms159741.aspx* to see the syntax to query a web service or embedded XML.

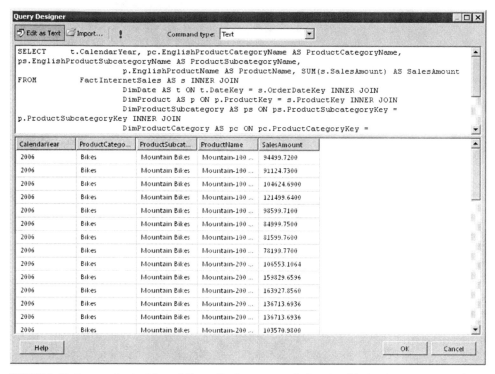

FIGURE 8-25 You use the text-based Query Designer to work directly with the dataset query string.

Understanding dataset properties

A dataset is more than a query. There are several dataset properties that you use to control the execution of the query and the appearance of the data. The fields of a dataset affect the way that you design the layout of data on a report, while dataset options affect the way that data displays in the final report. Dataset filters restrict the rows of data to display when the report renders, and parameters change the structure of a query at runtime.

Fields

When you test a dataset query, the query designer generates the fields collection for your dataset to match the data columns that you see in the query results. It also generates this collection when you save the dataset, even if you don't test the query first. The fields collection contains one field for every column retrieved by the query, but it can also contain *calculated fields*. A calculated field is a field that you add manually to the list in the Dataset Properties dialog box and is based on an expression that you define. You can use a calculated field in your report just like any other field, as we explain in Chapter 11.

Options

As shown in Figure 8-26, you can also specify options for the dataset, such as collation, case sensitivity, accent sensitivity, kanatype sensitivity, and width sensitivity. Each of these values affects sort order. The default collation is (Default), which relies on the data source to define the collation and uses the regional settings of the computer if the data source does not provide collation information. Otherwise, you can select a collation type, such as Latin1_General, in the Collation drop-down list. Similarly, the default value of Auto for the other options instructs Reporting Services to attempt to retrieve the correct setting for the option from the data source, but you can override this behavior by specifying True or False explicitly. An option is also included for specifying whether subtotal rows in your dataset should be treated as detail rows in your report, which is explained in more detail in Chapter 16.

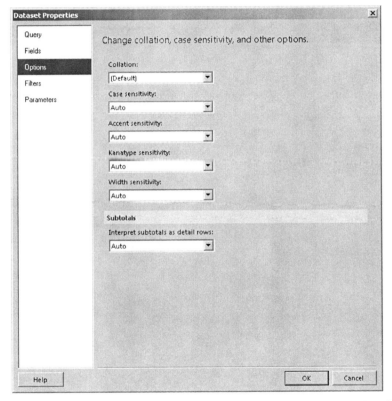

FIGURE 8-26 You change the dataset options to override the database settings for sort order.

Filters

A dataset also includes a filters collection, which doesn't always exist in every dataset like the fields collection does. If you cannot filter the data from your data source directly in the query—for example, by using a WHERE clause—you can filter the data in the dataset by defining filter rules. A dataset filter allows you to selectively exclude rows that don't meet a condition that you specify, but this exclusion takes place after the query executes. We explain dataset filters in greater detail in Chapter 14.

Parameters

Another collection in the dataset is the parameters collection. Not every dataset has a parameters collection, and not every data source supports query parameters, but if you create query parameters, they automatically appear in this collection. You can provide default values or link the query parameter to report parameters, as we explain in Chapter 14.

CHAPTER 9

Designing the report layout

Now that you know how to obtain data for a report, it's time to learn how to design the report layout. In this chapter, you learn how to use report items and data regions to structure your report. You also learn how to configure various properties that control the look and feel of your report. The examples in this chapter use the Report Designer in SQL Server Data Tools (SSDT), but the same report items, data regions, and properties are available to you when you use Report Builder.

Reviewing report items

A *report item* is a control that you use to add data or visual elements to a report. You can see all the report items available in the Toolbox window. Table 9-1 shows report items organized as three logical groups: general report items, tablix data regions, and graphical data regions.

 Note If you need a certain type of feature that is not available with the standard report items, you can implement a custom report item as we describe in Chapter 33, "Programming report design components."

TABLE 9-1 Report design elements

Type	Icon	Name	Description	Earliest Version Supported
General Report Items		Text Box	Static text or dynamic text from a dataset or an expression	2000
		Line	Graphic element with defined endpoints, color, and width	2000
		Rectangle	Graphic element or container for free-form layout of multiple report items	2000
		Image	Binary image data embedded in report, stored externally, or retrieved by a dataset	2000
		Subreport	External report embedded in a parent report	2000

Type	Icon	Name	Description	Earliest Version Supported
Tablix Data Regions		Table	Collection of text boxes with fixed columns and dynamic, data-driven rows	2000
		Matrix	Collection of text boxes with dynamic, data-driven rows and columns	2000
		List	Free-form structure with data-driven repeating section	2000
Graphical Data Regions		Chart	Graphical display of data in standard chart form	2000
		Gauge	Graphical display of performance data in gauge form	2008
		Map	Graphical display of spatial data	2008 R2
		Data Bar	Graphical display of a single point as a bar or column	2008 R2
		Sparkline	Graphical display of a data series over a defined period of time	2008 R2
		Indicator	Graphical display of conditional data using icon sets	2008 R2

General report items

The first group in the table contains general report items that can be used independently of a dataset. That is, you can create a report that does not contain a query by using any of these report items. Of course, you usually create a report to display data, and you can use the report items in this group to enhance the appearance of your report by adding titles, header text, footer text, and various types of images.

Text boxes

The most commonly used report item is the text box. The data in a text box can be static text or an expression, but unlike the other general report items, it can also display data from a dataset field. You can use a text box by itself or as a group of text boxes that are combined into a generic data region, such as a table or matrix.

Lines and rectangles

The line and rectangle report items are used completely independently of report data. These report items provide visual separation between report sections. You can also use the rectangle to contain other report items, which is useful to keep items together on the same page when the report renders.

Images

An image report item displays image data, as you might expect. You can use an image as a free-standing logo or picture in your report, or you can have pictures associated with rows of data, such as details for a product catalog. You can also use an image as a background for a text box, a data region, or the body of a report.

A common way to use an image is to display a corporate logo at the top of the report. You can import an image into the report definition to store the binary data locally in base64 format. However, this method increases the size of the report definition file and requires you to modify the report definition manually if you later want to change the image.

If you anticipate that an image might change in the future, you can configure the report item to reference an image stored at an external location, such as a URL on a web server. That way, you can update the file on the web server and all reports that use that image will use the new file automatically. One benefit of this approach is the smaller size of the report definition file because the image is not embedded into the report. Another benefit is the efficiency you gain from avoiding maintenance on each report that uses the new image.

Subreports

A *subreport* is a special report item that serves as a placeholder for another report that you want to embed in the report that you are currently developing, which is known as the *parent report*. You can build a report once and reuse it many times as a subreport. A popular way to use subreports is to combine many online reports into a single report for the purpose of producing a PDF document. You can pass parameter values from the report to the subreport to change the subreport's content dynamically, which you learn about in Chapter 13, "Adding interactivity." It's important to note that the page header and page footer sections of the subreport do not render in the parent report.

> **Tip** You might experience performance problems when using a subreport inside a data region because each instance of a subreport must execute its datasets separately from other subreport instances and datasets in the parent report. An alternative to using a subreport is the report parts feature introduced in SQL Server 2008 R2, which we explain in Chapter 29, "Reusing Report Parts." You also might consider using the new *Lookup* function introduced in Reporting Services 2008 R2 when you need to bring together data from different datasets. We explain the *Lookup* function in Chapter 12, "Using functions."

Tablix data regions

The next grouping in Table 9-1 contains tablix data regions. Tablix data regions are more complex report items than the general report items. In general, you use them to display data from a dataset by using repeating rows or columns. Each of the three types of tablix data regions—table, matrix, and list—are effectively the same report item behind the scenes, a tablix. Although the tablix data regions differ in how they display data, they are similar in behavior in that they each produce repeating sections of data based on the dataset rows.

> **Note** The tablix report item was introduced in Reporting Services 2008. We explain more about the nuances of a tablix in Chapter 10, "Working with the tablix." In this chapter, we introduce you to the basic concepts of each type of tablix and show how you can start working with each of them.

Table

The table data region displays a structure that has a fixed number of columns that you define, but the number of rows in the table depends on the number of rows in the dataset and the grouping definitions, if any, that you define. Much as a spreadsheet is a collection of cells, a table is a collection of text boxes organized as rows and columns. You can use a table to display detail data, summarized data, or both.

Matrix

The matrix data region has a dynamic number of rows and columns that are dependent on the dataset rows and defined groupings. Like a table, it is a collection of text boxes, but these text boxes are arranged only as groups. Therefore, you use a matrix to display summarized data.

List

The list allows you to define only one grouping, but you can place report items inside the data region. Whereas the table and matrix organize text boxes into rigid structures of rows and columns, the list can display text boxes in any arrangement, with or without alignment to the other text boxes in the same list. More commonly, you use a list to combine multiple views of the same data, such as a table and a chart.

Graphical data regions

The remaining report items are graphical data regions that you can use to visualize data. In most cases, the graphical data regions summarize data to allow easier comparison of values across categories or locations.

Chart

Reporting Services includes many standard types of charts, such as column, line, and pie charts, and also provides other types of charts with which you may not be as familiar, such as funnel and radar charts. We show you how to work with these chart types in Chapter 17, "Creating charts," and Chapter 18, "Working with chart elements."

Gauge

A gauge is useful for visual comparisons of a value to a target. The difference between a chart and a gauge is that a chart usually displays many values whereas a gauge usually displays one value, such as a key performance indicator using either a radial or linear gauge. You learn all about gauges in Chapter 19, "Comparing values to goals with gauges."

Map

For spatial data visualization, you can use maps. You can create a map to display points to highlight specific locations or to display lines if you need to show a route between two or more points. Another option is to create a map using simple polygon shapes to represent a floor plan or more complex polygon shapes for countries or continents. You can even use Bing integration to add more detail to your map. In Chapter 21, "Mapping data," you learn how to use the Map Wizard to start building basic maps, which you can then enhance with additional properties as described in Chapter 22, "Working with map elements."

Data bar

By using a data bar, you can use inline column or bar charts to display a single data point for a detail row or group in a data region. Chapter 17 provides you with more information about using the data bar report item.

Sparkline

You can use a sparkline to add inline charts for a series of data points. Although the term sparkline implies a line chart, you can use a column, line, area, pie, doughnut, or range chart to visually compare multiple values in a data region's detail row or group. Turn to Chapter 17 to learn more about this type of data visualization.

Indicator

Indicators provide another way to compare values to goals. You can choose indicators from built-in icon sets to display in a data region, and you can customize these sets to change properties like the color or size of an indicator icon. If you prefer, you can use your own images. We explain how to use indicators in Chapter 20, "Displaying performance with indicators."

Adding general report items to a report

In this section, you learn how to add each of the general report items to a simple report. You'll place a text box at the top of the report to display a static title, and then you'll add a line below the title to separate it from other items below the title. You'll also add a logo as an embedded image. Last, you'll include a subreport to reuse information from a different report.

Note In this book's companion content, you will find the files we use in the examples for this chapter. The Chapter 09 folder contains an image and a subreport, in addition to the final versions of the reports that we demonstrate in this section.

Adding a text box

You can use a freestanding text box to display static text as the report title at the top of the report, as you'll do in this example. Later, in Chapter 11, "Developing expressions," you'll learn how to use a text box to display an expression, as you might do when you want to display page numbers in the footer of each page.

If the Toolbox is not visible in SSDT, select Toolbox from the View menu to display it. The Toolbox, shown in Figure 9-1, contains all the built-in report items that we discuss in this chapter. From the Toolbox, drag the Text box onto the report design surface and position it in the upper-left corner of the report body. Instead of dragging the text box onto your report, you can double-click the Text box and then drag it from the default location in the report to the preferred location. When you have positioned it where you like, click inside the text box and type a title.

FIGURE 9-1 Select a report item to add to your report from the Toolbox.

Show the ruler

To make precision placement of report items easier, right-click in the empty design space surrounding the report, point to View, and then click Ruler. A vertical ruler now appears on the left side of your workspace, and a horizontal ruler displays across the top of the design surface. A line moves along on each ruler as you move your cursor so that you can easily see the current position of your cursor relative to the top-left corner of the report.

Click once anywhere in the report outside of the text box to clear the current selection, and then click inside the text box to select it. You can now resize the text box by dragging its right edge to the 3-inch mark on the horizontal ruler, as shown in Figure 9-2.

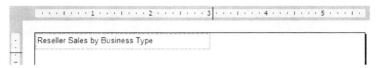

Reseller Sales by Business Type

FIGURE 9-2 You can use the ruler to gauge the height and width of a text box during resizing.

 Tip For more precise sizing of a text box, you can set its Height and Width properties, as we explain later in this chapter in the "Configuring the placement and size of a report item" section.

Adding a line

The primary purpose for a line is to add a visual effect to a report. A line has properties that you can set to define its length, width, and color, among others. Although you can configure many property values of a report item to change at report execution, as you learn later in this chapter, a line always has a fixed length that cannot be changed dynamically. You can also configure the *Bookmark* and *DocumentMapLabel* properties for a line, which means that you can use it as a navigation aid.

 Note We explain how to work with bookmarks and document maps in Chapter 13.

Adding a line to a report is very similar to adding a text box. You can drag it from the Toolbox or double-click it. Either way, a line appears as a diagonal line that you can change to a horizontal or vertical line if you prefer. Just drag the edges to create the desired line angle. For this example, place the line below the report title text box and then click the right end of the line. You can now drag the right edge of the line to create a horizontal line and to match the length of the report title text box. In the "Changing the appearance of a report item" section of this chapter, you will learn how to use properties to give the line an improved look.

As you move report items around on the design surface, a blue snap line appears when the edges of multiple items are in alignment, as shown in Figure 9-3. In this illustration, the horizontal snap line obscures the line, but you can see its endpoints at the left edge of the report and at the 3-inch mark. After you release your mouse button, the line disappears. You can use this feature to get perfect alignment without resorting to setting the location properties for each report item.

FIGURE 9-3 Use the blue snap lines to guide the placement of one report item relative to the edges of another report item.

Tip The problem with a line as decoration or as a visual separation between different sections of your report is that it cannot resize dynamically like other report items. As an alternative, you might consider using a rectangle to contain report items by section and then using the rectangle's *Border* property on one side only to produce the same effect as a line.

Adding a rectangle

A rectangle is nothing more than a container that you can use to group items together. If you need to rearrange items in your report but still keep together a group of items, you'll find it easier to move items as a group within a rectangle than to move them individually and realign them in the new location. Also, during rendering, a rectangle can prevent the items it contains from affecting the placement of items outside the rectangle. As long you leave enough space within the rectangle for its contents to grow, the items outside of the rectangle will not be pushed out of place by the expansion of the items inside the rectangle.

Drag the rectangle from the Toolbox onto the report design surface. You can then drag other items, either from the Toolbox or from another area on the report, into the report. After placing an item into the rectangle, you should check to make sure it's really inside the rectangle. You can do this by clicking the item to select it. In the Properties window, locate the *Parent* property and make sure its value is the name of the rectangle, such as Rectangle1. If the *Parent* property shows a different value, such as Body, the item is only overlapping the rectangle, which will not produce the desired effect.

Note When you have overlapping values, the rendering process determines what happens next. If the report renders as a PDF or TIFF file, the item with the highest *ZIndex* property is visible and displays on top of the other item. If the report renders as HTML, Excel, or Word, the rendering engine rearranges the items to prevent overlapping.

Tip You can place a rectangle inside a text box that itself is inside a tablix. When you use this technique, you can place multiple items inside the rectangle and arrange them freely.

Adding an image

You can add images to a report in a number of ways. The most straightforward way is to import an image into the report and store it as an embedded image. If you need to refer to the same image in many reports, such as a corporate logo, you can store the image on a network share or on a web server and embed a reference to the image in your report. Then, if the image later changes, you can update the image in one location, and all reports then use the new image. Finally, for the display of separate images in detail, you can retrieve images from a database.

You can use the following format types as images in reports:

- Bitmap (BMP)

- Graphics Interchange Format (GIF)

- Joint Photographic Experts Group (JPEG)

- Portable Network Graphics (PNG)

Embedded image

From the Toolbox, drag the Image report item to the top edge of the report at the 4-inch mark on the horizontal ruler. In the Image Properties dialog box, you can change the name of the image and keep the default value of Embedded in the Select The Image Source drop-down list, as shown in Figure 9-4. If you already have an embedded image in your report, you can use the Use This Image drop-down list to select the image and use it in this new location. Otherwise, click the Import button to import an image from a location that you have stored on your computer or a network share.

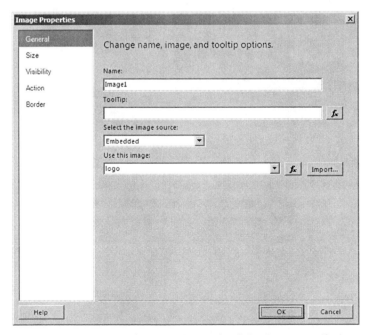

FIGURE 9-4 You can use the Image Properties dialog box to specify the source for an image in your report.

The Image Properties dialog box includes other pages to configure properties for the image. On the Size page, you can set the image size by choosing one of the following options:

- Use Original Size when you want to retain the actual image size, as shown in Figure 9-5.

- You can choose the Fit To Size option when you must restrict the image to the dimensions of a text box.

- The Fit Proportional option ensures that the image fits within the text box but preserves the original aspect ratio of the image.

- If you use the Clip option and the image is larger than the text box, only the top-left corner of the image displays.

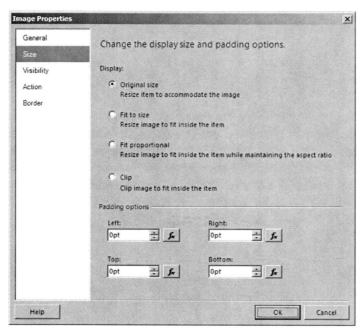

FIGURE 9-5 You can choose whether to retain the original size of an image or to make it fit inside the current report item size.

Note You use the other pages in the Image Properties dialog box to control the Visibility, Action, and Border of a report item. These properties are not unique to images but are available to most report items. We explain report item visibility and actions in Chapter 13.

After you close the Image Properties dialog box, the image displays on the design surface where you can make further adjustments to the fit. For example, the original height of the sample image is approximately 1.5 inches. When you drag the bottom edge of the image to the ½-inch mark of the vertical ruler, the image resizes proportionally, as shown in Figure 9-6.

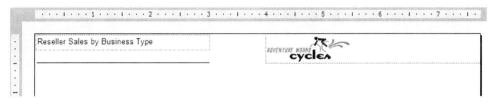

FIGURE 9-6 As you manually resize the height or width of an image, the report designer maintains the original proportions.

The Report Data pane now shows your newly added image in the Images folder, as shown in Figure 9-7. You can drag an image from this folder to another location on your report to reuse the same image. When you do this, an Image Properties dialog box displays for you to configure the properties for the new instance of the image. The report definition file stores the contents of the image file once, as a text string, but renders each instance of the image separately. That way, the size of the file will not grow too large when you reuse the same image repeatedly in the same report.

FIGURE 9-7 Each image that you add to your report appears in the Images folder in the Report Data pane.

Tip If you like, you can import images into your report and then add them to the layout. To do this, right-click the Images folder in the Report Data pane and select Add Image to bypass the Image Properties dialog box. Alternatively, you can click the New button in the toolbar of the Report Data pane and select Image. You can navigate to the folder containing the image and import it into the report.

External image

Rather than embed an image into your report, you can upload your file to a central location. You can use a web server, a network file share, or even a folder on your report server, but you must configure the report server to use an Unattended Execution Account, as described in Chapter 4, "Installing Reporting Services," so that the report server has a security context to use when accessing the storage location.

You start by adding the image to the report in the same way that we describe for an embedded image, but in the Select The Image Source drop-down list, select External. Then you type the location of the image in the Use This Image box. For example, if you uploaded the logo bitmap file to a folder called Images on the report server, the location is *http://<servername>/reportserver?/Images/logo.bmp,* where *<servername>* is the name of the server hosting Reporting Services.

> **Tip** The image might not display in the Design mode as it does when you use an embedded image. Furthermore, the size of the report item in Design mode might not match the size of the report item in Preview mode. You can check to make sure the correct image displays by switching to Preview mode. To adjust the size, when you have the external image report item selected in Report Designer, locate the *Sizing* property in the Properties window and change the value to *FitProportional.* Then you can resize the image to the height and width that you prefer.

Database images

When you have a data region in your report that you have already associated with a dataset (as we describe how to do in the "Binding data to a data region" section of this chapter), you can drag the Image report item from the Toolbox into an empty text box in a detail row. In the Image Properties dialog box, you must change the Select The Image Source selection in the drop-down list to Database. You can then select the dataset field that contains an image for each record in the Use This Field drop-down list. You must also choose an applicable value in the Use This MIME Type drop-down list: image/bmp, image/jpeg, image/gif, image/png, or image/x-png.

> **Tip** Be sure to change the display size to Original Size. You can always adjust the image size later if the original size is too large or too small.

Because the image for each row of the dataset varies, you see only a generic icon display in the data region. You can see the images display when you switch to Preview mode, as shown in Figure 9-8, which displays the top of the Database Images report.

FIGURE 9-8 You can view database images when you preview your report.

Adding a subreport

When you have an existing report that you want embed in your current report, you start by dragging the Subreport item from the Toolbox to the report body. A gray placeholder appears for your subreport, measuring 3 inches high by 3 inches wide, as shown in Figure 9-9. You can resize the placeholder if you like, but your subreport will not be confined to the dimensions of the placeholder, as you'll see when you preview the report.

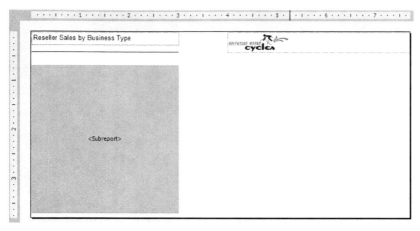

FIGURE 9-9 In Design mode, you see only a placeholder for a subreport.

Right-click the subreport item, and then select Subreport Properties. In the Subreport Properties dialog box, you can select a report in the Use This Report As A Subreport drop-down list, as shown in Figure 9-10, as long as the subreport exists in the same project as the parent report. However, you aren't required to store the subreport in the same project as the parent report. As you learn in Chapter 23,"Deploying reports to a sever," when you store reports in the same project, they deploy to the same folder on the report server. When your subreport is in a different folder than the parent report, you must identify the path to subreport's folder in addition to the name of the subreport.

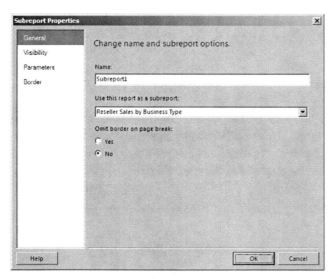

FIGURE 9-10 You specify only the name of the subreport when it is available in the same folder as the parent report.

After you configure the subreport properties, the subreport item in the report displays the name of the report you selected. If the subreport is available in one of the projects in your current solution, you can preview the report to verify that the subreport renders correctly, as shown in Figure 9-11.

Group	Country	Specialty Bike Shop	Value Added Reseller	Warehouse
Europe	France	$120,181		
			$399,159	
				$857,271
	Germany	$77,158		
			$299,827	
				$508,136
	United Kingdom	$92,952		
			$538,183	
				$645,970
	Group Total	*$290,292*	*$1,237,168*	*$2,011,377*
North America	Canada	$171,182		
			$884,996	
				$1,334,083
	United States	$712,180		
			$4,847,762	
				$3,802,117
	Group Total	*$883,362*	*$5,732,759*	*$5,136,200*
Pacific	Australia	$165,542		
			$400,571	
				$180,791

FIGURE 9-11 You can preview the subreport when it exists in the same solution as the parent report.

Troubleshooting subreport rendering

The addition of a subreport to your current report, known as the *parent* report, does not first require the existence of the subreport, although you won't be able to use SSDT to preview the parent report until the subreport exists in one of the projects in your current solution. If you prefer not to add the subreport to an open project, you can reference a report that exists on the report server, but then you must deploy the parent report the report server and then execute it on the server to verify that the subreport renders correctly.

When the subreport cannot render, the following message displays: "Error: Subreport could not be shown." The first thing you should do when you encounter this message is to open the report that you are using as a subreport to make sure that it renders when you view it directly. If it does not, you must resolve the problem, which might be an incorrect data source configuration or an authentication problem with the data source.

If the subreport renders correctly as a stand-alone report, the next thing to check is the path that you specified in the subreport properties. Make sure that you specify the path beginning with a forward slash (/) followed by the name of each folder name that you must open as you navigate from the Home folder of the report server (assuming a native-mode implementation) to the subreport. Separate each folder name with a forward slash. Also, do not include the RDL file extension with the subreport name.

Sometimes when you use multiple subreports in the same report, which render individually without a problem, the parent report does not display one or more of the subreports correctly. Try placing each subreport inside its own rectangle. Rectangles can cure many rendering problems!

Working with data regions

Because the table, matrix, and list report items are all based on the tablix, they have many common characteristics. In each case, you bind a dataset to a data region and then assign dataset fields or expressions to the data region's text boxes. The beauty of having these data regions derived from the tablix is that you're not stuck with your initial choice. The flexibility of the tablix allows you to start with a table, which you later convert into a matrix without having to start all over with a new matrix data region. In addition, you can group data more flexibly as we explain in the next chapter.

Nested data regions

A data region is a collection of text boxes. Although you typically place expressions into a text box, you can develop more advanced reports by inserting any type of report items into a text box inside a data region. For example, you can insert a subreport, an image, or even another data region into a text box.

You must have a clear understanding of the behavior and requirements of a data region to use this technique effectively. For example, if you nest a data region inside another data region, both data regions must be bound to the same dataset. The exception is when you place a subreport inside a data region, because the subreport renders separately.

A common technique requiring nested data regions is to put a list inside a list when your report layout requires a flexible arrangement of report items with multiple groupings. Another way to use a list is to place multiple data regions, such as a table and chart, side-by-side inside a list. If you define the list grouping as year, for example, the report displays one table and chart combination per year.

Adding a table

In the Toolbox pane, double-click Table to add a table to the report body. The Dataset Properties dialog box displays, prompting you to choose a data source and create a query. This is your hint that the data region requires your report to have a dataset. You can click Cancel to add the table to your report without first having a dataset in your report. The default table has three columns and two rows and is placed as near to the top-left corner of the design surface as possible, as shown in Figure 9-12. You can drag the table to another location if you like.

FIGURE 9-12 Default table layout with three columns and two rows.

You can also add or remove columns to suit your requirements. Before you can make changes to a table, you must click any of its text boxes to select the table. When you select a table (or any tablix data region), gray handles appear above the columns and to the left of the rows, as shown in Figure 9-13. To add a column, right-click the gray handle above a column, point to Insert Column, and click either Left or Right to position the new column to the left or right of the current column. To delete a column, right-click the column handle and click Delete Columns.

FIGURE 9-13 Select any text box in a data region to display its column and row handles.

Binding data to a data region

After you add a data region to your report, you must bind a dataset to the data region so that you can position fields from that dataset within the data region. When you bind a dataset to a data region, you create a relationship between the dataset and the data region. An easy way to do this is to drag a dataset field from the Report Data pane to a text box in the data region. If you prefer, you can set the *DatasetName* property for the data region in the Properties pane.

> **Note** After you bind a data region to a dataset, you cannot add fields from a different dataset to that data region.

When you add a field to a detail row in a table, the field name automatically displays in the column header, as shown in Figure 9-14. You can change the text if you prefer a different label. The report designer left-aligns string data but right-aligns the value in the text box when the data type is numeric.

FIGURE 9-14 The addition of a field to a table automatically generates the column header text.

Rather than drag fields from the Report Data pane into each text box, you might find it easier to point to each text box on the Data row, click the Field List icon that displays, and select a field. If you have not yet bound a dataset to the table, the Field List icon displays a list of available data sources and datasets from which you can select a field. After you select the first field, the Field List icon displays only the fields from the same dataset as the selected field.

When you preview the Data Regions report, as shown in Figure 9-15, you can see that the column headers display once and then the detail rows from the dataset display. In this example, the detail rows contain repeating business types: Specialty Bike Shop, Value Added Reseller, and Warehouse. The dataset contains additional fields for grouping, and each combination of business type and these additional fields for sales territories results in a separate row.

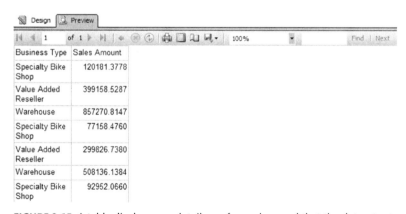

FIGURE 9-15 A table displays one detail row for each record that the dataset returns.

Grouping data

You can use groups to combine detail rows into related sets. For a table, you define row groups only. In a matrix, you set up both row groups and column groups.

To create a new group, you right-click a text box in a data region, and then select a dataset field or an expression to use for grouping. For example, right-click the Data row of the table and select Add Group. In the Row Group section, click Parent Group. There are other options for grouping that we cover in more detail in the next chapter. In the Tablix Group dialog box, in the Group By drop-down list, you select the field to use for grouping, as shown in Figure 9-16. Here you also have the option to add a group header or footer, which adds a row to the table above and below the details row, respectively.

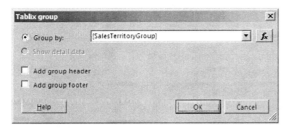

FIGURE 9-16 Use the Tablix Group dialog box to set the field to use for grouping detail rows, and optionally add a group header or group footer.

After you add a new parent group, a new column displays to the left of the existing columns in the table, as shown in Figure 9-17. Just as when you add a field to the Data row, the column header for the new group displays the field name that you selected for the group. You can replace the column header by typing a new value in the text box.

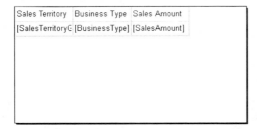

FIGURE 9-17 Addition of a parent group to the table adds a new column to the left of existing columns.

When you add a group to a data region that already contains at least one group, you must decide how the groups will relate to each other. If the new group will contain the existing group or detail rows, you create a Parent Group. If instead an existing group will contain the new group, you create a Child Group. To do this, right-click the Data row of the column containing the first group, select Add Group, click Child Group, and then select a field in the Group By drop-down list in the Tablix Group dialog box. The new child group, Country in this example, appears to the right of the first group, as shown in Figure 9-18.

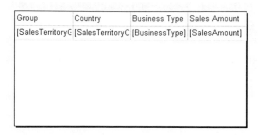

Group	Country	Business Type	Sales Amount
[SalesTerritoryC	[SalesTerritoryC	[BusinessType]	[SalesAmount]

FIGURE 9-18 Addition of a child group to the table adds a new column to the right of an existing group.

If you change the labels for the group columns, the corresponding group names do not change in the Grouping pane at the bottom of the report designer, shown in Figure 9-19. This Grouping pane makes it easier to see which groups are defined for the data region and, if multiple groups are defined, how the groups relate to one another hierarchically. Furthermore, in the Grouping pane, you can access properties for each group or add additional groups easily.

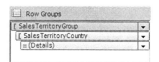

FIGURE 9-19 The Grouping pane displays the hierarchical relationship between a parent group, a child group, and detail rows.

Tip You can drag a dataset field from the Report Data pane to the Grouping pane and drop it above an existing group to create a parent group or drop it below an existing group to create a child group.

If you want to change the names of the groups, you must access the Group properties. For example, you might consider changing group names to make it easier to identify groups in the Grouping pane. To change the group name, right-click the group in the Grouping pane and click Group Properties. In the Name text box, type a new name for the group, as shown in Figure 9-20.

Note Just as with data sources and dataset names, the group name cannot contain spaces and must start with a letter.

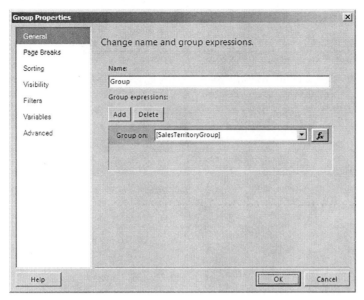

FIGURE 9-20 The Group Properties dialog box allows you to change the name of a group, define the group expressions, and set other properties related to an individual group.

Now when you preview the report, as shown in Figure 9-21, you can see the effect created by adding multiple groups to the table. The field value for each group displays in a cell that spans the child groups and the detail rows it contains.

Group	Country	Business Type	Sales Amount
Europe	France	Specialty Bike Shop	120161.3778
		Value Added Reseller	399158.5287
		Warehouse	857270.8147
	Germany	Specialty Bike Shop	77158.4760
		Value Added Reseller	299826.7380
		Warehouse	508136.1384
	United Kingdom	Specialty Bike Shop	92952.0660
		Value Added Reseller	538182.9649
		Warehouse	645970.2022

FIGURE 9-21 The group value displays in a text box spanning the child groups and detail rows it contains.

Adding a total to a table

When you use a table in your report, you can use the Add Total command to add a row to sum detail rows for a group or for the entire table. By default, the Add Total command inserts an expression using the *Sum()* function, but you can change the expression to use an alternative aggregate function such as *Average()* or *Min()*. To use the command, right-click a text box containing a field or expression with a numeric data type and select Add Total. If the table contains one or more groups, a new row appears as a group footer row for the innermost group, as shown in Figure 9-22.

 Note We provide a more detailed explanation of row types in Chapter 10, where we also include more examples of working with totals, and we show you how to work with all the aggregate functions in Chapter 12.

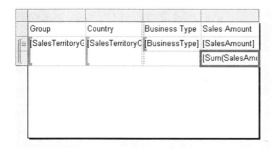

FIGURE 9-22 You can add a total row to sum the detail rows contained by a group.

When you select the new text box containing the *Sum()* function, an orange bar appears to the left of the group to which the aggregation applies. It's a visual indicator to help you see which rows and groups are in the same scope as the selected text box. An aggregation includes only the values in the detail rows for the current scope. In Figure 9-22, the sum of Sales Amount applies only to the detail rows for each Country group.

Because the aggregation expression in the text box on the group footer row returns a numeric data type, you can right-click it and use the Add Total command again to create another row to total detail rows contained by the next group, if one exists, or for the entire table if there are no more groups. You can also type labels in one of the text boxes to the left of an aggregation to clarify its contents. When you preview the report, as shown in Figure 9-23, you see the label and the group total for each group.

		Specialty Bike Shop	171182.2357
North America	Canada	Value Added Reseller	884996.2610
		Warehouse	1334083.0160
		Country Total	2390261.5127
	United States	Specialty Bike Shop	712179.9685
		Value Added Reseller	4847762.3092
		Warehouse	3802117.0880
		Country Total	9362059.3657
	Group Total		11752320.8784
Pacific	Australia	Specialty Bike Shop	165542.3580
		Value Added Reseller	400571.4995
		Warehouse	180790.5552
		Country Total	746904.4127
	Group Total		746904.4127

FIGURE 9-23 You can add a total row to sum the detail rows contained by a group.

Adding a matrix

Another type of data region that you will find useful is the matrix. Whereas a table has a fixed number of columns and a dynamic number of rows, both the rows and columns of a matrix are dynamic. A matrix displays data in a structure much like a crosstab or pivot table and can use groups on either rows or columns with optional subtotals.

The first step is to drag the Matrix from the Toolbox onto the design surface. If you need more room on the design surface, you can resize the body of the report before adding the matrix. The default matrix has a text box for columns, a text box for rows, and a text box for data, as shown in Figure 9-24. You use the fields or expressions that you add to the Columns and Rows text boxes to group detail data from your dataset. Because the matrix automatically groups the dataset rows, it applies the *Sum()* function to the field or expression that you add to the Data text box, although you can change this to any other aggregate function if you prefer.

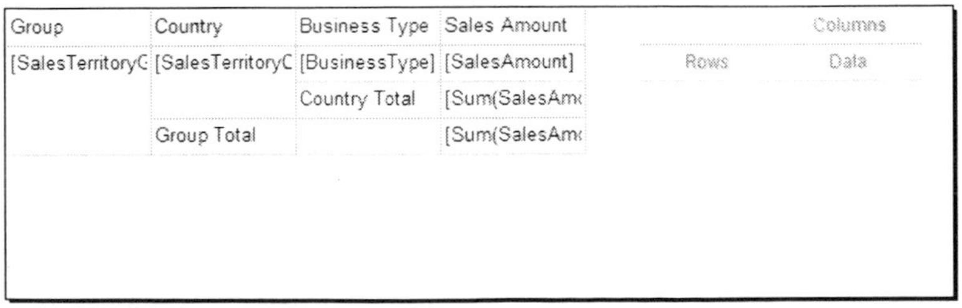

Group	Country	Business Type	Sales Amount		Columns
[SalesTerritoryC	[SalesTerritoryC	[BusinessType]	[SalesAmount]	Rows	Data
		Country Total	[Sum(SalesAm(		
	Group Total		[Sum(SalesAm(		

FIGURE 9-24 The matrix layout contains text boxes for a row group, a column group, and an aggregate value.

Just as you do with a table, you add fields to the matrix by dragging them into the data region from the Report Data pane or by clicking the Field List icon in each text box and selecting a field. The fields that you add to the Rows and the Columns text boxes display in the Grouping pane as groups, as you can see in Figure 9-25. Unlike a table, there are no detail rows in a matrix, which is one of the differentiating characteristics of the matrix.

FIGURE 9-25 A matrix contains at least one row group and one column group, as you can see in the Grouping pane.

When you preview the report, the matrix creates a row for each distinct value in the row group and creates a column for each distinct value in the column group, as shown in Figure 9-26. You can add fields to the Grouping pane to create more row or column groups if necessary. In addition, you can use the Add Total command to create group totals for rows or columns.

Group	Country	Business Type	Sales Amount
Europe	France	Specialty Bike Shop	120181.3778
		Value Added Reseller	399158.5287
		Warehouse	857270.8147
		Country Total	1376610.7212
	Germany	Specialty Bike Shop	77158.4760
		Value Added Reseller	299826.7380
		Warehouse	508136.1384
		Country Total	885121.3524
	United Kingdom	Specialty Bike Shop	92952.0660
		Value Added Reseller	538182.9649
		Warehouse	645970.2022
		Country Total	1277105.2331
	Group Total		3538837.3067

Sales Territory Country	2001	2002	2003	2004
Australia			847430.9640	746904.4127
Canada	1513359.4563	4822999.2021	5651305.4254	2390261.5127
France		857123.1784	2373804.0354	1376610.7212
Germany			1098866.6849	885121.3524
United Kingdom		841757.7607	2160145.8328	1277105.2331
United States	6552075.8490	17622549.5128	20071116.4827	9362059.3657

FIGURE 9-26 The rendered matrix repeats rows and columns for each distinct value in the respective groups.

Sorting groups

A matrix automatically sorts the row group and column group values in ascending order, thereby overriding an ORDER BY clause in your dataset if one exists. To change the sorting options, you can right-click a group in the Grouping pane and then select Group Properties. In the Group Properties dialog box, select the Sorting page, shown in Figure 9-27, and make the necessary changes. For example, you can click the Add button if you want to use a compound sort based on multiple fields, or you can select a Sort By row and click the Delete button.

Note You can also set sorting properties for groups in a table or list by using the Sorting page in the Group Properties dialog box.

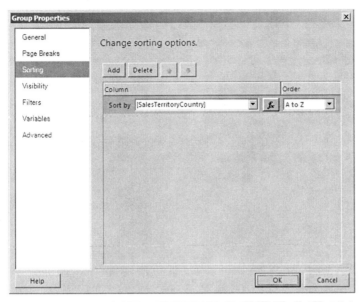

FIGURE 9-27 A matrix automatically sorts group values in ascending order.

While most often you use the group field as the field to sort by, you can select a different field in the Sort By drop-down list. For example, you can specify a field such as MonthName as the Group On field on the General page of the Group Properties dialog box, but use a field such as MonthNumber-OfYear as the Sort By field on the Sorting page. That way, you can display month names in the matrix in chronological rather than alphabetical order. Instead of using a dataset field for sorting, you can also use an expression, which you add by clicking the Expression button to the right of the Sort By drop-down list.

 Note You learn how to create expressions in Chapter 11.

You can also use other options on the Sorting page to modify the sort behavior of the group. When you add a new Sort By field, the default sort order is ascending, which is designated by A to Z in the Order drop-down list. You can change this to Z to A when you want to apply a descending sort. When you have a sort based on multiple fields, you can assign each field its own sort order, and you can use the up and down arrow buttons to control the order in which the sorts apply.

Adding a list

When you use a table or matrix, you present data in text boxes that are arranged in rows or columns, but a list can create a more flexible layout than the other two data regions. For example, you can use nothing but text boxes for a completely free-form layout, or you can use a combination of text boxes and other data regions to present some data in free form and other data in a structured layout. Unlike the table and matrix data regions, the list supports only one level of grouping, but you can implement multiple levels of grouping by nesting lists within lists.

When you drag a List item from the Toolbox window onto the design surface, as shown in Figure 9-28, the list resembles a rectangle. However, it behaves much differently. Whatever you place inside the list repeats for each distinct value of the group that you associate with the list.

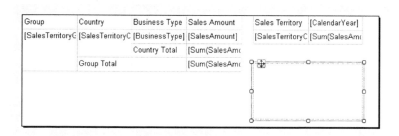

FIGURE 9-28 A list looks like a rectangle in Design mode.

You can drag a new report item from the Toolbox and drop it into the list, or you can move existing items in your report into the list. For example, to move a matrix into the list, you right-click any text box in the matrix, point to Select, and click the tablix name, such as Tablix2. Then use the crosshair to drag the matrix into the list, leaving some room at the top of the list if you want to add a label later, as shown in Figure 9-29.

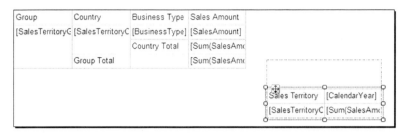

FIGURE 9-29 You can move other report items inside of a list, such as a matrix.

A list, like the other data regions, must be bound to a dataset. Adding an existing report item that is already bound to a dataset does not automatically update the list binding. You can manually set the binding by selecting the list tablix in the report designer and then changing the *DataSetName* property in the Properties window. Before you change this property, make sure that you have the correct report item selected by checking to see which item displays the resizing handles along its borders, as shown in Figure 9-30. The name of the selected item also appears at the top of the Properties window. To change the property, use the drop-down list in the DataSetName box to select the applicable dataset.

Important When you nest one data region inside another data region, such as a matrix inside a list as shown in Figure 9-30, you must bind both data regions to the same dataset.

You must also define a group for the list. By default, it has a details group that you must modify. Click anywhere in the list to see this group in the Grouping pane. Right-click the group, and select Group Properties. On the General page, click the Add button, and then select the field that you want to use for grouping in the Group On drop-down list.

It is usually helpful to viewers of your report to include a label somewhere in the list to indicate the grouping value. One way to do this is to add a freestanding text box to the list. You can drag a text box from the Toolbox, place it in the list, and then add a field to the text box. A shortcut method is to drag a field from the Report Data pane and position it in the list. The report designer automatically adds a freestanding text box to hold the field, as shown in Figure 9-31.

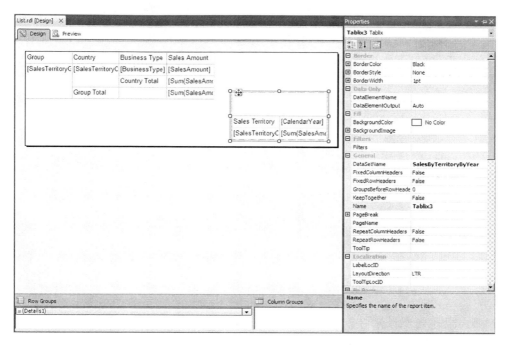

FIGURE 9-30 You can update the *DataSetName* property in the Properties window for the selected data region.

Group	Country	Business Type	Sales Amount		
[SalesTerritoryG	[SalesTerritoryC	[BusinessType]	[SalesAmount]	[First(SalesTerri	
		Country Total	[Sum(SalesAmc	Sales Territory	[CalendarYear]
	Group Total		[Sum(SalesAmc	[SalesTerritoryC	[Sum(SalesAmc

FIGURE 9-31 Use a freestanding text box in a list as a label for each distinct group value.

When you add a field to a freestanding text box, you must use an aggregate function, such as *Sum()* for a numeric field or *First()* for a string field. Usually, a label text box in your list contains a string field, so let's consider the effect of using the *First()* function. Because the dataset has multiple rows containing the same value in the field that you use for grouping, the label text box can use just one of those values from any row in that group. The *First()* function gets the value in the first row, but you could use the *Last()* function to get the value from the last row in the group and achieve the same result.

In Figure 9-32, you can see the labels for the Europe, North America, and Pacific groups appear above a matrix containing the sales by sales territory country in rows and by year in columns. The list defines the contents of each group, a label and a matrix, and repeats this group of report items for each distinct value of the list group. Notice also that because each group contains a different set of years, each matrix contains a different number of columns. In Chapter 10, you learn how to adjust this behavior to display the same set of years in each matrix.

Group	Country	Business Type	Sales Amount
Europe	France	Specialty Bike Shop	120181.3778
		Value Added Reseller	399158.5287
		Warehouse	857270.8147
		Country Total	1376610.7212
	Germany	Specialty Bike Shop	77158.4760
		Value Added Reseller	299826.7380
		Warehouse	508136.1384
		Country Total	885121.3524
	United Kingdom	Specialty Bike Shop	92952.0660
		Value Added Reseller	538182.9649
		Warehouse	645970.2022
		Country Total	1277105.2331
	Group Total		3538837.3067

Europe

Sales Territory Country	2002	2003	2004
France	857123.1784	2373804.0354	1376610.7212
Germany		1098866.6849	885121.3524
United Kingdom	841757.7607	2160145.8328	1277105.2331

North America

Sales Territory Country	2001	2002	2003	2004
Canada	1513359.4563	4822999.2021	5651305.4254	2390261.5127
United States	6552075.8490	17622549.5128	20071116.4827	9362059.3657

Pacific

Sales Territory Country	2003	2004
Australia	847430.9640	746904.4127

FIGURE 9-32 A list repeats the report items that it contains for each distinct group value.

Using properties to control appearance and behavior

After you finalize the data layout, you can improve your report by configuring properties to manage the location and size of report items or change the formatting of report items. Reporting Services also includes many properties that you can use to control the appearance of a report item, such as formatting and colors. You can access properties by opening the dialog box for the selected item, such as a tablix or a text box, or by selecting an item and viewing the Properties window.

Configuring the placement and size of a report item

You can use drag-and-drop to move a report item or a data region to a new location, and you can drag the edges of a report item to make it larger or smaller. However, using drag-and-drop to perform these tasks might not provide the precision you need for a pixel-perfect report. Instead, you can use the *Location* and *Size* properties to configure the placement and size of a report item to meet exact specifications.

Setting the *Location* property

Every report item has a *Location* property that defines its position relative to the top-left corner of the current section of the report, whether the item is in the report body, the page header, or the page footer. If a report item exists inside another report item, its location is relative to the top-left corner of the parent report item. You can change the location of any report item except text boxes that are part of a table or a matrix. Although you can specify the position of an item explicitly, its actual position in the report depends on whether the report contains data regions above it or to its left, because these items can expand vertically and horizontally as the dataset returns more data.

The *Location* property has two values, Left and Top. You can type the values in the Location box, separated by a comma, or you can click the plus symbol to the left of Location to access the two values separately, as shown in Figure 9-33.

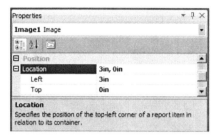

FIGURE 9-33 Use the *Location* property to set the position of a report item.

 Tip The default unit of measurement for the location values is inches, which you express by using the corresponding Cascading Style Sheets (CSS) length unit, in. You can use any valid CSS length unit instead of inches, such as cm or pt. You can find a complete list of CSS length units at *http://msdn.microsoft.com/en-us/library/ms531211(VS.85).aspx*.

Setting the *Size* property

Like the *Location* property, the *Size* property has two values. To adjust the size of an item, you can set Width and Height. As you change these values, the size of the item in the report adjusts to match the settings. Be aware that the size that you specify for an item might not be the actual size of the item when the report renders. There are two other properties that we discuss in the next section that determine whether the item's size can change dynamically if it is a text box or contains text boxes.

 Note You can use the *Size* property with any report item except the line, which instead has an *EndPoint* property for which you set the Horizontal and Vertical values, which are the coordinates for the rightmost point of the line. Also, be aware that the size settings for a subreport affect only the size of the placeholder in the design layout. The actual size of the subreport depends on the layout defined for that report.

For less precise sizing, you can drag the edges of a report item to make it smaller or larger as needed. You can also resize all text boxes in a data region column by positioning your cursor on the right-edge of the column and then dragging the mouse to the left or right, as shown in Figure 9-34. If the new size of the tablix is wider than the report body, the report body size widens automatically.

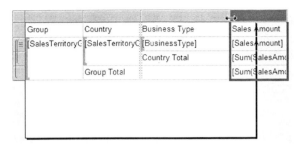

FIGURE 9-34 Drag a column handle to increase or decrease the width of all text boxes in the column.

Controlling text box growth

A text box can never grow wider than the width that you specify for its size. However, if the value to display cannot fit within that width, the default behavior of the text box is to grow vertically until the complete value of the field can display with wrapped text. If the field value fits within the text box without wrapping, the text box will be no smaller than the width and height that you specify. To produce different behavior, you can change the *CanGrow* or *CanShrink* properties of the text box as follows:

- Keep the default value of the *CanGrow* property as True when you want the text box to expand vertically and wrap the text, or set it to False when you want the height of the text box to remain fixed. In the latter case, the report truncates the text to fit the available width. Regardless of the setting you specify for the *CanGrow* property, the width of the text box never changes.

- Keep the default of the *CanShrink* property as False when you want the text box to remain at the specified height, even when the text to display does not fill the available space. Set the value to True when you want to reduce the height of the text box to the smallest size necessary to display the text.

 Note Although a text box usually contains text, as its name implies, you can nest other report items inside a text box, such as an image. If the nested report item size can change dynamically, the containing text box will also change height dynamically, but never width. For an example of this behavior, refer to Figure 9-8. In this report, the text box size is 5 inches wide and .25 inches high, but the report renders each database image at its original size, each of which you can see is taller than .25 inches.

Changing the appearance of a report item

Many properties are available for configuring the appearance of a report item. Most commonly, you define font sizes, styles, colors of text, and format strings, but you can also use properties related to borders, padding, and background colors, among others.

Setting font properties

If you have experience with word processing software, you already know about using properties for fonts. The process is very similar in Reporting Services, except that instead of selecting the text itself, you select the text box and set the font properties for the text box. When designing reports, you can select one or more text boxes and then use the Report Formatting toolbar, shown in Figure 9-35, to set the more commonly used font properties. For more options, you can use the Properties window to set the font properties. For example, the *TextDecoration* property allows you to specify not only Underline but also Overline and LineThrough.

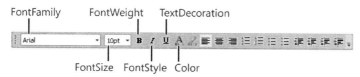

FIGURE 9-35 Use the Report Formatting toolbar to quickly change font properties.

 Tip You can apply the same properties to all text boxes in a row or column by selecting the corresponding handle in the data region rather than selecting each text box individually. After you select the row or column, you can use either the Report Formatting toolbar or the Properties window to set the properties.

Setting selected text properties

Most of the time, you set font properties for all characters in a text box. For those occasions when you want to use different formatting for some characters, you can highlight the portion of the text that you want to change. The Properties window will display Selected Text as the current item at the top of the window and allows you to access the following properties, listed here by property type:

- Action: *Action*

- Alignment: *HangingIndent, LeftIndent, RightIndent, SpaceAfter, SpaceBefore, TextAlign*

- Font: *Color, FontFamily, FontSize, FontStyle, FontWeight, TextDecoration, LineHeight*

- General: *ToolTip*

- Lists: *ListLevel, ListStyle*

- Localization: *Calendar, Language, NumeralLanguage, NumeralVariant, ValueLocID*

- Number: *Format*

If you set any of these properties at the text box level, the properties that you set at the selected text level override the text box properties. For example, in Figure 9-36, the text box properties use a bold, italic, black 10pt font, but the selected text uses a blue 14pt font without italics. The bold property continues to apply to the selected text because no change was made to the *FontWeight* property for that text.

Reseller Sales *by Business Type*

FIGURE 9-36 You can override text box properties by setting properties for selected text.

Setting alignment properties

There are several alignment properties that you can use to control how text displays in a text box. For example, by default, each text box has 2pt padding to prevent text from displaying too closely to the top, left, right, and bottom edges of the text box. In addition, the *TextAlign* property of Default applies left alignment to non-numeric data types and applies right alignment to numeric data types. The *VerticalAlign* property is also initially set to Default, which starts the display of text at the top of the text box.

Use the following properties to configure alignment, as shown in Figure 9-37:

- *HangingIndent*, to set the size of the indent for the first line of a string of text in a text box. You use CSS length units such as in or pt, as we describe in the "Setting the *Location* property" section earlier in this chapter.

- *LeftIndent*, to preserve space, as measured in CSS length units, on the left side of a text box when the text wraps as multiple lines.

- *RightIndent*, to preserve space, as measured in CSS length units, on the right side of a text box when the text wraps as multiple lines.

- *Padding* (Left, Right, Top, Bottom), to preserve space, as measured in CSS length units, on the specified side of a text box. You cannot use this property with selected text. The default padding is 2pt on each side.

- *SpaceAfter*, to insert white space, as measured in CSS length units, after the text displays.

- *SpaceBefore*, to insert white space, as measured in CSS length units, before the text displays.

- *TextAlign*, to align left, align right, or center text by using the values Left, Right, or Center, respectively.

- *VerticalAlign*, to align text at the top, middle, or bottom of a text box, using the values Top, Middle, or Bottom, respectively. This property is not available for use with selected text.

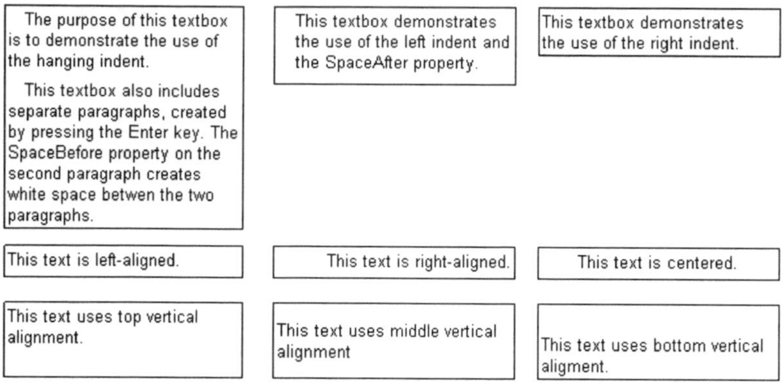

The purpose of this textbox is to demonstrate the use of the hanging indent.

This textbox also includes separate paragraphs, created by pressing the Enter key. The SpaceBefore property on the second paragraph creates white space between the two paragraphs.

This textbox demonstrates the use of the left indent and the SpaceAfter property.

This textbox demonstrates the use of the right indent.

This text is left-aligned.

This text is right-aligned.

This text is centered.

This text uses top vertical alignment.

This text uses middle vertical alignment

This text uses bottom vertical alignment.

FIGURE 9-37 This report contains text boxes that illustrate each type of alignment property.

Padding or Indent?

In some cases, you can use *LeftIndent*, *RightIndent*, *SpaceAfter*, and *SpaceBefore* to preserve white space on the left, right, bottom, and top sides of a text box and get the same results as you would by using the *Padding* property. However, padding applies to the entire text box, whereas indentation and spacing can apply either to the text box or to selected text. By using the indentation and spacing properties, you can display multiple lines of text in the same text box, separated into the equivalent of paragraphs by pressing the Enter key between paragraphs. You can then select each paragraph in the text box separately to apply different indentation and spacing properties.

Setting the *Format* property

When working with numeric or date/time data types, you might need to specify a formatting string in the *Format* property of a text box to display the value nicely in your report. You can use any Microsoft Visual Basic .NET format string for this property. The following list describes the more common formatting strings that you will use:

- For numeric data, use N0 to display a value with a thousands separator and without decimal places, so that 1234.5 becomes 1,235.

- For currency data, use C2 to display a value with the local currency setting and a thousands separator. In the United States, C2 translates 1234.5 to $1,234.50.

- For percentage date, use P1 to multiply a value by 100, add a thousands separator if necessary, and append a percent symbol so that .1234 becomes 12.34%.

Tip You can find a complete list of predefined numeric formats at *http://msdn.microsoft .com/en-us/library/y006s0cz(VS.71).aspx*. For a list of user-defined numeric formats, see *http://msdn.microsoft.com/en-us/library/4fb56f4y(VS.71).aspx*. Predefined date/time formats are available at *http://msdn.microsoft.com/en-us/library/362btx8f(VS.71).aspx* and user-defined date/time formats are at *http://msdn.microsoft.com/en-us/library/73ctwf33(VS.71) .aspx*.

As an alternative to looking up format strings when you need to adjust the *Format* property of a text box, you can right-click a text box and select Text Box Properties. On the Number page of the Text Box Properties dialog box, shown in Figure 9-38, you can select a category and options to use for formatting. The report designer translates your selections into the appropriate formatting string.

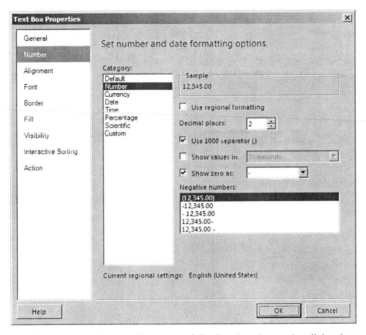

FIGURE 9-38 Use the Number page of the Text Box Properties dialog box to generate the correct format string.

Setting locale properties

The locale of the operating system of the report server (or your workstation when previewing reports in SSDT) determines the default formats that Reporting Service uses for regional-specific data such as dates and currency values. You can override the operating system locale for your report by setting the *Language* property at the report level, or you can override it at the text box level.

To change the *Language* property at the report level, click anywhere in the workspace outside the report design surface to view the report properties in the Properties window. Use the drop-down list in the Language box to set the property. For example, select fr-CA to set the locale to French-Canadian.

At the text box level, you can configure the following properties to override both the operating system locale and the report's *Language* property (if one is set):

- **Calendar**   You can select a Gregorian or GregorianUSEnglish calendar.

- **Direction**   You can choose LTR to display text left-to-right or choose RTL to display text right-to-left.

- **Language**   You can select a language to apply in general to values in the current text box. Other properties, such as *NumeralLanguage*, override this property.

- **NumeralLanguage**   Type the format string to apply to numbers.

- **NumeralVariant**   If the number format has a variant, specify the variant to use. The default is 1, which is a direction to use Unicode context rules. The value 2 represents the standard digits 0123456789.

 Tip A list of all numeral variants is available at *http://msdn.microsoft.com/en-us/library/ms154037(v=sql.90).aspx.*

- **WritingMode**   You can choose from Horizontal or Vertical to rotate the text 90 degrees, or Rotate270 to rotate the text 270 degrees. Figure 9-39 shows text boxes for which this property is set to Rotate270.

Group	Country	Business Type	Sales Amount
Europe	France	Specialty Bike Shop	$120,181.38
		Value Added Reseller	$399,158.53
		Warehouse	$857,270.81
		Country Total	$1,376,610.72
	Germany	Specialty Bike Shop	$77,158.48
		Value Added Reseller	$299,826.74
		Warehouse	$508,136.14
		Country Total	$885,121.35
	United Kingdom	Specialty Bike Shop	$92,952.07
		Value Added Reseller	$538,182.96
		Warehouse	$645,970.20
		Country Total	$1,277,105.23
	Group Total		$3,538,837.31

FIGURE 9-39 Set the *WritingMode* property to Rotate270 to change the text orientation.

Setting border properties

All report items, with the exception of a line, have border properties for which you can configure color, style, and width. Not only can you set these properties on the entire border of an object, but you can set these properties individually for the top, bottom, left, and right sides of an item's borders. Within a data region, you can set border properties for each text box as a group or separately.

The following list explains the options you have for each border property:

- **BorderColor**   You have the same color selection options here as you have for the *Color* and *BackgroundColor* properties. See the "Setting fill properties" section of this chapter for more details.

- **BorderStyle**   The style defines the type of line used for the border. Your choices include None, Dashed, Dotted, Double, or Solid.

- **BorderWidth**   You specify the width of the borderline by using a CSS length unit.

If you want to assign the same value to a border property for all four sides of a report item, you can set the value in the Default box. To override the default, set a different value in the Left, Right, Top, or Bottom boxes. For example, in Figure 9-40, you can see the text boxes in the Grand Total row have a border style set for the top and bottom sides of the text box but not for the left and right sides.

		Specialty Bike Shop	$165,542.36
Pacific	Australia	Value Added Reseller	$400,571.50
		Warehouse	$180,790.56
		Country Total	$746,904.41
	Group Total		$746,904.41
	Grand Total		**$16,038,062.60**

FIGURE 9-40   You can set border properties separately for each side of an item.

Setting fill properties

You can use fill properties to set either a color or an image as the background for most report items. By default, there is no color and no image. The No Color option is transparent, so anything behind the item is visible. For example, if you use the Fixed Header feature that we describe in Chapter 13, you should consider changing the *BackgroundColor* property of the column header rows to prevent users from seeing text box values scrolling behind the header text.

When you want to set the *BackgroundColor* property, you can select a color from the color picker that displays when you use the drop-down list for that property in the Properties window. The name of the color displays as a tooltip when you hover the cursor over it. For more options, you can click the More Colors link in the color picker to display the Select Color dialog box, shown in Figure 9-41.

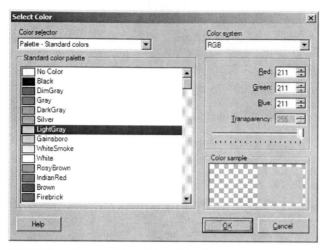

FIGURE 9-41 Use the Select Color dialog box to create a custom color, use alternate palettes, or set transparency.

In the Color Selector drop-down list, you can choose one of the following methods for viewing colors for selection:

- **Palette**   Standard Colors is the default option, which lists the colors by name next to a sample of the color. Colors are organized into families, such as blacks, reds, and so on.

- **Picker**   Color Circle is the option to choose when you want to view colors by spectrum in a circle. You can drag your cursor across the circle to change the current selection.

- **Picker**   Color Square allows you to focus on a single color family to allow you to get even more precise with color selection.

Sometimes you have a requirement to match a color exactly, such as when you have specific corporate colors to display. In the Color System drop-down list, you can select RGB and then specify decimal values for Red, Green, and Blue directly. If you prefer, you can select HSB as the color system and then specify decimal values for Hue, Saturation, and Brightness. The Color Sample box in the lower-right corner displays the current background color of the item on the left and your current color selection on the right so that you can compare the two colors side by side.

As an alternative to using a color as a background, by setting the *BackgroundImage* property, you can use an embedded image, an external image, or a database image. Just set the Source, Value, and MIMEType values for this property in the Properties window by using the same values that you would use for a freestanding image in your report.

The setting to use for Value is not obvious when you're new to Reporting Services. Use the following list to determine the correct setting to use by image type:

- For an embedded image, you must first add the image to the Report Data pane, as described in the "Embedded image" section earlier in this chapter. Then select the item for which you want to set the background image, open the Properties window for that item, and then type the image name that you see in the Report Data pane into the Value box.

- For an external image, set the Value to the path or URL reference for the image, such as *http://<servername>/reportserver?/Images/logo.bmp*.

- For a database image, set the Value to the field expression that contains the image, such as =Fields!LargePhoto.Value.

The default BackgroundRepeat value of the *BackgroundImage* property creates repeating tiles of the image across the entire body of the report. For example, consider a scenario in which the body of the report is 3 inches high and 7.5 inches wide, and you have an image that is 1 inch high and 3.5 inches wide. In this scenario, the default repeat behavior displays the image in three rows using slightly more than two copies of the image in each row, as shown in Figure 9-42. When you render the report, the number of image rows and the number of images displayed in each row increases to fill the actual size of the report.

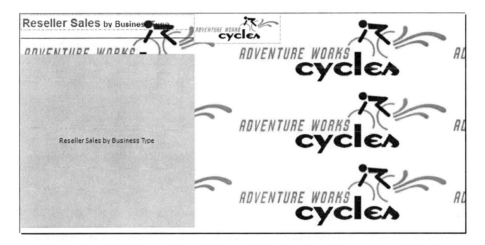

FIGURE 9-42 The default BackgroundRepeat value fills the report body with multiple copies of the same image.

Filling the background with so many images might create a report that is difficult to read. You have the following options for the BackgroundRepeat value:

- Default, to repeat the image both horizontally and vertically.

- Repeat, to repeat the image both horizontally and vertically, just like Default.

- RepeatX, to create a single row of repeating images along the top of your report.

- RepeatY, to create a single column of repeating images along the left edge of your report.

- Clip, to display the image once in the top-left corner of your report.

- Fit, applicable to a chart only, to resize the image to fit within the chart.

Setting list properties

Not to be confused with properties for a list report item, there are properties that you can set to control the display of text lists. As we describe in the "Setting alignment properties" section of this chapter, you can add multiple lines of text to a single text box and separate the lines by pressing the Enter key. You can set the text box's *ListLevel* property to 1 and then set the *ListStyle* property to numbered or bulleted to convert the separate text lines into list items. You can then select a line and increase the *ListLevel* property to indent the selected text relative to other items in the list, as shown in Figure 9-43.

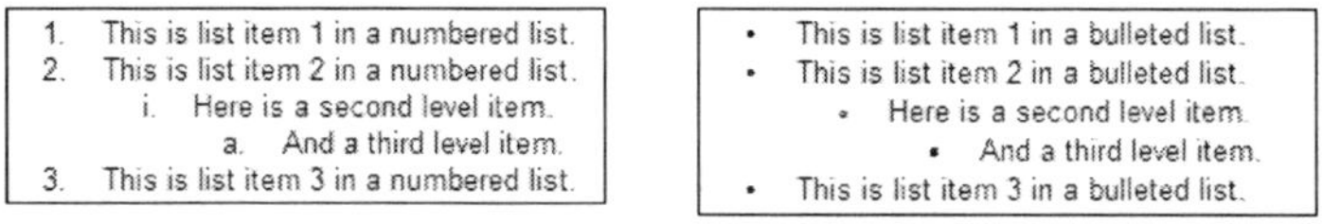

```
1.   This is list item 1 in a numbered list.          •   This is list item 1 in a bulleted list.
2.   This is list item 2 in a numbered list.          •   This is list item 2 in a bulleted list.
        i.   Here is a second level item.                     •   Here is a second level item.
             a.   And a third level item.                          •   And a third level item.
3.   This is list item 3 in a numbered list.          •   This is list item 3 in a bulleted list.
```

FIGURE 9-43 Use the *ListLevel* and *ListStyle* properties to create multilevel lists in a text box.

Setting line properties

After you add a line to your report, some additional properties that you can set to enhance its appearance include the following:

- **LineColor**   You can choose from the default color selection in the drop-down list or use the Select Color dialog box (described in the "Setting fill properties" section in this chapter) for a greater range of colors to choose from.

- **LineStyle**   The line can be Dashed, Dotted, or Solid.

- **LineWidth**   You must express the width of the line by using a CSS length unit, such as pt or in.

CHAPTER 10

Working with the tablix

The Toolbox window in Report Designer and the ribbon in Report Builder allow you to choose any of the three generic data regions for your report—a table, matrix, or list. Behind the scenes, these are all the same type of report item called a *tablix*. In this chapter, we explain how its name was derived and introduce important concepts that you must understand to develop more advanced layouts. To make report development easier, the design environment includes the three generic data regions as starting points to make it easier for you to lay out the report quickly. Each of these data regions includes preconfigured properties governing the behavior of rows or columns. However, if you find later that you need a different layout, you can easily modify these starting points to change a table to a matrix or a matrix to a table and so on. In addition, you can further enhance the layout by adding more groups, adding static columns, or arranging data in hierarchical structures and thereby take full advantage of the flexibility that the tablix provides.

Exploring the tablix

As you work with the report design surface, whether using Report Designer or Report Builder, you work with a graphical representation of elements that instruct Reporting Services how to arrange data on a report. These elements conform to a standard known as the Report Definition Language (RDL) specification. Each release of SQL Server Reporting Services (with the exception of SQL Server 2012) has introduced slight modifications to the specification, but the SQL Server 2008 release replaced the table, matrix, and list report items with a single report item called the tablix.

 Note You can download the specification for each version at *http://msdn.microsoft.com/en-us/library/dd297486(v=sql.100).aspx*.

What is a tablix?

Let's start by reviewing what we know so far about the table and the matrix. On the left, Figure 10-1 shows a table with fixed columns and dynamic rows. That is, the number of columns stays constant no matter how many rows the dataset query returns. The dataset query results can change over time as more data is inserted into or deleted from the source database. To the right of the table is a matrix with dynamic columns and rows. In this case, the number of both the rows and the columns is subject to change when the underlying data changes.

Product	Avg Sale
Accessories	**$18.34**
Helmets	$19.47
Locks	$14.94
Pumps	$11.96
Bikes	**$860.45**
Mountain Bikes	$1,079.25
Road Bikes	$738.05
Grand Total	**$689.66**

Category	Subcategory	2006	2007	Grand Total
Accessories	Helmets	$74,281.39	$113,443.66	**$187,725.05**
	Locks	$10,084.70	$6,140.52	**$16,225.22**
	Pumps	$8,369.26	$5,145.43	**$13,514.69**
Bikes	Mountain Bikes	$9,190,838.09	$8,854,263.03	**$18,045,101.13**
	Road Bikes	$10,765,176.58	$11,294,381.37	**$22,059,557.95**
Grand Total		**$20,048,750.03**	**$20,273,374.00**	**$40,322,124.03**

FIGURE 10-1 A table (left) has fixed columns and dynamic rows, and a matrix (right) has dynamic rows and columns.

Sometimes you might want to combine the static columns of a table with the dynamic columns of a matrix, as shown in Figure 10-2. We can combine the terms table and matrix to derive a name for this hybrid structure—tablix. The RDL specification for a tablix supports much more flexible structures than table or matrix structures could support in earlier versions of Reporting Services. You can start the layout with a table structure and then modify it to include repeating columns to produce a hybrid of a matrix. Or you can start the layout with the matrix structure and add in a static, non-repeating column like you find in a table. Regardless of which item you select from the Toolbox (or ribbon), you can easily change the structure of a tablix to suit your needs.

Subcategory	2006	2007	Grand Total	Avg Sale
Accessories	**$92,735.35**	**$124,729.60**	**$217,464.96**	**$18.34**
Helmets	$74,281.39	$113,443.66	**$187,725.05**	$19.47
Locks	$10,084.70	$6,140.52	**$16,225.22**	$14.94
Pumps	$8,369.26	$5,145.43	**$13,514.69**	$11.96
Bikes	**$19,956,014.67**	**$20,148,644.40**	**$40,104,659.07**	**$860.45**
Mountain Bikes	$9,190,838.09	$8,854,263.03	**$18,045,101.13**	$1,079.25
Road Bikes	$10,765,176.58	$11,294,381.37	**$22,059,557.95**	$738.05
Grand Total	**$20,048,750.03**	**$20,273,374.00**	**$40,322,124.03**	**$689.66**

FIGURE 10-2 A hybrid matrix, or tablix, combining dynamic rows and columns with a static column at far right.

Tablix data regions

The table, matrix, and list are simple variations of a tablix. It's important to understand their distinguishing characteristics before learning how to use them to create more advanced tablix structures. Understanding the basic behavior of these base data regions with regard to rows and columns and understanding the tablix properties in general can help you design some very flexible report layouts.

Table

When you add a table to the report design surface, the default layout that you start with is a tabular structure with three static columns and two rows, as shown in Figure 10-3. The top row of the table is a header row that appears only once at the top of the table when you render the report. The second row is the detail row and repeats once for each row in the dataset query results.

FIGURE 10-3 A tablix using a tabular structure starts with one detail row and three static columns.

You can add more static columns or remove one or more columns, as explained in Chapter 9. You can also add more header or detail rows to the table. When you right-click a header row, you click Insert Row, and then click Above or Below to add another row. You can then add an expression to cells in the new row or type static text, as shown in Figure 10-4.

Calendar	Sales Territory Group	Sales Amount	Order Quantity
		Tax Amount	Avg Sale
[CalendarYear]	[SalesTerritoryGroup]	[SalesAmount]	[OrderQuantity]

FIGURE 10-4 You can add another header row to a table.

When you right-click a detail row (and currently have no row groups defined for the table) and click Insert Row, you have the following options for positioning the new row:

- **Inside Group - Above**   Create a detail row above the selected row.

- **Inside Group - Below**   Create a detail row below the selected row.

- **Outside Group - Above**   Create a header row above the selected row.

- **Outside Group - Below**   Create a footer row below the selected row. A footer row is similar to a header row in that it appears only once in the table, but it appears after all detail rows.

If you configure the table with multiple detail rows, one set of detail rows appears in the table for each row in the dataset query results. You can use this technique when you have a lot of fields for each dataset record but have limited horizontal space in which to display the field data. Figure 10-5 shows a table to which a new detail row and two footer rows have been added.

Calendar	Sales Territory Group	Sales Amount	Order Quantity
		Tax Amount	Avg Sale
[CalendarYear]	[SalesTerritoryGroup]	[SalesAmount]	[OrderQuantity]
		[TaxAmt]	[AvgSale]
		SalesAmount)]	m(OrderQuantity)]
		Sum(TaxAmt)]	

FIGURE 10-5 You can also add detail rows and footer rows to a table.

Note Although the new row inherits properties such as font color and background color, it does not inherit numeric formatting. Therefore, you must take additional steps to correctly set the *Format* property in each text box in the new row.

The report preview, shown in Figure 10-6, displays the two header rows at the top of the table above the detail rows. Next, the body of the table contains a pair of detail rows for each of the five records returned by the execution of the dataset query. The last two rows of the table are the footer rows containing the totals for Sales Amount, Tax Amount, and Order Quantity.

Calendar Year	Sales Territory Group	Sales Amount	Order Quantity
		Tax Amount	Avg Sale	← Tablix Header Rows
2006	Europe	$1,698,880.94	5,123
		$135,910.47	$331.62
2007	Europe	$5,632,816.55	19,255
		$450,625.32	$292.54
2006	North America	$22,445,548.71	53,118
		$1,795,643.86	$422.56	← Detail Rows
2007	North America	$25,722,421.91	77,908
		$2,057,793.70	$330.16
2007	Pacific	$847,430.96	3,009
		$67,794.48	$281.63
		$56,347,099.08	158,413	← Tablix Footer Rows
		$4,507,767.83	

FIGURE 10-6 Header and footer rows in a table do not repeat, but detail rows repeat for each dataset record.

Matrix

The starting layout for a matrix, shown in Figure 10-7, has both a row and column group but does not include detail data. Instead, you define an expression that uses an aggregate function, such as *Sum*. You can add multiple row groups and column groups to a matrix. You can use the cells appearing above the row groups as static headers, whereas the column group values become dynamic headers for the columns that appear in the rendered report, as explained in Chapter 9.

FIGURE 10-7 A tablix using a matrix structure starts with one row group, one column group, and an aggregated data cell.

You can insert columns or rows into the matrix without adding a new column group or row group, but you must specify whether the new column or row is inside the selected column or row group or outside the group. For example, let's say that you want to display two numeric values in the matrix in separate rows. You can select the cell containing the first numeric value, use the Insert Row/Inside Group-Below command to add a new row, and then select a field or add an expression to add a numeric value to the new cell. Because the new numeric value is inside the group with the first numeric value, the two values repeat for each combination of row and column values in the matrix, as shown in Figure 10-8.

Category	2006	2007
Accessories	$92,735.35	$124,729.60
	5,207	6,651
Bikes	$19,956,014.67	$20,148,644.40
	22,231	24,378

FIGURE 10-8 You can add another value to repeat across row and column groups in a matrix.

When displaying multiple values in a matrix, you should consider including labels. One approach is to insert rows above the first numeric value, outside of the group, to repeat the labels in each column below the calendar year. Another approach is to insert a column outside of the group to the left of the numeric value to repeat labels for each row, as shown in Figure 10-9. Because the labels are independent of a column group, they do not repeat for each row and column value but repeat only for each row group.

Category		2006	2007
Accessories	Sales Amount	$92,735.35	$124,729.60
	Order Quantity	5,207	6,651
Bikes	Sales Amount	$19,956,014.67	$20,148,644.40
	Order Quantity	22,231	24,378

FIGURE 10-9 You can add a static column to display labels for repeating data.

Of course, you can add totals to the matrix by using a tablix footer for rows, for columns, or for both rows and columns, as shown in Figure 10-10. To do this, you can right-click a data cell and use the Add Total/Row or Add Total/Column command. As an alternative, you can select the last row or last column and then use the Insert Row/Outside Group – Below or Insert Column/Outside Group – Right command, respectively.

Group Headers

FIGURE 10-10 A matrix can include tablix headers and footers, group headers and footers, and repeating data values.

> **Note** If the matrix has multiple row groups or column groups, you can add total rows for the nested groups. These total rows are also known as group footer rows.

List

A common way to use a list is to group a collection of report items, such as a set of text boxes, or a combination of a table and a chart. You can put as many things inside the list as you like because the initial space inside is a rectangle. However, the starting layout for the list has one group only. Furthermore, the group is for details, which means the collection of items that the list contains repeats once for each row in the dataset query results. Because you start with a details group, you can use only the following non-repeating data regions inside the list: Text Box, Data Bar, or Indicator. You have more options with the list when you add groups, as we explain in the "Detail list to grouped list" section later in this chapter.

FIGURE 10-11 A tablix using a list structure starts with a details group as a single row.

You can add a new row to the list, but you must right-click the row or column handle to access the Insert Row or Insert Column command. If you insert a row inside the group, you can add only a single field to the new row because the row contains a text box. You can, of course, add a rectangle to this text box to if you want to place multiple items in the new row. You get a similar result when you add a new column to the list.

Tip You can also place data regions and other report items inside a text box of a table or a matrix like you can with a list. After all, a table and matrix are just alternate forms of a tablix and share all the same properties of a list. To place multiple free-standing text boxes or report items other than data regions inside a text box of a table or matrix, you must first insert a rectangle.

Figure 10-12 illustrates the effect of adding new columns and rows to a list without adding new groups. The initial detail row contains three staggered text boxes, and the new inside group row containing the Average Sale amount is another detail row. Each set of detail rows repeats for each dataset record. The additional column containing the data bar, like the original column, is static. The tablix also contains two outside group rows, one of which is a tablix header added above the initial row and a tablix footer added below the second detail row.

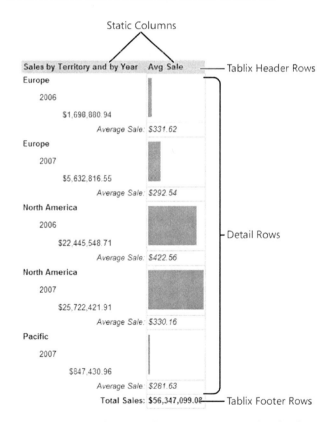

FIGURE 10-12 A tablix using a list structure starts with a details group as a single row.

Tablix cells

Regardless of which type of tablix you use in your report, it is a collection of one or more text boxes, or cells. In addition to understanding how these cells are organized as details or groups in rows and columns, you should understand what type of content you can place in a cell and how a cell's location in a tablix affects scope. Last, you should know how to modify tablix cells by using merge and sort operations.

Cell content

Besides deciding how to arrange rows and columns when you create a tablix, you also need to decide the content that should appear in each cell. Figure 10-13 shows examples of the following types of cell content:

- **Static Text**   You usually use static text as a label in the tablix and group header and footer rows. Static text often appears automatically in the tablix header when you add a field to the detail row in a table layout.

- **Field Reference**   Much of the time, you place fields into cells to display data directly from the dataset. In this case, the cell displays a field reference, such as [CalendarYear], [SalesTerritoryGroup], or [SalesAmount], which is the name of the field encapsulated in brackets. This abbreviated field reference style was introduced in SQL Server 2008 Reporting Services. In earlier versions of Reporting Services, the cell displays the full expression for the field. For example, instead of [CalendarYear], the cell displays =Field!CalendarYear.Value.

- **Expression**   A cell can also contain expressions, such as a subtotal in the group footer or a grand total in the tablix footer. For simple expressions, the cell displays an expression place-holder such as [Sum(SalesAmount)]. Although you see the same expression placeholder in the group footer and tablix footer, the expression resolves as a different value in each row based on its current scope. You can also add more complex calculations to the layout, such as the concatenation of the word Total and the current instance of the calendar year field, which display in the tablix with the generic placeholder <<Expr>>. To discover the syntax of the expression, you must open the Expression Editor for the text box.

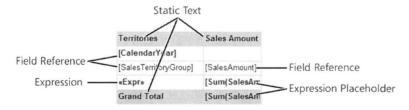

FIGURE 10-13 A tablix cell can contain static text, a field reference, or an expression.

Note In a group header or footer, the scope is the set of detail rows associated with the current group instance, while the scope of a tablix footer is the entire set of detail rows from the dataset and not the sum of the values that display in the tablix. This latter point is an important concept—expressions always apply to the data in scope and have no dependency on the visible data in the tablix.

Tip You can override the text that displays as a placeholder by providing a label. That way, you can see a more meaningful description of a tablix cell's contents instead of a generic placeholder label like <<Expr>>, although you can use this technique for any type of placeholder. To add a label, click twice in a tablix cell, right-click to open the context menu, and select Placeholder Properties. In the Placeholder Properties dialog box, type the label text to display in the tablix cell.

Cell scope

Getting the scope right is important for producing the correct result in expressions, so you need to pay close attention to the scope of a cell as you're building each expression. Fortunately, the report design surface provides visual cues for this purpose.

When you click on a cell in the tablix, as shown in Figure 10-14, a dark gray line appears as the border for the selected cell and an orange bracket displays on the interior left edge of the tablix to show the rows that belong to the same group as the selected cell. The icon with three horizontal lines in the row handle indicates that this cell is in a details row, so the expression in the Sales Amount column has detail row scope. Therefore, the rendered table displays the SalesAmount value for each dataset record, within each grouping defined for the table.

Territories	Sales Amount
[Category]	
[CalendarYear]	
[SalesTerritoryGroup	[SalesAmount]
«Expr»	[Sum(SalesAm
«Expr»	[Sum(SalesAm
Grand Total	[Sum(SalesAm

FIGURE 10-14 An orange bracket on the left edge of the details row indicates the scope for the highlighted cell.

You can identify cells having group scope by the lines spanning multiple rows in the row handles along the left edge of the tablix. In Figure 10-15, the smaller (and innermost) group line indicates that [CalendarYear] and an expression are the top and bottom rows of the same group. This group line shows you the section of rows that repeat for each instance of a group when the report renders. The expression of the selected cell, [Sum(SalesAmount)], evaluates once for each set of rows included in the group. In other words, the expression calculates the sum of SalesAmount values for the detail rows of each calendar year separately.

Territories	Sales Amount
[Category]	
[CalendarYear]	
[SalesTerritoryGrou|	[SalesAmount]
«Expr»	[Sum(SalesAm
«Expr»	[Sum(SalesAm
Grand Total	[Sum(SalesAm

FIGURE 10-15 Row handle lines spanning multiple rows indicate group scope.

When you click on the cell containing the grand total expression in the tablix footer, as shown in Figure 10-16, you don't see an orange line appear because there is no group scope for this cell. Instead, the cell scope is the entire dataset that is bound to the tablix. That is, the expression calculates the sum of the SalesAmount values for all rows in the dataset.

Territories	Sales Amount
[Category]	
[CalendarYear]	
[SalesTerritoryGrou|	[SalesAmount]
«Expr»	[Sum(SalesAm
«Expr»	[Sum(SalesAm
Grand Total	[Sum(SalesAm

FIGURE 10-16 A cell with no detail row or group scope has dataset scope.

Cell merge and split

Cells within a tablix are similar to cells within a Microsoft Excel workbook. By default, the dimensions of a cell are one row in height by one column in width. You can expand the size of a cell and force it to span multiple columns or rows by using the Merge Cell command. To do this, select two contiguous cells, right-click the selection, and click Merge Cells. Be aware that the merge operation discards data in all merged cells except the first cell. After the merge, you can update the contents of the cell with static text, a field reference, or an expression, as shown in Figure 10-17.

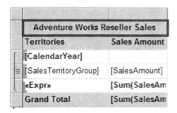

Adventure Works Reseller Sales	
Territories	Sales Amount
[CalendarYear]	
[SalesTerritoryGroup]	[SalesAmount]
«Expr»	[Sum(SalesAm
Grand Total	[Sum(SalesAm

FIGURE 10-17 You can merge contiguous cells to create a single cell that spans multiple columns or rows.

You can merge more than two cells at a time. You can also merge both horizontally and vertically, except in the tablix body, where you can merge only horizontally. The tablix body is the portion of the tablix that is to the right of row groups and below column groups, or the entire tablix if no row groups or column groups exist. If you want to merge cells in both directions in other parts of the tablix, you must perform the operation in two steps, one direction at a time.

If you later want to revert a merged cell to individual cells, right-click the cell and click Split Cells. The cell contents of the merged cell move to the first cell resulting from the split operation.

Transforming a tablix

Sometimes, you might start designing a layout using one structure and later decide that you need to use a different structure. The beauty of the tablix is that you don't need to start with a new structure, as was necessary prior to SQL Server 2008. Instead, you can transform the one you have.

Table to matrix

Strictly speaking, a table has no column groups. After you add column groups to a table, it becomes a type of matrix. Let's say you start with a table having three columns: CalendarYear, SalesTerritoryGroup, and SalesAmount. To convert the table to a matrix with CalendarYear as a column group, start by deleting the CalendarYear. Then, with the tablix selected (so that you see the Row Groups and Column Groups panes below the report), drag the CalendarYear field from the dataset field list to the Column Groups pane. Double-click the Details group in the Row Groups pane, and add a group expression using [SalesTerritoryGroup] in the Group On drop-down list.

Note If you omit this step, the tablix renders multiple rows for the same SalesTerritoryGroup value when the dataset result contains multiple rows.

Now take a close look at the new structure, shown in Figure 10-18. Notice the double-dashed line between the two tablix header rows. This line separates the group headers from the body of the tablix, which in this case includes not only the SalesTerritoryGroup and SalesAmount values but also the static column headers above these rows.

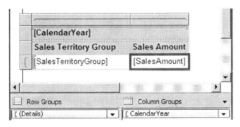

FIGURE 10-18 Adding a column group to a table creates a matrix with repeating static columns.

To display the SalesTerritoryGroup column only once, you must add a parent row group (as described in Chapter 9) based on SalesTerritoryGroup, and delete the static SalesTerritoryGroup column to the left of SalesAmount. It's important to right-click the SalesTerritoryGroup cell (or its header), and then select Delete Columns to eliminate only the static column and not the dynamic CalendarYear header. You can delete the Details group in the Row Groups pane if you like, but it doesn't change the rendering behavior in this case.

Notice in Figure 10-19 that there are now two double-dashed lines to the left of the SalesAmount value and above its header row. When a column or row appears to the left or above the double-dashed line, it appears only once in the rendered report, whereas a column or row appearing to the right or below the double-dashed line repeats for each combination of row and column group with which it is associated. For example, the SalesAmount header in the second column of the second row repeats in each for each CalendarYear value because it is within scope of that column group. However, it is not contained within any row group scope, so the value displays in one row only, immediately below the CalendarYear value.

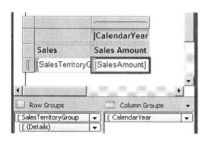

FIGURE 10-19 Columns and rows above or to the left of the double-dashed lines repeat once per group instance.

Matrix to table

To transform a matrix into a table, you must at minimum eliminate the column groups and optionally add a details group. Let's assume you're starting with a matrix that has a row group based on SalesTerritoryGroup (without a Details group as shown in Figure 10-19) and a column group based on CalendarYear. You must delete the CalendarYear group by right-clicking CalendarYear in the Column Groups pane, clicking Delete Group, and selecting the Delete Group And Related Rows And Columns. That way, you don't retain a header row that includes CalendarYear. If you choose the Delete Group option, you must edit the header row. Either way, you must modify the resulting table to achieve the result you want.

Next, if you want to add a details group as a child of SalesTerritoryGroup, right-click SalesTerritoryGroup in the Row Groups pane, point to Add Group, and click Child Group. In the Tablix Group dialog box, select the Show Detail Data option. A new column appears in the tablix for the new group, but because it appears to the left of the double-dashed line, you need to delete the new column, using the Delete Columns Only option. With the details group in place, the tablix renders one row per dataset record.

You can then delete SalesTerritoryGroup from the Row Groups pane, using the Delete Group And Related Rows And Columns option to remove the column to the left of the double-dashed line. Then you can insert static columns for CalendarYear and SalesTerritoryGroup and insert a header row to hold labels for each column (using the Outside Group – Above option), as shown in Figure 10-20. Notice that there are no double-dashed lines nor are there group lines in the row and column handles.

FIGURE 10-20 You remove column groups and insert static columns to transform a matrix into a table.

Detail list to grouped list

The default layout of a list uses a detail row without groups. However, an effective use of a list is to use it as a repeating container for other report items that also group data, such as a table or chart. Before you can add these types of report items to the list, you must transform it from a detail list to a grouped list. To do this, double-click the Details group in the Row Groups pane, rename it, and add a group expression in the Group Properties dialog box. You can now insert repeating report items, such as a Table, Matrix, List, Chart, Sparkline, or Map.

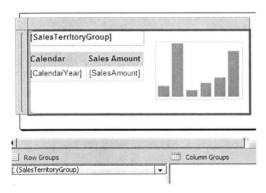

FIGURE 10-21 You can place repeating report items inside a list after converting the detail list to a grouped list.

Configuring tablix properties

In Chapter 9, you learn about properties that modify the appearance and behavior of report items. As a report item, a tablix shares many of the properties we describe in that chapter and includes other properties that we discuss in later chapters covering interactivity, pagination, and report parts. In this section, we review the remaining properties.

No data rows

One situation for which you should consider planning is the possibility that a dataset returns no data. In that case, any data region bound to the dataset does not render. Users might be confused if the data region does not appear where expected, so you can configure the tablix to display a message when this situation arises. To do this, select the Tablix to access its properties in the Properties window. Scroll to locate the No Rows section, which contains several properties, such as Color and Font, which you can use to configure the appearance of the message. The key property to configure here is *NoRowsMessage*. Simply type the message to display, such as **No data available**.

> **Tip** To select a tablix, you can click any cell in the tablix to display the row and column handles, and then click the top-left corner handle. As an alternative, you can right-click any cell in the tablix, point to Select, and then click the tablix name. A third option, if you know the name of the tablix, is to use the report item drop-down list at the top of the Properties window to select the tablix.

Groups before row header

The default behavior of a matrix is to display row group headers in the first column of the matrix, but you can display one or more of the other matrix columns first and then display the row group headers. As long as the first column in the matrix is not a static column and is truly a row group header, you can set the *GroupsBeforeRowHeaders* property to specify the number of columns to display to the left of the row group header.

For example, let's say that you want to compare three months of one quarter to three months of the next quarter, and your dataset returns six months. You can set the *GroupsBeforeRowHeaders* property to 3 to display the three month columns, followed by a column containing the row group header values. Then the remaining three month columns display to the right of the row group header column.

Sort

In Chapter 9, we explain how to configure sorting for a group. You can also configure sorting for the entire tablix by using the *SortExpressions* property in the Properties window. When you click the property box for *SortExpressions*, you see an ellipsis button. Click the button to open the Sorting page of the Tablix Properties dialog box. On that page, you can add one or more sort expressions by using the same interface that you use for sort expressions in the Group Properties dialog box. That is, you click the Add button to add a new sort expression, select a field in the Sort By drop-down, and then select A to Z in the Order drop-down list to set an ascending sort or select Z to A to set a descending sort.

Working with tablix groups

Now that you know how the basic tablix structure behaves with detail rows and basic row and column groups, you're ready to explore the variety of options possible with different arrangements of groups. In addition to working with groups that repeat rows or columns, you can also set up different layouts using static columns that don't repeat. You can also use adjacent groups to display multiple groups in the same tablix without using a hierarchical structure to nest one group inside another. Last, you can use group properties to handle issues with data alignment for nested data regions and recursive hierarchy groups.

Grouping in the database or in the report?

You can develop dataset queries that return detail data only and then use groups in the tablix to aggregate that data. Even when using a table structure, you can eliminate detail rows and display only row groups to have Reporting Services compute the aggregated values. Whether you should use the Database Engine to pre-aggregate details or leave the work to Reporting Services depends on reporting requirements. For example, as with sorting, you should leave the aggregation work to the Database Engine where possible because the Database Engine is optimized to perform this type of operation and can send a smaller set of data to the report server for rendering. However, if users want to move from summary to detail values quickly, you might prefer to return all data to the report and design drill-down navigation to support a faster interactive experience.

Row groups

When designing a tablix, you can create more than one row group. The default result of adding a new row group is the addition of a column in which to display the group's values, but you can modify the arrangement of fields and columns to display values from multiple groups in the same column.

Note In this section, we show you how to work with multiple row groups specifically, but the principles also apply to column groups. For example, as you add a new column group, the tablix contains multiple rows, with the parent, or outer group, values displaying in cells spanning the child, or inner group, columns. See the Row and Column Groups report in the Chapter 10 folder of the sample files for examples of column groups.

Separate columns for each group

As you add each additional row group to a tablix, a new column appears in the tablix to hold the group's values. By default, the values in the parent group do not repeat with each row of the child group. Instead, each parent group displays in a cell that spans the child group's rows in a blocked format, as shown in Figure 10-22.

Category	Sales Territory Group	2006	2007
Accessories	Europe	$8,976.30	$71,680.31
	North America	$83,759.05	$209,264.78
	Pacific		$15,587.79
	Total	$92,735.35	$296,532.88
Bikes	Europe	$1,300,926.54	$4,313,478.72
	North America	$18,655,088.13	$20,557,650.39
	Pacific		$680,645.96
	Total	$19,956,014.67	$25,551,775.07
Clothing	Europe	$52,003.83	$172,404.70
	North America	$433,583.32	$673,337.01
	Pacific		$26,122.48
	Total	$485,587.15	$871,864.19
Components	Europe	$336,974.26	$1,075,252.82
	North America	$3,273,118.21	$4,282,169.74
	Pacific		$125,074.73
	Total	$3,610,092.47	$5,482,497.29
Total		$24,144,429.65	$32,202,669.43

FIGURE 10-22 By default, parent group values span the rows containing the child group values.

Single column for each group

When you have limited horizontal space for a tablix, such as when you're designing a report for a printed page, you might want to place all row groups in a single column. When you structure your row groups this way, the parent group appears above the child group, as shown in Figure 10-23. To make it easier for people to distinguish values in separate groups, consider using different formatting or padding properties for each group.

To modify a tablix from the default layout for multiple row groups to a single column layout, right-click the parent group and click Delete Columns. Then click a cell in the child group row, click Insert Row, and click Outside Group – Above. Because the parent group already exists, the scope for the new row is properly set. Select the value from the field list to display in the new row, or add an expression to calculate the applicable value, and then apply formatting to each text box to distinguish values for each group.

Category / Sales Territory Group	2006	2007
Accessories		
Europe	$8,976.30	$71,680.31
North America	$83,759.05	$209,264.78
Pacific		$15,587.79
Category Total	$92,735.35	$296,532.88
Bikes		
Europe	$1,300,926.54	$4,313,478.72
North America	$18,655,088.13	$20,557,650.39
Pacific		$680,645.96
Category Total	$19,956,014.67	$25,551,775.07
Clothing		
Europe	$52,003.83	$172,404.70
North America	$433,583.32	$673,337.01
Pacific		$26,122.48
Category Total	$485,587.15	$871,864.19
Components		
Europe	$336,974.26	$1,075,252.82
North America	$3,273,118.21	$4,282,169.74
Pacific		$125,074.73
Category Total	$3,610,092.47	$5,482,497.29
Grand Total	$24,144,429.65	$32,202,669.43

FIGURE 10-23 You can display values for multiple row groups in a single column.

Static columns

The main difference between a table and a matrix is the column structure. In a table, the columns are static. They do not repeat and have no dependency on the dataset query results to change the number of columns. By contrast, the columns in a matrix are dynamic. The column definition appears once in the layout, but the actual number of columns in the rendered report depends on the results of executing the dataset query. You can modify a matrix to include static columns in one of two ways, either by repeating a set of static columns for each column group or by displaying a static column as a separate, adjacent column group.

> **Note** Just as you can apply row group principles to column groups, you can also apply static column principles to static rows. In this section, we discuss only static columns. See the Static Columns and Rows report in the Chapter 10 folder of the sample files for an example of static rows.

Repeating static columns

A common way to use static columns is to display a set of values for each combination of column groups, as shown in Figure 10-24. In this example, there is one column defined for Sales Amount that repeats once per column grouping instance, and a second column defined for Order Quantity that also repeats once per column grouping. The set of static columns is a set of two columns, the combination of Sales Amount and Order Quantity. Even though the set of columns repeats within a grouping, the columns won't repeat if they're not placed inside a grouping.

Sales Territory Group	2006		2007		Grand Total	
	Sales Amount	Order Quantity	Sales Amount	Order Quantity	Sales Amount	Order Quantity
Accessories	$92,735.35	5,207	$296,532.88	13,136	$389,268.23	18,343
Europe	$8,976.30	514	$71,680.31	3,111	$80,656.61	3,625
North America	$83,759.05	4,693	$209,264.78	9,450	$293,023.83	14,143
Pacific			$15,587.79	575	$15,587.79	575
Bikes	$19,956,014.67	22,231	$25,551,775.07	31,310	$45,507,789.75	53,541
Europe	$1,300,926.54	1,589	$4,313,478.72	5,333	$5,614,405.26	6,922
North America	$18,655,088.13	20,642	$20,557,650.39	25,123	$39,212,738.52	45,765
Pacific			$680,645.96	854	$680,645.96	854
Clothing	$485,587.15	16,927	$871,864.19	31,623	$1,357,451.34	48,550
Europe	$52,003.83	1,700	$172,404.70	6,262	$224,408.54	7,962
North America	$433,583.32	15,227	$673,337.01	24,420	$1,106,920.33	39,647
Pacific			$26,122.48	941	$26,122.48	941
Components	$3,610,092.47	13,876	$5,482,497.29	24,103	$9,092,589.76	37,979
Europe	$336,974.26	1,320	$1,075,252.82	4,549	$1,412,227.08	5,869
North America	$3,273,118.21	12,556	$4,282,169.74	18,915	$7,555,287.95	31,471
Pacific			$125,074.73	639	$125,074.73	639
Grand Total	**$24,144,429.65**	**58,241**	**$32,202,669.43**	**100,172**	**$56,347,099.08**	**158,413**

FIGURE 10-24 You can repeat a set of static columns for each column group value and use an adjacent column in the tablix footer.

To create a layout with static columns, start by creating a matrix and add at least one row group and at least one column group. Right-click the cell intersection of the row and column group (such as Sales Amount in the example shown in Figure 10-24), click Insert Column, and then click Inside Group – Right. Then add a field reference or expression to the new cell.

Adjacent columns

Another way to use static columns is completely independent of groupings. In fact, Figure 10-24 illustrates the use of an adjacent column in the tablix footer, which has no groupings, although it appears to be a repeating set of static columns like those you see for the column group. In the context of that example, the Order Quantity represents the grand total for the entire dataset, but it's the scope of the expression and not the position of the column that determines the value that displays here.

Consider another example in which you use an expression in a column of the tablix footer that has no corresponding columns in the body of the tablix. In Figure 10-25, the last column is a static column that appears alongside, or adjacent to, the other columns in the tablix. For both examples, you create the additional column in a similar way. If the rightmost cell is inside a group, click Insert Column and then click Outside Group – Right. Otherwise, click Insert Column, and then click Right.

Sales Territory Group	2006		2007		Total Sales	Avg Sales
	Sales Amount	Order Quantity	Sales Amount	Order Quantity		
Accessories	*$92,735.35*	*$5,207.00*	*$296,532.88*	*$13,136.00*	*$389,268.23*	*$21.22*
Europe	$8,976.30	514	$71,680.31	3,111	$80,656.61	$22.25
North America	$83,759.05	4,693	$209,264.78	9,450	$293,023.83	$20.72
Pacific			$15,587.79	575	$15,587.79	$27.11
Bikes	*$19,956,014.67*	*$22,231.00*	*$25,551,775.07*	*$31,310.00*	*$45,507,789.75*	*$849.96*
Europe	$1,300,926.54	1,589	$4,313,478.72	5,333	$5,614,405.26	$811.10
North America	$18,655,088.13	20,642	$20,557,650.39	25,123	$39,212,738.52	$856.83
Pacific			$680,645.96	854	$680,645.96	$797.01
Clothing	*$485,587.15*	*$16,927.00*	*$871,864.19*	*$31,623.00*	*$1,357,451.34*	*$27.96*
Europe	$52,003.83	1,700	$172,404.70	6,262	$224,408.54	$28.18
North America	$433,583.32	15,227	$673,337.01	24,420	$1,106,920.33	$27.92
Pacific			$26,122.48	941	$26,122.48	$27.76
Components	*$3,610,092.47*	*$13,876.00*	*$5,482,497.29*	*$24,103.00*	*$9,092,589.76*	*$239.41*
Europe	$336,974.26	1,320	$1,075,252.82	4,549	$1,412,227.08	$240.62
North America	$3,273,118.21	12,556	$4,282,169.74	18,915	$7,555,287.95	$240.07
Pacific			$125,074.73	639	$125,074.73	$195.74
Grand Total	**$24,144,429.65**		**58,241** **$32,202,669.43**		**100,172** **$56,347,099.08**	**$355.70**

FIGURE 10-25 You can add an adjacent column to display values independently of column groups.

Adjacent groups

A traditional grouping structure in a table or matrix combines multiple groups into a hierarchical structure that refers to a containing group as a parent group and a contained group as a child group. However, the flexibility of the tablix structure allows you not only to create an adjacent column, but also to create an adjacent group. One way you might use adjacent groups is to display data in a matrix with each adjacent group representing different views of data from the same dataset query, as shown in Figure 10-26. Each adjacent group is independent of other groups on the same axis but shares access to the same data.

Category	2006		2007		Total Sales	Avg Sales	Europe	North America	Pacific
	Sales Amount	Order Quantity	Sales Amount	Order Quantity			Sales Amount	Sales Amount	Sales Amount
Accessories	$92,735.35	5,207	$296,532.88	13,136	$389,268.23	$21.22	$80,656.61	$293,023.83	$15,587.79
Bikes	$19,956,014.67	22,231	$25,551,775.07	31,310	$45,507,789.75	$849.96	$5,614,405.26	$39,212,738.52	$680,645.96
Clothing	$485,587.15	16,927	$871,864.19	31,623	$1,357,451.34	$27.96	$224,408.54	$1,106,920.33	$26,122.48
Components	$3,610,092.47	13,876	$5,482,497.29	24,103	$9,092,589.76	$239.41	$1,412,227.08	$7,555,287.95	$125,074.73
Grand Total	$24,144,429.65	58,241	$32,202,669.43	100,172	$56,347,099.08	$355.70	$7,331,697.49	$48,167,970.62	$847,430.96

FIGURE 10-26 Use adjacent groups to display different views of the same data in one tablix.

To add an adjacent column group, right-click a cell in an existing group, point to Add Group, and click Adjacent Left or Adjacent Right. The Tablix Group dialog box displays, allowing you to select a field in the Group By drop-down list or to build an expression for grouping. You can create as many adjacent groups as you need.

Group properties

Some report layout scenarios require special handling. In this section, we show you how to use group properties to solve two specific design problems: missing group values in nested data regions and recursive hierarchy groups.

Missing group values in nested data regions

When you create a column group to generate columns dynamically in a tablix, each distinct value for that group appears in a separate column. If a value doesn't exist in the dataset query results, no column appears for that value. When the tablix appears multiple times because you are nesting it inside another data region, and group values are missing, the result is a misalignment of column values, as shown in Figure 10-27. This layout consists of a list, called Tablix1, and a matrix, called Tablix2, inside the list. Tablix1 has a single row group based on calendar year, while Tablix2 has a single column group based on month.

2005 Sales

July	August	September	October	November	December
$489,329	$1,538,408	$1,165,897	$844,721	$2,324,136	$1,702,945

2006 Sales

January	February	March	April	May	June	July	August	September	October	November	December
$713,117	$1,900,789	$1,455,260	$882,900	$2,269,117	$1,001,804	$2,393,690	$3,601,191	$2,885,359	$1,802,154	$3,053,816	$2,185,213

FIGURE 10-27 Columns in a repeating data region do not align properly when group values are missing.

To make it easier for users to compare a month's sales from one year to the next, the columns should align so that any given month appears in the same location relative to the left edge of the tablix, even when there are no sales for the month. You can use the *DomainScope* property for the nested data region's group to automatically generate columns for the missing group values. In this example, you click a cell in Tablix2 to view the Column Groups pane, and then click the group to set the focus for the Properties window. In the Properties window, expand the Group node, and then type the name of the parent group, as shown in Figure 10-28.

FIGURE 10-28 Assign the parent data region to the *DomainScope* property to fix data synchronization for a group.

Important The name of the data region, like all objects in Reporting Services, is case-sensitive. If you type a value that does not match the data region name exactly, the report generates an error and does not display when you try to preview it.

With the *DomainScope* property correctly set, the report now renders with additional columns appearing as placeholders for missing group values, as shown in Figure 10-29. This technique also works with nested data visualizations, such as charts and sparklines, as you learn in Chapter 17, "Creating charts."

2005 Sales

January	February	March	April	May	June	July	August	September	October	November	December
						$469,329	$1,538,408	$1,165,897	$844,721	$2,324,136	$1,702,945

2006 Sales

January	February	March	April	May	June	July	August	September	October	November	December
$713,117	$1,900,789	$1,455,280	$882,900	$2,269,117	$1,001,804	$2,393,690	$3,801,191	$2,885,359	$1,802,154	$3,053,816	$2,185,213

FIGURE 10-29 The column values synchronize correctly after the *DomainScope* property is set.

Recursive hierarchy groups

Hierarchical data comes from a table with a self-referencing join, which is sometimes referred to as a parent-child table. You can recognize a table of hierarchical data by the presence of a foreign key column with a relationship to a primary key column in the same table, as shown in Figure 10-30. This type of data structure is useful when multiple levels of data exist, such as you might find in an organizational chart of employees, but where a different number of levels exist in each branch from the top of the hierarchy.

FIGURE 10-30 A hierarchical table contains a column having a foreign key relationship to the table's primary key.

Reporting Services allows you to create a group to organize rows into hierarchical levels as defined by the foreign key relationships. The *Level* function is available to show the level of a row within the hierarchy, which can be useful for applying formatting. We explain more about this function in Chapter 11, "Developing expressions."

For example, Figure 10-31 shows a portion of a table of employees based on a simple query to a hierarchical table. The order of employees does not reflect the relationships between employees and their managers, nor is the list shown in alphabetical order. The employees display in the order in which the database returns records for the query.

Employee Name	Title
Gilbert, Guy	Production Technician - WC60
Brown, Kevin	Marketing Assistant
Tamburello, Roberto	Engineering Manager
Walters, Rob	Senior Tool Designer
D'Hers, Thierry	Tool Designer
Bradley, David	Marketing Manager
Dobney, JoLynn	Production Supervisor - WC60
Ellerbrock, Ruth	Production Technician - WC10
Erickson, Gail	Design Engineer
Johnson, Barry	Production Technician - WC10
Goldberg, Jossef	Design Engineer
Duffy, Terri	Vice President of Engineering
Higa, Sidney	Production Technician - WC10
Maxwell, Taylor	Production Supervisor - WC50
Ford, Jeffrey	Production Technician - WC10
Brown, Jo	Production Supervisor - WC60
Hartwig, Doris	Production Technician - WC10

FIGURE 10-31 The hierarchical table without grouping displays rows in the order received from the data source.

Unlike the groups described in the previous sections of the chapter, for which group properties are maintained separately from the details row, a recursive hierarchy group is defined by changing the detail row's group properties. In the Group Properties dialog box, add a group and define the initial grouping of the hierarchy by selecting the primary key column in the Group On drop-down list, and then select the foreign key column in the Recursive Parent drop-down list on the Advanced page of the Group Properties dialog box, as shown in Figure 10-32. No separate grouping for the recursive hierarchy group appears in the Row Groups pane.

Figure 10-33 shows a portion of the table after the recursive hierarchy grouping is defined. The Chief Executive Officer appears at the top of the list, followed by the Marketing Manager, after whom several employees reporting to the Marketing Manager display. Without conditional formatting or padding, it is difficult to see the relationships between managers and employees. That's where use of the *Level* function is useful, as you learn in Chapter 11. In addition, you can use the *Recursive* keyword with aggregate functions to correctly aggregate values in hierarchical groups like this, which we also explain in Chapter 11.

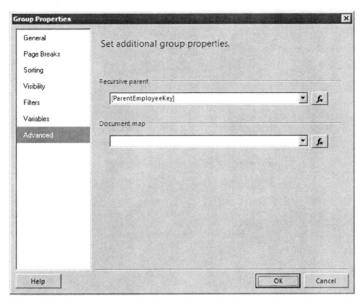

FIGURE 10-32 Use the foreign key column of a hierarchical table as the Recursive Parent in Group Properties.

Employee Name	Title
Sánchez, Ken	Chief Executive Officer
Bradley, David	Marketing Manager
Brown, Kevin	Marketing Assistant
Harnpadoungsataya, Sariya	Marketing Specialist
Gibson, Mary	Marketing Specialist
Williams, Jill	Marketing Specialist
Eminhizer, Terry	Marketing Specialist
Benshoof, Wanida	Marketing Assistant
Wood, John	Marketing Specialist
Dempsey, Mary	Marketing Assistant
Bradley, David	Marketing Manager
Duffy, Terri	Vice President of Engineering
Tamburello, Roberto	Engineering Manager
Walters, Rob	Senior Tool Designer
Walters, Rob	Senior Tool Designer
Erickson, Gail	Design Engineer
Goldberg, Jossef	Design Engineer

FIGURE 10-33 The rows in a hierarchical group display in correct order after the Recursive Parent is set.

CHAPTER 11

Developing expressions

You can build many reports that rely exclusively on data that comes straight from the data source by using the techniques described in Chapter 9, "Designing the report layout," but often the real value of information in reports comes from enhancing the data. You can include derived information in your report by creating expressions based on dataset fields. You can also enhance a report by including the name of a report, its location, and the date of execution in the report by using a special set of expressions. In addition, expressions are useful for changing properties based on predefined conditions. Expressions, in general, support a lot of flexibility in your report design, but you have even more options with variables at the report and group level and dynamic expressions for data sources and datasets. In this chapter, you learn about constructing and using expressions, while in the next chapter, you learn how to perform more advanced operations in expressions by using functions.

Introducing expressions

There are two types of expressions that you can use: simple and complex. You use a simple expression as an abbreviated version of the more common expressions that define the data to display in a text box. When a simple expression is not available, you use a complex expression. Both types of expressions require you to use a specific syntax that we introduce in this section.

Simple expressions

Technically speaking, each time you add a field from a dataset to the report design surface, you are adding an expression to the report. However, the process is streamlined to make it easy for you to work with field expressions by using a *simple expression* on the report design surface to display the field name enclosed in brackets. A simple expression is a reference to a single item, such as a dataset field, a built-in field, or a parameter.

Simple expressions display on the report design surface as *placeholders*. Placeholders were introduced in SQL Server 2008 Reporting Services to make it easier to see the expression that a text box contains. In prior versions, you saw only a portion of the expression that could fit in the space allocated unless you opened the Expression Editor, as we describe later in this chapter. Table 11-1 shows examples of each type of placeholder.

TABLE 11-1 Expression placeholders

Item	Placeholder	Expression Example
Dataset field	[SalesAmount]	=Fields!SalesAmount.Value
Aggregate function	[SUM(SalesAmount)]	=Sum(Fields!SalesAmount.Value)
Built-in field	[&PageNumber]	=Globals!PageNumber
Parameter value	[@BusinessType]	=Parameters!BusinessType.Value

Tip Notice that each type of placeholder encloses a string inside brackets. If you need to display text in a text box by using a string enclosed in brackets, you must use a back-slash as an escape character in front of each bracket. For example, if you want to display *[CalendarYear]* in a text box, you must use the following expression instead: *\[CalendarYear\]*.

Dataset field placeholder

When you drag a dataset field into a text box, the simple expression is created for you, like *[SalesTerritoryGroup]* or *[SalesAmount]*, as shown in Figure 11-1, but you can also type it directly into the text box. A simple expression, using brackets around the field name, is a placeholder for the full underlying expression, such as *=Fields!SalesTerritoryGroup.Value* or *=Fields!SalesAmount.Value*. Even if you type a full expression into the text box, the report designer displays the corresponding simple expression in the layout.

Group	Country	Business Type	Calendar Year	Product	Sales Amount	Cost
[SalesTerritoryGrou	[SalesTerritoryCoul	[BusinessType]	[CalendarYear]	[EnglishProductName]	[SalesAmount]	[TotalProductCost]

FIGURE 11-1 Simple expressions use the Fields placeholder when you add fields to the report layout.

The simple expression is only for display purposes. If you look at the XML in the report definition file or use the Expression dialog box to look at the text box expression, you see the underlying expression. To open the Expression dialog box, shown in Figure 11-2, right-click a text box and click Expression. The underlying expression for a field includes the name of a collection, Fields; the name of the field, SalesAmount, which is an item in the Fields collection; and the item property to display, Value. As we explain in Chapter 8, "Retrieving data for a report," the Fields collection contains one field for every column retrieved by the query and for each *calculated field*.

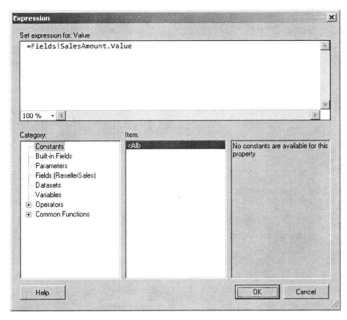

FIGURE 11-2 The Expression dialog box displays the underlying expression for a text box.

Aggregate function placeholder

You can also use a placeholder with an aggregate function, which the report designer creates when you use the Add Total command in a tablix or when you add a field to the body of a matrix. A simple expression for an aggregate function combines the function name followed by the field name enclosed in parentheses, and then encloses the result in brackets, such as *[Sum(SalesAmount)]* as shown in Figure 11-3. The underlying expression in this example is *=Sum(Fields!SalesAmount.Value)*.

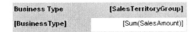

Business Type	[SalesTerritoryGroup]
[BusinessType]	[Sum(SalesAmount)]

FIGURE 11-3 A simple expression can include an aggregate function with a field.

When manually creating simple expressions, you can use the following aggregate functions (explained in Chapter 12, "Using functions") with a dataset field: *Aggregate, Avg, Count, CountDistinct, First, Last, Min, Max, StDev, StDevP, Sum, Var,* or *VarP*. The use of these functions with an expression, the use of any other aggregate function, or the addition of a scope argument to an aggregate function results in a complex expression.

Built-in field placeholder

The global collection contains a set of built-in fields, which we describe in more detail later in this chapter, and is useful for expressions referencing the environment, such as the report server's URL or the current page number of the report, as shown in Figure 11-4. You can recognize a simple expression for an item in the global collection by the ampersand preceding the item name, such as *[&PageNumber]*. The underlying expression for this simple expression is *=Globals!PageNumber*.

FIGURE 11-4 You can use a simple expression with a built-in field for a result specific to the current report execution.

Parameter value placeholder

You can also use placeholders with the Parameters collection, which stores labels and values for report parameters, as you learn in Chapter 14, "Creating dynamic reports with parameters." A common reason to use a parameters placeholder is to map a report parameter to a query parameter, which we describe in more detail in Chapter 14. The simple expression for a parameter value uses the @ symbol as a prefix for the parameter name and encloses the entire string in brackets, such as *[@CalendarYear]*. The underlying expression for a reference to the *CalendarYear* parameter value is *=Parameters!CalendarYear.Value*. You can use the expression as a text box value, a property value, or a query parameter value, as shown in Figure 11-5.

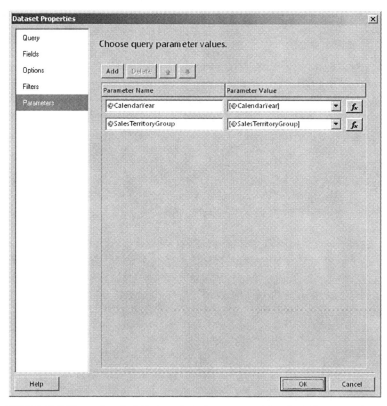

FIGURE 11-5 Use a placeholder to reference a parameter value when mapping a report parameter to a query parameter in the Dataset Properties dialog box.

Complex expressions

Many of the expressions that you add to reports are operations that perform mathematical or string manipulation operations on fields in a dataset and require you to build a longer *complex expression*, which was the only option for expressions in earlier versions of Reporting Services. A complex expression always starts with an equal sign (=) to differentiate it from static text and can reference multiple fields, parameters, or built-in fields, include operators to combine several expressions into a compound expression, and specify calls to functions. Usually, you open the Expression dialog box to create or edit an expression, but you can type it directly into a text box or property box as well. For example, you can concatenate a constant string with a dataset field by using an expression like *="Calendar Year " + CStr(Fields!CalendarYear.Value)*, which the Report Designer considers to be a complex expression and displays the generic placeholder, *<<Expr>>*, on the design surface.

Collection syntax

Whether you use simple or complex expressions, you interact with one or more of the built-in collections available in Reporting Services: data sources, datasets, dataset fields, globals, report items, parameters, user, and variables. To reference a collection item in an expression, you use standard Microsoft Visual Basic collection syntax. For example, to refer to the *SalesAmount* field, you use *Fields!SalesAmount.Value* in your expression.

Most objects that you use in expressions belong to a collection. There are multiple syntax options available to you when referring to collections and their objects in an expression. If you prefer, you can use any of the following syntax options when referencing a property of a collection object:

- *Collection!ObjectName.Property*

- *Collection!ObjectName("Property")*

- *Collection("ObjectName").Property*

Similarly, you have multiple options for referencing a member of a collection, such as *User!UserID*. You can use any of the following syntax options when referencing a member of a collection:

- *Collection!Member*

- *Collection.Member*

- *Collection("Member")*

Regardless of the syntax option you use, it's important to remember that the names of collections, objects, members, and properties are all case-sensitive. If you use an expression for which the case is incorrect, an error displays when you try to preview the report.

Using the Expression dialog box

You can use expressions in a variety of ways, as you will learn later in this chapter. Whether you want to create a complex expression for a text box or set a property value by using an expression, you can use the Expression dialog box as a graphical interface to help you build an expression.

Opening the Expression dialog box

The method you use to open the Expression dialog box depends on what you want to do. Follow the instructions for the applicable starting point in the following list:

- **Text Box Context Menu**   To edit the expression for a text box, right-click the text box, and click Expression on the context menu, as shown in Figure 11-6.

FIGURE 11-6 Use the Expression command on a text box context menu to open the Expression dialog box.

 Note Figure 11-6 illustrates the context menu for a freestanding text box. You will see a different set of commands on the context menu when you right-click a text box inside a tablix, but Expression remains one of the available commands.

- **Dialog Box**   Most dialog boxes that you use to configure properties for a dataset, parameter, text box, tablix, and other report items allow you to select a value from a list or to click a button to use an expression instead. When you have the option to use an expression, a button with the letters *fx* displays next to the property setting, as shown in Figure 11-7.

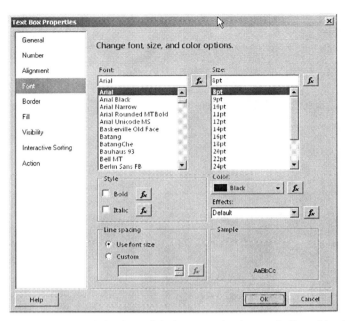

FIGURE 11-7 In a dialog box, click the expression button, indicated by the letters *fx*, to open the Expression dialog box.

- **Properties Window** In most cases, you can configure a property value by using an expression. A property for which an expression is permissible displays the Expression command in the property value drop-down list, as shown in Figure 11-8.

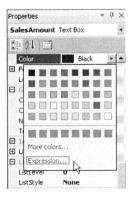

FIGURE 11-8 You can configure a property using an expression when the Expression option appears in the property value drop-down list.

Regardless of which method you use, the same Expression editor opens, as shown in Figure 11-9. You must create an expression that returns a valid value for the property you are configuring. You can type your expression directly into the code window, preceding the expression with the equal sign (=) like this:

```
="Calendar Year " + CStr(Fields!CalendarYear.Value)
```

Alternatively, you can use the Category tree, Item pane, or Values pane, shown in Figure 11-9, to help you build the expression. You can double-click a value in the Values pane or in the Item pane to add it to your expression.

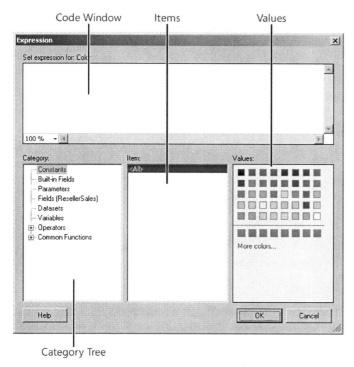

FIGURE 11-9 Use the Expression dialog box to create an expression.

> **Note** You are not required to use the Expression dialog box to build an expression. It is available to provide guidance if needed. You can type an expression directly into a text box or into a property value box in the Properties window (if it supports expressions) if you are certain of the syntax.

Exploring the Category tree

The contents of the Item and Values panes change according to the selection you make in the Category tree. The Values pane is visible only for some categories and is replaced by a Description pane and Example pane when you select certain categories and select an item, as shown in Figure 11-10.

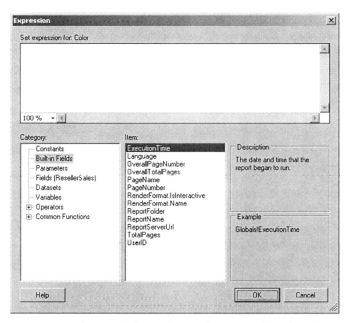

FIGURE 11-10 The Description and Example panes replace the Values pane when you select a category and item.

You can choose among the following categories in the Category tree:

- **Constants**   The Values pane displays a list of valid string values for the current property, such as Dashed or Solid for the *BorderStyle* property. When you are creating an expression for a property like *Color* or *BackgroundColor*, you can use the basic color picker in the Values pane or click More Colors to open the Select Color dialog box.

 Note   For more information about the Select Color dialog box, see the "Setting fill properties" section of Chapter 9.

- **Built-in Fields**   When you select this category, you can choose one of the items available in the global collection. These fields are useful for creating an expression using information about your report, such as the time the report is run or the total number of pages in the report. When you click on a field in the Item pane, you can view its description and an example of its usage.

- **Parameters**   Selection of this category displays a list of report parameters, if any, in the Values pane. You can use parameter values to set properties at report runtime or display parameter labels in a text box.

- **Fields**   You will see a separate Fields list for each dataset in your report, with the name of the dataset enclosed in parentheses and appended to the word Fields in the Category tree. When you select this category, the Values pane displays each field available in the dataset.

- **Datasets**   This category displays each dataset in the Item pane. When you select a dataset, you see its fields display in the Values pane in combination with aggregate functions. Numeric fields display with the *Sum* function, such as *Sum(SalesAmount),* and non-numeric fields display with the *First* function, such as *First(CalendarYear).* Typically, you use these values in a freestanding text box, which requires you to use an aggregate function with a field reference as described in Chapter 12.

- **Variables**   The Values pane displays report variables, if any exist in the report. Group variables do not display in this interface, although you can reference them in an expression. You use report and group variables to store values for use in expressions.

- **Operators**   You must expand the Operators category to view the subcategories for operators: Arithmetic, Comparison, Concatenation, Logical/Bitwise, and Bitshift. When you select a subcategory, you can view the available operators in the Item pane. When you click an operator, you can view a description and see an example of an expression using the operator. You can also type an operator directly into the code window, but the list of operators is helpful to remind you of your options. A complete list of operators appears in Table 11-2.

- **Common Functions**   As with Operators, you expand the Common Functions category to view groupings of common functions: Text, Date & Time, Math, Inspection, Program Flow, Aggregate, Financial, Conversion, and Miscellaneous. Click a function in the Item pane to view its description and an example of its usage. You learn how to use these functions in Chapter 12.

> **Tip**   You're not limited to the functions available in the Common Functions list. You can use any function available in the *Microsoft.VisualBasic, System.Convert,* and *System.Math* namespaces. You can use other .NET Framework Common Language Runtime (CLR) namespaces if you include the fully qualified namespace in the expression. Alternatively, you can create your own custom functions, as we describe in Chapter 33, "Programming report design components."

TABLE 11-2 Operators

Operator	Description	Example
Arithmetic		
^	Raises a number to the power of another number	=Fields!SalesAmount.Value ^ 2
*	Multiplies two values	=Fields!SalesAmount.Value * 10
/	Divides two values	=Fields!SalesAmount.Value / 4
\	Divides two values and returns an integer result	=Fields!SalesAmount.Value \ 3
Mod	Divides two values and returns the remainder	=Fields!SalesAmount.Value Mod 3

Operator	Description	Example
+	Adds two values	=Fields!SalesAmount.Value + Fields!TaxAmount.Value
-	Subtracts one value from another	=Fields!SalesAmount.Value – Fields!Cost.Value
Comparison		
<	Less than	=Fields!ProfitMargin.Value < Variables!Threshold.Value
<=	Less than or equal to	=Fields!SalesAmount.Value <= 100000
>	Greater than	=Fields!SalesAmount.Value > Fields!Quota.Value
>=	Greater than or equal to	=Fields!ProfitMarginPct.Value >= .15
=	Equal to	=Fields!SalesAmount.Value = 100
<>	Not equal to	=Fields!SalesAmount.Value <> 0
Like	Compares two strings, using * as a wildcard for multiple characters and ? as a wildcard for a single character	=Fields!EnglishProductName.Value Like "Mountain*"
Is	Compares two objects	=Fields!Category.Value Is Fields!EnglishCategory.Value
Concatenation		
&	Concatenates two strings	=Fields!FirstName.Value & " " & Fields!LastName.Value
+	Concatenates two strings	=Fields!FirstName.Value + " " + Fields!LastName.Value
Logical/ Bitwise		
And	Logical conjunction of two Boolean values or bitwise conjunction of two numeric expressions	=Fields!SalesAmount.Value < 100000 And Fields!DiscountAmountPct.Value > .25
Not	Logical negation of Boolean value or bitwise negation of numeric expression	=Not(Fields!SalesAmount.Value < 100000)
Or	Logical disjunction of two Boolean values or bitwise disjunction of two numeric expressions	=Fields!SalesAmount.Value < 100000 Or Fields!SalesAmount.Value > 5000000
Xor	Logical exclusive disjunction of two Boolean values or bitwise disjunction of two numeric expressions, also known as an exclusive OR, denoting "either one but not both"	=Fields!Cost.Value < 10 Xor Fields!Cost.Value > 50
AndAlso	Short-circuiting logical conjunction of two Boolean values, where evaluation of the second expression occurs only when the first expression is true	=Fields!SalesAmount.Value > 100000 AndAlso Fields!Cost.Value > 50000

Operator	Description	Example
OrElse	Short-circuiting logical disjunction of two Boolean values, where evaluation of the second expression occurs only when the first expression is false	=Fields!xxx.Value < 100000 OrElse Fields!xxx.Value > 5
Bitshift		
<<	Performs arithmetic left shift on a binary number	=Fields!BitField.Value << 1
>>	Performs arithmetic right shift on a binary number	=Fields!BitField.Value >> 1

Using IntelliSense

Another benefit of using the Expression dialog box to construct expressions is the IntelliSense feature. This feature helps you build a string to represent a collection member or property of a collection member and displays a tooltip to remind you of the syntax of a function. In addition, if your expression is invalid, a visual cue notifies you of a potential syntax error.

Member or property selection

Instead of using the expression lists to build an expression, you can type the expression directly into the expression box. As an aid to typing the expression, the Expression dialog box uses IntelliSense to display a list of valid fields when you begin an expression using collection syntax. This feature ensures that you get the correct name and case for the field name. However, the expression is not yet complete. You must still specify which member of the collection item to use in the expression, in addition to the property.

If you type the name of a collection, such as Fields, and then type an exclamation point, a drop-down list of the available members of that collection appears. If the list is long, you can type the first few characters of the member name, as shown in Figure 11-11, and then press Tab or double-click the member name to select it. Similarly, you can type a period (.) at the end of the expression, and then select a property from the drop-down list that appears.

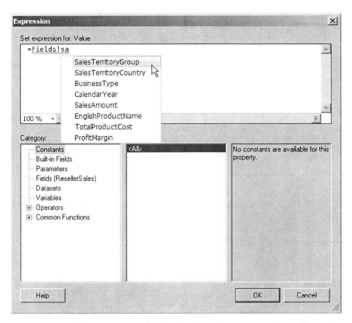

FIGURE 11-11 You can type the beginning of an expression using collection syntax to view a list of members or properties for selection.

Function tooltip

When you type a function name into the code window in the Expression dialog box and append a left parenthesis, a tooltip with the function syntax displays, as shown in Figure 11-12. The bold text in the tooltip indicates the next argument that you must supply in the code window and its data type. The tooltip disappears as you continue building the expression. You can type the argument directly into the code window or use the Category tree and other panes in the Expression dialog box to build the argument. If the tooltip disappears, it will display again when you type a comma (,) to end the current argument and prompt you with the syntax for the next argument.

FIGURE 11-12 You can see the function syntax as you type function arguments in the code window.

Syntax error

A red wavy underscore below an expression or operator is a visual cue that the expression currently contains a syntax error. In the expression shown in Figure 11-13, the syntax error is the result of an incomplete expression. When you correct the problem, the red wavy underscore disappears. The purpose of this feature is to alert you to a problem before you try to preview the report.

> **Note** Sometimes you'll see the red wavy underscore display when the expression is correct. For example, the expression *=DataSets!DataSource1.CommandText* displays in the Expression dialog box with a red wavy underscore beneath the *CommandText* property even though the expression is syntactically correct. You can execute the report to see the query string display in a text box as expected. Therefore, keep in mind that this indicator for a syntax error is not always accurate. If you double-check your expression and are certain it is correct, you can continue with report development. The best way to know for sure that the expression is correct is to preview the report. If it renders and you see the result you expected, you can safely ignore the red wavy underscore.

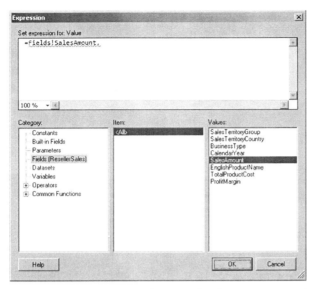

FIGURE 11-13 A wavy red underscore identifies a syntax error in an expression.

Using built-in collections

We first introduce collections in Chapter 8 when describing dataset properties. The fields and parameters collections associated with datasets are two of the built-in collections that you can reference in expressions. Table 11-3 contains a complete list of all built-in collections available for expressions. Some of these collections are available in the Category tree in the Expression dialog box, while others are not.

TABLE 11-3 Built-in collections

Collection	Description	Expression Example
DataSets	Datasets in report	=Datasets!DataSet1.CommandText
DataSources	Data sources in report	=DataSources!AdventureWorksDW.DataSourceReference)
Fields	Fields contained in a dataset	=Fields!SalesAmount.Value
Globals	Built-in fields	=Globals!ExecutionTime
Parameters	Report parameters	=Parameters!CalendarYear.Label
ReportItems	Text boxes in report	=ReportItems!SalesAmount.Value
User	User-specific fields	=User!UserID
Variables	Report and group variables	=Variables!GroupThreshold.Value

DataSets collection

The *DataSets* collection allows you to access information about the datasets that are included in a report. This isn't a particularly useful collection to use for displaying information to users, but it is useful if you're a developer troubleshooting report problems, particularly when using dynamic datasets. For example, you can add a text box that displays the command text and see the exact query that report execution sends to the data source.

Use the following properties to access query strings:

- **CommandText**   Use this property in an expression like *=DataSets!DataSet1.CommandText* to display the dataset's query string in a text box, as shown in Figure 11-14.

Expression: =DataSets!ResellerSales.CommandText

```
SELECT    st.SalesTerritoryGroup, st.SalesTerritoryCountry, r.BusinessType, d.CalendarYear, p.EnglishProductName, SUM(s.SalesAmount) AS
SalesAmount, SUM(s.TotalProductCost) AS TotalProductCost
FROM      FactResellerSales AS s INNER JOIN
              DimReseller AS r ON r.ResellerKey = s.ResellerKey INNER JOIN
              DimDate AS d ON d.DateKey = s.OrderDateKey INNER JOIN
              DimSalesTerritory AS st ON st.SalesTerritoryKey = s.SalesTerritoryKey INNER JOIN
              DimProduct AS p ON p.ProductKey = s.ProductKey
WHERE     (d.CalendarYear = @CalendarYear and st.SalesTerritoryGroup in (@SalesTerritoryGroup))
GROUP BY st.SalesTerritoryGroup, st.SalesTerritoryCountry, r.BusinessType, d.CalendarYear, p.EnglishProductName
ORDER BY st.SalesTerritoryGroup, st.SalesTerritoryCountry, r.BusinessType
```

FIGURE 11-14 Use the *CommandText* property of a *DataSets* collection member to view its query string.

- **RewrittenCommandText**   Use this property in an expression like *=DataSets!DataSet1 .RewrittenCommandText* to display the dataset's query string in a text box with query parameters replaced with actual values. For example, you can use it to see the query string generated by a report model data source. However, because some data providers do not populate this property, it has limited value. The data provider must support the *IDbCommandRewriter* interface for this to work.

DataSources collection

The *DataSources* collection is similar to the *DataSets* collection in that it's not commonly used except for troubleshooting purposes. You can use it to verify the reference to a data source.

Use the following properties to check data sources in your report:

- **DataSourceReference**   An expression like *=DataSources!DataSource1.DataSourceReference* returns a string value representing the name of a shared data source when applicable. If the data source in the expression is an embedded data source, the expression returns an empty string.

- **Type**   An expression like *=DataSources!DataSource1.Type* displays a string value representing the type of data provider used by an embedded data source, such as SQL for SQL Server or OLEDB-MD for Analysis Services. The expression returns an empty string for a shared data source.

Fields collection

Each dataset has its own *Fields* collection. When you assign a field to a tablix, you automatically assign the field's dataset to the tablix. As a result, in all other text boxes in the same tablix, you can reference only fields in the same dataset.

Use the following properties to work with dataset fields in your report:

- **IsMissing**   You can test for the existence of a field in the dataset by using an expression like *=Fields!CalendarYear.IsMisssing* as an argument in program flow function (described in Chapter 12). This property returns *True* or *False,* which you can use to hide or show a column for that field. (You learn how to work with visibility in Chapter 13, "Adding interactivity.") This property is useful when you are working with a stored procedure for which the columns returned for the dataset vary for each execution.

- **Value**   The expression you use for a field, such as *=Fields!CalendarYear.Value*, does not include the dataset name because the parent tablix for the text box determines which dataset's field collection applies to the expression. You can also use a simple expression for members of the *Fields* collection, such as *[CalendarYear]*.

When you use the Analysis Services data provider, you can replace the *Value* property in the expression with an extended field property, such as *Color* or *FontFamily*, to set values for corresponding text box properties. We explain more about working with extended field properties in Chapter 16, "Using Analysis Services as a data source."

Globals collection

The *Globals* collection contains many different members that are generic in nature. That is, they are available to provide values for use in the report, but they have no dependency on data. Table 11-4 lists the members of the *Globals* collection. When using a member of the global collection, you can use a simple expression or use *Collection!Member* syntax. For example, you can use either *[&ExecutionTime]* or *=Globals!ExecutionTime* to place the date and time of report execution into a text box.

TABLE 11-4 Globals collection

ExecutionTime	**The start date and time of report execution**
OverallPageNumber	The current page number counting from the report's first page. Use only in the page header or page footer.
OverallTotalPages	The total number of pages in the report, counting from the report's first page. Use only in the page header or footer.
PageName	The name of the current page, set initially by the *InitialPageName* property of the report and replaced by the *PageName* property of a rectangle, data region, data region group, or map, if applicable. Use only in the page header or footer.
PageNumber	The current page number counting from the report's first page or from the page on which the *ResetPageNumber* property is set to True for a rectangle, data region, data region group, or map, if applicable. Use only in the page header or footer.

ExecutionTime	The start date and time of report execution
RenderFormat.IsInteractive	A Boolean value, True or False, to indicate whether the current rendering format is interactive.
RenderFormat.Name	The name of the current rendering extension as represented in the RSReportServer .config file, such as RPL for online viewing or EXCELOPENXML for Excel 2010.
ReportFolder	The path to the report. For example, a report in the Sales folder (appearing in the Home folder of a native-mode report server) has the path /Sales, while a report in the Documents folder of a SharePoint site has the path *http://<server>/<site>/Documents*.
ReportName	The name of the report.
ReportServerUrl	The URL of the native-mode report server (such as *http://<server>/ReportServer*) or the URL of the SharePoint site (such as *http://<server>/<site>/_vti_bin/ReportServer*) where the report executes.
TotalPages	The total number of pages in the report counting from the report's first page or from the page on which the *ResetPageNumber* property is set to True for a rectangle, data region, data region group, or map, if applicable. Use only in the page header or footer.

Note Members of the *Globals* collection have a variant data type. To create an expression combining the result of an expression containing a member of the *Globals* collection with another expression having a different data type, you might need to use a data type conversion function, such as *CStr* or *CDate*. You learn how to use these functions to convert data types in Chapter 12.

Parameters collection

You typically use a report parameter when you want to prompt a user for information. You can pass the user's response to a dataset as a query parameter (as we describe in Chapter 14), or you can use it to change a property in the report. When you use the report parameter to assign a value to a query parameter, you might want to display the user's selection in the report so that if they print the report out or export it to another format for offline viewing, they will clearly see on the report how the data has been filtered.

Use the following properties when referencing a parameter in an expression:

- **Count**   Use this property in an expression like *=Parameters!Parameter1.Count* to return the number of values selected for a multivalue parameter. The result is always 1 for a single-value parameter.

- **IsMultiValue**   Use this property in an expression like *=Parameters!Parameter1.IsMultiValue* to return True if the parameter is multivalue or False if it is not. You can use the result of this expression to determine whether you must access the parameter value as an array of values or as a single value.

- **Label** Use this property in an expression like *=Parameters!Parameter1.Label* to return the parameter label for a single-value parameter. The parameter label is the value that the user sees in the parameter drop-down list, as we show you in Chapter 14. For a multivalue parameter, you must specify the array index to retrieve one of the values. For example, the expression *=Parameters!Parameter1.Label(0)* returns the label for the user's first selection.

- **Value** Use this property in a simple expression like *[@Parameter1]* or a complex expression like *=Parameters!Parameter1. Value* to return the parameter value for a single-value parameter. For a multivalue parameter, you must specify the array index to retrieve one of the values by using an expression like *=Parameters!Parameter1.Value(0)* to return the value for the user's first selection.

Tip You can return the entire set of selected labels or values as a comma-delimited string by using the *Join* function in an expression like *=Join(Parameters!Parameter1.Label, ", ")* or *=Join(Parameters!Parameter1.Value, ", ")*.

ReportItems collection

The *ReportItems* collection is not visible as a collection in the report data pane nor is it in the Expression dialog box. However, it can be useful when you need to reference the value in a particular text box that in turn might be the result of some calculation. Rather than copy and paste around the same calculation, you can define it once and then use the *ReportItems* collection to reference it.

The value of a member of the *ReportItems* collection is available only after the rendering of the page on which it appears. It's important to know that the report server renders the report body of a page first and then renders the page's header and footer. At that point, the dataset is no longer available, which means that you can no longer use the *Fields* collection to include a field value in an expression that you want to display in a page header or footer. By using the *ReportItems* collection creatively, you can solve this problem.

User collection

The *User* collection is a special collection containing members that you use when you need to create multilingual reports or implement row-level security.

Use the following members to create expressions based on the current user:

- **Language** Use an expression like *=User!Language* to get the language of the user currently running the report. You can then use this expression to set the *Language* property of the report or a text box. (We describe this property in Chapter 9 in the "Setting locale properties" section.) You can also use this expression to retrieve data from a different field of the dataset to display data in the current user's language.

- **UserID** Use an expression like *=User!UserID* to obtain the Windows login for the current user, using the format *domain\user*, when the report server is using Windows Authentication. A common reason to use this member of the *User* collection is to implement data security as we describe in Chapter 24, "Securing report server content."

> **Note** The *User!UserID* member is useful only when the user is viewing a report interactively. That is, you should not use it in an expression when the report is run on a schedule for a snapshot or a subscription because the report execution will not have access to the user's identity and will not be able to apply the correct security context.

Variables collection

You can create variables to store values at the report level or at the group level and then use the *Variables* collection to retrieve the current value of the variable. Regardless of whether the variable is a report variable or a group variable, you retrieve its value using a similar expression, such as *=Variables!Variable1.Value*. You learn more about variables later in this chapter in the section "Working with variables."

Working with expressions

There are many ways to use expressions in a report. In this section, we review many common examples. However, the range of possibilities is much more extensive than we can show in this book. Most expressions are references to a collection member, a concatenation of string values, or an arithmetic operation. You can also create more elaborate expressions by using functions or combining the results of multiple functions, but regardless of the specific operations performed by an expression, you can use expressions to perform certain tasks. More often, you use expressions to display the results of a calculation in a text box or to change the appearance or behavior of a report item. Less often, you can use expressions to reference values stored in group or report variables or to create dynamic strings at runtime for use as a data source connection or a dataset query.

Adding calculations to a report

Report calculations are expressions that you use to derive a value for display in your report based on dataset fields or user input. You can add expressions to a dataset as a calculated field to use it like any other dataset field. More often, you can add expressions to text boxes to perform operations on dataset fields and other built-in collections to produce a value for display in your report.

Calculated fields

A calculated field in your dataset is equivalent to adding an expression to the SELECT clause in a Transact-SQL (T-SQL) statement. In fact, ideally you create a derived column in your dataset query to get the desired value into the dataset from the data source, but in the case when you have no control over the source, such as when you're accessing a view or a stored procedure that you do not own, you can create the calculation you need for your report.

> **Tip** Another way to use a calculation in your report is to add it as an expression in a text box, as we describe next in this chapter. However, when you need to use the same calculation in multiple places in your report, it's better to add the calculation as a calculated field. That way, if a change is necessary later, you have only one place to make the change.

To add a calculated field to a dataset, right-click the dataset in the Report Data pane, and click Add Calculated Field. In the Dataset Properties dialog box, in the empty row at the bottom of the field list, in the Field Name text box, type a name for the calculated field.

> **Note** You cannot include spaces in the name of the calculated field, and you must use a letter as the first character.

To the right of the Field Source text box, click the Expression button. Create an expression in the Expression dialog box. For example, let's say that you need an expression that subtracts one field value from another, select the Fields category for your dataset in the Category list and then double-click the first field in the Values pane. In the Category list, expand Operators, select Arithmetic, and then double-click the minus sign (–), or you can simply type the minus sign directly into the code window. Then select the Fields category again, and double-click the second field in the Values pane to produce an expression like the one shown in Figure 11-15.

> **Important** The equal sign (=) is required in your expression. Be careful not to remove it when you begin creating the expression.

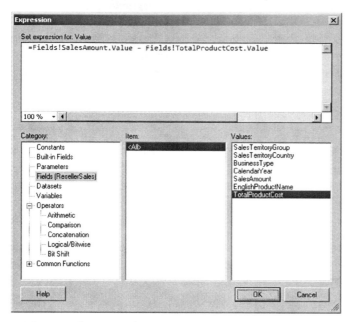

FIGURE 11-15 Create a scalar expression using dataset fields to add to your dataset as a calculated field.

When you close the Expression dialog box, you can see the complex expression placeholder in the Field Source box for the calculated field. You can now use the new calculated field just as you would use any other field that comes directly from the dataset. In fact, you cannot distinguish the calculated field from other fields by looking at the list of fields in the Report Data pane, as shown in Figure 11-16.

FIGURE 11-16 A calculated field displays in the dataset field list like all other fields returned by a dataset query.

The only way to know if a field is calculated is to open the Dataset Properties dialog box and review the contents of the Field Source text box, as shown in Figure 11-17.

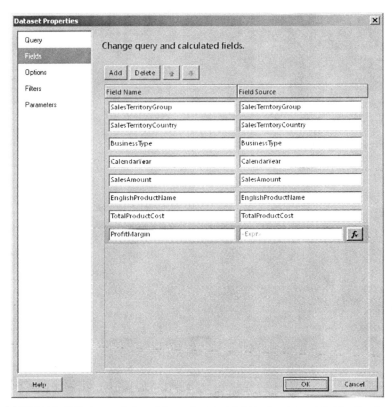

FIGURE 11-17 You can distinguish a calculated field in the dataset field collection by the expression placeholder in the Field Source text box.

Text box expressions

A tablix is comprised of text boxes, each of which displays either static text or an expression. In Chapter 9 and Chapter 10, "Working with the tablix," you learn how to use expressions to display a field value or an aggregate of a field value. You can add a calculated field to a dataset for use in your report just like any other dataset field, as many times as needed. When you intend to use an expression only once in the report, you can instead create an expression for the text box.

To create a text box expression, right-click the text box to which you want to add the expression, and click Expression. In the code window of the Expression dialog box, type an expression or use the panes at the bottom of the dialog box to build the expression. You can even use calculated fields as part of a text box expression. When you create a complex expression, such as the one shown in Figure 11-18, the complex expression placeholder displays in the text box. The only way to view the expression in this case is to open the Expression dialog box.

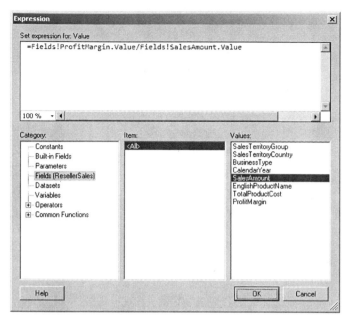

FIGURE 11-18 You can use calculated fields in other expressions, such as this text box expression.

Report item references

Sometimes you need to use the result of a text box expression in the expression for another text box. For example, you might use the aggregated value of detail rows in a group in a different text box. As described in Chapter 10, the total that appears in a group header or footer uses the *Sum* function to calculate the text box value. As an alternative to using the same expression over and over, which can often be quite long, the *ReportItems* collection provides you with a pointer to an expression in a specific text box.

> **Note** You cannot use a report item expression as a sort or group expression.

Before you use a report item expression, you should change the generic name for the text box you want to reference to make it easier to identify later. For example, let's say that your report contains a text box for the subtotal of a group called *BusinessType*. You can change the *Name* property of the text box from *Textbox14* to a more recognizable name such as *BusinessTypeTotal*, as shown in Figure 11-19. Then, you can reference the text box by name when you open the Expression dialog box for the text box, using an expression like this:

```
=Fields!SalesAmount.Value/ReportItems!BusinessTypeTotal.Value
```

> **Note** You cannot use the expressions list in the Expression dialog box to construct an expression that uses the *ReportItems* collection, but the IntelliSense feature prompts you with a list of available items.

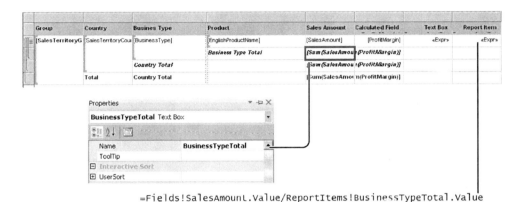

=Fields!SalesAmount.Value/ReportItems!BusinessTypeTotal.Value

FIGURE 11-19 You can use a report item expression to refer to a text box in the current or higher scope.

The *ReportItems* collection is dependent on the processing sequence and context of each text box in the report. In Figure 11-19, the text box containing the report item expression is in a detail row of a data region and can refer only to a text box in the same scope or in a higher scope. In this example, the *BusinessTypeTotal* text box is in the same data region, but in a parent group, and therefore has higher scope. A freestanding text box outside the data region in the report body or in a rectangle (but not a list) would also have higher scope. Conversely, you could not use reference *BusinessTypeTotal* in a report item expression for any text box in the *Country* group of this data region because the *BusinessType* group is a child group of *Country*.

Although using the *ReportItems* collection can be a simple way to refer to a text box value within a data region, it is the only way to refer to a text box value in an expression that is external to the data region. You can use this technique to display information in a page header or footer about the first and last items on each page. However, you can use only one member of the *ReportItems* collection in an expression, so you must use two text boxes to access the first and last item, as shown in Figure 11-20.

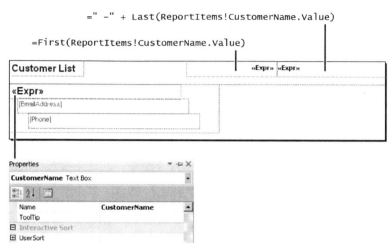

```
="  -" + Last(ReportItems!CustomerName.Value)

=First(ReportItems!CustomerName.Value)
```

FIGURE 11-20 You can use a report item expression in the page header or footer to reference a text box value on the same page.

> **Note** When using a report item expression in the page header or footer, the text box referenced in the expression must appear on the page when the report renders. Otherwise, the expression returns an error.

Built-in fields

In the Report Data window, the Built-in Fields folder contains thirteen fields that you can use to add an expression quickly to a text box when you want to display information that is specific to your report, such as the *Execution Time* or the *Report Name* field. These are the same fields available in the Built-in Fields category in the Expression dialog box.

> **Tip** By using the *Report Name* built-in field instead of static text for a report title, you make your report design more flexible. For example, you can modify the report title visible in Report Manager (or a SharePoint document library) after deploying the report to the report server, but a report title using static text would not reflect the modification. If you use the built-in field instead, the report title displaying in the report always matches the title displayed in Report Manager.

You can use a built-in field in any text box in your report, but you can use the built-in fields related to pagination (such as *Page Number* and *Total Pages)* only in the report's page header or page footer. You can easily add a page footer by selecting Add Page Footer on the Report menu. You can then drag a text box into the page footer, setting its *Location* and *Size* properties as needed.

You can create a compound version of a simple expression by combining multiple built-in fields in a single text box. For example, if you want to display both the current page number and the total pages in the page footer, add a text box to the page footer and drag *Page Number* from the Report Data pane, or type its simple expression, *[&PageNumber]*, into the text box. With the cursor at the end of the simple expression, press the Spacebar and type **[&TotalPages]** as shown in Figure 11-21.

FIGURE 11-21 Use the built-in fields related to pagination in the page header or footer only.

Applying conditional formatting

By using *conditional formatting*, you can change most format properties of a report item dynamically at run time based on specified conditions. These conditions can be determined by a value returned in the data, by a user selection for a parameter, or by the result of a calculation. For example, you can use an expression to set format properties affecting appearance, such as *BorderStyle*, *Color*, *FontFamily*, or *Padding*. Similarly, you can use an expression to set format properties affecting behavior, such as *Hidden* (which you learn about in Chapter 13). However, you cannot use expressions to set properties that specify size or location.

> **Tip** You can determine whether a property supports conditional formatting by checking the property's drop-down list in the Properties window. If <Expression...> is available in the drop-down list, you can use the property to apply conditional formatting.

To create an expression for conditional formatting, you use one of the program flow functions: *Choose*, *Iif*, or *Switch*. These functions evaluate an expression to determine the value to return. The *Iif* function, the mostly commonly used function, uses the following syntax:

```
=Iif(Expression as Boolean, TruePart as Object, FalsePart as Object)
```

For the first argument, you provide an expression that returns either a *True* or *False* value. The second argument contains the value to return if the first argument is true, while the third argument contains the value to return if the first argument is false. The second and third arguments can be static text or an expression that evaluates to a string, numeric, or Boolean value.

> **Note** You can learn more about the other program flow functions in Chapter 12.

For example, you can conditionally change the font color for values in a text box by updating the *Color* property to use an expression. For the second and third arguments, you provide the string values for constants that are valid for the property. For example, to display the text box value using a red font when sales are below $1,000 and a black font otherwise, you can use an expression like this:

```
=Iif(Fields!SalesAmount.Value < 1000, "Red", "Black")
```

Using *Me.Value*

Another way to reference a text box value, instead of using the *ReportItems* collection, is to use the Visual Basic built-in global *Me.Value*. You can use this global for the current text box. You might find it a handy way to reuse the same expression in multiple text boxes. For example, let's say you have two columns in a tablix in which you want to use a red font to emphasize values below a specific threshold. You can select all the text boxes at once by clicking each column handle while pressing the CTRL key, and then type the following expression in the *Color* property box:

```
=Iif(Me.Value < .05, "Red", "Black")
```

That way you can speed up report development by avoiding the need to enter the expression into the *Color* property individually. Furthermore, you avoid the need to modify the expression for the separate field references in each column or for the addition or removal of aggregate functions for detail and group rows.

Working with variables

As you learned earlier in this chapter, the location of an expression within a report affects when it is evaluated. In addition, the expression's location determines how many times it is evaluated. As you switch from page to page in a report, expressions on the requested page are evaluated when you open the page. You can manage the evaluation of expression-based values by using variables.

You can use a variable to store an explicit value or an expression that calculates at run time. You can scope a variable to a group or to the report. A group variable evaluates when the group instance changes, so it can potentially change even on the same page of a report. By contrast, a report variable evaluates only once and persists for the lifetime of the report. The primary purpose for variables is to address an architectural change in report processing introduced in SQL Server 2008 Reporting Services for the following scenarios:

- **Cache results for expensive calculations** If your report makes a call to an external assembly, you can store the results in a report variable and refer to the variable in expressions rather than repeatedly call the external assembly. Executing a single call should result in better performance.

- **Reference a consistent time value**   If text box appearing on multiple pages of a report has an expression using a function like *Now()* to get the current date and time, the expression can yield different results as the user pages through the report. You can use the time-dependent function in the report variable to evaluate once when the report begins executing and then refer to the report variable in the text box expression to obtain a consistent result on each page.

- **Custom aggregation**   In versions of Reporting Services prior to SQL Server 2008, you could use custom code to take advantage of the processing sequence of detail rows to derive a custom aggregation, such as median, at a group or data region scope. However, the new processing engine introduced in SQL Server 2008 Reporting Services invalidates that technique. For details of the problem and the solution, see the following post by Robert Bruckner, a member of the Reporting Services development team: *http://blogs.msdn.com/b/robertbruckner/ archive/2008/07/20/using-group-variables-in-reporting-services-2008-for-custom-aggregation .aspx*.

> **Important** Although you can reference a variable in most expressions by using the *Variables* collection, you cannot use it as an argument in an aggregate function nor can you use it in an expression for a calculated field.

Group variables

A group variable evaluates once for each distinct value defining a group. After you add a group variable to a group, you can reference it in an expression for any group or text box contained by the group for which the variable is defined.

Let's say that you create a group variable to assign a different conditional formatting threshold to each group. In the Row Groups pane, right-click a group, and click Group Properties. In the Group Properties dialog box, click Variables. Click Add, and then provide a variable name in the Name text box, as shown in Figure 11-22. Notice that you can create multiple group variables for the same group. To the right of the Value text box, click the Expression button and create an expression similar to this:

```
=Switch(Fields!SalesTerritoryGroup.Value="Europe", .13,
Fields!SalesTerritoryGroup.Value="North America", .15,
Fields!SalesTerritoryGroup.Value="Pacific", .09)
```

This expression assigns a value to the variable based on the current group instance. You can use this variable value to assign a value to the *Color* property and thereby change the threshold that changes the font color of the sales amount value according to sales territory group. That way, If the logic changes for the conditional formatting, you have only one place to make the change.

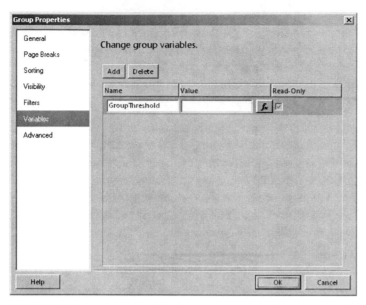

FIGURE 11-22 Use a group variable to store a separate reference value for each group instance to use in other expressions in the data region.

As long as a text box is at the same or lower scope of the group with the group variable, you can apply conditional formatting by setting the *Color* property by using an expression similar to this:

```
=Iif(Fields!Me.Value < Variables!GoupThreshold.Value, "Red", "Black")
```

> **Note** IntelliSense displays an error for the *Variables!GroupThreshold.Value* property, but you can safely ignore it.

Report variables

Because a report variable evaluates only once during report processing, it is especially useful in expressions closely linked to time, such as currency rates or time stamps. As you page through a report, you get consistent results in these types of calculations only if the expression calculating time is stored in a report variable.

To create a report variable, click Report Properties on the Report menu. In the Report Properties dialog box, click Variables, and click Add. Type a name for the function, and type an expression in the Value text box, as shown in Figure 11-23.

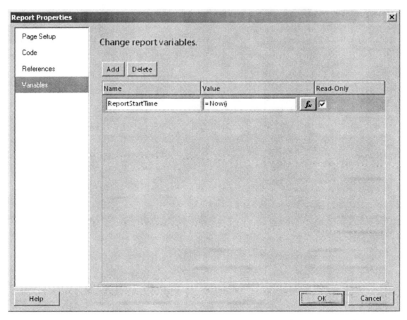

FIGURE 11-23 Use a report variable as a single consistent reference value for other expressions in the report.

You can use the report variable in any expression in your report using the *Variables* collection syntax. For example, to display the value of the report value illustrated in Figure 11-13, use the following expression:

```
=Variables!ReportStartTime.Value
```

In this example, the report variable value stays consistent from page to page. If you were to use the *Now* function in an expression (independently of the report variable) that returns a value for a text box that displays on multiple pages, you would observe a difference between the value of the text box on the first page and each subsequent page as you page forward. Furthermore, on returning to the first page, you would find the value on the first page is different from the value you initially saw.

DeferVariableEvaluation property

You can use the report property *DeferVariableEvaluation* to control when report processing evaluates variables. You can access this property only in the Properties window, after selecting the Report item in the drop-down list at the top of the window. This property is set to *False* by default, which means it will evaluate variable values when the report begins processing. If you change it to *True*, the evaluation occurs before the first usage of the variable. However, bear in mind that evaluation might never occur if the user views only the first page and the first use of the variable is on a separate page. Regardless of when the evaluation occurs, a report variable is evaluated only once during report processing, whereas a group variable is evaluated for each instance of the group.

Using expressions for dynamic connections and datasets

The data that displays in your reports will change as data is inserted into or deleted from your source database. But what if you need to change the actual source of the data at run time, or even the query string that executes to retrieve the data? All the reports in your project currently use a static data source and static datasets. The data source and the datasets remain the same no matter how many times you run each report and no matter who runs the report. You can use expressions to evaluate the connection string or the query string before processing the data for the report.

Dynamic connection strings

Although the creation of dynamic connections strings is not the most common way to use expressions, it does allow you to generate a connection string at run time so that you can specify the conditions under which one connection string might be used versus another. However, the downside of using dynamic connection strings is that you can use it only with an embedded data source, which means that you could have some administrative overhead with it if you need to make changes. Typically, you use a reference to the *Parameters* collection to get a value retrieved from a dataset, specified by a user, or evaluated from an expression, and then you incorporate this reference into a concatenation of static text and parameter references that resolves as a valid connection string.

> **Note** If your goal is simply to switch the server name from a development server to a production server, you would typically leave the data source connection string configured using a hard-coded value and then override this value by editing the data source object on the production server. You learn more about working with data sources on the report server in Chapter 23, "Deploying reports to a server."

Let's say that you want to use a report parameter to store a server name and then use the report parameter value to generate a dynamic connection string for the report's data source. You can prompt the user for the server name when viewing the report online, or you can choose to hide the parameter by selecting the *Hidden* value for parameter visibility. For example, you could build a table that maps user accounts from Active Directory directory service to specific servers (or from Active Directory Domain Services if you're using Windows Server 2008). You could store the result of retrieving the server name from the table in a report parameter but hide the parameter value so that the server name could not be changed on demand by the user. Regardless of how you provide a value for the report parameter, you can use it to build a dynamic connection string for the data source.

> **Note** You learn about report parameters in Chapter 14.

To use the report parameter value in a dynamic connection string, right-click the data source in the Report Data pane, and select Data Source Properties. In the Data Source Properties dialog box, select Embedded Connection. Select a provider, such as Microsoft SQL Server, in the Type drop-down list, select Microsoft SQL Server, and then click the Expression button to the right of the Connection String text box. There you can construct an expression similar to this:

```
="Data Source=" + Parameters!ServerName.Value + ";Initial Catalog=AdventureWorksDW2012"
```

You can replace any argument value in a connection string with a parameter item to create an expression that generates the applicable connection string when the report executes. In the Data Source Properties dialog box, click Credentials, and make sure to select Use Windows Authentication (Integrated Security).

> **Tip** Before you define an expression for the data source connection string, you should run your report with the static connection string to ensure that you have a valid connection string at the start and that you have connectivity to the source server and database.

Preview the report to test the expression. If the report displays, you know that the connection string for the data source was generated correctly.

Dynamic query strings

The use of query parameters, as you learn in Chapter 14, allows you to filter query results dynamically, but what if you need to modify the query itself dynamically? The ability to create a query dynamically provides enormous flexibility. However, with flexibility comes responsibility. You must take care that the structure of the result set is the same regardless of which version of the dynamic query executes. That is, the number of columns, the column names, and the column data types should match each and every time the query executes.

Where possible, you can create a stored procedure in your data source to ensure a consistent structure for query results. However, there might be situations in which you as a report developer require access to a data source but you have no ability to add a stored procedure to the source database. Creation of a dynamic dataset in the report itself allows you to define the right query without requiring a change in the database.

One way to generate a dataset dynamically is to use a report parameter. You can modify a previously tested dataset query by right-clicking it in the Report Data pane and selecting Dataset Properties. In the Dataset Properties dialog box, click the Expression button to the right of the Query text box and modify the static text to use an expression similar to this:

```
="SELECT st.SalesTerritoryGroup, st.SalesTerritoryCountry, r.BusinessType,
d.CalendarYear, p.EnglishProductName, SUM(s.SalesAmount) AS SalesAmount, "
+
Switch(Parameters!CostBasis.Value="Total", "SUM(s.TotalProductCost)",
Parameters!CostBasis.Value="Standard", "SUM(s.ProductStandardCost)")
+
" AS
TotalProductCost FROM FactResellerSales AS s INNER JOIN DimReseller AS r ON r.ResellerKey
= s.ResellerKey INNER JOIN DimDate AS d ON d.DateKey = s.OrderDateKey INNER JOIN
DimSalesTerritory AS st ON st.SalesTerritoryKey = s.SalesTerritoryKey INNER JOIN
DimProduct AS p ON p.ProductKey = s.ProductKey WHERE (d.CalendarYear = '2004') GROUP BY
st.SalesTerritoryGroup, st.SalesTerritoryCountry, r.BusinessType, d.CalendarYear,
p.EnglishProductName ORDER BY st.SalesTerritoryGroup, st.SalesTerritoryCountry,
r.BusinessType"
```

You must convert your query to a string expression by placing an equal sign at the beginning of the expression and enclosing the string with double quotes. In addition, you can replace a single column, such as *Sum(s.TotalProductCost),* with the *Switch* function (highlighted in bold) to return a string expression that resolves as the sum of a numeric column based on the current value of the *CostBasis* report parameter. Preview the report to ensure that the query string resolves successfully.

Important You should wait until you have finished your report design before you replace the static query string with an expression, because the field list will not update and you cannot access the query designer for the dataset. If the field list is not current, you cannot add fields to a data region.

CHAPTER 12

Using functions

Expressions are the key to informative, flexible, and dynamic reports. Chapter 11, "Developing expressions," provides an introduction to the use of expressions as calculations and for conditional formatting. In this chapter, you learn about the variety of built-in functions and how to use external functions. This chapter organizes the functions by using the same categories that you see in the Expression dialog box and then groups similar functions together. Although we cannot describe every possible scenario for using each function, we provide common reasons for using particular functions where applicable.

Note A few functions appear in more than one category in the Expression dialog box. In this chapter, we list such functions only once.

Getting help for functions

The Expression dialog box includes some features to help you learn how to use functions. First, you can view a description of a function and see an example of its syntax. Second, you can use the function tooltip as you build your function to select a syntax version and monitor your progress through the addition of arguments to the function.

Tip You can review examples of commonly used functions in expressions at *http://msdn .microsoft.com/en-us/library/ms157328.aspx.*

Function description and syntax

To discover the available functions, you can look through the Common Functions node of the Category tree in the bottom section. When you click a function in the Item list, the function's description displays above an example expression using the function, as shown in Figure 12-1.

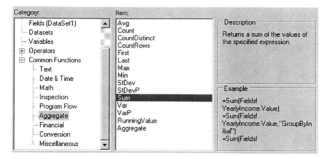

FIGURE 12-1 You can click the function in the item list to see its description and example.

Function tooltip

Whether you type a function or double-click a function in the Item list to add it to your expression, the IntelliSense feature displays syntax information to help you properly construct the expression. When the function has more than one possible syntax, you see a visual cue, such as "1 of 3," as shown in Figure 12-2. You can click the arrow icons to review each syntax example.

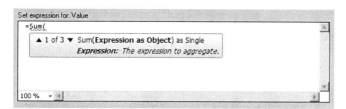

FIGURE 12-2 You click the up or down arrow in the tooltip to review a function's syntax options.

Using text functions

The text functions are among the most common functions you are likely to use in expressions. For this reason, this collection of functions is conveniently located at the top of the list of function categories. You can use character functions to compare characters or include control characters in a text string. You can also use search functions to find strings, characters, or character positions within a string. When you combine string data with other data types, you can use formatting functions to control the appearance of dates and numbers. Other functions allow you to manipulate the structure of a string in some way, whether working with arrays, case, or substrings. You can also use functions to evaluate the string length or sort sequence of two strings. Last, there are a few functions for cleansing data through substitution of one substring for another or elimination of leading or trailing spaces.

The character functions

This group of functions allows you to work with character codes, ASCII characters, Unicode characters, and an embedded space.

The *Asc* and *AscW* functions

The *Asc* and *AscW* functions both return an integer value representing a character that you provide as an argument. You use *Asc* to return ASCII (American Standards Committee for Information Interchange) character codes and *AscW* to return a Unicode character code. The value that *Asc* returns can change when run on different computers having different regional settings, whereas the value that *AscW* returns is consistent across all computers.

A common reason to use either of these functions is to compare characters in two different strings using the *Iif* function. You can use one of the string manipulation functions such as *Mid* or *Right* to locate a specific character within a string and use the result of that function as an argument for *Asc* or *AscW*. If you want to return the code for the first character of a string only, you can use the entire string as an argument because these functions operate the first character only. Thus, to compare the first character of strings found in two text boxes in a table, you use the following expression:

```
=Iif(Asc(ReportItems!String1.Value) = Asc(ReportItems!String2.Value), "Match", "No Match")
```

The *Chr* and *ChrW* functions

The *Chr* and *ChrW* functions both return a character represented by the integer that you provide as an argument, with *Chr* returning an ASCII character applicable to your regional settings and *ChrW* returning a Unicode character independent of regional settings. You can use either of these functions when you want to insert a character into a string and, more commonly, to insert control characters. For example, you can use the following expression using *Chr(13)* and *Chr(10)* for a carriage return and new line command to create a string that displays on separate lines:

```
=Fields!EnglishProductName.Value + Chr(13) + Chr(10) + Fields!EnglishDescription.Value
```

The *Space* function

You use the *Space* function when you want to add a specific number of spaces to a string. The number you pass as an argument to this function can be a constant integer or derived from an expression. The automatically generated list of available values for a report parameter from an Analysis Services–based dataset uses this technique to distinguish each level of a hierarchy in the list, as we describe in Chapter 16, "Using Analysis Services as a data source." The expression uses the level number of a dataset row to determine how many spaces to add as a prefix to the label string, like this:

```
=Space(3*Fields!ParameterLevel.Value) + Fields!ParameterCaption.Value
```

The search functions

The search functions give you different options for finding strings or characters. The *Filter* function is helpful for finding a matching string in a string array. The *GetChar* function finds a character at a location, whereas the *InStr* and *InStrRev* functions find the position of a character.

The *Filter* function

The *Filter* function returns a zero-based array containing matches found in a string array that you provide as an argument or returns an empty array if no match is found. The syntax of this function looks like this:

```
Filter(string_array, match_string [, include_substring] [, compare_method])
```

You use the *Filter* function to find one or more matches for a specific string in a string array. The first two arguments of the *Format* function are required. You can optionally add *True* or *False* as the third argument, to specify whether the function can match on a substring or must match the string entirely. You use the optional fourth argument to specify the comparison method, using *Compare-Method.Binary* to require a case-sensitive match or *CompareMethod.Text* to perform a case-insensitive match.

When you use multivalue report parameters, as we describe in Chapter 14, "Creating dynamic reports with parameters," Reporting Services stores the user's selections as a string array. You can use the *Filter* function to determine whether the user's selection includes a specific string, using an exact case-sensitive match by using an expression like this:

```
=Filter(Parameters!Product.Value,Fields!EnglishProductName.Value, True, CompareMethod.Binary)
```

> **Tip** Use the *Filter* function with the *Join* function to display the array it returns. Another option is to add *.Length* to the end of the expression to count the number of elements in the array. If the array is empty, the result is zero. You can then apply conditional formatting to a text box based on a zero or non-zero result of the combined expressions.

The *GetChar* function

You use the *GetChar* function to return a single character at the specified location in a string. An error results if you use an index for the second argument that is greater than the length of the string. An expression using the *GetChar* function looks like this:

```
="The 4th character of 'alphabet' is : " + GetChar("alphabet", 4)
```

The *InStr* and *InStrRev* functions

The *InStr* function searches one string for the starting position of another string. It also takes optional arguments for you to specify a character position within the first string to begin searching for the second string and the type of comparison. Like the *Filter* function, you use the optional fourth argument to specify the comparison method, using *CompareMethod.Binary* to require a case-sensitive match or *CompareMethod.Text* to perform a case-insensitive match. The syntax for the *InStr* function looks like this:

```
InStr([start_position, ] search_string, match_string [, compare_method])
```

The *InStrRev* function works similarly, but begins the search from the right side of the string. Although it takes the same arguments, the arrangement of arguments is different than the arrangement you use for the *InStr* function, as shown here:

```
InStrRev(search_string, match_string [, start_position] [, compare_method])
```

One way you might use the *InStr* function is to create a NOT IN filter for a data region. There is no NOT IN operator, but you can achieve the same result by creating an expression that evaluates as True or False, like this:

```
=Iif(InStr(Join(Parameters!Product.Value,","), Fields!EnglishProductName.Value)=0,True,False)
```

Then, in the Tablix Properties dialog box, you can set the Expression field of a new filter to *True*, use an = operator, and use the *InStr* expression for the filter definition in the Value field, as shown in Figure 12-3. The filter will keep rows where the value is *True* and exclude rows causing the value to be *False*. When you use the *InStr* function in the Value field to compare the current row's product name to the product string (converted from an array to a comma-delimited string by using the *Join* function in this example), the *InStr* function returns 0 if the category is not found, which is the equivalent of NOT IN. In that case, the expression returns *True*, which keeps the row in the data region.

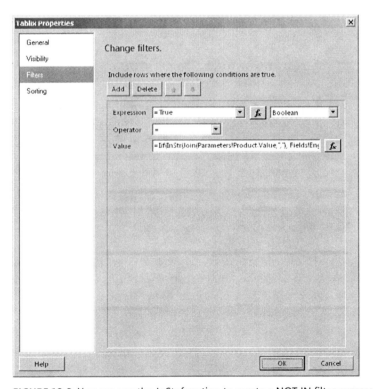

FIGURE 12-3 You can use the *InStr* function to create a NOT IN filter expression.

Important In Figure 12-3, note that the expression is =*True* and not just *True*. This is important because Reporting Services interprets *True* by itself as a string instead of a Boolean data type.

The formatting functions

Often you create new strings by combining string expressions with expressions returning other data types. When you work with currency, numeric, or date/time data, you can convert these data types to a string by using one of the formatting functions. Furthermore, you can use arguments with these functions to apply a specific style of formatting.

The *Format* function

The *Format* function returns a string formatted according to style argument that you provide. The style argument can be a predefined numeric or date/time format or a user-defined numeric or date/time format. If you use parameters to prompt a user for a date range, you can use this function to combine the selected date values into a string that you display in the report using an expression like this:

```
="From " + Format(Parameters!StartDate.Value, "d") + " to " + Format(Parameters!EndDate.Value,
"d")
```

Note You can learn more about predefined numeric formats at *http://msdn.microsoft.com/ en-US/library/y006s0cz* and about predefined date/time formats at *http://msdn.microsoft .com/en-US/library/362btx8f*. For similar information about user-defined numeric formats, see *http://msdn.microsoft.com/en-US/library/4fb56f4y*. Information about user-defined date/time format is available at *http://msdn.microsoft.com/en-US/library/73ctwf33*.

The *FormatCurrency*, *FormatNumber*, and *FormatPercent* functions

You might find using *FormatCurrency*, *FormatNumber*, or *FormatPercent* easier than the *Format* function, which requires you to know (or look up) the string to use as a style argument. The *FormatNumber* and *FormatPercent* functions use the same syntax as the *FormatCurrency* function, shown here:

```
FormatCurrency(string [, digits_after_decimal] [, leading_digit] [, parens] [, group_digits])
```

You can simply pass the value as a single argument to the function you want to use, or you can provide optional arguments to override your computer's regional settings. For example, you can specify the number of digits to display after the decimal place as the second argument and pass *True* or *False* as the third argument to indicate whether to display a zero in front of the decimal place when the value is less than one. As the fourth argument, you use *True* or *False* to require or omit parentheses when formatting negative values. Last, you use *True* or *False* as the fifth argument to use grouping or avoid grouping of digits according to your regional settings. For example, in United States English, the default grouping uses a comma as a thousands separator.

You use *FormatCurrency*, *FormatNumber*, and *FormatPercent* when you need to apply formatting to a currency, numerical, or percentage value, respectively, in a string, like this:

```
="Standard Cost: " + FormatCurrency(Fields!StandardCost.Value,0,,,False)
="Weight: " + FormatNumber(Fields!Weight.Value, 3)
="Dealer Pct of List: " + FormatPercent(Fields!DealerPrice.Value/Fields!ListPrice.Value,2)
```

> **Note** You should update the *Format* property of the text box when you want to format a value that is not part of a string, rather than use the formatting functions to achieve better performance of a large report.

The *FormatDateTime* function

The *FormatDateTime* function is another type of formatting function that you can use in place of the *Format* function when working with a value having a date/time data type. You use the following syntax for this function:

```
FormatDateTime(string [, format])
```

If you omit the second argument, the default formatting uses the *DateFormat.GeneralDate* format, which displays a date without time as a short date, such as 1/1/2012, and a time without date as a long time, such as 08:00:00 AM. For other formatting options, you can use *DateFormat.LongDate*, *DateFormat.ShortDate*, *DateFormat.LongTime*, or *DateFormat.ShortTime* as the second argument.

Like the other formatting functions, you use the *FormatDateTime* function to apply formatting to a date/time value that you use in a string expression such as this:

```
="Effective Date: " + FormatDateTime(Fields!StartDate.Value)
```

The array functions

When you create a report parameter that allows the user to make multiple selections, as we describe in Chapter 14, you can use the *Join* function to combine these selections into a single string. Conversely, you can create an array from a single string by using the *Split* function.

The *Join* function

The *Join* function is useful for combining the elements of an array into a single string value, such as you might want to do when you want to display the user's selection of multiple values for a parameter in your report. You pass the array as the first argument and then provide an optional second argument to specify the delimiter to use as a separator between array elements. If you omit this argument, Reporting Services uses a space between array elements. An expression to display parameter values in a list separated by a comma and a space looks like this:

```
=Join(Parameters!Product.Value, ", ")
```

The *Split* function

The *Split* function does the opposite of the *Join* function by creating an array from a string value by using a delimiter that you specify as the second argument to create separate elements in the array. You can use a third optional argument to specify the maximum number of substrings you want to add to the array. If the number of possible substrings is greater than the limit you specify, the last substring in the array combines the remaining substrings into a single substring. The fourth optional argument is the comparison method, using *CompareMethod.Binary* to require a case-sensitive match of the delimiter string or *CompareMethod.Text* to perform a case-insensitive match. You use the following syntax for the *Split* function:

```
Split(string [, delimiter] [, limit] [, compare_method])
```

A creative way to use the *Split* function is to create a filter based on an OR condition between multiple conditions as an alternative to the approach we describe in Chapter 14. For example, let's say that you have two report parameters that you use to prompt the user for two possible dates and you want to use these two values in a filter using an OR condition. That is, you want to filter either by the first date or by the second date. If you create two separate filters, one for each date, the report displays results only when both conditions are met, because it uses a logical AND operator to combine the filter expressions.

To handle this scenario, you create a single filter that uses the *In* operator and then set up the *Value* expression as an array, as shown in Figure 12-4. To create an array, you use the *Split* function after creating a string that concatenates the two values, as shown here:

```
=Split(CStr(Parameters!StartDate.Value) + "," + CStr(Parameters!SecondDate.Value), ",")
```

> **Note** In this example, you first apply a string conversion using the *CStr* function with each parameter value so that you can concatenate the two parameter values into a single string. You must use a comma delimiter for the result of the *Split* function to work correctly with the *In* operator. You also must change the expression value from *[StartDate]* (or *=Fields!StartDate.Value*) by using the *CStr* function so that the expression returns a string to compare with the values in the string array.

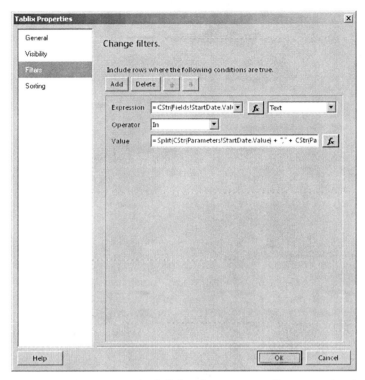

FIGURE 12-4 You can use the *Split* function to create a filter expression that uses OR logic.

The conversion functions

The conversion functions *LCase*, *UCase*, and *StrConv* are helpful for converting strings into lowercase or uppercase. You can also use *StrConv* to convert strings to proper case or from one type of international character to another for certain locales.

The *LCase* and *UCase* functions

The *LCase* and *UCase* functions work similarly, taking a string as a single argument. The *LCase* function converts the uppercase characters in the string to lowercase, whereas the *UCase* function converts the lowercase characters in the string to uppercase. For example, to return a string using uppercase characters only, you use an expression like this:

```
=UCase(Fields!EnglishProductName.Value)
```

The *StrConv* function

You can also use the *StrConv* function to convert a string to uppercase or lowercase, but the *StrConv* function can do much more. You can use it to convert a string to proper case or convert Simplified Chinese characters to Traditional Chinese, among others. You specify the conversion type as the second argument by using a *VbStrConv Enumeration* member. To override your computer's regional settings, you can provide a locale identifier as the optional third argument. You use the following syntax for the *StrConv* function:

```
StrConv(string, conversion [, locale])
```

To convert a string to proper case, you use an expression like this:

```
=StrConv(Fields!EnglishDescription.Value, VbStrConv.ProperCase)
```

> **Note** You can view a complete list of *VbStrConv Enumeration* members at *http://msdn .microsoft.com/en-US/library/3a1cfsz3*.

The string manipulation functions

String manipulation is a very common operation in reports. The string manipulation functions *Left*, *LSet*, *Right*, *RSet*, and *Mid* allow you to extract a portion of a string. The *StrDup* function creates a string by repeating a character multiple times, or use the *StrReverse* function to display a string's characters in reverse.

The *Left*, *LSet*, *Right*, and *RSet* functions

You can use the *Left* or *LSet* function to return a specified number of characters from a string, starting from the left side of the string, or use the *Right* or *RSet* function to do the same, starting from the right side of the string. These two functions require a string as the first argument and the number of characters to return as the second argument. For example, when you want to extract a user name from the value that *User!UserID* returns in domain\user name format, you can use an expression like this:

```
=Right(User!UserID, Len(User!UserID) - InStr(User!UserID, "\"))
```

The *Mid* function

Rather than start from the left or right side of a string to extract a substring, you can use the *Mid* function to start from a specified position that you pass as a required second argument. You can provide an optional third argument to restrict the length of the substring this function returns. If you omit the third argument, the *Mid* function returns the substring starting from the specified start position to the end of the string.

```
=Mid(Fields!EnglishProductName.Value, InStr(Fields!EnglishProductName.Value, " "))
```

If you prefer, you can use the *Substring* member of the .NET Framework *String* class to work with substrings, using the start position of the substring and number of characters to return, like this:

```
=Fields!EnglishProductName.Value.Substring(0,5)
```

The *StrDup* function

The *StrDup* function repeats a character a specified number of times. You can pass the character as a character, string, or object, but Reporting Services uses the first character only. An expression using the *StrDup* function looks like this:

```
=StrDup(len(Fields!EnglishProductName.Value), Fields!EnglishProductName.Value)
```

The *StrReverse* function

You use the *StrReverse* function to display each character of a string in reverse. That is, the rightmost character of a string displays first in the resulting string, and each successive letter to the left of that last character appears in sequence to the right of the new string's first letter. An expression using the *StrRev* function looks like this:

```
=Right("C:\Program Files\Microsoft SQL Server\MSRS11.MSSQLSERVER ", InStr(StrReverse("C:\Program
Files\Microsoft SQL Server\MSRS11.MSSQLSERVER"), "\")-1)
```

> **Note** You can achieve the same result by using the *InStrRev* function instead.

The string evaluation functions

The string evaluation functions provide information about strings. You use the *Len* function to discover the length of a string and use the *StrComp* function to compare the sort sequence of two strings.

The *Len* function

The *Len* function counts the number of characters in a string or the number of bytes required to store other data types in a file. For example, the length of a double data type is 8. The *Len* function takes a single argument, like this:

```
=Len(Fields!EnglishDescription.Value)
```

The *StrComp* function

The *StrComp* function compares two strings and returns -1 if the first string sorts before the second string, 0 if the strings are equal, and 1 if the first string sorts after the second string. You can include an optional third argument to set the comparison type as *CompareMethod.Binary* to perform case-sensitive sorting or *CompareMethod.Text* to perform case-insensitive sorting. An expression using the *StrComp* function looks like this:

```
=StrComp(Fields!EnglishProductName.Value, Parameters!Product.Value(1), CompareMethod.Text)
```

The cleanup functions

You can modify the data that a query returns by using the cleanup functions. You can use the *Replace* function to find a specified substring and replace it with another substring. The *LTrim* and *RTrim* functions are useful for eliminating spaces at the beginning or end of a string, respectively, whereas the *Trim* function eliminates both leading and trailing spaces.

The *Replace* function

You use the *Replace* function to substitute a substring in one or more places within a string with another substring. You can optionally define a start position from which to start searching for the substring to replace and can restrict the substitutions to a specified number rather than keep the default of all possible substitutions. Last, you can specify the comparison method as *CompareMethod.Binary* for a case-sensitive match or *CompareMethod.Text* for a case-insensitive match. The *Replace* function syntax looks like this:

```
Replace(search_string, replace_substring, replacement_substring [, compare_method]
```

For example, let's say you create a report that lists hierarchical data using an expression like the one shown in the section "The *Space* function" earlier in this chapter. If you render the report as HTML, you find that your browser eliminates the leading spaces. As an alternative, you can use the *Replace* function to substitute the space with a non-truncating space. You create a non-truncating space by pressing and holding the Alt key while you type **0160** on the numeric keypad. The resulting expression looks like this:

```
=Replace(Microsoft.VisualBasic.Strings.Space(3 * Fields!ParameterLevel.Value), " ", " ") +
Fields!ParameterCaption.Value
```

> **Note** In this example, the second argument is the substring to replace, which consists of a space. The third argument looks like a space but is the ASCII character code created by typing Alt-0160.

> **Tip** If you are working on a laptop without a numeric keypad, your keyboard might use a Fn key to change keys from letters to numbers as a numeric keypad emulator. Otherwise, you can use your operating system's Help feature to turn on the On-Screen Keyboard. Click the Options key, and select the Turn On Numeric Key Pad check box. Then on the keyboard that displays, click the NumLock key until you see numbers display in the numeric keypad. Next, press and hold the Alt key on your laptop's keyboard and type **0160** by using the numeric keypad on the On-Screen Keyboard. When you release the Alt key, a space displays in your expression.

The *Trim*, *LTrim* and *RTrim* functions

You use the *Trim* function to remove both leading and trailing spaces from a string. The *LTrim* function removes only leading spaces from a string, while the *RTrim* function removes only trailing spaces from a string. All three functions use the same syntax, taking a string value as a single argument. An example of an expression using the *LTrim* function looks like this:

```
=LTrim(ReportItems!LabelWithSpace.Value)
```

Using date and time functions

Many reports use date and time date in some way, whether in report parameters and query parameters to restrict the report content or to display transactional information or even report execution time. You can use date calculation functions to add or subtract intervals of time to or from dates. Or you can use data manipulation functions to extract a part of a date, such as a day or a year. There are date conversion functions you can use to transform a date from one format to another. Last, there is a group of functions to display information about the current date or time.

The date calculation functions

To perform arithmetic operations on dates, you can use the *DateAdd* function or the *DateDiff* function. The *DateAdd* function allows you to calculate a new date by adding an interval to an existing date. The *DateDiff* function finds the difference between two dates.

The *DateAdd* function

The *DateAdd* function calculates a date based on a starting date and an interval. An interval is a unit of time, such as a second or day. You can use a *DateInterval* enumeration value (with no quotes) or a string enclosed in double-quotes to specify an interval as an argument for the *DateAdd* function. Table 12-1 shows all the interval settings you can use. The syntax for the *DateAdd* function looks like this:

```
DateAdd(interval, number, date)
```

TABLE 12-1 Interval settings

Enumeration Value	String
DateInterval.Second	s
DateInterval.Minute	n
DateInterval.Hour	h
DateInterval.Day	d
DateInterval.DayOfYear	y
DateInterval.Weekday	w
DateInterval.WeekOfYear	ww

Enumeration Value	String
DateInterval.Month	m
DateInterval.Quarter	q
DateInterval.Year	yyyy

For example, if you use a parameter to prompt the user for a start date, you can use a function to calculate a date six months later by using the *DateAdd* function like this:

```
=DateAdd(DateInterval.Month, 6, Parameters!StartDate.Value)
```

You can use a negative value as the second argument when you need to calculate a date prior to the date you supply as the third argument. An expression to calculate the date six months prior to the *StartDate* parameter looks like this:

```
=DateAdd(DateInterval.Month, -6, Parameters!StartDate.Value)
```

The *DateDiff* function

The *DateDiff* function calculates the difference between two dates for the specified interval. The *DateDiff* function uses the same interval values that you can use with the *DateAdd* function, as shown in Table 12-1. The syntax looks like this:

```
DateDiff(interval, start_date, end_date [, FirstDayOfWeek] [, WeekOfYear])
```

When you use weekday or week of year intervals, you might need to apply rules to the calculation to derive the correct number of weeks between two dates. First, you can optionally use a *FirstDayOfWeek* argument with either an enumeration value, such as *FirstDayOfWeek.Sunday*, or a number of the week such as 1, which represents Sunday and is the default setting. Second, you can use the *WeekOfYear* argument with one of the following settings:

- **FirstWeekOfYear.Jan1**   Sets the first week of the year as the week in which Jan 1 occurs

- **FirstWeekOfYear.FirstFourDays**   Sets the first week of the year as the first week having at least four days in the new year

- **FirstWeekOfYear.FirstFullWeek**   Sets the first week of the year as the first full week in the new year

Let's say that you want to display a label in the report to represent the time span between the start date and end date parameter selections. You can use the following expression, which includes the *CStr* function to convert the integer to a string and allows you to concatenate the result of the *DateDiff* function with static text to create a label:

```
="Report time span (days): " + CStr(DateDiff("d", Parameters!StartDate.Value,
Parameters!EndDate.Value))
```

The date manipulation functions

The date manipulation functions allow you to access a portion of a date, such as the day of the month or the year. You can use the *DatePart* function to extract any interval from the date, but there are also interval functions, such as *Day* or *Year*, to perform the same function.

The *DatePart* function

The *DatePart* function returns an integer for the specified interval of a date. The syntax looks like this:

```
DatePart(interval, date [, FirstDayOfWeek] [, WeekOfYear])
```

Notice the similarity of the *DatePart* function to the *DateDiff* function. You can use optional arguments for *FirstDayOfWeek* and *WeekOfYear* if necessary.

Just like the DateAdd and *DateDiff* functions, the *DatePart* function allows you to specify the interval by using a *DateInterval* enumeration value, like this:

```
=DatePart(DateInterval.Day, Today())
```

Or you can use a string interval, like this:

```
=DatePart("d", Today())
```

> **Tip** If necessary, use the *CDate* function to convert a string representation of a date to a date data type. Otherwise, the *DatePart* function fails when it evaluates the expression.

The interval functions

When you use the *DatePart* function, you must remember (or look up) the valid values for the interval. You might find it easier to use one of the interval functions shown in Table 12-2. The syntax for each of these functions is the same. You pass an expression that returns a date data type as the single argument, like this:

```
=Day(Parameters!StartDate.Value)
```

TABLE 12-2 Interval functions

Function	Description
Second	Returns a value between 0 and 59 within an hour.
Minute	Returns a value between 0 and 59 for the minutes of an hour.
Hour	Returns a value between 0 and 23 for the hour of the day.
Day	Returns a value between 1 and 31 for the day of the month.

Function	Description
Weekday	Returns a value between 1 and 7 for the day of the week. Uses optional second argument FirstDayOfWeek enumeration value or numerical value from 0 to 7.
Month	Returns a value between 1 and 12 for the month in the year.
Year	Returns the year as 4-digit integer.

The date conversion functions

There are two types of date conversion functions. The first type, which includes the *DateSerial*, *TimeSerial*, *DateValue*, and *TimeValue* functions, return a date data type based on the input arguments. The other type, which includes the *MonthName* and *WeekdayName* functions, returns a string for the name of a month or day based on the integer you supply as input.

The *DateSerial* and *TimeSerial* functions

The *DateSerial* function takes three integer values as arguments. The first argument represents the year, the second argument represents the month, and the third argument represents the day. The *TimeSerial* function is similar, using three integer values as arguments for hour, minute, and second, respectively. You use this function to return a date data type from an expression, like this:

```
=DateSerial(ReportItems!Year.Value, ReportItems!Month.Value, ReportItems!Day.Value)
```

The *DateValue* and *TimeValue* functions

The *DateValue* function converts a date string in long or short format to a date data type. Similarly, the *TimeValue* function converts a time string to a Date data type. You use the *DateValue* function to return a date data type from an expression, like this:

```
=DateValue("1/1/2012")
```

The *MonthName* and *WeekdayName* functions

The *MonthName* function returns the name of the month based on the number you provide as an integer. You use the optional second argument to specify whether to allow the abbreviation of the month name. The syntax of this function looks like this:

```
=MonthName(integer [, true_or_false])
```

The *WeekdayName* function also takes an optional third argument to specify the first day of the week, as described for the *DateDiff* function, like this:

```
=WeekdayName(integer [, true_or_false] [, FirstDayOfWeek])
```

The current date and time functions

Table 12-3 lists the functions you can use to return a date or string data type for the current date or time. You can use these functions to display values in a text box or as input arguments for date and time functions. None of these functions require an argument, and they use similar syntax, like this:

=Today()

TABLE 12-3 Current date and time functions

Function	Description
DateString	Returns a string based on your computer's current date.
Now	Returns the current date and time.
TimeOfDay	Returns the current time.
Timer	Returns the number of seconds that have elapsed since midnight.
TimeString	Returns a string based on your computer's current time.
Today	Returns the current date.

Using math functions

You can choose from an assortment of math functions. Probably less commonly used for standard business reporting are the trigonometry functions. You might use one of the sign functions when working with key performance indicator data. You can use exponent functions for advanced mathematical operations or rounding functions when you do not require precise numbers in your report. Last, there are two miscellaneous functions that do not fit neatly into any other group, *BigMul* and *Rnd*.

The trigonometry functions

Table 12-4 lists the trigonometry functions available for you to use.

TABLE 12-4 Trigonometry functions

Function	Syntax	Description
Acos	Acos(cosine)	Returns the inverse cosine, also known as the arccosine, (in radians) of a number representing the cosine of an angle (in radians).
Asin	Asin(sine)	Returns the inverse sine, also known as the arcsine, (in radians) of a number between -1 and 1 representing the sine of an angle (in radians).

Function	Syntax	Description
Atan	Atan(tangent)	Returns the inverse tangent, also known as the arctangent, (in radians) of a number representing the tangent of an angle (in radians).
Atan2	Atan2(x, y)	Returns the arctangent (in radians) of the x-coordinate and y-coordinate of a point.
Cos	Cos(angle)	Returns the cosine (in radians) of a number representing an angle (in radians).
Cosh	Cosh(angle)	Returns the hyperbolic cosine (in radians) of a number representing an angle (in radians).
Sin	Sin(angle)	Returns the sine (in radians) of a number representing an angle (in radians).
Sinh	Sinh(angle)	Returns the hyperbolic sine (in radians) of a number representing an angle (in radians).
Tan	Tan(angle)	Returns the tangent (in radians) of a number representing an angle (in radians).
Tanh	Tanh(angle)	Returns the hyperbolic tangent (in radians) of a number representing an angle (in radians).

The sign functions

The sign functions, *Abs* and *Sign*, might be useful for key performance indicator calculations. Sometimes you might need to know the difference between two values expressed as a positive value, in which case you use the *Abs* function. Other times you might need to know whether one value is greater than another value, in which case you use the *Sign* function. You can see a more complete description for each function in Table 12-5.

TABLE 12-5 Sign functions

Function	Syntax	Description
Abs	Abs(number)	Returns the absolute value of a number. In effect, it returns a positive number whether you pass a positive or negative number as an argument.
Sign	Sign(number)	Returns -1 if the number is less than 0, 0 if the number is equal to zero, or 1 if the number is greater than zero.

The exponent functions

You can use the functions shown in Table 12-6 to perform exponential operations. This group of functions is useful for financial modeling and statistical analysis.

TABLE 12-6 Exponent functions

Function	Syntax	Description
Exp	Exp(power)	Returns the constant e (approximately 2.71828183) raised to the specified power.
Log	Log(number [,base])	Returns the natural logarithm of a positive number when you provide one argument or returns the logarithm of a positive number in the base specified as the second argument.
Log10	Log10(number)	Returns the base 10 logarithm of a positive number.
Pow	Pow(number, power)	Raises a number to the specified power.
Sqrt	Sqrt(number)	Returns the square root of a number.

The rounding functions

Rounding functions are useful when you do not need to display precise numbers in a report. Table 12-7 displays a list of functions that you can use for rounding.

TABLE 12-7 Rounding functions

Function	Syntax	Description
Ceiling	Ceiling(number)	Returns the smallest integer greater than or equal to a number.
Fix	Fix(number)	Returns the smallest integer after truncating the decimal part of a positive number and the largest integer after truncating the decimal part of a negative number (that is, returns -6 for -6.1).
Floor	Floor(number)	Returns the largest integer less than or equal to a number.
Int	Int(number)	Returns the smallest integer after truncating the decimal part of a number (that is, returns -7 for -6.1).
Round	Round(number)	Returns the nearest integer to a number. You can add a second optional argument to specify a rounding mode by using the *MidpointRounding.AwayFromZero* or *MidpointRounding.ToEven* enumeration values.

Other math functions

The *BigMul* and *Rnd* functions are unlike any other math function, so they appear in a group of their own. Table 12-8 shows the syntax and description for each of these functions.

TABLE 12-8 Other math functions

Function	Syntax	Description
BigMul	*BigMul(number1, number2)*	Returns the result of multiplying two 32-bit numbers.
Rnd	*Rnd([number])*	Returns a random number according to the number you provide: a number less than 0 returns the same random number every time, a number greater than 0 or no number returns a different random number every time, 0 returns the most recently generated random number.

Using inspection functions

The inspection functions are useful for investigating the result of an expression before proceeding with another operation. You typically use them as part of a compound expression using the *Iif* function, which we describe in the "Using program flow functions" section of this chapter. For example, you can use the *IsNothing* function to ensure that an expression returns a value before using it as a denominator in a division operations. Table 12-9 lists the inspection functions, provides an example of their usage, and includes a description of the function results.

TABLE 12-9 Inspection functions

Function	Example	Description
IsArray	*IsArray(Parameters!Product.Value)*	Returns a Boolean value to specify whether the input argument is an array.
IsDate	*IsDate(Fields!StartDate.Value)*	Returns a Boolean value to specify whether the input argument is a valid date.
IsNothing	*IsNothing(Fields!LargePhoto.Value)*	Returns a Boolean value to specify whether the input argument is null.
IsNumeric	*IsNumeric(Fields!Size.Value)*	Returns a Boolean value to specify whether the input argument is a number.

Note The *IsNumeric* function returns *True* for numeric input arguments as well as for certain characters: plus (+), minus (-), and currency symbols, such as a dollar sign ($).

Using program flow functions

You use the program flow functions to control the order of operations. The *Choose* function allows you to select an item from a list based on an index. Both the *Iif* and *Switch* functions rely on a Boolean expression to determine which argument to evaluate.

The *Choose* function

The *Choose* function uses an index that you pass as the first argument to select an item from an array that you pass as the second argument. You can specify an array by using the *Parameters* collection. For example, you can use the day of the month as an index to select a different product from a list stored as a parameter:

```
=Choose(DatePart("d", ParametersStartDate.Value), Parameters!Product.Value)
```

You can also pass the array as a comma-delimited string, like this:

```
=Choose(2, "1", "2", "3")
```

The *Iif* function

The *Iif* function evaluates a Boolean expression in the first argument and returns the result of the expression in the second argument if the Boolean expression evaluates as *True*. Otherwise, it returns the result of the expression in the third argument. A common use of the *Iif* function is to apply conditional formatting as described in Chapter 11. The syntax of the *Iif* function looks like this:

```
=Iif(expression, true_expression, false_expression)
```

You can also use the *Iif* function in combination with the *IsNothing* function to verify that an expression returns a non-null value before using it in an expression, like this:

```
=Iif(IsNothing(expression), true_expression, false_expression)
```

The *Switch* function

The *Switch* function is an alternative to using a series of nested *Iif* functions when you want to return different results for different conditions. You add arguments to the function in pairs, with the first item in the pair representing a Boolean expression and the second argument representing the result to return. For example, you can apply conditional formatting by using the *Switch* function like this:

```
=Switch(Fields!PctComplete.Value >= 10, "Green", Fields!PctComplete.Value >= 1, "Blue",
Fields!PctComplete.Value = 1, "Yellow", Fields!PctComplete.Value <= 0, "Red")
```

Using aggregate functions

In this section, you learn the general purpose of each aggregate function and how the use of a scope argument affects the result of an aggregate function. Most aggregate functions work similarly, taking an expression as the first input argument and scope as an optional second argument. However, the *RunningValue* function operates differently than the others, so we cover that function in greater detail.

The aggregate functions

You use aggregate functions, shown in Table 12-10, primarily to summarize many records of numerical data, such as giving a total or average value. You can also use aggregate functions to get the first or last string value in a group of records.

TABLE 12-10 Aggregate functions

Function	Description
Aggregate	Returns a custom aggregation of non-null values as defined by the data provider.
Avg	Returns the average of non-null numerical values in scope.
Count	Returns the count of values in scope.
CountDistinct	Returns the count of distinct values in scope.
CountRows	Returns the count of rows in scope.
First	Returns the first value in scope.
Last	Returns the last value in scope.
Max	Returns the highest value in scope.
Min	Returns the lowest value in scope.
RunningValue	Returns the current cumulative value of rows in scope.
StDev	Returns the standard deviation of non-null values in scope.
StDevP	Returns the population standard deviation of non-null values in scope.
Sum	Returns the sum of numerical values in scope.
Var	Returns the variance of non-null values in scope.
VarP	Returns the population variance of non-null values in scope.

Important To work successfully with aggregate functions, you must first understand how the location of an expression in the report affects when it is evaluated. An expression in the report body has access to the dataset and therefore can reference an object directly in the *Fields* collection. However, an expression in the page header or page footer is evaluated after the report body is processed when the dataset is no longer available. Although you can no longer use the *Fields* collection, you can access the results of the report processing by referencing an object in the *ReportItems* collection.

The *Scope* argument

An aggregate function uses scope to determine which detail rows to include in the aggregation. If you omit the *Scope* argument when using an aggregate function, the scope is inferred by the location of the expression. If the expression appears in a text box in a group (or a property of that text box), the scope is limited to the dataset rows associated with that group. If you want to use a scope other than the inferred scope, you must specify the scope explicitly in the aggregate function. To specify the scope, you provide the name of a dataset, data region, or group. Any reference to one of these objects must match the actual case used in the name, or the expression fails. You know if the expression succeeds or fails due to a case mismatch only if you attempt to preview the report, because no warning displays in the Expression dialog box to alert you to the mistake.

Figure 12-5 shows a portion of a report that includes two types of calculations. The first calculation uses the scope argument to display a grand total in a freestanding text box in the top right of the report. Because this text box is not bound to a dataset, you cannot use the Fields category in the Category list to select a specific field, nor can you use IntelliSense to prompt you for the field item, but you can use the following expression in which the ResellerSales data region is the scope for the aggregation:

```
="Total Sales: " & CStr(FormatCurrency(Sum(Fields!SalesAmount.Value, "ResellerSales"),0))
```

Note In Figure 12-5, because the freestanding text box is not bound to a dataset, IntelliSense detects an error related to *Fields!SalesAmount.Value*, but you can safely ignore the warning.

Reseller Sales Cumulative Sales   ADVENTURE WORKS **cycles**   Total Sales: $16,038,063

Group	Country	Busines Type	Product	Sales Amount	Pct of Business Type
Europe	France	Specialty Bike Shop	Mountain-200 Black, 38	$17,901	15 %
			Touring-1000 Yellow, 46	$15,735	13 %
			Road-350-W Yellow, 40	$15,309	13 %

FIGURE 12-5 You use the *Scope* argument to identify the range of detail rows to aggregate for an expression.

Another reason to use scope is to calculate the percentage contribution of a detail row to its group or to the overall dataset. In Figure 12-5, you can see the result of the calculation of each detail row as a percentage of the *BusinessType* group. In this case, the expression looks like this:

```
=Fields!SalesAmount.Value/Sum(Fields!SalesAmount.Value,"BusinessType")
```

The *RunningValue* function

The main difference between using an aggregate function in a freestanding text box and using one in a data region is the *Scope* argument. Whereas this argument is required in a freestanding text box, you can omit the *Scope* argument in a data region if Reporting Services can infer the scope correctly. An exception to this rule is the *RunningValue* function, which not only requires you to specify scope but also requires you to specify an aggregate function to use to accumulate values.

To better understand how you might use the *RunningValue* function, consider a request from a business user to facilitate comparisons of product mixes across reseller business types. More specifically, the business user wants to see which products contribute most to sales for each reseller business type. To support this analysis, your report must show the products grouped by reseller business type. You must calculate the cumulative sales for each product within the group and the cumulative percentage of total sales for the group. When the products are sorted in descending order, the user can see easily which products collectively contribute to a target percentage of sales, such as the top 20 percent of sales or the top 50 percent of sales.

To satisfy this requirement, you use the *RunningValue* function to compute the cumulative sales and percentage of cumulative sales by product for each business type, as shown in Figure 12-6. In the expression for the Cumulative Sales column, you use the following expression:

```
=RunningValue(Fields!SalesAmount.Value, Sum, "BusinessType")
```

 Important When using the *RunningValue* function, be sure to include the aggregate function without quotes.

Reseller Sales Cumulative Sales   Total Sales: $16,038,063

Group	Country	Busines Type	Product	Sales Amount	Pct of Business Type	Cumulative Sales	Cumulative Sales Pct
Europe	France	Specialty Bike Shop	Mountain-200 Black, 38	$17,901	15 %	$17,901	15 %
			Touring-1000 Yellow, 46	$15,735	13 %	$33,636	28 %
			Road-350-W Yellow, 40	$15,309	13 %	$48,945	41 %
			Touring-1000 Yellow, 60	$14,304	12 %	$63,249	53 %

FIGURE 12-6 You use the *RunningValue* function for cumulative calculations.

If you assign the name *CumulativeSales* to the text box in which you added the *RunningValue* function, you can add another column to divide that value by the total sales by business type (in the *BusinessTypeTotal* text box). In the new column, add the following expression to the detail row text box:

```
=ReportItems!CumulativeSales.Value/ReportItems!BusinessTypeTotal.Value
```

 Tip When working with cumulative sales data, you can sort the data in descending order by the value you are accumulating to easily see how each detail row represents a particular percentage of sales.

Using financial functions

If you create reports for depreciation or loan payment analysis, you might find the financial functions useful. You can see the available functions, their syntax, and descriptions in Table 12-11.

TABLE 12-11 Financial functions

Function	Syntax	Description
DDB	DDB(cost, salvage, life, period, factor)	Returns the double-declining balance depreciation of an asset based on its initial cost, the salvage value after full depreciation, the length of depreciation, the period for which to compute depreciation, and the factor to use (such as 2 for the double-declining method or 3 for the triple-declining method).
FV	FV(rate, periods, payment, value, period_type)	Returns the future value of an investment based on a constant interest rate, the length of the investment in periods, a constant payment, present investment value, and payment period type (such as 0 for end of period or 1 for beginning of period).
Ipmt	Ipmt(rate, period, periods, value, period_type)	Returns the interest payment based on a constant interest rate, the current payment period, the length of the investment in periods, present investment value, and payment period type (such as 0 for end of period or 1 for beginning of period).
NPer	NPer(rate, payment, value, future_value, period_type)	Returns the number of periods for loan amortization based on an interest rate, payment amount, present investment value, future investment value at end of term, and payment period type (such as 0 for end of period or 1 for beginning of period).
Pmt	Pmt(rate, periods, value, future_value, period_type)	Returns the period payment for loan amortization based on an interest rate, length of the investment in periods, present investment value, future investment value at end of term, and payment period type (such as 0 for end of period or 1 for beginning of period).
PPmt	PPmt(rate, period, periods, value, future_value, period_type)	Returns the principal amount of a loan payment based on a constant interest rate, the current payment period, the length of the investment in periods, present investment value, future investment value at end of term, and payment period type (such as 0 for end of period or 1 for beginning of period).

Function	Syntax	Description
PV	PV(rate, periods, payment, future_value, period_type)	Returns the present value of a series of constant payments based on an interest rate, length of the investment in periods, payment amount, future investment value at end of term, and payment period type (such as 0 for end of period or 1 for beginning of period).
Rate	Rate(periods, payment, value, future_value, due_date, guess)	Returns the rate of return of an investment based on the length of the investment in periods, payment amount, present investment value, future investment value at end of term, due date, and guess as an approximate interest rate.
SLN	SLN(cost, salvage, life)	Returns the straight-line depreciation of an asset based on its initial cost, the salvage value after full depreciation, and the length of depreciation.
SYD	SYD(cost, salvage, life, period)	Returns the sum-of-the-years'-digits method of depreciation of an asset based on its initial cost, the salvage value after full depreciation, the length of depreciation, and the period for which to compute depreciation.

Using conversion functions

The conversion functions are necessary when you must convert a data type before using it in an expression. Of all these functions, perhaps the *CStr* function is used most often because a common requirement is to create headings and labels based on fields or parameters with mixed data types. Each conversion function takes an expression as a single argument and converts it to the data type indicated by the function name. Table 12-12 lists the complete set of conversion functions.

TABLE 12-12 Conversion functions

Function	Description
CBool	Requires a char or string value as an input argument and returns a Boolean value. Valid values include yes or no, true or false, on or off, or 1 or 0.
CByte	Requires a value from 0 through 255 and returns a 1-byte integer.
CChar	Requires a char or string value (of which the function uses only the first character) or an unsigned value from 0 through 65535 and returns it as a Char data type.

Function	Description
CDate	Requires a string value representing a date (like "1/1/2012") or time (like "8:00 AM") and returns it as a Date data type.
CDbl	Requires a signed double-precision floating-point value ranging from -1.7969313486231570E+308 through -4.94065645841246544E-324 for negative values or 4.94065645841246544E-324 through 1.7969313486231570E+308 for positive values and returns a Double data type.
CDec	Requires a signed 128-bit value representing a 96-bit integer number ranging from +/- 79,228,162,514,264,337,593,543,950,335 for integers or +/-7.9228162514264337593543950335 for numbers with 28 decimal places and returns a Decimal data type.
CInt	Requires a signed 32-bit value ranging from -2,147,483,648 through 2,147,483,647 and returns an Integer data type.
CLng	Requires a signed 64-bit value ranging from -9,223,372,036,854,775,808 through 9,223,372,036,854,775,807 and returns a Long data type.
CObj	Uses any valid expression and returns an Object data type.
CShort	Requires a signed 16-bit value ranging from -32,768 through 32,767 and returns a Short data type.
CSng	Requires a signed IEEE 32-bit single-precision floating-point value ranging from -3.4028235E+38 through -1.401298E-45 for negative values and from 1.401298E-45 through 3.4028235E+38 for positive values and returns a Single data type.
CStr	Requires an expression that can be expressed in ASCII or Unicode characters and returns a String data type.
Hex	Uses any valid numeric or string expression and returns the hexadecimal value.
Oct	Uses any valid numeric or string expression and returns the octal value.
Str	Requires an object containing a valid numeric expression and returns a String data type.
Val	Requires a string expression that contains numbers and returns a number of the appropriate data type.

Using miscellaneous functions

This group of functions provides some unique functionality in reports. Although the *InScope* function was once commonly used for matrix reports, it is no longer necessary. The lookup functions were introduced in SQL Server 2008 R2 Reporting Services and are useful for overcoming the limitation of referencing only one dataset in a data region. Last, the row functions are useful for period-over-period types of calculations or for numbering rows of data in a data region.

The *InScope* function

Prior to SQL Server 2008 Reporting Services, in which the tablix data region made its debut, the only way you could apply conditional formatting to subtotal rows in a matrix was to use the *InScope* function, which was not always an intuitive operation to perform. The *InScope* function returns a *True* or *False* based on whether the group you use as an input argument is applicable to the current text box. With the availability of the tablix in the current release, you now have greater control over the formatting of subtotal rows for rows or columns in a matrix, rendering the *InScope* function less useful for this purpose today.

The lookup functions

The lookup functions enable you to combine data from two datasets in a single data region, which was not possible until SQL Server 2008 R2 Reporting Services. If all the data in a report comes from a single data source, you might find it easier to create a single dataset by using a SQL query that joins the data from multiple tables. However, there might be situations when you cannot write the query to join the data in advance. For example, you might have some data coming from a relational source and other data in a CSV file. Or perhaps you're taking advantage of shared datasets and need a way to link together data from two shared datasets in one data region. There are three lookup functions available: *Lookup*, *LookupSet*, and *MultiLookup*.

The *Lookup* function

The *Lookup* function has the effect of simulating a join between two datasets where there is a one-to-one relationship between the source and destination. Let's say that you want to produce a report of sales by state, but the dataset that you have for sales provides the two-letter code for state. Let's say also that you find another dataset that provides a list of states and the two-letter code for each state. Now you have two datasets available for the report, a portion of each of which is shown in Figure 12-7.

DataSet1

StateProvinceCode	SalesAmount
AL	45429.0290
AZ	1432585.5698
CA	9764270.7083
CO	2395913.8430
CT	1125700.4070
FL	2299888.8680

DataSet2

StateProvinceC...	Name
AK	Alaska
AL	Alabama
AR	Arkansas
AZ	Arizona
CA	California

FIGURE 12-7 You must have two datasets having common field data to use the *Lookup* function.

To connect the data from the two datasets, you use the *Lookup* function in an expression like this:

```
=Lookup(Fields!StateProvinceCode.Value,Fields!StateProvinceCode.Value,Fields!Name.Value,"State")
```

As a result of using this function, you can combine the two datasets in a single table, as shown in Figure 12-8. The *Lookup* function takes the following arguments:

- The first argument, *Fields!StateProvinceCode*, is a field (or expression based on a field) from the dataset that is bound to the data region, which is *Dataset1* in this example.

- The second argument is a field (or expression) from the dataset that you want to use for the lookup. In this example, the second dataset also contains a field called *StateProvinceCode*, but it's okay if the field names are different in each dataset. They should, of course, contain data that matches up, and they must have the same data type. You can think of the first and second arguments as analogous to two columns that you want to use to define a join between two tables.

- The third argument, which is *Fields!Name.Value* in this example, is the field (or expression) in the second dataset that you want to return as the function result.

- The fourth and final argument is the name of the second dataset, which must be enclosed in quotes and is case-sensitive.

State Province Code	State	Sales Amount
AL	Alabama	$45,429
AZ	Arizona	$1,432,586
CA	California	$9,764,271
CO	Colorado	$2,395,914
CT	Connecticut	$1,125,700
FL	Florida	$2,299,889

FIGURE 12-8 You can easily combine fields from two datasets in one table by using the *Lookup* function.

If you need to match two fields in the first dataset to two fields in the second dataset, that's okay. You simply create an expression to concatenate the pair of fields and use that expression in the argument in the *Lookup* function. However, your expression cannot include report or group variables, nor can it include another *Lookup* function.

> **Important** Reporting Services processes the *Lookup* function based on the scope of the expression, which is in this case comprises the detail rows of the table, which correspond to the rows of Dataset1. Using the *Lookup* function, Reporting Services uses a single value for the current row in the first dataset to find the first match in the second dataset and returns a single value. By contrast, the other two lookup functions, *MultiLookup* and *LookupSet*, work with arrays.

The *MultiLookup* function

Whereas the *Lookup* function evaluates one value per row in the source to find one value for that row in the destination, the *MultiLookup* function evaluates multiple values per row, finds each matching value in the destination, and returns the matches in a set. To better understand how to use it, let's look at an example of how to use this function. In this example, you want to produce a list of the sales of each salesperson and include a list of the states in each person's sales territory based on data from two datasets. In the first dataset, you have a comma-delimited list of two-letter codes for the states in each person's sales territory, as shown in Figure 12-9. In the second dataset, you have a list of states with their corresponding two-letter codes, just like the one in the example for the *Lookup* function.

SalesPerson	StateList	SalesAmount
David Campbell	ID,MT,OR,WA,WY,	3729945.3501
Jillian Carson	CT,IL,IN,MA,ME,MI,MN,MO,NH,NY,OH,RI,SD,TX,VA,WI,	10065803.5429
Linda Mitchell	AZ,CA,CO,NM,NV,UT,	10367007.4286
Michael Blythe	CT,IL,IN,MA,ME,MI,MN,MO,NH,NY,OH,RI,SD,TX,VA,WI,	9293903.0055
Pamela Ansman-Wolfe	ID,MT,OR,WA,WY,	3325102.5952
Shu Ito	AZ,CA,CO,NM,NV,UT,	6427005.5556

FIGURE 12-9 You can look up values for each item in a comma-delimited list that you later convert to an array.

You can use an expression in a text box to create an array from the comma-delimited list in the first dataset, look up the state corresponding to each value in the array, and then display the list by inserting a new line between each value, as shown in Figure 12-10. The expression to perform this operation looks like this:

```
=Join(MultiLookup(Split(Fields!StateList.Value, ","), Fields!StateProvinceCode.Value,
Fields!Name.Value,"State"), chr(10))
```

Salesperson	Territory	Sales Amount
David Campbell	Idaho Montana Oregon Washington Wyoming	$3,729,945
Jillian Carson	Connecticut Illinois Indiana Massachusetts Maine Michigan Minnesota Missouri New Hampshire New York Ohio Rhode Island South Dakota Texas Virginia Wisconsin	$10,065,804

FIGURE 12-10 You use the *MultiLookup* function to look up values for each item in an array.

The *MultiLookup* function takes the following arguments:

- The first argument, *Split(Fields!StateList.Value, ",")*, is an expression based on the *StateList* field found in the dataset that is bound to the data region, which is *Dataset1* in this example. The *StateList* field contains a comma-delimited list that is transformed into an array by using the *Split* function.

- The second argument is the *StateProvinceCode* field in *Dataset2* that you use as the lookup field. That is, you are matching each item in the array made from the *StateList* field in *Dataset1* with a *StateProvinceCode* in *Dataset2*. The values to match must have the same data type.

- The third argument, *Fields!Name.Value*, is the field (or expression) in the second dataset that you want to return as the function result. The difference here between the *Lookup* and *MultiLookup* functions is that the *Lookup* function returns a single value while *MultiLookup* returns an array.

- The fourth and final argument is the name of the second dataset, which must be enclosed in quotes and is case-sensitive.

Because this function returns an array of values, the *Join* function is used to convert the array back to a string of values. For presentation purposes, rather than use a comma separator, you can use *Chr*(10) to present each state on a separate line.

The *LookupSet* function

The *LookupSet* function evaluates data in two separate datasets in yet another way. You use this function to evaluate each row in the source and look for all matches in the destination, returning the resulting matches as a set. That is, a single row in the first dataset can produce no matches, one matching row, or multiple matching rows.

To illustrate how to use *LookupSet*, let's consider yet another example. This time you want to produce a list of sales by state and include a count of customers so that you can calculate an average sale per customer by state. In *DataSet1*, you have a list of the states' two-letter codes and total sales. In *Dataset2*, you have a list of customer IDs and the state associated with the customer. You can see a sample of data in each of these datasets in Figure 12-11.

DataSet1

StateProvinceC...	SalesAmount
AL	45429.0290
AZ	1432585.5698
CA	9764270.7083
CO	2395913.8430
CT	1125700.4070
FL	2299888.8680

DataSet2

StateProvinceC...	CustomerID
AL	44
AL	224
AL	296
AL	387
AZ	205

FIGURE 12-11 You can look up a value in a second dataset for each array associated with a single row in the first dataset.

In the Customer Count column, shown in Figure 12-12, you can see the result of matching customers by state. This count is based on an expression that includes the *LookupSet* function to retrieve the set of customers for the state on the current row and then uses a *Length* property of the array to get a count, like this:

```
=LookupSet(Fields!StateProvinceCode.Value,Fields!StateProvinceCode.Value, Fields!CustomerID.
Value,"CustomersByState").Length
```

Code	Customer Count	Sales Amount	Avg Sale Per Customer
AL	4	$45,429	$11,357
AZ	12	$1,432,586	$119,382
CA	65	$9,764,271	$150,220
CO	8	$2,395,914	$299,489
CT	8	$1,125,700	$140,713
FL	25	$2,299,889	$91,996

FIGURE 12-12 You use the *LookupSet* function to find all matching values in the second dataset for each value in the first dataset.

The *LookupSet* function takes four arguments, much like the *Lookup* function, except that *Lookup* returns a single value per row whereas *LookupSet* returns an array:

- The first argument, *Fields!StateProvinceCode.Value*, is a field in the dataset that is bound to the data region (*Dataset1* in this example).

- The second argument is the *StateProvinceCode* field in the *CustomersByState* dataset that you use as the lookup field. The *LookupSet* function matches each value in the *Dataset1* field with a value in the second dataset's field. The values to match must have the same data type.

- The third argument, *Fields!CustomerID.Value*, is the field in the *CustomersByState* dataset that you want to return as the function result. The difference here between the *Lookup* and *LookupSet* functions is that the *Lookup* function returns the first value it finds, but *LookupSet* returns an array of all matching values that it finds.

- The fourth and final argument is the name of the second dataset, which must be enclosed in quotes and is case-sensitive.

Important Remember that the *LookupSet* returns an array, so you can't use the results directly in the table but must use some other function to operate on the array to get a single value.

The row functions

The row functions are useful for those situations where the relationship between rows is important or the number of rows is important. You use the *Previous* function when you want to access a value in a previous row for use in a calculation. You use the *RowNumber* function to see row numbers in a long report and to help manage page breaks or set row color for even or odd rows only.

The *Previous* function

The *Previous* function returns the value of an expression by using fields from the previous row. An example might be when you display the sales by year for a product and want to see the percent change from the previous year. When using the *Previous* function, you must take care to sort the detail rows correctly to ensure that the previous row contains the value you expect. You can use an expression like this:

```
=Previous(Fields!SalesAmount.Value)
```

The *RowNumber* function

The *RowNumber* function is useful for assigning row numbers to a data region, such as a table. You use an optional argument to specify scope for row numbering. For example, if your report contains nested data regions, you can use the *Nothing* keyword to count each row in the table regardless of the data region to which it belongs, like this:

```
=RowNumber(Nothing)
```

Otherwise, you use the name of a data region or a group as the scope argument, like this:

```
=RowNumber("Group")
```

You can also use the *RowNumber* function to apply conditional formatting if you want to use alternating colors for each row in a table. You can use the following expression in the *BackgroundColor* property to evaluate whether the current row number is even and then assign one color to even row numbers or another color to odd row numbers:

```
=Iif(RowNumber(Nothing) Mod 2, "color1", "color2")
```

Another potential benefit of the *RowNumber* function is the ability to specify a maximum number of rows on a page. You start by adding a page break to a row group or a detail records group, and then you add a grouping expression to specify a number of rows. For example, if you want to display only 10 rows per page of the report, you can use the following expression:

```
=Ceiling(RowNumber(Nothing)/10)
```

Working with hierarchical data

Hierarchical data comes from a table with a self-referencing join, which is sometimes referred to as a parent-child table. You can recognize a table of hierarchical data by the presence of a foreign key column with a relationship to a primary key column in the same table. This type of data structure is useful when multiple levels of data exist, such as you might find in an organizational chart of employees, but where a different number of levels exist in each branch from the top of the hierarchy.

Reporting Services allows you to create a group to organize rows into hierarchical levels as defined by the foreign key relationships. A special function is available to show the level of a row within the hierarchy, which can be useful for applying formatting.

The *Level* function

The *Level* function returns a numerical value to specify the number of levels between the top of the hierarchy and the row for which the expression is being evaluated. You can include a *Scope* argument to limit the function to evaluating within a group, data region, or dataset. If you omit the argument, the function assigns a value of 0 to the top of the hierarchy and then increments this value by 1 for each level within the hierarchy until it reaches the evaluating row. Typically, you use this function to apply different formatting styles to different levels of a hierarchy.

In Chapter 10, "Working with the Tablix," we introduced the concept of recursive hierarchy groups. You can use the *Level* function to apply conditional formatting based on the level of a record in a recursive hierarchy. For example, in Figure 12-13, the text box in the Employee Name column uses two types of conditional formatting.

Employee Organization

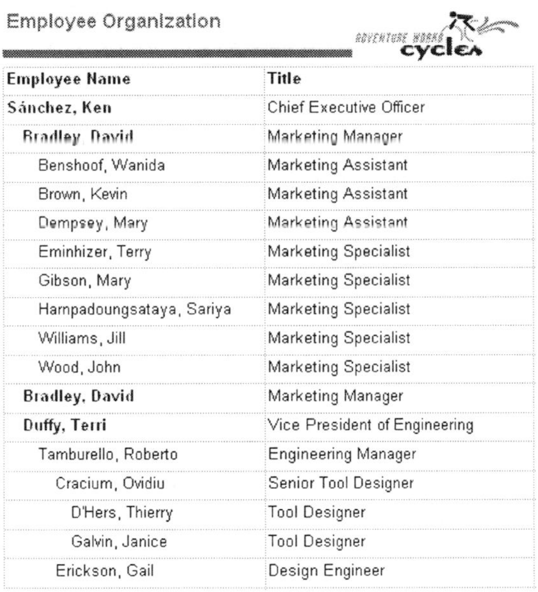

Employee Name	Title
Sánchez, Ken	Chief Executive Officer
Bradley, David	Marketing Manager
Benshoof, Wanida	Marketing Assistant
Brown, Kevin	Marketing Assistant
Dempsey, Mary	Marketing Assistant
Eminhizer, Terry	Marketing Specialist
Gibson, Mary	Marketing Specialist
Harnpadoungsataya, Sariya	Marketing Specialist
Williams, Jill	Marketing Specialist
Wood, John	Marketing Specialist
Bradley, David	Marketing Manager
Duffy, Terri	Vice President of Engineering
Tamburello, Roberto	Engineering Manager
Cracium, Ovidiu	Senior Tool Designer
D'Hers, Thierry	Tool Designer
Galvin, Janice	Tool Designer
Erickson, Gail	Design Engineer

FIGURE 12-13 You can use the *Level* function to apply conditional formatting in a recursive hierarchy.

First, the *Padding* property uses the following expression:

```
=CStr(2 + Level()*10) + "pt"
```

Second, the *FontWeight* property uses the following expression:

```
=Iif(Level() < 2, "Bold","Normal")
```

This expression displays all employees with a level below 2, using a bold font. As a result, the names of the chief executive officer and all employees reporting directly to the chief executive officer are bold.

The *Recursive* keyword

Because hierarchical data is structured into a recursive grouping, the process of aggregating values within the grouping differs from standard aggregation calculations. You can use the same aggregate functions, but to account for the difference in data structure, you include the *Recursive* keyword as a third argument in the aggregate function.

To continue the example in the previous section, you can add a column to a table with a recursive hierarchy group to count the number of employees for each manager by using the following expression:

```
=Count(Fields!EmployeeKey.Value, "Details", Recursive) - 1
```

When you use the *Recursive* keyword with an aggregate function, such as the *Count* function shown here, the aggregation applies to the scope of the specified group. In this example, the scope is the Details row group, which includes each instance of a manager record plus the number of employee records associated with that manager. To get the right count of employees for a manager, you must subtract 1 from the result returned by the *Count* function.

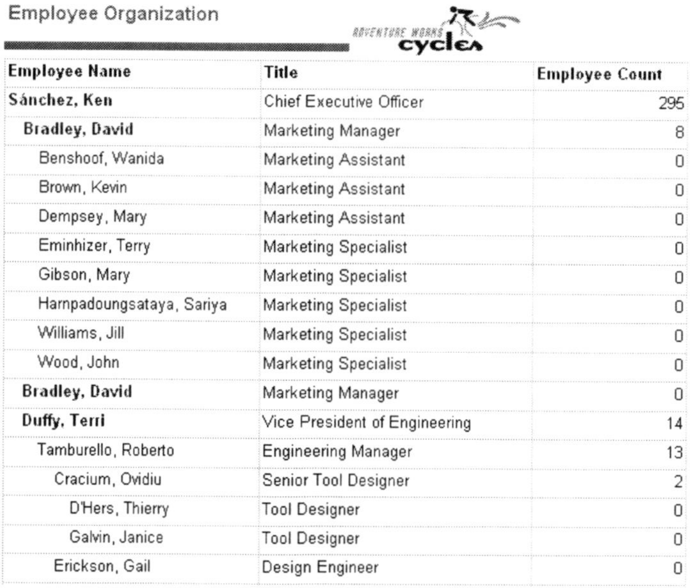

Employee Organization

ADVENTURE WORKS
cycles

Employee Name	Title	Employee Count
Sánchez, Ken	Chief Executive Officer	295
Bradley, David	Marketing Manager	8
Benshoof, Wanida	Marketing Assistant	0
Brown, Kevin	Marketing Assistant	0
Dempsey, Mary	Marketing Assistant	0
Eminhizer, Terry	Marketing Specialist	0
Gibson, Mary	Marketing Specialist	0
Harnpadoungsataya, Sariya	Marketing Specialist	0
Williams, Jill	Marketing Specialist	0
Wood, John	Marketing Specialist	0
Bradley, David	Marketing Manager	0
Duffy, Terri	Vice President of Engineering	14
Tamburello, Roberto	Engineering Manager	13
Cracium, Ovidiu	Senior Tool Designer	2
D'Hers, Thierry	Tool Designer	0
Galvin, Janice	Tool Designer	0
Erickson, Gail	Design Engineer	0

FIGURE 12-14 You can use the *Recursive* keyword with an aggregate function to correctly calculate subtotals at each level of a hierarchy.

Using external functions

Many of the functions available to you in Reporting Services are also Visual Basic functions, although a few, such as the lookup functions, are specific to Reporting Services. In general, you can use Microsoft Visual Basic .NET functions. Reporting Services automatically references *Microsoft.VisualBasic* and *mscorlib* for you and imports the following namespaces automatically so that you can use the members and functions without adding a namespace reference in your expression.

- **Microsoft.VisualBasic**   You can use any of the run-time library members and functions listed at *http://msdn.microsoft.com/en-us/library/c157t28f.aspx*.

- **System.Convert**   You can use this namespace to convert between data types, as opposed to using the functions discussed in the "Using conversion functions" section. For example, you can use an expression like this:

```
=System.Convert.ToString(Parameters!StartDate.Value)
```

- **System.Math**   Many of the math functions are available already in Reporting Services, but you can also use other math functions, such as *IEEERemainder* or *Truncate*.

You can also use other .NET Framework functions or your own custom functions (as we describe in Chapter 33, "Programming report design components") if you include the entire namespace. For example, to use the *Regex Replace* function in an expression, you must reference the function as *System.Text.RegularExpressions.Replace*.

CHAPTER 13

Adding interactivity

I f users access and view reports online most of the time, you can add interactive features to make it easier for them to use your reports. For example, you can allow the user to change the sort order of data, add tooltips, or make it possible to expand and collapse sections of your report. You can also employ navigation aids to help the user easily move to information located in the same report or to access information contained in a related report or webpage. In this chapter, you explore a variety of techniques for enhancing the interactive report experience.

Interacting with the report layout

When you design a report that contains many detail rows of data, spend some time thinking about how users might want to interact with the report. Although you define a specific sort order for report data based on an established specification, many users will want to view the data using a different sort order. Also, when the dataset contains several columns and a large number of rows, the column headers could move out of view as the user scrolls down the page. Finally, some users will want to see all the detail data, while other users might prefer to see only a summary of the detail data. In this section, you learn how to use the interactive features included in Reporting Services to address these particular issues.

Interactive sorting

You can give the user direct control over the sort order of report data by implementing the interactive sort feature. You implement this feature on any text box where you want the user to click to change sort order. Usually, the text box for which you enable this feature is a column header or row header in a data region. For example, when you have many numeric columns, you can configure each column header to use interactive sort, and the user can sort one column at a time or create a more complex sort by selecting multiple columns to sort.

To add interactive sorting, right-click the text box that you want to control the sorting action, and then click Text Box Properties. Select Interactive Sorting in the left pane of the Text Box Properties dialog box. Select the Enable Interactive Sorting On This Text Box check box, as shown in Figure 13-1. You have a number of options available to you, depending on how you want the interactive sorting to be applied. You can apply interactive sorting on detail rows independent of groups, or you can apply sorting to groups. You learn about each of these scenarios and how to apply them in the following sections.

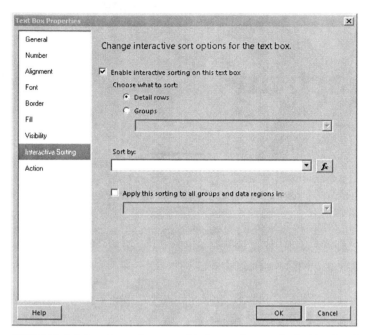

FIGURE 13-1 Select the option to enable interactive sort in the Text Box Properties dialog box.

After you've decided what you want to sort, you select what you want to sort by. In the Sort By drop-down list, you select a dataset field. You also have the option to sort by an expression, which we explain in a later section.

When you view the report, you see double arrows display in the text box for which you enabled the interactive sort, as shown in Figure 13-2. To apply the sort, you click the arrows.

FIGURE 13-2 Click the double arrows in the text box to use interactive sorting.

Click once on the double arrows icon to replace it with an up arrow and apply an ascending sort, as shown in Figure 13-3. Click a second time, and the up arrow changes to a down arrow and the sort changes to descending order. Each subsequent click toggles between these two sort directions.

Business Type	Sales Amount ⊙
Specialty Bike Shop	$77,158.48
Specialty Bike Shop	$92,952.07
Specialty Bike Shop	$120,181.38
Specialty Bike Shop	$165,542.36
Specialty Bike Shop	$171,182.24
Warehouse	$180,790.56
Value Added Reseller	$299,826.74
Value Added Reseller	$399,158.53
Value Added Reseller	$400,571.50
Warehouse	$508,136.14
Value Added Reseller	$538,182.96
Warehouse	$645,970.20
Specialty Bike Shop	$712,179.97
Warehouse	$857,270.81
Value Added Reseller	$884,996.26
Warehouse	$1,334,083.02
Warehouse	$3,802,117.09
Value Added Reseller	$4,847,762.31
	$16,038,062.60

FIGURE 13-3 Following a single click, the double arrows icon changes to a single arrow, and the values sort in ascending order.

Sort detail rows

Sorting detail rows is the most common and straightforward case. When you sort detail rows, the detail rows within each group sort in ascending or descending order independently of other groups. To sort detail rows, select the Detail Rows option in the Text Box Properties dialog box, and then in the Sort By drop-down list, select the field to use for sorting. You also have the option to sort by an expression, which we explain later in the "Sort by expression" section.

Sorting detail rows in a report with no groupings produces a result like the table shown in Figure 13-3, with the sorting applied across all rows. However, suppose you apply sorting to the detail rows of a table that has group instances. In that case, you'll see that the sorting is applied to the detail rows of each individual parent group instance, as shown in Figure 13-4, rather than across all detail rows.

Country	Business Type	Sales Amount
Australia	Value Added Reseller	$400,571.50
	Warehouse	$180,790.56
	Specialty Bike Shop	$165,542.36
	Country Total	$746,904.41
Canada	Warehouse	$1,334,083.02
	Value Added Reseller	$884,996.26
	Specialty Bike Shop	$171,182.24
	Country Total	$2,390,261.51
France	Warehouse	$857,270.81
	Value Added Reseller	$399,158.53
	Specialty Bike Shop	$120,181.38
	Country Total	$1,376,610.72
Germany	Warehouse	$508,136.14
	Value Added Reseller	$299,826.74
	Specialty Bike Shop	$77,158.48
	Country Total	$885,121.35

FIGURE 13-4 A sort of detail rows applies to each group instance separately.

Sort groups

Another option is to sort groups. When you sort groups, the sort uses the Sort By field value for the group to determine which group instance appears first in the report, which instance appears second, and so on. The detail rows continue to sort in the order in which the rows are returned in the query.

To sort groups, select the Groups option in the Text Box Properties dialog box. Then select the group you want to sort in the Groups drop-down list, as shown in Figure 13-5.

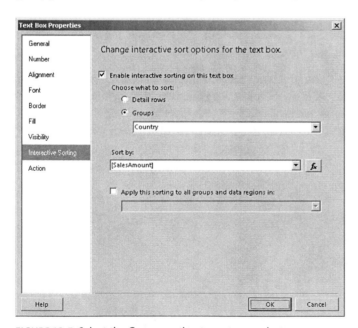

FIGURE 13-5 Select the Groups option to sort group instances.

In the report, shown in Figure 13-6, the group instances change order, but the detail rows for each group instance do not.

Country	Business Type	Sales Amount ⊙
United States	Specialty Bike Shop	$712,179.97
	Value Added Reseller	$4,847,762.31
	Warehouse	$3,802,117.09
	Country Total	$9,362,059.37
Canada	Specialty Bike Shop	$171,182.24
	Value Added Reseller	$884,996.26
	Warehouse	$1,334,083.02
	Country Total	$2,390,261.51
Australia	Specialty Bike Shop	$165,542.36
	Value Added Reseller	$400,571.50
	Warehouse	$180,790.56
	Country Total	$746,904.41
France	Specialty Bike Shop	$120,101.30
	Value Added Reseller	$399,158.53
	Warehouse	$857,270.81
	Country Total	$1,376,610.72

FIGURE 13-6 The countries sort in descending order by Sales Amount, while detail rows remain in ascending order by Sales Amount.

Sort by expression

Instead of sorting by a dataset field, you can also sort by an expression. Click the expression button to the right of the Sort By drop down list. You can then use the Expression dialog box (described in Chapter 11, "Developing expressions") to create an expression to use for sorting. For example, percentage values are often calculated in the report itself by using an expression similar to this:

```
=Fields!Numerator.Value/Fields!Denominator.Value
```

To sort the report by the percentage value, you can use the percentage expression as your sort expression.

Apply sort to other groups and data regions

In the Text Box Properties dialog box, select the Apply This Sorting To All Groups And Data Regions In check box when you want to apply the sort to other groups within the same data region or to a completely different data region. In this way, you can keep sorting consistent across the report, rather than limiting the sort to the current data region.

For example, use this option when you have a tablix and a chart in the same report and you want the interactive sort to apply to both data regions simultaneously. Make sure that the group you want to use for sorting has the same name in both the tablix and the chart and that both data regions contain the data field you want to sort by. Then, in addition to selecting the check box, select the name of the dataset used by both data regions from the drop-down list, as shown in Figure 13-7.

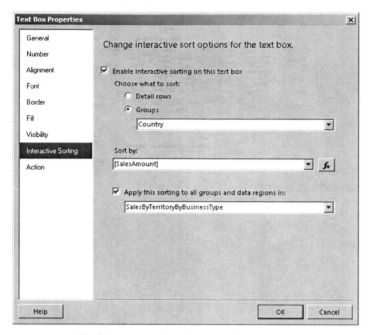

FIGURE 13-7 Check the appropriate box to apply sorting across groups and data regions.

When you click the interactive sort button while viewing the report, both data regions sort in ascending order, as shown in Figure 13-8.

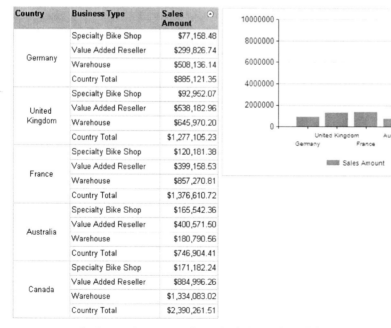

FIGURE 13-8 The interactive sort applies to both the table and the chart.

Tip Make sure to check that the sorting property is not set for the group to which you want to apply interactive sorting. The sorting specification for the groups in a tablix or for the categories in a chart overrides the interactive sorting specification and makes it appear that the interactive sort is not working.

Using fixed headers

When a full page of data in your report is larger than the vertical size of your screen, you must scroll to view the data near the bottom of the page. As a result, the column headers might scroll off the screen. You can pin the column headers into position at the top of the screen so that they remain visible as the user scrolls the page.

To pin a column header to the top of the screen, click the arrow at the far right of the Grouping pane and select Advanced Mode. In the Row Group section of the Grouping pane, click the Static group that corresponds to the far left text box of the column header row. This is usually the first Static group that appears in the Row Groups section. When you select a Static group, the corresponding text box is selected in the tablix. That way, you can confirm that your selection of the Static group is correct, as shown in Figure 13-9.

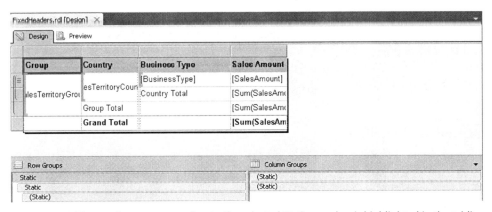

FIGURE 13-9 The text box corresponding to the selected Static member is highlighted in the tablix.

After selecting the proper Static group, locate the *FixedData* property in the Properties window and select *True* from the drop-down list, as shown in Figure 13-10. When you preview the report and scroll down, you can see that the column header row stays in place while you scroll.

FIGURE 13-10 Set the *FixedData* property to *True*.

Tip When using the *FixedData* property to pin a row or column into a fixed position, you should also set the *BackgroundColor* property of the row or column. If no color is defined, the background is transparent and you see the data scrolling behind the text in the fixed headers.

If you have many columns, such that a user must scroll horizontally to view all the data, you can also pin row headers in place. Instead of selecting a Static group from the Row Groups section, select the Static group from the Column Groups section of the column that you want to remain fixed, and then set the *FixedData* property to *True*. Now, when you preview the report and scroll horizontally, the column you selected remains in place.

Configuring visibility

When a report requires both summary and detail data, you might consider creating a *drilldown report*, in which only the summary data displays when the user opens the report and the detail data displays when the user clicks a text box that has been configured to toggle the visibility of details. To achieve this behavior, you configure an entire row, an entire column, or a specific text box using visibility properties to hide the selection when the document opens. You also configure the *ToggleItem* property of the selection to reference a text box in the report. When the report renders, a plus sign displays in that referenced text box to indicate to the user that the item can be expanded to show additional information.

Note In this section, we explain visibility in the context of rows, but you can use the same technique to configure visibility for columns.

Show or hide a row

Click anywhere in the tablix region to display its handles, then right-click the row handle for the row whose visibility you want to configure, and then click Row Visibility to open the Row Visibility dialog box, as shown in Figure 13-11. You can specify that you want the row to be visible upon initial rendering of the report by selecting the Show option. Otherwise, select the Hide option. Another option is to show or hide the row based on an expression. For example, you can create an expression that checks the country name and returns False if the country is the United States and returns True for all other countries. As a result, the report displays only the United States details and hides all other countries.

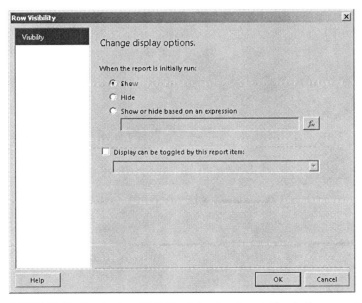

FIGURE 13-11 Use the Row Visibility dialog box to specify whether a row is visible when the report opens.

Drilldown

In general, when configuring drilldown reports, you'll likely set the Row Visibility to Hide when the report is initially run. You also select the Display Can Be Toggled By This Report Item check box, and then in the drop-down list, select the name of the text box you want to the user to click when toggling row visibility, as shown in Figure 13-12.

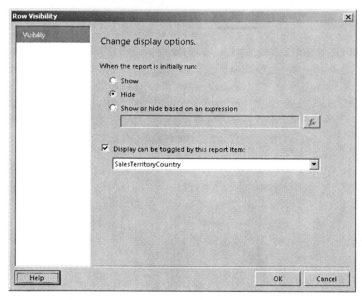

FIGURE 13-12 Configure drilldown by selecting Display Can Be Toggled By This Report Item, and choose a text box from the drop-down list.

When the report renders, the text box controlling visibility displays a plus sign, as shown in Figure 13-13. You click this plus sign to expand the row for which you configured visibility.

Group	Country	Business Type	Sales Amount
Europe	⊟ France	Specialty Bike Shop	$120,181.38
		Value Added Reseller	$399,158.53
		Warehouse	$857,270.81
		Country Total	$1,376,610.72
	⊞ Germany	Country Total	$885,121.35
	⊞ United Kingdom	Country Total	$1,277,105.23
	Group Total		$3,538,837.31
North America	⊞ Canada	Country Total	$2,390,261.51
	⊞ United States	Country Total	$9,362,059.37
	Group Total		$11,752,320.88
Pacific	⊞ Australia	Country Total	$746,904.41
	Group Total		$746,904.41
	Grand Total		**$16,038,062.60**

FIGURE 13-13 Use the plus and minus signs to toggle row visibility.

Tip If you plan to use a text box as a toggle item for report item visibility, be sure to give it a name to help you find the right text box in the drop-down list. In most cases, the text box name matches the field name added to the text box.

Adding tooltips

When you have information that doesn't require its own column but that users might want to see anyway, a tooltip is a useful feature to add. When you hover the mouse over a text box with a tooltip enabled, a message displays to further explain data or to supply additional information to the user.

You can add a tooltip to any text box by right-clicking it and selecting Text Box Properties. In the Text Box Properties dialog box, under the Name and Value boxes, you can enter static text directly into the ToolTip box, as shown in Figure 13-14, or click the Expression button to the right of the ToolTip box to open the Expression dialog box. There you can create a dynamic expression to display as your tooltip.

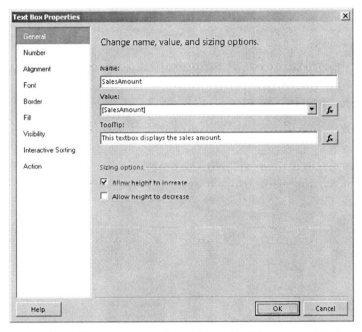

FIGURE 13-14 You can enter static text for the ToolTip value or click the Expression button to define an expression.

As you view the report, you can hover your mouse over the updated text box to view the tooltip, as shown in Figure 13-15.

Group	Country	Business Type	Sales Amount
		Specialty Bike Shop	$120,181.38
	France	Value Added Reseller	$399,15... This textbox displays the sales amount.
		Warehouse	$857,270.81

FIGURE 13-15 The tooltip appears when you hover your mouse over the configured text box.

Adding navigation features

Reporting Services includes several navigation features that you can implement to improve the usability of your reports. For example, you can configure a document map to help users go to a new location in the same report. In another example, you can also use Hypertext Markup Language (HTML) to create a link that opens a webpage or a mail application. Finally, you can define an action to go to a bookmark in the report, go to a URL, or go to another Reporting Services report.

Defining a document map

The document map feature allows you to configure bookmarks for each instance in a group and display this list of bookmarks next to the report. In effect, this list of bookmarks is a table of contents for the report that enables the user not only to see the group instances at a glance but also to jump to the location of a specific instance. When the report includes nested groups, the document map displays the list of bookmarks in a tree form. The user must expand a specific group instance to view the instances of groups contained by the selected group.

Creating a document map

To configure a document map, in the Row Groups pane, right-click the group that you would like to use for your document map, and then click Group Properties. In the Group Properties dialog box, in the left pane, select Advanced. In the Document Map drop-down list, select the group that you want to use for your document map, as shown in Figure 13-16.

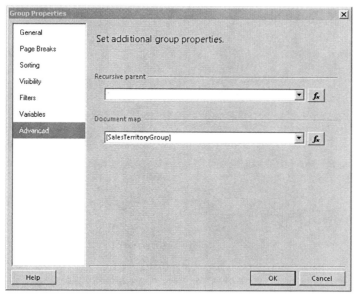

FIGURE 13-16 Choose the group you want to use for your document map from the drop-down list.

When you preview the report, the DocumentMap panel shown in Figure 13-17 appears to the left of the report body. This panel displays the group instance values for the group you configured. When you click one of the values of the group, the section of the report containing the selected instance displays.

Group	Country	Business Type	Sales Amount
	France	Specialty Bike Shop	$120,181.38
		Value Added Reseller	$399,158.53
		Warehouse	$857,270.81
		Country Total	$1,376,610.72

FIGURE 13-17 The document map appears to the left of the report.

If the group you selected has a child group, you can repeat the preceding steps to add the child group members to the document map. Then, when you preview the report, the document map displays as a hierarchical tree. You can expand and collapse group instances to see child group instance members, as shown in Figure 13-18. This ability to use parent and child groups in a document map gives you finer control over report navigation.

```
⊟ DocumentMap
  ⊟ Europe
      ⋯ France
        Germany
      ⋯ United Kingdom
  ⊞ North America
  ⊞ Pacific
```

FIGURE 13-18 Adding a child group to the document map creates an expandable hierarchy.

Customizing a document map

You are not limited to group instances to populate a node in the document map. You can add any report item to a document map by setting the *DocumentMapLabel* property of the report item to the name that you want to display in the document map. For example, let's say that you want to include the Group Total text box in the document map. First, you set the *DocumentMapLabel* property for the text box by using static text, as shown in Figure 13-19, or by using an expression.

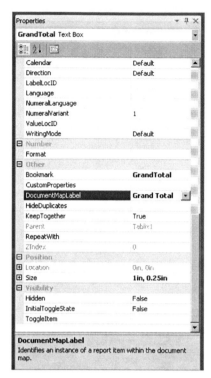

FIGURE 13-19 Set the *DocumentMapLabel* property to add a report item to the document map.

When you preview the report, you can see that the Grand Total item appears in the document map, as shown in Figure 13-20.

☐ DocumentMap
   ⊞ Europe
   ⊞ North America
   ⊞ Pacific
   └ Grand Total

FIGURE 13-20 The Grand Total member appears in the document map.

Showing and hiding a document map

You can toggle the display of the document map by clicking the Show/Hide Document Map button in between the document map and the report, as shown in Figure 13-21.

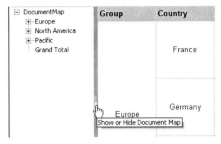

FIGURE 13-21 Click the arrow between the document map and report to toggle document map visibility.

You can also hide the document map upon initial rendering of the report by modifying the report URL. This is particularly useful if you link to the report using a Go To URL action, described later in the chapter, or if you are using URL access rather than Report Manager to make reports available to users (as described in Chapter 35, "Programming report access"). For example, you append *&rs%3aComm and=Render&rc%3aFormat=HTML4.0&rc%3aDocMap=False* to the end of the report URL to hide the document map when opening the report, although users can still toggle the visibility of the document map via the Show/Hide Document Map button.

Rendering a document map

The document map is primarily for use in the HTML viewer during online viewing. However, some rendering extensions also support the document map, although the appearance of the document map varies by rendering extension, as follows:

- **PDF** The document map is rendered as a Bookmarks pane.

- **Excel** The document map is rendered as a separate worksheet containing links to separate report sections. The report sections are rendered as individual worksheets in the same workbook as the document map.

- **Word** The document map is rendered as a table of contents.

- **Other** Other rendering extensions, such as the TIFF or CSV renderer, do not render the document map.

Using embedded HTML tags

You can use selected HTML markup tags in a report to control formatting in text to achieve a specific layout, but the <A href> tag in particular is useful for navigation. You can create a text expression that combines static text or an expression with HTML markup tags and evaluates as a URL or as a mail recipient. You assign this text expression to a placeholder, which you must also configure to interpret HTML tags as style commands.

The text value can be a field from a dataset, a parameter value, or a custom expression. You can use the HTML tags shown in Table 13-1 in placeholder text. Note that any HTML tag not shown in Table 13-1 is ignored when the report renders.

TABLE 13-1 HTML tags

For This Tag Type	Select From These Markup Tags
Font	<FONT>
Header, style, and block elements	<DIV>, <H{n}>, <HN>, <LI>, <P>, <SPAN>
Hyperlink	<A href>
List	<LI>, <OL>, <UL>
Text format	<B>, <I>, <S>, <U>

For example, you can create a table and place an HTML text expression in a text box. When you run the report, the HTML renders in plain text, as shown in Figure 13-22.

Customer
<a href="mailto:alejandro5@adventure-works.com">Li, Alejandro</a>
<a href="mailto:richard62@adventure-works.com">Johnston, Richard</a>
<a href="mailto:jordan19@adventure-works.com">Diaz, Jordan</a>
<a href="mailto:hannah30@adventure-works.com">Jenkins, Hannah</a>

FIGURE 13-22 The HTML-formatted text box values display as plain text.

To configure the report to interpret the text as HTML markup text, start by selecting the place-holder of the text box containing the HTML. To do this, click the placeholder (the text inside the text box) three times so that all the text inside the text box is highlighted. Right-click the highlighted placeholder, and then select Placeholder Properties. In the Placeholder Properties dialog box, select HTML – Interpret HTML Tags As Styles, as shown in Figure 13-23.

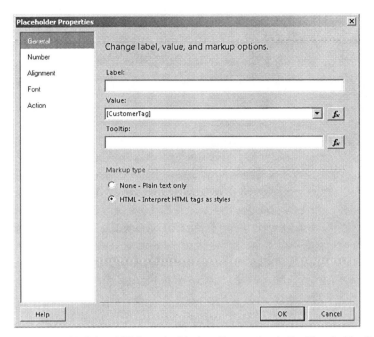

FIGURE 13-23 Select HTML as the Markup Type option in the Placeholder Properties dialog box.

When the report renders, the viewer interprets the HTML style tags correctly, as shown in Figure 13-24.

FIGURE 13-24 The text box values display as HTML.

Working with report actions

Each text box and image has an *Action* property that you can use to define a target location for display when the user clicks the text box or image. There are three types of actions you can set: Go To Report, which navigates to another Reporting Services report; Go To Bookmark, which navigates to another location in the current report; and Go To URL, which sends the user to the specified URL.

Go to report

To configure a Go To Report action, you define a target report, and if you want, you can also map expressions in the source report to parameters in the target report. Consequently, the target report can display information using the same context as the source report if the target report is designed to filter based on report parameter values.

To add a Go To Report action, right-click the text box you want to use for the action and select Text Box Properties. In the Text Box Properties dialog box, in the left pane, select Action. Click Go To Report. When the target report is contained in the same project as the report for which you are implementing the Go To Report action, you can specify what report you want the action to navigate to by selecting it in the Specify A Report drop-down list, as shown in Figure 13-25. Otherwise, you can type the name of the report in the box. As long as the two reports are stored in the same folder on the report server, you can simply use the report name. If the two reports are stored in separate folders, you must provide the folder path in addition to the report name. For example, if the target report Sales Analysis is stored in the Sales folder, you type **/Sales/Sales Analysis** to identify both the location and the name of the report. If you change the location of the target report, you must correct the path in the source report's *Action* property.

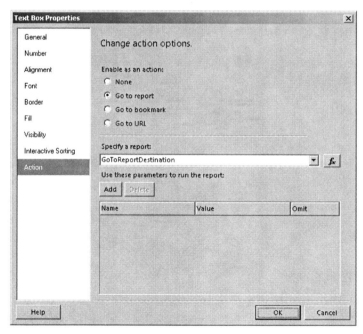

FIGURE 13-25 Specify the report you want the report action to link to in the drop-down list.

If your target report has parameters, click the Add button. Then select the report parameter name from the Name drop-down list. Select the value you want to map to that parameter from the Value drop-down list, or create the value as an expression. When configuring the Go To Report action, you can map any expression to a report parameter in the target report, such as a current field value or a report parameter selection, as you have done in this procedure, or you can develop a custom expression to map to a target report parameter. Repeat these actions for all the parameters that you want to map to the target report. For more information about parameters, see Chapter 14, "Creating dynamic reports with parameters."

> **Note** When you define a target report for the Go To Report action that is not in the current project, the target report's parameter name is not available in the Name drop-down list. You must type in the report parameter name manually. Remember that this property is case-sensitive, so be sure to match the case in the report parameter's name exactly.

When you preview the report and hover the cursor over the configured text box, the cursor icon changes to indicate that you can click a link, as shown in Figure 13-26. Clicking this link takes you to the target report. Although the text box now has an active link that opens the target report when clicked, it's important to note that the user has no visual cue that indicates that a link exists in the text box. Consider using *Font* properties to display the text in a blue font and with an underline effect to simulate the appearance of a hyperlink.

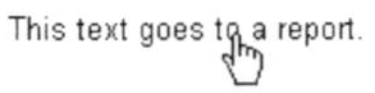

This text goes to a report.

FIGURE 13-26 The cursor changes to indicate that a report action is available.

If you want to return to the original report, simply click the Back To Parent Report button on the HTML toolbar, as shown in Figure 13-27.

FIGURE 13-27 The Back to Parent Report button.

Go to bookmark

You use the Go To Bookmark action to help the user quickly navigate to another location in the same report. For example, you could define a bookmark action on the Sales Amount values to quickly jump to the Grand Total row. You must first define a text box as a bookmark. In the *Bookmark* property, you type a string or select an expression to use as a label for the bookmark, as shown in Figure 13-28.

FIGURE 13-28 Create a bookmark by setting the Bookmark property for a report item.

After you have a text box defined as a bookmark, select the text box that you want to use to link to the bookmark. Right-click the text box, and then select Text Box Properties. In the Text Box Properties dialog box, in the left pane, select Action. Click Go To Bookmark. In the Select Bookmark drop-down list, you can type the name of the Bookmark that you want to navigate to, as shown in Figure 13-29. You can also use the drop-down list to select a field, or use the expression editor to create an expression that evaluates to the label of the bookmark you want to navigate to. When you view the report and click the text box that you configured with the Go To Bookmark action, the report jumps to the text box that you defined as the bookmark.

Tip It's important to note that the drop-down list does not populate with the names of bookmarks defined in the report. Only fields in the dataset connected to the tablix are shown. But unless you have a bookmark defined with a name that the field value resolves to, your action will not work.

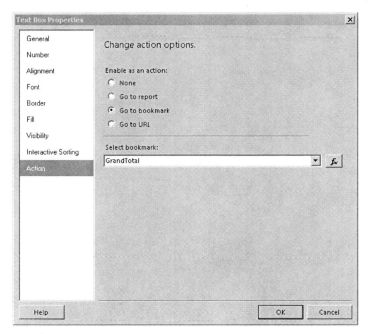

FIGURE 13-29 Type the name of the bookmark you want to link to in the Select Bookmark box.

Go to URL

A third option for navigation is the Go To URL action. You simply type a URL or select an expression that evaluates to a URL. When the user clicks the link, the target destination opens in the browser window.

Select the text box that you want to use to link to the URL. Right-click the text box, and then select Text Box Properties. In the Text Box Properties dialog box, in the left pane, select Action. Click Go To URL. In the Select URL box, you can type a URL, or you can click the Expression button to create an expression that evaluates to a URL, as shown in Figure 13-30. You can test the result by previewing the report and clicking the text box, which opens the browser window to the configured URL.

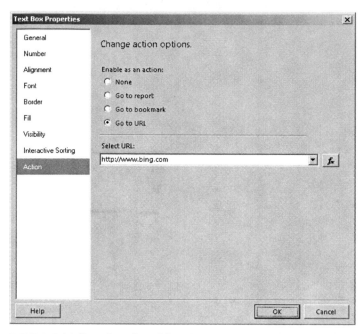

FIGURE 13-30 Type the value of the URL you want to navigate to in the Select URL box.

You can also force the Go To URL action to render in a new browser tab by using a JavaScript command. To do this, set the Select URL expression as follows:

```
javascript:void(window.Open('yourURLhere'))
```

Additionally, you can force the Go To URL action to render in a modal browser window by using the following expression:

```
javascript:void(window.showModalDialog('yourURLhere'))
```

> **Note** The JavaScript commands do not work in SSDT. You must deploy the report and test the action in Report Manager or SharePoint.

Creating dynamic reports with parameters

P arameters are another way to add interactivity as well as flexibility to your reports. A common way to use parameters is to prompt the user for input, although you can also use expressions or queries to set parameter values. Either way, you can use the parameters value to change the appearance or behavior of the report by using it in an expression to set a property, apply a filter, or send data to a related report.

Working with report parameters

Report parameters appear on the report toolbar and, if visible, allow users to select or enter values that the report uses when processing. You can reference a report parameter in an expression to control almost any report property by referencing the *Parameters* collection in the expression. Consequently, report parameters are a powerful way to customize reports for each user's unique experience. You can also change the content of a report by using a report parameter with a filter or as a query parameter, or you can pass a report parameter value to a drillthrough report or a subreport, all of which we explain later in this chapter.

Creating a report parameter

You use the Report Data pane to access and organize your report parameters. To create a new report parameter, right-click the Parameters folder in the Report Data pane and select Add Parameter. Alternatively, you can click New in the Report Data pane toolbar, and then select Parameter. In both cases, the Report Parameter Properties dialog box opens, as shown in Figure 14-1.

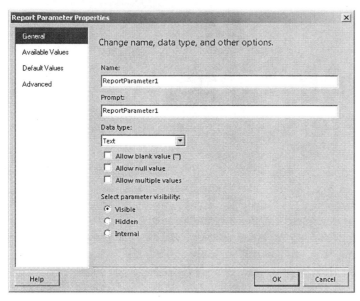

FIGURE 14-1 Use the Report Parameter Properties dialog box to define a new report parameter.

After you save the new report parameter, it appears in the Report Data pane in the Parameters folder, as shown in Figure 14-2. To make changes to it later, right-click the parameter name and then select Parameter Properties.

FIGURE 14-2 Report parameters appear in the Parameters folder of the Report Data pane.

Setting report parameter properties

There are many ways that you can use parameters. The possibilities are limited only by your imagination. The key to using report parameters effectively is in configuring each report parameter's properties correctly.

General properties

For a simple report parameter to prompt the user to type a value, you need only set the *Name*, *Prompt*, and *Data Type* properties on the first page of the Report Parameter Properties dialog box, but you should review the other properties on this page and other pages to ensure that the report parameter behaves as you expect. On the General page, you can configure the following properties:

- **Name** The parameter name identifies the parameter uniquely, and becomes a member of the *Parameters* collection for you to reference in expressions. The parameter name cannot contain spaces and must begin with a letter. It also cannot contain any characters other than letters, numbers, or underscores.

- **Prompt** If a report parameter is visible, the prompt text displays in the parameter section of the report viewer as a caption for the parameter input area. The prompt text can contain spaces and special characters but cannot be empty. Unfortunately, there is no way to format the prompt text.

- **Data Type** A report parameter must be one of the following data types: Boolean, Date/Time, Integer, Float, or Text. The default data type is Text. If you specify a Boolean data type, the user sets the report parameter value by using a radio button to select True or False, as shown in Figure 14-3.

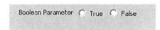

FIGURE 14-3 The user selects a radio button for a report parameter with the Boolean data type.

If the parameter type is Date/Time, the user has the option to select a date from a calendar control, as shown in Figure 14-4, although the user can also type a date in the text box.

FIGURE 14-4 The user selects a date from the calendar control for a report parameter with the Date/Time data type.

Note If you pass the report parameter value to a query parameter, the query fails if the report parameter's data type does not match the query parameter's data type. If you are unable to set the correct data type here for the report parameter, you must use an expression to convert the report parameter's data type as necessary when mapping the report parameter to the query parameter.

- **Allow Blank Value** Reporting Services interprets a blank value as an empty string. However, simply selecting these options does not add a blank value to the available values if you specify them. If you specify available values, you must add the blank value to the list for the user to be able to use it.

- **Allow Null Value** When you enable this option, you allow Reporting Services to accept a null value. If you do not specify available values, the user is not required to supply a value. Instead, the parameter input box is disabled and a NULL check box displays, as shown in Figure 14-5. To input a value, the user must clear the check box and type a parameter value.

FIGURE 14-5 You can use Allow Null Value when a report parameter is optional.

- **Allow Multiple Values** By default, the user can select only one value for the report parameter. You must explicitly enable support for multiple values, which will display in a drop-down list. If you enable this option, you cannot allow null values. When you allow multiple values for a report parameter, the user must select one or more check boxes from the drop-down list of available values (configured separately), as shown in Figure 14-6.

FIGURE 14-6 The user selects one or more check boxes for a multivalue parameter.

> **Note** If you do not configure available values for a multivalue report parameter, the user sees only an empty drop-down list, which is not very useful! We explain how to set up available values later in this chapter.

- **Select Parameter Visibility** If you want the user to provide a value for a report parameter, the parameter must be visible.

  You use the Hidden option if you don't want to display the prompt when the user views the report, but you still need the ability to set the parameter value. Common scenarios for using the Hidden option include setting up a linked report (described in Chapter 23, "Deploying reports to a server"), using URL access (described in Chapter 35, "Programming report access"), or creating a subscription (described in Chapter 27, "Working with subscriptions").

You use the Internal option when you need to use a parameter value in a report but can set the parameter value without user interaction. For example, you can get a parameter value by evaluating an expression or retrieving a value from a dataset, and thereby bypass the need to prompt the user. In a published report, internal parameters are visible only in the report definition of the published report.

Using a Date/Time report parameter

When you set the data type of a report parameter to Date/Time, the user can type a date into the report parameter text box or click a calendar icon to display a calendar control from which a selection can be made.

It is common practice to set a default value for a date parameter. You can set the current date as the default value by using *=Today()* as the expression. Alternatively, you can set a specific date relative to the current date, such as the last day of the previous month, which you define by using *=DateSerial(Year(Now()), Month(Now()), 0)* as the expression. We discuss default values in more detail later in this chapter.

Available values

You use the Available Values page of the Report Parameter Properties dialog box to control the method of capturing user input for the report parameter value. It's considered best practice to provide the user with a list of valid values, but you can also let the user simply type in a value. When you provide a list of valid values, you must specify whether the user can choose only one value or can select multiple values. You can type in a static list of valid values for the report parameter or generate a list of values from a dataset.

When you specify available values, regardless of whether you use a static list or a dataset, you specify both a parameter *value* and a parameter *label*. The value is the default item passed to a parameter expression or to a query parameter, whereas the label is the text that displays in the report parameter's drop-down list.

You configure available values by choosing one of the following options:

- **None**   When you select this option, as shown in Figure 14-7, the user must type a value of the proper data type into the parameter text box to run the report (unless you provide a default value).

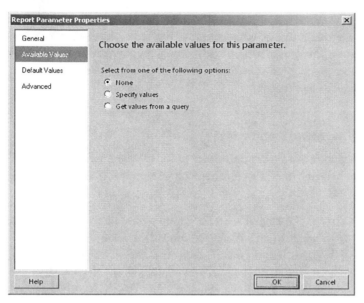

FIGURE 14-7 Use the default option of None for Available Values when you want the user to type a value.

In the report, the prompt text that you specified for your parameter displays first, and next to it is a text box where the user can input a value for the parameter, as shown in Figure 14-8. At this point, the parameter does not change anything in the report until you use it in a report expression or in a query as a query parameter.

FIGURE 14-8 A text parameter uses a text box to receive input from users when no available values are configured.

- **Specify Values** Choose this option to create a static list of available values. To add a value, click Add, and then type in values for the Label and the Value fields. Repeat these steps for as many parameter values as needed, as shown in Figure 14-9. In expressions referencing a report parameter, you access *Label* and *Value* as separate properties, as described in Chapter 11, "Developing expressions." Therefore, you must provide a value for both properties here, even if the values are the same.

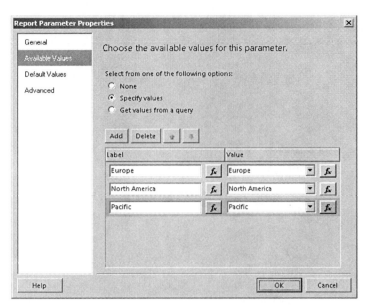

FIGURE 14-9 You can manually provide a pair of labels and values for each available value of a report parameter.

Notice that you can specify an expression rather than a static value for both Label and Value.

To delete a static value, simply click the row you want to remove, and then click Delete. You can also change the order of the parameter values by selecting a row and then using the up and down arrows.

- **Get Values From A Query**   Whenever possible, you should choose this option to use a dataset as the source for a list of available values for the report parameter. Ideally, your dataset should reference a view in your data source. By using a dataset, you can manage additions or deletions in the data source and can thereby avoid the need to edit a static report parameter list in each report using the same list. When you use a dataset to supply report parameter values, you typically have two columns in the dataset, one for the parameter value and one for the parameter label. You can, however, use a single column as both a value and a label, as shown in Figure 14-10.

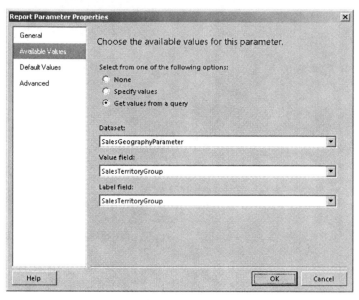

FIGURE 14-10 You can use a dataset containing Value and Label fields to provide available values for a report parameter.

There is no option to use an expression for the parameter value and label when using a dataset. You perform all value and label manipulation in the parameter dataset itself.

When available values are defined for a report parameter, the user chooses values from a drop-down list, even when the data type is Date/Time. When the Allow Multiple Values check box is not selected, the user can select only one value in the drop-down list, as shown by the image on the left in Figure 14-11. Otherwise, the user can select the (Select All) check box to include all values in the parameter value array or select one or more available values, as shown by the image on the right in Figure 14-11.

FIGURE 14-11 The user selects one or more check boxes for a multivalue parameter.

Default values

Whether you provide available values or not, the report does not execute until the user provides a parameter value, unless you define a default value. When all report parameters in a report have a default value specified, the report will run automatically on initial viewing. As with available values, you can specify a static default value or use a dataset to populate the default value. If you have a collection of available parameter values, you need to make sure that your default parameter value is a member of that collection, or else you will get an error when you try to run the report.

You configure a default value by choosing one of the following options:

- **No Default Value**   When you select this option, as shown in Figure 14-12, the user must provide a value for the report parameter (and each report parameter without a default value) before viewing the report.

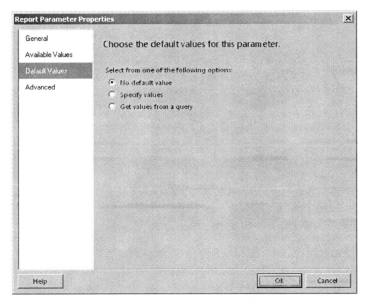

FIGURE 14-12 Use the default option of No Default Value to force the user to specify a parameter value.

- **Specify Values**   Choose this option to manually specify a default value or a set of values for a multivalue parameter. Click Add, and then type in the default value for the parameter, as shown in Figure 14-13, or create an expression for the default value. Notice that you do not specify a label here, because the label is only for display purposes when prompting the user to make a selection.

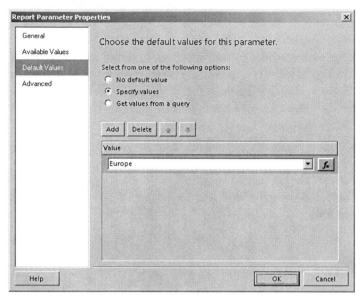

FIGURE 14-13 You can provide a static default value or an expression for the report parameter.

If your parameter is multivalued, you can add multiple default values by repeating these instructions. If your parameter is not multivalued but you try to add multiple default values, you will get an error when you click OK to close the Report Parameter Properties dialog box.

To delete a static default value, simply click the default value you want to remove, and then click Delete. You can also change the order of the default values by selecting a value and then using the up and down arrows.

■ **Get Values From A Query** Using this option to set default values for a report parameter can give you an extra level of control. For example, you might want different users to have different default values for a report. Or you can dynamically control defaults when using cascading parameters to avoid errors when a static default value would no longer be one of the available values.

Select the dataset you want to use in the Dataset drop-down list, and then select the field to use as a default value from the Value Field drop-down list, as shown in Figure 14-14. As with available values, there is no option to use an expression for the default value when using a dataset. You must instead perform any necessary value manipulation in the dataset itself.

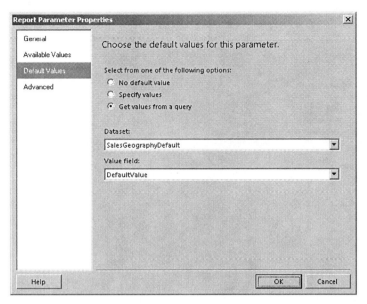

FIGURE 14-14 You can use a dataset to set the default value for a report parameter.

If the report parameter is configured to accept only a single value, the dataset must return only a single row. A multivalue report parameter can accept multiple rows. Either way, the field that you reference must contain a valid value as defined by the value column on the Available Values page.

If your dataset returns multiple values and the parameter is a multivalued parameter, all values returned in the dataset will be selected as the default values. If the parameter is not a multivalued parameter, only the first value returned in the dataset will be used as the default value.

Advanced parameter options

On the Advanced page of the Report Parameter Properties dialog box, shown in Figure 14-15, you set options controlling data refresh and report part notification. The first option applies only when your report parameter uses a dataset for available values, while the second option applies only if your report contains report parts (described in Chapter 29, "Reusing report parts").

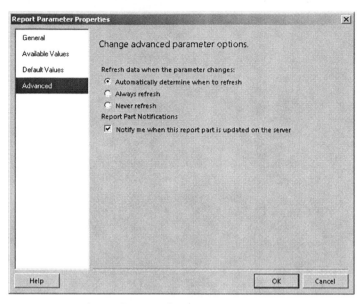

FIGURE 14-15 Advanced options for report parameters.

When a report parameter is dependent on a dataset query, you must decide what should happen when the user changes a parameter value causing any dataset in the report to execute. You can choose one of the following options:

- **Automatically Determine When To Refresh**   When you select this option, you let the report processor decide whether to refresh data if the user makes a new parameter selection. In that case, the refresh occurs when a dataset query has a direct or indirect reference to the report parameter or if the report has subreports.

- **Always Refresh**   Choose this option when you want the report parameter values to refresh when any dataset in the report refreshes.

- **Never Refresh**   Choose this option to prevent a refresh if any dataset in the report executes.

If you are developing your report in Report Builder, you can use the Report Part Gallery to add report parts, such as data regions and report parameters, to your report rather than building those items yourself. In the event that the author of the report parameter that you added as a report part makes a change to the report parameter's properties, you can decide whether you want a notification of the change. The default setting for Report Part Notifications is to display a notification when the author updates the report parameter on the server. When you next open your report after the change is made, a notification displays, which you can choose to apply to your report or ignore. If you prefer to always ignore such changes, you can clear the check box here to suppress all future notifications. You learn more about report part management and notifications in Chapter 29.

Deleting a report parameter

To delete a report parameter, locate the parameter in the Parameters folder in the Report Data pane, right-click it, and then click Delete. Make sure that the parameter you are deleting is not used elsewhere in the report, or you will get an error when you run the report.

Displaying parameter selections in a report

Because a report is often printed out or exported to another format, it is important to preserve the context of the report as specified by the report parameter selections. You can create a freestanding text box to display the parameter selections as a subtitle in the report or as a footnote in the page footer. By default, a parameter expression evaluates the value field of a report parameter, like this:

```
=Parameters!Quarter.Value
```

When the label field differs from the value field, you can modify the parameter expression to evaluate the label field instead, like this:

```
=Parameters!Quarter.Label
```

If you double-click the parameter name in the Values pane of the Expression dialog box when building the portion of the expression containing a *Parameters* collection (for example, *Parameters!SalesTerritoryGroup*), you discover that the default expression references the first item in an array, such as *Parameters!SalesTerritoryGroup(0)*. This behavior occurs only when you allow multiple values for the parameter. To display values in a multivalue parameter, you must use the *Join* function to concatenate the selected parameter values as a single delimited string that you can display in a text box, like this:

```
="Filters: " + Join(Parameters!SalesTerritoryGroup.Value, ",")
```

Notice that the delimiter string is the second argument of the *Join* function. In this case, the delimiter is a comma followed by a space, but you can use any characters you like as a delimiter.

Using filters

You can apply a filter to a dataset, a data region, or a group to limit the detail rows within the applicable scope to those rows satisfying the condition you define for the filter. To create a dynamic filter based on user input, you can use a report parameter to store the user's selection and then reference that parameter in the filter condition.

Because a filter is applied to the dataset rows after the query executes, even if you apply the filter to the dataset, the time to render the report after selecting a new report parameter value is quite low. When you want to both minimize the number of query executions against the source database and maximize report performance when changing report parameter values, use a report filter on the dataset. When you need access to all data in some data regions and filtered data in other data regions on the same report, use a report filter on the applicable data regions instead.

Creating a filter

You can create a filter on a dataset, a data region, or on a group. When the report is run, filters are first applied to datasets, then data regions, and then groups. If multiple groups are filtered, the filters are applied in a top-down order for group hierarchies. Row groups, column groups, and adjacent groups are all filtered independently of each other.

To create a filter, you open the properties window of the dataset, data region, or group that you want to filter, and then select Filters in the left pane, as shown in Figure 14-16. The steps to create and configure a filter are the same regardless of the object you are filtering.

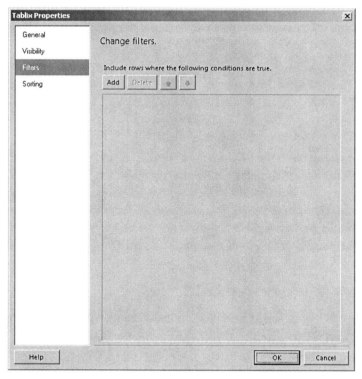

FIGURE 14-16 The Filters page is available in the Dataset Properties, Tablix Properties (shown here), Chart Properties, Map Layer Properties, or Group Properties dialog box.

On the Filters page, you can create one or more filters. A filter consists of three parts: Expression, Operator, and Value. Together, these parts construct a rule that Reporting Services uses to determine which detail rows in a dataset to keep when building a group, data region, or dataset. For example, let's say that you want your report to display information for Europe only. In that case, you assign the field, *[SalesTerritoryGroup]*, to Expression, use the equal sign (=) as Operator, and specify the string Europe as Value, as shown in Figure 14-17.

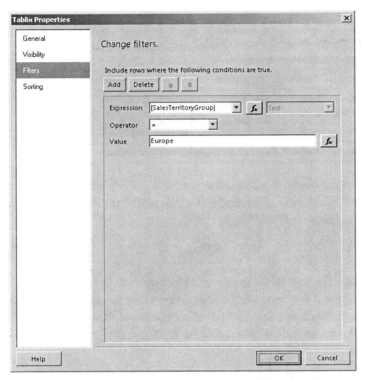

FIGURE 14-17 A simple filter compares a field to a static string value.

To create a new filter, click Add on the Filters page, and then select a field from the Expression drop-down list or click the expression button to enter an expression. If you select a field from a dataset, Reporting Services automatically sets the correct data type. Otherwise, you need to select a data type from the drop-down list. The data type must match both the field (or expression) that you assign to Expression and the value (or expression) that you assign to Value, except when using the *Top N*, *Bottom N*, *Top %* or *Bottom %* operators.

Next, select a filter operator from the drop-down list. The operators and their actions are described in Table 14-1. The operator you choose will affect whether you can use a single value or multiple values for comparison with the expression. Specifically, all operators other than *Between* and *In* accept only single values. The *Between* operator allows you to enter two separate values as boundaries for the comparison, whereas the *In* operator allows you to use multiple values for comparison.

TABLE 14-1 Filter operators

This Operator...	Performs This Action
=, <>, >, >=, <, <=, *Like*	Compares the expression to the value
Top N, Bottom N	Compares expression to Top (Bottom) set of N values (N = integer)
Top %, Bottom %	Compares expression to Top (Bottom) N percent of values (N = integer or float)
Between	Determines whether the expression is between two values, inclusive
In	Determines whether the expression is found in a list of values

Finally, in the Value box (or boxes if using the *Between* operator), input the value or expression (such as today's date) to compare against the expression in the Expression box. To use a static value, type the value without quotes, as shown in Figure 14-17.

Filtering a dataset

Adding a filter to a dataset applies the filter to the data in all data regions of the report that are associated with the dataset. For example, if you have a tablix and a chart using the same dataset and you add a filter to the dataset, both the tablix and the chart will show the same data. If you want different data regions based on the same dataset to have different filtering, you should apply a separate filter to each data region or group instead.

Filtering a data region

Adding a filter to a data region applies the filter only to the data that appears in that data region. For example, if you have a tablix and a chart that use the same dataset but you apply a filter to the tablix only, the chart data will include all data in the dataset, while the tablix data will be filtered.

Filtering a group

Filtering on a group gives you the finest control over the effect of filters on your data in a tablix or a chart. If you apply filters to hierarchical groups, Reporting Services applies the filters beginning with the topmost group and continuing successively to each child group. Filters apply to row groups, column groups, and adjacent groups independently of each other.

Using a report parameter as a filter

Because you can reference a parameter in an expression, you can use a report parameter as a filter value. You can use the simple expression *[@ParameterName]* (as shown in Figure 14-18) or the complex expression *=Parameters!ParameterName.Value* as the value. You can also combine the parameter expression with other functions to produce a compound expression for the value.

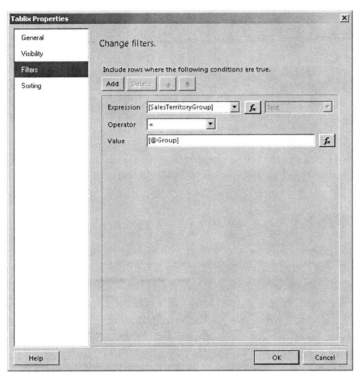

FIGURE 14-18 You can assign a report parameter to the Value field in a filter.

Understanding filter operators

To better understand how filter operators work, you might find it helpful to consider specific examples for each type of filter operator.

Equality and inequality

The construction of a filter using the equality and inequality operators (=, <>, >, >=, <, <=) is straightforward. Generally, you use any of these operators when the expression and the value are numeric values and use = or <> when the expression and the value are string values. Regardless of the data type, you can compare the expression to a single value only when using these operators.

Like

The *Like* operator is useful for pattern-matching, but it might not behave as you expect if you are accustomed to writing Transact-SQL queries with an operator having the same name. In that case, you might create a query using the percent symbol (%) as a wildcard for multiple characters, like this:

```
select * from DimProduct where EnglishProductName like '%Silver%'
```

Or you might create a query using the underscore symbol (_) as a wildcard for a single character, like this:

```
select * from DimProduct where EnglishProductName like '_L Mountain Frame - Black, 4_'
```

However, the *Like* operator in a Reporting Services filter does not work the same way. Instead, you use the asterisk symbol (*) as a wildcard for multiple characters, like this:

```
*Silver*
```

And you use a question mark (?) as a wildcard for a single character, like this:

```
?L Mountain Frame - Black, 4?
```

Top and bottom

In most cases, when you assign a static value to the Value field, you can omit quotes and the equal sign. However, when working with the *Top N* and *Bottom N* operators, you must assign a numeric value to Value. Let's say you want to filter your report to display the top five rows in the dataset based on *SalesAmount*. In that case, you assign *[SalesAmount]* to the Expression field, set Operator as *Top N*, and then type **=5** for Value. If you type 5 without the equal sign in front of it, Reporting Services interprets your entry as a string value and an error displays when you try to view the report. The same is true when using the *Bottom N* operator. When you use a report parameter to set Value, be sure to set the data type to Integer.

However, when using the *Top %* or *Bottom %* operators, you can type the numeric value without an equal sign. Apparently, Reporting Services automatically converts Value to the correct data type.

The value for *Top N* or *Top %* must reflect a number to use in a calculation, such as Top 5 or Top 50%, and the expression is the basis for determining rows to keep. That is, Reporting Services sorts the dataset rows by expression in descending order and then filters out everything except the topmost rows based on the operator you specify, either a specific number or a percentage of rows. The *Bottom N* and *Bottom %* works similarly. You provide a number for N or for the percentage, and Reporting Services works from the bottom up to determine which rows are kept and which are excluded.

Between

The *Between* operator prompts you to provide two values, as shown in Figure 14-19. This operator is inclusive, which means Reporting Services keeps rows for which the expression is both greater than or equal to the first value and less than or equal to the second value.

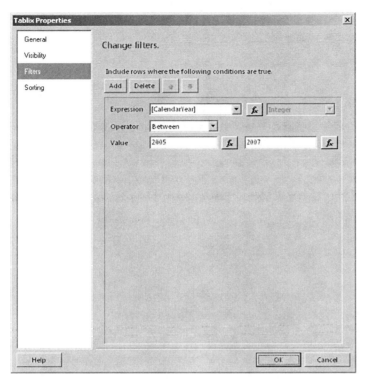

FIGURE 14-19 The *Between* operator requires you to specify a low value and a high value for a range of valid values.

In

To compare the expression to multiple values, use the *In* operator. For example, if you have a dataset that has a *BusinessType* field and the report includes a multivalue report parameter that prompts the user for the business type, you use the *In* operator and assign the report parameter, such as *[@BusinessType]*, to Value. The simple expression translates to =*Parameters!BusinessType.Value*, which represents the array of values.

> **Note** If you double-click the parameter name in the Expression dialog box, be sure to re-move the index array, (0), from the end of the expression. Otherwise, Value evaluates as the first value selected for the report parameter instead of the entire set of values.

If you have a static string representing a set of values that you want to assign to Value to use with the *In* operator, you must convert the string to an array. An easy way to do this to use the *Split* function. For example, let's say you have a string like this:

```
Specialty Bike Shop, Value Added Reseller, Warehouse
```

To use this string in a filter in which a detail row to keep in the report matches any of these business types, you assign Value an array expression like this:

```
=Split("Specialty Bike Shop, Value Added Reseller, Warehouse", ", ")
```

Not in

You can see in Table 14-1 that *Not In* does not appear the list of filter operators for filters. However, it's still possible to produce a filter that excludes items in the list, although this technique is not intuitive. To illustrate, let's use a scenario in which you have two tables, one for Bikes and Components, and one for everything else. For the first table, you have a filter that uses the *In* operator, and for the second table, you want to use a filter that excludes specific items as if you have a *Not In* operator.

To create the desired effect, you assign a Boolean value of True to the Expression field by using an expression that looks like this:

```
=True
```

It's important to use the equal sign in front of True. Otherwise, Reporting Services interprets it as a string. Also, you must set the data type to Boolean. Next, use the = operator.

Last, create an expression that resolves as True or False so that Reporting Services will keep rows where Value is True and exclude rows where Value is False. One way to do this is to use the *InStr* function to check whether the current category exists in the filter list, which in this example is in a report parameter array that you convert to a string to use with the *InStr* function. The complete expression looks like this:

```
=Iif(InStr(Join(Parameters!FilterList.Value,","),Fields!Category.Value)=0,True,False)
```

Applying OR logic to multiple filters

When you create multiple filters for a single dataset, data region, or group, Reporting Services requires a detail row to satisfy all conditions. That is, it uses AND logic when determining which detail rows to keep. But what if you want to use OR logic? The dialog box interface does not allow you to explicitly specify AND or OR logic between filter conditions, but you can create this logic in an expression that you assign to the Expression field.

To see how this works, consider a scenario in which you want to keep detail rows for Europe or detail rows for sales over $1,000. You can create an expression to combine these two conditions with OR logic, like this:

```
=Fields!SalesTerritoryGroup.Value = "Europe" OR Fields!SalesAmount.Value > 1000
```

Then set the data type for the filter to Boolean, and set Value using the following expression:

```
=True
```

Using parameters with subreports and drillthrough

Another way to use report parameters is to share data between reports. In particular, you can use the context of an item that the user clicks in one report to set a report parameter in another report, whether that report is a subreport or a drillthrough report.

Passing a parameter to a subreport

When you configure a report for use as a subreport (as described in Chapter 9, "Designing the report layout"), you have the option to configure its parameter properties as well. On the Parameters page of the Subreport Properties dialog box, click Add, select a report parameter in the subreport in the Name drop-down list, and assign that parameter a value, as shown in Figure 14-20.

> **Note** The report parameter name displays only if the subreport is available in the same project as the parent report. Otherwise, you must type the name. It's important to match the name exactly.

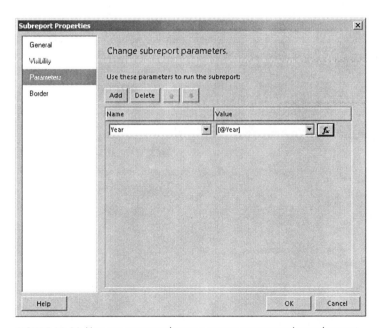

FIGURE 14-20 You can pass a value to a report parameter in a subreport.

Valid values that you can assign include a reference to a dataset field in the parent report, a parameter value in the parent report, or a custom expression. Repeat the process to add more parameter values as necessary. If you do not provide a valid value for a parameter, the subreport does not display correctly. However, if a report parameter in the subreport already has a default value that you do not want to override, you are not required to provide a value for that report parameter.

You can change the order of parameters by selecting a parameter and then using the up and down arrows to move the parameter in the list. To delete a parameter, select the parameter and click Delete.

Passing a parameter to a drillthrough report

You have the same options for configuring parameters when you define a drillthrough report as you do with a subreport. For drillthrough reports, all parameters must have a valid value specified or the drillthrough report does not render automatically. However, the user has the option to set the values for these report parameters on the drillthrough report, as long as they are visible and do not have a default value. If a report parameter in the drillthrough report has a default value specified, that value is used automatically unless you specify the report parameter in the parameters list of the report action. For more information about drill-through reports and the Go To Report action, see Chapter 13, "Adding interactivity."

Configuring the drillthrough report parameter value

To pass a parameter as part of the Go To Report action, click Add on the Actions page of the Text Box Properties dialog box where you have already added the drillthrough action. If the drillthrough report is in the same project as the parent report, you can select the report parameter in the Name drop-down list. Otherwise, you must type its name exactly. Then type the value you want to pass in the Value box, or click the expression button to build an expression that will resolve to the value you want to pass. You can also use the drop-down list to select a field value to pass, as shown in Figure 14-21. In that case, Reporting Services passes the value in scope when the user clicks to launch the action.

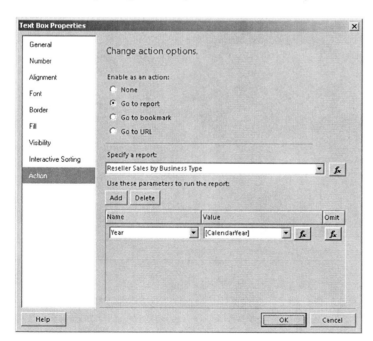

FIGURE 14-21 You can pass a value to a report parameter in a drillthrough report.

If you want to add more parameter values, click Add again. To delete a parameter, select the parameter and click Delete. You can also change the order of parameters by selecting a parameter and then using the up and down arrows to move the parameter in the list.

Omitting a parameter

You can control whether or not a parameter is passed to a drillthrough report by creating a Boolean expression to omit the parameter. In the report parameters section of the Action properties, notice the Omit column on the far right. When you click the expression button to open the Expression dialog box, you can change the default expression from False to another expression that conditionally evaluates as True or False. In that case, Reporting Services does not pass the parameter value that you configured but uses the default value defined in the drillthrough report. If the expression evaluates to False, Reporting Services passes the parameter value as defined in the parent report.

Note The Omit expression applies only to drillthrough reports, and not to subreports.

Working with query parameters

When it's important to reduce the amount of network traffic caused by returning a dataset's query results to a report, you should use a query parameter to filter the data at the source. You start by adding a query parameter to the WHERE clause of your dataset query, and then you associate the query parameter with an expression. This expression is typically a reference to a report parameter value, but it can also be an expression that evaluates current conditions in the report at execution, such as the date or the current user.

Creating a query parameter

You add a query parameter in the WHERE clause of a dataset query, as shown in Figure 14-22, by using the query designer or the Dataset Properties dialog box.

```
SELECT   st.SalesTerritoryGroup, st.SalesTerritoryCountry, r.BusinessType, d.CalendarYear, SUM(s.SalesAmount) AS SalesAmount
FROM     FactResellerSales AS s INNER JOIN
             DimReseller AS r ON r.ResellerKey = s.ResellerKey INNER JOIN
             DimDate AS d ON d.DateKey = s.OrderDateKey INNER JOIN
             DimSalesTerritory AS st ON st.SalesTerritoryKey = s.SalesTerritoryKey
WHERE    (d.CalendarYear = '2008') AND (st.SalesTerritoryGroup = @Group)
GROUP BY st.SalesTerritoryGroup, st.SalesTerritoryCountry, r.BusinessType, d.CalendarYear
```

FIGURE 14-22 The WHERE clause includes the query parameter *@Group*.

Note When the report parameter is configured to allow multiple values, you must use the *In* operator to use multiple values for comparison in the WHERE clause. In this case, the new WHERE clause would read WHERE (*st.SalesTerritoryGroup in (@Group)*). Don't forget the parentheses around the query parameter.

When you preview a query containing a query parameter, the query designer prompts you to input a value for the query parameter, as shown in Figure 14-23.

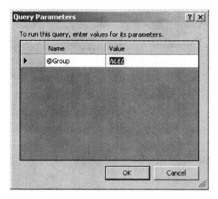

FIGURE 14-23 The query designer prompts you for a query parameter value when you preview the query.

After you add a query parameter to a dataset query, Reporting Services automatically links each query parameter to a report parameter with the same name. If no report parameter exists with the same name as the query parameter, Reporting Services automatically adds a report parameter with a String data type and links it to the query parameter. You can then modify the new report parameter by opening it from the Report Data pane, as described earlier in this chapter.

> **Note** You can also use query parameters with a stored procedure. The stored procedure must return a single result set. To configure a dataset to use a stored procedure instead of a query, change the Query Type to Stored Procedure in the Dataset Properties dialog box.

Linking report and query parameters

Reporting Services automatically links query parameters and report parameters that have the same name in the dataset. You can review this link by right-clicking the dataset in the Report Data pane and selecting Dataset Properties. Then in the Dataset Properties dialog box, select Parameters in the left pane to view the current relationship between query parameters and report parameters, as shown in Figure 14-24.

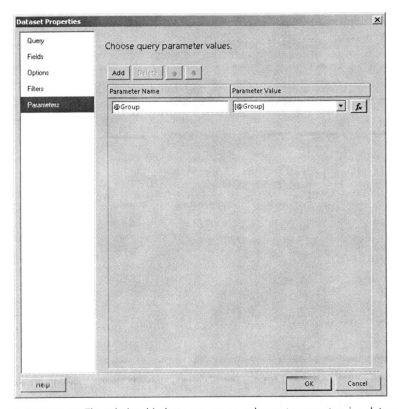

FIGURE 14-24 The relationship between query and report parameters is a dataset property.

You can also change the link between the query and report parameters here. If your report parameter has a different name than the query parameter, you can select a different parameter from the Parameter Value drop-down list. Notice that you can also use an expression for the parameter value. For example, you can concatenate the value selected by the user with static text, or you could use an expression that is completely independent of report parameters. For example, you could implement security at the data level by using a query parameter value that represents the current user (which we explain how to do in Chapter 24, "Securing report server content").

Deleting a query parameter

To delete a query parameter, you start by removing all references to the parameter in the query. Then, in the Dataset Properties dialog box, click Parameters in the left pane. Select the parameter in the list of parameters, and then click Delete.

Cascading parameters

Sometimes you might need to create the available values list for a report parameter based on the user's selection of a value for a different report parameter. This dependency between parameters is called *cascading parameters*. For example, let's say that you have two sales territory parameters, one for group and one for country, and you want the selection of a group value (the parent report parameter) to determine the set of available values for country (the child report parameter).

Creating a child report parameter dataset

When you want to implement cascading parameters, you create a dataset to retrieve the available values for the child report parameter. Furthermore, in the query for the parameter values, include a query parameter to filter the values, as shown in Figure 14-25.

```
SELECT DISTINCT SalesTerritoryCountry
FROM    DimSalesTerritory
WHERE   (SalesTerritoryGroup = @Group)
```

FIGURE 14-25 You use a query parameter to control a cascading report parameter's available values.

Linking a parent report parameter to a query parameter

Next, link the query parameter to the parent report parameter, as described in the previous section. When you run the report and select a value for the parent report parameter, the available values for the child report parameter change depending on your first selection, as shown in Figures 14-26 and 14-27.

FIGURE 14-26 The Country parameter displays one set of available values when the parent parameter value is Europe.

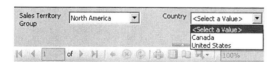

FIGURE 14-27 The available values for the Country parameter change when the parent parameter value changes.

Changing parameter order

Parameter order is important when you have cascading parameters, because you need users to see the default value for a parent parameter before they choose values for child parameters. A child report parameter contains a reference, in either its default values query or its valid values query, to a query parameter that points to a report parameter that is below it in the parameter list in the Report Data pane.

To change the order of a report parameter, select the report parameter in the Parameters folder of the Report Data pane. Use the up and down arrows to move the report parameter.

CHAPTER 15

Managing the page layout

When designing a report, it is important to keep in mind how the report is going to be displayed and distributed. Reports that users regularly print or export as PDF documents have different layout requirements than reports that users view only as HTML. You must plan not only how to structure data in a report but also how to arrange report items in relation to one another and in relation to the page. The structure of a page depends on rendering and various report properties. Some render formats use these properties, while other render formats ignore them. In this chapter, you learn how to factor rendering into the report development process, how to control the layout of items on a page, how to use properties to manage where page breaks occur, and how the type of page break affects the naming and numbering of pages.

Understanding rendering

Designing the page layout of a report is an important part of the report development process. Pagination affects the structure and count of pages within a report. However, pagination depends on the rendering extension used to produce the report. A report rendered in HTML can have a very different layout than a report rendered in PDF. Therefore, it is important to understand the differences among rendering extensions with regard to pagination.

Reviewing rendering formats by pagination type

Many organizations use Reporting Services primarily for online viewing of reports. But there are other ways that you might want to view the information contained in reports, and for that reason, Reporting Services allows you to export reports in multiple formats using a process called rendering. With regard to pagination, each of these rendering extensions belongs to one of the following three types:

- **Data** This group includes the XML, CSV, and ATOM rendering extensions. Formatting is ignored altogether because the output includes only data structures. Consequently, these rendering extensions do not support page breaks.

  The XML format is useful for integration with other applications. A CSV file includes a header row containing the names of each column and then includes the lowest level of detail in the report with a comma delimiter between each field and a carriage return and line feed at the end of each line. This format is also useful when data needs to be integrated with other applications. You can render the report as an ATOM service document. Each data region in the report becomes a separate data feed that you can import into PowerPivot for Excel or other applications that can consume data feeds.

- **Soft page-break** This group includes Excel, Word, and HTML rendering extensions. Users primarily view reports rendered in these formats online, viewing HTML in a web browser and Excel and Word within their respective applications. Of course, you can print the reports from within any of those three applications.

  When you use Report Manager or the SharePoint report viewer to access a report, the report renders in HTML format by default and all of the interactive features that you can possibly design into a report are fully supported. If you have a large report, Reporting Services inserts some page breaks automatically in strategic locations, or you can design the report with explicit page breaks in specific locations, which we explain in the "Configuring page breaks" section of this chapter. Using URL access techniques or a web service call, it's possible to render the report in an MHTML format, which is useful for consolidating a multipage report into a single file.

  When viewing a report online, you might notice a question mark display to the right of the page number, as shown in Figure 15-1. This number indicates that the report server has not yet fully rendered the report and that the total number of pages in the report is not yet available. The report server purposely renders one page at a time as a performance enhancement, which is especially noticeable when rendering a large report.

FIGURE 15-1 A question mark displays next to the page number when the report is not fully rendered.

Many users like to interact with the data in a report by using Excel, where they can add formulas and apply sorting or filtering to the data or combine it with other information as needed. When you export to Excel, Reporting Services tries to preserve as much of the formatting as possible. Some interactive features, like the document map and actions, are supported in Excel, but other interactive features, like report parameters and interactive sorting, are not.

Some users like to enhance the report with additional commentary and images from other sources. In this case, exporting the report to Word might be a good option. Hyperlinks and actions work in a Word document, but using visibility properties to toggle between showing and hiding items is not supported. The Word document imports most of the images in the report except for background images.

■ **Hard page-break** This group includes the PDF and TIFF rendering extensions. You can view a report in these formats online, but the main purpose of these rendering extensions is to create a pixel-perfect version of reports for printing. That is, you can be very precise about the appearance of the report items. Because they are intended primarily for print purposes, they have fewer interactive features, if any. If a report does not have explicit page breaks defined, Reporting Services inserts page breaks based on the report page height and width.

If users typically print out reports, a popular format is the PDF file. The only interactive feature that the PDF export supports is the document map feature. It's important when designing reports to consider how they will appear in PDF format if you know that users will be using this feature. What looks nice in an online format does not always look as nice in PDF format. So it's important during the report development process to preview the report in PDF format where applicable.

Another option for offline viewing in a format suitable for printing is to export the report as a TIFF file. The TIFF file is strictly an image, but it does support multiple pages. You can also use URL access or a web service call to generate a different type of image file for single page reports, using bitmap files, GIF, and other image file types. Just as with the PDF file, it's important to preview your report during the report development process if you know that users will be exporting reports as image files.

Using the *RenderFormat* global variable

In the report design, you need to plan ahead for the rendering format. Ideally, you can develop a report that users can render in multiple formats. However, because of the differences between rendering extensions, you might want some properties to change or you might want to hide selected report items depending on the rendering extension used to create the report. In SQL Server 2008 R2 Reporting Services, the *RenderFormat* global variable was introduced to allow you to create expressions that address these scenarios.

■ ***Globals!RenderFormat.Name*** Using this property of the *RenderFormat* variable returns the name of the current renderer. The *Name* property is case-sensitive and uses the following values: XML, CSV, ATOM, PDF, RGDI, HTML4.0, MHTML, EXCEL, EXCELOPENXML, RPL, IMAGE, WORD, and WORDOPENXML.

■ ***Globals!RenderFormat.IsInteractive*** The *IsInteractive* property returns a *True* or *False* value, depending on whether the current renderer is interactive.

A common reason to use the *RenderFormat* global variable is to conditionally hide a text box, depending on the rendering extension used. Some features that render nicely in HTML format do not render as nicely in Excel. For example, sometimes headers cause merged cells to appear in the Excel format, which then affects the user's ability to sort columns. In some cases, you can fix this by making sure that the edge of the page header text boxes align exactly with the right edge of a tablix column, but sometimes you don't have that option. Instead, you can hide a text box only when you render the report as an Excel 2010 (or higher) workbook by adding an expression to the *Hidden* property of the text box, like this:

```
=iif(Globals!RenderFormat.Name="EXCELOPENXML", True, False)
```

When you render the report in HTML, you can see the text box display, as shown in Figure 15-2.

This text box is not visible in Excel.

Country	Business Type	Sales Amount
Australia	Specialty Bike Shop	$165,542.36
	Value Added Reseller	$400,571.50
	Warehouse	$180,790.56
	Country Total	$746,904.41

FIGURE 15-2 You can conditionally display a text box by using an expression that makes it visible in HTML.

But when you render the same report in Excel, the text box is hidden, as shown in Figure 15-3.

	A	B	C
1	Country	Business Type	Sales Amount
2	Australia	Specialty Bike Shop	$165,542.36
3		Value Added Reseller	$400,571.50
4		Warehouse	$180,790.56
5		Country Total	$746,904.41

FIGURE 15-3 When you render the same report in Excel, the text box is now hidden.

> **Note** If you plan to render the report to Excel 2007-2010, use the render format name EXCELOPENXML. Similarly, use WORDOPENXML for a report rendered to Word 2007-2010. The render formats EXCEL and WORD apply only to Excel 2003 and Word 2003 respectively. Make sure to check that you are using the proper rendering format name in expressions when you are troubleshooting an expression that uses *RenderFormat*.

Dynamic positioning of text boxes

The position of a report item is fixed. That is, you cannot use an expression to dynamically set the location and size of a report item. However, you can dynamically set the padding properties of the text to display in a text box. In this way, you can achieve a result similar to dynamic positioning of text boxes.

To configure this behavior, create as many text boxes you need, using the same size and location. Then configure each text box by adding a dynamic expression for the applicable Padding properties: *Top*, *Left*, *Bottom*, and *Right*.

For example, let's say you have a parameter that passes a value for the orientation of the text boxes: Horizontal or Vertical. Then set the *Padding/Left* expression for one of the text boxes, like this:

```
=iif(Parameters!Orientation.Value="Horizontal", "50pt", "2pt")
```

Then set the expression for *Padding/Top* for the same text box, like this:

```
=iif(Parameters!Orientation.Value="Horizontal", "2pt", "32pt")
```

By adding these expressions to the text box padding properties, you can change the orientation dynamically at runtime. When the orientation parameter is set to Horizontal, the text box expands to the right with the extra padding, but when the orientation parameter is set to Vertical, the text box expands down. In a soft page-break renderer like HTML, as shown below, the vertical orientation does not display correctly because overlapping report items are not supported.

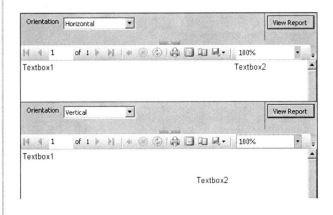

However, when you export the report to PDF, the correct layout is achieved with one text box displaying over the other text box, with the vertical orientation as shown below. Hard page-break renderers support overlapping report items, which allows you greater flexibility in designing the report layout.

```
Textbox1   Textbox2



Textbox1

Textbox2
```

Adjusting the report size

When developing a report for one of the hard page-break renderers, you should review and modify the report properties as needed to ensure a proper layout. For example, you might need to change page size and margin properties for reports that will be printed or exported to PDF format. You can also configure your report to display data in multiple columns. There is also a property to eliminate white space so that blank pages are not added to your report.

Understanding the page structure properties

A report has several properties related to page size, margin, and orientation that affect the structure of the page. These properties are ignored when you view a report online or in Excel (although the properties are used when you print the Excel workbook). The default page size is 8.5 inches wide by 11 inches high, which produces a portrait orientation. You can switch to landscape by setting the *Width* property to *11in* and the *Height* property to *8.5in*.

Report page structure

The height and width are not the only properties that determine how much of a report can fit on a page. Margins, body size, and the presence or absence of page headers and page footers, as shown in Figure 15-4, also have an effect. The renderer uses height and width as a starting point that defines the physical page size and then subtracts the margin properties from the page size to determine the width and height available for the report. Within the usable space for the report, sections are reserved for the page header and page footer, if you use them, and the remaining space is available to the body of the report.

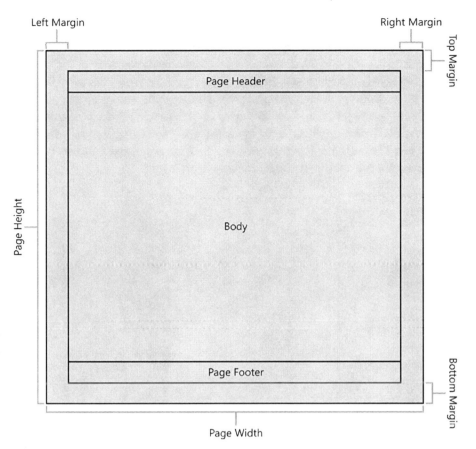

FIGURE 15-4 The structure of a report page.

If you don't use the page header and footer in your report, that space is usable by the body. The body contains all report items that you add to the report that aren't placed specifically in the page header and footer. The page header and footer repeat on each page of the report (unless you set a property to prevent the display of a page header or footer on the first or last page), and the body then displays report items in sequence from left to right and top to bottom.

Regardless of the use of page headers and footers, it's important to note that there are different properties that you use to define the page size and the body size. The page size is set by the report properties *Width* and *Height*. The usable space is restricted by the report properties for the margins: *Left*, *Right*, *Top*, and *Bottom*. The page header and page footer each have a *Height* property that further restricts usable space. Then the body of the report has *Width* and *Height* properties. If the body size plus the margins exceeds the page size, you can see problems occur in rendering. Typically, a report looks fine when you view it online but includes an extra blank page between pages containing report content.

Page size properties

You can change the page structure by changing several report properties. To access report properties, you first click anywhere in the document workspace outside the body of the report. This step selects *Report* in the drop-down list that displays at the top of the Properties window. You can also select it in the drop-down list. In the Page properties category, you have property groups for *InteractiveSize*, *Margins*, and *PageSize*, as shown in Figure 15-5. Expanding these property groups allows you to configure *Width* and *Height,* for both interactive and page sizing, and *Left*, *Right*, *Top*, and *Bottom* for the margins. The default unit of measurement for these properties is inches, but you can use other units, as described in Chapter 9, "Designing the report layout."

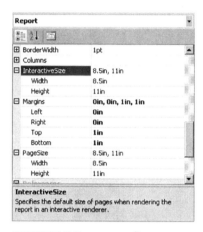

FIGURE 15-5 You can configure report properties to adjust the page size and usable space.

Interactive renderers, such as HTML, use the *InteractiveSize* properties. The renderer inserts page breaks using the interactive *Height* property but ignores the width. If you want the report to render as one long page, set the interactive *Height* property to 0in. However, if you do this, you will not be able to view the report until it is fully rendered, which might take a while if you have a large report.

Column properties

An alternative to the standard page layout is to have a report divided up into columns like a newspaper, as shown in Figure 15-6. The renderer treats each column as a separate a page of the report, and fills the columns in the same way. A report with columns simply has multiple report pages on a single physical page. The addition of column spacing to the page structure must be considered in your size calculations to ensure proper rendering.

To configure a report with columns, select Report from the drop-down list in the Properties window. In the *Page* group, expand *Columns*, and set the values for the *Columns* and *ColumnSpacing* properties, as shown in Figure 15-7. The *Columns* property controls the number of columns that render on each page layout of the report, while the *ColumnSpacing* property defines the space to reserve between columns.

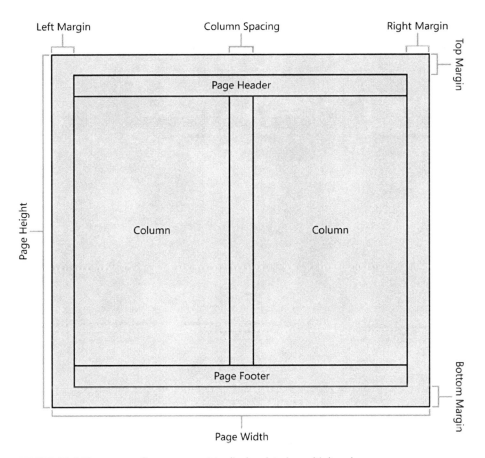

FIGURE 15-6 You can configure a report to display data in multiple columns.

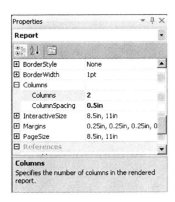

FIGURE 15-7 You use the *Columns* and *ColumnSpacing* properties to create a report with multiple columns.

Columns render only when you export a report to PDF or Image formats. You cannot see columns when you preview your report in HTML. When developing in SSDT or Report Builder, you can use the Print Layout mode to check the layout of columns in your report, as shown in Figure 15-8.

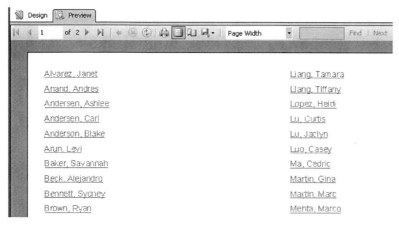

FIGURE 15-8 You must use the Print Layout mode to see the column layout when previewing your report in SSDT or Report Builder.

White space

The white space in the body of your report is preserved by default, which can extend the body size beyond the width of the report and cause blank pages to appear. For example, in a matrix, where columns are dynamic, any white space you have in your body to the right of the column group gets added on after all the columns are rendered. This results in blank pages, even though the matrix itself fits on one page. This problem with blank pages also occurs when you move report items around on the design surface and unintentionally expand the width of the body, as shown in Figure 15-9. You won't see this problem when previewing the report unless you switch to Print Layout mode or export the report using a hard page-break renderer.

You can disable this behavior by changing the value of the *ConsumeContainerWhiteSpace* property of the report. When this property is set to *True*, as shown in Figure 15-10, the white space to the right of the tablix in our example is removed. You can find this property in the Other category in the Properties window for the report.

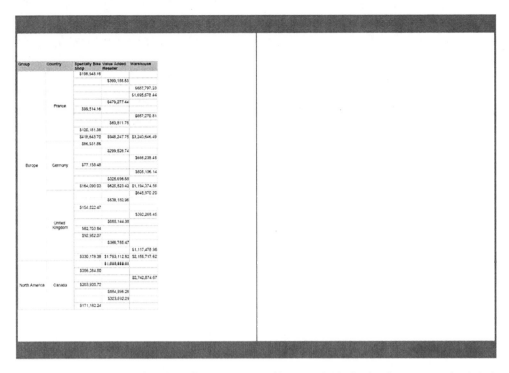

FIGURE 15-9 A hard page-break renderer preserves white space in the body of your report by default.

FIGURE 15-10 You can remove white space in a report by setting the *ConsumeContainerWhitespace* property to *True*.

After you set the *ConsumeContainerWhitespace* property, you can preview the report in Print Layout mode to check the results. As shown in Figure 15-11, the white space in the body of the report no longer affects the body width of the rendered report. As long as the size of the tablix and the margins fits within the defined page width, the blank pages no longer appear.

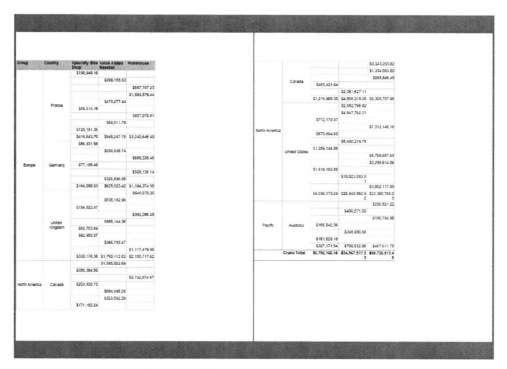

FIGURE 15-11 A report renders without blank pages after you set the ConsumeContainerWhitespace property to True.

Using device information to change page properties

Some rendering extensions allow you use device information settings to change how the report is rendered. For example, you can override the page margin sizes at runtime when rendering to PDF by using URL access, which we explain in more detail in Chapter 35, "Programming report access." In general, URL access allows you to request a report and provide additional information to the renderer. For example, you can create a report in PDF format with its default right margin width of 1 inch, as shown in Figure 15-12, by using a URL like this:

```
http://localhost/ReportServer?/Chapter 15/Sales&rs:Format=PDF
```

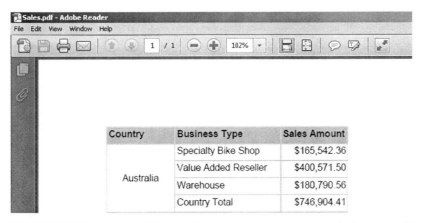

FIGURE 15-12 You can use URL access to render a report using its default margin of 1 inch.

To set device information settings by using URL access, you create a string that includes the device information tag and the value that you want to use by using the following syntax:

```
rc:<tag>=<value>
```

A list of useful tags is provided in Table 15-1. This is by no means an exhaustive list, but it includes tags that are applicable to pagination.

TABLE 15-1 Device information tags

Tag	Description	Renderers
Columns	The number of columns in the report.	PDF, IMAGE
ColumnSpacing	The spacing between columns in the report.	PDF, IMAGE
MarginBottom	The bottom margin value. This value is specified in inches and must include "in" after the value (example: 1in).	PDF, IMAGE
MarginLeft	The left margin value. This value is specified in inches and must include "in" after the value (example: 1in).	PDF, IMAGE
MarginRight	The right margin value. This value is specified in inches and must include "in" after the value (example: 1in).	PDF, IMAGE
MarginTop	The top margin value. This value is specified in inches and must include "in" after the value (example: 1in).	PDF, IMAGE
PageHeight	The page height value. This value is specified in inches and must include "in" after the value (example: 1in).	PDF, IMAGE
PageWidth	The page width value. This value is specified in inches and must include "in" after the value (example: 1in).	PDF, IMAGE

Tag	Description	Renderers
StartPage	The first page of the report to render. The default value is 1. If you set the value to 0, all pages will render.	PDF, IMAGE
EndPage	The last page of the report to render. The default value is the value of StartPage.	PDF, IMAGE
SimplePageHeaders	Specifies whether the report page header is rendered as an Excel page header. When set to false, the page header is rendered as the first row of the worksheet. The default value is false.	EXCEL
FixedPageWidth	Specifies whether the page width will grow to accommodate the width of the largest page in the report. The default value is false.	WORD

When you want to render a report to a PDF format with a modified page margin, as shown in Figure 15-13, you create a tag string for the *MarginLeft* tag and append it to the URL access request like this:

```
http://localhost/ReportServer?/Chapter 15/Sales&rs:Format=PDF&rc:MarginLeft=0in
```

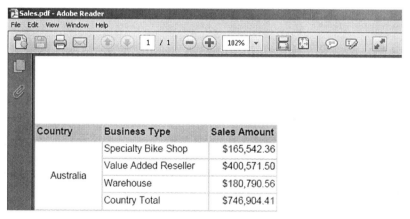

FIGURE 15-13 You can modify the margin settings by setting device information in the URL access request.

Working with the page header and footer

The page header and page footer sections of a report are optional and disabled by default. If you want to repeat information or images on all report pages, you can enable these report sections and then place a text box or image inside the desired section. However, you cannot add a dataset field to a text box in a page header or page footer, nor can you add a data region or subreport to these sections.

Adding a page header or footer

To add a page header or footer, simply right-click in the space outside the design area in the design tab and select Add Page Header or Add Page Footer. A space appears above the body of the report for a page header, as shown in Figure 15-14, or below the body of the report for a page footer. You can then add text boxes or images to this space.

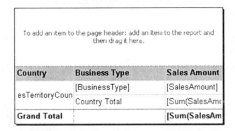

FIGURE 15-14 A new section appears above the body of your report in the design area when you add a page header.

Configuring page header or footer properties

The page header and page footer each have their own set of properties, including fill, border color, style, width, and background color and image. These are the same types of properties you can set for other report items, as we describe in Chapter 9. You can access the page header or footer properties by right-clicking inside the design surface for the page header or page footer and selecting Header Properties or Footer Properties to display the applicable dialog box, such as the one shown in Figure 15-15.

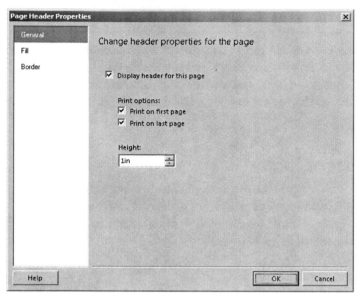

FIGURE 15-15 You configure the appearance of the page header by using the Page Header Properties dialog box.

You can set the following properties on the General page of the Page Header Properties dialog box and the Page Footer Properties dialog box:

- **Display Header (or Footer) For This Page** If you clear the Display Header (or Footer) For This Page check box, the page header (or footer) no longer appears in the report and its contents are deleted.

- **Print On First Page** You can include the contents of the page header (or footer) on the first page of the report by selecting this check box, or you can clear this check box to omit the page header (or footer) from the first page.

- **Print On Last Page** You can include the contents of the page header (or footer) on the last page of the report by selecting this check box, or you can clear this check box to omit the page header (or footer) from the last page.

- **Height** You can specify the height and unit of measurement for the page header or footer. You can resize the page header or footer by dragging the line that separates it from the body of the report.

 Note By default, the report items in the page header (or footer) display on each page of the report. However, even if you remove the page header or footer from the first or last page, the height allocated to that page section is still preserved on the printed page. If you want to omit the page header or footer from page other than the first page or the last page, you must use a conditional expression with the *Hidden* property for each report item in the page header or footer.

Using expressions in a page header or footer

Generally, you use the header and footer to display information related to the report page. The global variables to display page numbers are useful here, as well as the global variables related to the report name, report path, and report execution time.

You can also use the page headers and footers to show page and dataset aggregations. For example, you can use the page header to display the page total for a particular field or to display the grand total, as shown in Figure 15-16.

Although you cannot refer to a dataset field directly in a page header (or footer) expression, you can sum the values that display in a named text box to derive a page total on each page of the report, like this:

```
="Sales Amount Page Total: " & FormatCurrency(Sum(ReportItems!SalesAmount.Value), 2)
```

Sales Amount Page Total: $3,538,837.31

Sales Amount Dataset Total: $16,038,062.60

Group	Country	Business Type	Sales Amount
Europe	France	Specialty Bike Shop	$120,181.38
		Value Added Reseller	$399,158.53
		Warehouse	$857,270.81
		Country Total	$1,376,610.72
	Germany	Specialty Bike Shop	$77,158.48
		Value Added Reseller	$299,826.74
		Warehouse	$508,136.14
		Country Total	$885,121.35
	United Kingdom	Specialty Bike Shop	$92,952.07
		Value Added Reseller	$538,182.96
		Warehouse	$645,970.20
		Country Total	$1,277,105.23

FIGURE 15-16 The text boxes in the header contain page and dataset aggregations on sales amount.

Note You cannot reference more than one report item in a single expression that you use in a page header or footer.

You can use a dataset field in an expression only if you use it with an aggregate function for which the scope is set to a dataset. For example, you can display the grand total of the report by using an expression like this:

```
="Sales Amount Dataset Total: " & FormatCurrency(Sum(Fields!SalesAmount.Value,
"SalesByTerritoryByBusinessType"), 2)
```

Page headers and footers in Word

A page header and a page footer in a report are rendered as a header and footer in a Word document, as shown in Figure 15-17. However, the height of the page header or footer defined in the report does not set the height of the corresponding region in Word. Instead, the default height for these regions in Word is used. Furthermore, the *PrintOnFirstPage* and *PrintOnLastPage* properties are ignored in Word.

Sales Amount Page Total: $3,538,837.31

Sales Amount Dataset Total: $16,038,062.60

Header	Group	Country	Business Type	Sales Amount
	Europe	France	Specialty Bike Shop	$120,181.38
			Value Added Reseller	$399,158.53
			Warehouse	$857,270.81
			Country Total	$1,376,610.72
		Germany	Specialty Bike Shop	$77,158.48
			Value Added Reseller	$299,826.74
			Warehouse	$508,136.14
			Country Total	$885,121.36
		United Kingdom	Specialty Bike Shop	$92,952.07
			Value Added Reseller	$538,182.96
			Warehouse	$645,970.20
			Country Total	$1,277,105.23

FIGURE 15-17 A page header in a report renders as a header in Word.

Word also occasionally has problems with certain expressions in the header and footer regions. For example, take a look at the following two expressions:

```
="Page: " + Globals!PageNumber.ToString + " of " + Globals!TotalPages.ToString
```

```
="Page: " & Globals!PageNumber & " of " & Globals!TotalPages
```

Both expressions render the same in HTML, and the correct page number displays as you page through the report. However, when you render the report to Word, the first expression renders the same on every page, while the second expression has the correct behavior, as shown in Figure 15-18. Word handles only simple references to pagination variables and does not support calling a function such as *ToString*.

 Note If you use the pagination variables, such as *Globals!PageNumber* or *Globals!TotalPages*, in an expression in a page header or page footer and then render the report as a Word document, the render converts the pagination variables to the *Page* and *NumPages* fields, respectively, in the Word header or footer. That way, the correct page values and page counts display in the Word document.

		Specialty Bike Shop	$171,182.24
North America	Canada	Value Added Reseller	$884,996.26
		Warehouse	$1,334,083.02
		Country Total	$2,390,261.51
	United States	Specialty Bike Shop	$712,179.97
		Value Added Reseller	$4,847,762.31
		Warehouse	$3,802,117.09
		Country Total	$9,362,059.37

FIGURE 15-18 Header expressions that reference both pagination variables and functions are not supported when rendering a report as a Word document.

Page headers and footers in Excel

By default, a page header renders in Excel as part of the worksheet above other report items, as shown in Figure 15-19. However, you can render a header as an Excel header by using URL access and setting the *SimplePageHeaders* device information tag to *False*, as described in the "Using device Information to change page properties" section of this chapter.

	A	B	C	D
1				
2	**Page: 1 of 3**			
3				
4	**Page: 1 of 3**			
5				
6	**Group**	**Country**	**Business Type**	**Sales Amount**
7			Specialty Bike Shop	$120,181.38
8		France	Value Added Reseller	$399,158.53
9			Warehouse	$857,270.81
10			Country Total	$1,376,610.72
11			Specialty Bike Shop	$77,158.48
12	Europe	Germany	Value Added Reseller	$299,826.74
13			Warehouse	$508,136.14
14			Country Total	$885,121.35
15			Specialty Bike Shop	$92,952.07
16		United	Value Added Reseller	$538,182.96
17		Kingdom	Warehouse	$645,970.20
18			Country Total	$1,277,105.23

FIGURE 15-19 By default, a page header renders as part of the worksheet in Excel.

However, a page footer renders as an Excel footer, as shown in Figure 15-20. You cannot see the footer when viewing the worksheet. You can check the footer only by using Print Preview or printing the worksheet.

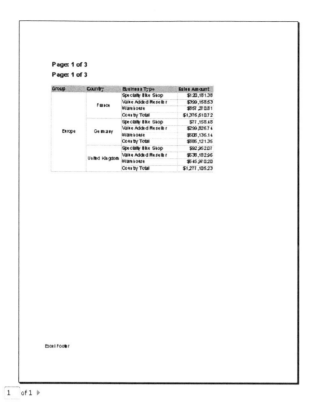

FIGURE 15-20 A page footer renders as an Excel footer and is visible only when you print the report.

Removing a page header or footer

To remove a page header or footer, right-click in that section of the design surface and select Remove Page Header or Remove Page Footer. Take care to move any report items that you want to save to another area of the report. Any report items remaining in the page header or footer are deleted when you remove the page header or footer from the report.

Configuring page breaks

By default, the report processing engine will fit as much of a data region onto a page as it can before creating a page break. You can override this behavior by inserting page breaks relative to a data region or when a group instance changes within a data region.

Note If you configure hard page breaks in your report, a rendering extension might continue to insert soft page breaks if necessary. For example, if the location of the page break that you add results in a page size larger than the report properties allow, the renderer adds a soft page break to adjust the page size accordingly.

Creating page breaks

You can create page breaks on most report items. To create a page break, select the data region to which you want to add a page break. In the Properties window, expand the *PageBreak* category to set the following properties, as shown in Figure 15-21:

- **BreakLocation** You use this property to specify the location of the page break relative to the selected report item: None, Start, End, or Start And End. You can set the break location at the start of a report item to force a page break before the report item renders. Or you can set the break location at the end of a report item. This might not make sense if nothing appears in the report after the report item that you set the page break on, because you'll end up with an extra blank page at the end. You can also have a page break before and after the report item renders.

- **Disabled** This property allows you to use a conditional expression to determine whether to apply a page break. For example, you might set it to *True* when the render format is HTML to prevent a page break but set it to *False* when the render format is PDF to add the page break.

FIGURE 15-21 You use the *BreakLocation* and *Disabled* properties to control the insertion of a page break before or after a report item.

Another option for configuring a page break is to open the applicable properties dialog box for a data region, such as the Tablix Properties dialog box shown in Figure 15-22. In the Page Break Options section, you can add a break before or after the data region or both before and after it renders. For the tablix, you can also select the Keep Together On One Page If Possible check box to set the *KeepTogether* property to true, which we explain further in the next section.

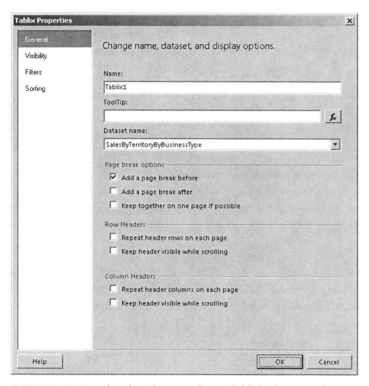

FIGURE 15-22 Page break options are also available in the report item properties dialog boxes.

Using the *KeepTogether* property

When you have a large table, you might find that the table is broken up in rendering, with some rows or columns ending up on a separate page from the bulk of the table. If you add a page break to the start of the table, the rendering pushes the entire table to the second page and keeps the table together. However, this page break setting always pushes the table to the second page, and this might not be what you want. Suppose you want to keep the table on the first page if it returns few enough rows that it will fit. Then you want to set the *KeepTogether* property to *True*.

By setting *KeepTogether* to *True*, if the table doesn't fit on the same page as the preceding items, the rendering engine pushes it to a new page. However, if the table is small enough, the rendering engine keeps the table on the same page as the preceding items. If the table doesn't fit onto its own page, the rendering engine will render as much of the table as possible on the first page and then continuing on subsequent pages.

To set this property, select the report item that you want to keep on one page, and then set the *KeepTogether* property to *True* in the Properties window, as shown in Figure 15-23. You must render the report in a paginated format to see the result of configuring the report item with *KeepTogether* set to *True*. You won't see the effect of this property when you view the report in HTML or Excel.

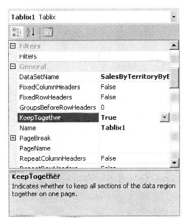

FIGURE 15-23 You use the *KeepTogether* property to move a report item to a new page if it cannot fit completely on the original page.

Adding page breaks by group

Another way to set page breaks is to use groups within a data region. The same properties that you have for setting page breaks by report item are applicable to groups: *BreakLocation* and *Disabled*. However, for *BreakLocation*, you have a new option available. Rather than create a page break only when a new group starts or ends, you can instead have a page break between group instances. That way, you don't create an unnecessary page break at the beginning or end of a report item and create a new page only when a new group starts.

To set the page break on a group, select the group in the Groupings Pane, and then expand the Group category in the Properties window to locate the PageBreak options. You can also right-click the group and open the Page Breaks page of the Group Properties dialog box, as shown in Figure 15-24, to set the appropriate page break options.

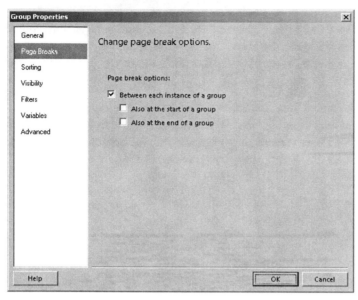

FIGURE 15-24 You can configure page breaks by group in the Group Properties dialog box.

You can also set the *KeepTogether* property for a group. This will ensure that, if possible, the entirety of a tablix group will appear on one page and not have a page break inserted in the middle. Simply select the group that you want to keep together in the Groupings pane, and then set *KeepTogether* to *True* in the Properties window.

Repeating headers

When a tablix spans multiple pages, you might want the column headers to repeat on each new page to make the tablix easier to read. By default, the column headers appear only once when the table renders, so when a table spans multiple pages, you lose that useful information on all following pages.

If you have a simple matrix type of tablix, you can configure repeating column headers. You can do this in one of two ways. One way is to open the Tablix Properties dialog box, as shown in Figure 15-25, and select the Repeat Header Column On Each Page check box. Another way is to set the *RepeatColumnHeaders* property to *True* in the Properties window. Reporting Services uses the group headers in the matrix as column groups.

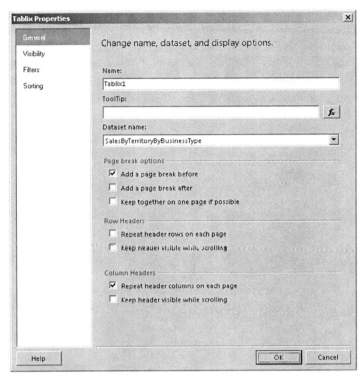

FIGURE 15-25 Select the Repeat Header Columns On Each Page check box to repeat column headers on each new page.

However, in a simple table, you do not have column groups. Although you can set the *Repeat-ColumnHeaders* property to *True*, it won't have the proper effect. To create repeating column headers in this scenario is a bit more complicated. First, you need to view the Row Groups in Advanced Mode. To open Advanced Mode in the Groupings pane, click the arrow to the right of the Column Groups and select Advanced Mode. Notice that Static Groups now appear in the Row Groups, as shown in Figure 15-26.

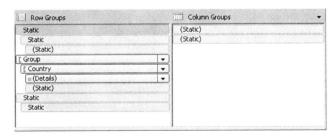

FIGURE 15-26 In Advanced Mode, the static members are visible in the Groupings Pane

To set the column headers, select the Static group that highlights the leftmost column header. This is generally the first Static group listed. In the Properties window, set the *RepeatOnNewPage* property to *True*. Also set the *KeepWithGroup* property to *After*, as shown in Figure 15-27. The *KeepWithGroup* property specifies which group the static member needs to stay with. If set to *After,* the static member stays with the group after, or below it, acting as a group header. If set to *Before*, the static member stays with the group before, or above it, acting as a group footer. If set to *None*, Reporting Services automatically decides where to put the static member.

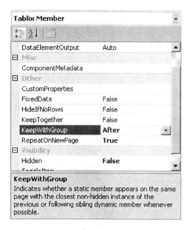

FIGURE 15-27 Set *RepeatOnNewPage* to *True* and *KeepWithGroup* to *After* to configure repeating headers for a table.

Numbering pages

Usually, it's helpful to add page numbers in a page header or page footer when you have a multipage report. You can reference the *PageNumber* global variable in an expression, but only in a page header or footer.

Global variables

When referencing page numbers in expressions, you can use the following global variables:

- **Globals!PageNumber**   The current page number relative to the last page number reset.

- **Globals!TotalPages**   The total number of pages in the current page numbering group.

- **Globals!OverallPageNumber**   The current page number in the report.

- **Globals!OverallTotalPages**   The total number of pages in the report.

> **Note** If you do not reset page numbers, the *OverallPageNumber* variable will be the same as the *PageNumber* variable, and the *TotalPages* variable will be equal to the *OverallTotalPages* variable.

ResetPageNumber property

A new concept for page numbering introduced in SQL Server 2008 R2 was the ability to reset the page number. Notice that there is a *ResetPageNumber* property in the set of page break properties for a report item or group, shown in Figure 15 21. You can set this property to *True* or *False*, and you can even use a conditional expression to set the property value.

For example, suppose you have page breaks between each Sales Country Group and each Sales Country Territory, and you set the page number to reset when the Sales Country Group changes. Then, for North America, you expect to have 2 total pages because North America has two countries in it, using the AdventureWorksDW2012 database. However, depending on the number of country groups in the dataset, the overall page number and actual page number could be different.

Figure 15-28 illustrates the difference between the page number global variables. The top text box in the report footer uses the following expression:

```
="Page: " & Globals!PageNumber & " of " & Globals!TotalPages
```

The bottom text box in the report footer uses the following expression:

```
="Overall Page: " & Globals!OverallPageNumber & " of " & Globals!OverallTotalPages
```

North America	Canada	Specialty Bike Shop	$171,182.24
		Value Added Reseller	$884,996.26
		Warehouse	$1,334,083.02
		Country Total	$2,390,261.51

Page: 1 of 2

Overall Page: 4 of 6

FIGURE 15-28 The page footer displays the different page number global variables.

Naming pages

Another feature introduced in SQL Server 2008 R2 was the ability to assign each page a unique name. The first page of a report is blank by default, and it's not necessary to set one. If you decide to assign a page name, you use the report property *InitialPageName*, as shown in Figure 15-29, which can be a constant value or an expression.

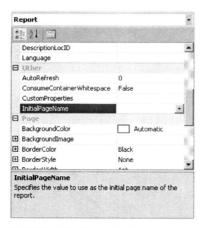

FIGURE 15-29 The *InitialPageName* property is empty by default.

You can reset the page name when you create a page break for a report item or group. For example, you might use the name of a group to reset the page name. You can set the page name property only by using the Properties window. Select the item that you want to use to control the page name, such as the tablix group, and then set the *PageName* property, as shown in Figure 15-30. The *PageName* property is located below the *PageBreak* properties, which appear in different places of the Properties location depending on the report item selected.

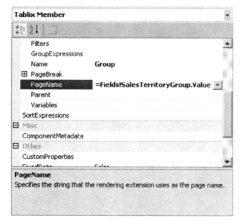

FIGURE 15-30 You can reset the page name by using the *PageName* property when a page break appears in the report.

You can reference the current page name in an expression, which can be useful in a page header or footer of a report and is the only place you can reference the page name. To reference the page name, use the global variable *Globals!PageName* in your expression.

When you export a report to Excel, the page name becomes the sheet name, as shown in Figure 15-31. If you set an initial page name for your report but do not set page names for the other pages in the report, all the sheets in Excel will have the initial page name.

	A	B	C	D
1	**Group**	**Country**	**Business Type**	**Sales Amount**
2			Specialty Bike Shop	$120,181.38
3		France	Value Added Reseller	$399,158.53
4			Warehouse	$857,270.81
5			Country Total	$1,376,610.72
6			Specialty Bike Shop	$77,158.48
7	Europe	Germany	Value Added Reseller	$299,826.74
8			Warehouse	$508,136.14
9			Country Total	$885,121.35
10			Specialty Bike Shop	$92,952.07
11		United	Value Added Reseller	$538,182.96
12		Kingdom	Warehouse	$645,970.20
13			Country Total	$1,277,105.23
14				
15				
16				
17				
18				
19				
20				
21				
22				
23				
24				
25				
26				

Europe / North America / Pacific

FIGURE 15-31 Page names appear as sheet names when you render the report as an Excel workbook.

CHAPTER 16

Using Analysis Services as a data source

When you have a large database to query or your reports contain complex calculations that are difficult to perform by using relational queries, you can move your data into an *online analytical processing* (OLAP) database managed by Analysis Services. An OLAP database is characterized by a multidimensional data structure known as a cube, which provides fast responses to queries and includes spreadsheet-style formulas to centralize and simplify the business logic used to perform calculations. To query a cube, you must use the Multidimensional Expression (MDX) query language, which many people find difficult to learn. The good news is that Reporting Services includes a query designer that you can use to create the MDX query if you're new to Analysis Services. If you're already experienced with MDX, you also have the flexibility to type your own MDX query or to modify the MDX query generated by the query designer.

In this chapter, you learn how to build reports that use an Analysis Services database. The examples rely on the sample database described in Chapter 4, "Installing Reporting Services." You also learn how to use the MDX query designer to create a dataset for a report. Furthermore, you learn how working with Analysis Services dataset fields and parameters differs from working with fields and parameters when using other data source types.

> **Note** You don't need any prior experience with Analysis Services before you begin this chapter. All the information that you need to build basic reports successfully by using Analysis Services as a data source is provided in this chapter, but you can learn more about Analysis Services by referring to *Microsoft SQL Server 2008 Analysis Services Step by Step* (Microsoft Press, 2009).

Creating an Analysis Services dataset

Before you can create an Analysis Services dataset, you must define a data source that stores the connection information for the Analysis Services server and database. Then, when you create the dataset, you provide an MDX query either by using a graphical interface to construct the query or by typing the MDX query directly into the query designer.

Analysis Services data source

The process to create an Analysis Services data source is very similar to building any other data source. Most often, you select the Microsoft SQL Server Analysis Services data source type. This provider allows you to use the MDX query designer, which simplifies the process of constructing an MDX query, particularly if you're still learning the MDX query language.

Note The instructions in this chapter assume that you are using the Microsoft SQL Server Analysis Services data source type.

If you're skilled in MDX and if your report specifications require you to build a dynamic expression for the MDX query, you can use the Object Linking and Embedding Database (OLE DB) data source type instead. With this data source type, you use the Microsoft OLE DB Provider for Analysis Services 10.0. However, this type of data source does not include a graphical designer, so you must be able to prepare the MDX query without assistance.

Note Regardless of which data source type you select, you must use Windows Authentication as the credentials to connect to the data source because this is the only type of authentication supported by Analysis Services.

Tip For an example of how to use the OLE DB data source type with an MDX query in Reporting Services, see *http://blog.datainspirations.com/2010/10/09/using-dynamic-mdx-in-reporting-services-part-2/.*

MDX graphical query designer

You use the MDX query designer to develop an MDX query to retrieve data from an Analysis Services cube. In the default Design mode, you can drag items from a list of OLAP database objects into a data pane to view the results incrementally. When you create a dataset based on the Analysis Services data provider, the MDX query designer, shown in Figure 16-1, displays by default.

Note You can also use the DMX query designer to develop a Data Mining Expression (DMX) query. A DMX query retrieves data from an Analysis Services mining model. To learn more about building a DMX query, refer to *http://technet.microsoft.com/en-us/library/ms155812(v=sql.100).aspx.*

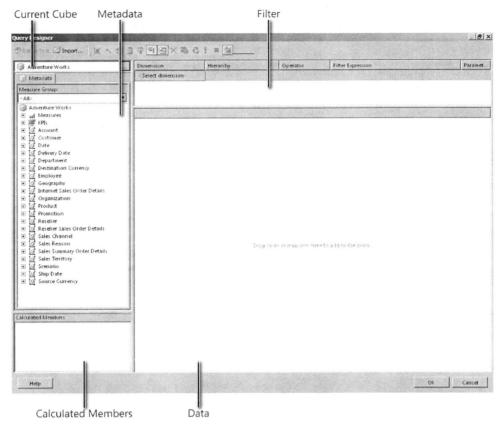

Current Cube   Metadata   Filter

Calculated Members   Data

FIGURE 16-1 You use the MDX query designer to retrieve data from an Analysis Services cube.

The query designer uses the following panes to help you construct an MDX query:

- **Current Cube**   The current cube displays in the upper-left corner of the query designer. In this example, the current cube is Adventure Works. When an Analysis Services database contains many cubes, click the button in the Current Cube pane to select a different cube.

- **Metadata**   The Metadata pane displays below the Current Cube pane on the left side of the query designer. A list of database objects displays in this pane, beginning with Measures and key performance indicators (KPIs) at the top of the list and continuing with dimensions associated with the current cube. You build a query by dragging objects from the list into the Data pane.

- **Calculated Members**   In the lower-left corner of the query designer, you find the Calculated Members pane. You can create calculations to extend the measures and dimensions available in the current cube. These calculations display in this pane. You can then drag a calculation from this pane into the Data pane to add the calculation to the query.

- **Filter**   The Filter pane displays across the top of the query designer, just below the query designer toolbar. You use the Filter pane to limit the data retrieved from the cube by the query.

- **Data**   The Data pane displays the results of the current query in the area below the Filter pane. You drag items from the Metadata pane and the Calculated Members pane into the Data pane to view the results of the query.

Metadata pane

You use items in the Metadata pane, as shown in Figure 16-2. At the top of the Metadata pane, the Measures folder contains one or more folders for measure groups. Each measure group folder contains measures, shown with a chart icon, or calculated measures, shown with a chart and calculator icon. Although measures and calculated measures differ in how the Analysis Services engine retrieves data in response to a query, you can use either type in a report query. In general, a measure is a numeric value that Analysis Services automatically aggregates based on the groupings you define in the query or in the report, such as Sales Amount. A calculated measure is a numeric value that Analysis Services computes at query time using the current context of the report.

Below the Measures folder, you find the folder containing KPIs, which are a special type of measure. Each KPI is really a collection of four measures: value, goal, status, and trend. The value is a number that represents a condition at a point in time or over a range of time periods, such as yesterday's sales or last year's sales. The goal is a target against which you compare the value. The status is a number that quantifies the progress towards the goal. It might be a percentage showing how close the value is to the goal, or it might be a flag to specify whether or not the goal is met. The trend is a number that compares the value or status at one point in time to the value or status at another point in time and reflects whether the change over time is positive.

Then the remaining folders contain dimensions. Each dimension folder contains attributes to use as groupings or detail rows in your report and hierarchies that organize attributes into a structure that allows you to move easily from summary to detail data. For reporting purposes, you can think of hierarchies as predefined groupings. If you expand the levels of an attribute or hierarchy, you can see the dimension members it contains. Dimension members become field values that display in your report.

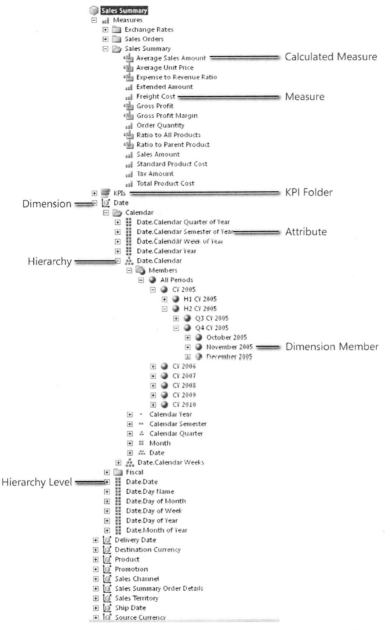

Sales Summary
- Measures
  - Exchange Rates
  - Sales Orders
  - Sales Summary
    - Average Sales Amount ══════════ Calculated Measure
    - Average Unit Price
    - Expense to Revenue Ratio
    - Extended Amount
    - Freight Cost ══════════ Measure
    - Gross Profit
    - Gross Profit Margin
    - Order Quantity
    - Ratio to All Products
    - Ratio to Parent Product
    - Sales Amount
    - Standard Product Cost
    - Tax Amount
    - Total Product Cost
- KPIs ══════════ KPI Folder

Dimension ══════ Date
- Calendar
  - Date.Calendar Quarter of Year
  - Date.Calendar Semester of Year ══════════ Attribute
  - Date.Calendar Week of Year
  - Date.Calendar Year

Hierarchy ══════ Date.Calendar
  - Members
    - All Periods
      - CY 2005
        - H1 CY 2005
        - H2 CY 2005
          - Q3 CY 2005
          - Q4 CY 2005
            - October 2005
            - November 2005 ══════════ Dimension Member
            - December 2005
      - CY 2006
      - CY 2007
      - CY 2008
      - CY 2009
      - CY 2010
    - Calendar Year
    - Calendar Semester
    - Calendar Quarter
    - Month
    - Date
  - Date.Calendar Weeks
  - Fiscal

Hierarchy Level ══════ Date.Date
  - Date.Day Name
  - Date.Day of Month
  - Date.Day of Week
  - Date.Day of Year
  - Date.Month of Year
- Delivery Date
- Destination Currency
- Product
- Promotion
- Sales Channel
- Sales Summary Order Details
- Sales Territory
- Ship Date
- Source Currency

FIGURE 16-2 The Metadata pane displays cube objects that you use to build your MDX query.

Data pane

To create a query, you drag measures, KPIs, attributes, or hierarchies from the Metadata pane to the Data pane (the area labeled Drag Levels Or Measures Here To Add To The Query). As you drag each item to the Data pane, the query automatically executes as long as you have at least one measure or KPI in the Data pane. The query results display as a table of unformatted data in the Data pane, as shown in Figure 16-3.

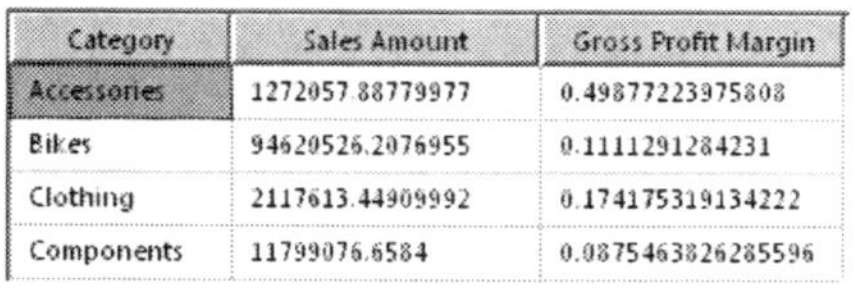

Category	Sales Amount	Gross Profit Margin
Accessories	1272057.88779977	0.49877223975808
Bikes	94620526.2076955	0.1111291284231
Clothing	2117613.44909992	0.174175319134222
Components	11799076.6584	0.0875463826285596

FIGURE 16-3 Query results display in the Data pane as you add items from the Metadata pane.

Filter pane

You can also apply a filter to the query by selecting a dimension, hierarchy, operator, and filter expression in the Filter pane above the query columns, as shown in Figure 16-4. You can drag an attribute or hierarchy from the Metadata pane to the Filter pane to begin constructing the filter, or you can use the Dimension and Hierarchy drop-down lists in the Filter pane. Then you can keep the default operator, which is Equal, or you can choose one of the other operators described in Table 16-1. Last, you use the Filter Expression drop-down list to set the expression to use for filtering. The contents of the Filter Expression drop-down list depend on the Operator selection.

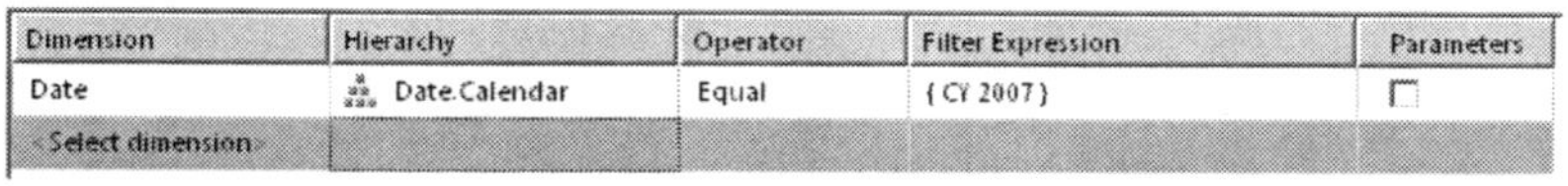

Dimension	Hierarchy	Operator	Filter Expression	Parameters
Date	Date.Calendar	Equal	{ CY 2007 }	☐
< Select dimension >				

FIGURE 16-4 You can create a filter expression to modify the query results.

In the example shown in Figure 16-4, the query results return data for calendar year 2007 only. After you create the filter, the query executes once more to apply the filter to the query results visible in the Data pane.

TABLE 16-1 Available MDX filter operators

Operator	Description	Example
Equal, Not Equal	Include or exclude the selected dimension members	{ CY 2007, CY 2008}
In, Not in	Include or exclude members that are part of a named set defined in the cube	Top 25 Selling Products
Contains, Begins With	Include members whose names contain or start with the string defined as the filter expression (that you type in the Filter Expression box without quotes)	Mountain

Operator	Description	Example
Range (inclusive)	Include members in a range between a beginning member and an ending member defined in the filter expression, and includes the beginning and ending members	Q1 CY 2007 : Q3 CY 2007
Range (exclusive)	Include members in a range between a beginning member and ending member defined as the filter expression, but excludes the beginning and ending members	Q1 CY 2007: Q4 CY 2007
MDX	Include members defined by an MDX expression	LastPeriods(12,[Date].[Calendar].[Month].&[2006]&[12])

Toolbar

The query designer also includes a toolbar, as shown in Figure 16-5, to help you as you build your MDX query.

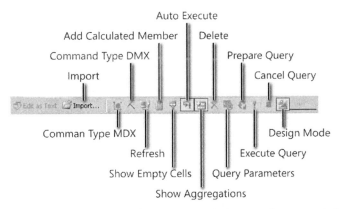

FIGURE 16-5 You can use the MDX query designer toolbar as you build a query.

The following is a description of each query designer toolbar button:

- **Import** Import an existing query from an MDX file or from another report, and then use the query designer to modify the query text.

- **Command Type MDX** Switch to the MDX query designer if the DMX query designer is currently active. The MDX query designer is initially active when you first open it, which disables this button in the toolbar.

- **Command Type DMX** Switch to the DMX query designer if the MDX query designer is currently active.

- **Refresh** Update the list of objects in the Metadata pane if changes have occurred in the data source since you opened the query designer.

- **Add Calculated Member**   Display the Calculated Member Builder dialog box, as described in the "Calculated Member Builder" section of this chapter.

- **Show Empty Cells**   Add or remove the NON EMPTY keyword in the query by using this toggle button, as shown in Figure 16-6. By default, the empty cells are hidden, which means that the NON EMPTY keyword is included, and any row for which no measure value exists is excluded from the query results.

Empty Cells Hidden

Category	Subcategory	Sales Amount	Gross Profit Margin
Accessories	Bike Racks	134868.468	0.38171582107687
Accessories	Bike Stands	18921	0.626
Accessories	Bottles and ...	27761.602100...	0.581897973388226
Accessories	Cleaners	9777.9388000...	0.439271884172574
Accessories	Fenders	19408.339999...	0.626000909918103
Accessories	Helmets	206027.19619...	0.455624938995317
Accessories	Hydration P...	58303.911899...	0.437022084276306
Accessories	Locks	6140.52	0.311438607805202
Accessories	Pumps	5145.426	0.312497915624479
Accessories	Tires and Tu...	103888.18360...	0.624483959116979

Empty Cells Visible

Category	Subcategory	Sales Amount	Gross Profit Margin
Accessories	Bike Racks	134868.468	0.38171582107687
Accessories	Bike Stands	18921	0.626
Accessories	Bottles and Cages	27761.602100...	0.581897973388226
Accessories	Cleaners	9777.9388000...	0.439271884172574
Accessories	Fenders	19408.339999...	0.626000909918103
Accessories	Helmets	206027.19619...	0.455624938995317
Accessories	Hydration Packs	58303.911899...	0.437022084276306
Accessories	Lights	(null)	(null)
Accessories	Locks	6140.52	0.311438607805202
Accessories	Panniers	(null)	(null)
Accessories	Pumps	5145.426	0.312497915624479
Accessories	Tires and Tubes	103888.18360...	0.624483959116979

FIGURE 16-6 Use the Show Empty Cells button in the toolbar to toggle between hidden and visible empty cells.

- **Auto Execute**   Switch between viewing results on demand or deferring query execution until explicitly requested. By default, Auto Execute is enabled when you open the query designer. When you disable Auto Execute, you must use the Execute Query button to update the query results after adding or removing items from the Data pane.

- **Show Aggregations**   Add or remove server aggregations in the Data pane. You learn more about this behavior in the "Show Aggregations button" section later in this chapter.

- **Delete**   Delete the currently selected column in the Data pane.

- **Query Parameters**   Display the Query Parameters dialog box when the query designer is in Query mode. For more information, see the "Designing parameters" section later in this chapter.

- **Prepare Query**   Validate the query syntax, and confirm the query completes successfully when the query designer is in Query mode.

- **Execute Query**   Run the query, and display the query results in the Data pane.

- **Cancel Query**   End a query that is currently executing.

- **Design Mode**   Switch between Query mode and Design Mode. In Design Mode, you drag objects to build the query, but in Query mode, you edit the MDX query directly.

Query mode

Because the MDX query designer automatically generates the MDX for you as you drag items from the Metadata pane into the Data pane, you are not required to know MDX before you can build a report using Analysis Services as a data source. However, if you learn MDX, you can fine-tune the query by using the Query mode of the query designer. In the MDX query designer toolbar, you can click the Design Mode button (the last button on the right side of the toolbar) to switch to Query mode to see the MDX generated by the query designer, as shown in Figure 16-7.

```
SELECT NON EMPTY { [Measures].[Gross Profit Margin], [Measures].[Sales Amount] } ON COLUMNS, NON EMPTY { ([Product].
[Category].[Category].ALLMEMBERS ) } DIMENSION PROPERTIES MEMBER_CAPTION, MEMBER_UNIQUE_NAME ON ROWS
FROM ( SELECT ( { [Date].[Calendar].[Calendar Year].&[2007] } ) ON COLUMNS FROM [Sales Summary]) WHERE ( [Date].
[Calendar].[Calendar Year].&[2007] ) CELL PROPERTIES VALUE, BACK_COLOR, FORE_COLOR, FORMATTED_VALUE,
FORMAT_STRING, FONT_NAME, FONT_SIZE, FONT_FLAGS
```

FIGURE 16-7 Switch to Query mode to see the MDX query syntax.

Toward the end of the query shown in Figure 16-7, notice that the MDX query designer automatically includes a request for cell properties that you can use to format values in the report. For example, in the sample database, both the Sales Amount and Gross Profit Margin measures have a property that defines the format string to be used by the client application when displaying the respective values. Unfortunately, the sample database does not implement the property controlling the font color based on the current value of the measure or other properties controlling the font appearance, such as bold or italics. Nonetheless, you should find out whether the cube you want to use as a source has such properties configured. Reporting Services does not automatically use these properties, but it includes them as extended field properties of the dataset as long as you include the CELL PROPERTIES clause in your query. You can then access these properties when designing the report layout, as described in the "Extended field properties" section of this chapter.

If you're comfortable with developing MDX queries, you can modify the query directly while in Query mode. However, after you make changes, you cannot switch back to Design Mode without losing any changes that you make in Query mode.

> **Important** The rule to follow when designing your own MDX queries for Reporting Services is to use only measures on the column's axis.

> **Tip** To work around the "measures only" limitation on the columns axis of an MDX query, you can create a calculated member by using the WITH clause. Create the new member as a member of the Measures dimension, and then include the new member in the set of measures defined for the columns axis in the SELECT statement.

Calculated Member Builder

If necessary, you can add calculations to the dataset if the calculation you need is not already defined in the cube. Although you can add calculations to the query in Query mode, you might find it easier to use the graphical interface in the Calculated Member Builder when the query designer is in Design mode. To open the Calculated Member Builder, click the Add Calculated Member button on the MDX Query Designer toolbar, or right-click the Calculated Members pane and select New Calculated Member.

In the Calculated Member Builder dialog box, shown in Figure 16-8, you type a name for the calculated member and assign it to a parent hierarchy. If you use a parent hierarchy other than Measures, you must also assign a parent member. Then you can type an MDX expression directly into the Expression text box, or you can use the Metadata and Functions panes to drag items into the Expression text box.

Tip You can define the formatting in your calculated member definition so that you can be consistent in using extended field properties for all values in the dataset, as shown in Figure 16-8.

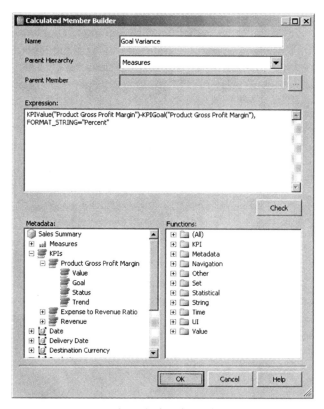

FIGURE 16-8 You use the Calculated Member Builder dialog box to construct an MDX expression for a calculated member.

Note A message box displays with a message regarding a syntax error in the calculated member if you include the *FORMAT_STRING* property. However, you can safely ignore this message. Just click OK to continue. If you later open the query designer, the message box displays again and removes the calculated member from your query. Simply drag it back again to the Data pane.

After you save the calculated member, it displays in the Calculated Members pane, as shown in Figure 16-9. You can then drag it to the Data pane to add it as a new field in your query.

FIGURE 16-9 You can drag a calculated member into the Data pane to add it to your query.

Building a report

After you have a dataset available, you are ready to build your report by arranging the dataset fields in data regions. For the most part, using fields from an Analysis Services dataset is no different from using fields from any other type of dataset. However, you'll find that there are a few notable differences when you need to format or aggregate field values, which you learn about in this section.

Analysis Services dataset fields

After creating an Analysis Services dataset, you're ready to develop the report layout. The columns returned by the MDX query are added as fields to the dataset, and you can use these fields in a data region in the same way that you learned to work with dataset fields in previous chapters. Like dataset fields from other data sources, the numeric fields are currently not formatted when you preview the report, as shown in Figure 16-10, even though these fields have formatting properties defined in the Analysis Service cube. Rather than use the format techniques you learned in Chapter 9, "Designing the report layout," you can use the extended field properties to apply the format properties defined in the Analysis Services cube, which we describe in the next section.

Category	Sales Amount	Gross Profit Margin	Goal Variance
Accessories	590242.586599887	0.480604538608472	0.0806045386084715
Bikes	34910877.6903989	0.0873928975592033	-0.0326071024407967
Clothing	1010112.15659997	0.15305987388601	-0.04694012611399
Components	5482497.28929999	0.075682978778629	-0.024317021221371
	41993729.7228988	0.796740288832314	-0.0232597111676862

FIGURE 16-10 Numeric fields are not automatically formatted in a data region.

Extended field properties

The cube developer can configure format strings for each numeric value in the cube. That way, you don't have to take the time to format these values when you display them in the report. When you include the CELL PROPERTIES clause in your MDX query, which Reporting Services adds automatically when you use the MDX query designer in Design mode, and include *FORMATTED_VALUE* as one of the cell properties to retrieve as part of the query, you can change the text box expression to use the *FormattedValue* extended property of the field, as shown in Figure 16-11.

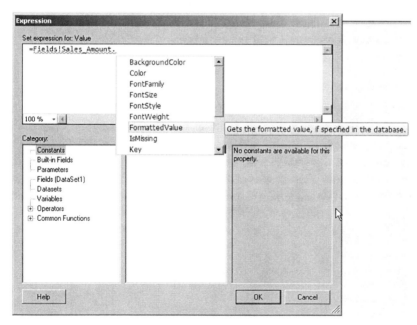

FIGURE 16-11 You can use the IntelliSense feature in the Expression dialog box to access a field's extended properties.

> **Important** When you use an aggregate function like *Sum*, you cannot use the *FormattedValue* property for a text box because this property returns a string value whereas the *Sum* function requires a numeric value. Therefore, whenever you use one of the aggregate functions, you must use the *Format* property for the text box to apply the desired formatting rather than use the *FormattedValue* extended property.

The developer of an Analysis Services cube can also define conditional formatting for calculations to set the font color, background color, font name, font size, and font flags to specify text decorations such as bold or underline. You can then use extended field properties to access these settings and configure text box properties, such as *Color* or *BackgroundColor,* using extended field properties having the same name.

For example, imagine that the Gross Profit Margin was defined in the cube to display the value by using a red font whenever the value falls below a specified threshold and by using a green font whenever the value falls above a different specified threshold. If that were the case, you could then use the definition stored in the cube to set the proper color of the value in your report by updating the *Color* property of a text box to the following expression:

```
=Fields!Gross_Profit_Margin.Color
```

> **Important** You must include the relevant properties in the CELL PROPERTIES clause of the MDX query to use extended field properties.

Aggregate function

When you add a total row to a table or matrix, the report designer uses the *Sum* function by default. However, if you look carefully, you will notice that the totals for some measures might not be correct. For example, as shown in Figure 16-12, the total rows for percentage values are incorrect when Reporting Services sums individual rows in the dataset. In this example, values for Gross Profit Margin and for Goal Variance are *nonadditive*. A nonadditive value cannot be summed because it is derived from a multiplication or division of other values that must be summed before the multiplication or division is performed, such as a ratio or percentage value. The cube can provide the correct percentage values for all product categories if you use the *Aggregate* function instead of the *Sum* function.

Category	Sales Amount	Gross Profit Margin	Goal Variance
Accessories	$590,242.59	48.06%	8.06%
Bikes	$34,910,877.89	0.74%	3.26%
Clothing	$1,010,112.16	15.31%	-4.69%
Components	$5,482,497.29	7.57%	-2.43%
	$41,993,729.72	79.67 %	-2.33 %

FIGURE 16-12 Use of the *Sum* function in a total row for nonadditive measures like Gross Profit Margin or Goal Variance produces incorrect results.

When you use a client application, such as Microsoft Excel, to retrieve nonadditive measures from a cube, the Analysis Services engine returns the correct aggregation because it knows to sum the constituent components of the measure before performing the calculation defined for the measure. In the case of Gross Profit Margin, the constituent components are Sales Amount and Total Product Cost. When you use Reporting Services, the MDX query returns the correctly aggregated value for each row in the results, but you might then design your report layout to include a total of these rows. To ensure that you get the proper results in the total row, you must replace the *Sum* function with the *Aggregate* function to instruct Reporting Services to retrieve the server aggregate instead of performing the calculation, as shown in Figure 16-13.

Category	Sales Amount	Gross Profit Margin	Goal Variance
Accessories	$590,242.59	48.06%	8.06%
Bikes	$34,910,877.69	8.74%	-3.26%
Clothing	$1,010,112.16	15.31%	-4.69%
Components	$5,482,497.29	7.57%	-2.43%
	$41,993,729.72	9.30 %	-2.70 %

FIGURE 16-13 Use of the *Aggregate* function produces correct results for nonadditive measures.

Aggregate values in detail rows

If you are able to write complex MDX queries in Query mode, you might want to use a dataset query that includes both detail and aggregate rows. One reason you might do this is to display different levels of aggregated data, as shown in Figure 16-14, in which the Bikes category values break down into subcategories but other categories do not. In this example, the rows in which the Subcategory column displays a null value are aggregate rows. For example, the first row is the total for all subcategories associated with the Accessories category.

Category	Subcategory	Sales Amount	Gross Profit Margin	Total Product Cost
Accessories	(null)	1272057.88779977	0.4987722397530B	637590.725999948
Bikes	Mountain Bi...	36445443.9409015	0.162788966193453	30512527.7993007
Bikes	Road Bikes	43878790.9970001	0.0994763678265337	39513888.2439989
Bikes	Touring Bikes	14296291.2698	0.0151981873969584	14079013.5560001
Clothing	(null)	2117613.44909992	0.174175319134222	1748777.45080002
Components	(null)	11799076.6584	0.0875463826285596	10766110.1786

FIGURE 16-14 You can develop a query that combines detail and aggregate rows in Query mode.

When you preview the report, you might find that the data region ignores the aggregate rows in the dataset. Only the rows having a value that is not null at the lowest level of detail display, as shown in Figure 16-15. Furthermore, an expression using the *Aggregate* function does not display results, as you can see in the Gross Profit Margin column.

Category	Subcategory	Sales Amount	Gross Profit Margin
Bikes	Mountain Bikes	$36,445,443.94	16.28%
	Road Bikes	$43,878,791.00	9.95%
	Touring Bikes	$14,296,291.27	1.52%
		$94,620,526.21	

FIGURE 16-15 Sometimes aggregate rows do not display with detail rows in a data region.

Fortunately, you can override this behavior that omits the aggregate rows by changing an option in the Dataset Properties dialog box. On the Options page, you can change the Interpret Subtotals As Detail Rows value to *True*. When the Interpret Subtotals As Detail Rows value is *Auto*, Reporting Services checks to see whether subtotal rows and detail rows are in the query results and adjusts the report display to include the subtotal rows. However, the structure of some query results causes subtotal rows to be ignored, as you see in Figure 16-15. By changing the value to *True*, Reporting Services instead includes the subtotal rows and ignores only the *Aggregate* function instead, as shown in Figure 16-16.

Category	Subcategory	Sales Amount	Gross Profit Margin
Accessories		$1,272,057.89	49.88%
Bikes	Mountain Bikes	$36,445,443.94	16.28%
	Road Bikes	$43,878,791.00	9.95%
	Touring Bikes	$14,296,291.27	1.52%
Clothing		$2,117,010.45	17.42%
Components		$11,799,076.66	8.75%
		$109,809,274.20	

FIGURE 16-16 You see aggregate rows after you set Interpret Subtotals As Details Rows to *True*.

To get the correct aggregate value in the total row, you could create an expression that sums the constituent components of the calculation first and then calculates the percentage. That is, you could construct the following expression:

```
=(Sum(Fields!Reseller_Sales_Amount.Value) - Sum(Fields!Reseller_Total_Product_Cost.Value))/
Sum(Fields!Reseller_Sales_Amount.Value)
```

Another option is to eliminate the total row in the data region and include the total row values in the query results, as shown in Figure 16-17. One benefit of this approach is that you maintain the logic for the calculation in the cube rather than in the report. Another benefit is the simplification of report development because you can use the *FormattedValue* property in all text boxes rather than in detail rows only.

Category	Subcategory	Sales Amount	Gross Profit Margin	Total Product Cost	CategoryName	SortOrder
Accessories	(null)	1272057.88779977	0.49877223975808	637590.725999948	Accessories	Accessories
Bikes	Mountain Bikes	36445443.9409015	0.162788966193453	30512527.7993007	Bikes	Bikes
Bikes	Road Bikes	43878790.9970001	0.0994763678265337	39513388.2439589	Bikes	Bikes
Bikes	Touring Bikes	14296291.2698	0.0151981873969584	14079013.5560001	Bikes	Bikes
Clothing	(null)	2117613.44909992	0.174175319134222	1748777.45080002	Clothing	Clothing
Components	(null)	11799076.6584	0.0875463826285596	10766110.1786	Components	Components
(null)	(null)	109809274.203	0.11430151359617	97257907.9547001	All Products	Z

FIGURE 16-17 You can modify the query to include values to display as totals on a separate detail row in a data region.

When you modify your query to include a row to display totals, you should also add a calculated member to display a label for each row because the query returns a null value in the column that you normally display. You might also need to add a calculated member to control sort order. After you change your query, you replace the old label field with the new label field and update the sort order of row groups to use the new sort field. Your report then displays all values correctly in the correct sequence, as shown in Figure 16-18, with the last row containing All Products as the grand total row.

Category	Subcategory	Sales Amount	Gross Profit Margin
Accessories		$1,272,057.89	49.88%
Bikes	Mountain Bikes	$36,445,443.94	16.28%
	Road Bikes	$43,878,791.00	9.95%
	Touring Bikes	$14,296,291.27	1.52%
Clothing		$2,117,613.45	17.42%
Components		$11,799,076.66	8.75%
All Products		$109,809,274.20	11.43%

FIGURE 16-18 A data region can display a grand total row as a detail row when the dataset query includes a row containing grand total values.

Show Aggregations button

The Show Aggregations button on the MDX query designer toolbar sometimes doesn't appear to do anything. You use this button to modify your MDX query to include aggregate values in the results. However, it works only under certain conditions.

Before we explain when you might use the Show Aggregations button, let's review aggregations in general. As we explained in the "*Aggregate* function" section, you cannot use the *Sum* function when working with certain types of measures. Specifically, the *Sum* function returns incorrect values for nonadditive measures (described in the "*Aggregate* function" section) and *semi-additive measures*. Examples of semi-additive measures include inventory counts or general ledger balances, both of which sum correctly across products or accounts, respectively, but not across time. That is, you cannot add the inventory available on the last day of January to the inventory available on the last day of February (and any days in between if you track inventory more frequently) to determine your total inventory for March 1.

In both cases, you can obtain the correct answer only by using server aggregations. After all, one of the key reasons to use a cube is to compute aggregated values correctly no matter what type of measure it is—additive, semi-additive, or nonadditive.

In the MDX query designer, you use the Show Aggregations button to see the server aggregates that are available to the report, but you will not see these aggregates in the MDX query designer until you add the dataset to a data region and add a grouping to that data region. If you look at the dataset at this point by opening the MDX query designer in Query mode, its query looks similar to the following query:

```
SELECT
NON EMPTY { [Measures].[Sales Amount], [Measures].[Gross Profit Margin] } ON COLUMNS,
NON EMPTY { ([Product].[Category].[Category].ALLMEMBERS ) }
DIMENSION PROPERTIES MEMBER_CAPTION, MEMBER_UNIQUE_NAME ON ROWS
FROM [Adventure Works]
CELL PROPERTIES VALUE, BACK_COLOR, FORE_COLOR, FORMATTED_VALUE, FORMAT_STRING, FONT_NAME,
FONT_SIZE, FONT_FLAGS
```

This query returns values for members of the Category level of the Category dimension. That is, the All member for each dimension is excluded from the query and no server aggregations are returned.

The addition of a group alone to the data region is not enough to trigger the display of the aggregates in the query designer. You must include the *Aggregate* function on at least one group or tablix header or footer row. After you add an expression with this function, you can open the MDX query designer and click the Show Aggregates button to see another row appear in the Data pane to hold the aggregate values, as shown in Figure 16-19.

Category	Sales Amount	Gross Profit Margin
(null)	109809274.203	0.11430151359617
Accessories	1272057.887799...	0.49877223975808
Bikes	94620526.20769...	0.1111291284231
Clothing	2117613.449099...	0.174175319134222
Components	11799076.6584	0.0875463826285596

FIGURE 16-19 The Show Aggregations button displays an aggregate row in the Data pane if the dataset is in a data region that includes a text box containing the *Aggregate* function in its expression.

The null value in the query results represents the All member for the Category attribute. If you switch to the Query mode, you can see that the MDX query now looks like this:

```
SELECT
NON EMPTY { [Measures].[Sales Amount], [Measures].[Gross Profit Margin] } ON COLUMNS,
NON EMPTY {{[Product].[Category].[All Products]}, ([Product].[Category].[Category].ALLMEMBERS )
}
DIMENSION PROPERTIES MEMBER_CAPTION, MEMBER_UNIQUE_NAME ON ROWS
FROM [Adventure Works]
CELL PROPERTIES VALUE, BACK_COLOR, FORE_COLOR, FORMATTED_VALUE, FORMAT_STRING, FONT_NAME,
FONT_SIZE, FONT_FLAGS
```

The query now explicitly includes the All member for the attribute that you use in the grouping of the table. You don't need to follow these steps to get the query right in the dataset before you deploy the report. Reporting Services creates the correct query when the tablix contains a grouping and the *Aggregate* function. However, as the report developer, you might want to see the query generated to retrieve server aggregates and make modifications to the query to suit your specific needs.

Designing parameters

Working with linked report parameters and query parameters when using an Analysis Services dataset is quite different from the process described in Chapter 14, "Creating dynamic reports with parameters," to set up linked parameters for a relational dataset. If you use dimension members from the Analysis Services cube to populate a list of available values for a report parameter, the process to create and configure the report parameter is quite easy. However, you're not limited to creating report parameters that are based on a cube. In this section, you learn how to work with both types of report parameters to filter a dataset and how to customize a query parameter linked to a report parameter.

Auto-generated query and report parameters

Chapter 14 describes how to create a report parameter by using a dataset to provide the list of available values and how to link a report parameter to a query parameter. When you use an Analysis Services data source, these steps are simplified. You need only to define the dimension on which the filter is based, specify a default value, and indicate that you want to create a parameter. The rest of the work required to build the report parameter and the query parameter is done for you.

Filter pane

To create both a report parameter and a query parameter when working with the MDX query designer in Design mode, add a filter to the Filter pane. Then select the Parameters check box to the right of the Filter Expression column, as shown in Figure 16-20.

Dimension	Hierarchy	Operator	Filter Expression	Parameters
Date	Date.Calendar	Equal	{ CY 2007 }	☑
<Select dimension>				

FIGURE 16-20 Select the Parameters check box in the Filter Pane of the MDX query designer to create a report parameter and query parameter In one step.

Report parameter

When you close the MDX query designer, a new parameter appears in the Report Data pane. If you open the Report Parameter Properties dialog box, you can see that its data type is Text and the option to allow multiple values is enabled, as shown in Figure 16-21.

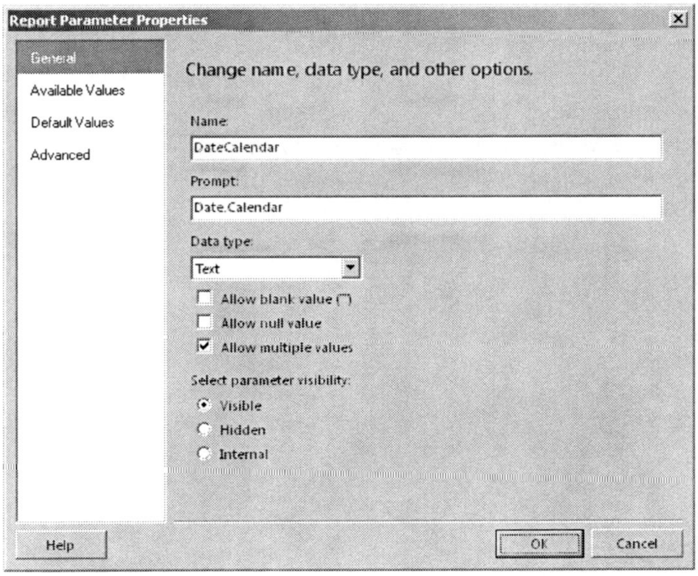

FIGURE 16-21 The automatically generated report parameter has a Text data type and allows multiple values.

The report parameter gets its list of available values from a new dataset, as shown in Figure 16-22. This new dataset is created automatically for you. It includes a value field used to filter the query results in the dataset and a label field used to display the available choices to the user.

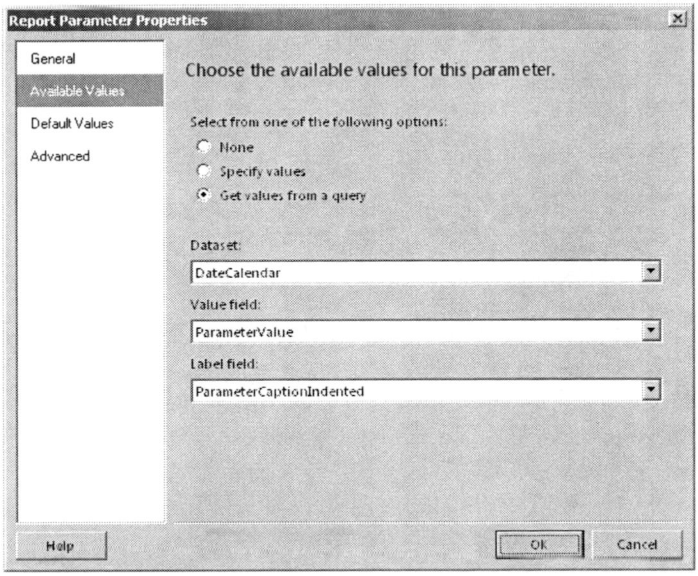

FIGURE 16-22 The report parameter uses an automatically generated dataset for its available values.

The default value defined for the report parameter is the same value you selected in the query designer, although the format of the value is not the same. When you supply a default value for a report parameter that is linked to an Analysis Services dataset, you must provide the unique name of a dimension member. The unique name includes the dimension, hierarchy, and member names. The key name can be used in place of the member name and is often preferred because the key doesn't usually change, whereas the member name might. In the current scenario, the label CY 2007 corresponds to the unique name [Date].[Calendar].[Calendar Year].&[2007] in the AdventureWorks cube.

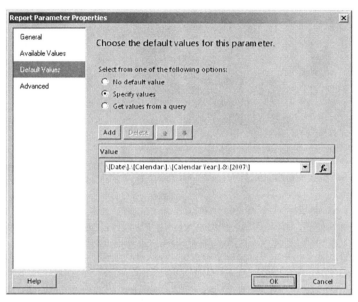

FIGURE 16-23 The value set for the Filter Expression in the dataset becomes the default value for the report parameter.

Reporting Services automatically includes a backslash (\) as an escape character in front of each bracket in the member name. However, in the expression editor for this value, the escape characters are not present. If you manually set the value, you can safely omit the escape characters.

Available values dataset

You might not see the dataset for the report parameter's available values in the Report Data pane because it is hidden by default. You can find it by right-clicking anywhere in the Report Data pane and then clicking Show All Hidden Datasets. When the dataset is visible, you can double-click it to open the Dataset Properties dialog box, and then click Query Designer to see the MDX generated by the query designer. An example of a dataset query for calendar years in the AdventureWorks cube looks like this:

```
WITH
MEMBER [Measures].[ParameterCaption] AS [Date].[Calendar].CURRENTMEMBER.MEMBER_CAPTION
MEMBER [Measures].[ParameterValue] AS [Date].[Calendar].CURRENTMEMBER.UNIQUENAME
MEMBER [Measures].[ParameterLevel] AS [Date].[Calendar].CURRENTMEMBER.LEVEL.ORDINAL
SELECT
```

```
{[Measures].[ParameterCaption], [Measures].[ParameterValue], [Measures].[ParameterLevel]}
ON COLUMNS ,
[Date].[Calendar].ALLMEMBERS ON ROWS
FROM [Sales Summary]
```

Notice that the fields used in the report parameter, *ParameterCaptionIndented* and *ParameterValue*, are defined in this query as calculations in the Measures dimension, even though these values are not the numeric values that are normally found in the Measures dimension. Nonetheless, to create the proper query structure, which requires you to use only measures on the columns axis, you can create calculations that evaluate as string values and assign the result to a new member in the Measures dimension as shown in the previous query. You can execute the query in the MDX query designer to see the data it returns, as shown in Figure 16-24.

Calendar Year	Calendar Semest...	Calendar Quarter	Month	Date	ParameterCaption	ParameterValue	ParameterLevel
(null)	(null)	(null)	(null)	(null)	All Periods	[Date].[Calendar].[All Periods]	0
CY 2005	(null)	(null)	(null)	(null)	CY 2005	[Date].[Calendar].[Calendar Year].&[2005]	1
CY 2005	H1 CY 2005	(null)	(null)	(null)	H1 CY 2005	[Date].[Calendar].[Calendar Semester].&[2005]&[1]	2
CY 2005	H1 CY 2005	Q1 CY 2005	(null)	(null)	Q1 CY 2005	[Date].[Calendar].[Calendar Quarter].&[2005]&[1]	3
CY 2005	H1 CY 2005	Q1 CY 2005	January 2005	(null)	January 2005	[Date].[Calendar].[Month].&[2005]&[1]	4
CY 2005	H1 CY 2005	Q1 CY 2005	January 2005	January 1, 2005	January 1, 2005	[Date].[Calendar].[Date].&[20050101]	5
CY 2005	H1 CY 2005	Q1 CY 2005	January 2005	January 2, 2005	January 2, 2005	[Date].[Calendar].[Date].&[20050102]	5
CY 2005	H1 CY 2005	Q1 CY 2005	January 2005	January 3, 2005	January 3, 2005	[Date].[Calendar].[Date].&[20050103]	5
CY 2005	H1 CY 2005	Q1 CY 2005	January 2005	January 4, 2005	January 4, 2005	[Date].[Calendar].[Date].&[20050104]	5
CY 2005	H1 CY 2005	Q1 CY 2005	January 2005	January 5, 2005	January 5, 2005	[Date].[Calendar].[Date].&[20050105]	5
CY 2005	H1 CY 2005	Q1 CY 2005	January 2005	January 6, 2005	January 6, 2005	[Date].[Calendar].[Date].&[20050106]	5
CY 2005	H1 CY 2005	Q1 CY 2005	January 2005	January 7, 2005	January 7, 2005	[Date].[Calendar].[Date].&[20050107]	5
CY 2005	H1 CY 2005	Q1 CY 2005	January 2005	January 8, 2005	January 8, 2005	[Date].[Calendar].[Date].&[20050108]	5
CY 2005	H1 CY 2005	Q1 CY 2005	January 2005	January 9, 2005	January 9, 2005	[Date].[Calendar].[Date].&[20050109]	5
CY 2005	H1 CY 2005	Q1 CY 2005	January 2005	January 10, 2005	January 10, 2005	[Date].[Calendar].[Date].&[20050110]	5
CY 2005	H1 CY 2005	Q1 CY 2005	January 2005	January 11, 2005	January 11, 2005	[Date].[Calendar].[Date].&[20050111]	5
CY 2005	H1 CY 2005	Q1 CY 2005	January 2005	January 12, 2005	January 12, 2005	[Date].[Calendar].[Date].&[20050112]	5

FIGURE 16-24 The dataset query for available values of a report parameter includes columns to use as values and labels.

Notice that the query also includes a *ParameterLevel* field, which is used to determine how many spaces to include as a prefix when displaying the list of available values in the parameter drop-down list. The use of spaces in the list of available values helps the user easily identify the hierarchical relationship between items in the list when multiple levels of a hierarchy are included in the list.

Calculated field

On the Fields page of the Dataset Properties dialog box, you can see the *ParameterCaptionIndented* field, which does not come from the dataset query but is a calculated field. The report parameter uses this field as the label for available values instead of the *ParameterCaption* field. The value for the *ParameterCaptionIndented* field is a concatenation of a dynamic number of spaces based on the *ParameterLevel* field and the *ParameterCaption* field. The expression for this calculated field looks like this:

```
=Space(3*Fields!ParameterLevel.Value) + Fields!ParameterCaption.Value
```

When the available values list contains values from multiple levels of a hierarchy, such as date, the spaces added to the caption help you better see the hierarchical relationship of date members, as shown in Figure 16-25.

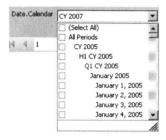

FIGURE 16-25 The labels displaying as a report parameter's available values include spaces to emphasize the hierarchical relationship of the date members.

Parameterized dataset

If you switch to Query mode in the MDX query designer, you can see the parameterized MDX query that Reporting Services generates automatically. The parameter appears both in a subselect statement in the FROM clause and in the WHERE clause, as shown here:

```
SELECT
NON EMPTY
{ [Measures].[Gross Profit Margin], [Measures].[Sales Amount] } ON COLUMNS,
NON EMPTY
{{[Product].[Category].[All Products]}, ([Product].[Category].[Category].ALLMEMBERS ) }
DIMENSION PROPERTIES MEMBER_CAPTION, MEMBER_UNIQUE_NAME ON ROWS
FROM
( SELECT ( STRTOSET(@DateCalendar, CONSTRAINED) ) ON COLUMNS FROM [Adventure Works])
WHERE
( IIF( STRTOSET(@DateCalendar, CONSTRAINED).Count = 1,
STRTOSET(@DateCalendar, CONSTRAINED),
[Date].[Calendar].currentmember ) )
CELL PROPERTIES VALUE, BACK_COLOR, FORE_COLOR, FORMATTED_VALUE, FORMAT_STRING, FONT_NAME,
FONT_SIZE, FONT_FLAGS
```

In both references to the query parameter, the *StrToSet* function converts the string value that the report parameter sends to the query parameter into a set that the MDX statement requires. The *CONSTRAINED* argument is optional, but it requires the query parameter value to correspond to an existing member of the dimension as a precaution against an MDX injection attack.

Note The use of a subselect statement in the FROM clause can be a useful way to optimize the performance of an MDX query. However, if the query includes a calculated measure that must evaluate across a large number of cells, it is possible that the subselect causes a performance problem for your report because it prevents Analysis Services from caching the calculation. In that case, if possible, you should rewrite the query to include the parameter in the ON ROWS portion of the query.

Tip If you create two parameters using two attributes that have a hierarchical relationship in the cube, Reporting Services automatically creates them as cascading parameters, as described in Chapter 14. The WHERE clause of the query for the child query parameter includes a subselect statement in the FROM clause that references the parent query parameter.

Custom query parameter

The Parameter check box in the Filter pane makes it easy to create a report parameter and linked query parameter, but you might have a situation in which you create a report parameter independently of the Analysis Services dataset. For example, when you require a report parameter that allows the user to select a specific day, you can use a calendar control instead of requiring the user to scroll through a list of date labels from the cube. However, when a date is selected by the user, the calendar control returns a string value that cannot be used in the MDX query as a query parameter value. You must convert the date string to the unique name of the date as it is represented in the Analysis Services cube, and then you can use the converted value as a filter on the dataset.

Query parameter

To create a custom query parameter, you start by opening the MDX query designer to display your dataset, switching to Query mode if the query designer is currently in Design mode. Then you click the Query Parameters button on the toolbar. As shown in Figure 16-26, you type a name for the parameter and specify a dimension and hierarchy. However, you do not want to allow the query parameter to accept multiple values. Although you use the report parameter to set the default value for the report, you must choose a default value from the Default drop-down list. Otherwise, you cannot save the query parameter. The calendar control does not use the default value that you set here because it cannot translate a date member name from a cube to the date format it requires.

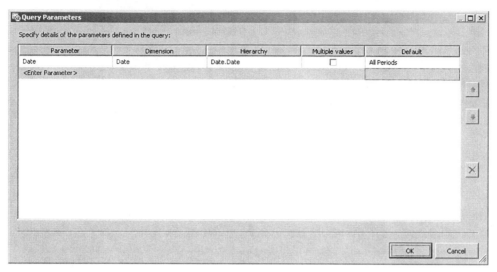

FIGURE 16-26 You can manually create a query parameter in Query mode by using the Query Parameters dialog box.

MDX query parameterization

Next you must manually update your query to reference the query parameter. You can use the query parameter in the WITH clause as a calculation, in the SELECT statement as a set or member expression, or in the WHERE clause as a partial tuple definition. If your report parameter allows only a single selection, as the calendar control does, you can use the *StrToMember* function in your query like this:

```
SELECT
NON EMPTY {[Measures].[Gross Profit Margin], [Measures].[Sales Amount]} ON COLUMNS,
NON EMPTY {{[Product].[Category].[All Products]}, ([Product].[Category].[Category].ALLMEMBERS)}
DIMENSION PROPERTIES MEMBER_CAPTION, MEMBER_UNIQUE_NAME
ON ROWS
FROM [Adventure Works]
WHERE
(STRTOMEMBER(@Date, CONSTRAINED))
CELL PROPERTIES VALUE, BACK_COLOR, FORE_COLOR, FORMATTED_VALUE, FORMAT_STRING, FONT_NAME,
FONT_SIZE, FONT_FLAGS
```

Query parameter value

In most cases, you map the report parameter directly to the query parameter on the Parameters page of the Dataset Properties dialog box. When you use a calendar control to get data for the report parameter, you must convert the report parameter value to a properly structured member unique name that you can use in the MDX query. For example, in the Adventure Works cube, the unique name for the first day of February 2007 is [Date].[Calendar].[Date].[February 1, 2007]. To convert the parameter value from the calendar control, which is in date/time format, to a string matching this unique name, you use an expression like this:

```
="[Date].[Calendar].[Date].[" + Format(CDate(Parameters!Date.Value), "MMMM d, yyyy") + "]"
```

Important Be sure to use *MMMM* instead of *mmmm* in the expression when you need to convert the month number to the full month name.

Report parameter

When you close the Dataset Properties dialog box, Reporting Services creates the new report parameter. You can then modify it to set the data type. To use a calendar control with the new report parameter, you must select Date/Time in the Data Type drop-down list.

When you create a new parameter in the Query Parameters dialog box, a new dataset is created automatically to supply the list of available values for the report parameter. However, when you use a calendar control, you must disable this list. On the Available Values page of the Dataset Properties dialog box, select None.

You can also set a default value if you like. A common default value to use is a dynamic expression such as =*Today()*, to allow the report to execute without forcing the user to make a date selection. Another option is to use the No Default Value option for this report parameter.

Calendar control

You can test the calendar control when you preview the report. Click the calendar icon to the right of the Date parameter box, and then choose a date. You can change the year by clicking the year in the calendar control and then clicking the left or right arrow to decrease or increase the year value. Then you can pick a month, and then pick a day, as shown in Figure 16-27.

FIGURE 16-27 You can use a calendar control to accept date values as a report parameter and then use an expression to convert the date into a member name.

PART III

Adding data visualizations

Reporting Services includes a wide variety of options for displaying information as a data visualization, as you learn in the chapters of Part III. We begin by describing how to work with chart controls and how to apply basic formatting to charts in Chapter 17, "Creating charts." Then we delve into more advanced chart layout options by exploring properties for controlling the color palette, vertical and horizontal axes, series, and pie slices in Chapter 18, "Working with chart elements."

A key performance indicator is a special type of data visualization that you can add to a report to monitor progress to goals. In Chapter 19, "Comparing values to goals with gauges," we show you the many options available for using a gauge as a key performance indicator. Next, in Chapter 20, "Displaying performance with indicators," we introduce the new indicator report item and explain how to configure and customize indicators.

Reporting Services also allows you to create spatial data visualizations. In Chapter 21, "Mapping data," you learn about working with spatial data in general and how to use the map wizard to create a map. Chapter 22, "Working with map elements," shows you how to fine-tune the appearance of a map by configuring properties for the map and adding multiple layers to a map.

CHAPTER 17

Creating charts

U sers can often gain better insights into data when visualization methods are used to display summarized data. With Reporting Services, you can choose from many different types of charts and gauges to provide rich data visualization. In this chapter, you learn about the basic chart types available to you, as well as how to configure chart elements.

Adding a chart to a report

Charts are a great way to summarize numerical information. If you apply good chart design principles, users can easily compare values, spot trends, and identify anomalies. You can create a report that contains only a chart, or you can combine a chart with other data regions to present data in multiple formats. You can even insert a chart inside a table, matrix, or list to repeat a chart within a data region. Reporting Services provides amazing flexibility in chart design.

Selecting a chart type

You add a chart to a report just as you add a table or matrix—by dragging the control from the Toolbox to the report design surface. You can also embed charts inside a tablix by dragging the chart control to the text box in the tablix where you want the chart to appear. Note that if you do this, the chart will repeat as the text box in the tablix repeats on rows and columns, so proper formatting is important to consider.

After dragging the chart control to the report design surface, the Select Chart Type dialog box appears, as shown in Figure 17-1. The chart displays in your report after you make your selection. If you later change your mind about what chart type you want, right-click the chart, select Change Chart Type to reopen the Select Chart Type dialog box, and then make a new selection.

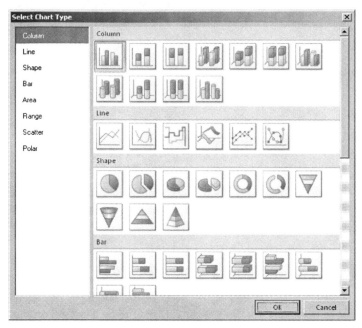

FIGURE 17-1 You must select a chart type before you can add a chart to your report.

Understanding chart types

The chart type determines how the numerical data displays in the report. A preview of each chart type appears in the Select Chart Type dialog box to help you match a chart type to your report specifications. When selecting a chart type, you should consider which chart types are best suited for the type of data you plan to show in the chart.

Linear data

Most charts that you use in business reporting display linear data using a coordinate system along an x-axis and y-axis. The following available chart types are used to display linear data:

- **Column chart**   The column chart is arguably one of the more common chart types that you'll use in your reports. Each series in the chart displays as a set of vertical bars. Use this chart type when you want to compare values in multiple series.

- **Line chart**   A line chart is also commonly used in business reports. A line represents the set of data points in a series, with the categories on the x-axis determining the relative position of data points horizontally. Often, time periods are used as categories in a line chart. If a category has an empty point in a series, Reporting Services adds a placeholder line, but you can disable this behavior, as we explain in Chapter 18, "Working with chart elements." You can combine a line chart with a column chart but not with other chart types. You can create a sparkline chart by removing all axis titles, axis labels, and the legend from the chart. (A sparkline chart, popularized by Edward Tufte, is a small condensed line chart that is presented inline and intended to show trends and variation rather than precise details.) As of the release of Reporting Services 2008 R2, sparklines are also available as a distinct report element, which we explain in more detail later in this chapter.

- **Bar chart**   A bar chart is similar to a column chart because it displays each series as a set of bars. However, the bar chart displays bars horizontally. In effect, the vertical axis becomes the category axis and the horizontal axis becomes the value axis. This type of chart is useful when the category labels are too long to read easily in a column chart format.

- **Area chart**   The area chart displays the data points in each series as a connected line and fills in the area between the line and the axis. You can also use a variation called the 100% stacked area chart to show how each series contributes to the total of the dataset. You typically use the area chart type to display data for a continuous period of time as categories. If your data has empty data points, you should avoid using this chart type.

- **Scatter chart**   A scatter chart displays numerical data as a set of points. Each category displays as a different marker on the chart. This type of chart is good for comparing thousands of data points across categories. You shouldn't add series groupings to the chart because the chart then becomes too visually complex. When used properly, this type of chart allows you to see value distributions and clusters in your data more easily.

Ratio data

When you want to compare values for individual categories to the value for all categories, you should choose a chart type designed to display ratio data. The available types are as follows:

- **Pie chart and doughnut chart**   The pie chart and the doughnut chart are shape charts that show data as a proportion of the whole to facilitate comparisons between categories. Reporting Services calculates each category value as a percentage of the total and sizes the category segment in the shape proportionally. You simply provide the raw data in your dataset.

> **Tip** In general, you should use no more than seven categories when using the pie chart and doughnut chart types because too many categories make the chart difficult to read. Null, negative, or zero values in your dataset are excluded from the chart.

- **Funnel chart and pyramid chart**   The funnel chart and the pyramid chart are another variation of shape charts that also display each category as a percentage of whole, but Reporting Services orders categories in the shape from largest to smallest. For best results, you should sort your dataset and, as with the other shape charts, use seven or fewer categories.

- **Polar chart**   The polar chart displays each series as a set of points grouped by category in a 360-degree circle. Higher values are farther from the center of the chart than lower values. Categories display along the perimeter of the chart. A variation of the polar chart is the radar chart, which shows series data as a circular line or a filled area. The radar chart is useful for comparing multiple categories of data, while a polar chart is best for graphing data coordinates consisting of angle and distance values.

- **Scatter chart** A scatter chart can also display ratio data as a set of points and is not restricted to linear data. You must provide the ratio values in the dataset.

Multivalue data

You can display multiple data points for each category and series combination in the chart by using the following chart types designed for multivalue data:

- **Range chart** A range chart must have a high and a low value for each category. The chart fills in the area between the two values for each data point. In addition to using this chart type to plot minimum and maximum values in a dataset by category, you can also use it to create a Gantt chart for tracking start and finish dates for a schedule.

- **Stock chart** A stock chart plots up to four values for each data point. For example, financial stock data has a high, low, open, and close value for each point in time.

Using the chart data pane

After you add a chart to your report design area, you click the chart to display the Chart Data pane, as shown in Figure 17-2. To define the chart layout, you add fields from your dataset to the Values, Category Groups, and Series Groups sections of the Chart Data pane.

> **Tip** If your dataset contains no rows of data, you can use the *NoDataMessage* property for the chart to display a message. However, if your dataset contains rows of data but has no values for the fields you add to the chart, Reporting Services renders an empty chart and ignores the *NoDataMessage* property.

FIGURE 17-2 You use the Chart Data pane to add dataset fields to the chart layout.

Values

As with a matrix, numeric values are aggregated automatically with an expression that uses the *Sum* function, but you can change the expression to use a different function. You can also use a non-numeric field in the Values section, in which case the *Count* function is applied. You can think of a chart as behaving very much like a matrix. Categories are like columns in the matrix, and series are like matrix rows.

Field selection

To add a value to your chart, drag a field from the Report Data pane to the Values area of the Chart Data pane. You can also click the plus sign above the Values drop zone to select a field from the dataset or create an expression. Regardless of how you add a value, the Chart Data pane displays two rows for it in the Values section of the Chart Data pane, as shown in Figure 17-3. The first row is the name of the series, and the second row is the expression defining the value to display in the chart.

FIGURE 17-3 The series name and series value expression.

You can add multiple values to a chart. If you do this, you might want to change the order in which they appear in the chart, which also changes the order that they are listed in the chart legend. To rearrange values within the list, select one of the values, and then use the up or down arrows in the Chart Data pane toolbar.

To delete a value, select it in the Chart Data pane and click the Delete button in the Chart Data pane toolbar. As an alternative, you can right-click the value in the Chart Data pane, and then click Delete Series.

Value aggregation

You can change the aggregate function applied to the value by clicking the arrow next to the value expression (the row under the series name in the Values drop zone). Point to Aggregate, and then select an alternate aggregate function, as shown in Figure 17-4. You can also change the aggregate function by clicking the arrow and then selecting Expression. In the Expression editor, you can edit the expression to manually change the aggregate function or adjust the expression as needed as long as the result returns a numeric value.

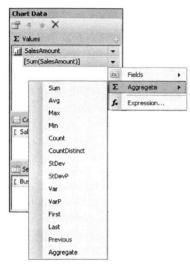

FIGURE 17-4 You can choose a different aggregate function for a value rather than use the default *Sum* function.

Fields

After adding a field to the Values section of the Chart Data pane, you can later change the chart to display another field. Click the arrow next to the value expression, select Fields, and then select the new field to use. The aggregate function reverts to *Sum*, and the name of the value does not automatically change to reflect the new field. You can adjust the aggregate function as described in the previous section, and change the name of the value by updating the *Name* property in the Properties window or by opening the Series Properties dialog box as described in the next section.

Series properties

To change the appearance or behavior of a chart value, you must edit the series properties. As with most report elements, you can open the Properties window and make any necessary changes. For example, you can change the *Name* property, as shown in Figure 17-5.

FIGURE 17-5 You can change the *Name* property for a selected chart value in the Properties window.

When you are first learning about series properties, you might find it easier to make changes by using the Series Properties dialog box, shown in Figure 17-6. To do this, right-click the value and select Series Properties in the context menu, or click the Properties button in the Chart Data pane toolbar. In the Series Properties dialog box, you have access to a variety of properties affecting the display of the selected value in the chart. Most properties can be set dynamically by using expressions. These properties are organized into the following pages:

- **Series Data** Here you can update the following fields: Value, Category, and Tooltip. The Value field is the same field or expression that you set directly in the Chart Data pane. You use the Category field to reference the field for the X coordinate in a scatter chart and leave it blank otherwise. The tooltip is a message that displays when you hover your cursor over a data point in the chart. For more information about tooltips, see Chapter 13, "Adding interactivity."

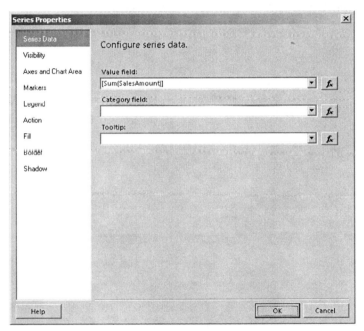

FIGURE 17-6 You can set the Value field, a Category field (for a scatter chart), and a tooltip on the Series Data page of the Series Properties dialog box.

- **Visibility** You can specify whether to show or hide a value in your chart conditionally, using the same visibility properties introduced in Chapter 13.

- **Axes And Chart Area** You use this page to place the value on either the primary or secondary axis of the vertical and horizontal axes. You learn more about using this property setting in Chapter 18.

- **Markers**   As shown in Figure 17-7, you can use the Markers page to define a style for markers that display in the chart as data points for each value. You can choose one of the following marker types: Square, Circle, Diamond, Triangle, 4 Point Star, 5 Point Star, 6 Point Star, 10 Point Star, or Auto. You can also set a specific size and color for the marker as well as a border width and border color.

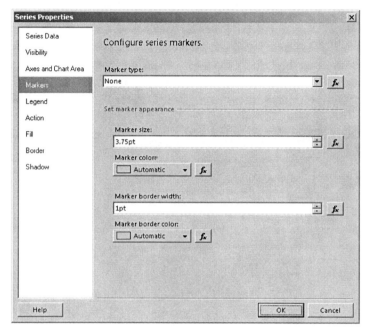

FIGURE 17-7 You can configure marker properties on the Markers page of the Series Properties dialog box.

- **Legend**   On the Legend page, shown in Figure 17-8, you specify how you want the series to appear in the chart legend or whether you want the series to appear in the chart legend at all. You can also specify Custom Legend Text in the appropriate text box, either as static text or as an expression. If your chart has multiple chart legends, you can specify which legend the value should appear in.

> **Note** If you use static text for a custom legend expression for a series and you have series groups, every instance of the series will have the same legend text. When using series groups, use a dynamic expression as your legend text, or to avoid duplicate legend members, use no legend text at all.

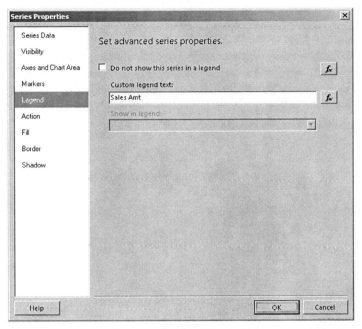

FIGURE 17-8 You use the Legend page of the Series Properties dialog box to specify whether and how a value displays in a chart legend.

- **Action** You can enable an action to launch when a user clicks a value in the chart. Actions are described in Chapter 13.

- **Fill** You can choose the fill style (Solid, Gradient, or Pattern) and set a specific color or use a conditional expression to set a color for the visualization of the value (such as a bar or pie slice).

- **Border** You can add a border to the value's visualization by specifying a line style (None, Dotted, Dashed, Solid, Dash-Dot, Dash-Dot-Dot), a line width, and a line color.

- **Shadow** You can add a subtle three-dimensional appearance to a chart by adding a shadow behind the value's visualization, specifying the shadow offset as a measurement unit (such as pt) and specifying a shadow color.

Category groups

You also use the Chart Data pane to set up category groups. For example, if you are using a column or line chart, category groups are the groupings of the values that you see on the horizontal (X-axis).

Field selection

By default, the category group is set as the Details group. If you leave this group in place and preview the report, the chart displays one value for each row in the dataset. If your dataset aggregates the data suitably for a chart, you do not need to add a category group. Otherwise, to add a new category group, drag a field into the Category Group section of the Chart Data pane, or click the plus sign and select a field. The addition of a new category group replaces the Details group. The chart displays one value per category group instance, as shown in Figure 17-9.

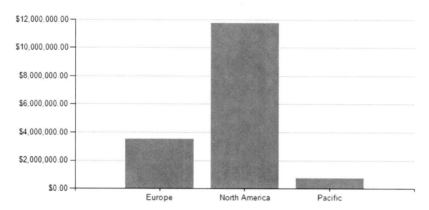

FIGURE 17-9 A chart displays one value per category group instance, shown here as Europe, North America, and Pacific.

You can continue adding other category groups if you like, but only after you first replace the Details group with a category group. As shown in Figure 17-10, the chart displays lines to show the relationship between category group instances. To rearrange category groups within the list, select one of the category groups, and then use the up or down arrows in the Chart Data pane toolbar.

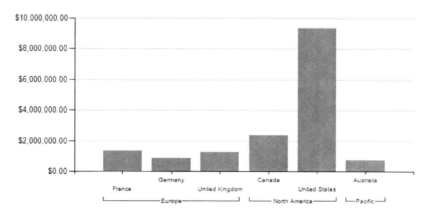

FIGURE 17-10 You can include multiple category groups in a chart.

If you want to revert to the Details group only, click the plus sign and select Use Details. To change a category group to a different field, simply click the arrow to the right of the category group, and then select a new field from the list.

You can delete a category group by selecting it in the Chart Data pane and clicking the Delete button in the Chart Data pane toolbar. Another option is to right-click the category group in the Chart Data pane, and then click Delete Category Group.

Category group properties

You can control many other category group properties by using the Category Group Properties dialog box. To do this, right-click the category group or select the arrow to the right of the category group, and then select Category Group Properties. The category group properties are organized into the following pages:

- **General** On this page, shown in Figure 17-11, you can modify the name of the category group, which you can later reference as a scope argument. The label is the field or expression to display in the chart for each category group instance. You select a category group in the Synchronize Groups In drop-down list when you embed shape charts in a tablix and want to ensure that the color assignments remain consistent by category group for each row in the tablix. Last, you specify the field or expression determining the category group instances. This often has the same value as the label.

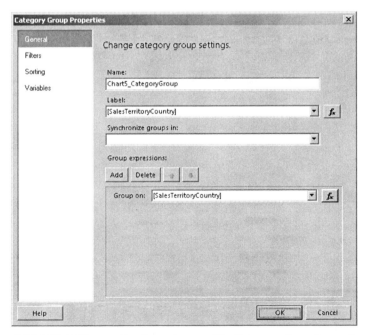

FIGURE 17-11 You use the General page of the Category Group Properties dialog box to identify the grouping expression and the corresponding label to display in the chart for each category group instance.

- **Filters**   You can use filter expressions, as explained in Chapter 14, "Creating dynamic reports with parameters," to filter data in a category group.

- **Sorting**   You can specify a sort expression and direction for the category group, as described for groups in general in Chapter 9, "Designing the report layout."

- **Variables**   You can use group variables with category groups, as covered in Chapter 11, "Developing expressions."

Series groups

You can add another layer of groups to your chart by adding series groups. For each category group, each instance of a series group appears as a separate color in the chart, as shown in Figure 17-12. The legend displays the color-coding of each series label so that you can easily interpret the chart.

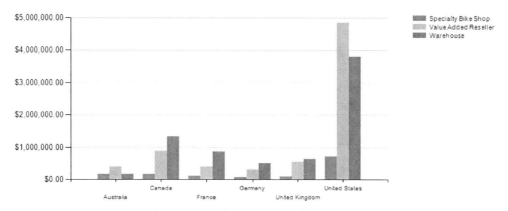

FIGURE 17-12 You can use series groups to show separate values as a subdivision of category groups.

Field selection

To add a series group to your chart, drag a field from the Report Data pane to the Series Group section of the Chart Data pane. You can also click the plus sign above the Series Group section to select a field from the list or to create an expression to use for grouping.

You can also use the Chart Data pane to reposition or remove a series group. To change the order that the series groups appear in the chart, select a series group, and then use the up and down arrows in the Chart Data pane toolbar to move the series group within the list. To delete a series group, select the series group in the Chart Data pane and click the Delete button in the Chart Data pane toolbar, or right-click the series group, and then click Delete Series Group.

Series group properties

Using the Series Group Properties dialog box, you have access to the properties that affect the way the chart displays a series group. To open the dialog box, right-click the series group in the Chart Data pane, or click the arrow to the right of the series group and then select Series Group Properties. You use this dialog box to access the following pages:

- **General**   The General page for a series group, shown in Figure 17-13, is similar to the General page for a category group. Here you can change the name of the series group, which you can later reference as a scope argument. The label is the field or expression to display in the legend for each series group instance. You select a series group in the Synchronize Groups In drop-down list when you embed shape charts in a tablix and want to ensure that the color assignments remain consistent by category group for each row in the tablix. Last, you specify the field or expression determining the series group instances, which often has the same value that is in the Label field.

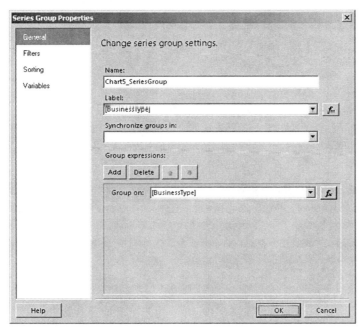

FIGURE 17-13 You use the General page of the Series Group Properties dialog box to identify the grouping expression and the corresponding label to display in the chart for each series group instance.

- **Filters**   You can use filter expressions, as explained in Chapter 14, to filter data in a series group.

- **Sorting**   You can specify a sort expression and direction for the series group, as described for groups in general in Chapter 9.

- **Variables**   You can use group variables with series groups, as covered in Chapter 11.

Formatting chart elements

Although you can use many different chart types, most chart types share some common elements. Figure 17-14 illustrates these various chart elements.

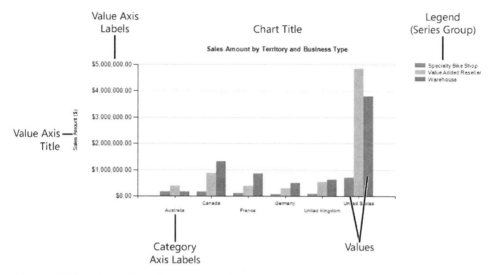

FIGURE 17-14 Each chart type has common elements.

Each of the following chart elements has a set of properties that you can use to fine-tune the appearance of the chart:

- **Value axis**   The value axis is also called the y-axis in a column chart. The value axis is a scale that shows the numerical values in the chart and includes a title that you can choose to remove. You can change many properties of the value axis, including the appearance of gridlines, the minimum and maximum values of the scale, the intervals between values on the scale, and the font and formatting of axis labels.

- **Chart title**   The chart title is an element that appears by default, but you can remove it, move it to a new location, or change its properties by specifying visibility, font, fill, border, and shadow options. You can also associate an action with the chart title.

- **Category axis**   The category axis is also called the x-axis in a column chart. This axis displays the grouping of numerical values in the chart. The category axis has most of the same properties available for the value axis, allowing you to customize its appearance. By default, the category axis includes a title that you can choose to remove, as the report author has done in Figure 17-14.

- **Series Group**   The series group is an optional chart element that allows you to add another level of grouping. When you have multiple sets of numerical data in a chart, such as Sales Amount and Order Quantity, each set of data is a series. You can also add a field explicitly, such as *Calendar Year,* as a series or to define an expression. You can apply a filter to a series group, specify a sort order, or define a group variable.

- **Legend**   The legend maps the colors in the chart to specific series values. You can configure the layout and position of the legend, set visibility properties, and specify font, fill, border, and shadow options.

In addition to properties for the chart that define its size and visibility, each chart element has properties that can customize the overall appearance of your chart. For example, you can control the location of the legend or choose to exclude it from the chart altogether. You can also customize the appearance of the horizontal and vertical axes and their labels. Although you can use the Properties window in the development interface to configure properties for a selected chart element, you might find it easier to open the element's Properties dialog box. Just right-click the element, and select the applicable Properties command from the context menu.

Chart

There are several properties that apply exclusively at the chart level. A chart is a data region like a tablix, so it has some properties in common, such as visibility and filters properties. These types of properties are discussed in more detail in Chapters 13 and 14, respectively. In addition, you can set fill and border properties for a chart. With the fill property, you can change the background color of the chart. This is the area of the chart in front of which display all other elements, such as the legends, titles, axes, and data values in the form of a column, line, pie, or other chart type. The border properties control the appearance of lines that enclose the entire area of the chart.

Another chart property is the color palette. You use the color palette to set the group of colors used to represent different values or different series groups in your chart. When you choose a color palette, you see some of the available colors in design mode, but you should preview the report to see the actual color scheme that Reporting Services applies to your values. You cannot control the color assignments from a built-in palette to a specific value or series group in your chart. Instead, you can either use expressions to set the fill property for a value or establish a custom palette as described in Chapter 18.

Chart title

To modify the chart title, click the chart title twice to select the chart title object, and then double-click the text to edit. If you prefer, you can remove the chart title. Just right-click it in the chart layout, and then select Delete Title. You can add a chart title again later by right-clicking the chart and selecting Add New Title. You can also use the Add New Title command to add multiple chart titles to the same chart.

You can also change the title, as well as access other properties, by right-clicking the chart title and selecting Title Properties. In the Chart Title Properties dialog box, shown in Figure 17-15, you can set the chart title by typing a static string in the Title Text field or by defining an expression. You can also choose a position for your chart title relative to the chart area.

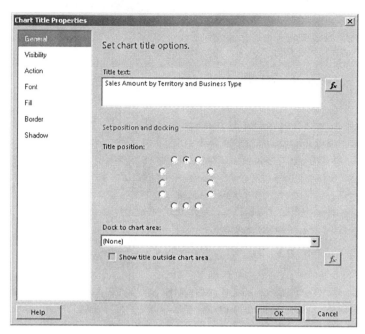

FIGURE 17-15 You use the Chart Title Properties dialog box to configure the chart title and its position relative to the chart.

If you have multiple chart areas (discussed in Chapter 18), you can choose to dock the title to a specific chart area by selecting it from the Dock To Chart Area drop-down list. When you select the Show Title Outside Chart Area check box, the report shows the chart title outside of the chart area to which you've docked the chart title. This option is available only when you dock the chart title to a chart area. By default, this option is selected to avoid overlapping items in the report and to maintain the visibility of the chart title. You can also set this option conditionally by using the expression button to the right of this option.

Notice all the other pages available for the chart title properties: Visibility, Action, Font, Fill, Border, and Shadow. You work with these properties (except for Font) in the same way as described earlier in this chapter for Series Properties. In addition, you have the option here to configure the font properties, including font family, font size, font style, font color, and font effects.

Axis title

Whether you're working with the horizontal axis or the vertical axis, you can easily toggle the visibility of the axis and its title by right-clicking the axis and selecting either Show Axis or Show Axis Title, respectively. If you decide to keep the axis, you can rename it by double-clicking the axis title text and typing a new name in place. You can also right-click the axis title and select Axis Title Properties to open the Axis Title Properties dialog box, shown in Figure 17-16. To change the text from here, simply type the text in the Title Text box, or create an expression.

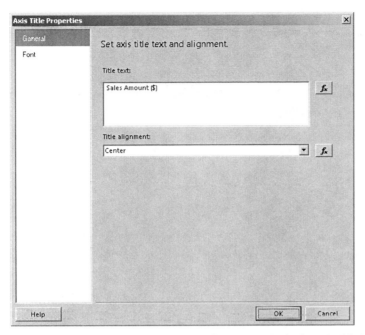

FIGURE 17-16 You can configure title and font properties in the Axis Title Properties dialog box.

By default, the axis title alignment is set to Center. You can also choose Near to move the axis title closer to the intersection of the value and category axes, or you can choose Far to move the axis title farther from the axis intersection. You can also configure font properties for the axis title by using this dialog box.

Axes

The properties for axes apply to every chart type except the shape charts—pie and doughnut. For chart types having axes, right-click an axis and select Vertical Axis Properties or Horizontal Axis Properties (depending on the one you click) to open the applicable Axis Properties dialog box. By using this dialog box, you can configure the following properties for the selected axis:

- **Axis Options** By default, Reporting Services automatically decides what range to use for your axes, as shown in Figure 17-17, but you can override these actions with options by clearing the Always Include Zero check box to prevent inclusion of a zero value on the axis if it is out of range or by setting Maximum and Minimum values to define a specific range. You can also specify interval properties and scale options, which we explain in more detail in Chapter 18.

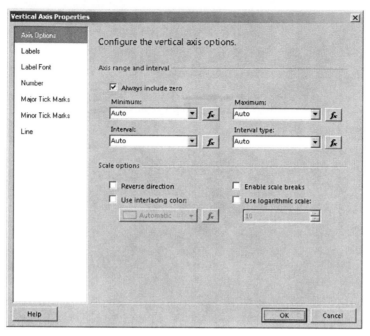

FIGURE 17-17 You can use the Axis Properties dialog box to set range, interval, and scale options for a vertical axis.

If you are configuring a category axis (also known as the horizontal axis in a column chart, for example), you have the additional option to set the axis type, category or scalar, as shown in Figure 17-18. Use a category axis type when the category group is based on fields like sales territory, product, or even month names. When you have numbers that represent days of the week or months of the year or hours of the day, use a scalar axis type. The chart automatically sets the minimum and maximum values and applies sorting for you.

■ **Labels** You also have fine control over the appearance of your axis labels, as shown in Figure 17-19. You can simply hide labels altogether by selecting a check box, use a conditional expression to hide them, or you can hide the first and last labels on the axis.

By default Reporting Services auto-fits your axis labels. You can set some limits on what Reporting Services does with auto-fit by setting minimums and maximums for font size, and whether labels can be offset, rotated, or wrapped.

Notice that the labels on the horizontal axis can rotate to display at a 90-degree angle. By default, the axis labels rotate to fit the chart. You can control the angle of the labels by setting the label angle explicitly. To do this, disable auto-fit and then set the Label Rotation Angle (Degrees) box to a value between –90 and 90, inclusive. When you specify a negative value, the label angles upward and the end of the label is close to the horizontal axis. A positive value displays each label with a downward angle with the beginning of each label close to the horizontal axis.

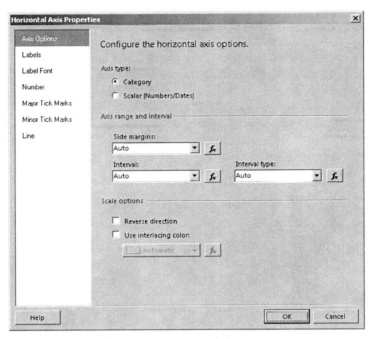

FIGURE 17-18 You can use the Axis Properties dialog box to set an axis type, intervals, and scale options for the horizontal axis.

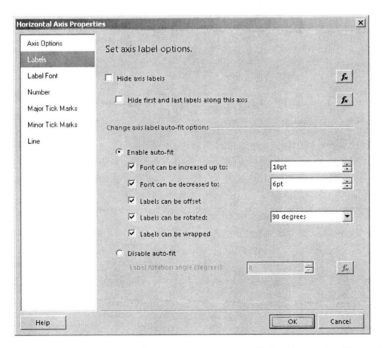

FIGURE 17-19 You can configure the appearance of labels in the Axis Properties dialog box.

- **Label Font**   Here you can specify the font family, font size, font style, font color, and font effects for the axis labels.

- **Number**   On this page, shown in Figure 17-20, you choose a category and select formatting options based on that category. For example, for the Number category, you can set the number of decimal places, show values in Thousands, Millions, or Billions, or choose how zero and negative numbers appear. Notice also the Use Regional Formatting check box, which allows you to localize numerical formatting for each user.

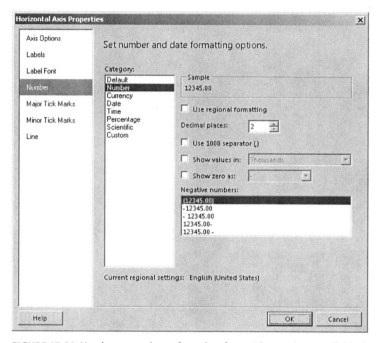

FIGURE 17-20 You have a variety of number formatting options available for an axis.

- **Major Tick Marks and Minor Tick Marks**   You also have options for the major and minor tick lines on your axis, by selecting the appropriate one from the left pane. Although only the Major Tick Marks page is shown in Figure 17-21, the options available are the same for both types of tick marks. You can simply hide tick marks by selecting the available check box, or if you retain them, you can choose a position, length, and line style for the tick marks. You can also set explicit intervals to selectively place tick marks along the axis. For example, if you define a category of days on the horizontal axis and need to display a label only for every seventh day, you set an interval of 7.

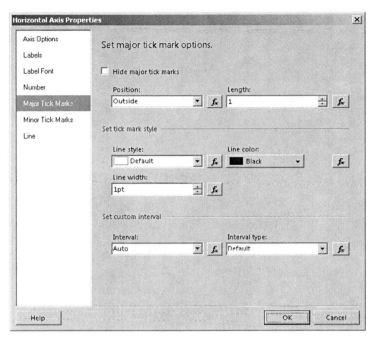

FIGURE 17-21 You can set position, style, and interval properties for major tick marks in the Axis Properties dialog box.

- **Line** On this page, you specify a line style (None, Dotted, Dashed, Solid, Dash-Dot, Dash-Dot-Dot), a line width, and a line color for the axis line.

Series labels

Sometimes you might want to display the actual values next to the value markers or bars in a chart. To do this, right-click the series in the chart or in the Chart Data pane, and click Show Data Labels. Labels will appear on your chart when you preview the report, as shown in Figure 17-22. The numbers displaying in design mode are placeholders intended to give you an idea of what the labels will look like and are not representative of the actual data in the chart.

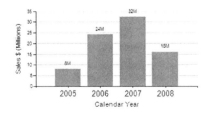

FIGURE 17-22 You can display data labels above each value in the chart.

After adding data labels to the chart, you can configure properties that further define the data to use for the labels as well as their appearance. Right-click any data label in the chart layout, and select Series Label Properties to open the Series Label Properties dialog box, shown in Figure 17-23.

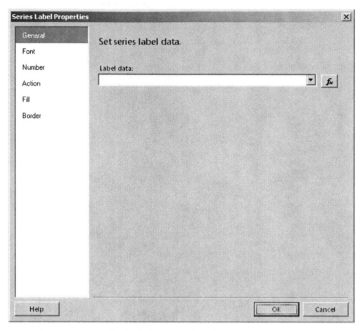

FIGURE 17-23 The Series Label Properties dialog box.

By default, the data used for the data label is the same as the field used for the series itself, and the Label Data text box is empty. You can display a different value by selecting a data label keyword from the Label Data drop-down list, or by creating an expression for your label data. The keywords available in the Label Data drop-down list are shown in Table 17-1. If you change the Label Data of the series to a keyword or expression, a message displays to explain that the new property value has no effect unless you set the *UseValueAsLabelData* property to *False*. The property change is made for you if you click Yes in this message box.

TABLE 17-1 Data label keywords

Data Label Keyword	Description
#VALX	The X-value of the data point
#VALY	The Y-value of the data point
#VALY, #VALY2, #VALY3, etc.	First Y-value, second Y-value, third Y-value, and so on, of the data point
#INDEX	The data point index within the series
#TOTAL	The total of all values in the current series
#PERCENT	The percentage value of the data point value within the series
#AXISLABEL	The category axis label for the data point

You also use the Series Labels dialog box to configure the font, number, action, fill, and border properties of the series labels. The available property settings for these additional pages in the dialog box are identical to the pages described for series and axis properties.

Legend

By default, a chart has a legend. To remove the legend, right-click the legend and click Delete Legend. To restore the legend later, right-click the chart and select Add New Legend. You can also select Add New Legend to add multiple legends, which might be useful when you are working with multiple chart areas and want to show separate legends for each chart area. Multiple chart areas are introduced in Chapter 19, "Comparing values to goals with gauges."

To manage legend properties, right-click the legend and select Legend Properties to open the Legend Properties dialog box, as shown in Figure 17-24. In addition to changing the legend object's name, you can choose the layout of your legend from the Layout drop-down list. The layout options are Column, Row, Auto Table, Wide Table, and Tall Table. Column and row describe whether the items in the legend display vertically in a column, horizontally as a row, or some variation of those options. Auto Table displays the legend contents in a table, but Reporting Services auto-fits the table to the area available. You can force the legend to expand vertically by choosing Tall Table or to expand horizontally by choosing Wide Table.

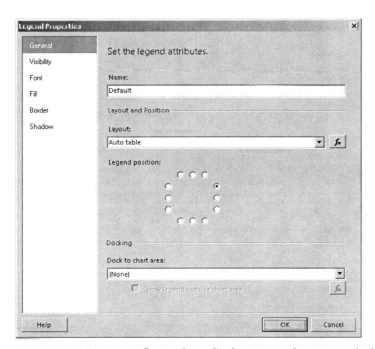

FIGURE 17-24 You can configure a legend's placement and appearance in the Legend Properties dialog box.

You can control the position of the legend in relation to the chart area by choosing the appropriate Legend Position. As with chart titles, you can also choose to dock the legend to a specific chart area. If you do so, you have the additional option to show the legend inside or outside the chart area by selecting or clearing the Show Legend Outside Chart Area check box.

Notice the other pages available in the Legend Properties dialog box to set properties for legend visibility, font appearance, the color and style of fill, border, and shadow effects. These property pages are the same as those explained earlier in this chapter for series and axis properties.

Working with data bars

You've always had the ability to put a chart inside another data region—a table, a matrix, or a list—to produce inline charts. But as of SQL Server 2008 R2 Reporting Services, you now have some new chart variations that you might find useful and much easier to configure. One of these new chart variations is the data bar. A data bar shows a single data point as a horizontal bar or as a vertical column. Typically, you embed a data bar inside of a tablix to provide a small data visualization for each group or detail group that it contains. A data bar has no axis titles, labels, gridlines, tick marks, and so on. This minimalist view allows you to compare each group's value to the minimum and maximum values within a range of values.

Adding a data bar

To add a data bar, drag the Data Bar report item from the Toolbox window into your report. You can add it as a stand-alone report item by dropping it onto the report design surface, but in that case it would be a single bar (or column) and would not communicate much information. More commonly, you drop it into a repeating text box in a tablix. After you drop it onto your report, the Select Data Bar Type dialog box appears, as shown in Figure 17-25. Here you select the variation of a data bar or data column chart that you would like to use.

After adding the data bar to the tablix, you can open the Chart Data pane by clicking the data bar, just as you do with other chart types. Although you can add fields to category groups and series groups, you typically add only a single value to the Values section of the Chart Data pane when setting up a data bar.

Like a bar chart, the horizontal axis of a data bar represents the value rather than category groups. When you place a data bar inside a tablix, it infers the applicable category from the current row scope, which ideally is clear to any viewer of the report. For example, if you place a data bar in a table column, the category of a data bar instance is the current detail row or current group row, as shown in Figure 17-26.

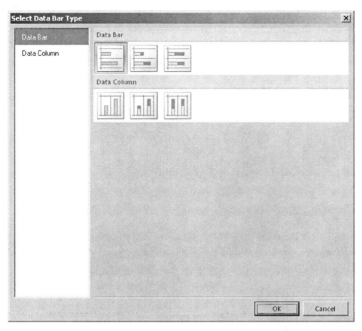

FIGURE 17-25 You can use only a bar or column chart as a data bar.

Group	Country	Business Type	Sales Amount	
Europe	France	Specialty Bike Shop	$120,181.38	
		Value Added Reseller	$399,158.53	
		Warehouse	$857,270.81	
	Germany	Specialty Bike Shop	$77,158.48	
		Value Added Reseller	$299,826.74	
		Warehouse	$508,136.14	
	United Kingdom	Specialty Bike Shop	$92,952.07	
		Value Added Reseller	$538,182.96	
		Warehouse	$645,970.20	
North America	Canada	Specialty Bike Shop	$171,182.24	
		Value Added Reseller	$884,996.26	
		Warehouse	$1,334,083.02	
	United States	Specialty Bike Shop	$712,179.97	
		Value Added Reseller	$4,847,762.31	
		Warehouse	$3,802,117.09	
Pacific	Australia	Specialty Bike Shop	$165,542.36	
		Value Added Reseller	$400,571.50	
		Warehouse	$180,790.56	

FIGURE 17-26 Each data bar derives its category group from the row context.

Configuring data bar properties

Because the data bar is a simplified variation of a chart, you use many of the same properties that you use with standard charts. However, one difference between a data bar and other chart types is the relative sizing of the data bar lengths, which is set as an axis property. Otherwise, you can use the same series properties and chart properties discussed previously in this chapter to adjust the look and feel of the data bar to suit your needs.

Data bar length

The purpose of a data bar is to show relative differences across categories (for example, rows in a table) with minimal distraction. There are no axes, lines, tick marks, legends, or series groups to configure. However, even with this minimalist appearance, there are a few properties you can set.

To access these properties, right-click the data bar, and then select Horizontal Axis Properties for a data bar having a bar chart type or select Vertical Axis Properties for a data bar having a column chart type. Although the properties affect different axes due to the different orientation of the data bar, the dialog box that displays allows you to configure the same properties, shown in Figure 17-27.

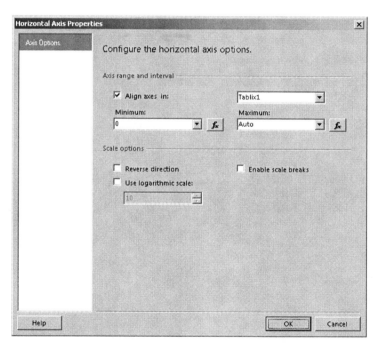

FIGURE 17-27 You can configure the axis alignment, range, and scale options for a data bar in the Horizontal Axis Properties dialog box.

By default, the data bar aligns the axes for the entire data region. That means that the default minimum value of 0 applies to each data bar, and the maximum value depends on the highest value found in the data region or is derived by aggregating detail records in a group. Each data bar's value displays as a ratio of this maximum value. You can also set scale options if necessary, although these are less likely to be necessary in a data bar.

If the data region contains groups, you can align the axes for a specified group, which you choose in the drop-down list. This option calculates the maximum value within each group, rather than across the entire data region. In Figure 17-28, you can see that the data bar for France has the maximum value for Europe and fills the width of the column, and likewise, the data bar for United States is the maximum value for North America even though the value for the United States is significantly higher than that of the France.

Group	Country	Sales Amount	
Europe	France	$1,376,610.72	
	Germany	$885,121.35	
	United Kingdom	$1,277,105.23	
	Group Total	$3,538,837.31	
North America	Canada	$2,390,261.51	
	United States	$9,362,059.37	
	Group Total	$11,752,320.88	
Pacific	Australia	$746,904.41	
	Group Total	$746,904.41	

FIGURE 17-28 You can change the axes alignment to display bars as a ratio of the maximum value within a group.

Tip Because it might be confusing to users to see bars of similar length in different groups for values that are considerably different, you might introduce some separation between groups as a visual cue to better distinguish one group from another and thereby discourage comparisons of bars between groups. One technique you could use is to place the table inside a list while leaving some white space between the bottom of the table and the bottom of the list, and then group the list based on the group you use for axes alignment.

Data bar appearance

You can control the appearance of the data bar by using the Series Properties dialog box to change visibility, markers, action, fill, border, and shadow properties. You can open this dialog box by opening the Chart Data pane, right-clicking the value in the Chart Data pane, and then selecting Series Properties.

You can also access chart-level properties such as the color palette, visibility, filters, fill, and border by right-clicking the data bar and selecting Chart Properties. The properties you set here affect the presentation of the chart rather than the data bars, which is an important distinction to understand. For example, if you set an expression to hide a chart, the border of the text box containing the hidden data bar disappears, whereas it remains visible if you use the same expression to hide the series. As another example, the fill property for the chart changes the background color within the text box, whereas the fill property for the series changes the color of the data bar itself.

Note If you ever find the minimalist nature of the data bar too restrictive for your requirements, you can change the data bar to one of the standard chart types. Simply right-click the data bar and click Convert To Full Chart. You then have all chart features available.

Working with sparklines

The sparkline is another new chart variation introduced in SQL Server 2008 R2 Reporting Services that allows you to include a data visualization alongside detailed data. Whereas a data bar generally shows a single point, a sparkline shows multiple data points over time by using a line, area, or range chart to show whether the measurement is trending up or trending down and with varying degrees of fluctuation over the represented time period. You are not required to use time periods to categorize data points, but you can use other fields to create category groups and then use a column or shape chart to compare these category groups. Like data bars, sparklines provide a minimalist view of your data; they do not include axis titles, labels, gridlines, tick marks, or legends.

Adding a sparkline

To add a sparkline, drag the Sparkline report item from the Toolbox window into your report. Just like the data bar, you can add a sparkline as an independent item on your report or drop it into a tablix. After you drop the sparkline, the Select Sparkline Type dialog box appears, as shown in Figure 17-29, to prompt you for the type of sparkline to add.

Note Because sparklines are intended to have multiple categories, where data bars do not, you cannot add a sparkline to a details row. If you try, you will get an error message.

You can then click the sparkline to open the Chart Data pane and add fields to the Values and Category Groups sections. Multiple values display using different colors, but you should include some explanatory text in the report to identify the values and limit the number of values to include. Multiple category groups are indistinguishable because there are no axis labels to identify the separate categories. Therefore, sometimes multiple categories are not useful unless they help sequence category instances properly, such as a combination of calendar year and month. You can add series groups to the sparkline also, but with no legend to identify the different series value, especially if you have multiple values in the sparkline, the result is a meaningless sparkline.

Sparklines are very useful as a line chart to show change over time. Place the sparkline in a tablix group associated with a dataset that includes multiple time periods, and then assign a category group for that time period (such as year, month, or day) to the sparkline. The tablix group must not be a grouping of time periods, but instead groups on another field in the dataset. The category group members will be determined by the row context, just as with data bars.

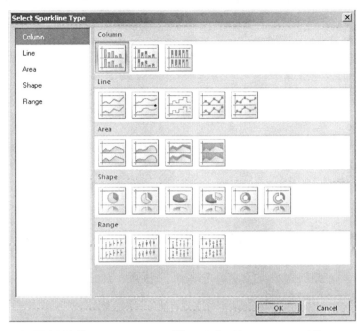

FIGURE 17-29 You can use many different chart types as a sparkline.

In Figure 17-30, the dataset includes fields for sales territory group, sales territory country, and calendar year. The tablix groups first by sales territory group and then by sales territory country and displays the sum of sales amount by sales territory country. Similarly, the sparkline shows the sum of sales amount by sales territory country but uses calendar year along the horizontal axis to show the sales amount by sales territory country and by calendar year using a line chart.

Group	Country	Sales Amount	Sales Amount by Year
Europe	France	$4,607,537.94	
	Germany	$1,983,988.04	
	United Kingdom	$4,279,008.83	
North America	Canada	$14,377,925.60	
	United States	$53,607,801.21	
Pacific	Australia	$1,594,335.38	

FIGURE 17-30 A sparkline uses multiple category groups based on the current row context.

Configuring sparkline properties

A sparkline shares many properties with the corresponding chart. However, it does not include properties controlling the appearance of axis labels, lines, tick marks, legends, and so on, because those chart elements do not exist in a sparkline. Besides setting properties for the elements that do exist, you should also consider whether configuring axes alignment is beneficial.

Sparkline appearance

To configure sparkline properties, you can use the Chart Data pane to access and configure the same properties described in the "Using the chart data pane" and "Formatting chart elements" sections of this chapter. You use the following dialog boxes to configure the applicable properties for a sparkline:

- **Series Properties**   Use this dialog box to configure tooltip, visibility, markers, action, fill, border, and shadow properties for the value's visualization, such as a column or a line.

- **Category Group Properties**   Use this dialog box to configure filters, sorting, and variables for each category group.

- **Vertical Axis Properties**   Use this dialog box to configure axis alignment, minimum and maximum scale ranges, and scale options.

- **Horizontal Axis Properties**   Use this dialog box to configure axis type, axis alignment, side margins, intervals, and scale options.

- **Chart Properties**   Use this dialog box to configure tooltip, color palette, visibility, filters, fill, and border properties at the chart level.

> **Note** You can always change the sparkline into a full chart if you find you want more detail to display than a sparkline provides. To do this, right-click the sparkline and click Convert To Full Chart.

Sparkline axes alignment

By implication, a category group has multiple members. For example, a category group of months should have twelve months as members. However, your dataset might not include all months for any given year. As a result, the horizontal axis of a sparkline can misrepresent trends if a user tries to compare one sparkline to another.

For example, in Figure 17-31, the sparklines in each row of the tablix expand to fill the entire column width. However, not every year for each sales territory country has data for every month of the year. The sales for France in 2006 begin in July and end in December, whereas 2007 sales begin in January and continue through December for a full twelve months. There is no way to see in these two rows of the tablix that the 2006 sparkline is for six months while the 2007 sparkline is for twelve months. Furthermore, the July 2006 value displays at the beginning of the line above the January 2007 value.

Group	Country	Calendar Year	Sales Amount	Sales Amount by Year
Europe	France	2006	$857,123.18	
		2007	$2,373,804.04	
		2008	$1,376,610.72	
	Germany	2007	$1,098,866.68	
		2008	$885,121.35	
	United Kingdom	2006	$841,757.76	
		2007	$2,160,145.83	
		2008	$1,277,105.23	

FIGURE 17-31 A sparkline can show trend directions correctly but might not show category members in the same position in each sparkline.

To fix this problem, right-click the sparkline and select Horizontal Axis Properties. Then select the Align Axes In check box, and select the lowest level group in the drop-down list. In the example shown, the lowest level group available in the check box is the group for sales territory country. When you preview the report, the sparklines now align each month in the same position, as shown in Figure 17-32. That is, July 2006 appears above July 2007, and so on, in each row of the tablix. You can now more easily detect when a sparkline represents a partial year rather than a full year.

Group	Country	Calendar Year	Sales Amount	Sales Amount by Year
Europe	France	2006	$857,123.18	
		2007	$2,373,804.04	
		2008	$1,376,610.72	
	Germany	2007	$1,098,866.68	
		2008	$885,121.35	
	United Kingdom	2006	$841,757.76	
		2007	$2,160,145.83	
		2008	$1,277,105.23	

FIGURE 17-32 You can configure axes alignment by group on the horizontal axis to ensure that category group members appear in the same location in each sparkline.

CHAPTER 18

Working with chart elements

When you understand the basics of chart design and configuration, you can use chart element properties to gain further control over the appearance of data visualizations in your report. In this chapter, you learn how to use color palettes and properties of the vertical and horizontal axes to enhance the readability of your charts. You also learn how to work with series properties to produce more advanced layouts using bubble charts, calculated series, secondary axes, multiple chart types, and multiple chart areas. Last, you learn about some hidden properties available to manipulate slices in pie charts.

Changing color palettes

When you create a chart, a default color palette applies to the values of bars, lines, slices, or other chart elements as applicable to the selected chart type. Rather than use the default color palette, you can select one of the other built-in color palettes as a static assignment, or you can use an expression to set the color palette dynamically. As an alternative, you can create your own custom color palette.

Built-in color palettes

You configure the color palette for a chart in the Chart Properties dialog box, as shown in Figure 18-1, which you open by right-clicking the chart. In the Color Palette drop-down list, you can choose one of the twelve preset color palettes, or you can select a custom color palette, which we discuss in the next section. As with other report item properties, you can also select the chart in the report layout and then use the *Palette* property's drop-down list to select your color palette in the Properties window.

Each instance in a series group gets a different color. Bear in mind that the color palette you see when the report is in design mode is not always representative of the actual palette of the rendered report; you must preview the report to see the actual color palette assignment. The sequence in which the colors get assigned in the series is fixed. That is, you cannot do anything to assign the palette colors in a particular sequence within the color palette.

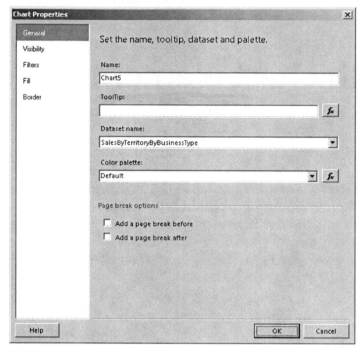

FIGURE 18-1 The Chart Properties dialog box.

Custom color palette

If you prefer, you can create a custom color palette to use in your chart. In the Chart Properties dialog box or in the Properties window, set the color palette to Custom, as shown in Figure 18-2. However, the Chart Properties dialog box does not include an interface for you to define the set of colors for your palette. You can perform this step only by using the Properties window.

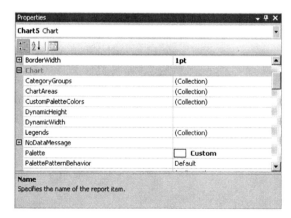

FIGURE 18-2 Set the *Palette* property to Custom when you want complete control over chart colors.

To assign colors to your palette, you must add collection members to the *CustomPaletteColors* property of your chart. In the Properties window, click the ellipsis button that appears when you select *(Collection)* for the *CustomPaletteColors* property to open the ChartColor Collection Editor, as shown in Figure 18-3. Use the Add button to create a new collection member, and then click in the *Color* property box to set a color for the new member. You can select a standard color or use the Select Color dialog box described in Chapter 9, "Designing the report layout." You can also use an expression to define the color dynamically.

FIGURE 18-3 Add colors to your custom palette by using the ChartColor Collection Editor.

The order of the collection members defines the order in which the chart assigns a color to each series instance. To change the order of the collection members, select a member, and then use the up and down arrows to rearrange the sequence of colors.

 Tip It's a good idea to alternate between light and dark colors to help the user distinguish between colors that appear side by side in the chart.

Working with vertical axis properties

In most charts, the vertical axis is your value axis. That is, the vertical axis represents the scale you use to measure your data. Depending on the range or type of values you have in your chart, you might want to change the scale the axis uses. You can simply change the range of your axis, setting specific minimum and maximum values and configuring the intervals displayed on the axis, as explained in Chapter 17, "Creating charts." However, for some situations, you might also consider using other properties affecting the scale on the vertical axis, such as a scale break or logarithmic scaling.

Scale break

Sometimes the range between high and low values in a chart is significant, as shown in Figure 18-4. When several values are low, it can be difficult to compare the differences in values between them. Because the value scale uses the maximum values in the chart to determine the intervals of the scale, the lower values in the chart might fall well below the first interval and you might not be able to easily interpret their relative values.

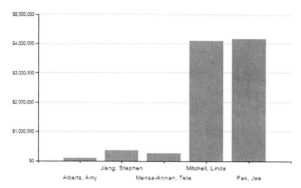

FIGURE 18-4 A chart with a wide range in high and low values can be difficult to interpret.

One way to solve this problem is to use a scale break to cut out sections of the scale. This approach makes it easier to read all the data in the chart. To add a scale break, right-click the value axis (the vertical axis in this case) and select Axis Properties. In the Vertical Axis Properties dialog box, select the Enable Scale Breaks check box, as shown in Figure 18-5.

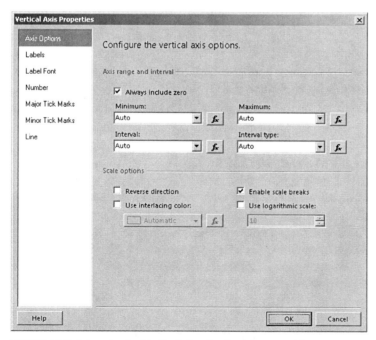

FIGURE 18-5 Select the Enable Scale Breaks check box to add one or more scale breaks to your chart.

You can see the scale breaks in your chart when you preview the report, as shown in Figure 18-6. Now you can more easily compare the lower values with one another. Notice the difference in scale intervals above and below the scale break.

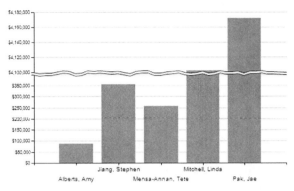

FIGURE 18-6 A chart with scale breaks allows you to more easily compare the lower values.

 Note You cannot enable a scale break in a three-dimensional chart, with a logarithmic value axis, or when you have specified minimum or maximum values for the axis. You also cannot enable a scale break with the following chart types: polar, radar, pie, doughnut, funnel, pyramid, or a stacked chart of any type.

In some cases, a chart might render with multiple scale breaks, as shown in Figure 18-7. Regardless, you cannot control the number of scale breaks, nor can you choose where the scale breaks appear. Reporting Services decides automatically where the breaks should go on the axis, or if they should be used at all.

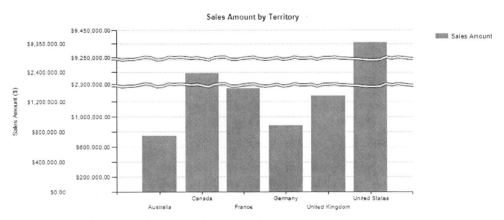

FIGURE 18-7 A chart can include multiple scale breaks.

Although you have no direct control over placement of the scale breaks, you can use properties to customize the appearance of the scale break. For example, you can change the color and width of the lines representing the scale break. To work with scale break properties, select the value axis in the chart, and then expand the *ScaleBreakStyle* category in the Properties window, as shown in Figure 18-8.

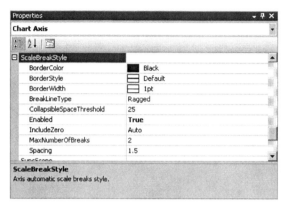

FIGURE 18-8 You can set *ScaleBreakStyle* properties to customize the appearance of scale breaks.

You can use any of the following properties to configure the scale break appearance:

- **BorderColor, BorderStyle, BorderWidth**   These properties control the color, style, and width of your scale break border. The options available here are the same as with other report element borders.

- **BreakLineType**   This property controls the shape of your scale break. By default, the scale break is Ragged, but you can also choose the any of the following options: Wave, Straight, or None.

- **CollapsibleSpaceThreshold**   This property controls how much of the axis can be collapsed. The number you enter (as an integer) is the minimum percentage of the axis that can be collapsed. Although you cannot control the placement of the scale break, you can set a threshold that must be exceeded for a scale break to appear. The default value is 25.

- **Enabled**   This property specifies whether a scale break is an option in the rendered chart. Instead of using the Axis Properties dialog box, you can simply change this property to *True* to enable scale breaks.

- **IncludeZero**   This property controls whether the axis segments should start the scale at zero. The default option is *Auto*, where Reporting Services decides the scale for you, but you can also set the property to *True* or *False*.

- **MaxNumberOfBreaks**   This property allows you to specify the maximum number of scale breaks that can appear in the chart. The default value is 2.

- **Spacing**   This property determines the size of the spacing of your scale break. The default value is 1.5.

Logarithmic scale

An alternative to using a scale break when your maximum and minimum series values are quite far apart is to use a logarithmic scale. A logarithmic scale can sometimes enable better comparisons than a linear scale, like the one shown in Figure 18-9. In this chart, the values for Europe in the first months of 2007 appear to be about the same as the values for Pacific in the later months of 2007. These values are low compared to the high values of North America and are difficult to compare to one another using a linear scale.

To use a logarithmic scale, click the vertical axis and select Vertical Axis Properties to open the Vertical Axis Properties dialog box. Then select the Use Logarithmic Scale check box, as shown in Figure 18-10. By default, the base value for the scale is set to 10, but you can change this to any positive value by using the up and down arrows in the value box below the Use Logarithmic Scale check box or by typing a value directly into the value box.

FIGURE 18-9 When a linear scale has a wide range of high and low values, the low values can appear similar.

It's important to understand that an interval value of 1 does not correspond to an increment of 1 unit of measurement, such as a dollar. Instead, the scale increases by one logarithmic unit. For example, if the interval value is set to 1 on a logarithmic scale of base 10, the intervals occur at 1, 10, 100, 1,000, and so on. Each interval is a multiple of 10. If you set the interval value in the Vertical Axis Properties dialog box to 3, the intervals occur at 1, 1,000, 1,000,000, and so on, where each interval is multiplied by 103.

As you can see in Figure 18-11, the intervals on the vertical axis for a logarithmic chart yield different results in the data visualization than you find in a linear chart. In this example, you can see the values for Europe were actually higher in the early months of 2007 than the values for Pacific in the later months of 2007. This distinction was not visible in the linear chart shown in Figure 18-9.

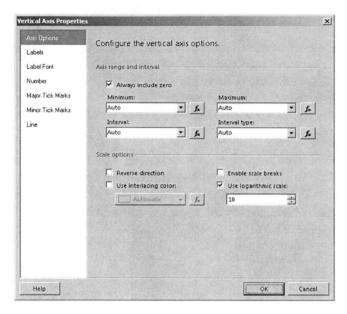

FIGURE 18-10 You can configure the vertical axis to use a logarithmic scale and define the logarithmic base.

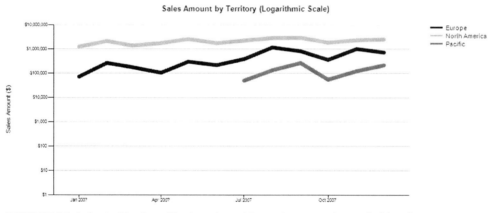

FIGURE 18-11 A chart with a logarithmic scale enables easier comparisons of wide value ranges.

In a logarithmic base 10 scale, each interval value is 10 times more than the previous interval, but the intervals are sized as equal lengths. Because of this, spatial differences between values at the higher end of the scale are actually much greater numerically than the same spatial difference between values at the low end of the scale. However, the same spatial differences between data points differ in magnitude by the same percentage. Thus, a data set that is proportional is a good candidate for a logarithmic scale. However, logarithmic scales are not intuitive to the average reader, so it is important to consider whether their use is appropriate and necessary to convey the information that you want to display.

Working with horizontal axis properties

The horizontal axis is usually your category axis. This axis displays your data according to the category groups in the chart data pane. In addition to the standard scale properties that you set for this axis as described in Chapter 17, there are some additional properties that you should learn how to use when appropriate. One of these properties is the axis type, which you use to control the display of numeric or date values as categories. The other set of properties affect the appearance of intervals when you do not want to display each category label on the horizontal axis.

Axis type

The default axis type for the horizontal axis is category. You use a category axis type when you want to display values for an entity such as a sales territory or product. However, when your chart category group contains numeric values representing days of the week, months of the year, or hours of the day, you should use a scalar axis type instead. With a scalar axis type, Reporting Service automatically determines the minimum and maximum values and applies the correct sort order. Furthermore, it accommodates gaps in your data.

To better understand how this works, consider the example in Figure 18-12, which shows a chart with a category axis type and a chart category group based on year. As you can see, there is no category for 2007. Because there is no data for 2007 in the report's dataset, a category for 2007 does not appear on the horizontal axis.

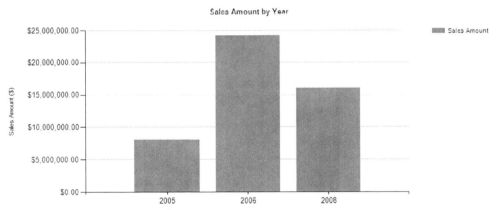

FIGURE 18-12 A category axis type based on numeric values such as years has gaps when the dataset does not include a specific time period.

If you change the axis type to scalar, Reporting Services automatically includes missing category values. To update the axis type, right click the horizontal axis on the chart, and select Horizontal Axis Properties. You can then change the Axis Type to Scalar (Numbers/Dates) in the Horizontal Axis Properties dialog box, as shown in Figure 18-13.

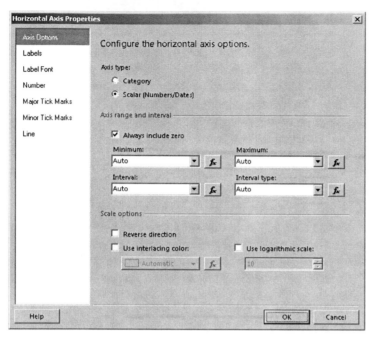

FIGURE 18-13 Set the Axis Type to Scalar when using numeric or date values as a chart category group.

After you change the axis type to scalar, the chart adjusts to include all possible categories for the instances defined by the category group, even if those categories do not exist in the data. For example, in Figure 18-14, the chart displays 2007, in addition to the minimum value of 2004 and the maximum value of 2009. You can manually override the minimum and maximum values in the Horizontal Axis Properties dialog box if you prefer.

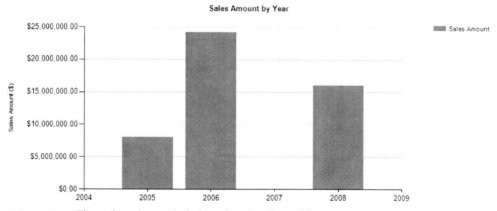

FIGURE 18-14 The scalar axis type includes values for all possible categories between the minimum and maximum values of the range.

Intervals

When you define values and category groups for a chart, Reporting Services creates a default layout of the horizontal and vertical axes based on the current dataset. When you use a report parameter to allow the user to dynamically change the dataset results, the chart layout might change as well. For example, notice the difference in the two charts shown in Figure 18-15. The top chart shows values for 2007, and the bottom chart shows values for 2008. In each chart, not only are the scales of the vertical axis different, but the intervals on the horizontal axis intervals also change. The chart for 2007 has intervals for every other month, while 2008 has intervals for every month. Reporting Services preserves the height and width of the chart but adjusts each axis to fit values into the vertical space and categories into the horizontal space.

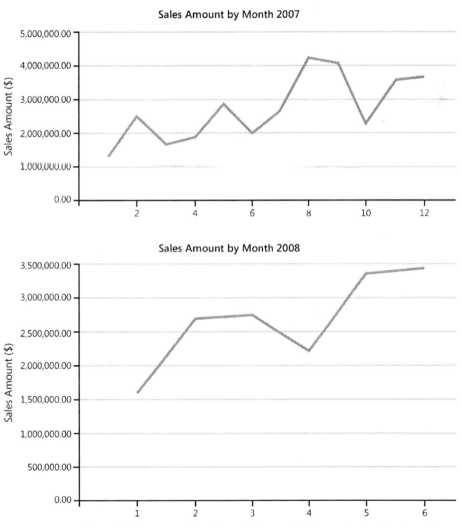

FIGURE 18-15 A change in dataset results affects the intervals of the vertical and horizontal axes but not the height and width of the chart.

Interval properties

If you prefer to maintain consistent intervals on the horizontal axis, you must configure its properties. Right-click the Horizontal Axis, and select Horizontal Axis Properties to open the Horizontal Axis Properties dialog box. Here you can change the Interval value, as shown in Figure 18-16.

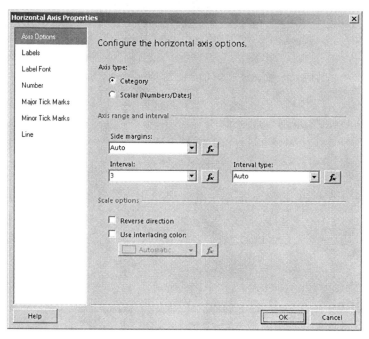

FIGURE 18-16 You can change the interval value of the horizontal axis to maintain consistency in the chart layout when the underlying data changes.

Even when you set a constant value as the interval, the horizontal axis layout still changes dynamically according to the categories that are in the dataset. For example, in Figure 18-17, the two charts now have consistent horizontal intervals. However, the top chart has twelve months of data as compared to six months of data in the bottom chart. Again, Reporting Services preserves the width of the chart and adjusts the layout of the horizontal axis within the available space.

FIGURE 18-17 Both charts have consistent horizontal intervals but have a different number of intervals when the underlying data changes.

Remember that you can use the scalar axis type when using numeric values, such as months, as categories on the horizontal axis. You can also set a fixed range for the axis. For example, if the chart always shows annual data, you can set the axis range Minimum to 0 and the Maximum to 12, as shown in Figure 18-18.

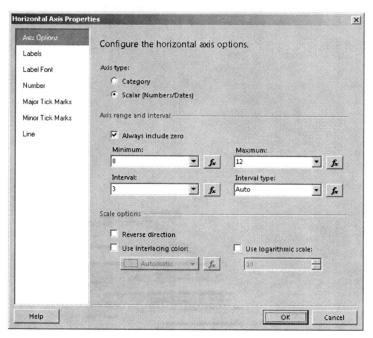

FIGURE 18-18 You can set the axis type to scalar and set minimum and maximum range values to maintain a consistent horizontal axis of time periods.

After adjusting the horizontal axis properties, the chart is more consistent when viewing different years that have a varying amount of data, as shown in Figure 18-19. Now the data values for each time period within the year align in the same place. That way, you can more easily make the comparison of data in one year to data in another year.

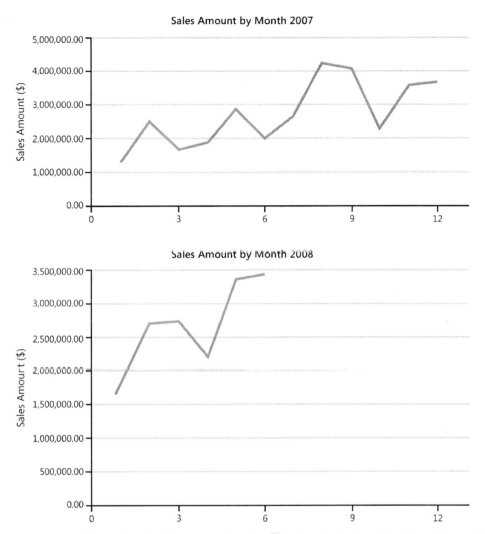

FIGURE 18-19 Comparing data in separate charts is easier when the horizontal axis layout is consistent.

Interlacing

You can also emphasize sections of a chart by adding interlacing, as shown in Figure 18-20. Interlacing adds alternating color strips to the chart to help you group data together. For example, if the category axis groups by month but you set the interval to 3, you can use interlacing to distinguish each quarter of the year. To do this, open the Horizontal Axis Properties dialog box, and select the Use Interlacing Color check box. You can then change the color from the default of gray or use an expression to set the color dynamically.

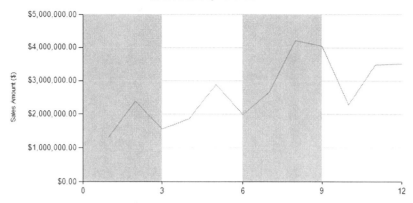

FIGURE 18-20 Use interlacing to highlight alternate intervals in a chart.

Working with series properties

Reporting Services also offers a lot of control over the appearance of series data. For example, you can use series properties to solve display problems when data is missing. Furthermore, you can use series properties to develop more complex charts using bubble charts or calculated series, such as rolling averages, to better visualize and compare trends in your data. You can also display values using different scales in the same chart by using a primary and secondary axis, or you can break each series into separate chart types or areas within a chart as alternate ways to compare data.

Empty points

When a category in a chart has null data, an empty point is the result. Empty points in a column or bar chart simply have no value, which is usually not a problem because the bars or columns are independent of each other. However, in line charts, where the values of each category connect to each other, you need to understand how Reporting Services handles empty points by default.

Consider the example shown in Figure 18-21. The dataset has values for 2005, 2006, and 2008. However, due to the empty point for 2007 and no data after 2008, the chart appears to have data only for 2005 and 2006 as represented by the line.

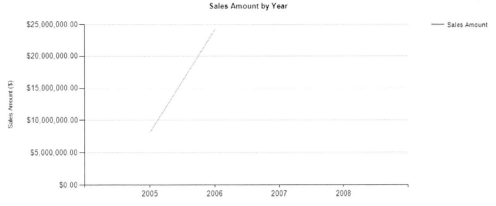

FIGURE 18-21 An empty point that exists at 2007 obscures the data point at 2008.

Marker

One way to ensure that missing data does not obscure single points of data on a line chart is to add a marker to the series, as shown in Figure 18-22. To add a marker, you use the Marker page in the Series Properties dialog box, as discussed in further detail in Chapter 17.

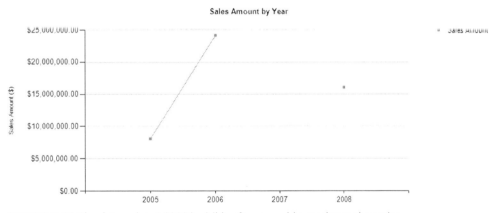

FIGURE 18-22 The data point at 2008 is visible after you add a marker to the series.

Empty point color

Another way to handle missing points is to reintroduce behavior from Reporting Services 2005 and earlier. In those earlier versions, Reporting Services connects the lines by calculating the average between the data points just before and just after the empty point. If you want to use this technique in your chart, you must set the color property for the empty point in the series. To do this, click the series in the chart layout. Then expand the *EmptyPoint* category in the Properties window, and select a color for the *Color* property as shown in Figure 18-23.

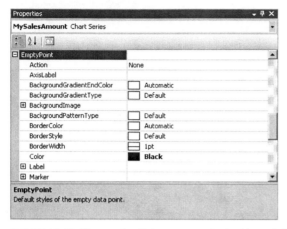

FIGURE 18-23 Change the *Color* property in the *EmptyPoint* category.

After you set the *Color* property for the empty point, you see a line connecting the data values before and after the empty point, as shown in in Figure 18-24. In this example, the color for the empty point does not match the series palette color, which can be a good way to highlight the existence of an empty point. However, you can also configure the empty point to match the chart's color palette.

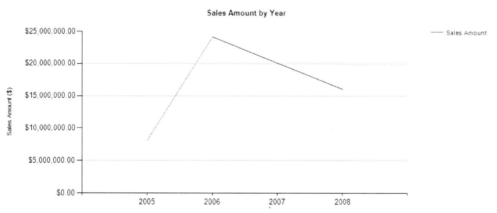

FIGURE 18-24 The chart treats the empty point at 2007 as the average between the 2006 and 2008 values.

Zero value

You might prefer to have the chart interpret the empty point as a zero value. In that case, select the series in the chart layout. In the Properties window, expand the *CustomAttributes* category and change the *EmptyPointValue* property from Average (the default) to Zero. With this setting, the existence of the empty point is more obvious, as shown in Figure 18-25.

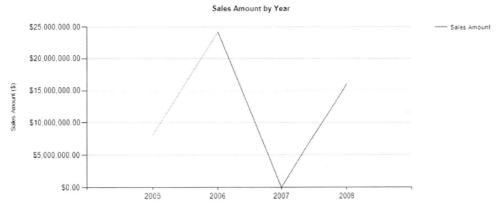

FIGURE 18-25 You set the *EmptyPointValue* to Zero to assign an explicit zero value to an empty point.

Bubble charts

A bubble chart is a special type of scatter plot chart that introduces a third dimension to data visualization. This third dimension is not a spatial third dimension but a third analytical dimension. That is, a bubble chart displays values as points in two-dimensional space using X and Y coordinates and uses a third value to set the size of the marker, or bubble, at each point.

To create a bubble chart, you select one of the two versions available to use from the Scatter category in the Select Chart Type dialog box, shown in Figure 18-26. You can choose from 2-D bubbles or 3-D bubbles.

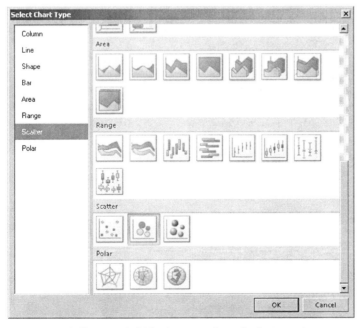

FIGURE 18-26 Choose a bubble chart type from the Scatter category.

You add a value to the chart the same as you do with other chart types, as described in Chapter 17. However, when you add a value to the chart data pane, there are additional properties for *Size* and *X Value* to configure, as shown in Figure 18-27. You click the arrow for these two properties to assign a numeric field or expression. Unlike a more traditional column or line chart, you do not specify a category group for a bubble chart, but you keep the Details grouping. Reporting Services calculates the horizontal scale from the minimum and maximum values of the field you assign as *X Value*.

FIGURE 18-27 You assign series value, size, and X value without category groups when configuring a bubble chart.

By default, the bubbles display in the chart using a square marker. To change the shape of the bubbles, you use the Markers page of the Series Properties dialog box, where you can select a more suitable marker type from the drop-down list, as shown in Figure 18-28. You can also set the color and border properties for the marker. However, changing the size of the marker has no effect because the marker size is determined by the *Size* value of the series.

An example of a bubble chart is shown in Figure 18-29. The value on the vertical axis is an expression to compute the profit margin, and the X Value on the horizontal axis is the sales amount. Using this style of chart, you can see whether high sales volumes have better or worse margins compared to lower sales volumes. The addition of a third analytical element is the bubble size, which in this case is the number of resellers associated with each combination of sales volume and profit margin. You can then see, in this case, that most low volume sales are associated with a lower count of resellers.

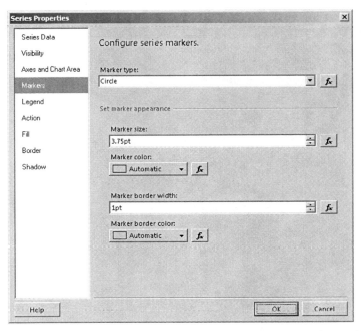

FIGURE 18-28 Choose a marker type from the drop-down list to change the shapes in the bubble chart.

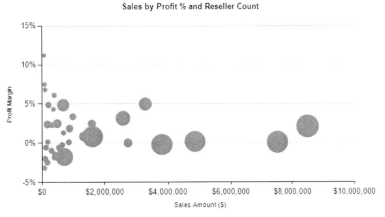

FIGURE 18-29 A bubble chart uses value ranges on both the vertical and horizontal axis as point coordinates and uses a third value to change the bubble size.

Calculated series

In addition to using dataset fields in the Values section of the Chart Data pane, you can also use expressions to define a series. For more complex expressions, you can add a calculated series based on built-in formulas, such as a moving average or median, which you apply to a dataset field. Reporting Services also includes several calculations for financial stock data, such as Bollinger bands and moving average convergence/divergence (MACD).

To create a calculated series, first add a value to the Values section of the Chart Data pane. Next right-click the value, and then click Add Calculated Series. The Calculated Series Properties dialog box appears, as shown in Figure 18-30.

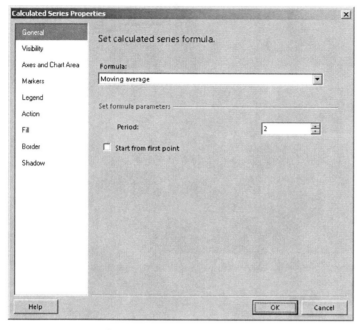

FIGURE 18-30 You select a built-in formula for a value in a chart in the Calculated Series Properties dialog box.

You can select one of the following built-in formulas from the Formula drop-down list:

- **Mean**   This formula calculates the mean of all values in the chart and displays the result as a constant value in a straight line across all categories.

- **Median**   This formula calculates the median of all values in the chart and displays the result as a constant value in a straight line across all categories.

- **Bollinger Bands**   This formula calculates a moving average for the values in the chart based on a time period you specify and then calculates shifts in value above and below the moving average based on the number of standard deviations you specify to define the upper and lower limits of a range. The calculated series displays as a range chart.

- **Moving Average**   This formula computes an average of values over a specified period of time and displays as a line chart.

- **Exponential Moving Average**   This formula is similar to a moving average but gives more weight to recent data points in the time series. In general, it calculates a percentage to apply to each time period's values with higher percentages allocated to recent periods.

- **Triangular Moving Average**   This formula is similar to a moving average but gives more weight to data points in the middle of the time series.

- **Weighted Moving Average**   This formula is similar to a moving average but gives more weight to recent data points in the time series. It calculates the weighting by assigning an index value to each time period and dividing this index value by the sum of all index values, thus giving higher weights to more recent time periods.

- **MACD**   This formula calculates two moving averages, one for a long time period and another for a short time period, and displays the result as a line.

- **Detrended Price Oscillator**   This formula calculates a simple moving average and then applies it in a formula that calculates the difference between a data point value and its moving average over a specified number of time periods in the past.

- **Envelopes**   This formula calculates a moving average for the values in the chart based on a time period you specify and then calculates shifts in value above and below the moving average based on a percentage value you specify to define the upper and lower limits of a range. The calculated series displays as a range chart.

- **Performance**   This formula compares each data point to the first data point to calculate the percent change, which displays as a line chart.

- **Rate Of Change**   Like the Performance formula, this formula calculates the change percentage between two values but uses a specified number of periods ago rather than the first data point.

- **Relative Strength Index**   This formula uses a special algorithm to derive a value from 0 to 100 that indicates whether trends are moving upward or downward.

- **Standard Deviation**   This formula compares the difference between a value and its moving average, with a high value indicating volatility and a low value indicating stability.

- **TRIX**   This formula is a triple moving average, usually used in comparison with the moving average as a buying signal for financial securities.

After you select a formula, you might need to configure additional parameters for the formula. The new calculated series displays in your chart and also appears as a new section in the Chart Data pane, as shown in Figure 18-31.

Note The Calculated Series Properties dialog box provides access to many other properties for the moving average. You can set visibility, reassign the calculated series to a different value or category axis, move the calculated series to a separate chart area, assign the calculated series to an action, or configure appearance properties such as markers, fill, border, and shadow settings.

A common type of calculated series to use in charts is a moving average, as shown in Figure 18-32. You can use a moving average to smooth out fluctuations in values within the number of periods specified for the calculated series. That way you can see whether values are trending up or down over the long term.

FIGURE 18-31 The calculated series appears in a new section of the Chart Data pane.

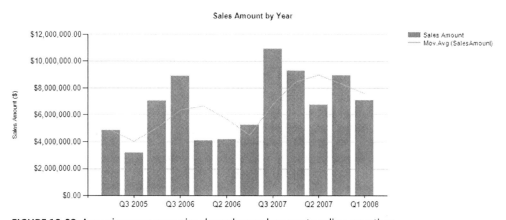

FIGURE 18-32 A moving average series shows how values are trending over time.

Secondary axis

When you want to compare values that use different units of measure, such as sales dollars versus order quantity, you can display the data in the same chart by placing each value on a separate axis. By default, a chart puts all items in the data drop zone on the primary value axis, but you can change the properties of any data item to assign it to the secondary value axis. Each axis has its own properties that you can use to apply formatting. You add a secondary axis both for values and for categories, although you will likely use the secondary value axis more often.

To add a secondary axis, right-click the series you would like to be represented on the secondary axis, and then click Series Properties to open the Series Properties dialog box. On the Axes And Chart Area page, select Secondary for the applicable axis, Horizontal or Vertical, as shown in Figure 18-33.

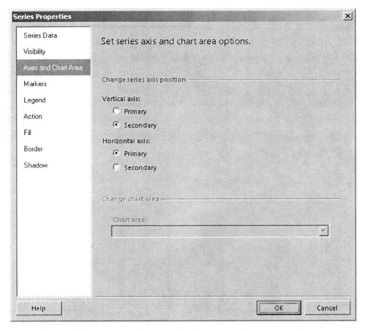

FIGURE 18-33 You can assign a series to a secondary value axis.

The secondary axis is visible in the chart layout after you move a value to the new axis. You can preview the report to check its appearance, as shown in Figure 18-34. In design mode, you can modify the properties of this new chart element, such as its title or number formatting, in the same way that you work with the primary axis.

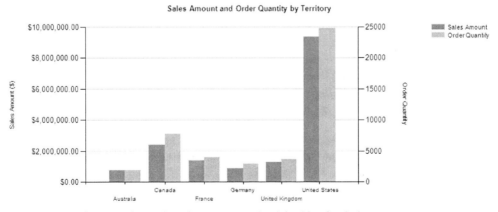

FIGURE 18-34 The secondary axis scale appears on the right side of a chart.

Multiple chart types

Another way to visualize data is to use different chart types within the same chart. For example, you can use a column chart to display the values of one series and a line chart to display the values of another series.

To change the chart type of a series, right-click the series in the Chart Data Pane, and then click Change Chart Type to open the Select Chart Type dialog box. There you can change the chart type you use for that series. For example, you can use a column chart for one series and a line chart for the other series, as shown in Figure 18-35.

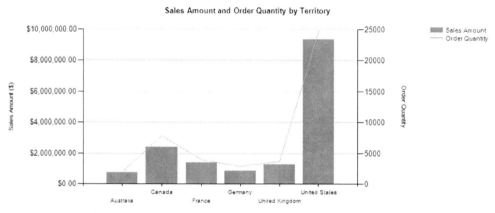

FIGURE 18-35 Order Quantity appears as a line chart, while Sales Amount uses columns.

Multiple chart areas

Instead of using a secondary axis, you might consider using separate chart areas for data that share categories but use a different scale for values. This approach is useful when you want to avoid visual comparisons of each series within a specific category and instead want to emphasize the series trend separately across a common set of categories, such as time periods. You can add as many chart areas as you need to display data, but you should resize the chart to ensure that each chart area has enough space to clearly view the data it contains.

To create a second chart area, right-click the chart, and then click Add New Chart Area. A new chart area appears below your current chart, although there is nothing in it, as shown in Figure 18-36.

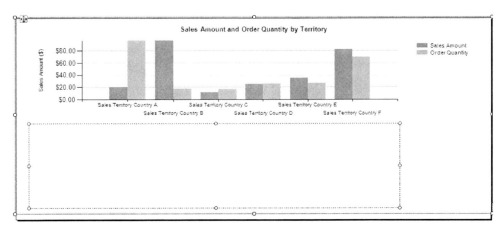

FIGURE 18-36 You can add a new chart area to an existing chart.

To add data to the second chart area, right-click the series you want to display in the new chart area in the Chart Data pane, and then click Series Properties. On the Axes And Chart Area page of the Series Properties dialog box, select the name of the new chart area from the Chart Area drop-down list, as shown in Figure 18-37.

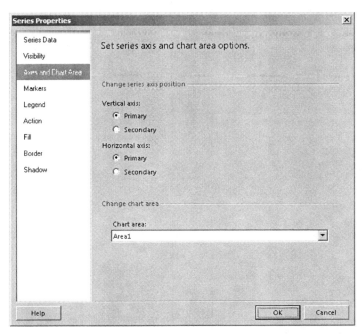

FIGURE 18-37 Select the name of the new chart area from the Chart Area drop-down list.

When you preview the report, you can see that the new chart area displays data values, as shown in Figure 18-38. You can modify the properties of the vertical axis, the horizontal axis, the series, and other elements of the new chart area to improve their appearance. One problem to watch for is the alignment of categories across chart areas. Notice in Figure 18-38 that the vertical axis labels of the top chart area reduce the horizontal space allocated to that chart area as compared to the bottom chart area.

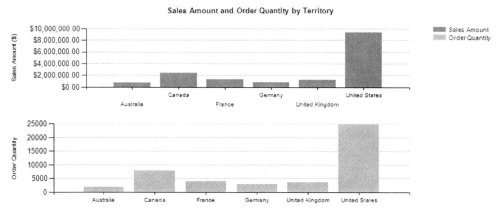

FIGURE 18-38 You can display each series of data in a separate chart area, but watch for category alignment issues.

Fortunately, you can fix this problem. Right-click the new chart area, and then click Chart Area Properties. On the Alignment page of the Chart Area Properties dialog box, select the name of the original chart area from the Align With Chart Area drop-down list, as shown in Figure 18-39.

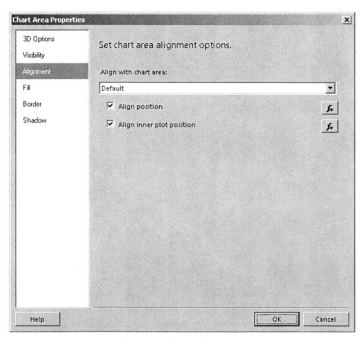

FIGURE 18-39 Use the Chart Area Properties dialog box to force alignment of multiple chart areas.

After you set the chart area alignment options, the chart has a better appearance, as you can see in Figure 18-40. The right edges of the vertical axes align properly, as do the individual category labels across the horizontal axis.

FIGURE 18-40 The chart layout is more appealing when the chart areas are aligned.

Working with pie charts

Problems arise in pie charts when the dataset returns too many categories, such as in Figure 18-41. Generally speaking, if there are more than seven categories, the pie chart tends to be difficult to interpret. To avoid this, you can consolidate slices to simplify the look of the chart and improve readability. As an alternative, you can create a secondary pie chart for which Reporting Services automatically breaks out the smaller pie slices as a second pie.

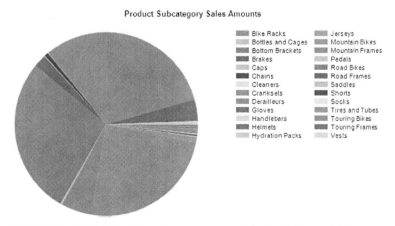

FIGURE 18-41 A pie chart can have too many categories to be useful for comparisons.

Slice consolidation

One method you can use to reduce the clutter in a pie chart is to consolidate all the smaller pieces of a pie chart into a single slice. To do this, select the series in the Chart Data pane. In the Properties window, expand the *CustomAttributes* section, and then set the *CollectedStyle* property to SingleSlice, as shown in Figure 18-42.

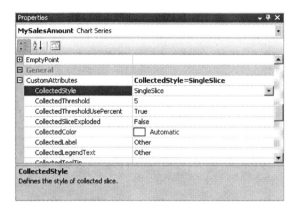

FIGURE 18-42 You can consolidate pie slices by setting the series' *CollectedStyle* property to SingleSlice.

After you configure the slice consolidation, your pie chart is easier to interpret, as shown in Figure 18-43. In this example, the smaller slices from the original pie chart are represented by a single slice. The legend refers to this slice as Other, but you can change this label by changing the *CollectedLegendText* property for the series in the Properties window. The Properties windows includes many other properties related to the collected slice, such as the color, tooltip, and visibility of the legend text.

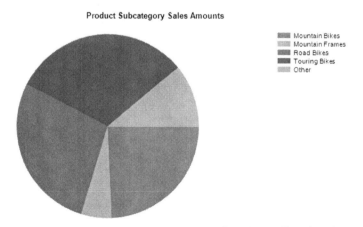

FIGURE 18-43 You can set a property to collect the smallest slices into one slice called Other.

You can also control the threshold at which slices are collected into a single slice. In the Properties window, in the *CustomAttributes* section, you can set the *CollectedThreshold* property. This value can be either a fixed value or a percentage. For example if the collected threshold is set to 10%, each pie slice that is 10% or less of the value of the total pie becomes part of the consolidated pie slice. When using a percentage as a threshold, set the *CollectedThresholdUsePercent* property to True. By default, the *CollectedThreshold* is 5%.

You can also use a fixed number, if you prefer. For example, if the threshold is set to 10,000, any slice with a value below 10,000 becomes part of the consolidated pie slice. In this case, make sure that *CollectedThresholdUsePercent* is set to False.

Secondary pie chart

Another option is to break out small pie slices into a secondary pie chart, as shown in Figure 18-44. In the *CustomAttributes* category of the Properties window, set the *CollectedStyle* property to Collected-Pie. Just as you can when you collect multiple slices into a single slice, you can specify a threshold by setting the *CollectedThresholdProperty*. However, unlike the single slice collection, you can specify the threshold of the secondary pie chart as a percentage only.

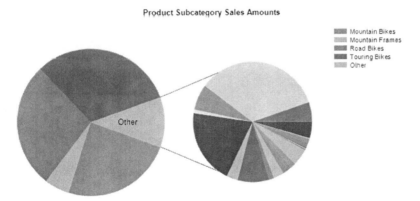

FIGURE 18-44 You can create a secondary pie chart to break out smaller pie slices.

The secondary pie chart does not allow you the same amount of formatting or configuration options that you have in the primary chart, although there are a few properties you can configure. These properties are available in the *CustomAttributes* section of the Properties window for the series. You can specify the color of the collected slice in the primary chart, the color, labels, legend text, and tooltips. You can also specify whether you want to show the legend for the collected chart. However, the labels appear in the same legend as the primary chart, and the legend does not distinguish colors by pie chart, as you can see in Figure 18-45.

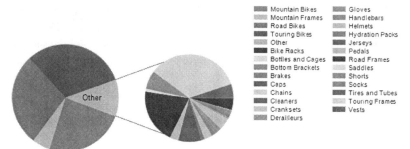

Product Subcategory Sales Amounts

Mountain Bikes	Gloves
Mountain Frames	Handlebars
Road Bikes	Helmets
Touring Bikes	Hydration Packs
Other	Jerseys
Bike Racks	Pedals
Bottles and Cages	Road Frames
Bottom Brackets	Saddles
Brakes	Shorts
Caps	Socks
Chains	Tires and Tubes
Cleaners	Touring Frames
Cranksets	Vests
Derailleurs	

FIGURE 18-45 You can include the secondary pie chart labels in the legend by setting the *CollectedChartShow-Legend* property to True.

CHAPTER 19

Comparing values to goals with gauges

A gauge is a special type of data visualization that you can use to display key performance indicators (KPIs). In many ways, a gauge is like a chart because you can choose among several different types. You can then configure the elements of the selected gauge type to fine-tune its appearance, as we explain in this chapter.

Adding a gauge to a report

Unlike a chart, which displays multiple data points in column or chart form, a simple gauge represents a single data value from your dataset that displays on a scale. You can think of it as analogous to a data point on a chart's value axis. A gauge uses a pointer to indicate the position of the data value on the scale. You can also add one or more ranges to the scale to identify areas on the scale that represent a warning zone or a target zone. You can also use multiple scales in a gauge and assign a separate pointer to each scale.

Understanding gauge types

Before adding a gauge to a report, you should have a clear understanding of your options. After you make a selection, you cannot change a gauge to a different type later. You can choose from the following two main types of gauges:

- **Radial Gauge**   This type of gauge has a circular or semi-circular shape and often uses a needle as a pointer to a value, much like a speedometer, as shown in Figure 19-1.

- **Linear Gauge**   This type of gauge is rectangular with a shape like a ruler, as shown in Figure 19-2. It can display a value by using a bar, like a thermometer, or by using a pointer. The linear gauge works well for comparisons of multiple data points, making it a good choice to include in repeating rows or columns in a tablix.

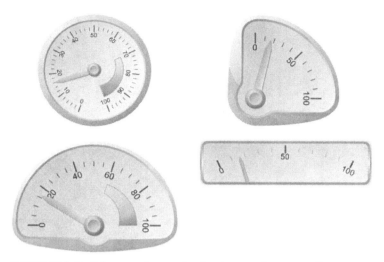

FIGURE 19-1 Radial gauges have a circular shape and use a needle to represent a value.

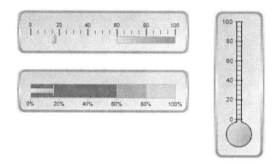

FIGURE 19-2 Linear gauges have a rectangular shape and use a bar or a needle to represent a value.

Creating a gauge

To create a gauge, you drag the control from the Toolbox into the report layout. Although you can add a gauge directly to the body of your report, a common way to display gauges is in groups, which you can achieve by placing a gauge inside a table, matrix, or list. You can also place multiple gauges in a single gauge panel to compare data between fields, as we explain later in the "Grouping gauges" section of this chapter. Regardless, the Select Gauge Type dialog displays when you add a gauge to your report, as shown in Figure 19-3.

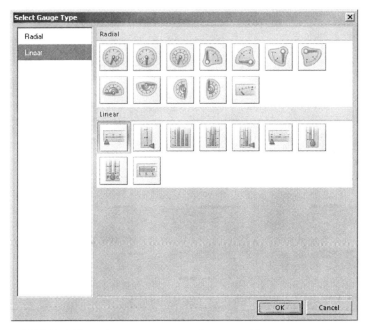

FIGURE 19-3 You select a gauge type when you add a new gauge to your report.

Radial gauges

You can choose any of the following twelve radial gauges for your report:

- **Radial**   The radial gauge is a full circular gauge.

- **Radial with Mini Gauge**   This gauge is a radial gauge that includes a second mini-gauge on the primary gauge face, which you can use to display a second value.

- **Two Scales**   This gauge type is a radial gauge with two scales.

- **90 Degrees Northeast/Northwest/Southwest/Southeast**   You can choose one of these four gauges when you want to use a radial gauge that displays a sweep of 90 degrees only. Each gauge in this set faces in a different direction.

- **180 Degrees North/South/West/East**   Another option is to use one of these half-circle gauges having a 180-degree sweep. You can choose from four orientations: north, south, east, and west.

- **Meter**   This gauge looks much like a linear gauge and uses a needle pointer by default. The radial scale curves according to the *StartAngle* and *SweepAngle* properties that you set, although the gauge face itself is linear.

Linear gauges

The following nine linear gauges provide a variety of KPI visualization options:

- **Horizontal/Vertical**   These two gauges are identical except for their orientation: horizontal or vertical.

- **Multiple Bar Pointers**   This gauge includes three bar pointers by default and looks similar to a column chart. You can add or remove pointers as needed.

- **Two Scales**   This linear gauge with a vertical orientation includes two scales by default.

- **Three Color Range**   This gauge includes three ranges, each spanning one-third of the gauge scale. By default, the range at the lower end of the scale is red, the middle range is yellow, and the top range is green.

- **Logarithmic**   This horizontal gauge has a logarithmic scale by default.

- **Thermometer**   You can use this gauge to display a value with a bar that increases in value beginning at the bulb end, like a traditional thermometer. The default values of the scale range from 0 to 100.

- **Thermometer Fahrenheit/Celsius**   This gauge is a thermometer gauge that includes both a Fahrenheit and Celsius scale.

- **Bullet Graph**   This gauge is an adaptation of the bar graph developed by Stephen Few and described in his book *Information Dashboard Design* (O'Reilly, 2006). You use it to easily compare a value to a target value against a background that defines whether the value represents bad, fair, or good performance.

Working with gauge elements

After you add a gauge to the report, you click the gauge to display the Gauge Data pane, as shown in Figure 19-4. The Gauge Data pane is similar to the Chart Data pane that you use to configure charts. However, a gauge has only a single drop zone that you use to assign a value to a pointer by selecting a dataset field or developing an expression. To further enhance the appearance of the gauge, you can configure properties for the pointer and scale, and you can add a range, a label, an additional scale, or even an additional gauge if you want.

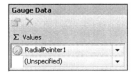

FIGURE 19-4 You use the Gauge Data pane to assign a value to a pointer and configure pointer properties.

Understanding gauge elements

Reporting Services provides you with a wide variety of gauge shapes and styles from which to choose. Regardless of the gauge type, all gauges share the following elements, shown in Figure 19-5, many of which are optional:

- **Gauge** The gauge element is the graphic that contains the scale, range, and pointer elements you use to convey information to the user. The gauge you choose determines the overall look and feel of the scale, range, and pointer elements associated with the gauge, although you do have some options for customizing these elements.

- **Pointer** The pointer is the gauge element that represents a data value. A pointer can be a needle, marker, or bar, although the needle pointer type is available for radial gauges only. After choosing a pointer type, you can further customize the look of the pointer by selecting a particular needle style or a specific marker shape. You can also use a custom image as a pointer. We explain how to configure the pointer in the "Pointer" section of this chapter.

- **Pointer cap** The pointer cap is the anchor from which a needle pointer extends. Pointer caps are an option with needle pointer styles only. You can choose from a range of styles for a pointer cap or use a custom image, as described in the "Pointer" section.

- **Scale** The scale is the element of the gauge that gives context to the value represented by the pointer. It functions just like a chart axis, supplying a range of values against which you compare the pointer value. You can customize the minimum and maximum values of the scale, the appearance and location of tick marks and scale labels, and the general appearance of the scale, as we explain in the "Scale" section of this chapter.

- **Major and minor tick marks** As on a chart axis, you have the option to display major and minor tick marks on your gauge scale. You can customize where and how these appear, explained later in this chapter in the "Scale properties" section.

- **Scale label** You can also add labels to your scale to help users understand the gauge. We explain how to add and configure scale labels in the "Scale properties" section of this chapter.

- **Range** A range is a highlighted portion of the scale. By using a range, you help users see when a data value falls within an important subset of values. You can add multiple ranges to a gauge, and you can customize the look and feel of a range with different colors and fill effects, as we explain in the "Range" section of this chapter.

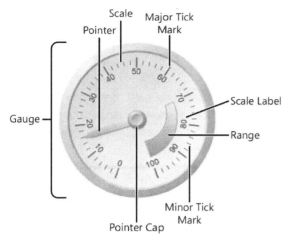

FIGURE 19-5 A gauge consists of many elements that you can configure individually to enhance its appearance.

Pointer

You associate a gauge's pointer to a data value you are measuring. To specify this value, you open the Gauge Data pane and select a field from the drop-down list for the second row of the pointer, which is labeled as Unspecified until you select a field. An alternative option is to drag and drop a field from the Report Data pane into the Values drop zone of the Gauge Data Pane. If you prefer to use an expression instead, you must select the Unspecified label for the pointer, click the Properties button in the Gauge Data pane toolbar, and then assign an aggregate expression to the *Value* property.

You can add another pointer to the same gauge by right-clicking the gauge and selecting Add Pointer. The new pointer displays in the Gauge Data pane. You then assign a value to the new pointer in the same way. A gauge can contain as many pointers as you like. If you decide later to delete a pointer, select it in the Gauge Data pane and click the Delete button. Or you can right-click the pointer in the gauge and select Delete Pointer.

Value

A gauge's pointer value can be a numeric field, which by default is summarized using the *Sum* function. Or it can be a non-numeric field, in which case it is aggregated using the *Count* function instead. You can change the default aggregation function by clicking the arrow next to the pointer expression. That is, click the arrow in the row below the pointer name in the Values drop zone, and then point to Aggregate, as shown in Figure 19-6. You can then select an alternate aggregate function to apply to the selected field.

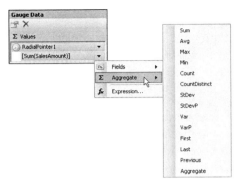

FIGURE 19-6 You can use any aggregate function to assign a value to a gauge pointer.

You can also change the pointer value by pointing to the expression below the pointer name and then selecting Expression. This selection displays the Expression editor, where you can change the aggregation in the expression or change the expression to any type of calculation that you need, as long as the result returns a numeric value.

Pointer properties

You can change pointer properties by selecting the pointer in the gauge and then locating and changing a property value in the Properties window, such as the *Name* property. However, until you become more familiar with pointer properties, you might find it easier to review current settings and make changes as necessary by opening the Radial Pointer Properties dialog box, shown in Figure 19-7, or the Linear Pointer Properties dialog box, depending on your gauge. To open this dialog box, right-click the pointer on the report layout, or select the arrow to the right of the pointer name in the Gauge Data pane and then select Pointer Properties.

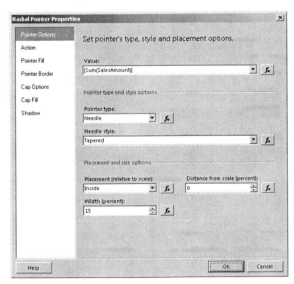

FIGURE 19-7 You can configure the Value expression, pointer type and style, and pointer placement on the Pointer Options page of the Radial Pointer Properties and Linear Pointer Properties dialog boxes.

The pointer properties are organized into the following pages:

- **Pointer Options**   Here you can update the expression to use as the pointer value, which you can also set directly in the Gauge Data pane. If you are working with a radial gauge, you can set the Pointer Type as Needle, Marker, or Bar. With a linear gauge, you can choose Marker, Bar, or Thermometer as the Pointer Type.

  Your selection of a pointer type determines the selection you can make for a pointer style. For example, for a needle type, you can select Triangular, Tapered, or Arrow, among others. Your options for Marker Style are the same as those you use in a chart, such as Rectangle, Circle, or Wedge. If you select Bar as a pointer, you set the *Bar Start* property by selecting either *ScaleStart* to use the minimum value on a dynamic scale or Zero to use an explicit start value if the scale has negative values or a subset of positive values. When using a Thermometer pointer type, you can set the Thermometer Style as Standard for a round bulb or Flask for a more triangular bulb shape.

  Many of the placement and size properties are common to all pointer types. For Placement (Relative To Scale), you can choose one of the following positions: Inside, Outside, or Cross. You can also set both the distance of the pointer from the scale and the pointer width as a percentage value. If you use a marker as a pointer, you can also set its length as a percentage value.

  A thermometer pointer has two additional properties: Offset (From Zero Position) and Size (Percent). The offset position determines the distance between the beginning of the scale and the top edge of the thermometer bulb, whereas the size setting increases or decreases the height and width of the thermometer bulb.

- **Action**   You can enable any of the standard action types (described in Chapter 13, "Adding interactivity") when a user clicks the pointer.

- **Pointer Fill**   On this page, you can choose one of the following fill styles: Solid, Gradient, or Pattern. If you choose Gradient or Pattern, you set both a color and a secondary color for the pointer. For a gradient fill, you specify a gradient style, such as Diagonal Left or Horizontal Center, to control the application of color to the pointer. For a pattern fill style, you must select a pattern such as Horizontal or Vertical, among others.

- **Pointer Border**   You can configure the pointer border by selecting a line style, a line width, and a line color.

- **Cap Options**   If you are working with a radial gauge, you have access to the Cap Options page, shown in Figure 19-8. Here you can choose to hide the pointer cap if you prefer. If you choose to show it, you can choose whether to show a reflection or position the cap above or below the pointer. You can also choose a specific style of pointer cap from the Cap Style drop-down list. Finally, you can set the width of the pointer cap as a percentage value.

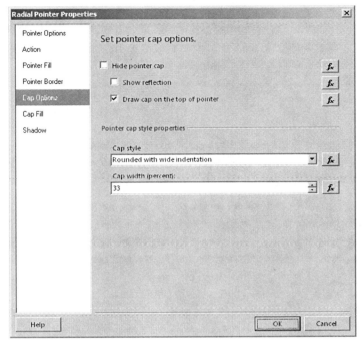

FIGURE 19-8 You can configure the appearance of the pointer cap on the Cap Options page of the Radial Pointer Properties dialog box.

■ **Cap Fill** Here you can specify the fill color of the pointer cap. This page is available only for a radial gauge.

■ **Shadow** You can add a subtle three-dimensional appearance to a gauge by adding a shadow behind the pointer (and cap, if applicable), specifying the shadow offset as a measurement unit, such as pt, and the shadow intensity.

Custom pointer

Instead of using one of the built-in pointers options, you can use a custom image instead. When using a custom image as a pointer, you should keep a few things in mind. The origin of the pointer must be at the top of the image, and the end of the pointer must be pointing down, regardless of how the pointer displays in the gauge.

After creating a suitable image, add it as an embedded image to your report (as described in Chapter 9, "Designing the report layout"). Then click the pointer on the gauge, and expand the *PointerImage* section in the Properties window. Set *Source* to Embedded, and then set *Value* to the name of your image. If you have areas of the image that you want to make transparent, set *TransparentColor* to the color that you want to remove from the image. Be sure to use a color that does not already appear on the gauge so as not to inadvertently hide portions of the gauge.

Note You are not limited to using an embedded image. If you store your image in an external location or in the database, set the *Source* property appropriately and proceed. Chapter 9 explains how to use all types of images in a report.

Snapping interval

By default, the pointer will point to the exact value specified on the scale. However, you can choose to have the pointer snap to a point if it is within a certain interval. This effectively rounds the value of the pointer to the value you desire.

To set a snapping interval, select the pointer on the gauge. Then, in the Properties window, set the *SnappingEnabled* property to True, as shown in Figure 19-9. Next, specify a value for *SnappingInterval*. For example, if you want the pointer to snap to the closest multiple of 5, set the interval to 5. If instead you want the pointer to snap to the closest multiple of 10, set the interval to 10.

FIGURE 19-9 You can use the *SnappingEnabled* and *SnappingInterval* properties to adjust the pointer's position on a gauge.

Scale

The gauge scale is the visual reference against which you measure the pointer value. Just as you can have multiple pointers on a scale, you can also have multiple scales in a gauge. However, a gauge has only one scale available by default, unless you select the Two Scale radial or linear gauge.

Scale properties

To configure the properties of a scale, right-click the scale and select Scale Properties to open the Radial Scale Properties dialog box, shown in Figure 19-10, or the Linear Scale Properties dialog box, according to the gauge type. In the Scale Properties dialog box, you have access to a variety of properties affecting the display of the scale in the gauge. Most properties can be set dynamically by using expressions.

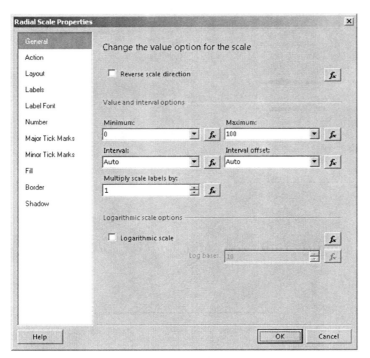

FIGURE 19-10 The Radial Scale Properties dialog box is similar to the Vertical Axis Properties dialog box for a column chart.

These properties are organized into the following pages:

- **General** The General page is the same for both linear and radial gauges. Here is where you set the Minimum and Maximum values for your gauge scale and specify the interval and interval type. You also have the option to multiply the scale labels by a value that you specify. By default, the Multiply Scale Labels By value is set to 1. This multiplier does not affect the values of the field or the scale but simply changes the labels on the scale, which can be a good way to avoid label collisions. If necessary, you can reverse the scale direction or use a logarithmic scale. These options are similar to settings you use to configure a vertical axis in a chart, as we explain in Chapter 18, "Working with chart elements."

- **Action** You can enable an action to launch when a user clicks on the scale. More information about actions is available in Chapter 13.

- **Layout** On this page, you can specify how to position the scale within the gauge. For a radial gauge, you have the option to set values for the Scale Radius, the Start Angle, the Sweep Angle, and the Scale Bar Width, as shown in Figure 19-11. The Scale Radius and Scale Bar Width are percentage values, whereas the Start Angle and Sweep Angle are expressed in degrees. For a linear gauge, you can set the Position, Start Margin, End Margin, and Scale Bar Width.

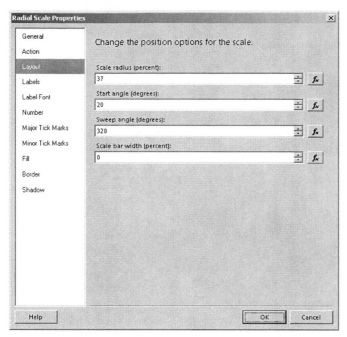

FIGURE 19-11 You can define the sweep and angle of a radial scale on the Layout page of the Radial Scale Properties dialog box.

- **Labels**   You also have fine control over the appearance of your scale labels, as shown in Figure 19-12. For both linear and radial gauges, you can simply hide labels altogether by selecting a check box or you can use a conditional expression to hide them. Another option is to hide the first and last labels on the scale. If you choose to display labels, you can specify Placement (Relative To Scale), Distance From Scale (Percent), Label Interval, and Label Interval Offset. For a radial gauge, you have the additional option to set whether you want the labels to rotate with the scale.

- **Label Font/Font**   Here you can specify the font family, font size, font style, font color, and font effects for the scale labels.

- **Number**   On this page, you choose a category and select formatting options based on that category. For example, for the Number category, you can set the number of decimal places, show values in Thousands, Millions, or Billions, or choose how zero and negative numbers appear. This page includes a Use Regional Formatting check box, which allows you to localize numerical formatting for users.

- **Major Tick Marks and Minor Tick Marks**   You can configure the appearance of the major and minor tick marks on your scale by opening the applicable page. Although only the Major Tick Marks page is shown in Figure 19-13, the options available are the same for both types of tick marks. You can hide tick marks, or you can choose a shape and set its placement relative to the scale if you choose to include the tick marks. You can also set the width and length by using a percentage value. Last, you can set explicit intervals to place tick marks along the axis.

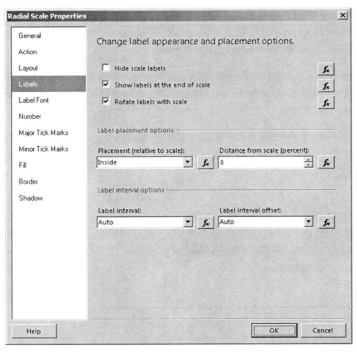

FIGURE 19-12 You can configure the appearance of labels in the Scale Properties dialog box.

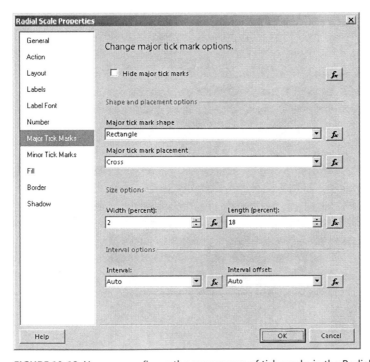

FIGURE 19-13 You can configure the appearance of tick marks in the Radial Scale Properties dialog box.

- **Fill** You can choose the fill style (Solid, Gradient, or Pattern) and set a specific color or use a conditional expression to set a color for the scale. You can set the fill properties only if the Scale Bar Width is not set to zero on the Layout page.

- **Border** You can add a border to the scale by specifying a line style, a line width, and a line color. As with fill, you can configure border properties only if the Scale Bar Width is not set to zero on the Layout page.

- **Shadow** You can add a shadow behind the scale by specifying the shadow offset as a measurement unit, such as pt, and a shadow intensity.

Multiple scales

To add a second scale, right-click the gauge and select Add Scale. A new scale appears on the gauge. You can now format this scale as described above. Further, you can then add a pointer to the new scale and compare multiple values side by side, as shown in Figure 19-14. If necessary, you can delete a scale by right-clicking it and selecting Delete Scale.

FIGURE 19-14 You can create a gauge with multiple scales and pointers.

Range

A range is a highlighted section of the gauge scale. You can define multiple ranges and use different colors to highlight multiple parts of a scale. Therefore, you can use a range to identify either an undesirable set of values, a desirable set of values, or both. Some gauges have a range by default.

Range properties

To configure the properties of a range, right-click the range and select Range Properties to open the Radial Scale Range Properties dialog box, shown in Figure 19-15, or the Linear Scale Range Properties dialog box. On the General page, you can specify the start and end values for the range. You can also define the placement of the range relative to the scale in addition to the starting and ending widths of the range as a percentage value. For example, if you have a larger starting width than ending width for your range, the range will taper down to the ending width over the length of the range. Other pages in the Range Properties dialog box allow you to set report actions on the range, the fill of the range, border properties, and shadow properties, which are similar to the properties for the scale.

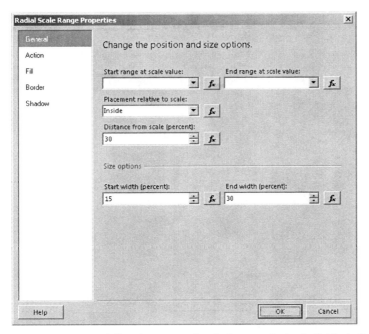

FIGURE 19-15 You define the start and end of a range in the Radial Scale Range Properties dialog box.

Multiple ranges

To add a second range, right click the gauge and select Add Range. A second range appears on the gauge, ready for you to format as described in the previous section. For example, you can display one range with a red color to represent a warning zone and a second range with a green color to represent a target zone, as shown in Figure 19-16. You can later remove a range by right-clicking it and selecting Delete Range.

FIGURE 19-16 You can add multiple ranges to the same gauge.

Gauge

The gauge face has a number of properties associated with it. To access these properties, right-click the gauge and click Gauge Properties to open the properties dialog box. Although several options are common to both radial and linear gauges, some properties are specific to each type.

Radial gauge properties

For a radial gauge, the dialog box that will open is the Radial Gauge Properties dialog box, shown in Figure 19-17. On the General page, you can give the gauge report element a specific name and you can define a tooltip, just as you can with a chart or other report item types.

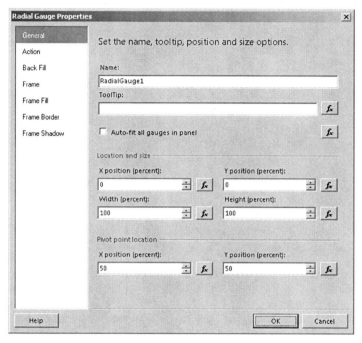

FIGURE 19-17 You use the Radial Gauge Properties dialog box to configure the location and size of the gauge, among other properties.

By default, the Auto-Fit All Gauges In Panel check box is selected. In that case, Reporting Services manages the size of the gauges that are grouped together in a single panel, as we describe in the "Grouping gauges" section of this chapter. If you prefer to resize the gauge yourself, you must clear this check box. Then you can set the location of the gauge by configuring its X and Y position, and you can adjust the width and height as necessary.

A radial gauge also includes an X and Y position for the pivot point location. The pivot point location is the point around which the gauge elements rotate. The default location for the pivot point is the center of the gauge.

Linear gauge properties

When you open up the Gauge Properties for a linear gauge, you have many of the same options as for a radial gauge on the General page, as you can see in Figure 19-18. Here you can set the name of the gauge, a tooltip, and size the gauge within the gauge panel. Unique to the linear gauge are the Gauge Orientation Options. The Aspect Ratio is automatically determined unless you provide an explicit value to set the width as a multiple of height. That is, an aspect ratio of 2 creates a linear gauge with a width that is always twice the height of the gauge, no matter how you resize the gauge. You can also set the gauge orientation as Auto, Horizontal, and Vertical.

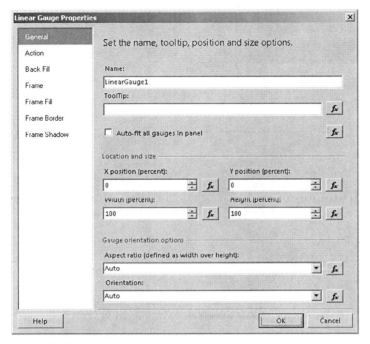

FIGURE 19-18 You can configure the aspect ratio and orientation of a linear gauge in the Linear Gauge Properties dialog box.

Common gauge properties

The following pages in the Gauge Properties dialog box are common to both radial and linear gauges:

- **Action**   You can set a report action for the gauge.

- **Back Fill**   You can specify the fill and color for the background of the gauge face.

- **Frame**   Here you can choose a style of frame (None, Simple, or Edged) for your gauge as well as a particular shape of frame from the Shape drop-down list, as shown in Figure 19-19. You can also set the width of the frame as a percentage value. Another option is to add a Glass Effect, which adds highlights and shadows as if the gauge face were made of glass.

- **Frame Fill**   You can specify the fill and color for the gauge frame.

- **Frame Border**   You can select a line style, color, and width for the frame border.

- **Frame Shadow**   You can add a shadow to the frame by specifying the shadow offset and intensity.

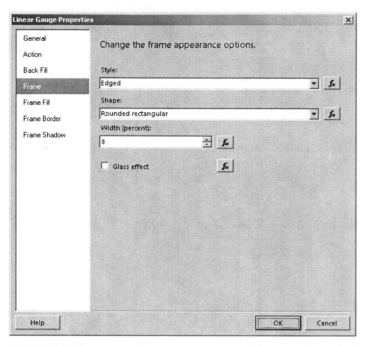

FIGURE 19-19 You can configure the appearance of the gauge frame in the Linear Gauge Properties dialog box.

Gauge label

You can add a label to the gauge face by right-clicking the gauge and clicking Add Label. After you add a label, you can configure its properties. Just right-click the label, and click Label Properties to open the Label Properties dialog box, shown in Figure 19-20.

In the Label Properties dialog box, you can specify the text to display as a label and set the vertical and text alignment of the text. You can anchor your label to a specific element by selecting that element in the Anchor Label To drop-down list. You can also specify the placement relative to the top-left corner of the gauge and set width, height, and angle properties. As with most report elements, you can also set actions on the label, as well as control font, fill, border, and shadow of the label on other pages of the properties dialog box.

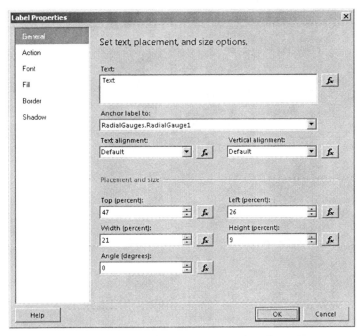

FIGURE 19-20 You can add a label to a gauge and configure its appearance, placement, and size in the Label Properties dialog box.

Gauge panel

The gauge panel is the container for a gauge, having properties of its own. Furthermore, a gauge panel is a type of data region to which you can apply visibility, filtering, and pagination options. To access the gauge panel properties, as shown in Figure 19-21, right-click inside the gauge control but outside of the face of the gauge, and click Gauge Panel Properties.

On the General page of the Gauge Panel Properties dialog box, you can specify a name for the gauge panel element and add a tooltip. Here you can also associate the gauge with a particular dataset. Just like other report items, the gauge panel has properties defining the visibility of the gauge, applying filters on the data used by the gauge, and setting the location of a page break. It also includes generic properties for setting the fill of the gauge panel and configuring its border.

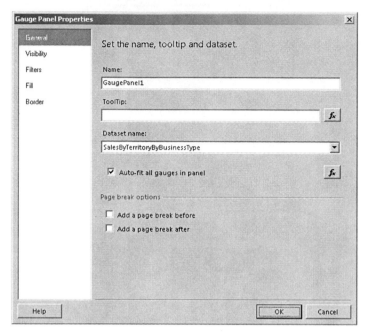

FIGURE 19-21 You can configure visibility, filtering, and pagination options in the Gauge Panel Properties dialog box.

Grouping gauges

Rather than use a gauge as an independent report item, you can combine it with other gauges to facilitate comparisons of KPI values. You can include multiple gauges in a single panel, or you can use repeating behavior in a tablix to dynamically generate multiple gauges.

Multiple gauges in a gauge panel

Similar to how you can create multiple chart areas in a chart, you can add multiple gauges to a gauge panel. When you do this, you can add an adjacent gauge to display gauges side by side. Or you can nest a child gauge inside a parent gauge.

Adjacent gauges

To add a new gauge adjacent to the current gauge, right-click the gauge, select Add Gauge, and then click Adjacent. At that point, the Select Gauge Type dialog box appears for you to make a selection. Then the second gauge displays adjacent to the first gauge. Both gauges are resized to fit next to each other in the gauge panel, as shown in Figure 19-22.

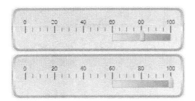

FIGURE 19-22 You can create adjacent linear gauges for easier comparison of values.

You can reposition adjacent gauges by right-clicking a gauge and selecting Gauge Properties. In the Gauge Properties dialog box, clear the Auto-Fit All Gauges In Panel check box. After you do this, you can then set the location and size properties of the gauge.

Child gauges

A child gauge displays inside the parent gauge, as shown in Figure 19-23. To add a child gauge, right-click a gauge, select Add Gauge, and then click Child. Make your gauge selection in the Select Gauge Type dialog box, and then the child gauge appears in the top-left corner of the parent gauge. You can later reposition the child gauge by right-clicking the child gauge and then setting the location and size of the child gauge relative to the parent. If you change your mind later, right-click the child gauge and then click Delete Gauge.

FIGURE 19-23 You can place a child gauge inside a parent gauge.

Repeating gauges

Gauges can be placed inside a tablix, repeating across rows for easy comparison. To do this, drop a gauge into the text box of the tablix in which you want it to appear, and then select the gauge type you want to use in the Select Gauge Type dialog box. The gauge now appears in your tablix and can be configured like any other gauge. You can assign the pointer to a field value that is determined by the row on which the gauge appears.

When you run a report, the pointer changes, depending on the row, as shown in Figure 19-24. As with charts, data bars, or sparklines in a tablix, the row context determines the data values used in the gauge.

Group	Country	Business Type	Sales Amount	
Europe	France	Specialty Bike Shop	$120,181.38	
		Value Added Reseller	$399,158.53	
		Warehouse	$857,270.81	
		Country Total	$1,376,610.72	
	Germany	Specialty Bike Shop	$77,158.48	
		Value Added Reseller	$299,826.74	
		Warehouse	$508,136.14	
		Country Total	$885,121.35	

FIGURE 19-24 You can add a gauge to a table to view repeating gauges in a tablix.

CHAPTER 20

Displaying performance with indicators

Another type of data visualization you can use in a report is an indicator. A more common way to display key performance indicators (KPIs) in a report is to use an indicator rather than a gauge. Prior to SQL Server 2008 R2 Reporting Services, the only way to display KPIs without using a gauge was to upload multiple images and then use a conditional expression to determine which image to display. Beginning with SQL Server 2008 R2, you can now choose from several built-in indicator types and define the value ranges applicable to each indicator. If you still prefer to use your own images, you can adapt the indicator to use those images, too.

Adding an indicator to a report

Indicators are a similar to gauges. In fact, indicators display inside a gauge panel just as a gauge does. Like a gauge, an indicator displays a single data value. Furthermore, you configure an indicator state in much the same way that you configure gauge ranges. However, unlike a gauge, an indicator does not have pointers or scales to give context to its data value.

Understanding indicator types

The following four main categories of indicators are available to you in Reporting Services:

- **Directional** Arrows pointing in the direction a value is trending.

- **Symbol** Easily recognizable graphics such as flags, check marks, and exclamation points representing an indicator state.

- **Shape** Assorted shapes such as circles, diamonds, squares, and traffic lights delineating different indicator states.

- **Ratings** Shapes showing a progression, such as one star up to five stars, or bars and quadrants that use progressive shading to represent an increasing value.

Creating an indicator

To create an indicator, drag the control from the Toolbox into the report layout. The Select Indicator Type dialog box, as shown in Figure 20-1, displays examples of indicators to guide you in making a selection. You must make a selection here even if you plan to use your own images as indicators. If you decide later to use a different indicator type, you can right-click the indicator in your report, select Change Indicator Type to reopen the Select Indicator Type dialog box, and then make a new selection. Or you can simply change the icon by opening the Indicator Properties dialog box. It's very easy to change the appearance of the indicator when the need arises.

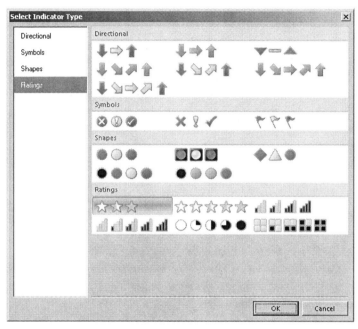

FIGURE 20-1 You must select an indicator type in the Select Indicator Type dialog box to add an indicator to your report.

Configuring an indicator

After adding an indicator to your report, double-click the indicator to display the Gauge Data pane, as shown in Figure 20-2. An indicator, like a gauge, displays inside a Gauge Panel and provides access to its value and properties through the Gauge Data pane. An indicator has a single drop zone that you use to assign a data field or expression to the indicator. You can then configure properties for the states of the indicator. To delete an indicator, simply right-click the indicator and then click Delete Indicator.

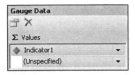

FIGURE 20-2 You can use the Gauge Data pane to configure an indicator value.

Assigning an indicator value

Click the arrow next to the Unspecified label to select a field from a dataset in your report, or drag the dataset field from the Report Data pane and drop it on the Unspecified label. The report design adds the Sum function for a numeric value and the Count function for a non-numeric field, just like a chart or gauge.

After you add a field to the Gauge Data pane, you can change the field. If you click the arrow next to the field name, you can point to Fields and choose a different field or point to Aggregate and apply a different aggregate function, in the same way we described for a chart in Chapter 17, "Creating charts." Another option is to click the arrow next to the field, click Expression to open the Expression editor, and then create an expression that returns a numeric value.

Unlike a gauge, you cannot set up multiple values for a single indicator. Although the single value of an indicator is analogous to a gauge pointer, an indicator can have only one value, unlike a gauge, which can have multiple pointers, one for each data value. However, you can have multiple indicators in a gauge panel, which we will explain in the "Grouping indicators" section of this chapter.

Defining indicator properties

The indicator properties determine how the indicator displays in your report. To open the Indicator Properties dialog box, right-click the indicator and then click Indicator Properties. You can also access this dialog box by clicking the arrow next to the indicator in the Gauge Data pane and selecting Indicator Properties.

General properties

On the General page of the Indicator Properties dialog box, shown in Figure 20-3, you configure the name for an indicator and optionally specify static text or set an expression to display as a tooltip. The default setting for the indicator layout in the gauge panel is to use auto-fit. You can clear this selection to configure the indicator's location and size within the gauge panel, as we explain later in the "Customizing indicators" section of this chapter.

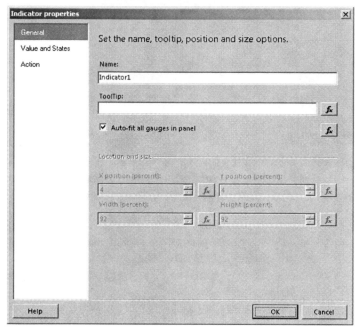

FIGURE 20-3 You configure the indicator name, tooltip, location, and size properties on the General page of the Indicator Properties dialog box.

Value and states

The key to the configuration of an indicator is the set of properties that you configure on the Value And States page of the Indicator Properties dialog box, shown in Figure 20-4. Here you establish the rules that determine the icon and the icon color to use when the report executes.

You use the Value And States page to configure the following properties:

- **Value** Yet another way to change the indicator value is to select a field expression in the Value drop-down list or configure an expression for the *Value* property.

- **States Measurement Unit** Before you can configure the start and end values of the state, you need to decide whether to define them as straight numeric values or percentages of a range by choosing the applicable unit type in the drop-down list: Numeric or Percentage.

- **Indicator States** A new indicator has default states based on the icon set you selected when you created the indicator, but you are not limited to that icon set. You can use different icons, change colors, and adjust the start and end values of each state.

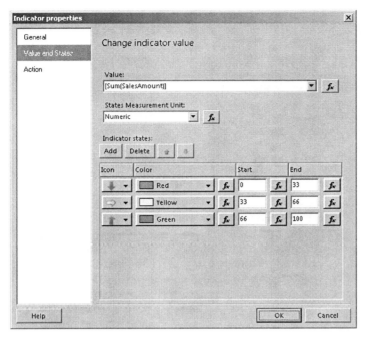

FIGURE 20-4 You use the Value And States page of the Indicator Properties dialog box to define the rules for displaying an icon at report execution time.

The indicator state is a collection of properties unique to indicators and differentiates it from all other data visualization types. You can think of the indicator states for an indicator as a conditional expression that determines the image to display at run-time. For each indicator state, you specify the following properties:

- **Icon**   Click the drop-down list for the icon to select a different icon from the set of built-in icons, and select No Icon or select Image for your own icon. You are not limited to the icon set you initially selected when creating the indicator. We explain more about working with your own images in the "Customizing indicators" section of this chapter. You can also use an expression to determine which icon to assign to a state.

- **Color**   Click the color to display the color picker, from which you can choose a different color, or click the More Colors link to open the Select Color dialog box to choose from a broader spectrum of colors. Click the fx button to the right of the color button to use an expression to set a color.

- **Start and End**   All states have a start and ending value that you set to define a range. You can also use the expression button to enter an expression for the start and ending values. Your States Measurement Unit selection affects the way that Reporting Services applies these values.

With a numeric measurement unit, the start and end values are explicit and easy to understand. You define a numeric start and end value for each state, just like you set a range in a gauge. For example, if a numeric indicator state has a start value of 0 and an end value of 1,000,000, a data value of 885,121.13 is assigned to this indicator state, as shown in Figure 20-5.

Country	Sales Amount	
Australia	$746,904.41	↓
Canada	$2,390,261.51	⇨
France	$1,376,610.72	⇨
Germany	$885,121.35	↓
United Kingdom	$1,277,105.23	⇨
United States	$9,362,059.37	↑

FIGURE 20-5 You can set an explicit numeric range for each indicator state, such as 0 to 1,000,000 for the down arrow.

With a percentage measurement unit, you define a start and end percentage for each state relative to a minimum and maximum value. By default, Reporting Services automatically calculates the minimum and maximum value found in the dataset, as shown in Figure 20-6, but you can explicitly set a specific minimum and maximum value.

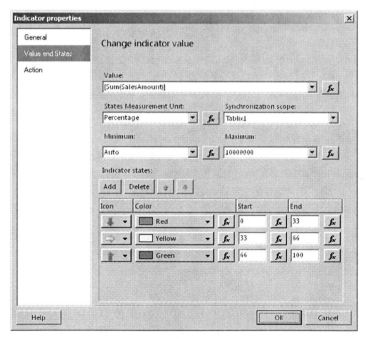

FIGURE 20-6 You can base an indicator state on a percentage of a range defined by the Minimum and Maximum fields, which can be calculated automatically at run-time or set explicitly.

Consider a scenario in which you have a target value for a key performance indicator. You can set the maximum value to this target and then create indicator states that represent progress toward that goal as a percentage. For example, if you set the target value as 10,000,000 for each country, you can see in Figure 20-7 how each country's sales amount compares to this target.

Country	Sales Amount		
Australia	$746,904.41	↓	7 %
Canada	$2,390,261.51	↓	24 %
France	$1,376,610.72	↓	14 %
Germany	$885,121.35	↓	9 %
United Kingdom	$1,277,105.23	↓	13 %
United States	$9,362,059.37	↑	94 %

FIGURE 20-7 You can use percentage-based indicator states to measure proximity to a target.

Note If you use a Percentage state measurement unit in an indicator that is not contained in a data region, you must specify a minimum and maximum range value. Otherwise, a Transformation Scope error displays when you run the report. When the indicator is inside a data region, Reporting Services can use scope to automatically calculate a minimum and maximum value within a group but lacks this scoping ability outside of a data region.

You can add another indicator state by clicking the Add button. The new state appears at the bottom of the indicator state list, as shown in Figure 20-8. The new indicator state is assigned No Color by default and has blank start and end values. You can then configure this new indicator state as needed. Conversely, to delete a state, click any property of the indicator state and then click the Delete button.

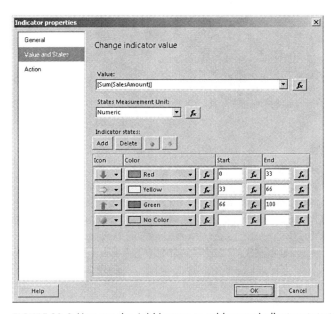

FIGURE 20-8 You use the Add button to add a new indicator state to the bottom of the indicator states list.

As you add or remove indicator states and make adjustments to start and end values, bear in mind that the sequence of indicator states is important, especially when the end value of one indicator state is also the start of another indicator state. For example, suppose you have a set of indicator states like those shown in Figure 20-9. The down arrow has an end value of 100, and the up arrow has a start value of 100. The indicator that displays in the report if the value is 100 depends on the order of the indicator states. Because the down arrow appears in the list of states before the up arrow, the report displays the down arrow for a value of 100. If you want the up arrow to be used instead, you must move that indicator state above the down arrow state in the indicator states list. To change the order of the indicator states, select the one to move and then use the up or down arrow buttons to move it within the indicator states list.

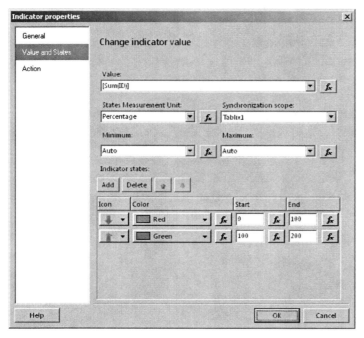

FIGURE 20-9 A data value of 100 uses the first indicator state that includes that value in the specified range of start and end values.

Synchronization scope

When using indicators in a tablix, the group context can change the range of data values available to you. For example, the minimum and maximum sale amounts for businesses in one sales territory might be different from the minimum and maximum sales amounts for businesses in another sales territory. If you use percentage-based indicator states and allow Reporting Services to automatically determine the range, you need to be aware that the minimum and maximum range can change for each group in a data region. Consequently, the indicator state calculations produce different results, which you might not intend.

You can synchronize the scope of the indicators to prevent this range variance by group. Right-click the indicator, and then select Indicator Properties. In the Indicator Properties dialog box, open the Values And States property page. When your indicator appears inside a data region, the Synchronization Scope drop-down list box displays on this page, as shown in Figure 20-10.

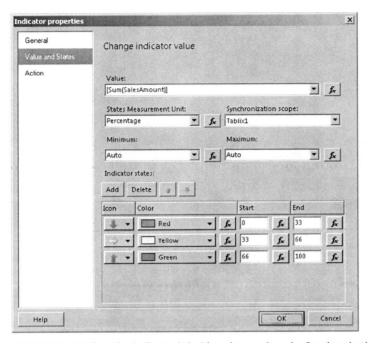

FIGURE 20-10 When the indicator is inside a data region, the Synchronization Scope drop-down list appears next to the States Measurement Unit drop-down.

The default scope is the data region itself, which in this example is the entire tablix. Consequently, Reporting Services uses the same range for all groups, based on the maximum and minimum values of all data in the tablix, as shown in Figure 20-11.

Country	Business Type	Sales Amount	
Australia	Specialty Bike Shop	$165,542.36	
	Value Added Reseller	$400,571.50	
	Warehouse	$180,790.56	
	Country Total	$746,904.41	
Canada	Specialty Bike Shop	$171,182.24	
	Value Added Reseller	$884,996.26	
	Warehouse	$1,334,083.02	
	Country Total	$2,390,261.51	

FIGURE 20-11 You can set the synchronization scope to evaluate each row against the minimum and maximum values of the entire tablix.

If you prefer, you can change the scope by selecting a different scope from this drop-down list. For example, if you change the scope to Country, Reporting Services calculates the minimum and maximum values for the indicator separately for each group, as shown in Figure 20-12.

Country	Business Type	Sales Amount	
Australia	Specialty Bike Shop	$165,542.36	⬇
	Value Added Reseller	$400,571.50	⬆
	Warehouse	$180,790.56	⬇
	Country Total	$746,904.41	
Canada	Specialty Bike Shop	$171,182.24	⬇
	Value Added Reseller	$884,996.26	➡
	Warehouse	$1,334,083.02	⬆
	Country Total	$2,390,261.51	

FIGURE 20-12 You can change the synchronization scope to evaluate each row against the minimum and maximum values of its group.

You can also select the scope option of None from the drop-down list to remove synchronization completely. However, this selection produces an error in the report unless you supply an explicit minimum and maximum value. The automatic calculation of minimum and maximum value requires you to specify group or data region scope.

Note If you use numeric states or specify a minimum and maximum value when you use percentage states, scope synchronization has no effect. That is, Reporting Services uses the scope option of None automatically for these scenarios and ignores any other scope setting you choose. Numeric states use static values for each indicator state and do not change by group. Similarly, by specifying a static range with an explicit minimum and maximum value, the indicator states cannot change dynamically by group.

Grouping indicators

Just as you can have multiple chart areas in a single chart, you can also have multiple indicators in a single gauge panel. You can place indicators adjacent to one another as one option. Or you can combine an indicator with a gauge, either side by side or by creating a child indicator for a gauge.

Adjacent indicators

You can use multiple indicators when you need to visualize multiple data points at once. For example, you might want to use one icon to represent the direction of a trend and another icon to represent whether a value is on target, as shown in Figure 20-13. To achieve this layout, you can position multiple indicators within the same gauge panel.

FIGURE 20-13 You can use one gauge panel to display adjacent indicators.

After you create an indicator, you can right-click the gauge panel and then select Add Indicator to display the Select Indicator Type dialog box and make a selection. The second indicator then appears adjacent to the first indicator, as shown in Figure 20-14. Both indicators are resized to fit next to each other in the space allocated to the gauge panel. If you decide you don't like the effect, you can click the arrow that displays to the right of the indicator name in the Gauge Data pane and then click Delete Indicator.

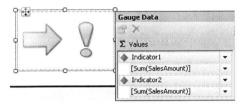

FIGURE 20-14 You can use one gauge panel to display adjacent indicators.

Gauge and indicator

A gauge panel can contain a gauge, an indicator, or both, as shown in Figure 20-15. If you create an indicator first and then want to add a gauge, just right click the gauge panel, select Add Gauge, and then select the type of gauge you want in the Select Gauge Type dialog box. The gauge displays in the Gauge Data pane next to the indicator, and you can proceed to configure its properties, as we explained in Chapter 19, "Comparing values to goals with gauges."

FIGURE 20-15 You can display both a gauge and an indicator in a single gauge panel.

Gauge with child indicator

If you already have a gauge in your report, you can add a child indicator to the gauge, as shown in Figure 20-16. To do this, right-click the gauge, point to Add Indicator, and then select Child. Next you select an Indicator Type. The child indicator displays by default in the upper-left corner of the gauge and is ready for you to set its properties.

FIGURE 20-16 You can enhance a gauge by adding a child indicator.

Customizing indicators

As with most objects in Reporting Services, there are many ways to fine-tune the appearance of an indicator. You can use customized images to add more variety to your use of indicators, and you can add labels to provide additional context. You can also control the layout of an indicator by adjusting its location and size.

Using customized images

Reporting Services includes a variety of icons that you can use as indicators and also provides you with the flexibility to use your own customized images. Your customized image can be an embedded image, external image, or database image, each of which we describe in Chapter 9, "Designing the report layout." To use a customized image as an indicator state icon, open the Values And States page of the Indicator Properties dialog box, and select Image in the icon drop-down list of an indicator state. In the Select The Image Source drop-down list, select External, Embedded, or Database. You then provide the additional information about the image, such as the URL for an external image, the name of the embedded image (which you can import if it's not already embedded), as shown in Figure 20-17, or the field name containing the image and its MIME type.

 Note The color specified for an indicator state is ignored when you use a customized image.

You can use a customized image for each indicator state that you configure for an indicator, as shown in Figure 20-18, or you can use a combination of customized images and built-in icons. You might need to resize the image to display it correctly. You can do this by adjusting the size of its container, such as a text box, or by changing its width and height as we explain in the "Adjusting location and size" section of this chapter.

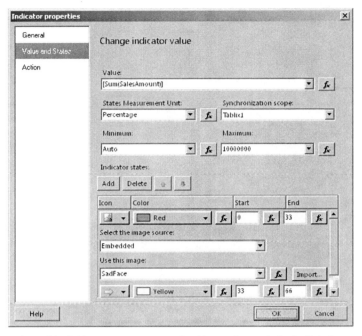

FIGURE 20-17 You can use a customized image instead of a built-in icon.

Country	Sales Amount		
Australia	$746,904.41		7 %
Canada	$2,390,261.51		24 %
France	$1,376,610.72		14 %
Germany	$885,121.35		9 %
United Kingdom	$1,277,105.23		13 %
United States	$9,362,059.37		94 %

FIGURE 20-18 Your report displays the applicable customized image based on the indicator properties.

Adding labels

You can add clarity to an indicator by including a label. To do this, right-click the indicator and then click Add Label. A label displays on top of your indicator with default settings. You can customize the label, including the text it displays, by right-clicking the label and then clicking Label Properties to open the Label Properties dialog box, shown in Figure 20-19.

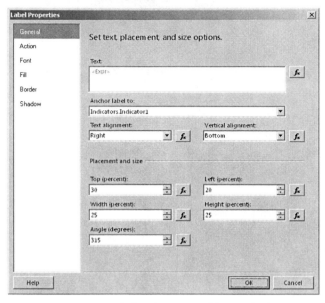

FIGURE 20-19 You can define the text, position, and other properties of an indicator label in the Label Properties dialog box.

Because indicators and gauges are related objects, the Label Properties dialog box is the same. Here you can specify the text of the label as static text or as an expression. You can anchor the label to the indicator and set the alignment of the text. You can also use percentage values to set the placement of the label within the gauge panel and to define its size. Additionally, you can specify an angle for the text. You might need to experiment with these properties to display a legible label without obscuring the indicator, as shown in Figure 20-20. You can use the other pages of the Label Properties dialog box to customize the font, color, border, and shadow for the label or to configure an action.

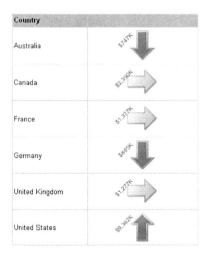

FIGURE 20-20 You can include a label with an indicator.

An indicator can have multiple labels. Just right-click the indicator, and click Add Label to add another label to the indicator. To remove a label, right-click it and then click Delete Label.

Adjusting location and size

If an indicator is too small or too large, you can customize its size. Additionally, you can position it within the gauge panel more precisely. Right-click the indicator, and select Indicator Properties to open the Indicator Properties dialog box. On the General page, clear the Auto-Fit All Gauges In Panel check box to make the Location And Size properties section available, as shown in Figure 20-21. You can now set a specific X and Y position, as well as the width and height of the indicator within the panel.

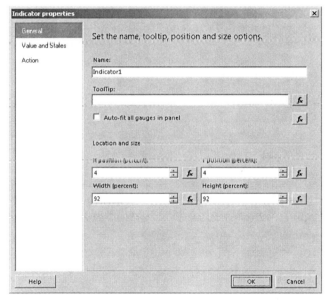

FIGURE 20-21 You can customize the location and size of an indicator on the General page of the Indicator Properties dialog box.

If you have adjacent indicators in the same gauge panel, you can reposition them individually. Be sure to clear the Auto-Fit All Gauges In Panel check box for each indicator. You can then set properties for each indicator's location and size relative to the gauge panel.

Dynamic sizing

When you set the width and height in the Indicator Properties dialog box, you define a static size for the indicator. As an alternative, you can change the size of the indicator according to the indicator state. For example, as the data value gets bigger, you can make the size of the icon bigger. This gives you another visualization technique to use when you want to differentiate more clearly between various indicator states, in addition to using icon type and color.

To set the indicator state size, first select the indicator. In the Properties window, locate the States category, and click the ellipses button next to (Collection) for the *IndicatorStates* property to open the IndicatorState Collection Editor, shown in Figure 20-22. Select the indicator state member to configure in the Members list. Then, in the properties on the right, you can specify a value for the *ScaleFactor* property.

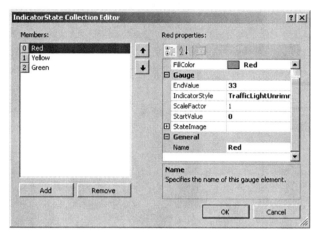

FIGURE 20-22 You can configure the indicator size by setting the *ScaleFactor* property in the IndicatorState Collection Editor.

Reporting Services uses the scale factor value to adjust the size of the icon, making it larger or smaller depending on your needs. You can specify a static number, or click the down arrow in the property box to select Expression and open the Expression editor to set the *ScaleFactor* property dynamically with an expression. For example, you can use a scale factor of 1 for Red, .6 for yellow, and .3 for green to display the largest icon when the indicator state is red and the smallest icon when it's green, as shown in Figure 20-23.

Country	Business Type	Sales Amount	
	Specialty Bike Shop	$120,181.38	
France	Value Added Reseller	$399,158.53	
	Warehouse	$857,270.81	

FIGURE 20-23 Resizing the icon by using the *ScaleFactor* property emphasizes the difference in indicator states.

CHAPTER 21

Mapping data

Charts, gauges, and indicators all provide useful ways to visualize data, but there is one more option that you have in Reporting Services. You can combine reporting data with spatial data in a map and thereby overlay data visualizations such as color-code points or lines onto a map or even a custom polygon shape. By incorporating a spatial aspect to data visualization, you can provide a new way to deliver insights to your users. For example, you can create maps to monitor changes in sales activity in different locations in response to promotional campaigns or show where your customer base is growing. The Map Wizard, which you learn to use in this chapter, simplifies the development of these types of spatial data visualizations. In Chapter 22, "Working with map elements," you learn how to enhance and customize the appearance of your maps by working with individual map elements.

 Note To work with the sample files for this chapter, you must restore the SpatialData database as described in the "Installing the code samples" section of the Introduction.

Understanding spatial data

Fortunately, you do not need to be an expert in *spatial data* to create maps in Reporting Services. Spatial data is information about the location and shape of objects in space. However, you might find it helpful to understand some key concepts. That way, you have a better idea of the types of maps that you can create and the type of data that you need to have available before you get started with report development.

Types of spatial data

There are three types of spatial data that we can use to describe the shape of objects—points, lines, and polygons. The general term for these shapes is *geometries*. Beginning with SQL Server 2008, you can store spatial data in a SQL Server database using any of these three geometries.

> **Note** More accurately, SQL Server stores LineStrings rather than Lines. The Open Geospatial Consortium (OGC) Simple Features for SQL Specification defines a line as a connection between exactly two points, but a LineString is a connection of two or more points. SQL Server implements only the LineString geometry, but conceptually, we refer to this geometry as a line throughout this chapter to correspond to the term you see in the user interface.

Points

A point represents one location in space using either an (X,Y) coordinate system or latitude and longitude. When using a point in maps, a point can have varying degrees of precision. It might be a specific latitude and longitude that you can locate by using a Global Positioning System (GPS), or it could represent a greater area such as a city. By using Reporting Services, you can create a map that displays a set of points, as shown in Figure 21-1. However, a map that displays only points lacks the spatial context that a user needs to understand where the points are located.

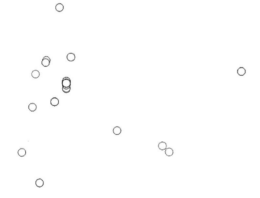

FIGURE 21-1 You can display multiple points in a map.

You can use Reporting Services to combine point data with other shapes to provide context, such as the shape of the state containing these points and where these points are situated relative to the state's borders or key landmarks. As an alternative, Reporting Services allows you to add a Bing Maps tile layer to your map to provide the necessary context without storing the additional spatial data in your database (as explained in the "Choosing spatial data and map view options" section later in this chapter).

Furthermore, Reporting Services allows you to combine a spatial dataset with another dataset to provide analytical context. That is, you can enhance these points by using a range of colors to reflect variances in quantitative data, such as sales volumes or customer counts. You can also use different images to represent a point, such as a pushpin or a star, and then use quantitative data to change the size of each point's image according to rules that you define.

Lines

A line connects multiple points or coordinates. You can use lines across a continent to represent a flight path for shipments or perhaps a suggested street-level route for a salesperson to use when planning customer visits. Just as you can with points, you can create a map containing lines only, as shown in Figure 21-2, but you typically provide additional spatial data to your map to provide context or add a Bing Maps tile layer. You can also support analysis by adding quantitative data to your map and defining rules to set the color or width of lines.

FIGURE 21-2 Geographic lines connect multiple points by using an arc.

Polygons

A polygon is an object composed of four or more coordinates in which the first and last coordinates represent the same point and create a closed area. A polygon shape can define geographical boundaries such as counties, provinces, or states, as shown in Figure 21-3, or structural shapes, such as a floor plan. Even when a polygon represents a recognizable geographical object, you can still combine it with a Bing Maps tile layer in Reporting Services to add features such as roads, city names, or satellite imagery. You can also use colors or bubbles to represent quantitative date within each polygon that you include in your map.

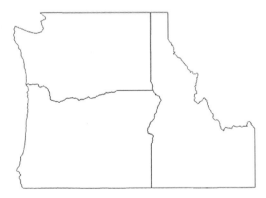

FIGURE 21-3 Of all the geometries, polygons typically provide the most spatial context when used alone.

SQL Server spatial data types

You can store spatial data in a SQL Server database by using the geometry and geography data types. Both of these data types store a stream of binary data in the same format. To insert geographical or geometrical data into a spatial data column, you use *CLR* methods to translate points, polygons, or lines into a spatial data type. You also use *CLR* methods to translate the spatial data to a human readable form. For our purposes in this chapter, we simply assume that the spatial data you want to map exists in a table already. You do not need to know *CLR* methods to use spatial data with Reporting Services.

> **Note** You cannot combine geometry and geography data in the same query. Although there is no restriction for creating a map using different datasets to superimpose one type of data over the other, if you are using different coordinate systems for each data type, the result might not make sense.

Geometry

The geometry data type is the simpler of the two data types. It works with data on a flat plane using simple (X,Y) coordinates. The use of geometry data eliminates the need to account for the curvature of the earth and is better suited for storing information about small-scale shapes. For example, you can use geometry data to identify locations of products in a warehouse or to define the shape of equipment in a factory.

Geography

The geography data type works with data that factors in the ellipsoidal shape of the earth. Geographic data can accommodate a three-dimensional model in contrast to the two-dimensional flat plane that geometric data supports. As a result, lines between two points are calculated as an arc rather than as a straight line. Typically, geographic data is expressed using latitude and longitude angles. Therefore, it's logical to use geographical for data that references any place on earth, ranging from a specific location to multiple continents.

Using the Map Wizard

You can start the Map Wizard and then cancel out if you want to build up layers of a map manually. However, you will likely find it easier to step through the Map Wizard to build the foundation for a map. You can then later add more map layers and configure map element properties to fine-tune the appearance of your map, much like you configure elements in a chart.

To get started, you select a spatial data source, and then you configure map view options to center and zoom the map as necessary. Your next step is to decide whether to include analytical data. If you do, you must specify the type of visualization to use for the analytical data and map it to the spatial data. Last, you select a theme for the map if you like and options for the data visualization, such as whether to add labels and which color scheme to use. If you change your mind later about a choice you make in the wizard, you can always adjust the map to add or remove an element as needed.

Selecting a spatial data source

After you drag the map from the Toolbox and drop it onto the report design surface, the first page of the Map Wizard displays, as shown in Figure 21-4. On this page, you must specify the spatial data source to use in your map. You can work with only one spatial data source at a time in the Map Wizard. If you want to combine multiple data sources in a single map, you must add each source as a separate map layer, which you learn how to do in Chapter 22. You have three choices for a spatial data source: the Map Gallery, an Environmental Systems Research Institute (ESRI) shapefile, or a SQL Server spatial data query.

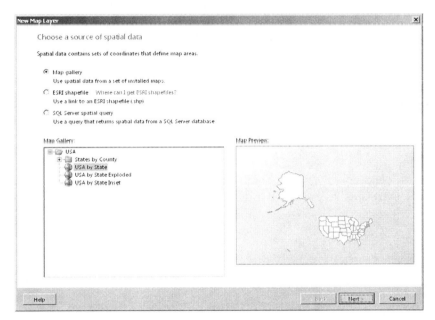

FIGURE 21-4 The first page of the Map Wizard prompts you to select a spatial data source.

Map Gallery

The Map Gallery contains a variety of maps for the United States. In the top-level folder, there are three maps that depict the entire country, showing outlines for each state. USA By State shows all states with true proportions, whereas USA By State Inset, shown in Figure 21-5, moves Alaska and Hawaii to an inset position and adjusts their size disproportionately to the mainland states. USA By State Exploded is a variation of USA By State Inset and adds some space between each state to make their boundaries more distinct. In the States By County folder, there are fifty-one maps—one for each state and one for the District of Columbia. These maps are actually a collection of reports with embedded spatial data obtained from the United States Census Bureau (*http://www.census.gov*). You can select a map in the tree view to see a preview of the map in the wizard.

FIGURE 21-5 One of the Map Gallery options is the USA By State Inset map.

The Map Gallery is an easy way to start working with maps if your data is based in the United States, because it does not require you to add spatial data to your databases or to know where to find ESRI shapefiles. Reporting Services does not include other countries in the Map Gallery due to potential political sensitivities over boundaries. However, you can add your own spatial data reports to the Map Gallery for other countries as described in the sidebar "Customizing the Map Gallery."

Customizing the Map Gallery

Although Reporting Services does not give you international maps in the Map Gallery, you can add your own maps for frequently used spatial data. The maps included in the Map Gallery are simply reports created using TIGER/Line shapefiles available free from the United States Census Bureau and stored in the Program Files\Microsoft Visual Studio 10.0\Common7\ IDE\PrivateAssemblies\MapGallery folder (or the same path beginning from the Program Files (x86) folder if you're developing on a 64-bit computer).

You cannot add just any report to the Map Gallery for this technique to work. The report must contain a map with embedded spatial data. You can create such a report by creating a map using any of the three options for spatial data—Map Gallery, ESRI shapefile, or a SQL Server spatial query. Then, on the Choose Spatial Data And Map View Options Page of the Map Wizard, you must select the Embed Map Data In The Report option. Continue through the wizard and make any necessary adjustments to the map, and then save the report to the MapGallery folder on your development computer. If there are multiple developers in your organization who need to use this map, you must provide them the resulting report and have them add it to the MapGallery folder on their respective computers.

If you prefer not to make your own map reports for the Map Gallery, you might find a map you need in the list of maps freely available at *http://mapgallery.codeplex.com/releases*. You can download an RDL file from this collection and add it to the MapGallery folder as described above.

ESRI shapefile

Another option as a spatial data source is an ESRI shapefile. A *shapefile* is a special file format developed by ESRI to store points, lines, and polygons for use in geographic information systems. When you obtain a shapefile, you actually get two files, an SHP file containing the geometric or geographic data and a DBF file containing additional attributes. When you select this option in the Map Wizard, you supply a path to the SHP file, but you must also store the DBF file in the same folder. If you do not plan to embed spatial data in your report (as explained in the "Choosing spatial data and map view options" section), you must first upload these files to a location accessible to the report server, and then use the Map Wizard to add the reference to that location in your report.

> **Note** There are a variety of sources for ESRI shapefiles, some free and some at a price. At the time of this writing, you can obtain free ESRI shapefiles from the United States Census Bureau (*http://www.census.gov/geo/www/tiger*), Global Administrative Areas (*http://www .gadm.org/*), and VDS Technologies (*http://www.vdstech.com/map-data.aspx*). Whenever downloading shapefiles, be sure to read and comply with the terms of use.

Spatial query

Yet another option available as a spatial data source is a SQL Server spatial query. When you choose this option, the wizard prompts you for a dataset on the next page. If you have a dataset already added to your report, you can select it from the list. Otherwise, you must select the Add A New Dataset With SQL Server Spatial Data option and continue to the next page of the wizard. There you can select a data source that exists in your report, or you can click the New button to open the Data Source Properties dialog box and add a shared data source or embedded data source. After you select the data source, you continue to the Design A Query page of the wizard, which allows you to use the graphical query designer (shown in Figure 21-6), switch to the generic query designer by using the Edit As Text button, or use the Import button to import a query from a SQL file or from another report.

You can execute the query to confirm that it retrieves spatial data in the form of a point, linestring, or polygon. If you click the Next button when the query does not contain spatial data, an error message displays, and you cannot continue to the next step of the wizard until you modify the query to include at least one column with a geometry or geography data type.

Each dataset row becomes a unique element in your map. For example, the query shown in Figure 21-6 returns three rows of linestring data. The resulting map displays three separate lines.

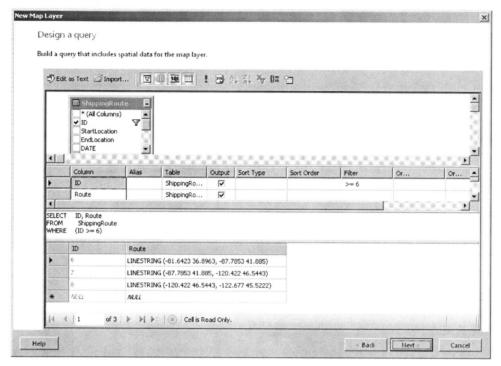

FIGURE 21-6 You can design your spatial query as a step in the Map Wizard.

Note The query you create in the Map Wizard becomes an embedded dataset. If you prefer to use a shared dataset, you must create the shared dataset prior to starting the Map Wizard, and then select the shared dataset on the Choose A Dataset With SQL Server Spatial Data page of the wizard.

Choosing spatial data and map view options

After you select the spatial data source or create a spatial query, you continue to the next page of the wizard, shown in Figure 21-7, where you select the spatial data field and layer type as well as configure various map view options. You use these options to center, zoom, and optimize properties of the viewport (the visible map area), to specify whether to embed spatial data in the report, and to optionally add a Bing Maps tile layer.

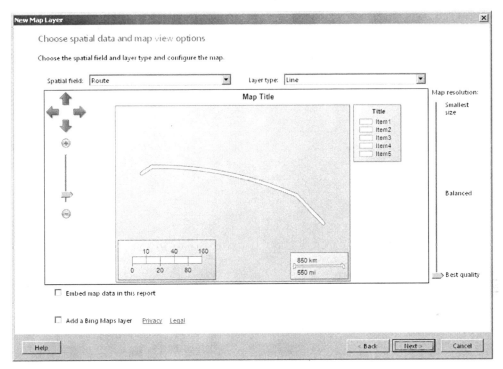

FIGURE 21-7 The Map Wizard provides a preview of your map and allows you to configure viewport and layer properties.

Spatial field and layer type

If you have only one spatial field in your data source, the Spatial Field and Layer Type values are set correctly. However, if your source contains multiple spatial fields, you must select one spatial field on this page of the wizard because you can associate only one spatial field with a single map layer. You can add multiple layers when you need to combine points, lines, and polygons in the same map (as described in Chapter 22), but the Map Wizard allows you to create only one map layer at a time. If you change the Spatial Field selection, the Layer Type selection changes automatically to the applicable data type.

Center point

On the left side of the page, you can use the four directional arrow buttons to change the center point of the map. Each time you click one of these buttons, the preview of your map changes so that you can easily observe the effect of your changes. You might choose to do this when you want to focus only on a particular section of the map.

Zoom factor

Similarly, there is a slider control beneath the directional buttons to adjust the zoom level of the map, which you can see change in the map preview. For example, if you decide to add a Bing Maps layer and then increase the zoom factor, you can display map with street level detail, as shown in Figure 21-8.

FIGURE 21-8 You can use the directional and zoom controls to control the center point and level of detail of your map.

Map resolution

On the right side of the Choose Spatial Data And Map View Options page (shown in Figure 21-7), you can use a slider control to set the map resolution. You can choose one of the following options:

- **Smallest Size**   If you choose this option and spatial data is embedded in the report, a smaller number of map elements are stored in the report, which produces less detail when you later view the report. However, if the spatial data is not embedded in the report, Reporting Services does not calculate all possible detail. Either way, the report renders faster with this option.

- **Balanced**   You can use this option to produce a report that strikes a balance between how many map elements are stored or calculated at runtime and the amount of time required to render the report.

- **Best Quality**   If you do not want to sacrifice detail and if the report rendering time is satisfactory, you can use this option. The report stores all map elements if you embed the spatial data or performs more calculations at runtime if spatial data is not embedded.

Embedded map data

If you select the Embed Map Data In This Report check box, the Map Wizard embeds all spatial data from the spatial data source in your report. Consequently, the size of the Report Definition Language (RDL) file is much larger, but the report renders much faster.

If you use the center and zoom options to reduce the amount of spatial data visible in the report, you can select the Crop Map As Shown Above to reduce the amount of data stored in the report. For example, if you have three lines in the report but crop the map to show only one line, the complete spatial data for that line remains in the report. That means you can add interactivity to the map by enabling dynamic changes to the zoom factor when viewing the report so that you can see a portion of the line or the entire line. That is, cropping the map does not limit the data storage to the portion of the spatial data visible in the preview.

If the spatial data source is static, such as a shapefile, you should embed the map data in your report. When you embed map data, you can see the actual spatial data in both the design and preview modes when working in SSDT. You should also use this option if you are creating a custom map to store in the Map Gallery, as described in the "Customizing the Map Gallery" sidebar earlier in this chapter.

Note If you choose to embed spatial data in your report, it does not automatically embed the Bing Maps tile data. However, you can update the Bing Maps tile layer properties later to embed it. That way, you can achieve faster report rendering time. Although you can embed the Bing Maps tile in your report, that data is not available from the Map Gallery if you save your report as described in the "Customizing the Map Gallery" sidebar. Only the data that you embed from other spatial data sources is available when you add your report to the Map Gallery.

Bing Maps layer

You also have the option to add a Bing Maps layer to your map. This is a useful and easy way to add context to points and lines that are based on geographic coordinates. Instead of adding another map layer later with polygons, you can select the Add A Bing Maps Layer check box and then select one of the following tile types: Road, Aerial, or Hybrid (which is a combination of road and aerial views). The Bing Maps tile layer provides a background for you automatically, as shown in Figure 21-9, which gives context to your spatial data.

FIGURE 21-9 The Bing Maps layer adjusts to the spatial data coordinates and displays below the spatial data layer.

To build the Bing Maps layer, Reporting Services analyzes the spatial locations in your map to determine the coordinates that it can match to a Bing Maps tile at the same zoom level and resolution. The advantage of using a Bing Maps layer is that you can include show point data for locations all over the world very easily, as long as your report server is configured to access the Bing Maps Web Service. You can add a Bing Maps layer during development without a connection to the Internet, but you see the following message display in design and preview mode, "The remote name could not be resolved: 'dev.virtualearth.net'."

 Note To avoid this error message on the report server, you should take care to configure the report server properly. For details, see *http://msdn.microsoft.com/en-us/library/ms157273.aspx#bkmk_MapTileServer*.

Choosing map visualization

The choice you have on the Choose Map Visualization page of the wizard depends on the spatial data type you use for the current map layer. You can choose either a basic map to show only the points, lines, or polygons in your dataset, or you can choose one of the available analytical map options to modify the appearance of your spatial data based on *analytical data* that you supply separately. Analytical data is a dataset that contains one or more fields sharing values with one or more fields in the spatial data source and usually includes numeric data that the report server can aggregate by map element.

Point data maps

If your spatial data set contains point data, the Choose Map Visualization page displays your options for using point data in a map.

For point data, you can choose one of the following map types:

- **Basic Marker Map**   This is the simplest of the point data map types. With this map type, you can use only one type of marker, such as a circle or a star. You can use a single color for all markers, as shown in Figure 21-10, or you can allow the report server to assign colors randomly. You can change these settings after you close the wizard.

- **Bubble Marker Map**   This map type requires you to include analytical data in the report. You can optionally use the size of the bubble in the map to represent the relative size of the analytical data value. You can instead use the color of the bubble to represent different ranges of values. As an alternative, you can use both color and size, using the same analytical field value, as shown in Figure 21-11, or different analytical field values.

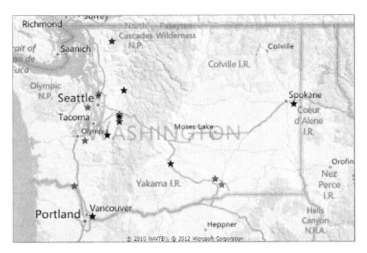

FIGURE 21-10 A basic marker map displays points on the map with no difference in marker size or shape and no meaning attributed to marker color.

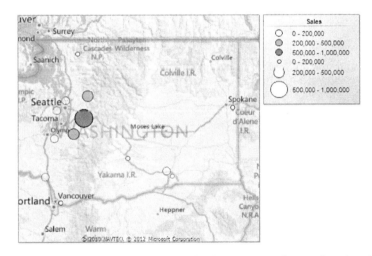

FIGURE 21-11 A bubble marker map displays points on the map by using size and color to differentiate value ranges associated with each point.

■ **Analytical Marker Map** With this type of map, you can use values in the analytical data set to configure the style, size, and color of markers. You can use the same value to configure each of these properties, as shown in Figure 21-12. More commonly, you use three separate values to configure the marker properties. The marker styles are initially assigned randomly, but you can adjust the markers by changing the marker type rule after you complete the wizard.

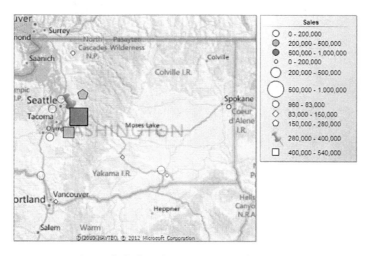

FIGURE 21-12 An analytical marker map uses marker style, size, and color to differentiate value ranges associated with each point.

Line data maps

You have different maps to choose from if your spatial data set contains line data. In that case, the Choose Map Visualization page of the wizard displays the following two choices:

- **Basic Map**   This map uses only one line color and one width, as shown in Figure 21-13, both of which are configurable after you exit the wizard.

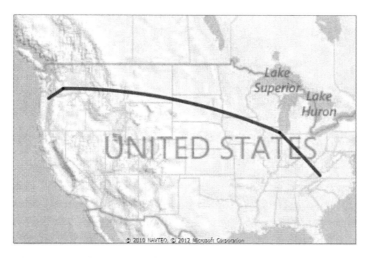

FIGURE 21-13 A basic map with line data displays each line with no difference in line size or shape and no meaning attributed to line color.

- **Analytical Map**   You can create an analytical map to specify different line colors and widths based on values in your analytical data set, as shown in Figure 21-14.

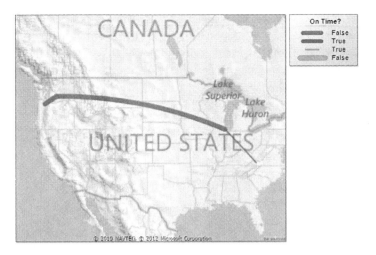

FIGURE 21-14 An analytical map for lines uses line size and color to differentiate value ranges associated with each line.

Polygon data maps

As with the other spatial data types, the Choose Map Visualization provides multiple options when you use polygon data.

You have the following choice of map types for polygon data:

■ **Basic Map**   In this case, you can use one color for all polygons in the map or you can use randomly assigned colors. In this map type, the color assignments have no relationship to data.

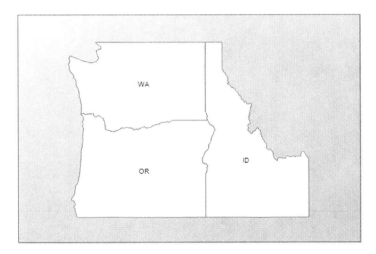

FIGURE 21-15 A basic polygon map uses the same color for each polygon by default and optionally includes labels.

- **Color Analytical Map** When you have analytical data, you can create a color analytical map, in which case the color of the polygon is determined by the range in which an analytical data value for that polygon falls. For example, in Figure 21-16, the report server determines the color for each state by aggregating the total sales for the state and applying the color rule for the range in which the value falls.

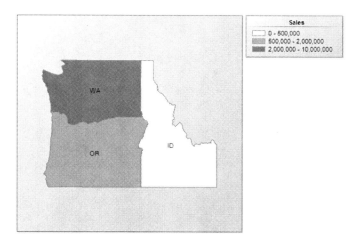

FIGURE 21-16 A color analytical map assigns a color to a polygon based on the aggregated analytical value associated with the polygon.

- **Bubble Map** A bubble appears at each polygon's center point with this type of map. The size of the bubble depends on a single data value from your analytical data set. You can also assign color to each polygon based on the same value that you use for the bubble size, or you can use a different value, as shown in Figure 21-17.

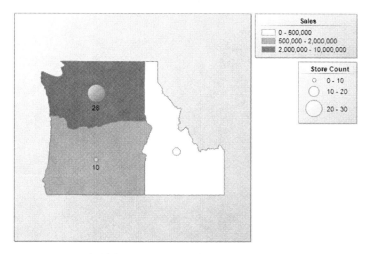

FIGURE 21-17 A bubble map assigns colors to each polygon based on the aggregated analytical value associated with the polygon and includes bubbles at the center point of each polygon, using size to differentiate values.

Adding an analytical data set

The purpose of the analytical data set is to provide quantitative data that Reporting Services can use to superimpose colors and shapes onto a map to aid in comparing this analytical data by location. For example, you can use color to illustrate the population density or other demographic information for selected geographical areas. A map always has a spatial data set, but an analytical data set is an optional data set that you associate with a map.

The analytical data set must include at least one field that corresponds to a single row in the spatial data set. Not only must that field match a value found in the spatial data set, but it also must have the same data type and the same formatting. The analytical data must also include a field containing numeric data that Reporting Services can aggregate using a sum function, for example, to produce an analytical value. As an alternative, the analytical dataset can include a non-numeric field that Reporting Services can count to produce an analytical value.

If you select a map type that requires an analytical data set, the Map Wizard opens the Choose The Analytical Dataset page, which is similar to the page you see when you choose to use a spatial query to get data for your map. You can select an existing dataset in the report (which can be the same dataset as the one you use for a spatial query), or you can select the Add A Dataset That Includes Fields That Relate To The Spatial Data That You Chose Earlier option. In the latter case, you select a data source for the new dataset (or create one if necessary) and then use the Design A Query page to create the query.

Note Although a spatial data query must use a SQL Server database as its source, you can use any data source that Reporting Services supports for the analytical dataset query. The only requirement is to include a field that matches a field in the spatial data.

Your next step after designating an analytical data set, whether you select an existing dataset or create a new one, is to match the fields between the analytical dataset and the spatial dataset, as shown in Figure 21-18. At the top of the page, you see the Spatial Dataset Fields list. If the wizard detects a column having the same name and the same data type in the analytical dataset, it creates the match selection for you. As you match fields at the top of the page, the wizard highlights the corresponding fields in each dataset so that you can visually confirm that the match is correct.

Note The wizard does not display this page if you use the same dataset as both the spatial dataset and the analytical dataset.

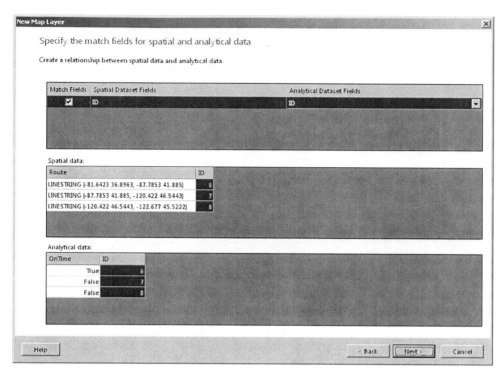

FIGURE 21-18 You must identify the matching fields in the spatial and analytical datasets.

Setting theme and data visualization options

The final step of the wizard, shown in Figure 21-19, allows you to set the data visualization options. Here you can apply a theme to the map, which sets properties like fonts, border, fill, and others, or you can use the Generic theme if you prefer to configure the appearance properties later. If you added an analytical dataset to the map, you use this page to configure options that affect the data visualization in the map. The specific options you see depend on the type of analytical map you are creating. In general, you can select a field for the report server to use to set color, size, or marker style properties. The map includes a legend to help you understand the values associated with each color, size, or marker style.

When you have the option to specify a color rule, you can select either a two-color or three-color palette to provide a spectrum of colors for the range of values. The report server assigns the first color to the lowest values in the analytical field that you specify and assigns the last color to the highest values. For example, if you select the Light-Dark palette, the map displays low values with a light color and high values with a dark color, but it also includes several shades between the light and dark colors for multiple value ranges between the low and high values.

 Note You can always change the settings later by using the wizard or by setting properties for the applicable map elements.

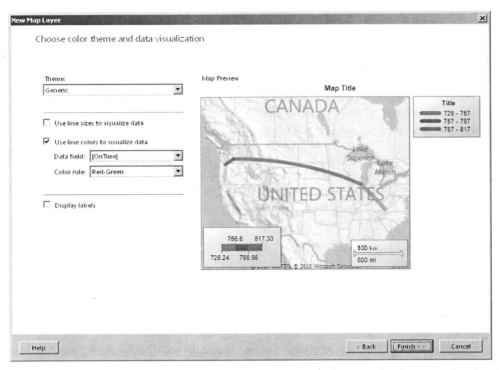

FIGURE 21-19 The final page of the wizard allows you to select a color theme for the map and optionally configure data visualization options.

Basic marker map

You use this map type with point data without analytical data. On the final page of the wizard, you can set the following options:

- **Marker**   You can specify the marker that the map uses to display a point. The default is Circle, but you can change this by selecting Rectangle, Diamond, Triangle, Trapezoid, Star, Wedge, Pentagon, PushPin, or Image. If you select Image, after you complete the wizard, you must edit the point properties to associate an image with the point.

- **Display Labels**   You can select this check box and then select a field from your spatial data set to display information next to a point.

- **Single Color Map**   The default setting is to use a single color for all lines in the current map layer. If you clear this check box, the map uses random color assignments for each line.

Bubble marker map

When you add analytical data to the map, you can use this map type with point data. As you finalize the Map Wizard, you can set the following options:

- **Use Bubble Sizes To Visualize Data**   To change the relative size of the bubble marker, you can select a non-numeric field from either the dataset or an aggregation of numeric fields, using the *Sum* or *Count* function from your analytical dataset. The map displays larger bubbles for higher field values and smaller bubbles for smaller field values.

- **Use Bubble Colors To Visualize Data**   You can also select a field to change the color of the bubble marker, using either non-numeric fields from either dataset or an aggregation of a numeric field from your analytical dataset by using the *Sum* or *Count* function. You can also select a color rule.

- **Display Labels**   You can select this check box and then select a field to display information next to a bubble. The label can be one of the non-numeric fields from either dataset or an aggregation of a numeric field from the analytical dataset by using the *Sum* or *Count* function.

Analytical marker map

You can also combine point data and analytical data to create an analytical marker map. In that case, you can set the following options:

- **Use Marker Types To Visualize Data**   You can select a non-numeric field from either dataset or an aggregation of numeric fields, using the *Sum* or *Count* function, from your analytical dataset to change the type of marker representing each point. The report server randomly assigns marker types for a range of values when you use a numeric field or for a specific value when you use a non-numeric field.

- **Use Marker Sizes To Visualize Data**   As an alternative to markers or in combination with markers, you can select a non-numeric field from either dataset or an aggregation of a numeric field, using the *Sum* or *Count* function, from your analytical dataset to change the relative size of the marker. The map displays larger markers for higher field values and smaller markers for smaller field values.

- **Use Marker Colors To Visualize Data**   You can also select a field to change the color of the marker, using either non-numeric fields from either dataset or an aggregation of a numeric field from your analytical dataset by using the *Sum* or *Count* function. You also select a color rule.

- **Display Labels**   You can select this check box and then select a field to display information next to a bubble marker. The label can be one of the non-numeric fields from either dataset or an aggregation of a numeric field from the analytical dataset by using the *Sum* or *Count* function.

Line map

You can set the following options when you have a line map without analytical data:

- **Single Color Map**   The default setting is to use a single color for all lines in the current map layer. If you clear this check box, the map uses random color assignments for each line.

- **Display Labels**   You can select this check box and then select a field from your spatial data-set to display information next to a line.

Line analytical map

After adding an analytical dataset to a map containing line data, you can set the following options on the last page of the wizard:

- **Use Line Sizes To Visualize Data**   When you select this check box, you can select a non-numeric field from either dataset or an aggregation of a numeric field from your analytical dataset, using the *Sum* or *Count* function. The map displays larger lines for higher field values and smaller lines for smaller field values.

- **Use Line Colors To Visualize Data**   Selection of this check box allows you to specify the data field to use for applying a color to a line. This field can be a non-numeric field from either dataset or an aggregation of a numeric field from the analytical dataset by using the *Sum* or *Count* function. You can also specify a color rule.

- **Display Labels**   You can specify a field from your spatial or analytical dataset to display with a line if you select this check box when you want to provide more information about the line.

Basic polygon map

For a simple map containing only polygon data, you can complete the wizard by setting the following options:

- **Single Color Map**   The default setting is to use a single color for all polygons in the current map layer. If you clear this check box, the map uses random color assignments for each line.

- **Display Labels**   You can select this check box and then select a field from your spatial data set to display information inside a polygon.

Color analytical map

The addition of analytical data to a polygon map allows you to finalize the Map Wizard by setting the following options:

- **Field To Visualize**   You select a non-numeric field from either dataset or an aggregation of a numeric field from your analytical dataset by using the *Sum* or *Count* function.

- **Color Rule**   You select a color rule to apply to the field to visualize.

- **Display Labels**   You can select this check box and then select a field from either dataset to display information inside a polygon.

Bubble map for polygons

The last style of map you can create includes adding bubbles and assigning colors to polygons based on analytical data after you set the following options:

- **Use Bubble Sizes To Visualize Data**   You can select a non-numeric field from either dataset or an aggregation of a numeric field from your analytical dataset, using the *Sum* or *Count* function, to change the relative size of the bubble marker. The map displays larger bubbles for higher field values and smaller bubbles for smaller field values.

- **Use Polygon Colors To Visualize Data**   You can also select a non-numeric field from either dataset or an aggregation of a numeric field from your analytical dataset, using the *Sum* or *Count* function, to change the color of the bubble marker. In addition, you can select a color rule.

- **Display Labels**   You can select this check box and then select a field to display information inside the polygon. The label can be one of the non-numeric fields or an aggregation of a numeric field by using the *Sum* or *Count* function.

Finalizing the map

After you complete the wizard, the map data region appears in your report design layout. In design mode, the features you see on the map and in the legend might not represent actual data. You should always preview the report to check the actual results and determine the additional changes to make.

Map preview

When you preview the report, the spatial data and analytical data, if any, render according to the current center point, zoom factor, and resolution properties. In addition, data visualization properties affect the appearance of the map, as shown in Figure 21-20.

FIGURE 21-20 You should preview the map after completing the Map Wizard to determine the additional adjustments to make.

Simple adjustments

The Map Wizard does not allow you to assign a title to the map or to the legend. Furthermore, the Map Wizard does not allow you to specify whether you want to include the color scale and distance scale appearing along the bottom edge of the map. At minimum, you should make simple adjustments to the map to modify or remove these map elements to make the report more attractive.

Map title

If you prefer not to have a map title, you can right-click the map title and select Delete Title. To change the text instead, click once to select the map, click again to select the title, and then click a third time to put the map title in edit mode. You can then replace the existing text with a new title.

Legend

You can remove the title of a legend by right-clicking it and clearing the selection for Show Legend Title. You can also change the title by using the same technique that you use for editing the map title. Click three separate times to put the legend title in edit mode, and then type the replacement text. If you prefer to remove the legend entirely, you can right-click the legend and select Delete Legend.

Scales

Related to the legend is the color scale in the lower-left corner of the map. You can remove it by right-clicking the color scale and then clearing the selection for Show Color Scale.

The distance scale displays in the lower-right corner of the map by default. If it is not helpful information, you can also remove it. Right-click the distance scale, and then clear the selection for Show Distance Scale.

After making all your changes, you can preview the report to assess the results, as shown in Figure 21-21. If you want, you can continue refining the map, which you learn to do in the next chapter.

FIGURE 21-21 You can make simple adjustments to a map after creating it with the Map Wizard by adjusting the title and removing elements such as the legend and color scale.

CHAPTER 22

Working with map elements

As with most aspects of Reporting Services reports, you have many options for configuring the appearance and behavior of map elements. You can create a map by using a wizard and then enhance it by adding additional map layers. You can configure properties that control the layout and look of the map, and you can position supporting elements like legends and scale. You can also access a collection of properties to link data to each map layer and control colors, line widths, marker sizes, or marker types of spatial elements in each layer based on analytical data. You can even add custom points to your map without using a spatial data source. By understanding how to work with individual map elements, you can easily produce informative and attractive maps.

Configuring map elements

The Map Wizard is a useful tool for adding common map elements and configuring their properties quickly. However, you might find later that you want to make changes to these settings. Furthermore, there are many more properties available to configure than are accessible in the Map Wizard. Table 22-1 shows you the map elements and dialog boxes to use when you want to update settings. In this section, we explore the properties for elements that all maps have in common and then we explore the properties related to spatial data in the "Working with map layers" section.

TABLE 22-1 Map element property pages corresponding to Map Wizard settings

Map Wizard Step	Map Wizard Setting	Map Element	Toolbar or Context Menu Command	Dialog Box / Page
Choose A Spatial Data Source				
	Spatial data selection	Map layer	Layer Data	Map <Data Type> Layer Properties / General
Choose Spatial Data and Map View Options				
	Spatial field	Map layer	Layer Data	Map <Data Type> Layer Properties / General
	Center	Viewport	N/A	Map Viewport Properties / Center And Zoom

Map Wizard Step	Map Wizard Setting	Map Element	Toolbar or Context Menu Command	Dialog Box / Page
	Zoom	Viewport	N/A	Map Viewport Properties / Center And Zoom
	Map resolution	Viewport	N/A	Map Viewport Properties / Optimization
	Embed map data	Map layer	Embed Spatial Data	N/A
	Add Bing Maps layer	N/A	Add Layer	N/A
Choose Map Visualization				
	Map type	N/A	N/A	N/A
Choose the Analytical Dataset				
	Analytical data selection	Map layer	Layer Data	Map <Data Type> Layer Properties / Analytical Data
Specify The Match Fields For Spatial And Analytical Data				
	Match fields	Map layer	Layer Data	Map <Data Type> Layer Properties / Analytical Data
Choose Color Theme And Data Visualization				
	Theme	N/A	N/A	N/A
	Display labels	Map layer	Point Properties, Line Properties, or Polygon Properties	Map Point Properties / General or Map Line Properties / General or Map Polygon Properties / General
	Marker	Map layer	Point Properties	Map Point Properties / General
	Single color map (point)	Map layer	Point Properties	Map Point Properties / Fill
	Bubble sizes (point)	Map layer	Point Size Rule	May Layer Size Rules Properties / General
	Bubble colors (point)	Map layer	Point Color Rule	Map Color Rules Properties / General
	Marker types (point)	Map layer	Marker Type Rule	Map Marker Type Rules Properties / General
	Marker sizes (point)	Map layer	Point Size Rule	Map Layer Size Rules Properties / General
	Marker colors (point)	Map layer	Point Color Rule	Map Color Rules Properties / General

Map Wizard Step	Map Wizard Setting	Map Element	Toolbar or Context Menu Command	Dialog Box / Page
	Single color map (line)	Map layer	Line Properties	Map Line Properties / Fill
	Line sizes	Map layer	Line Width Rule	Map Layer Width Rules Properties / General
	Line colors	Map layer	Line Color Rule	Map Color Rules Properties / General
	Single color (polygon)	Map layer	Polygon Properties	Map Polygon Properties / Fill
	Field to visualize	Map layer	Polygon Color Rule	Map Color Rules Properties / General
	Color rule (polygon)	Map layer	Polygon Color Rule	Map Color Rules Properties / General
	Bubble sizes (polygon)	Map layer	Center Point Size Rule	Map Layer Size Rules Properties / General
	Bubble colors (polygon)	Map layer	Center Point Color Rule	Map Color Rules Properties / General
	Polygon colors	Map layer	Polygon Color Rule	Map Color Rules Properties / General

Like charts, maps share many common elements, regardless of the type of spatial data they contain. Of the map elements shown in Figure 22-1, only the viewport is a required element. You can remove the map title, legend, color scale, and distance scale if you prefer. Each of these elements has a comprehensive set of properties allowing you to control the appearance of your map and to use conditional formatting to adjust the appearance based on a user's parameter selections or dataset values. In addition, the map contains one or more layers of spatial elements: points, lines, or polygons.

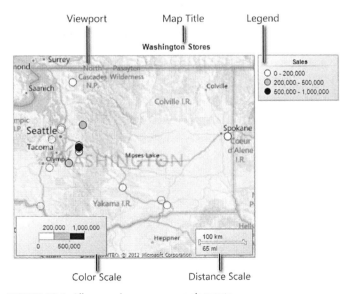

FIGURE 22-1 All maps share common elements.

The following map elements are common to all maps:

- **Map Title**   The map title appears above the map, but you can relocate it or remove it altogether. If you keep it, you can set visibility, font, fill, border, shadow, and action properties.

- **Legend**   The legend displays colors for value ranges to correspond to analytical data represented by location on the map. You can configure the layout and position of the legend, and you can configure visibility, font, fill, border, and shadow properties. You can create multiple legends and assign different color rules to different legends.

- **Viewport**   The viewport is the container for all spatial elements. You configure properties for the center point, zoom level, and map resolution. You can also configure fill, border, and shadow properties for the viewport itself.

- **Color Scale**   The color scale is a specialized legend that shows value ranges in a scale format. The color scale has many of the same properties as a legend, although you can have only one color scale in a map.

- **Distance Scale**   The distance scale is another specialized type of legend with similar properties. It displays the units of measurement in the map to allow you to assess distances between areas in the map.

Map

There are a few properties that you configure for the map as a whole, much like a chart or a tablix. Like these other data regions, you can configure visibility and action properties, as described in Chapter 13, "Adding interactivity." There is no option to define filters (described in Chapter 14, "Creating dynamic reports with parameters") at the map level because you can associate multiple datasets with separate map layers. Other properties you can set include a tooltip, page break, fill, and border properties. The fill properties affect only the background of the map outside of the viewport, whereas the border properties affect the lines that you use to enclose the entire map area. To set the map properties, right-click the map, point to Map, and then select Map Properties.

Viewport

The viewport properties control the overall appearance of the map. It contains the area in which spatial data displays and includes supporting elements such as meridians and parallels. You can set some of its properties in the Map Wizard, such as the centering and zoom level. There are several other viewport properties available to control the way Reporting Services uses two-dimensional space to display spatial data.

Center and zoom

A quick way to adjust the map's center point and zoom level is to open the Map Layers pane, shown in Figure 22-2. To open the Map Layers pane, click twice on the map in design mode. Just as you can in the Map Wizard, you can use the four directional arrow buttons near the bottom of the Map Layers pane to shift the visible portion of the map in the direction you choose. With each click of a button, you can observe the change to the center point in the map preview. Similarly, you can use the slider control at the bottom of the Map Layers pane to increase or decrease the zoom level.

FIGURE 22-2 You can use the controls at the bottom of the Map Layers pane to change the center point and zoom level of the map.

For greater precision, you must open the Center And Zoom page in the Map Viewport Properties dialog box, shown in Figure 22-3. To do this, right-click the viewport, select Viewport Properties, and then click the Center And Zoom page. The default setting, Set A View Center And Zoom Level, allows you to specify values controlling the center point and zoom factor. You provide a horizontal and vertical location (x and y, respectively) of the center point as a percentage of the map's width and height, using values between 0 and 100. You also specify the zoom level as a percentage, with 100 percent representing no change to the current magnification. You can decrease the magnification by using a value between 0 and 100 and increase it by using a value greater than 100.

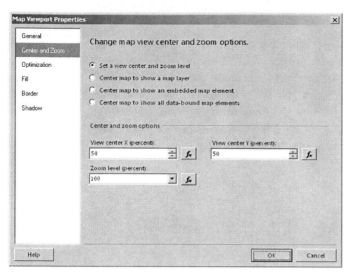

FIGURE 22-3 Use the Center And Zoom page of the Map Viewport Properties dialog box to adjust the center point and zoom level of the map.

In the Map Viewport Properties dialog box, you also have the following options for working with center point and zoom level settings:

- **Center Map To Show A Map Layer**   You can automatically center a map based on the spatial data contained in a map layer that you specify and then set a zoom level percentage.

- **Center Map To Show An Embedded Map Element**   If your map includes both analytical data and embedded spatial data, you can center the map on a specific dataset value, as shown in Figure 22-4. You can also set the zoom level percentage.

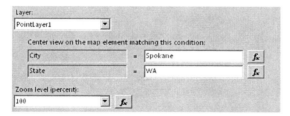

FIGURE 22-4 You can center the map to focus on a specific spatial data map element.

 Important The condition you specify is case sensitive and defaults to a string data type, even if you type a numeric value. For example, if you are matching an identifier field with a value of 1, you must type **=1** to instruct Reporting Services to interpret the value as a number rather than a string. If the matching field uses a different data type, you must create an expression to convert the condition value to the applicable data type.

■ **Center Map To Show All Data-Bound Map Elements**   If your map includes analytical data, you can select this option to adjust the center point of the map based on the current map elements that have analytical values. For example, if a map contains a single point layer for which it displays markers for cities by sales, the calculation of the center point includes only those cities with sales. Because you can configure the map to dynamically change the display of visible points, you can use this option to dynamically adjust the center point at the same time. With this option, you specify only the zoom level percentage to apply.

Parallels and meridians

When you use a geographic data type for spatial data, you use latitude and longitude as coordinates for points that display individually or as part of lines or polygons. When you use the Map Wizard, the resulting map does not display the geographic lines representing latitude and longitude, known as parallels and meridians, respectively. You can add these features to the viewport, as shown in Figure 22-5, by right-clicking the map and selecting Show Parallels and then selecting Show Meridians.

FIGURE 22-5 You can add parallels and meridians to your map.

After you add parallels and meridians, you can right-click the map again to access the Parallels Properties or Meridians Properties commands. The dialog box that displays when you select either of these commands allows you to change any of the following types of properties:

■ **Labels**   Reporting Services automatically computes the intervals between lines as measured in degrees, but you can override this setting. You can also specify whether to display labels for each line. If you choose to display the lines, you can specify the placement of the labels relative to the lines: Near, One Quarter, Center, Three Quarters, Far. Near displays the labels above meridian lines and left of parallel lines, while Far displays the meridian labels below the lines and right of parallel lines. The other options move the labels progressively from top to bottom for meridians and from left to right for parallels.

■ **Label Fonts**   You can set font family, size, style, color, and effects options for the labels.

- **Line** You can also set line style, line width, and line properties for the parallels and meridians.

- **Visibility** You can set visibility options to conditionally hide or show parallel or meridian lines.

Viewport coordinate system, projection, and boundaries

Another set of important viewport properties is available on the General page of the Map Viewport Properties dialog box, as shown in Figure 22-6. Here you specify the coordinate system to correspond to the type of spatial data you associate with the map, the cartographic projection method, and the minimum and maximum values of the coordinate system to define the boundaries of the visible map.

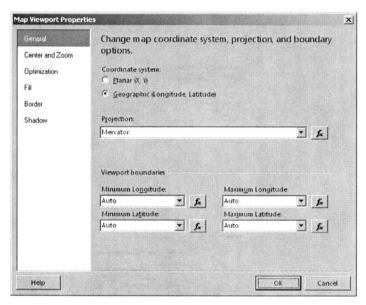

FIGURE 22-6 You can change the appearance of the map in the viewport by changing the coordinate system, projection, or boundary properties.

When you use the Map Wizard to create your map, the coordinate system for the viewport defaults to match the spatial data type you use. Therefore, the only time you should override this setting is when you change the contents of the spatial dataset. You can create a map by using one of the following coordinate systems:

- **Planar (X, Y)** This option is applicable when your spatial data has a geometry data type using x and y coordinates, such as you might have for a floor plan.

- **Geographic (Longitude, Latitude)** You use this option for spatial data that references latitude and longitude, the more common type of data for maps.

Reporting Services uses projection to convert three-dimensional coordinates to a two-dimensional format by using various standards developed for cartography. The default projection is Mercator, which is suitable if your map applies to a single country. However, it introduces a lot of distortion when your spatial data applies to a map of the world because it exaggerates the size of the land areas that are further away from the equator. For example, when you look at the map shown in Figure 22-7, Greenland appears to be similar to the size of Africa, but actually Africa is approximately 14 times the size of Greenland. This distortion is not as dramatic when you view a single country, which is why it is a reasonable default. You should consider other options for projection when you need to display world maps.

FIGURE 22-7 The Mercator projection exaggerates the size of land areas that are far from the equator.

There following four main types of projections are available in Reporting Services:

- **Cylindrical** A cylindrical projection has equally spaced meridians, and parallels are mapped across these meridians as horizontal lines.

- **Pseudocylindrical** With a pseudocylindrical projection, only the central meridian and all parallels are straight lines.

- **Pseudoconic** A pseudoconic projection uses curved lines for all parallels.

- **Azimuthal** An azimuthal projection identifies a point of perspective as its central point and uses concentric circles and radial lines to project great circles as straight lines.

You can choose any of the following projections for your map:

- **Equirectangular** This projection uses constant spacing between latitude and longitude lines, which also introduces distortions. It is better for showing coastlines and boundaries as a point of reference rather than for precision mapping and is typically used for showing aggregated data patterns in a region.

- **Mercator**   This is the default projection, suitable for smaller land areas, such as a single country rather than multiple continents, due to the distortion it introduces. Despite this potential problem, it is a useful map for marine navigation purposes due to its preservation of angles as a line crosses multiple meridians. It is also useful for interactive zooming because the transition from one magnification to another introduces little to no distortion.

- **Robinson**   As a compromise approach to projection, it introduces a slight curve to the meridians but displays high distortion at the poles in a world map. Rand McNally has been using this pseudocylindrical projection for decades.

- **Fahey**   This projection is another pseudocylindrical representation of the earth, similar to Robinson, which has high distortion at the poles. It is also a non-equal area map, which means that the area of the quadrilateral formed by meridians and parallels is not proportional to the corresponding area on earth.

- **Eckert1**   This pseudocylindrical projection equally spaces parallels and uses straight lines for the meridians, with the poles occupying half the space of the equator.

- **Eckert3**   As another pseudocylindrical projection, this version also equally spaces parallels but uses curved lines for the meridians instead.

- **HammerAitoff**   This projection is an equal area azimuthal map for use with polar maps or world maps. All meridians and parallels, except for the equator, display as curved lines.

- **Wagner3**   Here is another non-equal area pseudocylindrical compromise projection used for world maps with equally spaced parallels.

- **Bonne**   This is a pseudoconic equal area map atlas with little distortion except for areas distant from the center. All parallels are equally spaced curved lines. Only the central meridian is a straight line.

Regardless of which coordinate system you use, the default settings for the viewport boundaries are all Auto. That means Reporting Services uses the spatial data in all map layers in combination with the zoom and center properties for the viewport to determine the boundaries of the map. In the case of a geographic coordinate system, Reporting Services calculates the minimum and maximum of both latitude and longitude, whereas it calculates minimum and maximum X and Y coordinates for a planar system. You can override these settings with a hard-coded or expression-based value.

Optimization

On the Optimization page of the Map Viewport Properties dialog box, you can use a slider control to adjust the value that appears in the Map Resolution box. The default setting of the control is Quality, which stores more data in your report when you embed spatial data or renders the report more slowly when you do not embed spatial data, but with greater detail. As you slide the control's pointer to the right towards Performance, Reporting Services renders the report more quickly, but with progressively less detail. You can also directly set the map resolution value without using the slider.

Map title

The Map Title properties are just like the Chart Title properties discussed in Chapter 17, "Creating charts." You can change the default map title by clicking it twice to select the object and then double-clicking the text to edit it. You can also remove the map title by right-clicking it and then selecting Delete Title. If you decide to add it back again later or if you want multiple map titles, right-click the map and select Add Title.

In the Map Title Properties dialog box, which you open by right-clicking the map title and selecting Title Properties, the properties are nearly identical to those available for chart titles as described in Chapter 17. One difference is the Show Title Outside The Viewport option, which is selected by default. You can clear this selection to superimpose the title across the top of the viewport. You can also set the alignment of the title text, and you can specify an angle in degrees to use for displaying the title. All other pages available for the map title properties should be familiar: Visibility, Action, Font, Fill, Border, Shadow, and Action.

Legend

A map can have one or more legends or no legend at all. To remove the legend, right-click the legend and then click Delete Legend. You can restore the legend later or add a new legend by right-clicking the chart, and selecting Add Legend. When a map has multiple legends, you can associate a map layer's color rule with a specific legend, as we describe later in the "Color rules" section.

To manage legend properties, right-click the legend and select Legend Properties to open the Legend Properties dialog box. For the most part, the legend properties are the same as those described in Chapter 17 for chart legend properties. An exception is the Show Legend Outside The Viewport option, which is the default selection. Furthermore, the legend displays at the top-right corner of the map area outside the viewport, but you can drag it to another location if you prefer. As you drag the legend from its current position, the available drop positions display in the map control, such as the lower-right corner, as shown in Figure 22-8, or in the viewport.

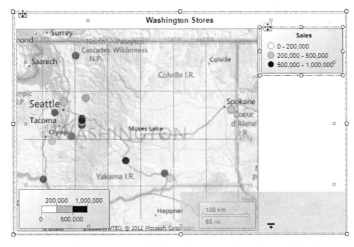

FIGURE 22-8 You can drag the legend to a new location within the map area.

Tip For greater precision, you can set the Location properties for the legend in the Properties window. There you can specify the distance from the top left of the map to position the element. To set the position explicitly, the docked property needs to be set to False. The location unit of measurement can be a percentage of the map size or sizes in specific measurements of inches or millimeters.

As for properties similar to chart legends, you can choose the layout of your legend and set the position of the legend relative to the map area. You can also set properties for visibility, fonts, fill, border, shadow, and action properties.

Scales

By default, a map includes a color and distance scale inside the viewport. Just like the legend, you can drag either of these map elements to a predefined docking location along the edges inside or outside the viewport. Each of these scales has its own location and appearance properties, including the same type of layout options available for legends, for which you can set position explicitly.

You can also remove the color and distance scales by right-clicking the item and then clearing the applicable selection—Show Color Scale or Show Distance Scale. Similarly, you can open the dialog box to set the scale properties by right-clicking the scale and selecting either Color Scale Properties or Distance Scale Properties, as applicable.

Color scale

Unlike the distance scale, the color scale has an optional title, which does not display by default. You can also add a title by right-clicking it and selecting Show Color Scale Title. After the title is added, you can right-click it and select Color Scale Title Properties to configure the alignment of the title text and font properties.

As for the color scale properties, you can set the following properties that are unique to this scale type:

- **General** Here you can set the position of the scale within the viewport or map area, specify whether to display the color scale inside or outside the viewport, and then select the color to use as the border for the color scale.

- **Labels** You can set a display property to allow the labels to generate automatically or to use the middle or border value for each color. You can also specify whether the labels should display along the bottom of the scale, across the top, or alternate from top to bottom for each value. Another option you have is to change the interval value from the default of 1. Next, you can select the Hide End Labels option to remove labels from the left and right edges of the scale. Each value on the scale displays with a tick mark for which you can specify a length.

The Map Color Scale Properties dialog box includes several other properties, all of which are similar to those you find for other map and chart elements. There are pages here you use to configure number formatting, visibility, font, fill, border, shadow, and action properties.

Distance scale

The distance scale properties are very similar to those available for the color scale, except that there is no option to set a title nor do you have any control over the units of measurement or intervals in the scale. Reporting Services adjusts the distance scale as necessary according to the current zoom level of your map. As with the color scale, you can use the General page of the Map Distance Scale Properties dialog box to set the position of the distance scale relative to the map and whether the scale displays inside or outside the viewport. In addition, you can set the border color options and the color of the distance scale's lines and tick marks. You cannot set number formatting properties for a distance scale, but you can set visibility, font, fill, border, shadow, and action properties.

Working with map layers

Map layers are containers for spatial data that display within the viewport. When you use the Map Wizard, you create one spatial data map layer from point, line, or polygon data. Optionally, you can add a Bing Maps tile layer also. After you complete the Map Wizard, you can add another map layer either by using the New Layer Wizard, which is a variation of the Map Wizard, or by manually adding a new layer and configuring its properties directly. Even if you choose not to add another map layer, you should be familiar with the properties associated with a map layer in case you need to make changes to the existing map layer.

 Note Each map layer can use a different spatial and analytical dataset.

Map Layers pane

To work with map layers, you use the Map Layers pane, shown in Figure 22-9. The toolbar contains several buttons for you to add a new map layer, delete an existing layer, access properties, or re-arrange layers. You can also see the set of layers in the current map, and you can use each layer's buttons to change its visibility or show its context menu.

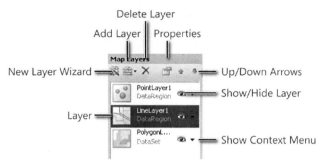

FIGURE 22-9 You can add a new map layer or set map layer properties by using the Map Layers pane.

The toolbar in the Map Layers pane contains the following buttons:

- **New Layer Wizard**   You can add a new layer to the map by using the New Layer Wizard. Similar to the Map Wizard, it walks you through similar steps, from choosing a spatial data source to selecting a map visualization, adding an optional analytical dataset, and setting data visualization options. When you complete the wizard, the new layer displays in the Map Layers pane above the previously existing layers.

- **Add Layer**   You can add a new layer manually by using this button and selecting one of the following options: Tile Layer, Polygon Layer, Line Layer, and Point Layer. The new layer displays in the Map Layers pane, and you can then access its shortcut menu to associate it with a spatial dataset and configure other properties.

- **Delete Layer**   You can select a layer and then use this button to remove it from the map. Removing the layer does not remove the query-based spatial dataset or the analytical dataset from the report.

- **Properties**   You can access the general properties for the layer by using this button. These properties are described in greater detail in the "Map layer properties" section of this chapter. This button opens the same dialog box that displays when you use the Layer Data command on the layer's shortcut menu.

- **Up / Down Arrows**   When you add multiple layers to a map, Reporting Services renders the map from bottom to top according to the sequence displaying in the Map Layers pane. You can use these buttons to adjust the rendering sequence.

 Important Items that cover a smaller spatial area, such as points, should display above large spatial areas such as polygons; otherwise, the larger items cover the spatial data points.

You can also interact directly with each layer by using the following techniques:

- **Show/Hide Layer** You can quickly change the visibility of a layer by using this button. You might do this while working in preview mode so that you can better see other layers. For dynamic visibility (with more options than you usually have with visibility), you can change the visibility properties as described in the "Map layer properties" section.

- **Show Context Menu** The context menu allows you to access the various properties available for each layer, including the dataset properties and properties controlling appearance and behavior of spatial data, such as line widths or polygon colors. Alternatively, you can right-click the layer to open the context menu. The context menu changes by spatial data type but always includes the Layer Data command to access the general layer properties, the Layer Wizard command to add a new layer, and the Delete Command to remove the selected layer. You can also use the Refresh command to update the spatial data in the map preview or use the Embed Spatial Data command to embed data into the report, as described in Chapter 21, "Mapping data."

Note At any time, you can also select a map element in the map control and then access its properties directly in the Properties window or right-click the map element to open its shortcut menu.

Map layer properties

There are properties common to every layer that you access by selecting a layer in the Map Layers pane and then clicking the Properties button or by right-clicking the layer and then selecting Layer Data. Either way, this action opens a dialog box corresponding to the spatial data type of the layer: Map Point Layer Properties, Map Line Layer Properties, Map Polygon Layer Properties, or Map Tile Layer Properties.

With the exception of the Map Tile Layer Properties dialog box, which we explain in more detail in the "Tile layer maps" section of this chapter, the other dialog boxes contain the following pages:

- **General** Here you specify the source of the spatial dataset: embedded spatial data, ESRI shapefile, a spatial field from a specified dataset, or a spatial field from an analytical dataset bound to the map.

- **Analytical Data** On this page, you add a reference to an analytical dataset in your report and then match the fields from your spatial data to the analytical data.

Note You might be surprised to find your spatial dataset appear on the Analytical Data page without field matches after using the wizard to create the map layer. The map displays data correctly even with this setting.

- **Filters**   You can apply filters to the spatial data using expressions or parameters, as described in Chapter 14.

- **Visibility**   The visibility options for a map layer are similar to the options you see for other report items, as described in Chapter 13. However, you have some additional options for a map layer, as shown in Figure 22-10. In particular, you can choose the Show Or Hide Based On Zoom Value option and then set the Minimum Zoom (Percent) and Maximum Zoom (Percent) values to define a range of magnification for which the layer is visible. You use this setting only when you allow the user to dynamically change the zoom level in the report by changing a parameter value.

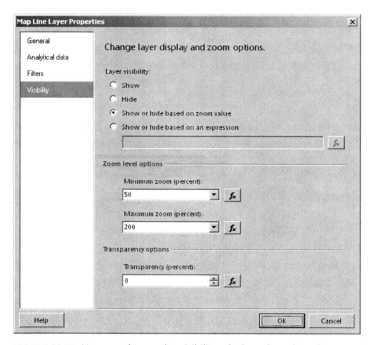

FIGURE 22-10 You can change the visibility of a layer based on the current zoom level.

Notice also the Transparency (Percent) value. The default value of 0 produces a map layer that is completely opaque. If your map includes multiple layers, with some map elements in one layer overlaying map elements in a lower layer, you can increase the transparency percentage for the top layer to allow the lower layer to be visible despite the presence of the top layer.

Common spatial element properties

The shortcut menu for each layer includes a command to open the general properties for the spatial element: Point Properties, Line Properties, and Polygon Properties. Although there are properties you can change that are specific to a spatial data type, which we discuss in the sections of the same name later in this chapter, you can use the respective dialog boxes to access standard settings for tooltip, font, fill, border, shadow, and action properties. You generally use the fill properties only when you do not link the spatial data to an analytical dataset. If you are using an analytical dataset, you configure color rule options as we describe in the next section.

Note If you embed spatial data in your report, you can right-click a specific spatial element in the viewport and select Embedded Point Properties, Embedded Line Properties, or Embedded Polygon Properties as applicable. You can then select the check box to override options for the layer and then change general, labels, font, fill, border, shadow, or action properties for the selected spatial element.

In addition, these dialog boxes for common properties include a General page where you configure properties related to labels. You can select a field or provide a string expression to use as a label for each spatial element. Each spatial data type also has its own properties related to placement or visibility of label text.

Note In the Label Text drop-down list, you see keywords (string text preceded by the pound symbol, #) in addition to aggregate expressions for fields in your analytical dataset, if applicable. The keywords are simply a placeholder for field expressions referencing your spatial dataset.

Color rules

When you add analytical data to your map, you have the option to apply a color rule. Whether you are applying rules to point, line, or polygon data, the process of defining a color rule is the same. You start by right-clicking the layer in the Map Layers pane, and then you select the applicable command: Point Color Rule, Line Color Rule, or Polygon Color Rule. You then select the colors to use for the rule, define the distribution of values across ranges, and configure properties for displaying the color rule in a legend.

Colors

On the General page of the Map Color Rules Properties dialog box, shown in Figure 22-11, you have the following options for assigning colors to spatial elements in your map:

- **Apply Template Style** This is the only option available when your map does not include analytical data. You can also use this option if you prefer to have Reporting Services use the color palette associated with the theme selection made in the Map Wizard or Layer Wizard. You have no control over the color assignments with this option.

- **Visualize Data By Using A Color Palette** You identify the analytical data field to use for visualization and select one of the available color palettes: Random, Light, Semi Transparent, or Bright Pastel. In that case, Reporting Services assigns each range of values to a separate color, but you have no additional control over the color assignments.

- **Visualize Data By Using Color Ranges**   You select the field to visualize and then set up color ranges by defining a spectrum with a start, middle, and end color. Although you specify only three colors here, Reporting Services uses one color per distribution bucket that you define on the Distribution page. You should use a natural progression from the start color to the end color, using a light color first and a dark color last, or using common colors for key performance indicators like red, yellow, and green. When you set No Color for the Middle Color value, Reporting Services selects a color between the start and end color.

- **Visualize Data By Using Custom Colors**   For greater control over the colors, you can create a custom collection using as many colors as you like. You might use this option when you want to use a particular color spectrum or when you have specific color scale requirements to match.

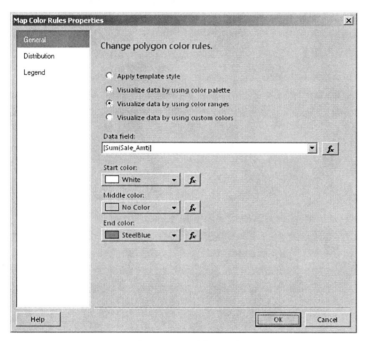

FIGURE 22-11 You can set the start, middle, and end color when basing the color rule on color ranges.

Distribution

The number of colors you see in the map depends on the number of distribution buckets, or *sub-ranges*, that you define on this page of the Map Color Rule Properties dialog box. Reporting Services assigns a distinct color to each subrange. You can select one of the following distribution options:

- **Optimal**   With this selection, you configure the number of subranges you want to use in the map for color assignment purposes. You can optionally configure values for Range Start and Range End if you want to eliminate outliers from the color scale. If the analytical dataset has fewer than four data points, Reporting Services uses the equal distribution option. Otherwise, it uses an algorithm to find natural breaks in the data as boundaries for each subrange.

- **Equal Interval**   If you want the interval of values to be the same in each subrange, you select this option. For example, if you want to group values in your map by using five different colors, you set Number Of Subranges to 5. If your minimum and maximum values are set to 0 and 100, respectively, this option produces the following ranges: 0–20, 20–40, 40–60, 60–80, and 80–100.

- **Equal Distribution**   If you prefer to have the number of rows in your analytical dataset distributed evenly, more or less, across a specified number of subranges, you should use this option. For example, let's say you have 35 records in the dataset to spread across 5 subranges and you set the minimum and maximum values to 0 and 100, respectively. Reporting Services might create the 35 records like this: 0–3, 3–6, 6–9, 9–15, and 15–100. Most of the subranges reflect values for 8 records, while others might reflect values for 6 or 7 records.

- **Custom**   You can manually configure each subrange, as shown in Figure 22-12. Just click the Add button to add a new subrange and provide the Start Value and End Value. You can remove a subrange by clicking in the Start Value box and then clicking the Delete button. Use the arrow buttons to rearrange the sequence of subranges if you prefer. Reporting Services uses this sequence for the visualization by color range.

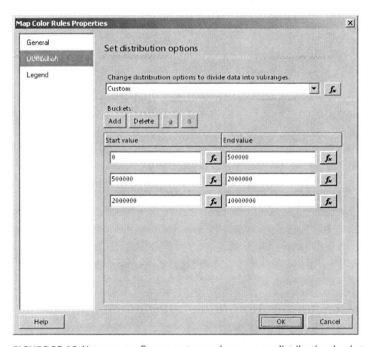

FIGURE 22-12 You can configure custom subranges, or distribution buckets, to group values by color.

Legend options

By default, a map displays both a legend and a color scale to show you the value range that applies to a spatial element. On the Legend page of the Map Color Rules Properties dialog box, as shown in Figure 22-13, you can choose whether to include the current color rule in either the legend or the color scale. You can clear the Show In Color Scale option to remove the color rule from the color scale, or you can select the blank option to exclude it from all legends in the map.

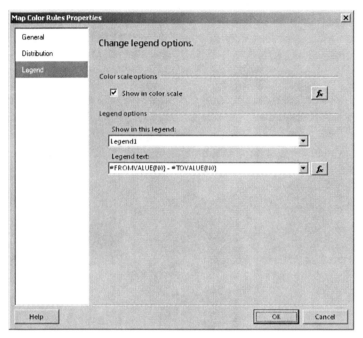

FIGURE 22-13 You can specify whether to display the color rule subranges in the color scale or assign the color rule to a particular legend and define the expression for the legend labels.

If you decide to show the color rule in a legend, you can assign it to a specific legend. You must first add the legend as described in the "Legend" section of this chapter, and then you can select the legend in the Show In This Legend drop-down list. Unlike most properties, the assignment to a legend is not dynamic. You can also modify the keywords in the Legend Text box to restructure or apply formatting to the subranges, as shown in Table 22-2.

TABLE 22-2 Legend text format options

Legend Text Expression	Example
#FROMVALUE {C0}	$1,000,000
#FROMVALUE {C2}	$1,000,000.00
#TOVALUE	2000000
#FROMVALUE {N0} - #TOVALUE {N0}	1,000,000 – 2,000,000

Point maps

For a map layer based on point data, you can configure general point properties. You can configure a point color, marker size, or marker type to use for all points, or you can use rules to change any of those properties based on values in an associated analytical dataset.

Point properties

You can right-click a map layer in the Map Layers pane and select Point Properties to configure label and marker options in addition to the properties we described in the "Common spatial element properties" section of this chapter. Not only can you specify the label text here, but you can also set the label placement relative to the point as Top, Bottom, Left, Right, or Center.

If you do not have an analytical dataset associated with the point map layer or if you choose not to use it to set the marker color only, you can select the marker type and marker size on the General page of the Map Point Properties dialog box. Your marker type options include Circle, Rectangle, Diamond, Triangle, Trapezoid, Star, Wedge, Pentagon, PushPin, or Image. If you select Image, you must specify whether the image is embedded or comes from an external or database source (as described in Chapter 9, "Designing the report layout"). You can add an image from any of these sources directly within the Map Point Properties dialog box.

Point color rule

You can change the marker color for a point based on a color rule that you define. For more information, see the "Color rules" section of this chapter.

Point size rule

To set a rule for marker sizes based on analytical values, right-click the layer in the Map Layers pane and select Point Size Rule. On the General page of the Map Layer Size Rules Properties dialog box, you select Visualize Data By Using Size, select a field to visualize, and define the Start Size and End Size, as shown in Figure 22-14. The default size applies to a value that does not fall within the range you specify, as described in the "Distribution" section of this chapter.

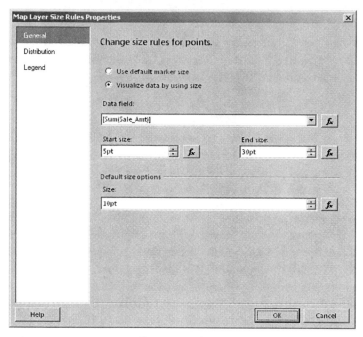

FIGURE 22-14 You can specify a range of marker sizes to visualize a data field.

Marker type rule

You can also use marker types for visualizing data points in a map layer. To do this, right-click the layer in the Map Layers pane and select Marker Type Rule. On the General page of the Map Marker Type Rules Properties dialog box, you select the Visualize Data By Using Markers option and select a field to visualize. You can then add or delete marker types in the Markers list, as shown in Figure 22-15. Use the arrow buttons to rearrange the sequence of markers. Reporting Services assigns the first marker type to the lowest values in the analytical dataset and assigns each subsequent marker type to successive subranges.

> **Note** Take care to adjust the number of subranges on the Distribution page to match the number of marker types you define on the General page of the Map Marker Type Rules Properties dialog box.

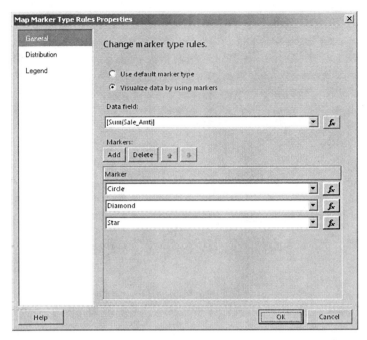

FIGURE 22-15 You can customize the set of markers to use for visualizing a data field.

Line maps

A line map has general properties related to the line. Specific to the line map are the line color and line width properties. If you have analytical data associated with the line data, you have the option to set the line color, line width, or both, based on the values in the analytical data.

Line properties

To configure basic properties like the ones we described in the "Common spatial element properties" section of this chapter, right-click a map layer in the Map Layers pane and select Line Properties to open the Map Line Properties dialog box. If you choose to display label text, you can use this dialog box to set the label placement relative to the line as Above, Center, or Below. You can also use this page to change the line width from its default of 3.75 pt if you are not using analytical data to adjust the width at runtime. To set the line color, use the properties on the Fill page.

Line color rule

You can set a color for line data based on analytical data by right-clicking the map layer and selecting Line Color Rule. You can then define the colors to apply to lines as described in the "Color rules" section of this chapter.

Line width rule

To override the width that you specify in the Map Line Properties dialog box, you can right-click the map layer and select Line Width Rule. The Map Layer Width Rules Properties dialog box that displays is similar to the one you use for point size rules. For lines, you select Visualize Data By Using Line Width, select a field to visualize, and define the Minimum Line Width and Maximum Line Width. You also set the default size for values outside a specified range, as described in the "Distribution" section of this chapter.

Polygon maps

Like the other spatial data types, a polygon map has general properties and properties affecting polygon color. In addition, you can enable center points and then configure a variety of center point properties.

Polygon properties

The general properties for a polygon are available in the Map Polygon Properties dialog box that you open by right-clicking the map layer and selecting Polygon properties. Most of these properties are described in the "Common spatial element properties" section of this chapter. In addition to setting the label text here, you can allow Reporting Services to decide whether to display the label if you select Auto in the Visibility drop-down list, or you can explicitly set the behavior by selecting True or False. You can also use an expression to dynamically control the label visibility. To control polygon color without setting up a color rule, you can use the fill properties.

Polygon color rule

Open the Map Color Rules Properties dialog box for a polygon by right-clicking the layer and selecting Polygon Color Rule. In this dialog box, you configure the rules for assigning a color to a polygon, as described in the "Color rules" section of this chapter.

Center points

Center points are a feature unique to polygons. You can right-click a polygon layer and select Show Center Points to add a marker to the center of each polygon. These center points have the same default properties as a point layer, so you should take some time to modify the center point properties if your map includes both center points and spatial data points. That way, users can clearly distinguish between the two types of points. Center point properties are identical to point properties. You can access the following commands on the polygon layer's context menu after you enable center points: Center Point Properties, Center Point Color Rule, Center Point Size Rule, and Center Point Marker Type Rule.

Tile layer maps

A Bing Map tile layer displays information that Reporting Services retrieves from the Bing Maps servers at runtime, but only when the viewport is configured to use a geographic coordinate system and a Mercator projection. Reporting Services adjusts the contents of the tile layer to correspond to the boundaries defined by the spatial data in each map layer, with no additional configuration required. You can adjust the type of tile layer to Road, Aerial, or Hybrid. You can also configure the visibility of the tile layer in the same way as described in the "Map layer properties" section of this chapter.

Inserting custom points

For special situations, you can enhance a map by adding custom points without getting the data from the supported spatial data sources. Reporting Services makes it very easy to add a new point. You can add a new point layer to the map to store the custom point, or you can add a point to an existing layer. The latter option is available only if you first embed spatial data in the report. Remember that embedding spatial data in the report allows it to run faster but requires that the spatial data is constant each time the report executes.

After selecting the point layer to which the point will belong, right-click and select Add Point on the shortcut menu. When you do this, a special cursor appears when you hover it over the viewport. You can then click on the map and thereby set the location for the custom point, as shown in Figure 22-16.

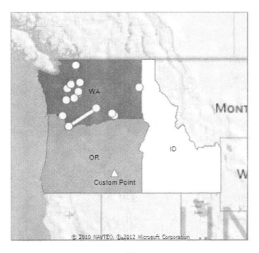

FIGURE 22-16 You can add a custom point to a map.

You can set point properties for the new point by using any of the point layer properties discussed in the "Point maps" section of this chapter. You can also override properties for the single point by right-clicking it in the map, selecting Embedded Point Properties, and selecting the Override Point Options For This Layer check box. Use the Properties window to fine-tune the coordinates for the point's location, as shown in Figure 22-17, when you need greater precision.

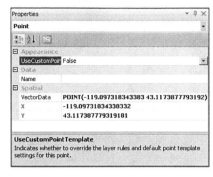

FIGURE 22-17 Use the Properties window to set the X and Y coordinates for precise placement of a custom point.

Understanding order of precedence

If multiple properties apply to the same element, Reporting Services uses an order of precedence to render a map, as shown in Figure 22-18. Rendering begins with the properties that you specify for the map layers. These properties remain unchanged unless a property for a specific map element overrides the layer setting. Usually, you do not encounter any conflict between map layer and map element properties. However, you might have conflicting settings for points, lines, or polygons when you have rules for analytical data. These properties supersede settings in map layers or map elements. Properties for a custom point or for a specific embedded spatial element that you override specifically are last to render.

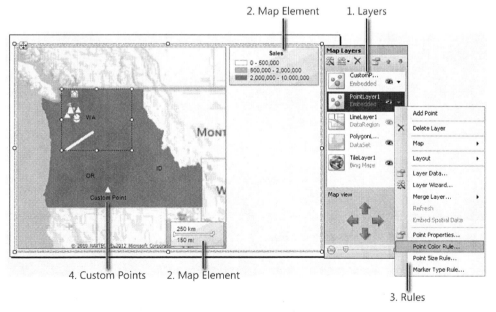

FIGURE 22-18 Reporting Services uses an order of precedence to resolve conflicting properties for the same area of a map.

PART IV

Managing the report server

In Part IV, you learn how to deploy reports to the report server and how to manage the reporting environment. In Chapter 23, "Deploying reports to a server," you learn several ways to move reports from a report developer's computer to the report server. You also learn how to organize content on the report server and configure properties that control data source access and report execution behavior. You explore security options in detail in Chapter 24, "Securing report server content." Then, in Chapter 25, "Performing administrative tasks," you review the management tools included in Reporting Services, explore the server configuration files that you can change, and learn about the tools that you can use to monitor report server performance. These chapters explain all aspects of managing the report server.

CHAPTER 23

Deploying reports to a server

The process of deploying reports includes a variety of tasks that are covered in this chapter. At minimum, you place report definition files on the report server to make reports available to users. Typically, you also configure data sources to associate reports with a different test or production database. You might create alternate versions of a base report by setting up linked reports or generating report copies. You can also configure report properties, such as report parameter default values, execution options, or history management properties, to control what data displays in a report, the amount of time before the user request that the data is retrieved for the report, and the amount of time a snapshot of a report is saved on the report server.

The deployment process copies the report definition into the *ReportServer* database described in Chapter 2, "Introducing the Reporting Services environment." A shared data source or any other file type that you want to store centrally for user access can also be deployed to the report server and is similarly stored in the *ReportServer* database. Report developers typically deploy a report directly from SSDT, while report server administrators often deploy a report manually by using Report Manager or programmatically by using the rs utility (described more fully in Chapter 34, "Programming report server management").

Deploying content

There are multiple ways that you can deploy content to the report server. The approach you take might depend on the standard operating procedures and security policies you choose to enforce within your environment, the number of items to deploy to the report server, or the degree of automation you prefer to use. For example, you might allow report developers to deploy directly from SSDT to a development report server but require an administrator to programmatically deploy approved reports to a production report server.

> **Important** Regardless of which method you use to deploy content, you must be assigned to the Content Manager role on a native-mode report server or to the Owners role on an integrated-mode report server. To learn more about roles, see Chapter 24, "Securing report server content."

Deploying a report project

A solution in SSDT can contain one or more report projects, each of which can contain one or more reports. Each project has a set of properties to define the target location for the reports and data sources that it contains. After you define these properties, you can deploy all reports in all report projects in the solution, all reports in a single report project, a selected set of reports, or a specific report.

Deployment from SSDT

To deploy a report server project by using SSDT, you must first configure the project properties to specify the target report server's web service endpoint and the folders for each report project item type. You can find a description and valid values for each project property in Chapter 7, "Working with report server projects." If a target folder does not exist, the deployment process creates it for you.

For a SharePoint integrated-mode report server, the targets must be fully qualified folder URLs, with some exceptions. The TargetServerURL requires no Virtual Directory and must point to the top-level site or subsite containing the document library prepared for deployment, as outlined in Chapter 4, "Installing Reporting Services," such as *http://<servername>*, *http://<servername>/<site>*, or *http://<servername>/<site>/<subsite>*. Integrated mode requires folders as target locations for reports, data sources, and datasets, unlike native mode, which allows you to deploy items to the home folder of the Report Manager web application if you leave these targets blank.

> **Important** If you are deploying to a SharePoint site on your local computer, you must specify the server name in the URL rather than localhost. Otherwise, the deployment fails with the following error: "Report Server has encountered a SharePoint error."

You first select the file or files to deploy in Solution Explorer, including report files, data source files, dataset files, or any other file type your project contains. You can select an individual file, or you can use the Ctrl key to select multiple files. If you select a project, all the files it contains will deploy. After making your selection, use the Deploy command on the Build menu, or right-click anywhere in Solution Explorer and select Deploy.

The progress of deployment displays in the Output window, as shown in Figure 23-1, which displays at the bottom of your screen in the default layout. The Output window shown here is for deployment to a native-mode report server. An integrated-mode report server deployment looks very similar but instead displays each file's complete URL reference as each file deploys.

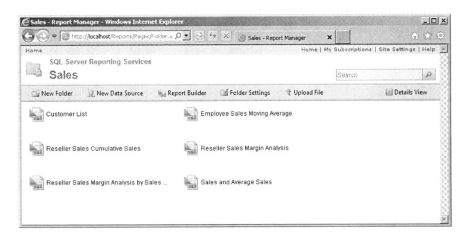

FIGURE 23-1 Review the Output window to check the deployment status of each file.

Note Even when you use SQL Server 2012 Reporting Services, the Output window indicates that each report is built for SQL Server 2008 R2 Reporting Services.

Deployment verification

After deployment completes successfully, you can open Internet Explorer and navigate to the web application hosting Reporting Services to verify deployment as follows:

- **Native mode** Type the URL for the Report Manager, such as *http://<servername>/Reports*, to open the Home page, and then click the applicable folder link to view the deployed reports, as shown in Figure 23-2. All files are physically stored as binary files in the Catalog table in the *ReportServer* database. For a native-mode report server, Report Manager queries this table to retrieve a list of the items for the current folder and displays the results in two columns, in alphabetical order.

FIGURE 23-2 Open Report Manager to verify report deployment on a native-mode report server.

- **Integrated mode**   Navigate to the document library specified in the project properties for your reports, such as *http://denali:37780/sites/ssrs/Documents*. In integrated mode, the list of current items in the Document library is stored in the SharePoint Web Application content database. All physical files are also stored as binary files in the Catalog table of the Reporting Services Service Application database. The SharePoint engine queries the content database to retrieve a list of items for the current folder within the document library, as shown in Figure 23-3.

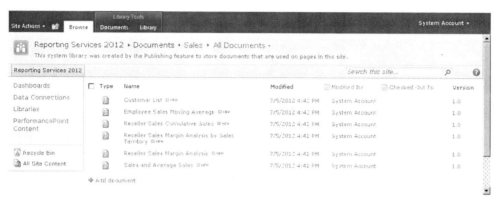

FIGURE 23-3 Open the SharePoint document library to verify report deployment on an integrated-mode report server.

Saving a report from Report Builder

If you use Report Builder to create a report, you have the option to save the report to your computer for personal use or to the report server. Even if you save your report to the report server, you can save it for personal use if you save it to the My Reports folder, as we describe in Chapter 26, "Accessing reports online." If you have the appropriate permissions, you can save a report to a shared folder on the report server. To do this, click the Report Builder button in the top-left corner, click Save As, and then navigate to the applicable folder on the report server. You can click the Recent Sites And Servers button in the Save As Report dialog box to locate the report server's URL, or you can type the URL in the Name box and press Enter. You can then open a folder and type a name for the report, as shown in Figure 23-4.

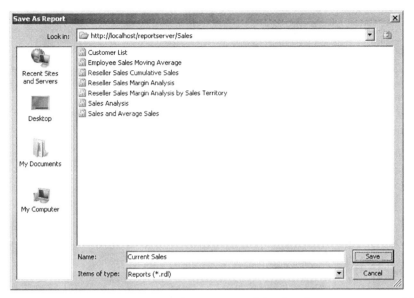

FIGURE 23-4 You can save a report from Report Builder directly to a report server folder.

Uploading a report

In some organizations, certain users might be report server administrators who have permission to add content to the report server, but do not develop content. In that case, it's likely they won't have SSDT installed on their computers. If you are in this group of users, you can upload reports directly to the report server using the web application interface as follows:

- **Native mode** In the web browser, open Report Manager (*http://<servername>/Reports*) and navigate to the folder into which you want to upload the report. Click the Upload File button on the Report Manager toolbar, click Browse, navigate to the report definition file on your computer, select it, and click Open to add the file location to the File To Upload text box, as shown in Figure 23-5. In the Name text box, you can change the file name if you like. You must select the Overwrite Item If It Exists check box if a file of the same name already exists in the folder.

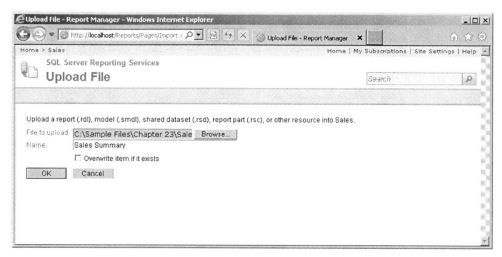

FIGURE 23-5 Use Report Manager to upload a single report to a native-mode report server.

- **Integrated mode**   In your web browser, navigate to a document library on a SharePoint site (such as *http://denali:37780/sites/ssrs/Documents*), and then click the Upload button on the Documents tab of the ribbon. Navigate to the report definition file on your computer, select it, and click Open to add it to the Upload Document page, as shown in Figure 23-6. In the Name text box, you can change the file name if you like. You can check the box to add a new version if a file of the same name already exists in the folder.

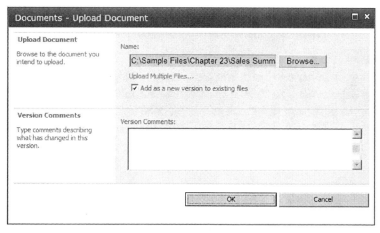

FIGURE 23-6 Use the Upload Document page to add a file to an integrated-mode report server.

Note By default, the uploaded document in SharePoint adds the report definition as new content to support the versioning feature in SharePoint. In-depth coverage of generic features of SharePoint is beyond the scope of this book. However, you can learn more about versioning in SharePoint at *http://technet.microsoft.com/en-us/library/cc262378*. In the case of Reporting Services reports, versioning applies only to the report definition file itself. You cannot use versioning to store different copies of the report as data changes. You can instead use report history, as we explain in the "Saving report snapshots in report history" section of this chapter.

After you upload your report to a document library, SharePoint prompts you to assign one of the content types that are applicable to the document library, as described in Chapter 4. When you assign the Report content type to your report, SharePoint prompts you for additional properties to assign to the report, as shown in Figure 23-7. On this form, only the Name property is required. You can optionally supply a title, report description, owner, report category, and report status.

 Tip Report properties are useful for creating custom views in a SharePoint document library.

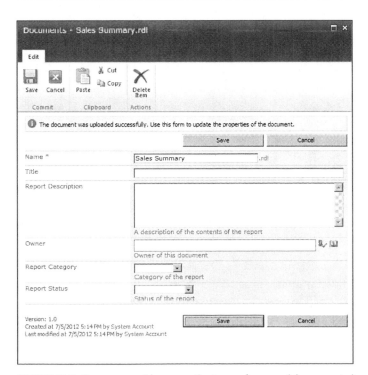

FIGURE 23-7 You can provide properties to use for organizing reports in a SharePoint view.

Important The upload process to a report server in native mode or integrated mode does not associate the report definition file with a shared data source, which prevents you from viewing the report immediately after upload. In the "Configuring data source properties" section of this chapter, you learn how to correctly associate a report with its data source.

Tip You can upload other file types to the report server. For example, you can use Word or Excel documents to store documentation or metadata. You can also upload images for use in reports. For example, you might place the corporate logo in a file that you reference in a report as an external image. That way, you can replace the logo once on the report server if it ever changes, rather than open every report as you do when you need to change an embedded image. However, an image is subject to a 2-GB size limitation.

Activating the file sync feature

If you frequently upload published report items directly to SharePoint document libraries, the report server file sync feature will be beneficial. This feature synchronizes the report server catalog with items in document libraries on a more frequent basis and aids report server performance. Otherwise, the report server must copy a report definition from the SharePoint content database to the report server catalog at report execution time, which adds unnecessary overhead at runtime. You must activate this feature at the SharePoint site level. To do this, click Site Settings on the Site Actions menu, click the Manage Site Features link, and then click the Activate button for Report Server File Sync.

Using the rs utility

A report administrator can run Reporting Service script files (.rss) with the rs utility to manage many activities on a native-mode or SharePoint integrated-mode report server, including report deployment. The rs utility allows administrators to utilize any of the Reporting Services web service operations, such as deploying items to the report server, moving or deleting items, creating subscriptions, and much more.

When you want an administrator to deploy reports in bulk, you develop a script file using Microsoft Visual Basic .NET and save the file as a Unicode or UTF-8 text with an .rss file name extension. Then you provide the administrator with the script file and report definition files to be uploaded. The report administrator can then use the script file as an input file for the rs utility (described in more detail in Chapter 34).

Important Beginning with SQL Server 2008 R2, you can use the rs utility with both native-mode and integrated-mode report servers.

For example, to execute the rs utility with the DeploySalesReports.rss script to deploy reports to a local native-mode report server, you type the following command in a command prompt window:

```
rs -i DeploySalesReports.rss -s http://localhost/ReportServer -e Mgmt2010
```

The URL that you use for a SharePoint integrated-mode report server references the SharePoint site to which you are deploying reports. The syntax then looks like this:

```
rs -i DeployReports_SP.rss -s http://denali:37780/sites/ssrs/_vti_bin/ReportServer -e Mgmt2010
```

The results of executing the utility display in the command prompt window, as shown in Figure 23-8. The messages that display during execution of the rs utility depend on the instructions in the script and whether errors occur.

```
Administrator: Command Prompt                                    _ □ ×
C:\Sample Files\Chapter 23>rs -i DeploySalesReports.rss -s http://localhost/repo
rtserver -e Mgmt2010
Parent folder Sales and Order Quantity Analysis created successfully
Report: Sales and Order Quantity by Year published successfully
Report: Sales and Order Quantity Summary published successfully
The command completed successfully

C:\Sample Files\Chapter 23>
```

FIGURE 23-8 You can use the rs utility to deploy reports to a report server from the command line.

Deploying a report model

Although you can no longer create report models by using SQL Server 2012 Reporting Services, you can deploy a report model to a SQL Server 2012 report server to continue using it as a data source for reports. You cannot open the report model project in SSDT to deploy it, but you can deploy the report model manually by uploading the SMDL file directly to the report server. However, errors display when you attempt to use the report model without modification.

Before you manually deploy a report model, you must first edit the SMDL file to include the contents of its corresponding data source view file. That is, you must open the data source view file in a text editor such as Notepad. The first node of the XML begins with the *DataSourceView* element, which contains several attributes. Replace this first node with the following code:

```
<DataSourceView xmlns="http://schemas.microsoft.com/analysisservices/2003/engine"
xmlns:xsi="RelationalDataSourceView">
```

After making this change, copy all the XML elements in the revised data source view file. Then open the report model file in a text editor, and paste the data source view's XML just before the closing *SemanticModel* tag at the end of the file. Save the SMDL file, and then use the Upload File button in the Report Manager toolbar to upload the report model to the report server.

The last step is to update the data source associated with the report model. You can add a data source manually or upload a data source that you create in SSDT, but it must exist on the report server before you can proceed. Point to the newly uploaded report model, click the down arrow to display the submenu, and click Manage. Click the Data Sources link, and then click the Browse button. Navigate to the folder containing the applicable data source, expand the folder, select the data source, and click OK. Next, click the Apply button. Your report model is now ready to use as a data source in reports.

Managing content

One way to manage content on a report server is to store every report in a single location, such as the Home page, but before long, you'll find that the number of reports becomes so large that it is difficult to manage security and to find content. You can use folders to simplify report management and usage. You can move content to a new folder later and, on a native-mode server, use a linked report to set up variations of a single report for applying different properties such as security or parameters.

Using folders to organize content

Folders are useful for organizing content into logical groups by subject matter, target audience, security, or any combination of these. For example, you can easily create report locations for Development, User Acceptance Testing, and Production by using folders with separate security settings. You can also nest folders to create a hierarchical structure. A child folder inherits the security settings of its parent folder, unless you explicitly override security. We describe folder security in Chapter 24.

> **Tip** A common approach to managing content in folders is to create one report project in SSDT for each folder on the report server. You can then configure the target report folder in the project properties for easy deployment to the intended folder. Of course, you can subsequently move a report another folder if necessary.

Although deployment from SSDT creates a folder on the report server if a target does not yet exist, you can also manually create a folder as follows:

■ **Native mode** In Report Manager, go to the Home folder or navigate to the folder in which you want to create a new folder, and then click the New Folder button on the Report Manager toolbar. You must provide a name for the new folder, as shown in Figure 23-9, and optionally, you can include a description to provide users with more information about the folder content.

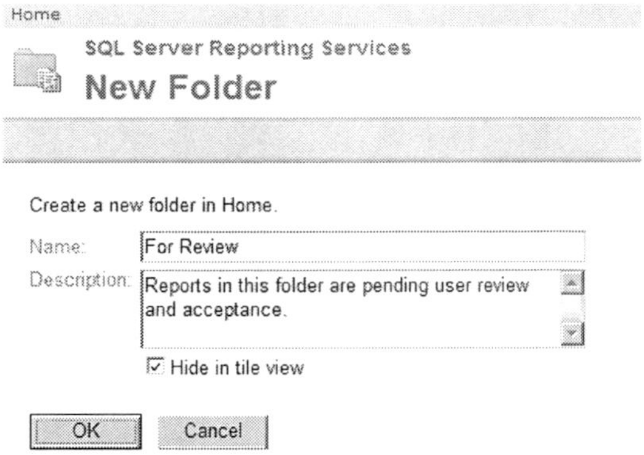

SQL Server Reporting Services

New Folder

Create a new folder in Home.

Name: For Review

Description: Reports in this folder are pending user review and acceptance.

☑ Hide in tile view

[OK]   [Cancel]

FIGURE 23-9 You can add a new folder to organize content on a native-mode report server.

You can view folders in two different ways in Report Manager: Detail View and Tile View. The default is Tile View, which keeps hidden folders from view. To hide a folder from this view, just select the Hide In Tile View check box, as shown in Figure 23-9. Each report also has a Hide In Tile View check box, which you might want to use to hide drill-through reports or subreports. Whether you use this technique to hide an entire folder or individual reports, you should not rely on this feature as a security measure. When a user changes the view to Tile View, all hidden folders and reports are grayed out but visible, and they can still be selected and opened.

- **Integrated mode** You have another level of organization possible by using document libraries, which you can subdivide by using folders. Open the document library in your SharePoint site, and then click the New Folder button on the toolbar, shown in Figure 23-10.

FIGURE 23-10 You use the New Folder button on the SharePoint ribbon to add another folder to a document library on an integrated-mode report server.

Moving content

Getting the right folder structure established for reports might take some time. You can move reports (or other items deployed to the report server) individually or as a block by moving the containing folder. You can move an item from one folder to another folder as follows:

- **Native mode** In Report Manager's Tile View, you can point to the item, click the down arrow to display the submenu, and then click Move. To move multiple items, switch to Details View, select the check box to the left of each item In Report Manager, and then click the Move button on the Report Manager toolbar. Either way, your next step is to type the path for the new parent folder or select the target location in the tree control, as shown in Figure 23-11.

FIGURE 23-11 You can select a new parent folder in the tree view of folders on a native-mode report server.

■ **Integrated mode** In the upper-left corner of the browser, click Site Actions, select Manage Content And Structure, and then, in the tree view on the left, select the document library and navigate to a folder to view its contents, as shown in Figure 23-12. Select the check box to the left of items to move (or select the topmost check box to the left of Type to select all items), click the Actions menu, and then click Move.

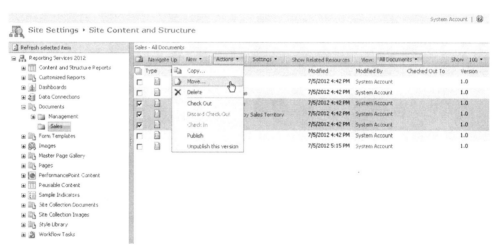

FIGURE 23-12 You use the Site Content And Structure page to move content on a SharePoint integrated-mode report server.

In the Move… Webpage Dialog box, you can navigate to a different folder on the SharePoint site, select it in the folder list, as shown in Figure 23-13, and then click OK. The items you selected in the previous step move to the new location.

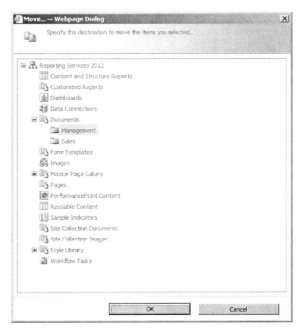

FIGURE 23-13 You can select another folder on the same SharePoint site as a target for relocating content on an integrated-mode report server.

Important When you move reports to a new folder on an integrated-mode report server, the link between the data source and the report breaks. You must reset the link on each report manually before users can view the reports. See the "Configuring data source properties" section later in this chapter to learn how to reset this link for moved reports.

Creating a linked report

On a native-mode report server, by creating a *linked report,* you can create a variation of a report without the need to create and maintain multiple report definition files. A linked report is a separate report item on the report server that uses a report definition file as a base but has separate execution, parameter, subscription, and security properties. A common reason to use a linked report is if you want to build a report that contains data for multiple departments and includes a parameter to filter the report content by department. You can then deploy the report to a folder that none of the users can access, create one linked report per department, set the report parameter default to a specific department, and configure security such that users can access only the linked report for their department.

Important The linked report feature is not supported on a SharePoint integrated-mode report server.

To create a linked report, point to a report in Report Manager, click the down arrow to display the submenu, as shown in Figure 23-14, and then click Create Linked Report.

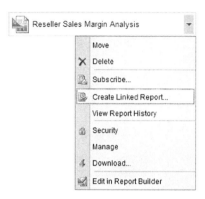

FIGURE 23-14 You can use a report's submenu to launch the process to create a linked report on a native-mode report server.

On the Properties page, provide a name and an optional description for the linked report. By default, the linked report is created in the same folder as the base report. You can click the Change Location button to select a target folder for the linked report. The Properties page then displays the location for the linked report, as shown in Figure 23-15.

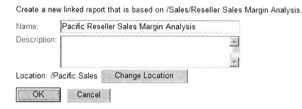

FIGURE 23-15 You must provide a name for the new linked report and specify a location on a native-mode report server.

After you click OK, the linked report displays in the browser window. You can now customize other properties of the linked report and not affect the base report. For example, to display only data for the Pacific sales territory in the report, you can change the parameter properties as described in the "Configuring report parameters" section of this chapter.

Copying a report

Although you cannot create linked reports on an integrated-mode report server, you can create a copy of a report to achieve a similar result. That is, you can reproduce the same report definition as a separate file on the report server and set different execution, parameter, subscription, and security properties on the new file. However, any changes to the base report definition do not update the copy.

You begin the process by pointing to the report to copy, clicking the down arrow to display the submenu, pointing to Send To, and selecting Other Location. In the Copy dialog box, as shown in Figure 23-16, type the URL for the document library or folder into which you want to copy the report and provide a name for the new report.

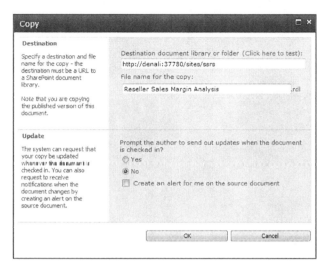

FIGURE 23-16 You can copy a report definition to another location on a SharePoint integrated-mode report server.

> **Note** Because the Reporting Services deployment process does not depend on checking items in and out on a SharePoint integrated-mode report server, setting the Prompt The Author To Send Out Updates When The Document Is Checked In? option to Yes does not lead to an update of the report copy when the base report changes. You should select Yes only when you require report developers to check in reports.

> **Important** Even if you copy a report that has a valid data source reference, the copy process does not include the link between the data source and the report copy. You must manually add this link before users can view the report copy, as described in the "Configuring data source properties" section later in this chapter.

Configuring report parameters

Besides managing the location of reports on the report server, you can also manage the default values that are configured for the report parameters. Additionally, you can control the visibility of the parameter, whether or not it has default values, and what text the user prompt will display. Any changes made to the report parameters directly in Report Manager or a SharePoint library will persist even if you deploy the report multiple times from SSDT or upload the report directly to the server after originally setting the parameter properties. The steps you follow depend on the report server type, as follows:

- **Native mode**   In Report Manager, point to a report, click the down arrow to display the submenu, and select Manage. Next, click the Parameters link on the left side of the page to display the report parameter properties, as shown in Figure 23-17. This link is visible only when a report has one or more report parameters.

Select the parameters that all users can change, and choose a default value for each.

Parameter Name	Data Type	Has Default	Default Value	Null	Hide	Prompt User	Display Text
CostBasis	String	☑	Total		☐	☑	Cost Basis
Year	String	☑	Query Based		☐	☑	Year
Quarter	String	☑	Query Based		☐	☑	Quarter
SalesTerritoryGroup	String	☑	Europe, North America, ▼ Pacific		☐	☐	SalesTerritoryGroup

Apply

FIGURE 23-17 You can modify the report parameter properties after deploying a report or creating a linked report.

On the Parameters page, you can change the following report parameter properties:

- **Has Default**   If you clear this check box, the report cannot execute until the user provides a parameter value. In this case, be sure not to remove the user prompt for the same report parameter. If you select this check box, you must set the *Default Value* property.

- **Default Value**   If the report definition uses a query to select the default value for the report parameter, you see the Query Based label appear for this property. You cannot modify the query here, nor can you see the results of the query. Otherwise, you can type a value to set a default for the report parameter. If the report parameter accepts multiple values, you can expand the drop-down list and add or remove values. Each value must appear on a separate line.

> **Important**   If the *Default Value* property is set to Query Based and you clear the Has Default check box, you lose the association with the query that sets the default value. If you later change your mind and select the Has Default check box, you have no way to restore the associated query. You must manually supply default values, or delete the report and redeploy the original report definition with the default query.

- **Hide**   If you select this check box, the Prompt User and Display Text properties are disabled. You must supply a default value. The user does not see this parameter when viewing the report online and cannot set a different parameter value when creating a subscription for this report.

- **Prompt User**   When you select this check box, the user can change the parameter when viewing the report online. If you do not set the *Default Value* property, the user must specify a parameter value before the report can execute. If you clear the Prompt User check box, the user cannot see or change the parameter when viewing the report online. However, the user can set an alternate value when creating a subscription for the report.

- **Display Text**   If you select the Prompt User check box, you must type a value in this box to display as a label for the report parameter.

■ **Integrated mode**   The interface differs somewhat from the one for a native-mode report server, but the method you use to manage report parameters is similar. Start by pointing to a report in a document library, clicking the down arrow to display the submenu, and then selecting Manage Parameters. A list of report parameter links displays, as shown in Figure 23-18. Click a link to view or change the report parameter properties.

Use this page to manage parameters used in this report.

| | | | | Close |
Prompt Order ↑	Parameter Name	Default Value	Data Type	Display
1	CostBasis	Total	String	Prompt
2	Year	(Query based)	String	Prompt
3	Quarter	(Query based)	String	Prompt
4	SalesTerritoryGroup	Europe, North America, Pacific	String	Prompt
				Close

FIGURE 23-18 You must click a report parameter link on the Manage Parameters page on a SharePoint integrated-mode report server to view or edit its properties.

When you click a report parameter link on the Manage Parameters page, a new page displays the selected report parameter's properties, as shown in Figure 23-19. Here you can change the following report parameter properties:

- **Default Value**   If you select the Use This Value option, you can type a value if the parameter is not query-based. If the parameter is query-based and accepts multiple values, you can select one or more values in the drop-down list. Otherwise, you can select Do Not Use A Default Value to require the user to supply a parameter value.

- **Display**   If you select the Prompt option, you must type a value to display as a label for the report parameter. The Hidden option allows you to specify a default value for a report parameter without allowing the user to view or change the report parameter value when viewing the report, but the user can change the value when creating a subscription. The Internal option also hides the parameter from a user viewing the report and creating a subscription.

Use this page to manage parameter information for a report.

Parameter Name	SalesTerritoryGroup
Data Type	String

Default Value
Specify a default value for the parameter. If all defaults are specified, the report runs immediately when you open it.

• Use this value:
 Pacific
○ Do not use a default value

Display
Specify how the parameter value is provided to the report.

Show the default value defined for this parameter or prompt the user for a value when the report is run.

• Prompt
 SalesTerritoryGroup
○ Hidden
○ Internal

FIGURE 23-19 You can modify the *Default Value* and *Display* properties for a report parameter on a SharePoint integrated-mode report server.

Enabling personalized folders

On a native-mode report server, you can enable My Reports to give each user a personal workspace in which the user can store reports that are created by using one of the report development tools. A user with appropriate permissions can also create a linked report to personalize a report, such as setting a specific parameter value when the report opens. To enable My Reports using SQL Server Management Studio, connect to Reporting Services, right-click the server in Object Explorer, select Properties, and then select the Enable A My Reports Folder For Each User check box. The tasks that a user can perform in this folder are controlled by the role settings that are described in Chapter 24.

On an integrated-mode server, you can also provide a personal workspace for report storage by setting up a My Site host site collection as described at *http://technet.microsoft.com/en-us/library/ee624362.aspx*. A user with appropriate permissions can then click the My Site link in the Announcements section of a top-level website and then click My Content on the My Site page to create a personal workspace. Then the user can use the Send To command (as described in the "Copying a report" section earlier in this chapter) to copy a report and personalize the parameter settings.

Configuring data source properties

You will likely design and test reports in SSDT by using a local data source that contains a representative subset of production data. By limiting the data used for report development, you can avoid long waits for report execution. However, on the server, you want reports to retrieve data from the production data sources. You can maintain one data source for your development environment and another for your server environment.

Important The *OverwriteDataSources* property for the project controls whether the data source in your project gets copied to the server. By default, the deployment process copies the data source file on the first deployment, but ignores the data source file on subsequent deployments, allowing you to change the properties on the server without affecting the data source on your development computer.

Selecting a data source for a report

You can configure the data source settings for a report after deployment by choosing an existing shared data source on the report server or by specifying the connection information for a custom data source. Of the two options, a shared data source is preferred because you have only one place to update connection information later if necessary rather than opening each report individually to change connection information. We explain about data sources in greater detail in Chapter 8, "Retrieving data for a report."

Note You cannot change properties for a shared data source by opening the report's data source management page as described in this section. Instead, you must navigate to the folder containing the shared data source and click its link to display the properties. The properties for a shared data source are the same as the properties available for a report's custom data source.

Tip When you change the connection information or credentials for a data source, you can use the Test Connection button to make sure that the data source definition correctly connects to the data source. This button is not enabled if you set the data source to use prompted credentials.

The process to select a data source for a report is similar for both report server types, as follows:

- **Native mode** In Report Manager, point to a report, click the down arrow to display the submenu, and select Manage. Click the Data Sources link to view the current data source selection, and make changes as necessary, as shown in Figure 23-20. If a report has multiple data sources, they all display on the same page. You must scroll to view the properties for each data source. For a shared data source, click the Browse button to navigate to the folder containing the data source and select it from the tree view that displays. If you choose to create a custom data source, you select a data source type and then supply the applicable connection string. There is no editor to help you build the correct connection string like you have in SSDT. Click Apply to save the setting.

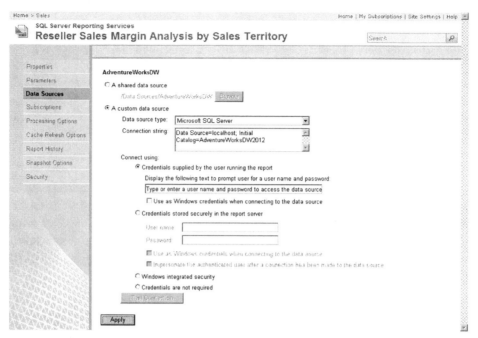

FIGURE 23-20 You access the Data Sources properties as one of the management pages for a report on a native-mode report server.

- **Integrated mode**   Point to a report in a document library, click the down arrow to display the submenu, and select Manage Data Sources. On the Manage Data Sources page, a list of each data source defined in the report displays, but the presence of a data source in this list does not mean the data source is correctly configured. Click the applicable data source link to open its properties.

  To assign a shared data source to a report, you must supply a valid URL, such as *http://denali:37780/sites/ssrs/Data Connections for PerformancePoint/AdventureWorksDW.rsds*, as shown in Figure 23-21. You can click the ellipsis button to open the Select An Item dialog box, and navigate through the site folders to find the data source if you don't know the URL.

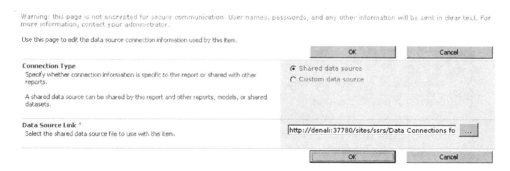

FIGURE 23-21 You must supply the data source URL when configuring a shared data source for a report on an integrated-mode report server.

You can also configure a custom data source for the report, as shown in Figure 23-22. When you select this option, you must select a data provider in the Data Source Type drop-down list and type in the applicable connection string. You must know the correct connection string to use because there is no builder here to help you.

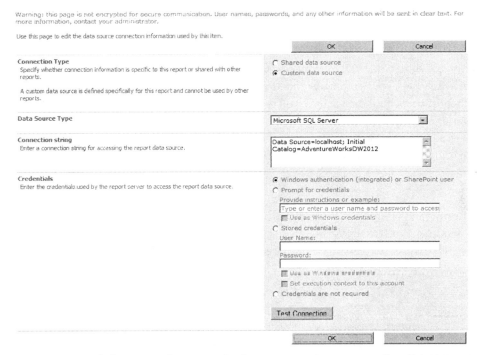

FIGURE 23-22 Each data source for a report has its own properties page on a SharePoint integrated-mode report server.

Sending credentials to a data source

In addition to setting the connection information, you must specify the credentials to use when connecting to the data source. You can select any of the same options that you have when defining a data source in SSDT (as described in Chapter 8), or you can specify stored credentials. There is no way to set stored credentials in a data source within SSDT. You must first deploy the report, if using a custom data source, or the shared data source and then edit the data source properties on the report server.

Windows integrated security

The simplest type of security to implement is Windows integrated security, which passes the user's Windows account to the data source, where the user's account must have Read permissions. The data source must be located on the same computer as the report server. If it's located on a remote computer, you must configure the Kerberos protocol on the network to allow the report server to forward the user's credentials.

On a SharePoint integrated-mode report server, you can configure a reporting-enabled web application to use claims-based authentication. In that case, the report server uses the SharePoint user token to authenticate rather than the Windows account.

You can use this setting for credentials only when users execute the report on demand. It is not a valid option for reports run as snapshots or subscriptions.

Prompted credentials

You might have data sources that don't use Microsoft Windows credentials for authentication. For these situations, you can prompt the user for credentials, which then pass to the data provider for authentication at the data source. You should use this authentication method only for reports that the user can access on demand because the report cannot execute without user input. When the user opens a report having a data source configured to use prompted credentials, the user must provide a valid log-in name and password in a prompt such as the one shown in Figure 23-23, before the report displays.

> **Important** If the user must supply a Windows user account, be sure to select the Use As Windows Credentials When Connecting To The Data Source check box in native mode, or select Use As Windows Credentials in integrated mode.

FIGURE 23-23 Native mode prompt for user credentials.

No credentials

Most data sources require some level of security. However, for those reports containing public data that you want to make accessible to everyone, you can configure the data source with the Credentials Are Not Required option. If the report server must connect to another computer to reach the data source, Reporting Services uses the Unattended Execution Account (described in Chapter 4) to authenticate the connection to the remote computer.

Stored credentials

You must configure a data source to use stored credentials when a report is cached, runs on a scheduled basis, or produces a report snapshot. That is, the report server requires stored credentials for any execution option other than on demand. The stored credentials are stored in the *ReportServer* database by using reversible encryption. The account used for stored credentials must be granted Read permission on the source database and Execute permission on a stored procedure if the account is not assigned a default database role, such as *db_datareader*.

On a native-mode report server, select the Credentials Stored Securely On the Report Server option, or select the Stored Credentials option on a SharePoint integrated-mode report server. Then provide the user name and password. If you are using Windows authentication, include the domain name (or computer name if there is no domain) with the user name and select the Use As Windows Credentials when connecting to the data source check box, as shown in Figure 23-24. Otherwise, provide the application login name and password without selecting that check box.

If the credentials saved on the report are no longer valid due to a change in database security or because the user account has been deactivated, you will see a Logon failure and will need to return to this screen again and modify the account being used.

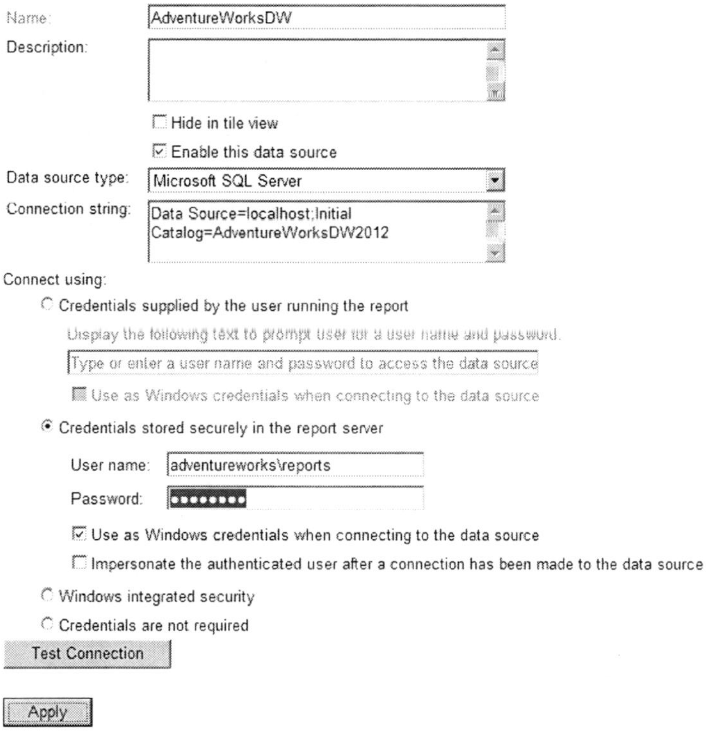

FIGURE 23-24 You can configure a single account to use as stored credentials for a data source.

If the database server supports impersonation, you can configure the data source to use this method to authenticate. For example, on a SQL Server database, impersonation sets the *SETUSER* function. To do this, select the Impersonate The Authenticated User After A Connection Has Been Made option on a native-mode report server or the Set Execution Context To This Account option on a SharePoint integrated-mode report server.

Important If you type an incorrect user name and password for a data source's stored credentials, no error message displays. You can click the Test Connection button after entering the credentials to ensure that you have a good connection. A message will appear indicating that the connection was created successfully.

Configuring report processing options

Report processing transforms a report stored in the ReportServer database into a rendered report that the user views. As part of the execution process, the queries defined in the report's datasets execute and return data to the report server, which then uses the report definition file to determine how to construct the report with the retrieved data. At this point, the report is in an intermediate format that is sent to the applicable rendering extension to produce the final rendered report.

Report performance is determined largely by how much data is retrieved by the dataset query and how much processing is required to produce the rendered report. If the users don't need the most current data in the database each time the report executes, you should consider any execution option that generates the report's intermediate format in advance of the user viewing the report to achieve optimal performance. The following sections in this chapter explain the relationship between each execution option and generation of the intermediate format.

Executing a report on demand

All new reports execute on demand by default. When a user clicks the link for a report, the report executes on demand, returning the most current data to the report server, which then produces an intermediate format. The intermediate format is stored in the *ReportServerTempDB* database in a session cache to speed up subsequent requests by the same user for the same report during the current session. For example, after the user views the report online, the user might export the report to an Excel format. By having the intermediate format in session cache, the online version and the Excel version of the report match. Furthermore, the Excel version renders very quickly from the intermediate format of the report because the report server does not need to wait for the query to execute again.

To configure a report to execute on demand, you must set the report's properties as follows:

- **Native mode**   In Report Manager, point to a report, click the down arrow to display the submenu, and select Manage. Click the Processing Options link, and select both the Always Run This Report With The Most Recent Data and the Do Not Cache Temporary Copies Of This Report options, as shown in Figure 23-25.

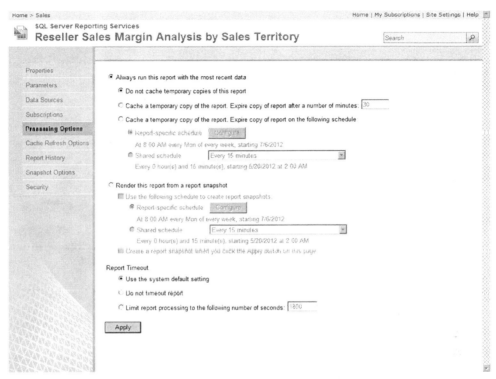

FIGURE 23-25 A report executes on demand by default, but you can change execution behavior on a report's Processing Options when working on a native-mode report server.

- **Integrated mode**   Point to a report in a document library, click the down arrow to display the submenu, and select Manage Processing Options. On the page that displays, select the Use Live Data option, as shown in Figure 23-26.

Use this page to specify how and when report processing occurs.

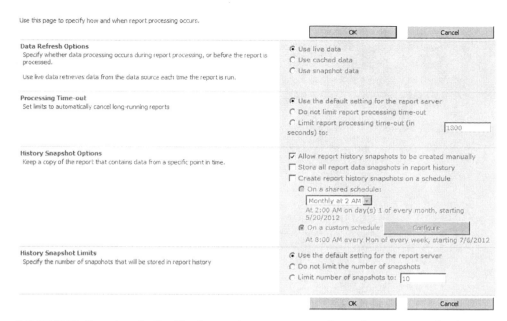

FIGURE 23-26 You select the Use Live Data option to execute on-demand report processing for a report on a SharePoint integrated-mode report server.

Caching reports

Caching a report is helpful when you want to strike a balance between having current data in the report and having faster access to the online report. The first time a user clicks the link for a report configured to cache, the report execution process is identical to the on-demand process. However, the intermediate format is flagged as a cached instance and stored in *ReportServerTempDB* until the time specified by the cache settings expires. Meanwhile, if any user requests the report during the time that it still resides in cache, the report server retrieves the intermediate format and renders the report, as long as the user requests the same combination of parameter values. This process is much faster than retrieving the data, producing the intermediate format, and then rendering the report.

If a user requests a different set of parameter values for a cached report, the report processor treats the request as a new report executing on demand but flags it as a second cached instance. If users are constantly looking at different parameter combinations and not reusing parameter values, using cached reports is not helpful.

When you configure caching, you define the expiration schedule so that cached instances don't remain in the *ReportServerTempDB* database indefinitely. One option is to expire the cache after a specified number of minutes after the report server creates the cached instance. Another option is to expire the cache on a schedule. The schedule can be specific to the report, or you can select a shared schedule that has already been established on the report server, as described in Chapter 27, "Working with subscriptions."

Important You must configure all data sources for a report to use stored credentials before you can configure caching.

To set up caching, you first need to open the processing options page for the report and configure the applicable properties as follows:

- **Native mode** You must first select the Always Run This Report With The Most Recent Data option. Then you choose either of the Cache A Temporary Copy Of The Report options. One of the caching options expires the report after a specified number of minutes, and the other option expires the report according to a schedule. You can select a shared schedule set up on the report server or a report-specific schedule.

- **Integrated mode** When you select the Use Cached Data option, the Cache Options section of the Manage Processing Options page displays, as shown in Figure 23-27. You can then select one of the following expiration options: Elapsed Time In Minutes, On A Shared Schedule, or On A Custom Schedule.

FIGURE 23-27 The Caching Options section displays when you select Use Cached Data on the Manage Processing Options page of a report on a SharePoint integrated-mode report server.

Configuring report time-out

Regardless of the method you use to execute a report, you can control the report time-out period to limit the amount of time the report server takes to process the report. Table 23-1 lists the options you have for configuring the report time-out property by report server type. The System default setting or Site Default setting is 1,800 seconds, unless you override this value at the report level. If you want to override this value for all reports, you can change the server (or site) setting as we describe in Chapter 25, "Performing administrative tasks."

TABLE 23-1 Report time-out configuration

Native-Mode Option	Integrated-Mode Option	Description
Use The System Default Setting	Use The Default Setting For The Report Server	The report times out when the default setting for the report server (native mode) or site (integrated mode) elapses.
Do Not Timeout Report	Do Not Limit Report Processing Time-Out	The report never times out.
Limit Report Processing To The Following Number Of Seconds	Limit Report Processing Time-out (In Seconds) To	The report times out after the specified number of seconds for the current report.

Refreshing the cache

When you configure caching, the cached instance does not exist until a user opens the report. You can use cache refresh to automate the process of generating the cached instance instead. That way, the first user to request the report doesn't have to wait for the time required to generate the query results.

 Important If SQL Server Agent is not running, creation of the cache refresh plan fails.

You must first configure the report for caching. If the report is not yet set up for caching, a message displays and allows you to set up caching with default values before proceeding with the creation of a cache refresh plan. Just like the expiration schedule for caching, you can use a report-specific schedule for the cache refresh or you can select a shared schedule. Furthermore, you can set up a cache refresh plan for each parameter combination that you expect to be used most commonly by users, as follows:

- **Native mode** Instead of opening the processing options page as you do when configuring caching, click the Cache Refresh Options page and then click the New Cache Refresh Plan button on the toolbar. Assign a description and a schedule, as shown in Figure 23-28, and optionally change parameter values.

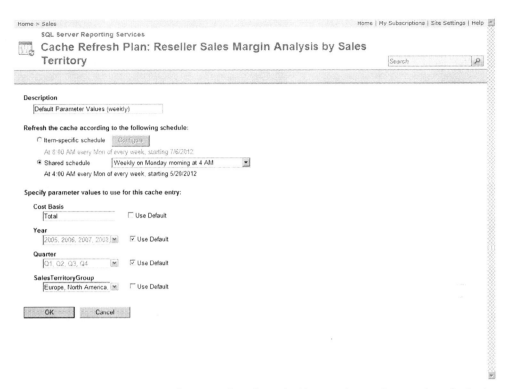

SQL Server Reporting Services

Cache Refresh Plan: Reseller Sales Margin Analysis by Sales Territory

Search

Description

Default Parameter Values (weekly)

Refresh the cache according to the following schedule:

○ Item-specific schedule   Configure

At 8:00 AM every Mon of every week, starting 7/6/2012

● Shared schedule   Weekly on Monday morning at 4 AM

At 4:00 AM every Mon of every week, starting 5/20/2012

Specify parameter values to use for this cache entry:

Cost Basis
Total   ☐ Use Default

Year
2005, 2006, 2007, 2008   ☑ Use Default

Quarter
Q1, Q2, Q3, Q4   ☑ Use Default

SalesTerritoryGroup
Europe, North America   ☐ Use Default

OK   Cancel

FIGURE 23-28 You can automate the generation of a cached instance by creating a cache refresh plan.

- **Integrated mode** From the document library, you point to a report, click the arrow to display the submenu, select Manage Cache Refresh Plans, and click the link for an existing plan or click the New Cache Refresh Plan link. On the Cache Refresh Plan Properties page, shown in Figure 23-29, you specify a description and choose a shared schedule or a custom schedule. You can also use report parameter default values, or you can select the option to override a default and supply an alternate value.

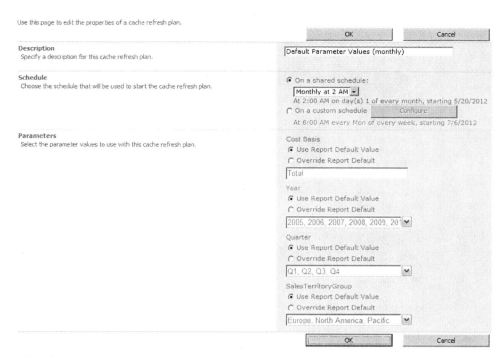

Use this page to edit the properties of a cache refresh plan.

Description
Specify a description for this cache refresh plan.

Default Parameter Values (monthly)

Schedule
Choose the schedule that will be used to start the cache refresh plan.

○ On a shared schedule:
Monthly at 2 AM ▾
At 2:00 AM on day(s) 1 of every month, starting 5/20/2012
○ On a custom schedule   Configure
At 8:00 AM every Mon of every week, starting 7/6/2012

Parameters
Select the parameter values to use with this cache refresh plan.

Cost Basis
○ Use Report Default Value
○ Override Report Default
Total

Year
○ Use Report Default Value
○ Override Report Default
2005, 2006, 2007, 2008, 2009, 201 ▾

Quarter
○ Use Report Default Value
○ Override Report Default
Q1, Q2, Q3, Q4 ▾

SalesTerritoryGroup
○ Use Report Default Value
○ Override Report Default
Europe, North America, Pacific ▾

FIGURE 23-29 You use the Cache Refresh Plan Properties page to generate cached instances on a schedule basis on a SharePoint integrated-mode report server.

Working with snapshots

You can use report snapshots to manage the processing of large reports or resource-intensive reports during off-peak hours. The report server stores report data and layout information in the intermediate format in the *ReportServer* database. That way, users can view reports more quickly during normal business hours, although the data in the report might not reflect the most current data in the data source. You can also use report snapshots to save data at a point in time for historical purposes, such as month-end or year-end reporting.

Important You must configure all data sources for a report to use stored credentials before you can configure report snapshots or save snapshots to report history.

Creating report snapshots

When data volumes are high, server performance is a concern, or when you need to save historical records of report data, you can use report snapshots. A report snapshot executes the query and produces the intermediate format in advance of the user's request to view the report. You can configure a report to generate a snapshot on demand, or you can set up a recurring schedule to replace a snapshot periodically with a more current version. The intermediate format of the report has no expiration time like a cached instance, and it is stored in the *ReportServer* database as part of permanent storage.

> **Important** If you have limited disk space, you should monitor the growth in your *ReportServer* database, as described in Chapter 25.

If you decide to create a report snapshot on a recurring schedule, you can choose between a report-specific schedule and a shared schedule. The benefit of using a shared schedule is the ability to apply the schedule to several different activities, such as creating snapshots, expiring caches, refreshing caches, or delivering subscriptions. We explain how to create a shared schedule in Chapter 27.

To configure a report as a schedule snapshot, you open the same processing options page that you use to configure on-demand execution or caching, as follows:

- **Native mode** Select the Render This Report From a Report Snapshot option, as shown in Figure 23-30. You can then select the Use The Following Schedule To Create Report Snapshots check box when you want to use either a report-specific schedule or a shared schedule. For a report-specific schedule, you click the Configure button to open the schedule definition page, which uses the same settings as a shared schedule. You can also select the Create A Report Snapshot When You Click The Apply Button On This Page check box if you want to create a snapshot right away.

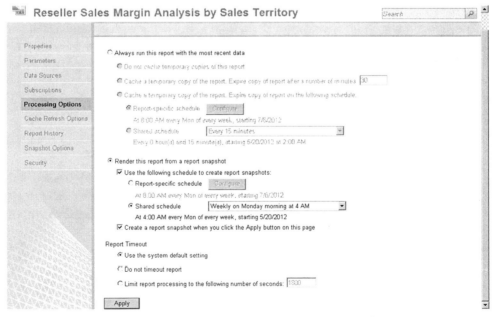

FIGURE 23-30 You use the Processing Options page on a native-mode report server to configure report snapshot settings.

- **Integrated mode** Select the Use Snapshot Data option in the Data Refresh Options section to open the Data Snapshot Options section of the Manage Processing Options page, as shown in Figure 23-31. You can then select the Schedule Data Processing check box, and then select the On A Shared Schedule option or the On A Custom Schedule option. If you choose to use a custom schedule, you can click the Configure button to open the schedule definition page, which you set up the same way that you create a shared schedule. You can also select the Create Or Update The Snapshot When The Page Is Saved check box if you want to create a snapshot right away.

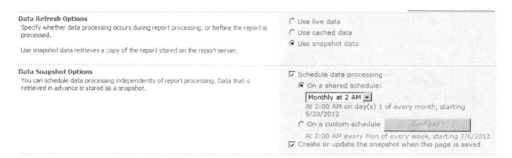

FIGURE 23-31 You must select Use Snapshot Data to display the Data Snapshot Options section on the Manage Processing Options page for a report on a SharePoint integrated-mode report server.

Saving report snapshots in report history

By default, a new report snapshot replaces the previous report snapshot. You can choose to accumulate report snapshots in report history to preserve a record of the report contents at specific points in time. To add a report snapshot to report history, you can click a button to add it manually or you can add to report history each time a new report snapshot is created according to the defined schedule.

The list of report snapshots in history includes the date and time the report snapshot was created and the total size of the report. You can delete a report by selecting its check box and clicking the Delete button on the toolbar.

The report snapshot settings you use depend on the report server type, as follows:

- **Native mode** If you want to accumulate report snapshots, you must open the Snapshot Options page, shown in Figure 23-32, which you can access after you select the Manage command on a report's submenu. Here you control how and when snapshots are added to report history.

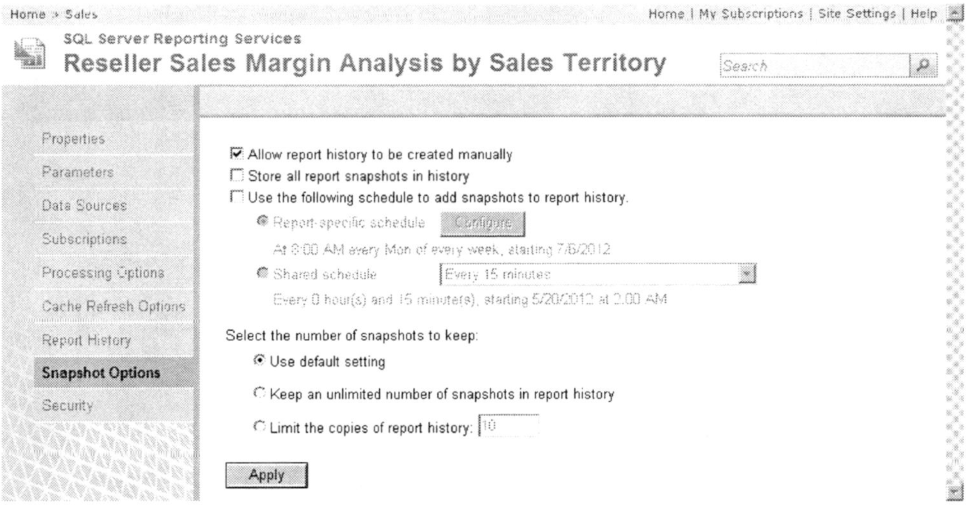

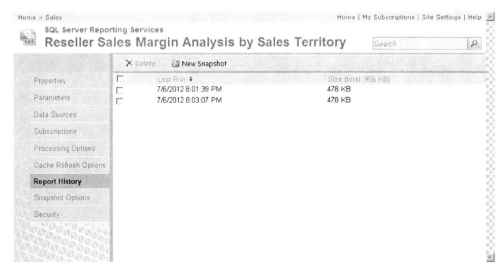

FIGURE 23-32 You manage settings for snapshots on the Snapshot Options page for a report on a native-mode report server.

By default, the report settings allow manual creation of report history only, but you can disable this option by clearing the Allow Report History To Be Created Manually check box. Select this check box to enable users to create a report history snapshot on demand. The report history snapshot is different from a scheduled snapshot because it is accessible only on the Report History page for the report, where you can accumulate multiple snapshots in report history, as shown in Figure 23-33. The New Snapshot button appears on the History tab when this option is enabled. You can click a date-time link to view the associated report snapshot.

FIGURE 23-33 You can view accumulated report snapshots on the Report History page for a report on a native-mode report server.

All other settings on the Snapshot Options page that are related to report snapshots are disabled by default. As an alternative to creating report history manually, you can select the Use The Following Schedule To Add Snapshots To Report History check box on a native-mode report server. If you already have a schedule established for generating a report snapshot, you can select the Store All Report Snapshots In History check box.

- **Integrated mode** You configure report snapshot settings on the Manage Processing Options page in the History Snapshot Options and History Snapshot Limits sections of the page, as shown in Figure 23-34. The only selection that appears here for a new report is Allow Report History Snapshots To Be Created Manually. This selection enables the New Snapshot option on the Report History page for the report. You also select the Store All Report Data Snapshots In Report History check box to automatically add to history when the report server creates a report snapshot according to the schedule you set in the Data Snapshot Options section. You can also set up a separate schedule for accumulating history by selecting the Create Report History Snapshots On A Schedule check box, and then you can select a shared schedule or set up a custom schedule.

FIGURE 23-34 You use the Manage Processing Options page to configure report snapshot settings for a SharePoint integrated-mode report server.

To manually create a report snapshot or to view accumulated snapshots, open the document library containing the report, point to the report, click the arrow to display the submenu, and then select View Report History. You can then see a link for each existing snapshot by date and time, as shown in Figure 23-35, which you click to view the report. Click the New Snapshot button (if it is available) to create a new snapshot using current data.

FIGURE 23-35 You open the Report History page on a SharePoint integrated-mode report server to access the accumulated report snapshots.

Because report history consumes storage space in the *ReportServer* database, you should carefully manage the number of snapshots that accumulate in report history. Your options for applying a snapshot limit are described in Table 23-2. When the report server generates a new report snapshot and exceeds the limit, it deletes the oldest snapshot and adds the new one to history.

TABLE 23-2 Report snapshot limit configuration

Native-Mode Option	Integrated-Mode Option	Description
Use Default Setting	Use The Default Setting For The Report Server	The report server limits snapshots to the number set at the server level (native-mode) or site level (integrated-mode).
Keep An Unlimited Number Of Snapshots In History	Do Not Limit The Number Of Snapshots	The report server accumulates report snapshots indefinitely.
Limit the Copies Of Report History	Limit Number Of Snapshots To	The report server retains the most current snapshots up to the number specified for the report.

Tip Because snapshots can require a lot of storage space, you might want to impose a server-wide limit to the number of snapshots that can accumulate for a report instead of setting a limit specific to each report. Refer to Chapter 25 to learn how to change the server-wide limit.

Managing shared datasets

A shared dataset is a catalog item that you create in SSDT or Report Builder and deploy to the report server just like a report. You can also configure several properties by using techniques that we have described in this chapter. Just click the dataset link to access the following properties:

- **Data Source**   Change the shared data source with which the dataset is associated.

- **Caching**   Configure caching and define the schedule by which the cache expires, but only if the dataset's shared data source uses stored credentials for authentication. Using caching is effective for reducing the impact of executing commonly used queries on the report server. If you use queries to populate default values for report parameters in several reports, you can improve the performance of these reports by relying on a cached dataset.

- **Cache Refresh Options**   Create a new cached instance of the dataset automatically on a schedule.

- **Security**   Control who can use the dataset by assigning role-based security, as we describe in Chapter 24.

Managing change in the reporting life cycle

When report modifications are required for fixing issues during testing or to accommodate changing business requirements, you must edit the report definition file and then redeploy the report. You can redeploy the report by using any of the methods described previously in this chapter. The deployment process replaces the original report definition in the *ReportServer* database with the new report definition. All existing report properties are preserved, so you won't need to change execution settings or security permissions when you redeploy a report, for example.

It's important to keep in mind that because parameter properties are preserved, any changes you make to report parameters in the report definition in SSDT do not deploy and replace the report server parameter properties. Deployment adds only new report parameters and leaves previously existing report parameters as they were on the report server. If you need to implement new default values for existing report parameters, you have two options:

- You can manually make the change on the report server.

- If you prefer to keep the report definition in SSDT synchronized with the report definition on the report server, you must delete the report from the report server and then deploy the report to the report server to enable access to report parameter settings in the report definition.

CHAPTER 24

Securing report server content

Whether everyone in your organization can access all reports on the report server freely or whether groups of users are restricted to viewing specific sets of reports, you must implement security to allow access to the content that you deployed to the report server in Chapter 23, "Deploying reports to a server." In this chapter, you learn how to use security to manage user access to folders, reports, and report models and to grant specific administrative privileges for managing the report server. You also learn how to restrict the data that displays in a report based on the current user.

> **Important** To perform the tasks described in the "Configuring report server security policies" section in this chapter, you must be a local system administrator on the report server. You must also deploy reports to your report server as described in Chapter 23 so that you have content available on the report server to secure.

Configuring report server security policies

Before a user can access content on the report server, Reporting Services uses *authentication* to confirm the user's identity through the use of a login name and password. The default authentication method is Windows integrated security. This authentication method requires you to create a Microsoft Windows account for each user who will access the report server. If you want, you can organize these user accounts into Windows groups.

> **Note** As we describe in Chapter 25, "Performing administrative tasks," you can configure your report server to support basic authentication in native mode and to support custom forms authentication in both native mode and SharePoint integrated mode. The focus of this chapter is how to work with Windows integrated security.

Understanding authentication types

With Windows integrated security, the report server uses either the NT LAN Manager (NTLM) or Kerberos protocol, depending on the configuration of your network. When using NTLM, the report server never passes the user's credentials to another server, as would be the case when the report server needs to connect to a data source on a separate server. In that case, you always need to use stored credentials with data sources to connect successfully. If you use Kerberos instead, the report server uses Kerberos ticketing to authenticate the user when connecting to data sources and consequently maintains the user's security context when retrieving data from a remote server.

Another option is to use basic authentication. Using this configuration, the report server passes the user's credentials across the network. In that case, you should require the user to connect to the report server by using the Secure Sockets Layer (SSL) protocol to protect the credentials in transit. You can configure SSL support in the Reporting Services Configuration Manager for a native-mode report server or in Central Administration for a SharePoint integrated-mode report server, as described in Chapter 4, "Installing Reporting Services."

When you want to bypass the Windows authentication, a third option is custom authentication by setting up Forms authentication. With custom authentication, you can allow users without a Windows account on your network to access your report server. You must develop a logon form for the user to supply a user name and password that you authenticate and authorize by using a custom security extension that you develop and install on the report server. This custom security extension replaces the report server's default security extension and cannot coexist with it.

> **Note** You cannot implement a custom security extension for a SharePoint integrated-mode server. Instead, you must use SharePoint Forms-Based Authentication, which is explained at *http://blogs.technet.com/b/speschka/archive/2009/11/05/configuring-forms-based-authentication-in-sharepoint-2010.aspx*. Another option for a SharePoint integrated-mode report server is Claims Authentication, which you can learn more about at *http://msdn.microsoft.com/en-us/library/hh231678.aspx*.

Reviewing default authorization policies

After authentication, the process of *authorization* grants permissions to the user to access content on the report server and to perform specific actions. In native mode, Reporting Services uses a role-based authorization system to control what users can see and do on the report server. In SharePoint integrated mode, all authorization is managed through Microsoft SharePoint security policies, but it is conceptually similar to the role-based system in native mode. To implement authorization, you map Windows users or groups to a set of tasks that they can perform on the server. This set of tasks is called a *role* in native mode and a *permission level* in SharePoint integrated mode.

Important Before you can implement security on the report server by using Windows integrated security, you must create Windows user accounts. You can also create Windows groups to combine many users that require the same role or permissions-level assignments into a set.

The authorization policy that you implement depends on your report server topology. A native-mode report server uses roles to restrict the activities of users, while a SharePoint integrated-mode server uses SharePoint groups. Table 24-1 compares the default authorization policies defined by roles and SharePoint groups.

TABLE 24-1 Comparison of default authorization policies

Native-Mode Roles	SharePoint Groups
Content Manager Permission to perform all content management tasks, including security configuration	Owners Full Control permission to change site content, pages, or functionality
Publisher Permission only to view and manage all content except subscriptions and security	Members Contribute permission to view and manage content and submit changes for approval
Browser Permission only to view reports and manage individual subscriptions	Visitors Read permission to view content and create subscriptions
Report Builder Permission only to view reports, manage individual subscriptions, and start Report Builder	No equivalent group—Owners and Members can start Report Builder
My Reports Permission to perform all content management tasks within the My Reports folder only	No equivalent group—Enable the My Site features of SharePoint to support similar functionality within My Site

You can change the activities associated with each role or SharePoint group or add new roles or SharePoint groups to customize the authorization policies. The activities that users can perform are called *tasks* on a native-mode report server and *permissions* on a SharePoint integrated-mode server. Table 24-2 compares the native-mode tasks to SharePoint permissions.

TABLE 24-2 Comparison of activities

Native-Mode Task	SharePoint Permission	Activity
Consume reports	View Items	Open a report
Create linked reports	Not applicable	Create a copy of a report that remains linked to a base report
Manage all subscriptions	Manage Alerts	View and manage all users' subscriptions
Manage data sources	Add Items, Edit Items, Delete Items, View Items	Add, change, or delete data sources
Manage folders	Add Items, Edit Items, Delete Items, View Items	Add, change, or delete folders

Native-Mode Task	SharePoint Permission	Activity
Manage individual subscriptions	Create alerts	Add, change, or delete subscriptions owned by the user
Manage models	Add Items, Edit Items, Delete Items, View Items	Add, change, or delete report models
Manage report history	Edit Items, View Versions, Delete Versions	Add or delete report history snapshots and change report history properties
Manage reports	Add Items, Edit Items, Delete Items, View Items	Add or delete reports and change report properties
Manage resources	Add Items, Edit Items, Delete Items, View Items	Add, change, or delete resources and change resource properties
Set security for individual items	Not applicable	View and change security properties for folders, data sources, reports, report models, and resources
View data sources	View Items, Edit Items	View data sources in a folder and view the data source properties
View folders	View Items	View folders in the folder hierarchy and view folder properties
View models	View Items	View report models and report model properties and use report models as data sources
View reports	View Items	View reports in a folder
View resources	View Items	View resources in a folder and view resource properties

Native-mode roles

Reporting Services in native mode includes five default roles that will likely satisfy most of your authorization requirements. For example, the Browser role lets users view reports, but they cannot add or delete reports. Each default role definition includes a predefined group of tasks that the user can perform. You can modify a default role to add or remove tasks, or you can create a new role to define a customized set of tasks.

You can review the existing default role definitions by opening SQL Server Management Studio. In the Connect To Server dialog box, select Reporting Services in the Server Type drop-down list, and then type the name of your report server in the Server Name text box.

 Important You can use only Windows Authentication to connect to the report server. You must be a local Windows administrator on the report server or be assigned to a System Administrator role to view or change role definitions in SQL Server Management Studio.

You can find the roles in a dedicated folder inside the Security folder in Object Explorer, as shown in Figure 24-1. After installing Reporting Services, the five default roles are available: Browser, Content Manager, My Reports, Publisher, and Report Builder. To review or edit any of these roles, double-click the role. You can also add your own role or delete a role, by right-clicking the Roles folder and selecting New Role or Delete Roles, respectively.

FIGURE 24-1 You can review or modify the default roles and add new roles by connecting to a native-mode report server in SQL Server Management Studio.

Whether you add a new role or edit an existing role, you select tasks to assign to the role in the User Role Properties - Browser dialog box, as shown in Figure 24-2. You can add permissions to the role by selecting the applicable check boxes, or you can remove permissions by clearing the check boxes. However, you cannot add custom tasks to the role.

FIGURE 24-2 You can review or modify task assignments for a role in the User Role Properties dialog box.

SharePoint integrated-mode groups and permission levels

If you have a SharePoint integrated-mode report server, you can use one of the three basic Share-Point groups to manage authorization. You assign most users to the Visitor group to let them view reports and prevent them from adding or removing content. The default SharePoint groups are associated with specific permission levels that you can change, or you can add new SharePoint groups.

> **Important** You must be assigned Full Control permissions to configure security settings for a SharePoint site or document library. Your permission level might vary in different sections of a SharePoint site if you are not the site administrator.

You manage security by assigning users to default SharePoint groups and permission levels for each SharePoint site separately. For example, you can manage Reporting Services activities by using the site's Members group, with Contribute permissions; the Owners group, with Full Control permissions; and the Visitors group, with Read permissions. You can view the current site permissions by clicking Site Actions, selecting Site Settings on the menu, and then clicking Site Permissions to view the permission levels assigned to each group, similar to the page shown in Figure 24-3.

> **Note** The default group names for a site include the name of the site (in this case, Reporting Services 2012) and the type of group, such as Members, Owners, or Visitors. There are a few other specialized groups to support other SharePoint features unrelated to Reporting Services.

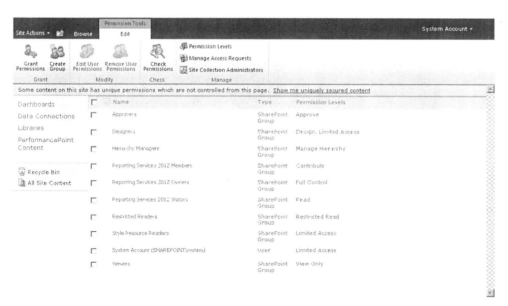

FIGURE 24-3 On the SharePoint site's permissions page, you can review and edit permission levels for groups and individual users.

You can modify the permission levels for a SharePoint group. Select the check box for the group, and then click Edit User Permissions on the ribbon to open the Edit Permissions dialog box, as shown in Figure 24-4. A group can have one or more permission levels assigned. In this example, the group has Read permission only.

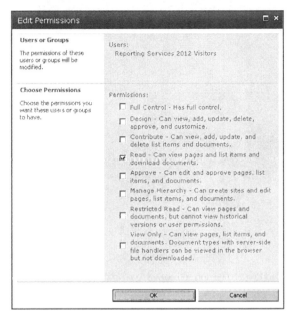

FIGURE 24-4 Permission levels define the types of activities a group or user can perform.

The specific activities that are associated with the Read permission are defined on the Permission Level page. To reach this page, click the Permission Levels button on the ribbon, and then you can review the available permission levels, as shown in Figure 24-5, or create a new permission level.

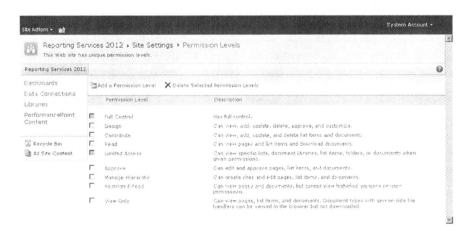

FIGURE 24-5 You can modify the existing SharePoint permission levels or add a custom permission level.

Click the Read link to open the Edit Permission Level page to review its settings, as shown in Figure 24-6. You can add or remove permissions to customize the authorized activities for groups and users assigned to this permission level.

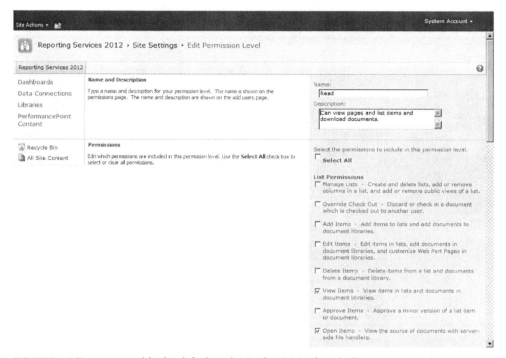

FIGURE 24-6 You can override the default authorized activities for a built-in permission level.

Assigning user permissions

The report server content is secure by default. You must grant access to the report server content before users can use the reports that you have deployed. You can then implement item-level security for more specific control over which reports that users can access and what activities they can perform.

The procedure that you follow to grant access to report server content depends on your server architecture. Conceptually, the process is similar for both server types. You map users or groups to the activities they can perform at the upper-level folder for report server content. The upper-level folder is the Home page on a native-mode report server, and it is the document library folder on a SharePoint integrated-mode server.

Native-mode role assignments

A *role assignment* is the mapping of a Windows user or group to a role for a selected item on the native-mode report server. An item can be a folder, a report, a report model, or any other resource uploaded to the report server, such as image or spreadsheet files. Although you can specify a role assignment on each individual item for each user, most administrators use role assignments for Windows groups at the folder level to simplify administration.

Even if you want everyone to have access to all report server content, you must configure a role assignment on the Home folder that allows users to view reports. All folders below the Home folder inherit its role assignments, but you can override inheritance for any item to specify a new role assignment for that item. To do this, open Report Manager and click the Folder Settings button to see that the local Administrators group is assigned to the Content Manager role on the Home folder by default, as shown in Figure 24-7. Only local administrators have access to the report server after installing Reporting Services and must grant access to other non-administrators through role assignments before these other users can deploy reports or access deployed content.

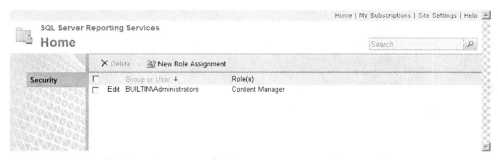

FIGURE 24-7 You add role assignments to folders to grant access to its contents.

You add other groups or users by clicking the New Role Assignment button. Type the Windows login for the user in *domain\username* format, or type the name of a Windows group in the Group Or User Name text box, as shown in Figure 24-8. You can then select the check box for each role that you want to assign. In this example, members of the Sales Analysts groups have access to the report server but can only browse the folders and open reports. Because security of the Home folder is inherited by all other folders, they also have access to the other folders on the server. You can remove access to other content on the report server at the folder or report level, as we describe in the "Configuring item-level security" section of this chapter.

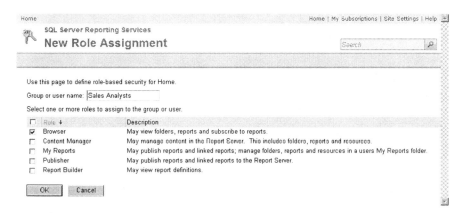

FIGURE 24-8 You use the New Role Assignment page to assign a Windows user or group to a role on a native-mode report server.

Note If you do not assign a user to a role, the user sees the following message when attempting to open Report Manager: User '<*DOMAIN\user*>' does not have required permissions. Verify that sufficient permissions have been granted and that Windows User Account Control (UAC) restrictions have been addressed.

SharePoint permission-level assignments

You can use SharePoint groups to map a Windows user or group to a permission level. You then define the SharePoint groups that can access the Reports Library in your Report Center site (or any document library for which you have enabled Reporting Services content types). All folders below the upper-level folder inherit its role assignments, but you can override inheritance for any item to specify different users or groups with permission to access that item.

When you're ready to give a Windows user or group access to report server content, you start by opening the SharePoint group page. To do this, click Site Actions, Site Permissions, and then click the Visitors link for the site. Click New to open the Grant Permissions dialog box, and type the name of the group. Click the Check Names icon below the text box to validate the group names, as shown in Figure 24-9. The web application prefixes each group name with the domain or server name applicable to the Windows group names that you entered.

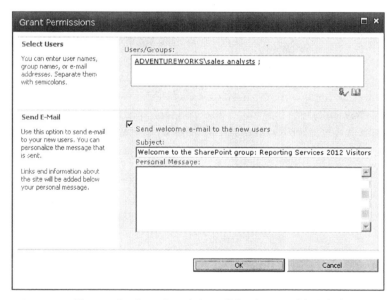

FIGURE 24-9 You use the Grant Permissions dialog box to add a Windows user or group to a SharePoint group.

Configuring item-level security

After granting access to the report server content, you then configure security to control which items each user can see and open. If a user's role does not permit access to an item, the item is not visible to the user. Similarly, if the user cannot perform a certain task, the user interface does not include the option or buttons required to perform that task. Because security is inherited from the parent folder, you change the security settings only for those items requiring a different role assignment than the one configured for the upper-level folder.

Securing folders and document libraries

Folder-level security is easier to implement and maintain than report-level security because you can then take advantage of security inheritance. At minimum, you should secure the folder containing data sources to control who can add, change, or delete them. Then you need to consider on a folder-by-folder basis how to manage access and configure user permissions accordingly.

Native-mode folder security

You must give everyone access to the Home folder in Report Manager so that they can access reports available in that folder or any other folder on the report server. However, it is likely that you want to prevent all users from seeing all reports. In that case, you should create folders in the Home folder to separate reports into logical groupings based on security requirements.

For example, you might require report developers to deploy all new reports to a common folder for review by a report server administrator who then moves reports to the intended target folder. This common folder should be highly restricted to prevent users from inadvertently opening a report containing malicious code. The report server administrator must have the Content Manager role for this folder, while report developers must have the Publisher role. As another example, you should protect access to folders containing data sources so that only authorized people can view and edit the connection strings they contain.

Because a folder inherits its settings from its parent folder, you start by removing permissions for folders in the Home folder, which itself has the least restrictive permissions of all folders. In Report Manager, click the folder to restrict, click the Folder Settings button on the toolbar, and then click the Security link on the left side of the page. The same role assignments that you configured for the Home folder appear in the selected folder because security is currently inherited. To disable security inheritance, click the Edit Item Security button, and then click OK in the message box to confirm that you want to apply different security settings for this item.

After you disable security inheritance, any permission changes made to the parent folder do not apply to the current folder. Select the check boxes next to any user or group, as shown in Figure 24-10, and click the Delete button to remove access to the folder. You must click OK in the message box to confirm the deletion.

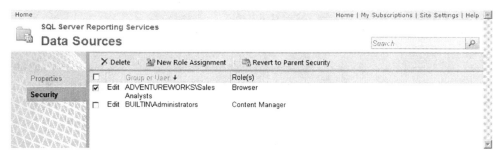

FIGURE 24-10 After disabling security inheritance, you must remove a role from a folder to prevent members of the role from accessing the folder.

 Note Notice the Revert To Parent Security button on the page shown in Figure 24-10, which allows you to discard the item-level role assignments and restore security inheritance from the Home folder.

When a user that is a member of a group to which folder access is denied, the user does not see that folder in Report Manager, as shown in Figure 24-11. In this example, the user cannot see the Data Sources folder. Furthermore, the user would not be able to open that folder by using URL access, as we describe in Chapter 35, "Programming report access." The folder security you implement in Report Manager applies to all access methods, whether using Report Manager, URL access, or a custom application that uses the report server's web service to retrieve report server content.

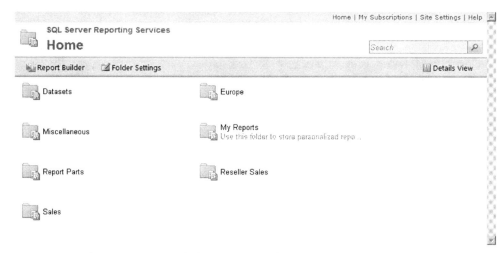

FIGURE 24-11 The user cannot see folders without a role assignment, such as Data Sources in this example.

SharePoint integrated-mode document library security

The primary container for reports in SharePoint is a document library. One option is to give the document library the least restrictive permissions of all the folders it contains and then remove permissions from child folders. However, you should assign the data sources document library or folder the most restrictive settings. For example, if you are using the Business Intelligence Center template for your site, you might store data sources in the Data Connections document library. You can require users to store all reports in a single document library, or you can create multiple document libraries on the site with different security settings. The process you follow for securing report document libraries and the Data Connections document library are the same.

To remove permissions from the library, navigate to the document library in your browser, click the Library tab on the ribbon, and then click the Library Settings button. Next, click the Permissions For This Document Library link appearing in the Permissions And Management section of the Document Library Settings page. If you have never changed permissions for this document library, the following message displays, "This library inherits permissions from its parent. (<*Site Name*>)." You also see all the SharePoint groups or users and permission levels assigned to each group for this document library.

Your first step is to click the Stop Inheriting Permissions button on the toolbar. A message box displays to warn you that changes to the parent site permissions will no longer apply if you continue. After you click OK, you see check boxes appear next to each SharePoint group and user. In addition, the message below the ribbon indicates that the document library now has unique permissions. Select the check box next to each group or user to remove, as shown in Figure 24-12, click the Remove User Permissions button on the ribbon, and click OK to confirm the deletion of permissions.

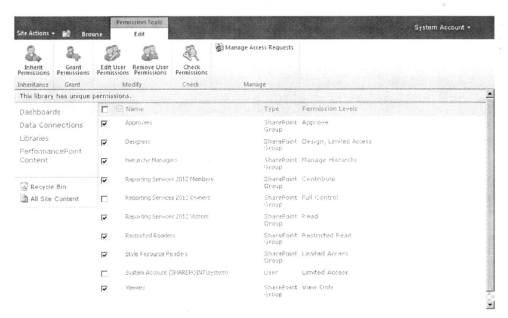

FIGURE 24-12 After disabling security inheritance from the site settings, you can remove groups or users from a document library to prevent access.

Note You can restore the original site permissions for the document library by clicking the Inherit Permissions button on the toolbar.

If you keep the default link to a document library in the Quick Launch (on the left side of the page), such as Data Connections, a user without permissions to open the library continues to see the link. However, when the user clicks the link, an Access Denied message displays. However, if the user clicks the Site Actions button and then selects View All Site Content, the library does not display in the list of document libraries, as shown in Figure 24-13.

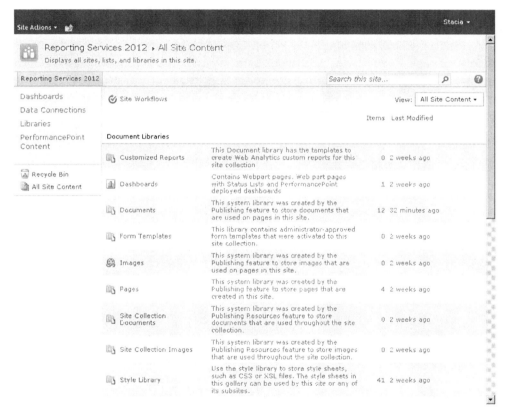

FIGURE 24-13 A user having no access to the Data Connections library does not see its folder appear in the list of all site content, although the link continues to display in the Quick Launch.

To add a user or group to a document library, you use the Grant Permissions toolbar button on its permissions page. The Grant Permissions dialog box, shown in Figure 24-14, allows you to identify a Windows group or user and then assign permissions. When you assign permissions, you can associate the group or user with a SharePoint group for which you already have a set of defined permissions, or you can explicitly assign a custom set of permissions. Optionally, you can automatically send an email message to welcome members of the group or the user to the document library.

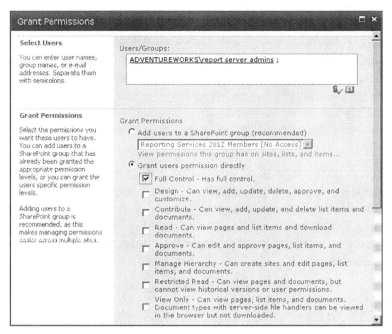

FIGURE 24-14 You use the Grant Permissions page to assign permissions to a Windows user or group on a SharePoint integrated-mode report server.

SharePoint integrated-mode folder security

Rather than use separate document libraries to secure reports, you can allow people with different levels of security access to view reports in the same document library by organizing reports into separate folders and assigning permissions as necessary. As we describe in the "Native-mode folder security" section, you might centralize the deployment of all new reports to a common folder and then require a report server administrator to review and move approved reports to the intended target folder. The report server administrator must have the Full Control permissions for this folder, while report developers must have Contributor permissions. Similarly, you should allow only authorized users to view or edit the contents of data sources.

Like folders on a native-mode server, each SharePoint folder in a document library inherits its settings from its parent folder. If you decide to use folder-level security in a document library, you open the permissions page by pointing to the folder and opening the folder menu by clicking the down arrow that appears. Then click Manage Permissions on the folder menu. On the permissions page, you click Stop Inheriting Permissions, click OK to confirm, and then make changes as described in the "SharePoint integrated-mode document library security" section to remove user permissions or grant permissions.

Approving data sources in SharePoint integrated mode

When you deploy data sources from SQL Server Business Intelligence Development Studio to the report server, the data source is added as a minor version. As the owner of the data source, you can view reports that use this data source. Users with the Manage Lists permission can also view reports associated with the data source, but all other users receive an Access Denied message when they try to view the report. To enable the data source for all users, you must publish a major version. In addition, you must give users Restricted Read permissions on the data source (or its document library, if you prefer).

In the data sources document library, point to the data source, click the down arrow to open its submenu, and click Publish A Major Version, as shown in Figure 24-15. You can then select Manage Permissions on the data source's submenu to open the permissions page, select the group or user, and click Edit User Permissions, as described in the "SharePoint integrated-mode groups and permission levels" section earlier in this chapter. Then grant Restricted Read permissions to the selected group or user to enable the data source.

FIGURE 24-15 You must use the Publish A Major Version command to make a data source available to reports.

Note If you neglect to both publish a major version of a data source and assign the Restricted Read permissions to users, they see the following message when opening the report: "The permissions granted to user are insufficient for performing this operation."

Securing an item

The process of securing a report (or any other file on the report server) is similar to securing a folder. By default, the report inherits the security settings of its parent folder. You can disable inheritance and configure different role assignments for an individual report when necessary. Any changes to the parent folder security do not change the report's security settings.

To secure an item on a native-mode report, point to the item name to open its shortcut menu, and then click Security, as shown in Figure 24-16. You must then click the Edit Item Security button to disable security inheritance from the parent folder. You can remove users or add a new role to the folder just as you do for folder security.

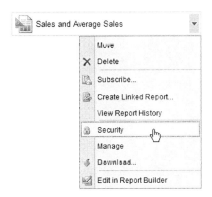

FIGURE 24-16 You can configure security at the item level by using the Security command on its shortcut menu.

Similarly, for a SharePoint integrated-mode report server, you can configure permissions on individual files in a document library. Just point to the file, click the down arrow that appears, and then click Manage Permissions, as shown in Figure 24-17. Then click Stop Inheriting Permissions on the ribbon, and click OK to confirm. You can then click Grant Permissions to add permissions for new users. You can also select one or more groups or users already assigned to the file, and then click either Edit User Permissions or Remove User Permissions to change or delete permissions as necessary.

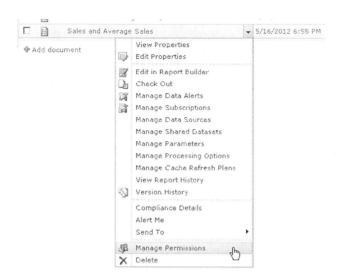

FIGURE 24-17 You use the Manage Permissions command on the report server item's shortcut menu in SharePoint to configure security at the item level.

Assigning a system role

System role assignments are used to assign users to tasks related to system administration tasks on the report server. Assigning a user to a system role does not grant access to report server content. Two default system roles, System Administrator and System User, are defined with different sets of administrative tasks. You can change the system role definitions or create a custom system role definition by using Management Studio. The set of administrative tasks that you can use in a system role definition are shown in Table 24-3. To assign users or groups to the system role, you use Report Manager.

> **Note** System roles apply only to a native-mode report server. The capabilities authorized by System Administrator are available to SharePoint farm administrators and site administrators by default. You can also assign Full Control permission level at the site to grant other users access to the report server settings for that site, but not at the same task granularity that is possible in native mode.

TABLE 24-3 System roles

Use This Task...	To Allow This Activity
Execute Report Definitions	Execute a report independently of a report server, such as in Report Builder
Generate Events	Generate events in the report server namespace (applicable to applications, not to users)
Manage Jobs	View and cancel running jobs

Use This Task...	To Allow This Activity
Manage Report Server Properties	Change report server properties
Manage Report Server Security	Add or delete users assigned to system roles
Manage Roles	Add, change, or delete role definitions
Manage Shared Schedules	Add, change, or delete shared schedules used to execute reports or subscriptions
View Report Server Properties	View report server properties
View Shared Schedules	View shared schedules used to execute reports or subscriptions

You can think of system roles that allow users to manage a task as offering a means by which you can delegate report server administration responsibilities. Rather than allow access to all management tasks, you can segregate the responsibilities by role. For example, let's say you want to give a group of users the task of managing shared schedules. To do this, you open SQL Server Management Studio and connect to Reporting Services. In Object Explorer, expand the Security folder, and then expand the System Roles folder. Right-click the System User folder, select New System Role, and then type a name for the new role. Reporting Services automatically assigns three default tasks to new System User roles: View Report Server Properties, View Shared Schedules, and Execute Report Definitions. You can then select the Manage Shared Schedules check box, as shown in Figure 24-18.

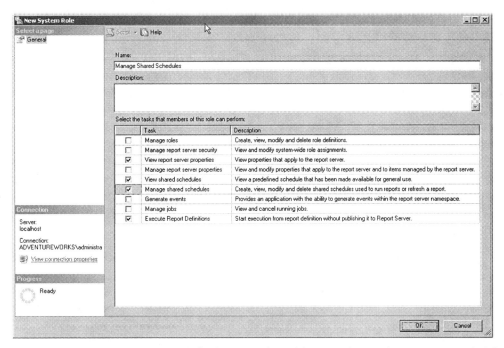

FIGURE 24-18 You can create a customized system role to delegate native-mode report server administration tasks.

After you create the role, you can assign a group or user to the role. In Report Manager, click the Site Settings link in the upper-right corner, click the Security link on the left side of the page, and then click New Role Assignment. Type a name of a Windows group or user in the Group Or User Name text box, and select the check box for the new role, as shown in Figure 24-19. After you save this role assignment, the members of the role can create a new schedule, edit or delete existing schedules, or pause or resume schedules on the Schedules page of the Site Settings area of Report Manager, as described in Chapter 27, "Working with subscriptions."

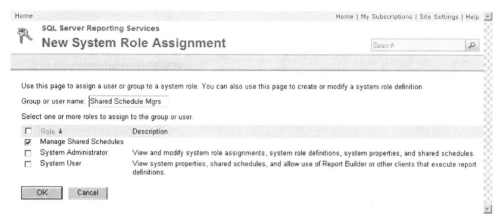

FIGURE 24-19 After creating a system role, you assign a group or user to the role in Site Settings.

Securing a report model

Although you can no longer develop a report model in the current version of Reporting Services, you can deploy a report model that you develop using an earlier version for use as a data source as described in Chapter 8, "Retrieving data for a report." You can control who can access a report model through role assignments or permissions just as you can control access to folders and reports. On a native-mode report server, users must first be assigned to the System User and Report Builder roles to use the report model in Report Builder. In addition to securing access to the report model, you can secure entities, attributes, and roles in the report model to limit access to specific items in the report model. Refer to Table 24-4 to learn which role assignments are required on a native-mode report server to deploy or use a report model. If you're using a SharePoint integrated-mode server, a user must have Full Control or Contribute permissions to deploy a report model. Read permissions are sufficient to access the report model as a data source.

TABLE 24-4 Role assignments required for using report models

Assign These Roles...	To Allow This Activity
System User, Browser	View reports created with Report Builder (but the user is not able to start Report Builder to create ad hoc reports)
System User, Report Builder	View reports created with Report Builder, start Report Builder to create ad hoc reports, and save reports to the report server
System User, Publisher	Deploy a report model to the report server

To set the model permissions on a native-mode report server, point to the model name, click the down arrow, and then click Security. On a SharePoint integrated-mode report server, point to the model, click the down arrow, and select Manage Permissions. You then configure permissions in the same way that you would any other item on the report server.

In addition to enabling access to the report model through item permissions, you can also configure security of specific model items. To do this, click the Model Item Security link from the model's Security page on a native-mode report server. On a SharePoint integrated-mode server, you use the Manage Model Item Security command on the model's shortcut menu. Then on either server type, you select the Secure Individual Model Items Independently For This Model check box to continue. In the model item tree, select the model name in the root node, and then type the name of a Windows group or user in the Assign Read Permission To The Following Users And Groups text box, as shown in Figure 24-20. In SharePoint integrated mode, you can click the Check Names icon to validate each name you enter. These users have access to the model when you click Apply (in native mode only).

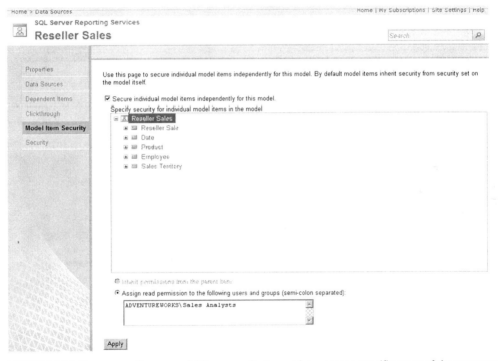

FIGURE 24-20 You can configure model item security to restrict access to specific areas of the report model.

 Note The Model Item Security page in SharePoint integrated mode looks similar to the page shown in Figure 24-20.

The default behavior of items within the model is to inherit from the parent item. If you want to prevent users from accessing a specific entity or attribute, you can navigate to that portion of the model and change the selection from Inherit Permissions From The Parent Item and select Assign Read Permissions To the Following Users And Groups. You must explicitly name the groups or users for each entity or attribute in the model if you do not want the item to inherit settings from its parent. There is no way to exclude one group that has permission to access a parent item while retaining the permissions for other groups.

Implementing data security

It's important to remember that giving a user access to a report does not necessarily mean that a user has access to the data retrieved by the dataset queries. If you're using Windows integrated security, you must also give users Read permission on the source data.

Furthermore, when you need to give users access to the same report but must manage how much data displays in the report for each user, you must implement data security. There are several ways to implement data security, but all methods achieve the same result. For example, consider a report having a parameter that allows a user to select multiple values. You can configure security to allow one user to view all selections and then limit the data in the report to a single selection for other users. In this section, we describe three different ways to restrict data by user.

> **Important** Local administrators on the report server always have access to the report server, even if you remove the built-in administrators' role assignments on folders and reports. If you need to prevent local administrators from viewing reports, you need to implement data security.

Using a query parameter and a role to secure data

One way to implement data security is to create a linked report, set the parameter value used to filter the report, hide the parameter, and then use role assignments to control access to each linked report. In Chapter 23, we describe how to create a linked report (or a copy of the report if you're using Share-Point integrated mode) and configure a default parameter value for the linked report. To build on this concept of using linked reports for data security, you secure this linked report to allow only a specified role to view the report. Then you repeat the entire process by creating linked reports from the same report by using different parameter values for separate linked reports and securing each linked report as applicable. You can secure the linked reports individually or place them in separate folders if you prefer to manage security at the folder level.

> **Note** Although a SharePoint integrated-mode server does not support linked reports, you can achieve similar results by creating a copy of a report, as explained in Chapter 23. Similarly, you can create report copies for each parameter value and secure each copy individually.

The benefit of using this approach is that you can implement data security for any report that uses parameters to filter content. The other approaches we discuss in the next two sections require you to modify the report definition in Report Designer and maintain a permissions table.

Using a permissions table to secure data

Another approach to implementing data security is to modify the dataset query to join to a permissions table that maps the current Windows user to a value that filters the dataset results. The user mapping is made possible by the use of a query parameter to which you assign the expression *=User!UserID* to get the current user from the operating system. This approach ensures that even local administrators on the report server, who always have access to report server content, cannot view confidential data. The disadvantage of this approach is the requirement to maintain the permissions table, such as the one shown in Figure 24-21, which at minimum must include a column for the user's Windows account and a column for the value filter. Another problem is that you cannot use this report for subscriptions because the report server runs the report instead of the user, losing the security context of the current user.

	UserId	ParameterValue
1	ADVENTUREWORKS\stacia	Europe
2	ADVENTUREWORKS\stacia	Pacific
3	ADVENTUREWORKS\erika	North America
4	ADVENTUREWORKS\administrator	Europe

FIGURE 24-21 You must create a table that maps users to values that you use to filter a dataset query.

Modify the dataset query to include a join between a table in the dataset and your permissions table. You can manually adjust the query text or use the diagram pane to create the join if you are using the graphical query designer. In that case, click Add Table (the last button) on the query designer toolbar. Select the permissions table in the Add Table dialog box, click Add, and then click Close. Then drag a field from the table in your dataset query to the corresponding field in the permissions table to create the join, as shown in Figure 24-22, which depicts a join between the st and UserPermission tables.

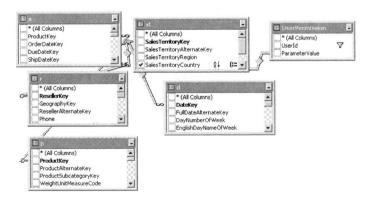

FIGURE 24-22 You must join the permissions table to a table in the dataset query and then update the WHERE clause of the query to use the permissions table as a filter at the source.

After you add the join, you modify the WHERE clause to include a reference to the user column in the permissions table so that you filter the query using a query parameter like this:

```
and UserPermission.UserID = @UserID
```

Next, on the Parameters page of the Dataset Properties dialog box, as shown in Figure 24-23, type the following expression in the Parameter Value box on the same row as the new query parameter:

```
=User!UserID
```

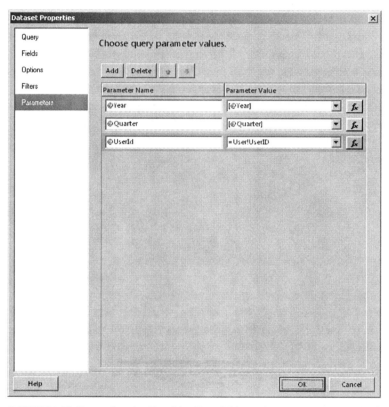

FIGURE 24-23 You assign the *User!UserID* variable to the query parameter in the Dataset Properties dialog box.

Important Your Windows account must be in the permissions table to test the report in SSDT. Otherwise, you must deploy the report to the report server and have the named users log on to the report server and execute the report using their own credentials.

Using a dataset filter to secure data

The third way to implement data security also uses the *=User!UserID* expression to filter the dataset, but it uses the expression in the dataset filter property rather than as a value assigned to a query parameter. You also add a join to a permissions table in the dataset query, but you select the UserId column from the permissions table and compare its value to the current user to filter the dataset. The benefit of using this approach as compared to using the query parameter is the ability to use a data source configured to use stored credentials. Because the user expression is evaluated only when the filter is applied, all data is retrieved during report execution, which allows you to set up the report as a scheduled snapshot.

To use this technique, you must first create a permissions table similar to the one shown in Figure 24-21, and you join that table to a table in your dataset query as described in the previous section. However, instead of referencing the permissions table in the WHERE clause of the query, you add the user column to the query by selecting the UserId check box in the diagram, as shown in Figure 24-24, or by including the column name in the SELECT statement and the GROUP BY clause, if applicable.

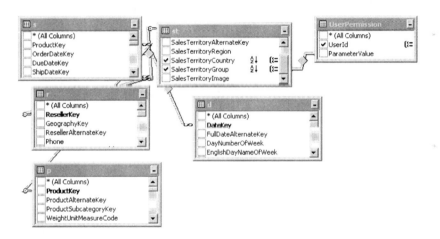

FIGURE 24-24 You must join the permissions table to a table in the dataset query and include the user column in the query's SELECT statement so that you can filter the dataset in the report.

Then open the Filters page in the Dataset Properties dialog box, and add a new filter, as shown in Figure 24-25. You can select the field containing the user name in the Expression drop-down list, and then type the following expression in the Value text box:

```
=User!UserID
```

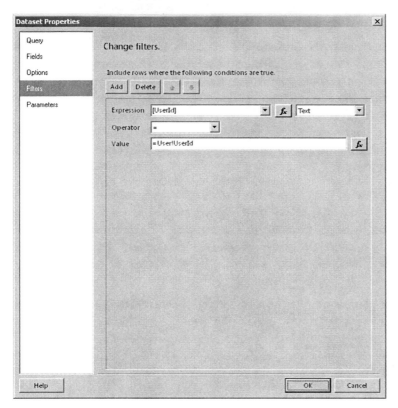

FIGURE 24-25 You assign the *User!UserID* variable to the filter value for comparison to the user field in the Dataset Properties dialog box.

Important You cannot preview the report to test the filter unless your Windows account is in the permissions table. Instead, you must deploy the report to the report server and have the named users log on to the report server and execute the report using their own credentials.

CHAPTER 25

Performing administrative tasks

Reporting Services provides three tools for managing your report server: SQL Server Management Studio (SSMS), a web application interface (Report Manager or a Microsoft SharePoint site), and Reporting Services Configuration Manager for a native-mode report server or SharePoint Central Administration for an integrated-mode report server. In most cases, there is no overlap in functionality between the tools. We introduce Reporting Services Configuration Manager and SharePoint Central Administration in Chapter 4, "Installing Reporting Services," for the initial set up of the report server. In Chapter 23, "Deploying reports to a server," we describe how to use Report Manager and the SharePoint site to manage data source authentication and to configure report properties. Then, in Chapter 24, "Securing report server content," we explain how to set up roles by using SSMS, how to set up role assignments by using Report Manager, and how to assign permissions in the SharePoint site. But management of a report server is more than the initial configuration and security implementation. In this chapter, you discover how to use the management features in SSMS, Report Manager, and SharePoint to perform other administrative tasks on your report server.

Configuring the report server

As described in Chapter 4, you use the Reporting Services Configuration Manager to set the values required to run a native-mode report server. In that chapter, we explain how to configure the service account, the virtual directories and URLs for the web service and Report Manager, database connection information, Simple Mail Transfer Protocol (SMTP) server information, and the execution account. The settings you specify by using the Configuration Manager are stored in the Rsreportserver.config file, which you can find in the Program Files\Microsoft SQL Server\MSRS11.<*Instance*>\Reporting Services\ReportServer folder, where <*Instance*> is the instance identifier for your report server. (If you use the default instance, the default instance identifier is MSSQLSERVER.)

On a SharePoint integrated-mode report server, you use the Manage Service Applications link in SharePoint Central Administration to access a link, for each Reporting Services service application, that takes you to management pages that are similar to the Configuration Manager. Some of these settings update the SharePoint configuration database, which you should not edit directly. There is also an Rsreportserver.config file for SharePoint, which you can find at Program Files\Common Files\Microsoft Shared\Web Server Extensions\14\WebServices\Reporting.

Not all settings are stored in the configuration file. Many properties that govern the behavior of the report server are set by using the Server Properties dialog box in SSMS. You can use SSMS to manage both native-mode and SharePoint integrated-mode report servers, although there are some properties that you cannot set for a SharePoint integrated-mode report server. Those properties are disabled in the Server Properties dialog box.

Rsreportserver configuration file

The Rsreportserver.config file is an XML file that contains settings used to run the report server, to control options in Report Manager, and to manage scheduled operations. In most cases, you use the Configuration Manager to update the setting that you want to change because, apart from the configuration file, there might be other updates required on the report server that the Configuration Manager performs for you. Furthermore, you must use the Configuration Manager or command-line utilities to update connection information because that information is encrypted and cannot be edited directly in the configuration file. Although you can manage many settings by using the Configuration Manager, you might need to change some default settings in the configuration file, such as authentication or memory management settings, by editing the file directly. To edit the configuration file, you can use Notepad, an XML editor, or SSDT.

 Note For a full description of each element in the Rsreportserver.config file, refer to the topic "RsReportServer Configuration File" in SQL Server Books Online at *http://msdn.microsoft.com/en-us/library/ms157273*.

Updating report server properties

SSMS allows you to configure several types of properties for your report server. Some properties enable specific features, such as My Reports, report execution logging, and client-side printing. Other properties define global values for report execution time-out or the amount of report history that can accumulate for a report.

When you open SSMS, you can select Reporting Services in the Server Type drop-down list in the Connect To Server dialog box. If SSMS is already open, click Connect in the Object Explorer window, and click Reporting Services. In the Server Name text box, if necessary, type the name of your report server, or type **localhost** if you are connecting to a native-mode server. If you are connecting to a SharePoint integrated-mode server, type **the URL** of your SharePoint site, such as *http://denali:37780/ sites/ssrs*. In the Authentication drop-down list, select Windows Authentication, and then click Connect. The report server now appears in the Object Explorer window, as shown in Figure 25-1.

 Important You cannot use localhost as the server name for a SharePoint integrated-mode report server even if you are connecting to a report server on your local machine. SSMS requires you to name the server to connect successfully to the report server.

FIGURE 25-1 You can access report server properties from the server node in the Object Explorer window of SSMS.

After connecting to the report server, separate folders are available for managing report execution jobs, security, and shared schedules. To access report server properties, right-click the server node at the top of the tree and click Properties.

General properties

The General page of the Server Properties dialog box, shown in Figure 25-2, provides important information about the version and edition of Reporting Services you have installed. The report server's authentication mode and the URL for the web service also display on this page. On a native-mode report server, you can change the report server site name from SQL Server Reporting Services to another name of your choosing.

By default, the My Reports folder feature is disabled, but the ActiveX client print control is enabled. The My Reports folder feature allows users of a native-mode report server to create a personalized folder on the report server, where they can store reports and other resources. The ActiveX client print control adds a button to the toolbar in Report Manager that permits users to print the report they are viewing, without first downloading the report to their computers.

Note The My Reports folder feature is not supported for a SharePoint integrated-mode server. In that case, the Enable A My Reports Folder For Each User check box is disabled in the Server Properties dialog box.

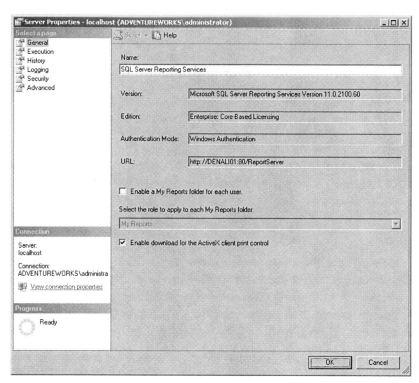

FIGURE 25-2 You configure My Reports and the client print control on the General page of the Server Properties dialog box for a native-mode report server.

If you are working on a native-mode report server and want to enable the My Reports feature, select the Enable A My Reports Folder For Each User check box. Next, select the desired role, such as My Reports, in the Select The Role To Apply To Each My Reports Folder drop-down list. The role you select gives users the functional equivalent of the Content Manager role, but only for the user's My Reports folder, as described in Chapter 26, "Accessing reports online." This permission allows users to add or delete content in a folder that only they can access.

> **Important** If you enable My Reports and then later disable it after users have added reports to their folders, the reports remain in the report server catalog. That is, they continue to consume space in the *ReportServer* database. Furthermore, snapshots and subscriptions associated with these reports continue to execute on schedule. Therefore, you should work with users to delete unwanted reports and to transfer desired reports to a shared folder before disabling My Reports.

For both a native-mode and a SharePoint integrated-mode report server, you can control whether to enable or disable the ActiveX print control on this page. We explain the use of this print control in Chapter 26. If you disable the print control, users will not have the ability to print a report from the report page in Report Manager or from the Report Viewer in SharePoint.

Execution properties

You use the Execution page of the Server Properties dialog box to control whether a time limit applies to report execution at the server level. The default setting is to limit report execution to 1800 seconds, as shown in Figure 25-3. You can select Do Not Timeout Report Execution if you anticipate that some reports could require a long time to execute and prefer not to impose a static limit on the execution time required by the report server.

Tip The report execution time-out setting here applies globally to all reports on the report server, unless you specify a time-out setting in the execution properties of an individual report. Report time-out can be a result of a long-running query at the source or of complex processing and rendering by the report server. You can place a time-out on the dataset query only by modifying the report and editing the dataset properties.

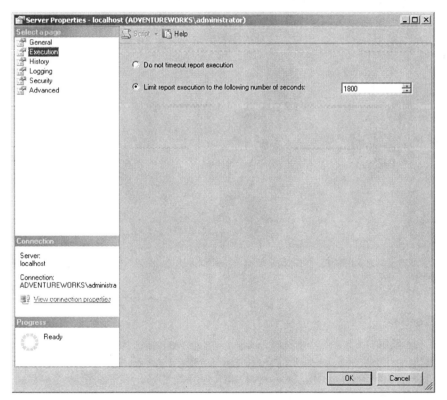

FIGURE 25-3 You can impose a time limit on report execution time on the Execution page of the Server Properties dialog box.

History properties

The History page of the Server Properties dialog box, shown in Figure 25-4, gives you the option to allow an unlimited number of snapshots to accumulate in report history or to define a limit. This setting is a global default only. You can override the value for an individual report, as described in Chapter 23.

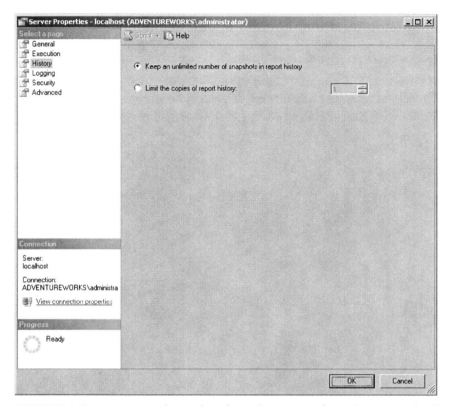

FIGURE 25-4 You can manage the number of snapshots to store for each report on the History page of the Server Properties dialog box.

Logging properties

By default, report execution logging is enabled, but log entries are removed automatically after 60 days, as shown in Figure 25-5. You can disable execution logging if you prefer not to capture this data, or you can increase or decrease the number of log entries to retain on the server if you plan to periodically review execution log data.

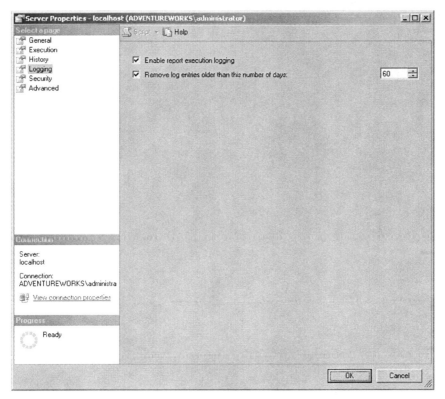

FIGURE 25-5 You can enable or disable report execution logging on the Logging page of the Server Properties dialog box.

The report execution log is a different mechanism from the trace logging that you learn about later in this chapter. As reports are executed, information about the execution, such as query processing time, report rendering time, parameter selections, and user name, are collected in a log. The format of the log in the *ReportServer* database does not lend itself well to reporting, but you can extract this data and load it into a separate log database with a schema that is much better suited for reporting, as described in the "Execution logging" section of this chapter.

Security properties

The settings on this page, shown in Figure 25-6, allow you to enable or disable Microsoft Windows integrated security for report data sources. In earlier versions of Reporting Services, you could disable the ad hoc report execution to turn off the click-through feature for report models, but this ability is not supported in the current version on a native-mode report server. However, it is possible to configure this feature on a SharePoint integrated-mode report server.

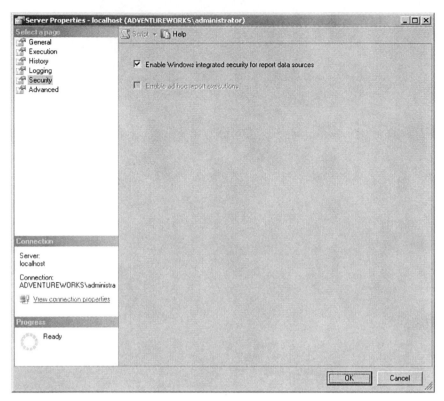

FIGURE 25-6 You control whether Windows integrated security is supported for data sources on the Security page of the Server Properties dialog box.

Advanced properties

The Advanced page, shown in Figure 25-7, provides access to many of the properties that you can set on other pages of the Server Properties dialog box. However, there are several additional properties to configure here. The following properties are accessible only on this page:

- **EditSessionCacheLimit**　You can apply a limit to the number of data cache entries active for a report edit session. The default is 5.

- **EditSessionTimeout**　You can change the duration of a report edit session here. By default, a report edit session is active for 7200 seconds.

- **EnableRemoteErrors**   By default, this property is set to False, which means that error information is captured only by the trace log and details do not display to the user. That is, the user sees only a general message that remote error information is not available and does not see the actual text of the error.

- **SessionTimeout**   By default, a session is active for 600 seconds, but you can change this setting here.

- **EnableTestConnectionDetailedErrors**   By default, a detailed error message is sent to the client when a user clicks the Test Connection button for a data source. If you change this property to False, the report server sends a generic error message instead.

- **ExecutionLogLevel**   The default setting is Normal, but you can change it to Verbose to include more detail in the execution log.

- **ReportBuilderLaunchURL**   This property is blank by default. If you want to use a custom URL to launch Report Builder, you can supply it here. For example, if you want to use Report Builder 1.0 as a client interface for use with report models, you can provide the URL to launch it here. When a user clicks the Report Builder button in Report Manager or the Report Builder Report button on the SharePoint document library ribbon, the report server uses the URL that you supply here.

- **RDLXReportTimeout**   This property sets the number of seconds that an RDLX report session remains active. RDLX reports are specific to Power View on a SharePoint integrated-mode report server. The default setting is 1800 seconds.

- **SessionTimeout**   By default, a session is active for 600 seconds, but you can change this setting here.

- **SnapshotCompression**   The report server can compress snapshots for storage. You can set this property to SQL to compress snapshots in the report server database only, None to disable compression for all snapshots, or All to compress snapshots for storage in both the report server database and the file system. The default is SQL.

- **StoredParametersLifetime**   You can specify the number of days to keep a stored parameter. The default is 180 days.

- **StoredParametersThreshold**   You can specify the maximum number of parameter values that the report server can store. The default is 1500. The maximum is 2,147,483,647.

- **UseSessionCookies**   By default, the report server uses session cookies to communicate with the client browser, but you can disable this feature by setting this property to False.

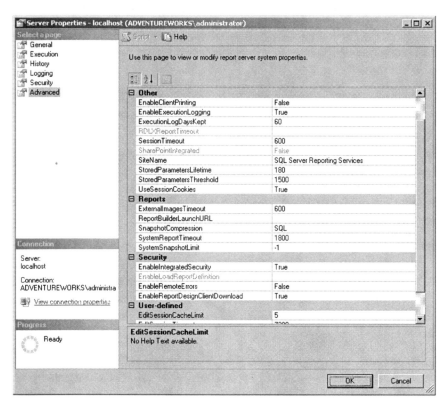

FIGURE 25-7 You have access to a variety of properties on the Advanced page of the Server Properties dialog box.

Managing encrypted information

The Rsreportserver.config file contains the connection information that the report server uses to connect to the application databases (*ReportServer* and *ReportServerTempDB*), but it encrypts the information to protect the security of the database. You must update this connection information when you need to change the credentials used to connect to the application databases, change the name of the databases, or relocate the databases to a new server. The configuration file also includes the domain user account and password defined as the execution account in the Reporting Services Configuration Manager (described in Chapter 4). You might need to update this information if you want to use a different account or update an expired password. Many administrators prefer to use command-line utilities to perform administrative tasks like these. To meet this need, Reporting Services includes the Rsconfig command-line utility to update encrypted information in the configuration file.

To use the Rsconfig utility, you must be a member of the local Administrators group on the report server. To view the syntax help, use the /? argument after the utility name, like this:

```
rsconfig /?
```

Here is the complete syntax for using this utility on the Report Server using Windows authentication:

```
rsconfig -c -m computername -s SQLServername -d ReportServerDatabaseName -a windows -u [domain\]
username -p password
```

You use the Rsconfig utility with the following arguments:

- **-c** This argument specifies that the utility will update the report server connection information.

- **-m** You use this argument when you run the utility on your local computer for a remote report server. If you omit this argument, *localhost* is used by default.

- **-s** This argument is required to supply the server name when the *ReportServer* database is located in a default SQL Server instance.

- **-i** You include this argument to specify the instance only when the *ReportServer* database is located in a named instance of SQL Server.

- **-d** You must include the name of the report server database, which by default is *ReportServer*. However, this argument is not case-sensitive.

- **-a** This argument specifies the authentication method as either sql or windows.

- **-u** Here, you provide the login for the authentication method that you specify in the previous argument. If you use Windows authentication, the argument value is a domain name (or computer name if there is no domain) followed by a backslash and the user name. You omit this argument if you are using the Report Server Windows service account or a built-in account such as NT AUTHORITY\NetworkService.

- **-p** Next, you provide the password for the user account if you use the –u argument.

- **-t** You can optionally add this argument (with no value) to add trace information to error messages that might occur when the utility executes.

For example, let's say you need to update encrypted connection information in the configuration file. Before you start, the Rsreportserver.config file contains encrypted data in the *<Dsn>* element, as shown in Figure 25-8. The encrypted data stores information required by the report server to connect to the application databases, such as the server name and credentials for authentication. Because this information is encrypted, you cannot edit the file directly when connection information changes.

```
rsreportserver.config  ×
    <Configuration>
        <Dsn>AQAAANCMnd8BFdERjHoAwE/Cl+sBAAAAStZ+Yqlzx0elKP6bI4IMWwQAAAAiAAAAUgBlAHAAbwBy
AHQAaQBuAGcAIABTAGUAcgB2AGUAcgAAAANmAADAAAAAEAAAAGo2erSVy+Onn0QuhID5d0AAAAA
BIAAAKAAAAAQAAAAN1dEhx5pkvmDhZ6TP6a7gdgAAAD//+UtWx2sKRLomO4CWOX7M+L0NzPkcEe0
OQSCt9Uz3lIh4LprIo4hkbPLmHlMPhh5DT9WoXM1fJzLeXrP+GYITpdWkxy5lOiiPEWBlj8kqA7C
eVruVdyYCgApWOB320UHrw7od3aD9AAesGmdlWP6lZl+20akNnc3A4IAeDanIeyRmYFEgZcawuBK
BHj+WPFwoF6M5lShN/WiibrGAQPrm/7+yNYG2TCWpVSutNOKMh1Se8/tP08t6cXRYF+XqbBQ4PgQ
KYwhuOGlw37W9fkUzbpHitVVGU4UAAAA9wFflPzw0AnrYLjNN12Koyk2ZSE=</Dsn>
        <ConnectionType>Default</ConnectionType>
        <LogonUser></LogonUser>
        <LogonDomain></LogonDomain>
        <LogonCred></LogonCred>
        <InstanceId>MSRS11.MSSQLSERVER</InstanceId>
```

FIGURE 25-8 You cannot directly edit the encrypted data in the *<Dsn>* element of the Rsreportserver.config file.

If you want to use a specific Windows account, you can use the Rsconfig utility to change the configuration. In a command prompt window, type the following command (where *<domain\account>* is the login domain and Windows account and *<password>* is the password for this account):

```
rsconfig -c -s <servername> -d reportserver -a windows -u <domain\account> -p <password>
```

 Important In a production environment, you should use only a least-privilege Windows account created for the purpose of creating a connection to the Reporting Services database.

To assign a built-in account, such as NT AUTHORITY\NetworkService, use the following syntax:

```
rsconfig -c -s <servername> -d reportserver -a windows "NT AUTHORITY\NetworkService"
```

If you prefer to use the Report Service Windows account, you omit any reference to an account from the arguments, like this:

```
rsconfig -c -s <servername> -d reportserver -a windows
```

When you change the login for the report server database, the configuration file changes to include the login information. However, this information is encrypted, as shown in Figure 25-9. Notice that the value of the *<ConnectionType>* element is now *Impersonate*. And the *<LogonUser>*, *<Logon-Domain>*, and *<LogonCred>* elements have encrypted values where previously they were empty.

```
rsreportserver.config  X

⊟<Configuration>
⊟    <Dsn>AQAAANCMnd8BFdERjHoAwE/Cl+sBAAAAtr8WaDPkfkOM1bCh1UjKoQQAAAAiAAAAUgBlAHAAbwBy
AHQAaQBuAGcAIABTAGUAcgB2AGUAcgAAAANmAADAAAAAEAAAADi74XmZ5PNAyawe6NF9qZwAAAAA
BIAAAKAAAAAQAAAAS1tsAmbLvoRzZRNQLSQTLdgAAABc0eHPd2uiqppycJlI2wKrfLq1MG4EHK9D
o3mVo/GgJC28YnYDtq2/3uzgOpaXwDly4sYMZdS90RzOMj7kv4EaAVv8oF9GmKlH+bQvLCbhzGcs
9KDwirGNbH8ca+eBD7B001ADJHZ9mYj7rXj6uYkJgU8vOxp8NDzuwZ1ia8qMi8BwExrBA6q5Jh9H
mwi6dCl6HOLG5/YTJIAySmwMD5ktBSBMzdFnmOPqpY4ll9SquWx8udYAZ7P34G2Bgv83bzSgLtvV
qss4mJECLBmwn6uXpfMGG9UA3agUAAAA4t9aLlzVZbF/UX4UaQSWIug8XLU=</Dsn>
    <ConnectionType>Impersonate</ConnectionType>
⊟    <LogonUser>AQAAANCMnd8BFdERjHoAwE/Cl+sBAAAAtr8WaDPkfkOM1bCh1UjKoQQAAAAiAAAAUgBlAHAAbwBy
AHQAaQBuAGcAIABTAGUAcgB2AGUAcgAAAANmAADAAAAAEAAAAPNUs7u+pkDrWjpehP6uhwoAAAAA
BIAAAKAAAAAQAAAA15RzGADjh6Le12ZDyOOoOiAAAABqXX2mykLJRhnINTo89NbHjRDSyA/K/fXQ
SfJ3rUSmZhQAAACskCn16e5njy+/6MC+wlrqiX5QLA==</LogonUser>
⊟    <LogonDomain>AQAAANCMnd8BFdERjHoAwE/Cl+sBAAAAtr8WaDPkfkOM1bCh1UjKoQQAAAAiAAAAUgBlAHAAbwBy
AHQAaQBuAGcAIABTAGUAcgB2AGUAcgAAAANmAADAAAAAEAAAAGnOT5DY2pi5OzzedV9+9gwAAAAA
BIAAAKAAAAAQAAAAgMsu6bkjv/pGYAQE1zrgQSAAAAAwwMd9W8ljh1K8S4IsrrEnmanC+0vOLwAe
vdk4Z0iOPBQAAACfGWO37iJ+OJNli0ozn1As3RpYDg==</LogonDomain>
⊟    <LogonCred>AQAAANCMnd8BFdERjHoAwE/Cl+sBAAAAtr8WaDPkfkOM1bCh1UjKoQQAAAAiAAAAUgBlAHAAbwBy
AHQAaQBuAGcAIABTAGUAcgB2AGUAcgAAAANmAADAAAAAEAAAAM88t3Qk/GOP//E1OwczkX0AAAAA
BIAAAKAAAAAQAAAAs+kQ/9u//qpjGCet3AW6YBgAAADNxgUc09yilannEyL3NZhxBDhRHF+RkAIU
AAAALc2LkfPjI8qkau0NCtCDM2keA8s=</LogonCred>
    <InstanceId>MSRS11.MSSQLSERVER</InstanceId>
```

FIGURE 25-9 The report server database logon information is encrypted in the Rsreportserver.config file.

You can also use the Rsconfig utility to update the unattended execution account information in the configuration file as encrypted data. Simply replace the –c argument with –e. For example, in a command prompt window, you use the following syntax (where *<domain\account>* is a login domain and Windows account and *<password>* is the account password):

```
rsconfig -e -m computername -s SQLServername -u [domain\]username -p password
```

Configuring authentication

The Rsreportserver.config file also contains settings to control how the report server authenticates users. If you are using Reporting Services in SharePoint integrated mode, you must keep the default authentication settings in the configuration file. If you need to change authentication, you must do so by changing the web application's authentication settings.

There are several different types of authentication that you can use in Reporting Services. The account under which you are running the Reporting Services service determines the default authentication method that you find in the configuration file by default, but you can change the authentication at any time on a native-mode report server. If you configure Reporting Services to use the RSWindowsNegotiate authentication type, Reporting Services tries to use Kerberos authentication first. If Kerberos is not enabled in your network, Reporting Services then reverts to NTLM security automatically. You can force Kerberos authentication by using the RSWindowsKerberos authentication type or force NTLM authentication by using the RSWindowsNTLM authentication type, as shown in Figure 25-10. Another option is to use RSWindowsBasic authentication if you are using client applications connecting to the report server using Basic authentication.

```
rsreportserver.config  ×
        <Authentication>
            <AuthenticationTypes>
                <RSWindowsNTLM/>
            </AuthenticationTypes>
            <RSWindowsExtendedProtectionLevel>Off</RSWindowsExtendedProtectionLevel>
            <RSWindowsExtendedProtectionScenario>Proxy</RSWindowsExtendedProtectionScenario>
            <EnableAuthPersistence>true</EnableAuthPersistence>
        </Authentication>
```

FIGURE 25-10 You can specify the authentication method to use for your report server in the Rsreportserver .config file.

It's possible to configure multiple authentication types in the configuration file. For example, your configuration file might not include the *<RSWindowsNegotiate />* element if you configured the Reporting Services service account as NetworkService or LocalSystem.

> **Important** If you configure a domain account as the Reporting Services service account, RSWindowsNegotiate authentication fails if Kerberos is not enabled on your network or a service principal name (SPN) has not been registered for the Reporting Services service. A user attempting to open Report Manager is prompted for credentials several times and then fails to authenticate. To solve this problem, you can either change the authentication type in the configuration file or register the SPN. To change authentication, you edit the configuration file to include only RSWindowsNTLM in the Authentication section. To regis-ter the SPN, have your domain administrator execute the following two commands:
>
> ```
> setspn -a http://<servername> <domain>\<accountname>
> setspn -a http://<fully qualified domain name> <domain>\<accountname>
> ```

The authentication type determines only whether a user can access the report server. It does not directly affect whether a user can authenticate on the server hosting the data source if the data is hosted on an external server. However, the type of authentication that you choose to implement can affect data source authentication as follows: If you configure the report server to use either RSWin-dowsNegotiate or RSWindowsKerberos, and if Kerberos and delegation are enabled in the domain, the report server can connect to the external data source by impersonating the user. If you imple-ment RSWindowsNTLM, you must configure data sources to use stored credentials because the report server cannot forward the user's credentials or impersonate the user.

> **Important** The browser that you use to access report server content must support Kerberos if you implement the RSWindowsKerberos authentication type. If you are using Internet Explorer, you must use RSWindowsNegotiate. You must also configure Internet Explorer to use Windows integrated security.

You can also implement ASP.NET forms authentication by specifying the Custom authentication type in the configuration file. However, you cannot use Custom authentication in combination with either of the Windows authentication types. Custom authentication requires you to change the Web.config file (found in the same folder as the Rsreportserver.config file) by setting the authentication mode to Custom and the impersonation flag to False.

> **Important** Because there is no validation of the authentication settings that you define in the configuration file, you should take care to test security before allowing users to access the report server. If you incorrectly configure authentication, attempts to open Report Manager fail with the HTTP 401 Access Denied error. For more information about authentication, refer to "Authentication with the Report Server" in SQL Server Books Online at *http://msdn.microsoft.com/en-us/library/bb283249.aspx.*

Managing memory

Report rendering can be a very memory-intensive process on the report server. Reports that must render a high volume of data require more RAM and increase the memory pressure on the report server. As memory pressure increases, the operating system must resort to paging to continue operations. If the memory requirements exceed the page file size, an out-of-memory exception occurs and report execution stops. Other processes that put memory pressure on the report server are model processing and background operations such as snapshots and subscriptions.

To reduce the possibility of out-of-memory exceptions, you can configure memory management settings in the Rsreportserver.config file to establish thresholds defining low, medium, and high memory pressure. Reporting Services uses the Memory Broker in SQL Server to detect memory pressure and responds to changes in memory pressure, as follows:

- **Low memory pressure**   All current requests made to the report server continue, new requests are accepted, and background processing is given lower priority than on-demand report rendering.

- **Medium memory pressure**   All current requests continue processing, new requests are accepted if existing reports can continue executing with reduced memory, and memory allocated to background processing is reduced most.

- **High memory pressure**   Current requests continue more slowly, new requests are denied, memory is reduced further across all running operations, and memory switches from RAM to the paging file.

The configuration file includes two settings that define the boundaries of medium memory pressure expressed as a percentage of memory. The lower boundary of medium memory pressure is defined by the *<MemorySafetyMargin>* element, which has a default value of 80. The *<MemoryThreshold>* element defines the upper boundary of medium pressure and has a default value of 90. Therefore, high memory pressure occurs when running processes consume more than 90 percent of server memory and low memory pressure exists when processes require less than 80 percent of memory.

You can tune the memory management settings by changing the boundaries of medium pressure and by adding two more settings to the configuration file to specify the minimum and maximum memory available to report server processes. These elements, *<WorkingSetMinimum>* and *<WorkingSetMaximum>*, are expressed in kilobytes (KB). If you don't include *<WorkingSetMinimum>* in the configuration file, Reporting Services assumes that its processes can be allocated 60 percent of the available memory and does not release memory below this threshold. If you don't explicitly assign a value in the configuration file, the default value for *<WorkingSetMaximum>* is the total server memory.

Only the *<MemorySafetyMargin>* and *<MemoryThreshold>* elements are configured by default. You must manually add the other settings to the configuration file. For example, you can reduce the minimum allocation of memory to Reporting Services to 50 percent instead of the default value of 60 percent. For a server with 4 gigabytes (GB) of available memory, the minimum allocation should be 2 GB. In this scenario, you would change the configuration file to look like this:

```
<MemorySafetyMargin>80</MemorySafetyMargin>
<MemoryThreshold>90</MemoryThreshold>
<WorkingSetMaximum>4000000</WorkingSetMaximum>
<WorkingSetMinimum>2000000</WorkingSetMinimum>
```

Disabling report server features

If you aren't using all report server features, you can disable those features as part of a lockdown strategy to reduce the surface area of a production report server that is at risk for attack. For example, if all report processing is performed as scheduled operations, you can disable all features except background processing. However, if you use interactive reporting only, disable all features except the report server web service. Refer to Table 25-1 to learn how to disable report server features.

> **Note** Background processing cannot be fully disabled because it must provide database maintenance functions.

TABLE 25-1 Disabling report server features

Feature	Steps to Disable
Report Manager	In the Rsreportserver.config file, set IsReportManagerEnabled to False.
On Demand Processing	In the Rsreportserver.config file, set IsWebServicerEnabled to False.
Scheduled Events and Report Delivery	In the Rsreportserver.config file, set the following elements to False: IsSchedulingService, IsNotificationService, and IsEventService.
Report Builder	In SSMS, open the Security page of the Server Properties dialog box, and clear the Enable Ad Hoc Report Execution check box.
Report Server Windows service	In SQL Server Configuration Manager, open the Service page of the SQL Server Reporting Services (MSSQLServer) Properties dialog box, and change Start Mode to Disabled.

Disabling an extension

You can disable a rendering or delivery extension if you prefer not to make it available to users. Rather than remove the extension from the Rsreportserver.config file, you can simply comment out the applicable lines by adding `!--` to the beginning tag and `--` to the ending tag of the extension, like this:

```
<!--Extension Name="MHTML" Type="Microsoft.ReportingServices.Rendering.HtmlRenderer.
MHtmlRenderingExtension,
Microsoft.ReportingServices.HtmlRendering">
  <Configuration>
    <DeviceInfo>
      <DataVisualizationFitSizing>Approximate</DataVisualizationFitSizing>
    </DeviceInfo>
  </Configuration>
</Extension-->
```

Another option is to eliminate a specific rendering format for use with subscriptions. In this case, you can add it to the *ExcludedRenderFormats* element for a delivery extension, like this:

```
<Extensions>
  <Delivery>
    <Extension Name="Report Server FileShare"
     Type="Microsoft.ReportingServices.FileShareDeliveryProvider.FileShareProvider,
     ReportingServicesFileShareDeliveryProvider">
      <MaxRetries>3</MaxRetries>
      <SecondsBeforeRetry>900</SecondsBeforeRetry>
      <Configuration>
        <FileShareConfiguration>
          <ExcludedRenderFormats>
            <RenderingExtension>HTMLOWC</RenderingExtension>
            <RenderingExtension>NULL</RenderingExtension>
            <RenderingExtension>RGDI</RenderingExtension>
          </ExcludedRenderFormats>
        </FileShareConfiguration>
      </Configuration>
    </Extension>
```

Managing the report server

Besides configuring the report server, other administrative tasks to perform include canceling jobs that are running on the report server or temporarily suspending report execution. These tasks are usually performed only as needed, but regular management of a report server should include performing backups consistently.

Canceling jobs

As an alternative to using time-outs to stopping a report that is taking too long to process, you can manually cancel an executing report, also known as a *job*. A job can be initiated either by a user viewing a report online and executing it on demand or by background processing for a subscription or a snapshot. If many jobs are running currently, you can cancel all the jobs in one step by using the Cancel All Jobs command. To see all running jobs, expand the Jobs folder in the Object Explorer window. If you need to cancel an individual job, right-click the job, and then select Cancel Job(s).

Important Canceling a job on the report server does not necessarily stop the corresponding process for a dataset query on the source data server.

Note The report server configuration file contains settings that control the frequency with which the report server checks for running jobs and the time that must elapse before a job transitions from a status of New to Running. The *RunningRequestsDbCycle* setting, with a default value of 60, is the number of seconds between checks for running jobs. The *RunningRequestsAge* setting changes the job status. The default is 30 seconds.

Suspending report execution

When you need to stop users from executing reports, such as when you are performing maintenance tasks on a source database, you can disable the shared data source. Not only are users prevented from executing reports, but scheduled snapshots and subscriptions for reports that depend on the disabled shared data source cannot execute reports. You can use this technique only for reports that depend on a shared data source. There is no way to stop users or other jobs from executing a report with a dataset that uses an embedded connection.

Tip Another way to suspend snapshot and subscription jobs temporarily is to pause a shared schedule on which these jobs are dependent. You learn how to work with a shared schedule in Chapter 27, "Working with subscriptions."

Note This technique affects only reports that execute on demand. Snapshot reports continue to be accessible because a snapshot report does not execute the report on demand. However, if the snapshot is created on a schedule and the data source remains disabled at the next scheduled execution of the report snapshot, the job fails.

To disable the data source, open the data source page in Report Manager or on your SharePoint site. Clear the Enable This Data Source check box, type the password for the stored credentials in the Password text box, and click Apply on a native-mode report server or OK on a SharePoint integrated-mode report server.

> **Note** Because this data source uses stored credentials, you must type the password each time you make changes to the data source properties.

You can confirm that the data source is disabled by reviewing the dependent items. To do this on a native-mode report server, click the Dependent Items link to view the reports using the shared data source, and then open one of the reports. You should see an error message display, as shown in Figure 25-11. On a SharePoint integrated-mode report server, you can click the View Dependent Items command on the data source's context menu in the document library, and then open one of the reports to confirm that you see a similar message.

Home > Sales > Reseller Sales Margin Analysis by Sales Territory   Home | My Subscriptions | Site Settings | Help
A data source associated with the report has been disabled. (rsDataSourceDisabled)

FIGURE 25-11 An error message displays when you try to view a report with a disabled data source.

Performing backup and recovery

As with any application on which your organization depends, you should have a disaster recovery plan in place, including a regular backup schedule of your Reporting Services environment. On a native-mode report server, there are no built-in tools for backup and recovery of the application databases like you have for a SharePoint integrated-mode report server. Your disaster recovery plan should also include management of encryption keys and configuration files.

Native-Mode report server database

Reporting Services has two application databases, named *ReportServer* and *ReportServerTempDB* by default. Only *ReportServer* requires a regular backup because this database contains the deployed reports, data sources, schedules, permissions, and other information required to run Reporting Services. It uses the Full recovery model so that you can back up both data and logs for point-in-time recovery if necessary. You can use the same backup process that you use for any other SQL Server database that you manage with a Full recovery model.

You do not need to perform a backup of *ReportServerTempDB* because it stores only session caches and cached instances of reports for use with on-demand execution and cached reports. If you later need to restore the *ReportServer* database, you can manually create a new *ReportServer-TempDB* and then execute the CatalogTempDB.sql script in the Program Files\Microsoft SQL Server\ MSRS11.<*instance*>\Reporting Services\Report Server folder. This script creates all the necessary objects required for the *ReportServerTempDB*.

SharePoint integrated-mode report server database

Because Reporting Services runs as a shared service application in SharePoint, you use the backup and restore tools built into SharePoint to manage Reporting Services disaster recovery. In SharePoint Central Administration, click the Backup And Restore link in the Quick Launch panel and then click the Perform A Backup link. In the Shared Services section, if you expand Shared Services Applications, you find your Reporting Services implementation listed. Select its check box, and click the Next button to advance to the Backup Options page. Here you specify the backup type (Full or Differential) and a backup location, and then click the Start Backup button. The location you specify must exist, and both the SQL Server and Reporting Services service accounts must be able to read and write to this folder.

Encryption keys

Reporting Services uses a symmetric key and a public key to encrypt and decrypt the connection information in the configuration file. One way to back up the encryption keys is to use the Reporting Services Configuration Manager, as described in Chapter 4. If you move the application databases to a new server, the encryption keys are invalidated as a security measure to prevent someone from opening an unauthorized copy of the databases. Invalidation of the encryption keys also occurs when you rename the report server or the report server instance, change the service account running the Reporting Services Windows service, or change the service account's password.

In addition to the commands in the Reporting Services Configuration Manager to manage the encryption keys, Reporting Services includes the Rskeymgmt command-line utility, which uses the following syntax:

```
rskeymgmt -e -f [drive:][folder\]filename -p password
```

After you store the encryption key in an external file, you can move it to a secure location.

 Important You must run the Rskeymgmt utility locally on the report server, and you must be a member of the local Administrators group.

You use the Rskeymgmt utility with the following arguments:

- **-e** This argument indicates that the operation extracts the encryption key. When you use this argument, you also supply the -f and -p arguments.

- **-a** When you need to replace an existing encryption key on the report server with a copy from a password-protected file, you use this argument and include the -f and -p arguments.

- **-d** You delete encryption keys and encrypted data in the report server database with this argument.

- **-s** You generate a new encryption key and re-encrypt data in the report server database by using this argument.

- **-r** You use this argument and supply the GUID representing the installation identifier (found in the Rsreportserver.config file) to remove a symmetric key from a report server instance when you want to remove it from a scale-out deployment.

- **-j** When you have a scale-out deployment, you use this argument to join a server instance to a report server database. You must also supply the -m argument for a remote server and the -n argument for a named instance. You include the -i argument when the local report server is set up as a named instance. You must also include the -u and -v arguments if your credentials are not set up with administrator privileges on the remote server.

- **-f** You use this argument when you run the Rskeymgmt utility with the -e argument to identify the target folder and file for the encryption key. If you exclude this argument, the encryption key is stored in the folder in which you execute the command.

- **-p** This argument specifies the password to the file. You must use this password if you later need to restore the encryption key to the report server.

- **-i** This argument specifies the local report server instance and is required only when you are referencing a named instance.

- **-m** You use this argument to specify the server name of a remote computer that you are joining to a scale-out deployment when using the -j argument.

- **-n** If the report server instance on a remote computer is a named instance, you must include this argument when using the -j argument.

- **-u** You use this argument to supply the administrator account on the remote computer when using the -j argument. If you omit this argument, your credentials are used.

- **-v** You must supply the administrator password when using the -u argument.

- **-t** You can optionally add this argument (with no value) to add trace information to error messages that might occur when the utility executes

To restore the encryption key using the Rskeymgmt utility, use the following syntax:

```
rskeymgmt -a -f [drive:][folder\]filename -p password
```

If you forget the password for the encryption key or if you lose the file to which you extracted the encryption key, you can delete encrypted information from the report server by using the following syntax:

```
rskeymgmt -d
```

You must perform this operation on each report server in a scale-out deployment. You must then update each shared and report-embedded data source with the applicable connection string information and authentication method.

If you have a remote report server to join to a report server scale-out deployment, you can use the Rskeymgmt utility on any computer that is already a member of this deployment by using the following syntax:

```
rskeymgmt -j -m <servername> -n <instancename> -u <administratoraccount> -v
<administratorpassword>
```

The syntax of this command is different when the report server instance to join to the scale-out deployment is installed on the same computer with another report server instance that is already a member of the deployment. In this case, you use the following syntax:

```
rskeymgmt -j -i <existinginstance> -m <computer name> -n <newinstance>
```

Configuration files

Both before and after you make adjustments to the configuration of your environment, you should make a backup of the configuration files so that you can restore Reporting Services to a working state if you make an incorrect change or if you need to completely rebuild your environment due to a server problem. You can use your favorite file backup tool to save the configuration files. Table 25-2 lists each configuration file to back up by location.

TABLE 25-2 Configuration files to back up

File Location	Configuration File
Program Files\Microsoft SQL Server\MSRS11.instance\ Reporting Services\ReportManager	RSMgrPolicy.config Web.config
Program Files\Microsoft SQL Server\MSRS11.instance\ Reporting Services\ReportServer	RSReportServer.config RSSrvPolicy.config Web.config
Program Files\Microsoft SQL Server\MSRS11.instance\ Reporting Services\ReportServer\Bin	ReportingServicesService.exe.config
Windows\Microsoft.NET\Framework\version\CONFIG	Machine.config

Monitoring the report server

Administration of a report server includes monitoring the server to ensure that adequate system resources are available and that operations are running smoothly and error-free. You can use built-in reports in SSMS to track the size of the Reporting Services application databases and take action to reduce the database size or add disk space as needed. You can review the Windows application event log and Reporting Services log files to monitor and troubleshoot activity on the report server. Finally, you can use performance counters to assess the impact of Reporting Services operations on server resources and to monitor trends over time.

Checking the application database size

Reporting Services uses two application databases, *ReportServer* and *ReportServerTempDB*. The *ReportServer* database is the primary storage used by Reporting Services to store the content, subscription, and schedule information, snapshots, and report history. Report definition files and most information stored on the server don't require a lot of space. However, if your reporting requirements depend on the availability of snapshots and report history, you should periodically check the size of the ChunkData table in the *ReportServer* database. As explained in Chapter 23, snapshots and report history are stored in the intermediate format, which can include a large volume of data.

> **Note** Although the SharePoint web application stores reports, models, data sources, permissions, and properties in its content database, report snapshots and history continue to be stored in the *ReportServer* database.

The *ReportServerTempDB* database is used only for temporary storage of session and caching information and therefore frequently fluctuates in size, based on user activity. Nonetheless, if users frequently request large reports, the session cache and cached instances can require a lot of space to store these reports in intermediate format. These temporary intermediate formats are found in the ChunkData table of the *ReportServerTempDB* database.

You can easily monitor the size of the report server databases by using reports in SSMS. In Object Explorer, expand the Databases folder, right-click ReportServer, select Reports, select Standard Reports, and select Disk Usage By Top Tables. On a new report server instance, the ChunkData table size is typically insignificant. In a production environment, this table grows at a faster pace than other tables in the database as snapshots and report history are added to the server. You can use the Disk Usage By Top Tables report to monitor its size periodically. If you have disk space constraints that require that you prevent unlimited growth, work with your users to decide how best to limit the amount of report history or the number of reports with snapshots.

Monitoring the Windows application event log

Reporting Services uses the Windows application event log to record errors, warnings, and miscellaneous information events. You can review this log by opening the Administrative Tools program group, which might be accessible only from Control Panel, depending on your operating system. Then open Event Viewer and locate the Application log. You can use the Source column to identify events from the report server, Report Manager, and the Scheduling and Delivery Processor.

Using the trace logs

When you need to troubleshoot report server operations, you can review the trace logs generated by Reporting Services. After midnight each day, the first traceable activity triggers the creation of a new file for the trace log in the Program Files\Microsoft SQL Server\MSRS11.<*instance*>\Reporting Services\ ReportServer folder on a native-mode report server. You can find the trace log on a SharePoint integrated-mode report server at Program Files\Common Files\Microsoft Shared\Web Server

Extensions\14\WebServices\LogFiles. A new file is also created when Reporting Services is restarted. The trace log records application log events, errors and exceptions, low resource warnings, report delivery details, and other details about Reporting Services operations.

You can configure the level of detail available in the trace log in addition to the maximum file size per log file and the number of days to persist a log file on the report server. You can even disable the trace log if you want. The configuration settings for a native-mode report server trace log are stored in the ReportingServerService.exe.config file, which is in the Program Files\Microsoft SQL Server\ MSRS11.instance>\Reporting Services\ReportServer\Bin folder. On a SharePoint integrated-mode report server, these configuration settings are in the Rsreportserver.config file at Program Files\ Common Files\Microsoft Shared\Web Server Extensions\14\WebServices\Reporting.

For a native-mode report server, the *DefaultTraceSwitch* setting has a default value of 3, as shown in Figure 25-12, which logs most report server operations. You can add more information by changing this value to 4 for Verbose mode, or you can log less information by using a lower value. For example, a value of 2 means that the log stores exceptions, restarts, and warnings, but a value of 1 means that the log stores only exceptions and restarts. To disable logging altogether, set the value to 0.

```
ReportingServicesService.exe.config  ×
        <switches>
            <add name="DefaultTraceSwitch" value="3" />
        </switches>
    </system.diagnostics>
    <RStrace>
        <add name="FileName" value="ReportServerService_" />
        <add name="FileSizeLimitMb" value="32" />
        <add name="KeepFilesForDays" value="14" />
        <add name="Prefix" value="appdomain, tid, time" />
        <add name="TraceListeners" value="file" />
        <add name="TraceFileMode" value="unique" />
        <add name="Components" value="all:3" />
    </RStrace>
```

FIGURE 25-12 The *DefaultTraceSwitch* setting in the ReportingServiceService.exe.config file controls the level of detail available in a trace log.

The name of the log file is determined by two of the settings found in the RStrace section of the configuration file, *FileName* and *Prefix*. By default, all trace log files begin with ReportServerService_ and end with a date and time stamp, as indicated by the *tid* and *time* values for the *Prefix* setting. Trace log files on a SharePoint integrated-mode report server also include a GUID. The application domain is included in the file name when you configure the Components setting to use specific component categories. For example, you can update the Components setting to add the HTTP component category, as described in the next section of this chapter.

The default file size limit, specified by the *FileSizeLimitMb* setting, is 32 megabytes (MB). You can increase or decrease this limit as needed. If you set this value to 0 or less, it evaluates as 1. Reporting Services creates a new log file after server activity logging exceeds the file size limit.

Typically, you use the most current log files for troubleshooting. Consequently, Reporting Services includes a mechanism to remove log files after an age threshold has been crossed. The *KeepFilesFor-Days* setting uses a default value of 14, but you can change this value to a more suitable value for your environment. If you set the value to 0 or less, Reporting Services considers it to be a value of 1.

In addition to logging trace information to a file, which is the default behavior as defined by the *TraceListeners* setting, you can specify additional output modes, such as *DebugWindow* or *StdOut*, for the trace listener by using a comma separator in the value list.

The *TraceFileMode* setting of *unique* requires Reporting Services to generate one unique trace file per day. Microsoft recommends that you don't change this setting.

You use the Components setting to specify the components to monitor and also specify the applicable trace level for that component by using a value from 0 to 4. You can use any of the following components as values:

- **All**   Capture trace messages for any component not listed (except HTTP).

- **HTTP**   Capture HTTP requests to Reporting Services. You must use a trace level of 4 to capture these requests. Otherwise, Reporting Services disables this component.

- **RunningJobs**   Capture messages about report and subscription execution.

- **SemanticQueryEngine**   Capture messages about queries executed by using the report model.

- **SemanticModelGenerator**   Capture messages about the generation of report models.

Adding the HTTP log

HTTP activity is not logged by default. You can create a second type of trace log by modifying the ReportingServicesService.exe.config file to include settings for HTTP logging. This file is in the Program Files\Microsoft SQL Server\MSRS11.<*instance*>\Reporting Services\ReportServer\Bin folder. To do this, modify the Components setting to look like this:

```
<add name="Components" value="all:3,http:4" />
```

This setting produces a log for all components by using the default trace level and a separate log for HTTP activity by using the verbose level as specified by the value of 4. Any other trace level disables the HTTP logging.

After this capability is enabled, all HTTP requests to the report server are recorded in the trace log. You must also specify which fields to log, such as client Internet Protocol (IP) address or HTTP status. You can use many of the same fields found in the World Wide Web Consortium (W3C) extended log file that is managed by Internet Information Services (IIS), which means that you use IIS log viewers to read the HTTP log file generated by Reporting Services.

To configure HTTP logging, add the following code to the Rstrace section of the ReportingServicesService.exe.config file, above the *<add name="Components" value="all:3"* line:

```
<add name="HTTPLogFileName" value="ReportServerService_HTTP_" />
<add name="HttpTraceSwitches" value="date,time,activityid,sourceactivityid
,clientip,username,serverip,serverport,host,method,uristem,uriquery,protocolstatus
,bytessent,bytesreceived,timetaken,protocolversion,useragent,cookiereceived,cookiesent,referrer"
/>
```

This code defines part of the trace log file name using the *HTTPLogFileName* setting. As you can see by reviewing the *HttpTraceSwitches* settings, the information in the trace log includes many fields related to an HTTP request. You have the option to customize the log by removing fields from the HttpTraceSwitches folder.

After updating the ReportingServicesService.exe.config file, you must restart the Reporting Services Windows service. An easy way to do this is to open the Reporting Services Configuration Manager and then connect to your report server. Next, on the Report Server Status page, click Stop, and then click Start. After HTTP logging is enabled, you can check the log file after enough time has elapsed for users to generate some trace log updates.

You can find the HTTP logs in the Program Files\Microsoft SQL Server\MSRS11.*<instance>*\Reporting Services\LogFiles. You can double-click a ReportServerService_HTTP_ log file to review its log entries. In the fifth row, you can see the list of fields included in the HTTP log file. You can use this list to interpret the data in the subsequent data rows even though the labels are not aligned with the columns. You must match the sequence of the field labels with the sequence of fields in the data rows. Each field is separated by a single space.

A common reason to review this file is to troubleshoot a client connectivity issue. For example, by checking the client's IP address in the third column (labeled *c-ip*), you can confirm whether a client is communicating with the server. You can also confirm the user identity used to connect to the report server by checking the user name in the fourth column (labeled *cs-username*). The *sc-status* field (in the eleventh column) shows the HTTP status code, such as 200 for OK or 401 for unauthorized, which helps you determine whether the client connectivity issue is related to the HTTP request.

> **Tip** You can find a list of definitions for HTTP status codes at *http://www.w3.org/Protocols/ rfc2616/rfc2616-sec10.html*.

SharePoint diagnostic logging

On a SharePoint server, you can take advantage of the diagnostic logging features to monitor and troubleshoot Reporting Services activity. To do this, you must first enable this feature in SharePoint Central Administration. Click the Monitoring link in the Quick Launch panel, and then click the Configure Diagnostic Logging link. In the Category list, you can select the SQL Server Reporting Services check box to log all events, or you can expand it to select any of the following individual events:

- Power View
- Report Server Alerting Runtime
- Report Server App Domain Manager
- Report Server Buffered Response
- Report Server Cache

- Report Server Catalog

- Report Server Chunk

- Report Server Cleanup

- Report Server Configuration Manager

- Report Server Crypto

- Report Server Data Extension

- Report Server DB Polling

- Report Server Default

- Report Server Email Extension

- Report Server Excel Renderer

- Report Server Extension Factory

- Report Server HTTP Runtime

- Report Server Image Renderer

- Report Server Memory Monitoring

- Report Server Notification

- Report Server Processing

- Report Server Provider

- Report Server Rendering

- Report Server Report Preview

- Report Server Resource Utility

- Report Server Running Jobs

- Report Server Running Requests

- Report Server Schedule

- Report Server Security

- Report Server Service Controller

- Report Server Session

- Report Server Subscription

- Report Server WCF Runtime

- Report Server Web Server

- Service Application Proxy

- Shared Service

- Configuration Pages

- HTTP Redirector

- Local Mode Processing

- Local Mode Rendering

- SOAP Client Proxy

- UI Pages

You can specify the least critical event to add to the event log and for your selection. The default event level is Information, but you can set it to None, Critical, Error, or Warning to restrict logging to fewer entries, or you can set it to Verbose for the highest level of logging. You can also set the least critical event to add to the trace log. Your options include None, Unexpected, Monitorable, High, Medium, and Verbose. The default trace Level is Medium, except for Power View, which is set to Monitorable.

When you configure diagnostic logging, you can change the path of the logs from %CommonProgramFiles%\Microsoft Shared\Web Server Extensions\14\LOGS\. You can also specify the number of days to retain logs if you don't want to keep the default of 14 days. If you want to restrict the amount of disk space allocated to logs, you can select the Restrict Trace Log Disk Space Usage check box and set a maximum number of gigabytes to use for trace log storage.

Execution logging

On the Codeplex site, Microsoft has a download for Server Management Report samples accessible from *http://msftrsprodsamples.codeplex.com/downloads/get/86580*. Included in this download is a sample Integration Services package for moving execution data from the *ReportServer* database into a log database and sample reports to help you get started quickly with analyzing the log data. These sample files are available for use with SQL Server 2008, but you can upgrade them to use with SQL Server 2012 if you open the files in SSDT and make some adjustments to make them functional. Or you can use the upgraded and modified versions that we included in the sample files download for this book.

Before you start using these files, you must first create a database named *RSExecutionLog,* in which to store the execution log data, and then use the Createtables.sql script to create the necessary database objects. Be sure to set the current database to *RSExecutionLog* before executing this script. Although the table names do not reference dimensions and fact tables like you find in a data mart or data warehouse, the *RSExecutionLog* tables are organized as a star schema containing a fact table, *ExecutionLogs*, and the following dimension tables:

- ExecutionParameters

- FormatTypes

- Machines

- Reports

- ReportTypes

- RequestTypes

- SourceTypes

- StatusCodes

- Users

To update these tables, open the RSExecutionLog_Update.dtsx package in SSDT. You can manually execute the package in SSDT by pressing F5. Or you can deploy the package to the SSIS catalog and execute it on a scheduled basis.

Note You can execute the package by using the Dtexec utility described at *http://msdn .microsoft.com/en-us/library/hh231187.aspx* or by using one of the other tools described in "Execution of Projects and Packages" at *http://msdn.microsoft.com/en-us/library/ms141708 .aspx*.

Tip If you use this book's sample files, you can instead open the RSExecutionLog solution in SSDT. This solution contains the Integration Services package as well the sample reports.

You can create your own reports to review the data in the *RSExecutionLog* database. You can also use the following sample reports as a starting point for analyzing the execution log data:

- **Execution Status Codes**   Within a user-specified date range, this report lists report execution count and percent of total by status code and lists each report with a count of successes and failures.

- **Execution Summary**   Within a user-specified date range, this report lists total executions, successes, failures, and average executions per day. It also includes charts to compare the number of executions by day of month and by day of week. The charts are followed by the following top 10 lists: Top 10 Most Executed, Top 10 Longest Running, Top 10 Largest Reports, and Top 10 Users.

- **Report Summary**   Within a user-specified date range for a selected report, this report provides execution statistics (total, successes, failures, average executions per day, average size in bytes and rows) and lists the number of executions by parameter name and value.

You might not want to accumulate data in this database indefinitely, but there is nothing built into the Integration Services package to remove data. You can modify the Cleanup.sql script to delete data prior to a specific date, or you can use an expression to calculate a date.

Using the ExecutionLog3 view

If you prefer not to set up a separate data mart for tracking execution log information, you can use the *ExecutionLog3* view in the report server database. You can query this view on an ad hoc basis in SSMS or create reports to review specific performance information on demand or via a subscription. The *ExecutionLog3* view contains the following columns:

- **InstanceName**   The instance name of the report server.

- **ItemPath**   The folder path and name of the item executed, such as a report or dataset.

- **UserName**   The identifier of the user account executing the item.

- **ExecutionID**   An internal identifier for the execution request. All requests from the same user sessions share a common *ExecutionID*.

- **RequestType**   The type of request: Interactive or Subscription.

- **Format**   The rendering format of a report.

- **Parameters**   The parameter values used for report execution.

- **ItemAction**   The action performed by the report server: Render, Sort, BookMarkNavigation, DocumentNavigation, GetDocumentMap, Findstring, Execute, or RenderEdit.

- **TimeStart**   The start time of the action.

- **TimeEnd**   The end time of the action.

- **TimeDateRetrieval**   The number of milliseconds required to retrieve data.

- **TimeProcessing**   The number of milliseconds required to process the report.

- **TimeRendering**   The number of milliseconds required to render the report.

- **Source**   The source of the request to execute the report: Live, Cache, Snapshot, History, AdHoc, Session, or Rdce.

- **Status**   Success or failure indicated by rsSuccess or the first error code causing the failure.

- **ByteCount**   The number of bytes required to store the rendered report.

- **RowCount**   The number of rows returned by queries for the report.

- **AdditionalInfo**   An XML structure containing more information about the execution.

The *AdditionalInfo* column can contain the following values:

- **ProcessingEngine**   The engine used to process the report, 1 for SQL Server 2005 and 2 for the newer on-demand processing engine.

- **ScalabilityTime**   The number of milliseconds required to scale operations. If this value is 0, no additional time was spent and the request was not executed under memory pressure.

- **EstimatedMemoryUsageKB**   The estimated peak memory in kilobytes reported by component, such as Processing.

- **DataExtension**   Each data extension or data source used in the report, including the number of occurrences per data source.

- **ExternalImages**   The number of milliseconds required to retrieve images from an external source. A count of images and the bytes retrieved is also reported.

- **Connections**   An XML structure of information about the connection, including the data source name, the duration of the connection, the dataset name, the number of rows retrieved per dataset, the total retrieval time per dataset, the query preparation and execution time per dataset, the *ExecuteReader* time per dataset, the datareader mapping time per dataset, and the datareader disposal time per dataset.

Using performance counters

You can use the Windows Performance Monitor to monitor report server activity. The Reporting Services installation adds several ASP.NET performance counters to monitor the current state of the server, the trend of report server operations over time, and the cumulative total of a counter since the service was last started. These counters can help you understand how Reporting Services is using system resources during on-demand or scheduled report execution.

To open Performance Monitor, click the Start button, type **perfmon** in the Search Programs And Files box, and press Enter. Expand the Monitoring Tools folder, and select Performance Monitor. Right-click the chart, and select Add Counters. You can then expand performance objects on the server and select the counters to monitor from the following performance objects:

- The *MSRS 2011 Web Service* and *MSRS 2011 Web Service SharePoint Mode* objects include performance counters for activity related to online interactive viewing.

- The *MSRS 2011 Windows Service* and *MSRS 2011 Windows Service SharePoint Mode* objects include performance counters for report processing by scheduled operations, such as subscriptions, snapshots, and report history.

- The *ReportServer:Service* and *ReportServerSharePoint:Service* objects include performance counters for HTTP activity related to Reporting Services and for memory management.

Tip A useful resource for learning how to run performance tests is "Planning for Scalability and Performance with Reporting Services," which you can view at *http://www.microsoft .com/technet/prodtechnol/sql/2005/pspsqlrs.mspx*. Although this white paper was written for use with Reporting Services 2005, much of the information is still applicable to Reporting Services 2012. However, the *ReportServer:Service* object was introduced in Reporting Services 2008 and is not discussed in the white paper. You can learn more about the performance counters included in that collection in the SQL Server Books Online topic "Performance Counters for the ReportServer:Service and ReportServerSharePoint:Service Performance Objects" at *http://msdn.microsoft.com/en-us/library/cc627471.aspx*.

You can use the performance counters listed in Table 25-3 to establish a baseline of performance statistics and then monitor these statistics over time to assess how increasing demand affects the report server. You rarely need to monitor all counters continuously. Instead, focus on key counters such as Requests/Sec and Memory Pressure State. If the report server is frequently in the high pressure or exceeded pressure state, you can tune the memory configuration settings and then reassess the performance statistics after making the configuration change.

TABLE 25-3 Reporting Services performance counters

Performance Counter	Description	Web Service	Windows Service	Report Server Service
Active Connections	Number of connections active against server		✓	✓
Active Sessions	Number of active sessions	✓	✓	
Bytes Received Total	Number of bytes received			✓
Bytes Received/Sec	Rate of bytes received per second			✓
Bytes Sent Total	Number of bytes sent			✓
Bytes Sent/Sec	Rate of bytes sent per second			✓
Cache Flushes/Sec	Number of cache flushes per second		✓	
Cache Hits/Sec	Number of report server cache hits per second	✓	✓	
Cache Hits/Sec (Semantic Models)	Number of times per second that models can be retrieved from the cache	✓	✓	

Performance Counter	Description	Web Service	Windows Service	Report Server Service
Cache Misses/Sec	Number of times per second that reports cannot be retrieved from cache	✓	✓	
Cache Misses/Sec (Semantic Models)	Number of times per second that models cannot be retrieved from cache	✓	✓	
Delivers/Sec	Number of deliveries per second		✓	
Errors Total	The total number of errors that occur during the execution of HTTP requests (error codes 400s and 500s)			✓
Errors/Sec	Number of errors that occur during the execution of HTTP requests (error codes 400s and 500s) per second			✓
Events/Sec	Number of events per second		✓	
First Session Requests/Sec	Number of new user sessions that are started per second	✓	✓	
Logon Attempts Total	Number of logon attempts for RSWindows* authentication types; returns 0 for Custom authentication			✓
Logon Attempts/Sec	Rate of logon attempts			✓
Logon Successes Total	Number of successful logons for RSWindows* authentication types; returns 0 for Custom authentication			✓
Logon Successes/Sec	Rate of successful logons			✓
Memory Cache Hits/Sec	Number of times per second that reports can be retrieved from the in memory cache	✓	✓	

Performance Counter	Description	Web Service	Windows Service	Report Server Service
Memory Cache Misses/Sec	Number of times per second that reports cannot be retrieved from the in memory cache	✓	✓	
Memory Pressure State	A number from 1-5 indicating the current memory state of the server (1-No pressure, 2-Low pressure, 3-Medium pressure, 4-High pressure, 5-Exceeded pressure)			✓
Memory Shrink Amount	Number of bytes the server requested to shrink			✓
Memory Shrink Notifications/Sec	Number of shrink notifications the server issued in the last second; indicates how often the server believes it is under memory pressure			✓
Next Session Requests/Sec	Number of requests per second for reports that are open in an existing session	✓	✓	
Report Requests	Number of active report requests	✓	✓	
Reports Executed/Sec	Number of reports executed per second	✓	✓	
Requests Disconnected	Number of requests that have been disconnected due to a communication failure			✓
Requests Executing	Number of requests currently executing			✓
Requests Not Authorized	Number of request failing with HTTP 401 error code			✓

Performance Counter	Description	Web Service	Windows Service	Report Server Service
Requests Rejected	Total number of requests not executed because of insufficient server resources; this counter represents the number of requests that returns a 503 HTTP status code, indicating that the server is too busy			✓
Requests/Sec	Number of requests per second; represents the current throughput of the application	✓	✓	✓
Requests Total	The total number of requests received by the report server service since service startup			✓
Snapshot Updates/Sec	Number of snapshot updates per second		✓	
Tasks Queued	Total number of tasks waiting for a thread to become available for processing (not tasks that are currently running)			✓
Total App Domain Recycles	Total number of application domain recycles		✓	
Total Cache Flushes	Total number of report execution server cache updates		✓	
Total Cache Hits	Total number of report server cache hits	✓	✓	
Total Cache Hits (Semantic Models)	Total number of cache hits made in the model cache	✓	✓	
Total Cache Misses	Total number of cache misses	✓	✓	
Total Cache Misses (Semantic Models)	Total number of cache misses made in the model cache	✓	✓	
Total Deliveries	Total number of deliveries		✓	
Total Events	Total number of events		✓	

Performance Counter	Description	Web Service	Windows Service	Report Server Service
Total Memory Cache Hits	Total number of cache hits made in the in-memory cache	✓	✓	
Total Memory Cache Misses	Total number of cache misses made in the in-memory cache	✓	✓	
Total Processing Failures	Total number of processing failures	✓	✓	
Total Rejected Threads	Total number of rejected threads as a result of thread pressure	✓	✓	
Total Reports Executed	Total number of reports executed	✓	✓	
Total Requests	Total number of requests being processed	✓	✓	
Total Snapshots Updates	Total number of report execution snapshot updates		✓	

PART V

Viewing reports

The third and final stage of the reporting life cycle is report access. In Chapter 26, "Accessing reports online," you learn how to use a browser to locate and open managed reports from a central repository, how to export reports to alternate formats, and how to create and manage a personalized folder for selected reports. Then, in Chapter 27, "Working with subscriptions," you learn how to create and manage report subscriptions as an alternative method for viewing reports. Last, in Chapter 28, "Data alerting," you learn about another type of subscription that sends you a notification only when data in a report matches criteria that you specify so that you can selectively view reports on a SharePoint integrated-mode report server.

CHAPTER 26

Accessing reports online

This chapter introduces you to Reporting Services from the perspective of a user who uses either Report Manager or a SharePoint web application to find and view reports online. You learn how to use the available online functions to change pages in a report, to change the page size, to change visibility of a report's document map or parameters, or to print a report. If you're running a native-mode report server, you continue by learning how to save your favorite reports to a personalized folder. If you're running an integrated-mode report server, you learn how to create a dashboard to display multiple reports on a single page. For both server modes, native and integrated, you learn about the different export formats that enable you to use report data in other applications.

Using Report Manager

Chapter 23, "Deploying reports to a server," explains how to use Report Manager to organize and view reports deployed to the native-mode report server. But you should learn a few more features in Report Manager to understand the functionality available to users who access reports online. Opening a report in Report Manager is fairly straightforward if you know where to find the report link. Instead of navigating through the folder hierarchies to locate its link, you can search for a report. After you open a report, you can use the HTML Viewer to manage the report display. The HTML Viewer also includes a print control that you can use to print one or more pages of the report for offline reference.

> **Note** You learn how to access reports on a SharePoint integrated-mode report server in the "Accessing reports in SharePoint" section of this chapter.

Searching for a report

When you aren't sure where to find a report, you can search for it by name or by description. The Search feature in Report Manager not only finds reports, but also folders, linked reports, shared data sources, report models, and other items stored on the report server, as long as you have permissions to view those items. Regardless of the current folder you are viewing in Report Manager, the search begins at the Home folder and searches through all nested folders to which you are assigned at least the Browser role. The search results do not include any item or folder that you don't have permission to see (as described in Chapter 24, "Securing report server content").

Every folder in Report Manager contains a Search box in the top-right corner of the page, as shown in Figure 26-1. You can type a word or phrase in this box to locate content on the report server having a name or description containing the search criteria. The search feature uses simple pattern matching. That is, you can type **sales** to find any item containing the word *sales*, or type **reseller sales** to find any item containing those two words consecutively. You can also type a word like **resell** to find any item containing that word, such as *reseller, reselling*, or any word that begins with *resell*. However, a search for reseller sales would not find a report named "Reseller Report of Sales."

FIGURE 26-1 You use the Search box in Report Manager to find report server content.

Note The search feature does not support Boolean logic or complex conditions using AND or OR operators.

After you click the button with the magnifying glass icon, you see the Search Results page display a list of reports, as shown in Figure 26-2. The search retrieves reports, folders, and report models containing the search term and displays the results in alphabetical order.

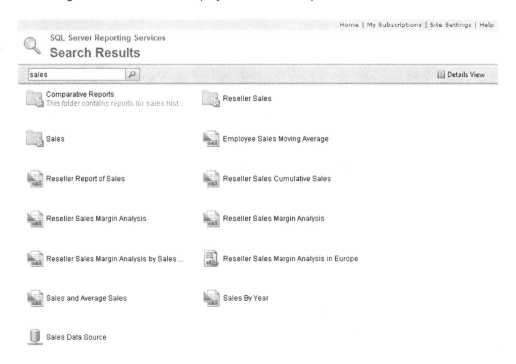

FIGURE 26-2 The Search Results page lists all content matching the search term.

If the set of reports that your search returns is large, you might find it useful to sort the list in other ways. You can click the Details View button to display the item names in a single column. The Details View, shown in Figure 26-3, also includes the following columns: Type, Description, Folder, and Last Run. You can click any of these columns to sort the list of items in ascending order and then click it again to reverse the sort. To view an item, click its link in the Name column to open an item or click the link in the Folder column to open that folder.

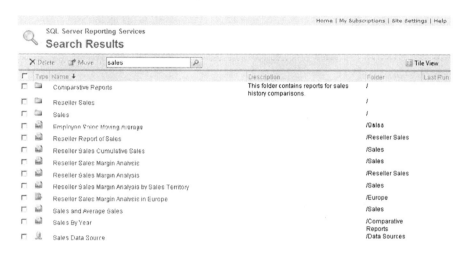

FIGURE 26-3 You can view the Search Results page in the Details View to sort the list of results by type, name, description, folder, or last run date and time.

Using the HTML Viewer

When you open a report in Report Manager, a special toolbar called the HTML Viewer displays above the report. You can use the HTML Viewer, shown in Figure 26-4, to navigate between pages, to change the zoom factor of the report, to search for text within a report, to refresh the report, to export to a different format, or to print the report. You also use the HTML Viewer to change the parameter selections for the report if parameters are enabled and visible on the report.

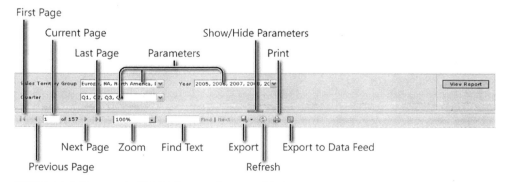

FIGURE 26-4 You use the HTML Viewer to interact with the report.

The HTML Viewer includes the following functions for managing the report view:

- **First Page**   Use this button to jump to the beginning of the report when viewing any page other than the first page.

- **Previous Page**   Use this button to open the previous page of the report when viewing any page other than the first page.

- **Current Page**   Type a page number in this text box, and press Enter to jump to the specified page. Afterwards, you can view a different page of the report by using the HTML Viewer buttons to page forward or backward, to jump to the first page or last page of the report, or to jump to a specific page.

- **Next Page**   Use this button to open the next page of the report when viewing any page other than the last page.

- **Last Page**   Use this button to jump to the last page of the report when viewing any page other than the last page.

- **Zoom**   Select any of the following options in the drop-down list to reduce or enlarge the size of the report: Page Width, Whole Page, 500%, 200%, 150%, 75%, 50%, 25%, or 10%.

- **Parameters**   Use the drop-down list(s) to select a new value, or type a new value in a text box, as applicable, and then click View Report to change a parameter selection. Parameters do not display if they are hidden in the report definition or the report properties.

- **Find Text**   Type a search string, and click the Find link to find and highlight the first instance of the string following the current position in the report. Click the Next link to find each subsequent instance of the string. If you click the Next link after the last instance has been displayed, a message box displays the message, "The entire report has been searched." The Find and Next links are disabled when the Find Text text box is empty.

- **Show/Hide Parameters**   Use this button to toggle the display of the parameters section of the HTML Viewer so that you can see more of your report on the page. This function is not available if the report contains no parameters. The direction of the arrow on the Show/Hide Parameters button reverses after you click the button. You can click the button to show the parameters again later when you want to change a parameter selection.

- **Export**   Click the Export button, and then select one of the alternate file types to export your report. You learn more about the export feature in the "Exporting reports" section of this chapter.

- **Refresh**   Use this button to reload the report definition and re-execute the dataset queries.

- **Print**   Print one or more pages of the report to a selected printer.

Note The Print button does not appear if the report server administrator has disabled the ActiveX print control feature on the report server, as described in Chapter 25, "Performing administrative tasks."

■ **Export to Data Feed** Use this button to create a data feed document to import data into a Microsoft PowerPivot for Excel workbook or to share as part of a data feed service.

Using the document map

A document map is a report navigation feature that the report author can include in a report, as described in Chapter 13, "Adding interactivity." It works like an interactive table of contents, allowing you to expand group labels in the tree view and click a label to jump to the corresponding section in the report, as shown in Figure 26-5. If necessary, you can click the Show/Hide Document Map button that appears in the center of the line separating the document map from the report to hide the map and give more screen space to the report. You can click the button again to open the document when you want to locate a different section of the report. The Document Map pane and the Show/Hide Document Map button are not visible if a document map does not exist for the report.

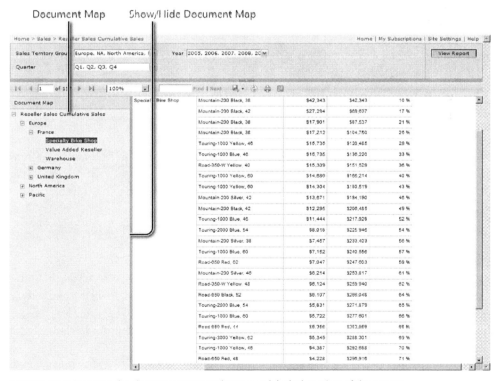

FIGURE 26-5 You use the document map to jump to a labeled section of the report.

Printing a report

The print feature of the browser includes web elements of the Report Manager application, so you should use the Print button on the HTML Viewer when you want a printed copy of the report that you are currently viewing online. This button opens an ActiveX control that you can use to preview the layout, change the orientation, define new margins, and select a range of pages to print if you don't want to print the entire report.

The first time you try to use this feature, an Internet Explorer – Security Warning message box displays. You must click Install to install the print control. After installation, the Print dialog box displays, as shown in Figure 26-6, so that you can select a printer in the Name drop-down list. You can choose to print all pages of the report, specify a range of pages, and select the number of copies to print. Use the Properties button to open a dialog box that allows you to choose between portrait or landscape orientation.

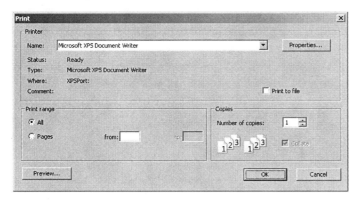

FIGURE 26-6 The print control allows you to select a printer, print range, and number of copies to print.

The Preview button allows you to check the layout of the report before printing. In the preview window, you can use the Margins button to increase or decrease margins as necessary. You can also use the Next and Previous buttons to preview different pages of the report or use the Page spinner control to jump to a specific page. When you're ready, you can click the Print button to print the report.

Using the My Reports folder

The My Reports folder is a user-specific folder available in Report Manager where you can publish and manage reports separately from reports available to other Reporting Services users. Only you and report server administrators have access to your My Reports folder. The My Reports feature is disabled on the server by default and must be enabled by a report administrator before you can start using it, as described in Chapter 25. The My Report folder is visible on the Home page of the Report Manager if the feature is enabled and if you have been assigned to the My Reports role (or to the role assigned to users of this feature).

The My Reports folder does not exist until the first time you open Report Manager after the My Reports feature has been enabled. At that time, the report server adds the folder for you and adds the role assignment for My Reports (as specified by the report server administrator) to the folder's security. The report server performs this process for each user, but only when they open Report Manager.

After your My Reports folder is added, you add content to your My Reports folder in the same way that content managers add content to other folders on the report server. By saving reports to the My Reports folder, you can keep all your favorite reports in a common location rather than having to remember where to find these reports in the Reporting Services folder hierarchy.

You can upload report definition files directly to this folder (or a folder that you create within that folder) if a report author has provided you with files via email or a network file share. You can instead create a linked report from an existing report on the report server and then store the linked report in the My Reports folder. More likely, you use Report Builder or SSDT to develop your own report and deploy it to the My Reports folder, with Report Builder the easier option to use due to its integration with Report Manager. To deploy to the My Reports folder, use the steps described for the applicable report design tool that you use, as follows:

- **Report Builder**   Click the File button, and then click Save As. In the Save As Report dialog box, click the arrow button in the top-right corner to navigate to the top-level folder of the report server (such as *http://<servername>/ReportServer*), double-click the My Reports folder to open it, and then click Save. Of course, you can change the name of the report before you save it.

- **SSDT**   Use the following value in the TargetReportFolder text box in the project properties: Users Folders/*<servername>* *<username>*/My Reports. Replace *<servername>* with the name of the report server if no domain exists or the domain name on your network, and replace *<username>* with your Microsoft Windows account.

> **Note** You cannot deploy a report into another user's My Reports folders from SSDT, even if you are the report server administrator. If you try to do this, deployment fails and an error message displays to explain that the permissions granted to your account are insufficient for performing this operation.

After you save a report to the My Reports folder, you have administrative privileges for the report. You can use the Manage command on the report's shortcut menu and configure parameters or execution properties, as described in Chapter 23. You can also use the Subscribe command on the report's shortcut menu to create a subscription as described in Chapter 27, "Working with subscriptions," if you prefer to access the report in your email inbox rather than online.

If you are a report server administrator, you can view the contents of the My Reports folder for any user when you open the User's Folders folder. If a user has developed a report that you both agree should be available to additional users, you can move the report from this folder to a different folder on the report server. You can also delete reports from this folder if necessary, such as when a user leaves the organization.

Accessing reports in SharePoint

A report in SharePoint is commonly accessible in a document library for which the Reporting Services content types are enabled. Just like any other document in SharePoint, you find the report and click its link to open it. If the SharePoint Server Search service has been configured on the SharePoint server, you can search for reports if you don't know which reports library contains the report that you want to access. A toolbar in the SharePoint Report Viewer allows you to manage the report display much like the HTML Viewer in Report Manager, with some slight differences. You can view a report in isolation by clicking its report link in the document library, or if you have the necessary permissions, you can combine multiple reports for display on a single page by creating a dashboard.

Searching for a report

If the Search service is enabled on your SharePoint server and this service browses the site containing reports in document libraries, you can search for reports by using keywords used in the report name or its properties. The Search service also finds data sources, report models, and other items stored on the SharePoint site that meet the search criteria as long as you have permission to view these items.

To start a search, you open a site and then open a content page. For example, you can click the Libraries link in the navigation pane to open a page from which you can search content in all document libraries in the site, or you can open a specific document library to limit the scope of the search. You can type a search word whenever you see the Search This Site box in the upper-right corner of the browser window, as shown in Figure 26-7, and then press Enter or click the magnifying glass icon to the right of the search box.

FIGURE 26-7 You use the Search This Site box in a SharePoint library to find content.

The search retrieves any content in SharePoint that matches your search, including Reporting Services content such as reports and folders containing content matching your search. The search considers both the name of the report as well as its properties (if these were updated after the report was deployed). Unlike a search in Report Manager, the search in SharePoint must match a word exactly. For example, a search for sale does not return reports containing the word *sales*.

The results display on the Site Search Results page, as shown in Figure 26-8. When you click the name of the item found, a page containing its properties displays. To view the report, click the View In Browser link below the report title.

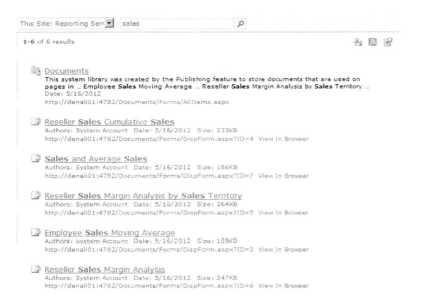

FIGURE 26-8 The Site Search Results page lists all content matching the search term.

Configuring Search in SharePoint

Because the search feature in SharePoint is not enabled by default and is independent of Reporting Services integration, you must complete several steps before users can search for reports. You must be a SharePoint farm administrator to enable search. For in-depth information about this feature, refer to the topic "Create and Configure a New Search Service Application" at *http://technet.microsoft.com/en-us/library/gg502597.aspx*.

In SharePoint's Central Administration, click the Manage Service Applications link in the Applications Management section. Click the New button on the ribbon, and click Search Service Application. At minimum, assign a name, select a service account for the Search service, select service accounts to use as application pool identities for the Search Admin Web Service and for the Search Query And Site Settings Web Service, and create new application pools or select existing application pools for these two web services.

If the Search service already exists, click the new service application in the Manage Service Applications page in Central Administration, and note the default content access account. You must give this account Read permission to any SharePoint site in which reports exist so that they can be indexed. More information about granting Read permission is available in Chapter 24.

Click Content Sources in the navigation pane on the left side of the screen, and then click Local SharePoint Sites if you want to enable search for all sites on your server. As an alternative, you can create a new content source here if you prefer to focus the search on specific sites. Either way, you can edit the content source to define the start addresses for crawling. You also define the crawl schedules on this page. If reports are deployed to the report server between crawl schedules, the new reports do not appear in a search results list. A full explanation of content crawling is beyond the scope of this book, but you can find more information at "Manage Crawling (SharePoint Server 2010)" at *http://technet.microsoft.com/en-us/library/ ee792876.aspx*.

Using the SharePoint Report Viewer

The SharePoint Report Viewer, as shown in Figure 26-9, includes all the same functionality for controlling the display of the report as the HTML Viewer that you use in Report Manager. However, arrangement of features is different, and the toggle to show or hide the parameters is not included on the toolbar. Parameters appear in a pane that displays on the right side of the screen, while the document map appears on the left side of the screen as it does in Report Manager. If your document does not contain a document map or parameters, the applicable pane does not display on the screen.

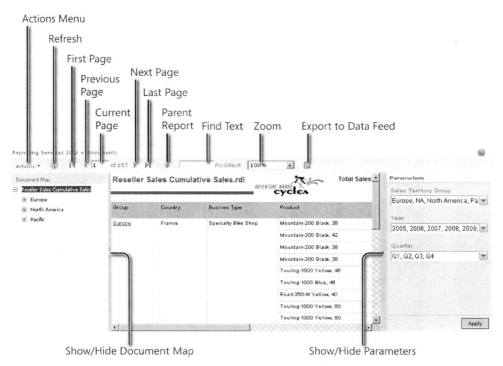

FIGURE 26-9 You use the SharePoint Report Viewer to interact with the report.

Note Notice that the report name in Figure 26-9 includes the RDL file extension because the text box uses the built-in field *ReportName*. A native-mode report server ignores the file extension, but a SharePoint integrated-mode report server does not. Therefore, to use the same report in both environments, you should consider creating an expression to remove the final four characters of the report name when these characters are ".rdl".

The SharePoint Report Viewer includes the following functions for managing the report view:

- **Actions Menu**   This menu accesses the following commands: Open With Report Builder, New Data Alert, Subscribe, Print, and Export. You learn about data alerts in Chapter 28, "Data alerting," subscriptions in Chapter 27, and exports in the "Exporting reports" section later in this chapter. The Print command opens the same Print dialog box described in the "Printing a report" section earlier in this chapter.

- **Refresh**   Use this button to reload the report definition and re-execute the dataset queries.

- **First Page**   Use this button to jump to the beginning of the report when viewing any page other than the first page.

- **Previous Page**   Use this button to open the previous page of the report when viewing any page other than the first page.

- **Current Page**   Type a page number in this text box, and press Enter to jump to the specified page. Afterwards, you can view a different page of the report by using HTML Viewer buttons to page forward or backward, to jump to the first page or last page of the report, or to jump to a specific page.

- **Next Page**   Use this button to open the next page of the report when viewing any page other than the last page.

- **Last Page**   Use this button to jump to the last page of the report when viewing any page other than the last page.

- **Parent Report**   This button is available when you use the drillthrough action in one report (known as the parent report) to open a second report. Use this button to return to the parent report.

- **Find Text**   Type a search string, and click the Find link to find and highlight the first instance of the string following the current position in the report. Click the Next link to find each subsequent instance of the string. If you click the Next link after the last instance has been displayed, a message box displays the message, "The entire report has been searched." The Find and Next links are disabled when the Find Text text box is empty.

- **Zoom** Select any of the following options in the drop-down list to reduce or enlarge the size of the report: Page Width, Whole Page, 500%, 200%, 150%, 75%, 50%, 25%, or 10%.

- **Export To Data Feed** Use this button to create a data feed document to import data into a Microsoft PowerPivot for Excel workbook or to share as part of a data feed service.

- **Show/Hide Document Map** Use this button to toggle the display of the document map, if one exists for the report.

- **Show/Hide Parameters** Use this button to toggle the display of the parameters, if any exist for the report.

Creating a dashboard

You can combine multiple reports on a single page by creating a dashboard. A *dashboard* in Share-Point is a special type of report that includes several Web Parts that you can configure to display a Reporting Services report, a Microsoft Office Excel spreadsheet, or other items. The Business Intelligence Center site collection type includes a document library for dashboards that you can use to store dashboards, although you can add the Web Part Page or Web Part Page With Status List content type to a document library that you create instead.

Create a Web Part page

You can create a new dashboard by opening a document library having the Web Part Page content type, clicking the New Document arrow button in the ribbon, and selecting one of the Web Part Page content types. You then give the dashboard a name and select a layout option. Then the Web Part page opens in edit mode, ready for you to add reports and other content types as Web Parts. When the dashboard is in edit mode, you can see multiple zones on the page, such as Top Left Zone, Middle Left Zone, or Header, Left Column, Footer, and so on. Each zone can contain one or more Web Parts. Empty zones do not display in the published dashboard page.

Add a SQL Server Reporting Services Report Viewer Web Part

Choose a zone for your report, and then click the Add A Web Part link. A list of Web Part categories displays at the top of the page for you to browse. Scroll down if necessary, and then click the SQL Server Reporting folder. Click SQL Server Reporting Services Report Viewer in the Web Parts list, and click Add. At this point, the Web Part displays in the dashboard, as shown in Figure 26-10, but is not yet associated with a specific report. A message containing instructions displays until you configure the Web Part correctly.

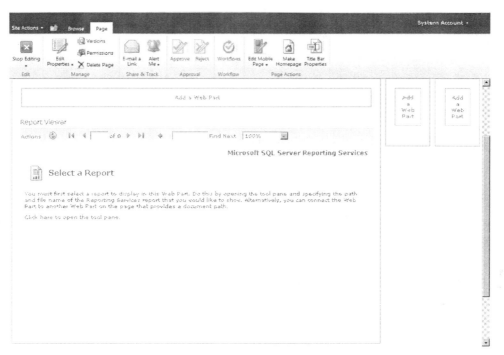

FIGURE 26-10 After you add the Report Viewer Web Part to the dashboard, you must select a report to display in the Web Part.

Configure the Web Part

To configure the Web Part to display a specific report, click the Click Here To Open The Tool Pane link. The Report Viewer tool pane displays at the right side of the browser. You might need to scroll horizontally and then scroll to the top of the page to see the tool pane.

You use the tool pane to select a report, to configure parameter default values if applicable, and to configure the appearance and layout properties of the Web Part. For example, you can change the height and width of the Web Part from its default size of 400 x 400 pixels. The View and Parameters sections of the tool pane can be expanded by clicking the arrows to the right of the section name, and the Appearance, Layout and Advanced sections of the tool pane can be expanded by clicking the plus sign to the left of the section name.

To select a report, click the ellipsis button to the right of the Report text box. A list of reports in the current document library displays, or you can navigate to a different document library if necessary. You can click OK to apply the selection and close the tool pane if you want to keep the default settings for the Web Part.

To reopen the tool pane after you add a report to the Web Part, click the down arrow in the top-right corner of the Web Part and select Edit Web Part, as shown in Figure 26-11. The other sections in the tool pane that you might consider changing include the Web Part title or the toolbar buttons to display in the Web Part that you set in the View section, parameter defaults in the Parameters section, and height and width of the Web Part in the Appearance section. You can make changes to settings and then click the Apply button to keep the tool pane open while you observe the effect your changes have on the Web Part.

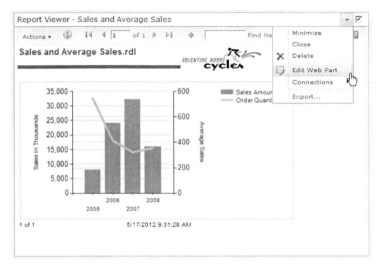

FIGURE 26-11 You can reopen the Web Part's tool pane by selecting Edit Web Part from its drop-down menu in the top-right corner.

In the View section of the tool pane, you can change the following settings:

- **Auto-Generate Web Part Title** This selection overrides the text that you enter in the Title box in the Appearance section of the tool pane. You must clear this selection if you want to supply your own title for the Web Part. Otherwise, the Web Part displays a title constructed from the concatenation of static text, "Report Viewer – ", and the report name.

- **Auto-Generate Web Part Title Link** This selection adds a hyperlink to the Web Part title to open the report in its own browser page using the SharePoint report viewer. You cannot test this link when editing the dashboard page. It works only when you are viewing the dashboard in Browse mode.

- **Show Report Builder Menu Item** The Web Part includes an Action menu that includes the Open With Report Builder command. Clear this selection if you do not want users to open the report in Report Builder from the dashboard page. If you keep this selection, users can edit the report and save a version of the report in their own document library without affecting the version that displays in the dashboard.

- **Show New Data Alert Menu Item** The Web Part's Action menu includes a New Data Alert command so that users can create a personal data alert to receive a notification when data matches specified criteria. Clear this selection if you prefer not to enable this feature in the dashboard.

- **Show Subscription Menu Item** This selection includes the Subscribe command in the Action menu of the Web Part for users to create a personal subscription to the report on a scheduled basis. Clear this selection to remove the command from the menu.

- **Show Print Menu Item**   The Action menu of the Web Part includes the Print command by default to allow users to print the report. You can remove this command from the menu by clearing the selection.

- **Show Export Menu Item**   The Web Part's Action menu also includes the Export menu for users to export the report into Excel, PDF, or other formats. You can clear this selection to prevent users from exporting the report from the dashboard.

- **Show Refresh Button**   By default, the Web Part's toolbar includes a Refresh button for the user to reload the report definition and re-execute the dataset queries. You can remove this button from the toolbar by clearing this selection.

- **Show Page Navigation Controls**   The Web Part's toolbar includes the First Page, Previous Page, Next Page, and Last Page buttons and the Current Page box to allow users to navigate from page to page in a report. If the report contains only a single page, you should consider clearing this selection to remove the controls from the toolbar.

- **Show Back Button**   This selection displays the Back button (also known as the Parent Report button) in the Web Part's toolbar. This button is disabled unless the user views a report after using a drillthrough action from its parent report. You can clear this selection to remove the Back button from the toolbar.

- **Show Find Controls**   This selection displays the Find text box and the Find and Next links in the Web Part's toolbar. For a single page report, you might consider clearing this selection to remove these items from the toolbar.

- **Show Zoom Control**   This selection adds the Zoom drop-down list to the Web Part's toolbar for the user to reduce or enlarge the size of the report. Clear this selection if you prefer not to support this feature in the Web Part.

- **Show ATOM Feed Button**   The Web Part includes the ATOM Feed button (also known as the Export To Data Feed button) on the toolbar by default. You can remove it by clearing this selection.

- **Toolbar Location**   By default, the toolbar displays above the report in the Web Part. Your other option is to display it below the report.

- **Prompt Area**   If the report has parameters, you can choose whether the parameter displays when the user first opens the dashboard page or you can hide it altogether. You can choose one of the following options for this setting: Displayed, Collapsed, or Hidden.

- **Document Map**   Like parameters, you can choose whether the document map displays (if one exists in the report) when the user first opens the dashboard page or stays hidden. You can choose one of the following options for this setting: Displayed, Collapsed, or Hidden.

- **Document Map Area Width**   If the report has a document map and you select Displayed or Collapsed for the Document Map setting, you can specify the width of the document map area. The default is 200 pixels.

- **Asynchronous Rendering**   Select this option to render the Report Viewer Web Part independently of other elements on the dashboard page. That way, if the report renders slowly, the remainder of the dashboard displays without interruption.

- **Ping Server To Maintain Session**   Select this option when you want the Report Viewer Web Part to ping the report server to keep a user session active. The user session preserves information about the current report, such as the parameter selection and visibility state of report items. This option is usually necessary only when a report takes a long time to execute.

If your report contains parameters, you can change the parameter selections in the tool pane. Expand the Parameters section, and click the Load Parameters button to retrieve the parameter list for the report. You can then select the Override Report Default option for any parameter and type a new value, or you can select a value from the parameter drop-down list, as shown in Figure 26-12.

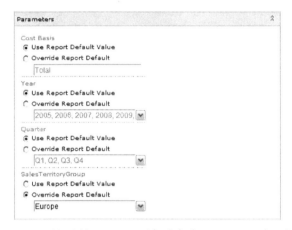

FIGURE 26-12 You can override default parameter values in the report by making a new selection in the tool pane.

In the Appearance section of the tool pane, you can set more general Web Part properties controlling its appearance. Here you can set the following options:

- **Title**   The default title is auto-generated, but you can clear the Auto-Generate Web Part Title check box in the View section of the tool pane and type your own title here.

- **Height**   You can assign a fixed height to the Web Part or allow the dashboard page to adjust the height automatically within the space allocated to the zone containing the Web Part. The default setting is a fixed height of 400 pixels.

- **Width**   You can assign a fixed width to the Web Part or allow the dashboard page to adjust the width automatically within the Web Part zone. The default setting is automatic adjustment.

- **Chrome State**   By default, this setting is Normal, which displays the entire Web Part when the user opens the dashboard page. You can change this setting to Minimized, in which case the user sees only the title bar and must expand the Web Part to see its contents.

- **Chrome Type**   This setting controls whether the title bar and border of the Web Part displays. You can choose the following settings: Default, None, Title and Border, Title Only, and Border Only. These settings rely on Cascading Style Sheets (CSS) to define the appearance of these elements.

Note   You can adjust more settings in the Layout and Advanced sections of the tool pane. These settings are common to all SharePoint Web Parts. You can learn more about at these settings at *http://office.microsoft.com/en-us/sharepoint-foundation-help/change-the-appearance-of-a-web-part-HA101790461.aspx.*

You can continue adding Web Parts to the dashboard page, and you can remove unwanted Web Parts. When you finish, your next step is to publish the page. On the toolbar above the dashboard page, click Stop Editing to make the dashboard page available to all users, similar to the one shown in Figure 26-13.

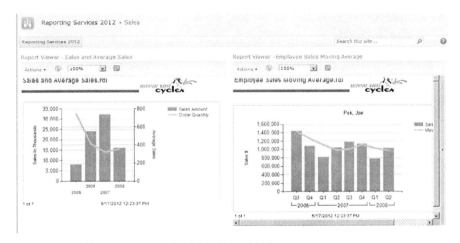

FIGURE 26-13 You can create a simple dashboard with reports.

More Info   There are many features that you can use in a SharePoint dashboard in SharePoint Server 2010, but these features are beyond the scope of this book. You can learn more about creating SharePoint dashboards and using other SharePoint business intelligence features by reading "Getting Started: Introduction to the Business Intelligence Center" at *http://office2010.microsoft.com/en-us/sharepoint-server-help/getting-started-introduction-to-the-business-intelligence-center-HA101809949.aspx.*

Native-mode Web Parts

You can incorporate Reporting Services reports into a SharePoint dashboard even if you are running a native-mode report server. To do this, you must install the SharePoint 2.0 Web Parts Report Explorer and Report Viewer by copying the RSWebParts.cab file from the Program Files (x86)\Microsoft SQL Server\110\Tools\Reporting Services\SharePoint folder to a folder on your SharePoint server. For example, let's say you place this file in the C:\cab folder. Then you can either use a SharePoint Management PowerShell script or the Stsadm.exe tool to install the Web Parts.

To use Windows PowerShell, open the SharePoint 2010 Management Shell using administrator privileges and run the following command:

```
Install-SPWebPartPack -LiteralPath "C:\cab\RSWebParts.cab" -GlobalInstall
```

To use Stsadme.exe, open a command prompt window using administrator privileges and run the following command:

```
STSADM.EXE -o addwppack -filename "C:\cab\RSWebParts.cab" -globalinstall
```

After the Web Parts install successfully, you can use them in a dashboard, as shown in Figure 26-14. When you edit a dashboard page, click Add A Web Part and locate the Web Parts in the Miscellaneous category. You can use the Report Viewer Web Part alone to display a specific report. Open the tool pane by opening the Web Part's drop-down menu and clicking Edit Web Part. In the Report Manager URL box, type the URL for Report Manager, such as *http://<servername>/Reports*. In the Report Path box, type the folder path and report name. For example, if you have a report called *Sales and Average Sales* in the *Sales* folder, type **/Sales/Sales** and **Average Sales**. You have the following options for toolbar size in the Web Part: None, Small, and Full. The small toolbar includes only the page navigation controls, whereas the Full toolbar is the entire HTML Viewer toolbar.

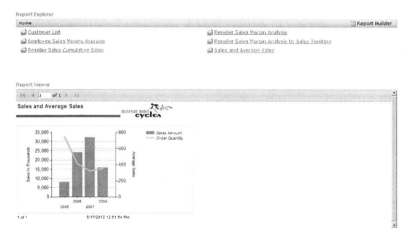

FIGURE 26-14 You can use SharePoint 2.0 Web Parts Report Explorer and Report Viewer to use native-mode reports in a SharePoint dashboard.

You can use the Report Explorer Web Part to display the contents of the native-mode report server. In the tool pane, set the Report Manager URL. By default, the Report Explorer displays the folders and reports available to the user on the Home page. If you prefer, you can display contents in a specific folder by providing a start path. For example, you can display the reports in the Sales folder by using */Sales* as the start path. You can choose Detail or List as the view mode, which corresponds to Details View or Tiles View in Report Manager, respectively.

If you like, you can connect the two Web Parts so that the user can see a selected report in the Report Viewer Web Part when clicking a link in the Report Explorer Web Part. To do this, click the arrow in the top-right corner of the Report Explorer Web Part, point to Connections, point to Show Report In, and then click Report Viewer.

Exporting reports

Online report access is a common way to provide information to a wide variety of users, but sometimes users need to view information when they are disconnected from the network or when they want to use the information in different ways. They might need to share information from a report in an email, or they might want to analyze report data by using a spreadsheet. Users might want to use a report as a mechanism for retrieving corporate data that they then can import into a document for rich formatting. They might want to share report information in a print-ready paginated file, or they might simply need access to raw data to import into another application. Reporting Services includes seven different rendering formats as alternatives to the online HTML format used to display reports. In this section, you learn the differences between these formats and how some report design features are more compatible with certain formats than with others.

Using soft page-break renderers

Reporting Services can render a report as a document that retains as much of the report layout as possible. This type of rendering, known as *soft page-break rendering,* is useful when users interact with the report onscreen rather than print the document. There are three rendering extensions that use soft page-break rendering: Excel, Word, and MIME Encapsulation of Aggregate HTML Documents (MHTML).

Excel format

Many users like to export data into Excel to perform analysis with added formulas or to combine the data with information from other sources. This output format, using a file extension of XLSX, is compatible with Excel 2007 and higher versions. You can also use it with Excel 2003 if you install the Microsoft Office Compatibility Pack for Word, Excel, and PowerPoint.

Note The rendering extension to support Excel 2003 natively is also available but disabled by default. You can modify the RsReportServer.config file to enable it.

The Excel renderer creates a range of cells for data regions, subreports, rectangles, and the report body itself. However, it creates a single cell for each text box, chart, sparkline, data bar, gauge, indicator, map, and image. To do this, the renderer might merge multiple cells together to contain these items, depending on where other report items requiring a range of cells appear in the report in relation to the single-cell report items.

Tip This automatic merging of multiple cells is a common problem for reports that you export to Excel and requires the report developer to take care to align report item edges in the report where possible.

Note The Excel workbook contains only images for charts, sparklines, data bars, gauges, indicators, and maps and provides no access to the underlying data if the report does not include that data in another data region.

Background images for report items are not supported in Excel and are consequently eliminated. However, if you use a background image for the body of the report, the renderer assigns it as the worksheet background image.

Formatting in the report is preserved in the worksheet wherever possible. If a report contains only soft page breaks, all data is rendered to a single worksheet in the Excel file. However, explicit page breaks in the report definition produce one worksheet per page. If you configure unique page names in the report, as described in Chapter 15, "Managing the page layout," the renderer assigns the applicable page name as the worksheet name. If you set up only an initial page name without configuring names for subsequent page breaks, the renderer appends a unique number to the initial page name to use as each worksheet name.

Each worksheet contains the page header items in the cells of the top rows, except for the document map cover worksheet if it exists. However, page footer items move to the Excel footer section. The renderer includes only text boxes in the page footer. If the text in the page footer exceeds 256 characters, the renderer truncates the text.

If your report includes a document map, the first worksheet in the file includes the document map links, as shown in Figure 26-15, which you can then use to jump to the target location in the worksheet containing the report data. Other interactive features, such as the hyperlink and bookmark actions, are also supported in the Excel version of the report.

FIGURE 26-15 The Excel renderer generates a cover worksheet for a document map.

The rendering process converts the hidden rows in the report into Excel outlines. The renderer supports a maximum of 7 levels in outline. You can click the row level button, as shown in Figure 26-16, to expand or collapse a level in the outline.

Row Level

FIGURE 26-16 Use the row level buttons to expand a level in Excel.

Document maps and visibility settings are not the only interactive features available in the Excel workbook. Other interactive features that the Excel renderer preserves includes explicit hyperlinks as well as hyperlinks generated for drillthrough reports and bookmarks. However, interactive sort is not supported.

All data that you see in the worksheet has been converted from expressions to a constant value. If your report uses conditional formatting to change properties such as font color, the font color displays correctly in Excel but it does not become a conditional formatting rule in the worksheet.

Note You can modify Excel rendering behavior by updating the device information settings in the RSReportServer.config file. Specifically, you can render the page header as an Excel header rather than as rows in each worksheet. In that case, the Excel header includes only text boxes from the report's page header up to a maximum of 256 characters. You can also exclude document maps and formulas from rendering. For more information, see *http://msdn.microsoft.com/en-us/library/ms155069.aspx*.

Word format

You can easily create a Microsoft Office Word document that presents data from your organization's databases by exporting a report to Word. The exported file has a file extension of DOCX and is compatible with Word 2007 and higher versions. You can also use it with Word 2003 if you install the Microsoft Office Compatibility Pack for Word, Excel, and PowerPoint.

Note If you require the Word 2003 rendering extension, you can modify the RsReportServer.config file to enable it.

After you export the report to Word, as shown in Figure 26-17, you can then enhance it with additional information or modify the formatting. Interactive features such as hyperlinks and actions are preserved after export, but unlike an Excel file, the ability to use a document map or toggle the visibility of items is not preserved. The detail rows in a report are visible only if you expanded a group in the online report before exporting to Word. There is no way to expand the group rows after export. Likewise, Word does not support interactive sort and displays the report using the sort applied at the time of export.

If your report contains a document map, the Word renderer creates Word Table of Contents (TOC) labels using the document map label text. The renderer does not build the TOC for you, but you can use the References tab of the Word ribbon to create one.

The page header and page footer in the report are converted to a header and footer in the document, but the *Height* property for each of these items is not converted. Otherwise, the Word document uses the same page size settings as defined in the report for the body and margins.

Note The maximum width of a report that Word supports is 22 inches.

Report items render as nested items inside a Word table. Both a text box and a rectangle render as a single cell inside the table. Like Excel, the Word document also includes a single cell for to hold a static image for each chart, sparkline, data bar, gauge, indicator, map, and image. The Word document includes most images found in the report definition, such as a logo, but excludes the background images in the report body or the report.

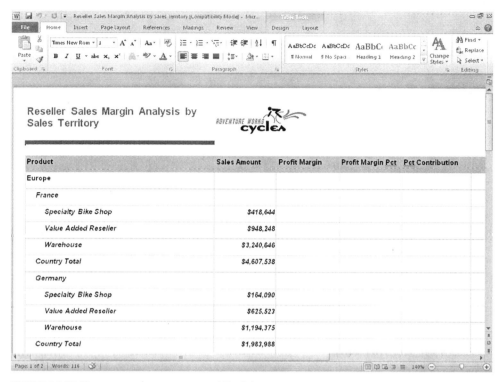

FIGURE 26-17 You can render a report as a Word document.

Note There are a few changes you can make to the RSReportServer.config file to change the Word rendering extension's default behavior. For example, you can automatically expand groups to display hidden items. You can also change the autofit behavior or always exclude hyperlinks and drillthrough actions. For more information, see *http://msdn.microsoft.com/en-us/library/cc281123.aspx*.

MHTML format

When you access a report online by using Report Manager or the SharePoint Report Viewer, the report is rendered as HTML by default and all interactive features in the report definition are supported. An HTML report might have multiple pages if explicit page breaks have been defined or if the HTML rendering extensions inserts soft page breaks to improve the viewing of large reports. When you want to save a multipage report as a one-page HTML file or embed it as a single page into an email message, you can export the report as a web archive file to save the report as an MHTML file, as shown in Figure 26-18.

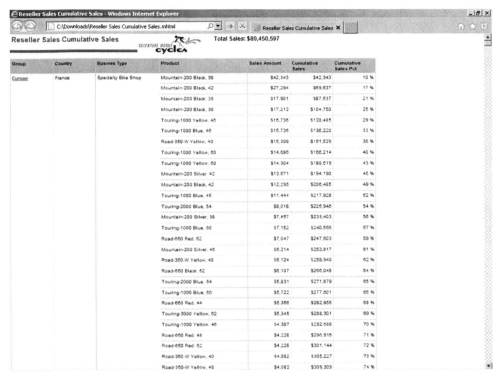

FIGURE 26-18 You can preserve multiple pages as a single-page HTML file by using the MHTML export format.

The exported file does not include the interactive features to expand or collapse the rows as is possible in Report Manager or the SharePoint Report Viewer. If you want to display the hidden rows in the exported file, you must toggle the desired items manually to display them in the report before exporting the report.

> **Note** You can change the rendering behavior of HTML and MHTML reports. One change you can make is the consolidation of charts, gauges, indicators, and maps as a single image to improve rendering performance. Another change is the method used to fit nested data visualization items, from Approximate to Exact, which could adversely affect rendering performance but improve the layout. You can also change a setting to improve the appearance of a report when opening it in Outlook. For more information about these settings and several other options, see *http://msdn.microsoft.com/en-us/library/ms155395.aspx*.

Using hard page-break renderers

For offline viewing in a print-ready format, you can save a report as a Tagged Image File Format (TIFF) or PDF file. When designing reports that will be primarily accessed by users in one of these printable formats, you should be sure to set correctly the report size properties *Width* and *Height* and the margin properties *Left*, *Right*, *Top*, and *Bottom*.

PDF format

It is not necessary to have Adobe Reader to export a report to this format, but you must have it installed on your computer to view the exported report. The report renders what you see online when you export the report. That is, report items in a hidden state are not visible in the PDF file and you cannot toggle their visibility in the PDF file. You also cannot use interactive sort, bookmarks, and drillthrough in the PDF. However, explicit hyperlinks in the report are supported.

The PDF renderer also supports the document map feature, as shown in Figure 26-19, which is useful for large reports. Each group label renders as a separate bookmark in the PDF file, which you use by opening the Bookmarks pane. The report might be difficult to read at this resolution, but you can use the magnification button or change the zoom percentage to increase the resolution for a more legible report.

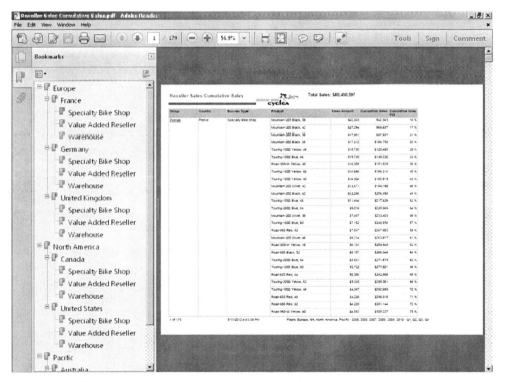

FIGURE 26-19 The PDF format preserves the document map as bookmarks.

 Important The fonts used in the report must exist on the report server to render correctly in the PDF file. The renderer replaces missing fonts with a box character. You cannot rely on testing PDF rendering from the report development computer. You must test rendering after deploying the report to the report server and then exporting the report to the PDF format.

> **Note** You can customize the PDF rendering behavior if necessary. Some of the changes you can make include adjusting the dots-per-inch (DPI) settings, the first page of the report to render, and overrides for report margins, page height, and page width. For more information, see *http://msdn.microsoft.com/en-us/library/ms154682.aspx*.

TIFF format

You can render a report as a multiple-page image file in the TIFF format, as shown in Figure 26-20. As an alternative, you can use the TIFF rendering extension to render a report one page at a time in any of the following formats that Windows Graphics Device Interface Plus (GDI+) supports:

- Bitmap image file (BMP)
- Enhanced Metafile (EMF)
- Enhanced Metafile Format Plus Extensions (EMFPlus)
- Graphics Interchange Format (GIF)
- Joint Photographic Experts Group (JPEG)
- Portable Network Graphics (PNG)

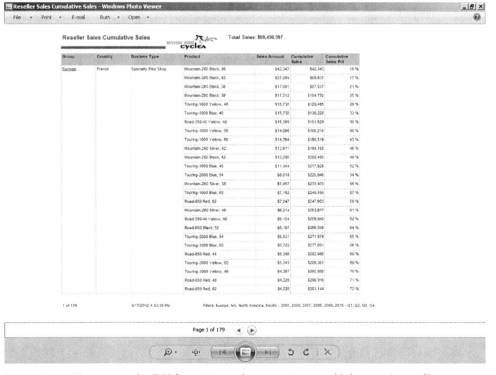

FIGURE 26-20 You can use the TIFF format to render a report as a multiple-page image file.

The TIFF renderer supports none of the interactive features. To see hidden items in the rendered image file, you must toggle the display before the export. Likewise, you must change the default sort by using the interactive sort feature (if the report has it) before the export.

> **Note** Customization options for the TIFF rendering extension are similar to those available for the PDF rendering extension. To learn more, see *http://msdn.microsoft.com/en-us/library/ms155373.aspx*.

Exporting a report for data exchange

Some users simply want the raw data in a Comma Separated Values (CSV) format to import into a spreadsheet or other analytical application. Or your organization might want to provide information in Extensible Markup Language (XML) format, such as a purchase order or sales invoice, for integration into a partner's business processes. Another option is to use the ATOM format to render a report as a data feed, which you might use when you want to import data into a Microsoft PowerPivot for Excel workbook. For these formats, the export file contains only data and excludes all the formatting that makes a report more readable for users.

CSV format

When you export a report to a CSV file, the Reporting Services rendering extension converts the report data to the lowest level of detail with a comma delimiter between each field and a carriage return and line feed at the end of each record. It includes all detail rows, including those that are hidden if they can be toggled to a visible state. A header row in the file provides the names of each column. If a text string contains a comma delimiter or if the value includes a line break, the output includes a quotation mark at the beginning and end of the text string as a text qualifier. The text qualifier is doubled if the original text string also includes quotation marks.

Because the CSV format exports only data, the new file does not include the page header, page footer, lines, images, rectangles, or custom report items. It also ignores any totals calculated by using expressions in a group or tablix footer. Furthermore, interactive features are ignored, including hyperlinks, visibility settings, the document map, actions, interactive sort settings, and fixed headers.

Each item in the report renders as a separate group of rows and columns in the output file, as shown in Figure 26-21. Each report item type has its own rendering behavior, as follows:

- **Freestanding text box**   A freestanding text box renders with a column header and a row value of its contents.

- **Table**   A table includes a row and column at the lowest level of detail it contains, which is not necessarily the level of detail visible in the report. Total rows or columns in footers are not included.

- **Matrix**   A matrix includes a row and column at the lowest level of detail it contains, which is not necessarily the level of detail visible in the report. Total rows or columns in footers are not included.

- **List**   A list includes a row for each detail row or group instance it contains. If the list contains nested items, the parent group instance value repeats in each row of the nested item.

- **Subreport**   If the subreport is nested inside another report item, the parent item values repeat for each row of the subreport contents.

- **Chart**   A chart includes a row for each combination of value and category, typically represented as a single data point in the chart. If the chart contains multiple series, the label for each series is included in the rows preceding the value for that series. Data bars and sparklines have the same rendering behavior but do not include series labels.

- **Gauge**   A gauge includes a single row containing the scale's minimum and maximum values, the range's start and end values, and the pointer value.

- **Indicator**   An indicator includes a single row with the current indicator state, available states, and the indicator value.

- **Map**   A map includes a row for each spatial data value and its corresponding label.

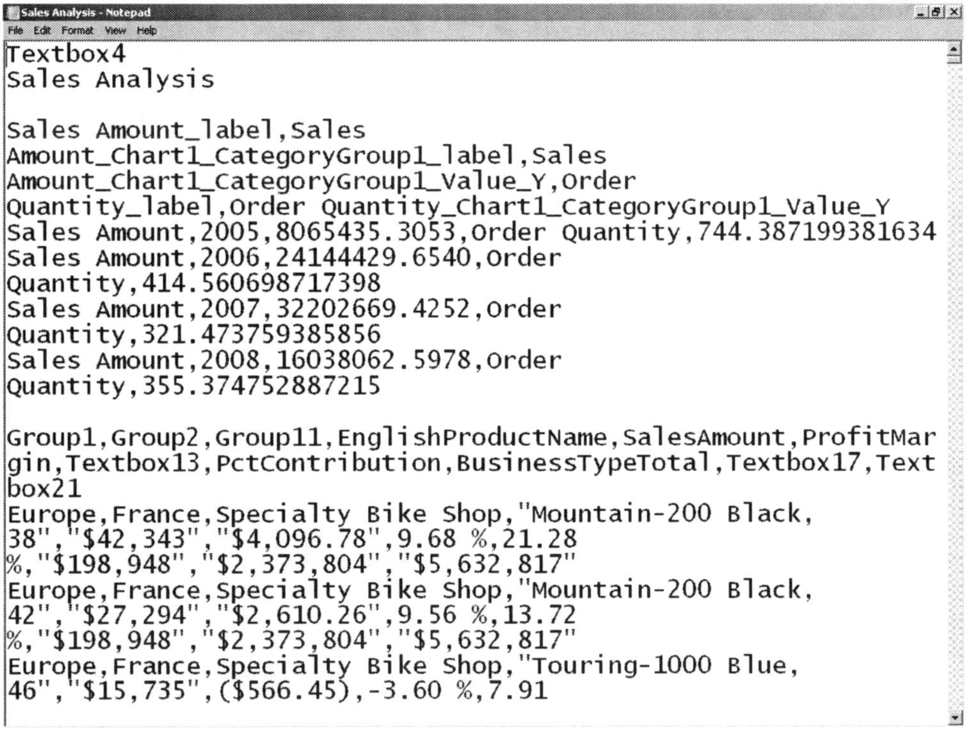

```
Sales Analysis - Notepad
File  Edit  Format  View  Help
Textbox4
Sales Analysis

Sales Amount_label,Sales
Amount_Chart1_CategoryGroup1_label,Sales
Amount_Chart1_CategoryGroup1_Value_Y,Order
Quantity_label,Order Quantity_Chart1_CategoryGroup1_Value_Y
Sales Amount,2005,8065435.3053,Order Quantity,744.387199381634
Sales Amount,2006,24144429.6540,Order
Quantity,414.560698717398
Sales Amount,2007,32202669.4252,Order
Quantity,321.473759385856
Sales Amount,2008,16038062.5978,Order
Quantity,355.374752887215

Group1,Group2,Group11,EnglishProductName,SalesAmount,ProfitMar
gin,Textbox13,PctContribution,BusinessTypeTotal,Textbox17,Text
box21
Europe,France,Specialty Bike Shop,"Mountain-200 Black,
38","$42,343","$4,096.78",9.68 %,21.28
%,"$198,948","$2,373,804","$5,632,817"
Europe,France,Specialty Bike Shop,"Mountain-200 Black,
42","$27,294","$2,610.26",9.56 %,13.72
%,"$198,948","$2,373,804","$5,632,817"
Europe,France,Specialty Bike Shop,"Touring-1000 Blue,
46","$15,735",($566.45),-3.60 %,7.91
```

FIGURE 26-21 The CSV export separates data from each data region with a blank row.

When you export a report to the CSV format, the file opens by default in Excel if you have that program installed on your computer. To view the export file in Notepad or other text viewer, you must first save the file to disk and then open the file with the desired application.

In Figure 26-21, notice that the report title and the name of the text box containing the report title, Textbox4, display at the top of the file because all data is exported even if the data is not found within a data region. The fourth row of the file is the header row for the data region containing a chart. The data following the blank row after the chart data is for a tablix data region. Notice the quotation marks used as a text qualifier when a field contains an embedded comma, and notice the formatting of values in the tablix data region as compared to the lack of formatting of values in the chart data region.

Note You can override some rendering behavior for CSV output. For example, you can disable the setting for Excel optimization when you need strict CSV standards compliance, by returning the number of columns in each row and ignoring the formatting. You can also choose a different field delimiter, record delimiter, or text qualifier and choose a character encoding other than UTF-8, such as ASCII. You change these settings only at the report server level. For more information, see *http://msdn.microsoft.com/en-us/library/ms155365 .aspx*.

XML format

A report exported to XML format tags the hierarchical structure of the data, as shown in Figure 26-22. The names of report items in the report definition become XML elements in the exported file, so you should take care to rename report items rather than keep the default names (such as Textbox1). All detail rows are included, including hidden data if it can be toggled to a visible state. Each report item type has its own rendering behavior, as follows:

- **Report** The report is the top-level element in the XML file.

- **Freestanding text box** A freestanding text box renders as an attribute in the element of its parent container.

- **Data region and rectangle** In this context, a data region is a table, matrix, list, chart, data bar, or sparkline. Data regions and rectangles render as child elements of their parent containers. In a chart, each series is a child element of the chart.

- **Group and details** Each instance renders as child element of its parent data region. Group instances include both row groups and column groups.

- **Text box inside data region** A text box that is not freestanding renders as a child element of its parent data region.

- **Map** The map renders as a child element of its parent container. Each map layer renders as a child element of the map and includes elements for each spatial member.

- **Gauge** A gauge renders as an element of its parent container and renders the scale's minimum and maximum values, the range's start and end values, and the pointer value as attributes of the gauge element.

- **Indicator** An indicator renders as an element of its parent container and renders the current indicator state, available states, and the indicator value as attributes of the indicator element.

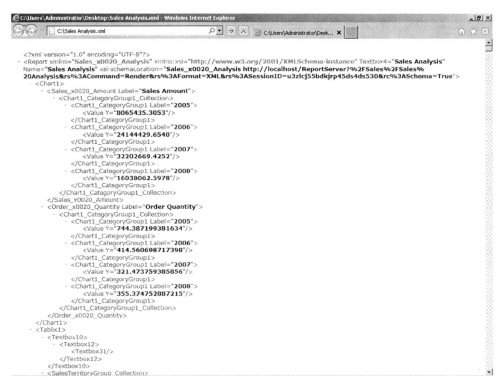

FIGURE 26-22 The XML export generates nodes for each data region.

> **Note** There are a few settings that you can change for the XML renderer. For example, you can require the renderer to produce formatted values where applicable or you can prevent the renderer from producing indented XML, among other settings. For more information, see *http://msdn.microsoft.com/en-us/library/ms154691.aspx*.

ATOM format

The ATOM renderer produces one or more data feeds that you can use with any client that consumes ATOM-compliant data feeds, such as PowerPivot for Excel. Each data region in the report becomes a separate data feed, and in some cases, a data region can render as multiple data regions. The export process produces an ATOM service document having a file extension of ATOMSVC. This document details the data feeds available to a client application, which in turn uses this information to request the data feeds.

The ATOM service document is an XML document. It describes each data feed in a collection element using a URL, as shown here:

```
<?xml version="1.0" encoding="utf-8" standalone="yes"?>

<service xmlns:atom="http://www.w3.org/2005/Atom" xmlns:app="http://www.w3.org/2007/app"
xmlns="http://www.w3.org/2007/app">
 <workspace>
  <atom:title>Sales Analysis</atom:title>
   <collection href="http://localhost/ReportServer?%2FSales%2FSales%20Analysis&amp;rs%3ACommand=
Render&amp;rs%3AFormat=ATOM&amp;rc%3AItemPath=Chart1.Chart1_CategoryGroup1">
    <atom:title>Chart1</atom:title>
   </collection>
   <collection href="http://localhost/ReportServer?%2FSales%2FSales%20Analysis&amp;rs%3ACommand=
Render&amp;rs%3AFormat=ATOM&amp;rc%3AItemPath=Tablix1">
    <atom:title>Tablix1</atom:title>
   </collection>
 </workspace>
</service>
```

The URL for each data feed is a render request using the URL access method for the web service, described in greater detail in Chapter 35, "Programming report access." The report server returns an XML document with an ATOM file extension. This file contains the report data using much the same rendering rules as those used by the CSV renderer. The values that appear as columns in the same row in a CSV file appear as separate child elements of an *entry* element, which represents one rowset.

FIGURE 26-23 The ATOM file contains one *entry* element for each rowset.

Tip To render the ATOM file to view its contents for yourself, you can replace the encoding of the URL that you see in the ATOMSVC document to produce a URL like this: *http://localhost/ReportServer?/Sales/Sales Analysis&rs:Command=Render&rs:Format=ATOM&rc:ItemPath=Chart1.Chart1_CategoryGroup1*. When you open this URL in your browser, the report server generates an ATOM file.

 Note You can change the rendering extension default to use an alternate character encoding instead of the default UTF-8 encoding. For more information, see *http://msdn.microsoft.com/en-us/library/ee210577.aspx*.

CHAPTER 27

Working with subscriptions

Rather than require users to connect to the report server to view reports, you can use Reporting Services to send reports to users via email or to a network folder. If you're running a report server in SharePoint integrated mode, you can also send reports to a Microsoft SharePoint document library. Regardless of which delivery method you use, you can send a report in any rendering format so that users can get reports when they want them and in the file type they want. Furthermore, you can send the subscription on a recurring schedule that you define for the report server and that can serve multiple uses (including snapshots) or that can be solely for a single report subscription.

Creating a shared schedule

A shared schedule makes it easier for anyone to assign a subscription to a schedule. You can edit the schedule for a subscription at any time. You can also pause all subscriptions associated with a schedule at one time whenever you need to perform server maintenance. When a schedule is no longer needed, you can delete it.

> **Tip** Your use of a shared schedule is not limited to subscriptions. You can also use shared schedules to generate a report snapshot, to expire the report cache, or to refresh a report cache.

Schedules list

You can view all schedules on your report server as a single list on the Schedules page. There is only one list of schedules on a native-mode report server, whereas a separate list exists for each SharePoint site for which you have enabled the Reporting Services integration feature. Use the following steps to open the list of schedules as applicable to your report server:

- **Native mode** In Report Manager, click the Site Settings link in the top-right corner, and then click the Schedules link on the left side of the page.

- **SharePoint integrated mode** In a SharePoint site, click Site Actions, select Site Settings, and select Modify All Site Settings. In the Reporting Services section, click the Manage Shared schedules link.

On this page, as shown in Figure 27-1, you can view the existing schedules for a native-mode report server, as long as you are a member of the System User or System Administrator role. The corresponding page in SharePoint is nearly identical, which requires you to have the Manage Alerts permission to view it. The schedule list shows you the name of the schedule, the frequency and execution time of the schedule, the creator (which does not display in SharePoint), the last time the schedule ran, the next time the schedule will run, and its current status. You can click any column header to sort the list by that column in ascending order, and then click it again to sort the list in descending order based on the selected column's value.

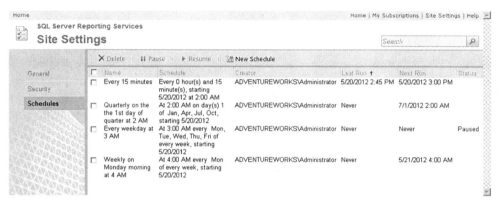

FIGURE 27-1 You can view shared schedules as a list on the Schedules page in the Site Settings section of Report Manager.

Note You cannot use the schedule list to see whether subscriptions, snapshots, or report caching are associated with a shared schedule. You must open the applicable report management page, such as its Subscriptions page, and edit the job to check its schedule assignment.

If you are a member of the System Administrator role or have Owner permissions in SharePoint, you can temporarily disable a subscription by selecting its check box in the schedules list and then clicking the Pause button in the Schedules toolbar. Its status changes to Paused, and the schedule execution does not occur at its designated frequency. Even when you pause a schedule, a user can select it from the list of shared schedules when creating a report job for background processing, such as a subscription. However, the report will not run as long as the schedule is in a paused state.

You can later resume a paused schedule by again selecting its check box and then clicking the Resume button on the toolbar. The Next Run date calculates the next date and time applicable to the schedule's frequency.

You can remove a subscription permanently by selecting its check box and clicking the Delete button. Any reports using this schedule continue using the same schedule, although the schedule is now specific to the report. If you need to make any subsequent changes to the schedule, you must edit the subscription directly.

New schedule

To add a new schedule, click the New Schedule button on the Schedules page if you are working in Report Manager. If you are working in SharePoint, click the Add Schedule button.

You must provide a name for the schedule, and then select one of the following frequencies: Hour, Day, Week, Month, or Once. The selection of schedule type determines the schedule options you can specify. For example, you can select specific days of the week, every weekday, or an interval of a specified number of days when you select a daily schedule, as shown in Figure 27-2.

FIGURE 27-2 You configure frequency options and optionally the start and end dates for a shared schedule.

Note The SharePoint schedule options are not identical to those available to a native-mode report server. For example, the Every Weekday option is not available in SharePoint for a daily schedule. In addition, the On Week Of Month option is not available in SharePoint for a monthly schedule.

You can change the Start Time to any time you like. The schedule begins running on the current date and continues indefinitely, unless you explicitly define a stop date by selecting the Stop This Schedule On check box in Report Manager or the Stop Running This Schedule On check box if you are creating a shared schedule on SharePoint. If you select this check box, you must provide a stop date by typing a date into the box or clicking the calendar icon to select a date by using a calendar control.

Creating standard subscriptions

A *standard subscription* is a subscription that delivers a specific report to a destination on a scheduled basis. By default, the Browser role (described in Chapter 24, "Securing report server content") gives users permission to manage individual subscriptions on a native-mode report server. On a SharePoint integrated-mode server, users must be in the Visitors group, which by default has the Create Alerts permission. These users can create, view, modify, and delete the subscriptions that they own. Users in the Content Manager role or Owners group can manage subscriptions created by anyone.

> **Important** The SQL Server Agent service must be running before you start creating a subscription. If the service is not running, an error message displays when you attempt to save the subscription settings.
>
> Each data source for the report must use stored credentials, as described in Chapter 24, before you create a subscription. Otherwise, an error message displays when you try to save the subscription.

New subscription

To send a report on a scheduled basis from a native-mode report server, you use Report Manager to create a subscription. Navigate to the folder containing the report. Point to the report name, and then click the down arrow that appears next to it to display the submenu, and then select Subscribe, as shown in Figure 27-3.

FIGURE 27-3 You use the report's submenu in Report Manager to open the Subscriptions page.

If your report is on SharePoint integrated-mode report server, you create a subscription by opening the document library containing the report. There you point to the report name, open its submenu by clicking the report's down arrow, and click Manage Subscriptions, as shown in Figure 27-4. On the Manage Subscriptions page, you click the Add Subscriptions link.

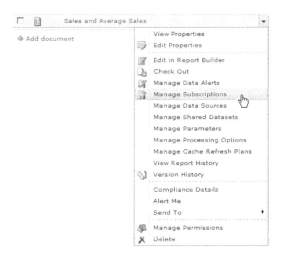

FIGURE 27-4 You use the report's submenu in a SharePoint document library to open the Subscriptions page.

Delivery providers

Reporting Services uses delivery providers to manage the process of sending a report from the report server to a designated destination. On a native-mode report server, you have two different options for sending reports on a recurring schedule, email and storage on a Windows file share. These two options are also available on a SharePoint integrated-mode report server, but that server environment also includes null delivery and a SharePoint document library as additional delivery providers. You can also develop or purchase third-party delivery extensions to provide additional delivery methods to users.

Email delivery

Recipients of a report created by an email subscription receive an identical copy of the report. When you define the subscription, you provide a list of recipients and specify the contents of the email. For example, you can specify whether the email includes the report as an attachment for offline viewing in addition to or instead of a link to the report on the report server. At a minimum, you can send just a notification that the report is ready for viewing on the report server. You then establish a schedule for the subscription by using either a schedule specific to the report or a global schedule established on the report server. If you want, you can override the report's default parameter values.

Important Before you can create an email subscription, Reporting Services requires you to specify a Simple Mail Transport Protocol (SMTP) server in the report server configuration settings. To do this for a native-mode report server using the Reporting Services Configuration Manager (described in Chapter 4, "Installing Reporting Services"), you configure the SMTP server address and an email address to use as the From: address. You do the same in the Manage Service Applications area of Central Administration on a SharePoint integrated-mode report server. If you skip the configuration, the email delivery option is not available when you try to create a subscription.

The content of the subscription page changes according to your selection of subscription delivery method. For an email subscription, you must at minimum specify one recipient of the email. If you choose to include the report in the email, you must specify a render format for the report, as shown in Figure 27-5 for a native-mode report server. The appearance of this page on a SharePoint integrated-mode server is very similar, although the order of fields differs somewhat.

FIGURE 27-5 You specify the recipients and report format for an email subscription.

When you select email as the delivery method, you specify the following report delivery options:

- **To** If you are a member of the Browser role on a native-mode report server or in the Visitors group on a SharePoint integrated-mode report server, you can create a subscription only for yourself and you cannot add other recipients to the subscription. In that case, your Microsoft Windows account displays in the To: text box and cannot be changed. If you are a member of the Content Manager role, you can create a subscription for recipients by adding one or more email addresses to this text box. Separate each email address with a semicolon (;).

Important Reporting Services does not validate the email address when you create the subscription.

- **Cc**   Use this text box to send a copy of the subscription email to designated recipients. You can add one or more email address to this text box if you are a Content Manager. It does not display if you are a member of the Browser role.

- **Bcc**   Use this text box to send a blind copy of the subscription email to one or more designated recipients. This text box displays only if you are a Content Manager.

- **Reply-To**   The subscription email from the report server uses the sender address that you configure for the report server (as described in Chapter 4). However, you can use this text box to provide an alternate reply-to email address to subscription recipients in case they have questions about the report. This text box displays only if you are a Content Manager.

- **Subject**   The default subject line of the email message is "@ReportName was executed at @ ExecutionTime." The report server replaces the @ReportName and @ExecutionTime placeholders with the actual report name and the background processing execution date and time. You can override this subject line with custom text.

- **Include Report (SharePoint: Show Report Inside Message)**   Select this check box to send a copy of the report as part of the email message. You use the Render Format setting to control whether the report server includes the report as an attachment or embeds it into the body of the email message. This option is useful when you need to send reports to recipients who have no access to the report server.

> **Tip** If you want to send the report as an attachment only, you select the Include Report check box and clear the Include Link check box. Conversely, if you want to send only a link to the report, you select the Include Link check box and clear the Include Report check box. You also can select these two check boxes to include both the report and the link, which is the default configuration for the email subscription.

- **Include Link (SharePoint: Include A Link To The Report)**   Select this check box to send a link to the report in the body of the email message. This option is useful when you want users to execute the report on the report server to view the most current data.

- **Render Format**   If you intend to send the report in the attachment, you must specify a render format. All the render formats available for export when viewing a report are also available for the email subscription. However, the MHTML (Web Archive) format is not sent as an attachment but is embedded into the body of the email message.

- **Priority**   You can choose one of the following options to set a priority for the email message: Normal, Low, or High.

- **Comment**   You can optionally include a comment to include in the body of the email message.

Windows file share delivery

Another commonly used method for sharing reports is to make them accessible on a Windows file share that you identify by using the Universal Naming Convention (UNC) for the folder. For example, you might store a PDF version of files on a web server for access by external users who do not have access to your internal network. A single copy of the report created by a Windows file share subscription is placed in the target location. You must configure the subscription to use a Windows account that has permissions to write to the target location. If you create a recurring subscription, you can specify whether an existing file on the file share is overwritten by the new file or if you want to append a number to the file name that automatically increments as each new file is added to the file share. Just as you do with email subscriptions, you define a schedule for Windows file share subscription by using a report-specific schedule or a shared schedule. You can also override the report's default parameter values, if you want.

Creating a Windows file share

Before you can create a subscription using the Windows File Share delivery method, you should create a Windows file share. You can successfully create a subscription without a valid file share location, but the subscription fails if the file share does not exist at the time of subscription processing.

To create a Windows file share, open Windows Explorer, navigate to the folder you want to share, right-click the folder, point to Share With, and then click Specific People. If the subscription is for yourself only, your account probably already has Read/Write or Owner permissions, so no further action is required.

If you want to use credentials other than your own when executing the report, you can select Find People in the drop-down list. In the Select Users Or Groups dialog box, click Advanced, and then click Find Now. In the Search Results list, double-click the name of the account, and click OK. In the Permission Level column for the newly added account, click the arrow next to Read, select Read/Write, and click Share.

When you specify the Windows File Share delivery extension for a subscription, the screen changes to prompt you for the settings specific to file shares, as shown in Figure 27-6 for a native-mode report server. The corresponding page for a SharePoint integrated-mode report server is very similar but arranges the fields in a different order.

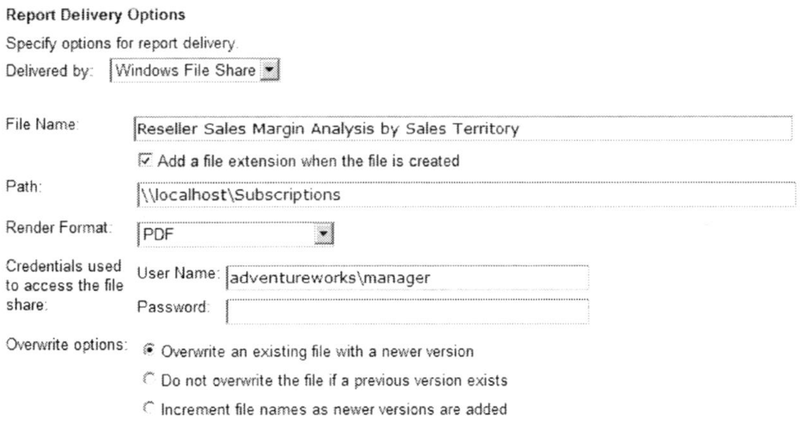

Report Delivery Options

Specify options for report delivery.

Delivered by: [Windows File Share ▾]

File Name:	[Reseller Sales Margin Analysis by Sales Territory]
	☑ Add a file extension when the file is created
Path:	[\\localhost\Subscriptions]
Render Format:	[PDF ▾]
Credentials used to access the file share:	User Name: [adventureworks\manager]
	Password: [ ]
Overwrite options:	⦿ Overwrite an existing file with a newer version
	○ Do not overwrite the file if a previous version exists
	○ Increment file names as newer versions are added

FIGURE 27-6 You specify the file share path, report format, and authorized credentials for a Windows file share subscription.

The Windows File Share delivery method requires you to specify the following report delivery options:

- **File Name**   The file name defaults to the name of the report, but you can change it to another name if you prefer.

- **Add A File Extension When The File Is Created (SharePoint: File Extension)**   In native mode, you select the check box to include the applicable file extension when the report server saves the report to the file share, while in SharePoint integrated mode, you select True for this setting. For example, if you create a subscription using Excel as the render format, the report server appends the file extension XLSX to the file name you specify on this page.

- **Path**   Here you type the name of the file share using the UNC naming convention. For example, if you have a file share called Subscriptions, you type **\\<*servername*>\Subscriptions**, replacing <*servername*> with the name of your server.

- **Render Format**   The same render formats are available for the Windows file share subscription as are available for the email subscription. There is also an additional render format called RPL Renderer, which is a special format that combines the report layout and the data in an intermediate format that can be used by the ReportViewer web server control.

- **User Name**   In the User Name text box, type the account name that has permissions to write to the designated file Share. Use the format *domain\user name* (or *servername\user name* if your computer is not part of a domain).

- **Password**   If you intend to create a report-specific schedule, you should leave the password blank until after you configure the schedule because the password disappears when you leave the current screen. Add the password just before you save the subscription settings.

- **Overwrite Options**   Choose Overwrite An Existing File With a Newer Version when you want to retain only one copy of a report at a time in the designated file share. You can protect an existing file on the file share by choosing Do Not Overwrite The File If A Previous Version Exists, but in that case, you must manually remove a report from the file share on a regular basis. As a third option, you can choose Increment File Names As Newer Versions Are Added to retain all copies of a report in the same file share until you are ready to move or delete them.

Null Delivery Provider

The Null Delivery Provider is available on a report server running in SharePoint integrated mode for standard or data-driven subscriptions, whereas it is available on a native-mode report server for data-driven subscriptions only. This delivery extension doesn't actually deliver a report; instead, it executes the report so that the report can be cached and ready for viewing on demand. By using this delivery extension, all your users can experience the benefits of a cached report, not just the users that view the report after someone else viewed it.

 Tip   As an alternative to using the Null Delivery Provider, you can create a Cache Refresh Plan for a report. The Cache Refresh Plan was introduced in SQL Server Reporting Services 2008 R2 as an alternative to the Null Delivery Provider for standard subscriptions only.

SharePoint Document Library

The SharePoint Document Library delivery extension is available only on a report server running in SharePoint integrated mode. It delivers a copy of the report to the specified document library, which must be on the same SharePoint site as the report on which the subscription is based. Because the report is a copy, the user experience might not be as fully interactive as the source report. If you have enabled versioning in the document library, the subscription always creates a major version of the report copy unless you specifically choose no versioning. If you limit the retention of versions, the oldest report version is removed with the newest subscription delivery.

When you select SharePoint Document Library as the delivery method, you configure the following subscription settings:

- **Document Library**   Here you type the full path of the document library, such as *http://<SharePointSite>/Documents*, replacing *<SharePointSite>* with the name of your SharePoint site. You can click the ellipsis button to open a dialog box that allows you to navigate through the SharePoint site and select the folder for the document library in which you want to save the report.

- **File Name**   The file name defaults to the name of the report, but you can change it to another name if you prefer.

- **Append File Extension To Name**   Select the check box to include the applicable file extension when the report server saves the report to the file share. For example, if you create a subscription using Excel as the render format, the report server appends the file extension XLSX to the file name that you specify on this page.

- **Title**   You can type a title for the report to store in the document properties.

- **Output Format**   You must specify one of the standard render formats. There is also an additional render format called RPL Renderer, which is a special format that combines the report layout and the data in an intermediate format that can be used by the ReportViewer web server control.

- **Overwrite Options**   Choose Overwrite Existing File Or Create New Version Of File when you want to retain only one copy of a report at a time in the designated document library. You can protect an existing file on the file share by choosing Do Not Overwrite File With A Newer Version, but in that case, you must manually remove a report from the document library on a regular basis. As a third option, you can choose Create A File With A Unique Name to retain all copies of a report in the same file share until you are ready to move or delete them.

Report parameter values

If your report has report parameters, you can specify the values to use when executing the report for the subscription, as shown in Figure 27-7. You can select the Use Default check box when you want the report to use the default report parameter values from the report definition. Otherwise, clear the check box and type the desired value in a text box, or select it from a list of available values.

FIGURE 27-7 You can change parameter values to use when the report subscription processes.

Subscription processing options

After you define the settings for the delivery provider, you select one of the following subscription processing options to define the schedule:

- **Report schedule (SharePoint: Custom schedule)**   A report schedule applies only to the subscription that you are creating. If you have several subscriptions, each with its own report schedule, any change that you might want to make to the schedules later requires you to open each subscription and modify the schedule settings. When you click the Select Schedule button, you have access to the same scheduling options that you have for a shared schedule (as described in the "Creating a shared schedule" section earlier in this chapter).

- **Shared schedule**   If you create a shared schedule, you can select it in the shared schedule drop-down list when you create a subscription. If you associate multiple subscriptions with the same shared schedule, you need only to change the settings of the shared schedule to update the schedule for all subscriptions.

- **Report snapshot creation**   On a SharePoint integrated-mode report server only, you also have the option to send a report to its destination on the same schedule that the report server uses to create a report snapshot, as described in Chapter 23, "Deploying reports to a server."

Creating data-driven subscriptions

A *data-driven subscription* is a subscription that delivers the same report to many destinations, each of which might receive a different render format of the report and a different set of parameter values on a recurring basis. The recurrence of a subscription can be defined by a schedule or by the creation of a report snapshot. As explained in Chapter 23, a report snapshot can be created manually or on a schedule.

You must be assigned to the Content Manager role (native mode) or the Owners group (SharePoint integrated mode) to configure a data-driven subscription. You must also have a relational table that stores the mapping between destinations (an email address or a file share), report settings, and parameter values. When you configure the data-driven subscription, you provide the query to this table and then assign the values in the query results to specific settings in the subscription configuration.

 Important To create a data-driven subscription, you must be using Microsoft SQL Server 2012 Enterprise Edition, SQL Server 2012 Business Intelligence Edition, or SQL Server 2012 Developer Edition.

Creating a subscription delivery table

Because Reporting Services does not include a table for you to use for storing subscription delivery information, you must create and maintain a table to use the data-driven subscription feature, such as the one shown in Figure 27-8. You can create a table that contains a single column of email addresses for the simplest data-driven subscription, or you can define columns for every subscription setting that can be changed by a value from this table. This flexibility allows you to manage customized subscriptions for individual users easily.

	SubscriptionType	ReportName	To	IncludeReport	RenderFormat	IncludeLink	ReportParameter1	ReportParameter2
1	email	Reseller Sales Margin Analysis by Sales Territory	EuropeMgr@adventureworks.com	1	Excel	1	Total	2012
2	email	Reseller Sales Margin Analysis by Sales Territory	PacificMgr@adventureworks.com	1	PDF	0	Cost	2011
3	fileshare	Sales and Average Sales	\\server01\Subscriptions	NULL	PDF	NULL		

FIGURE 27-8 You must create a table containing columns for data-driven subscription settings.

When you create the subscription delivery table, you can assign different render formats and the default report parameters for recipients. Also, you can add an IncludeLink column to determine whether the user can click a link in the email message to open the report on the web server. When you create a data-driven subscription later, you map the data in this table to specific subscription settings.

Configuring data-driven subscription settings

When you create a standard subscription as described earlier in this chapter, you set the subscription settings manually. In a data-driven subscription, these settings are set dynamically and might change for each row retrieved from the subscription delivery table.

Native mode

On a native-mode report server, you point to a report for which you want to create a data-driven subscription, click the arrow that appears to open the report submenu, and click Manage. Then click the Subscriptions link on the left side of the page. On the Subscriptions page, click New Data-Driven Subscription. The process to configure the data-driven subscription requires you to step through a series of pages.

On the first page of the data-driven subscription settings, you name the subscription, specify the type of subscription that you want to create, and identify the type of data source by using the following fields:

- **Description** The description appears in the list of subscriptions on the Subscriptions page for a report. When you need to change or delete a subscription, you can use the description to help you identify it.

- **Specify How Recipients Are Notified** You must select one of the following delivery methods: Windows File Share, Email, or Null Delivery Provider.

- **Specify A Data Source That Contains Recipient Information**   You must select either Specify A Shared Data Source or Specify For This Subscription Only. Reporting Services uses this data source to retrieve data from the subscription delivery table only.

On the second page, you provide data source information. If you selected Specify A Shared Data Source on the first page, you see a tree view of folders available in Report Manager. You can navigate through these folders to locate and select the shared data source to use for the data-driven subscription. Otherwise, if you selected Specify For This Subscription Only, you must provide the following data source details:

- **Data Source Type**   Your data source must be accessible by using a data provider that can return schema information to the report server. Your best option is to store subscription data in a relational database, such as Microsoft SQL Server.

- **Connection String**   Type the connection string that allows the report server to connect to the data source server and database.

- **Connect Using**   You can provide the user name and password that has read permission for the subscription data, or you can specify that credentials are not required.

On the third page, you provide the query to retrieve the subscription data. For example, your query might look like this:

```
Select
 [To] as Recipient,
 IncludeReport,
 RenderFormat,
 ReportParameter1,
 ReportParameter2
from
 DataDrivenSubscription
where
 SubscriptionType = 'email' and
 ReportName = 'Reseller Sales Margin Analysis by Sales Territory';
```

You can also optionally increase the query time-out value if necessary. To make sure your query works before continuing to configure the subscription settings, you can click the Validate button on this page. A success message displays if the report server can connect successfully to the data source and execute the query.

On the fourth page of the subscription settings, you specify the delivery extension settings. For example, if you are creating an email subscription, you must provide an email address for each recipient, specify a render format, and so on, as shown in Figure 27-9, much like you configure the email delivery extension for a standard subscription.

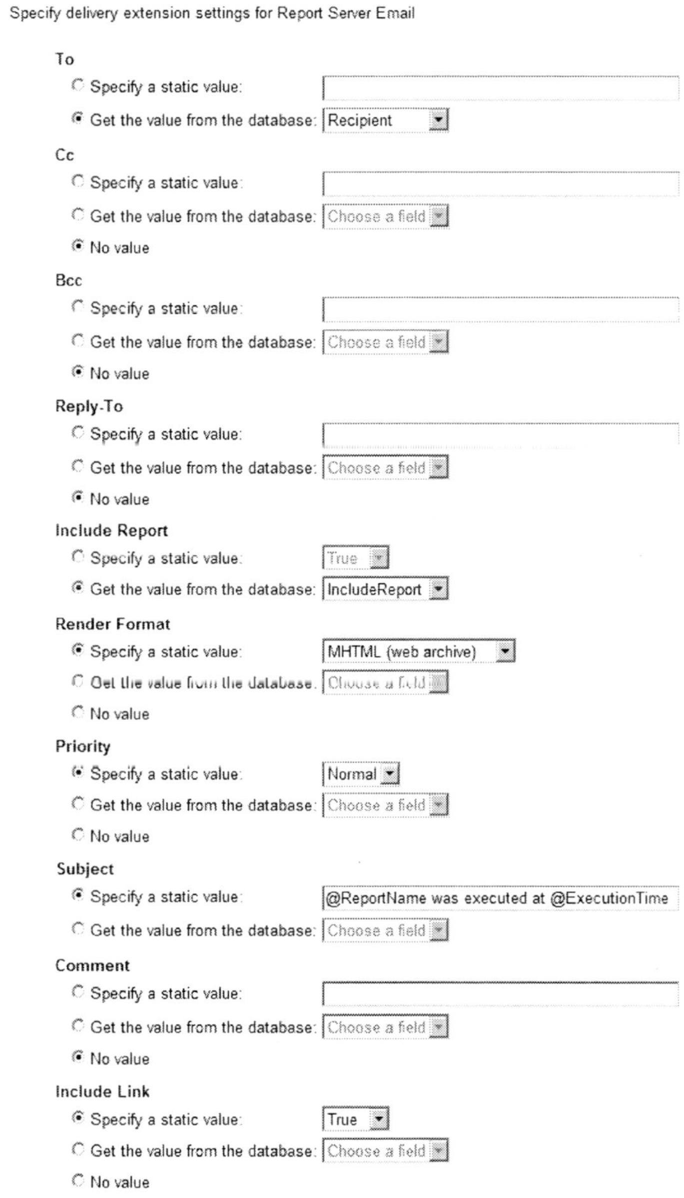

Specify delivery extension settings for Report Server Email

To
- ○ Specify a static value: [   ]
- ◉ Get the value from the database: [Recipient ▼]

Cc
- ○ Specify a static value: [   ]
- ○ Get the value from the database: [Choose a field ▼]
- ◉ No value

Bcc
- ○ Specify a static value: [   ]
- ○ Get the value from the database: [Choose a field ▼]
- ◉ No value

Reply-To
- ○ Specify a static value: [   ]
- ○ Get the value from the database: [Choose a field ▼]
- ◉ No value

Include Report
- ○ Specify a static value: [True ▼]
- ◉ Get the value from the database: [IncludeReport ▼]

Render Format
- ◉ Specify a static value: [MHTML (web archive) ▼]
- ○ Get the value from the database: [Choose a field ▼]
- ○ No value

Priority
- ◉ Specify a static value: [Normal ▼]
- ○ Get the value from the database: [Choose a field ▼]
- ○ No value

Subject
- ◉ Specify a static value: [@ReportName was executed at @ExecutionTime]
- ○ Get the value from the database: [Choose a field ▼]

Comment
- ○ Specify a static value: [   ]
- ○ Get the value from the database: [Choose a field ▼]
- ◉ No value

Include Link
- ◉ Specify a static value: [True ▼]
- ○ Get the value from the database: [Choose a field ▼]
- ○ No value

FIGURE 27-9 You assign values from the query to delivery extension settings where applicable.

For each setting, you can choose whether to specify a static value or to use a value from the subscription data query. If you choose to specify a static value, you type the value in the box provide or select an option from the drop-down list. For a value from the subscription data query, you select the applicable column name in the drop-down list. As you can see, you do not have to store all settings in the subscription data table. The data-driven subscription can use both manually configured settings that are constant for all recipients and dynamic values that come from the subscription data query.

If your report has report parameters, the fifth page of settings prompts you for report parameter values, as shown in Figure 27-10. You can use the default values from the report definition, specify a static value, or you can specify column name from the subscription data query to use as the source of the report parameter value. Just like the delivery extension settings, you can manually configure some of the report parameter values and retrieve the remaining values from the subscription data query.

Specify report parameter values for Reseller Sales Margin Analysis by Sales Territory

Cost Basis
- ○ Specify a static value: `Total` ☐ Use Default
- ● Get the value from the database: `ReportParameter1 ▾`

Year
- ○ Specify a static value: `2005, 2006, 2007, 2008 ▾` ☑ Use Default
- ● Get the value from the database: `ReportParameter2 ▾`

Quarter
- ● Specify a static value: `1, 2, 3, 4 ▾` ☑ Use Default
- ○ Get the value from the database: `Choose a field ▾`

SalesTerritoryGroup
- ● Specify a static value: `Europe, North America, ▾` ☐ Use Default
- ○ Get the value from the database: `Choose a field ▾`

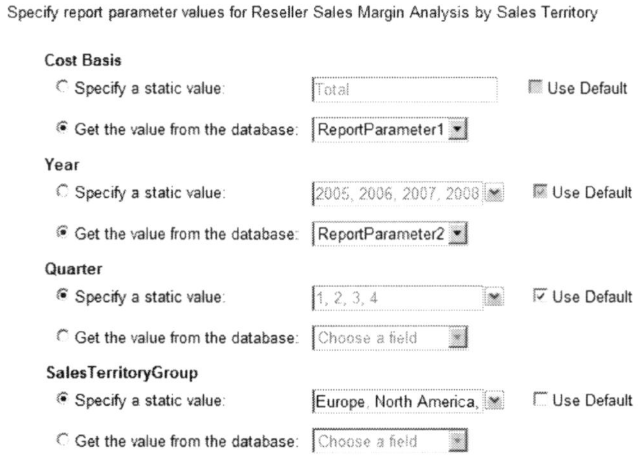

FIGURE 27-10 You have the option to set report parameter values by using values from the data-driven subscription query.

On the final page, you specify the subscription processing options. That is, you can choose when the report server executes the report and sends the subscription to its destination. You can choose the following options on a native-mode report server:

- When report data is updated on the report server

- On a schedule created for this subscription

- On a shared schedule

SharePoint integrated mode

Although the pages lay out differently and the field names do not match up, the process of configuring a data-driven subscription on a SharePoint integrated-mode report server is similar to the process you use for a native-mode report server. To start, point to a report for which you want to create a data-driven subscription, click the arrow that appears to open the report submenu, and click Manage Subscriptions. Then click the Subscriptions link on the left side of the page. On the Manage Subscriptions page, click Add Data-Driven Subscription to begin stepping through the configuration pages.

On the first page of the data-driven subscription settings, as shown in Figure 27-11, you name the subscription, specify the type of subscription that you want to create, identify the type of data source, and provide the subscription data query by using the following fields:

- **Description**   The description appears in the list of subscriptions on the Subscriptions page for a report. When you need to change or delete a subscription, you can use the description to help you identify it.

- **Connection Type**   Here you choose Shared Data Source or Custom Data Source. Reporting Services uses this data source to retrieve data from the subscription delivery table only. Your data source must be accessible by using a data provider that can return schema information to the report server, such as Microsoft SQL Server.

   If you select Custom Data Source, you must also select a data provider in the Data Source Type drop-down list, type in a connection string, and specify credentials to use when connecting to the subscription query's data source.

   If you select Shared Data Source, you must provide a value for the Data Source Link field. You can type a path to the data source, such as *http://<SharePointSite>/Data Connections for PerformancePoint/Subscriptions.rsds*, or click the ellipsis button to open the Select An Item – Webpage Dialog window and then locate and select the data source.

- **Query**   Here you provide the query to retrieve the subscription data, like the example shown in the preceding section for native-mode report server settings.

- **Query Timeout**   You can increase the query time-out value if the data source does not respond to the subscription data query quickly enough.

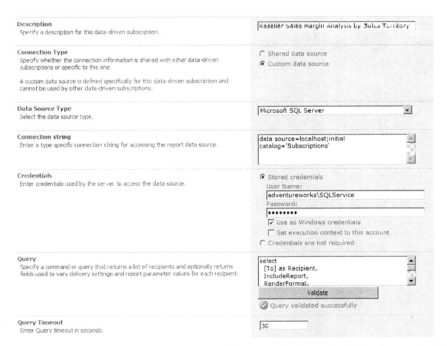

FIGURE 27-11 You define the data source and the query for the subscription data on the first page of the data-driven subscription settings.

On the second page of the data-driven subscription settings, you configure the report parameter values, as shown in Figure 27-12. You can use the report default value (as defined in the report definition), set a static value, or override the report default with a value from the subscription data query. If you choose the latter option, you must select the applicable column name in the drop-down list for the report parameter.

FIGURE 27-12 You assign values from the query to report parameters where applicable.

On the third page, you specify the delivery extension settings. First, you select the delivery type: Windows File Share, Email, SharePoint Document Library, or Null Delivery Provider. Next, for each setting, you specify a static value or select a value from the subscription data query.

On the final page, you choose when the report server executes the report and sends the subscription to its destination. You can choose the following options on a SharePoint integrated-mode report server:

- When a report snapshot is created
- On a shared schedule
- On a custom schedule

Managing subscriptions

Your options for managing subscriptions include viewing active subscriptions and deleting subscriptions. You can see when the subscription was last run and the status of the last subscription execution. If you are running a native-mode report server, you can also open the My Subscriptions page to view all subscriptions on the server in a single location.

Using the My Subscriptions page

If you create many subscriptions, you might find it challenging to locate each report on the report server to check the status of each subscription. If you are running a native-mode report server, you can use the My Subscriptions page to see all your own subscriptions. (There is no equivalent available in SharePoint integrated mode.) The My Subscriptions link to this page appears at the top of every page in Report Manager.

Note If you are a Content Manager, you cannot use the My Subscriptions page to manage subscriptions for other users. Instead, you must open each report individually and then open the report's subscription page to manage subscriptions created by other users.

Each time the subscription runs, the Last Run column displays the date and time of the subscription execution, and the Status column shows the action taken, such as Mail Sent, and the target of the delivery, such as the email recipient, as shown in Figure 27-13. When you have many subscriptions, you might find it useful to sort the subscriptions in ascending or descending order by clicking the Last Run link to change the sort order of the subscriptions. Each time you click the Last Run link, the sort order reverses.

FIGURE 27-13 You can review the status of your subscriptions on the My Subscriptions page.

Tip When you see a subscription status with a message stating that access to the file share is denied, you should probably check the permissions for that folder. After fixing the permissions issue, you can open the subscription, edit the schedule, and then save the subscription. The error message does not clear until the subscription executes successfully.

You can change the settings or schedule for an existing subscription by clicking the Edit link to the left of the subscription. The description on the My Subscriptions page changes accordingly.

SMTP relay restrictions

If the Status displays The Email Address Of One Or More Recipients Is Not Valid and you know that you have specified a valid email address, you should check the SMTP server properties. If you have implemented an SMTP server by using Internet Information Services (IIS), in the Administrative Tools program group on the SMTP server, open Internet Information Services (IIS) Manager. Right-click Default SMTP Virtual Server, and select Properties. In the Default SMTP Virtual Server Properties dialog box, click the Access tab, and then click Relay. In the Relay Restrictions dialog box, if Only The List Below is selected but the list is empty, you can change the selection to All Except The List Below and click OK until all dialog boxes are closed. By making this change, the SMTP server should accept the email addresses defined in the subscription. If the relay restrictions list is not empty, you should work with your network administrator to diagnose and resolve the problem.

Deleting a subscription

When you no longer need a subscription, you can delete it from the report's subscription page or the My Subscriptions page. In the latter case, you can delete subscriptions by selecting all the subscriptions you want to delete and then clicking the Delete button. The Delete button is not active until you select at least one subscription.

Native mode

On a native-mode report server, find the report with the subscription you want to delete, point to it, click the arrow that appears, and on the report submenu, click Manage. Then click the Subscriptions link on the left side of the page. To delete a subscription, select its check box in the subscription list, click the Delete button on the toolbar, and click OK to confirm.

SharePoint integrated mode

Point to a report for which you want to delete a subscription, click the arrow that appears, and on the report submenu click Manage Subscriptions. Then click the Subscriptions link on the left side of the page. Select the check box next to the subscription to delete, click the Delete button on the toolbar, and click OK to confirm.

CHAPTER 28

Data alerting

In Chapter 27, "Working with subscriptions," you learned about the options you have for scheduling the execution of a report, with the option to email the report each time the schedule runs. However, you might prefer to limit the email delivery of a report. Rather than receive a report every Monday morning, which you must then review to determine whether a condition in the report requires you to take action, you can set up a data alert to send an email notification only when that condition is true, as long as you are running a report server in SharePoint integrated mode. The report server continues to execute the report on a scheduled basis and tests the data values in the report against the rules that you specify when you create the data alert. In this chapter, you learn about the supporting architecture for the data alerting feature and how to create and manage data alerts.

Understanding the data alerting architecture

Data alerts in Reporting Services are different from SharePoint alerts. You use SharePoint alerts to send a notification when a document changes. When you save a report to a SharePoint document library, you save the report definition only, not the data that displays when you execute the report. You can set up a SharePoint alert to send a notification when someone makes a change to the report definition, but this alerting process does not monitor changes to the data that the report retrieves during report execution. For notification of data changes in reports, you use data alerting in Reporting Services.

Data alert workflow

The workflow for creating a data alert is shown in Figure 28-1. After opening a report in the Share-Point Report Viewer, you select the option to create an alert, which opens the Data Alert Designer. There you define the rules for monitoring changes in the report data and the schedule to use for evaluating those rules. Reporting Services saves your data alert definition in the alerting database and then schedules a SQL Server Agent job to execute the report and test the rules periodically.

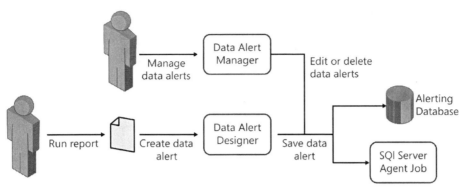

FIGURE 28-1 Reporting Services saves your data alert definition in the alerting database and schedules a SQL Server Agent job.

The Reporting Services components supporting this process include the SharePoint Report Viewer, the Data Alert Designer, Data Alert Manager, and the alerting database. These components install automatically into your SharePoint environment when you install the Reporting Services add-in and create a new shared service application for Reporting Services. Data alerting is enabled by default, although SQL Server Agent must be running and provisioned, as described in Chapter 4, "Installing Reporting Services."

The default name of the alerting database is *ReportingServices<guid>_Alerting*. Each shared service application has its own alerting database. It stores alert definitions, alert metadata, execution history, and stored procedures that Reporting Services uses to manage the alerting workflow.

Reporting Services creates a SQL Server Agent job when you save or update an alert schedule. If you look in the *AlertDefinition* table of the alerting database, you can see the *ScheduleId* column containing the name of each alert's corresponding SQL Server Agent job. The owner of the job is the application pool identity running the shared service application. This job contains one job step to execute a Transact-SQL script that adds a *FireSchedule* event record to the *Event* table in the alerting database. It also includes a job schedule using the frequency you define for the alert. If the job fails, SQL Server Agent updates the Windows application event log.

Alerting service

The Reporting Services alerting service is the component that uses a polling mechanism to monitor the *Event* table in the alerting database and respond to events, as shown in Figure 28-2. The *FireSchedule* event starts alert processing. When the alerting service finds this event in the *Event* table, it creates the *GenerateAlert* event to get the data feeds and evaluate the alert rules using this data. Then the alerting service records the result of the evaluation in the *AlertInstance* table in the alerting database. If the data values in a report's data feeds satisfy the alert rules or if an error occurs during processing, the alerting service creates the *DeliverAlert* event to generate an email to the recipients listed in the alert definition.

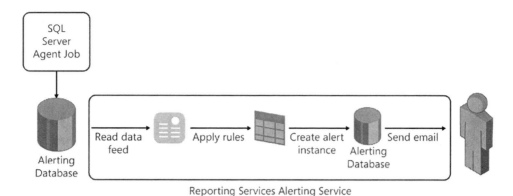

FIGURE 28-2 The Reporting Services Alerting Service refreshes report data, applies rules, and sends email notifications when applicable.

Creating data alerts

You can create a data alert for any report that you create in SSDT or Report Builder, as long as it contains at least one data region of any type. However, you cannot create a data alert for a Power View report or for a report that you access only as part of a custom application. The report must also exist in a SharePoint document library. You cannot store it on a native-mode report server and then access it through SharePoint Web Parts.

Note You must have the Create Alert permission to create a data alert. This permission is granted by default by the Read permission level.

SharePoint Report Viewer

Before you create a data alert, you must successfully open a report in the SharePoint Report Viewer. That is, you must have permission to open the report and the report must execute successfully and display data. If the report has parameters, you must execute the report by using the parameter values that you want to apply when Reporting Services executes the report on a scheduled basis to check whether the alert rules apply at that time. You can set up multiple data alerts if you want to use different combinations of parameter values or apply different rules at different times or for different recipients.

To open the Data Alert Designer, you open the report's Actions menu and select New Data Alert, as shown in Figure 28-3. If this command is not available on the menu, the alerting service is disabled or not installed. However, if the command is disabled, it indicates that you have not yet run the report because a parameter value is missing or one of the report's data sources does not support data alerts. That is, the data source uses Windows integrated security or prompts for credentials, both of which require user credentials at the time the report executes. Because data alerts run on a scheduled basis like subscriptions, report data sources must use stored credentials or no credentials.

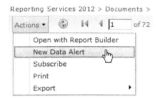

FIGURE 28-3 You use the Actions menu in the SharePoint Report Viewer to create a new data alert.

Data feeds

When the Data Alert Designer opens, as shown in Figure 28-4, the report server creates and caches data feeds for each data region in the same way that it does when you use the Export To Data Feed option, as described in Chapter 26, "Accessing reports online." Then the Data Alert Designer displays the first 100 rows of the first data feed. If the report has multiple data feeds, you can use the Report Data Name drop-down list to select a different data region and view the first 100 rows of its corresponding data feed. The Data Alert Designer includes vertical and horizontal scroll bars for you to review the portions of the data feed that cannot fit within the space allotted.

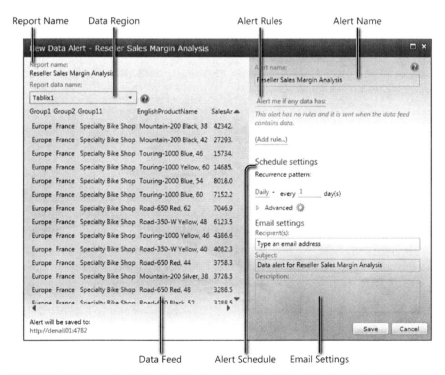

FIGURE 28-4 You use the Data Alert Designer to define data alert rules, schedule frequency, and recipients of data alerts.

Tip The alert name defaults to the report name. You should change this name to include information about the alert rules or schedule. That way, if you set up multiple alerts for the same report, you know which alert triggered the email notification. Otherwise, you see the same alert name appear in the Data Alert Manager and must open each one to determine which is safe to delete.

Data alert rules

By default, a new data alert has no rules. If you save the data alert after defining the schedule and email settings, Reporting Services sends an email notification according to the defined schedule if the report contains data. In this case, the data alert behaves more like a subscription. However, this option is more useful than a subscription when you have a report that contains data only under specific conditions.

Rule scope

A common reason to use data alerts is to receive a notification when conditions that you define arise in the data. You define the scope of the data alert by clicking the link in the top right of the Data Alert Designer and selecting one of the following options:

- **Alert Me If Any Data Has**   The rules that you specify must be true for at least one value in the data.

- **Alert Me If No Data Has**   The rules that you specify cannot be true for any value in the data.

Rule condition

Next you create one or more rules. A rule condition consists of three parts: a data field, a comparison operator, and a field or value for comparison, as shown in Figure 28-5. To create a rule, click the Add Rule link and select a field from the data feed currently visible in the left side of the Alert Designer. The default comparison operator is *Is*, which you can change by clicking its link to choose another comparison operator.

FIGURE 28-5 You can create a simple rule to compare a field to a specified value, as shown, or to another field.

If the data feed field is a numeric data type, you choose one of the following comparison operators:

- Is
- Is Not
- Is Less Than
- Is Less Than Or Equal To
- Is Greater Than
- Is Greater Than Or Equal To

You choose one of the following comparison operators if the data feed field is a string data type:

- Is
- Is Not
- Contains

The comparison operators for a date time data type include the following choices:

- Is
- Is Not
- Is Before
- Is After

 Note You cannot create a rule for a field having a Boolean data type.

You can type in a value to use for comparison in the text box to the right of the comparison operator, as shown in Figure 28-5, or you can click the down arrow that appears to the right of this text box and switch to Field Selection Mode. After you do this, you can click the comparison text box to see a list of fields from the current data feed and make a selection. The field list contains only fields with a compatible data type. If the field you select has a date time data type, an icon for the calendar control displays next to the value text box. You can type a date in the text box or select a data from the calendar control.

Multiple rules

After you create the first rule, you can continue adding more rules to a data alert by following the same steps. Reporting Services evaluates multiple data alert rules by using a logical AND operator only. If the data feed field you select for a rule is a string data type and you use the Is operator, you can compare the field to multiple values by using an OR operator, as shown in Figure 28-6. To add the additional field, click the ellipsis button that appears to the right of the comparison value.

Note You cannot change the logical AND operator between rules to an OR operator. You must create a separate data alert to test for the additional condition.

FIGURE 28-6 You can combine multiple rules by using a logical AND operator and compare a string data type to multiple values by using a logical OR operator.

Data alert condition removal

If you change your mind later about one of the rules or one of the comparison values in a rule, you can point to that section of the rule to display the X button, as shown in Figure 28-7. Click the button to remove the selected condition from the data alert rules.

Note You might need to use the horizontal scroll bar that displays below a rule to view the X button.

FIGURE 28-7 You can remove a data alert condition by pointing to the condition and clicking the X button.

Schedule settings

The default schedule for a data alert is daily at 2:00 AM starting on the current date, which you can see when you expand the Advanced section of the Data Alert Designer, as shown in Figure 28-8. You can change the start date and time by editing the text box or by using the calendar or date controls that display when you click the respective icon to the right of the text box. You can also set an end date for the schedule by selecting the Stop Alert On check box and specifying a date.

 Note Reporting Services does not delete a data alert when the schedule stops. You must manually delete the data alert by using the Data Alert Manager to remove it from your report server.

FIGURE 28-8 You can change the schedule frequency, interval, start date and time, and end date in the Schedule Settings section of the Data Alert Designer.

If you prefer a different frequency of email notifications, click the current frequency link (such as Daily) and choose one of the following options:

- Daily

- Weekly

- Hourly

- Minute

After you select a frequency, you can then specify an interval. If you choose a weekly frequency, you can specify the number of weeks between alert processing and you can specify the day of week on which to process alerts, as shown in Figure 28-9.

Schedule settings
Recurrence pattern:

Weekly ▾ every 1 week(s) on Monday

FIGURE 28-9 You can specify the number of weeks and the week day to process alerts when you choose the weekly frequency.

> **Important** A higher frequency for the data alert schedule has a potentially adverse impact on the overall performance of the report server.

If conditions in the report data satisfy the rules when the schedule runs, Reporting Services sends an email notification to the data alert's recipients, but only the first time the data alert schedule runs or when the data in the report changes from the last interval of the schedule. That way, you are not inundated by multiple email notifications containing the same data results. If you prefer to receive the email notification whenever the schedule runs, you must open the Advanced section of Schedule Settings and clear the Send Message Only If Alert Results Change check box.

> **Tip** If you suspect data in the report has changed and you don't want to wait until the next alert schedule interval to receive notification, you can run the alert on demand by using the Data Alert Manager, as explained in the "Run command" section later in this chapter.

Email settings

The final section to configure for data alerts is Email Settings. If SharePoint has access to your email address, it appears automatically in the Recipient(s) text box. Otherwise, this text box is empty. Either way, you can add one or more recipients to this text box, separating each email address by using a semicolon, as shown in Figure 28-10. As an alternative to email addresses, you can use the name of a distribution group.

Email settings
Recipient(s):
stacia@adventureworks.com;erika@adventureworks.com
Subject:
Data alert for Low Profit Margin Percent
Description:
Watching for low profit margins in Australia and Canada.

FIGURE 28-10 At minimum, you specify one or more recipients in the Email Settings section of the Data Alert Designer, but optionally, you can change the Subject and add a description.

Both the email subject and description are static strings. The subject line includes the name of the alert by default, but you can change it to another value if you prefer. You should use a meaningful subject line to help users easily recognize a data alert in their email inbox.

Receiving data alerts

Reporting Services sends an email notification to a data alert's recipients if either of two possible scenarios occurs. First, if the report data satisfies the data alert rules when the schedule runs, the email is sent. Second, if a failure occurs during alert processing, such as might happen when a report definition change removes a column in the report's data feed, an email describing the error is sent. In both scenarios, the email message contains the following information:

- **From**   The account that you specify in the email delivery configuration, as described in Chapter 4.

- **To**   The email addresses of each recipient that you specify in the alert definition.

- **Subject**   The subject text that you specify in the Email Settings section of the alert definition, which includes the report name unless you change the subject when creating or editing the alert.

Successful alert

When alert processing runs successfully and conditions in the report data trigger an email notification, each recipient specified in the alert definition receives an email similar to the one shown in Figure 28-11. The body of the email identifies the purpose of the alert and the raw data values that satisfy the alert rules.

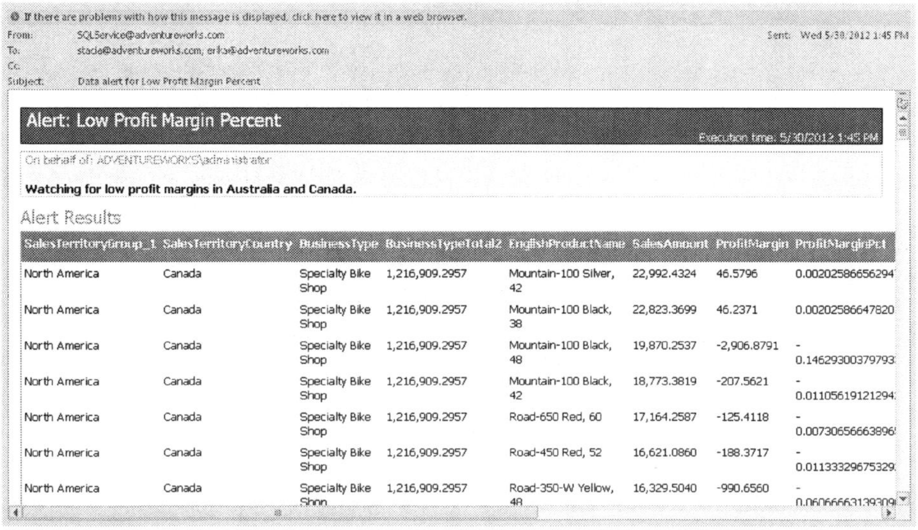

FIGURE 28-11 An email notification for a successful data alert includes data values that triggered the alert.

If the email notification contains many values, you might need to scroll to review the entire body of the message. For example, you can click the report link to open the report on the report server. The email also includes information about the alert rules and applicable parameter values at the bottom of the message, as shown in Figure 28-12.

Go to report
Reseller Sales Margin Analysis by Sales Territory

Rule(s):
Alert me if any data has:ProfitMarginPct is less than 0.05
and SalesTerritoryCountry is 'Australia'
    or 'Canada'

Report Parameters

CostBasis	Total
Year	2005,2006,2007,2008,2009,2010
Quarter	1,2,3,4
SalesTerritoryGroup	Europe,North America,Pacific

FIGURE 28-12 An email notification also includes a link to the report on the report server and other relevant information.

More specifically, the body of the email contains the following information:

- **Alert Title**   Reporting Services constructs the alert title by concatenating the word Alert with the Alert Name that you specify in the alert definition.

- **On Behalf Of**   Here you see the domain and Windows account of the user who created the alert.

- **Description**   If you include a description in the Email Settings section of the alert definition, it displays in the same yellow rectangle as the alert creator's account.

- **Alert Results**   The message also includes each row of data in the report's data feeds that meet the conditions that you defined in the alert rules.

- **Go To Report**   You use this link to view the current contents of the report, which might be different from the alert results if data changes frequently in the source database. If you create the alert using an SSL connection to the SharePoint server, the alert's report link requires an SSL connection using the HTTPS protocol in the report link. Otherwise, the report link uses the HTTP protocol.

Important If you later change the connection protocol on the report server after creating the data alert, the original setting is preserved. That is, if the report server used SSL prior to creating the data alert and you later change the report server configuration, the data alert's report link continues to use the HTTPS protocol. However, the alert continues to work. On the other hand, if you add the SSL requirement after creating the data alert, the link does not include HTTPS and fails.

- **Alert Rules** You can see all conditions specified in the alert definition that triggered the email notification.

- **Report Parameters** Because you can set up multiple alerts with varying combinations of parameters, the email notification includes the report parameters and corresponding values that caused the report data to trigger the alert.

Alert failure

When an error occurs during alert processing, the alerting service saves the alerting instance to the alerting database and sends the recipients an email describing the error, similar to the one shown in Figure 28-13. The bottom of the email notification includes the report link, rules, and report parameter information just as it does for a successful email notification.

FIGURE 28-13 An email notification is sent when an error occurs during alert processing.

Managing alerts

You own the data alerts you create, which means you can review the status of your data alerts, make changes to an existing data alert, or delete it if necessary by using the Data Alert Manager. You can also run the data alert on demand without waiting for the schedule to start alert processing. If you have the Manage Data Alerts permission, you can perform these tasks not only for your own data alerts but also for any data alert on the SharePoint site.

Alert status

You can check the status of your alerts by pointing to a report in a document library, clicking the down arrow to the right of the report name, and selecting Manage Data Alerts. The Data Alert Manager lists the existing alerts for that report, or you can use the View Alerts For Reports drop-down list to switch to a different report or view alerts for all reports. The left side of the page is similar to the one shown in Figure 28-14. Here you can see the alert name, the report with which the data alert is associated, the creator of the report, and the number of data alerts sent by Reporting Services since you created the alert.

Last Run	Last Modified	Status
5/30/2012 1:45:11 PM	5/30/2012 1:42:18 PM	Last alert ran successfully and the alert was sent.
5/30/2012 2:03:34 PM	5/30/2012 1:56:23 PM	Last alert failed Details: The data feed column, 'Order Quantity_Chart1_CategoryGroup1_Value_Y', was not found. The log file contains detailed information about the error. Refer to the log entry with the identifier: 36b1c197-b27e-4d02-8e8d-037b8dcf6bc2..

FIGURE 28-14 You can view the data alerts you create on the Manage Data Alerts page.

The right side of the page (which you might need to scroll to see), similar to the partial page shown in Figure 28-15, shows you when the alert processing last ran for each alert and when you last made a change to the alert definition. The last column shows the status, where you can see whether alert processing was successful or not. If the alert failed, additional information displays about the reason for the failure.

FIGURE 28-15 The Manage Data Alerts page also shows the last run date and status for data alerts.

If you are a data alert administrator on the SharePoint site, having the Manage Alerts permission, you can view all data alerts on the SharePoint site that have been created by any user. To view all data alerts, click the Site Actions button in the top-left corner of the page, click Site Settings, and then click Manage Data Alerts in the Reporting Services section. The same Data Alert Manager page displays as you see when managing your personal data alerts, except that you can switch the view to a different user by using the View Alerts For User drop-down list. You can also use the View Alerts For Report drop-down list to view data alerts for all reports or for a specific report.

Edit command

You can edit only your own alerts on the Data Alert Manager page. When you right-click a data alert, you can choose the Edit command on the submenu. Although a data alert administrator can see your data alerts listed on the Data Alert Manager page, the administrator can neither edit the data alert nor view its contents. When you use the Edit command, the Data Alert Designer displays and you can change any rule, schedule, or email setting as needed. However, you cannot change parameter values associated with the data alert.

If the report author has made any structure changes to the report definition by removing a field from a data region, an error displays in the Data Alert Designer. You must then delete and re-create the alert. Similarly, if the report author has added a new data region to the report, you cannot access the new data region in the Data Alert Designer. Instead, you must create a new alert.

Delete command

If you no longer require a data alert, you can delete the data alert. On the Data Alert Manager page, right-click the data alert and select the Delete command. You can delete only your own data alerts, unless you are a data alert administrator on a SharePoint site. In that case, you can delete any data alert on the site when you open the Data Alert Manager page from the Site Settings page. Although the data alert no longer appears on the Data Alert Manager page immediately after you perform this action, the alert definition remains in the alerting database until a periodic cleaning process removes it, although the alerting service does not process the alert definition during this time.

Run command

If you find a need to check the data values in a report using the data alert rules, you can run a data alert rule on demand. Right-click the data alert on the Data Alert Manager page, and click the Run command. A *FireAlert* event appears in the *ExecutionLog* table in the alerting database, and alert processing starts in the same way that it starts when SQL Server Agent job adds the *FireSchedule* event to the table.

Configuring data alerting

The report server configuration includes settings that manage some of the default behaviors of data alerting. You can change some of these settings by editing the RsReportServer.config file or by running a Windows PowerShell script to update the shared service application.

RsReportServer.Config file settings

As described in Chapter 25, "Performing administrative tasks," the RsReportServer.config file contains several settings that modify the behavior of the report server. You can use the graphical user interface in SharePoint Central Administration to update the more common settings, but you cannot use Central Administration to change settings related to data alerting. Instead, you must manually update the configuration file, which is located in the Program Files\Common Files\Microsoft Shared\Web Server Extensions\14\WebServices\Reporting folder.

IsAlertingService flag

The data alerting service is enabled by default right after installation of Reporting Services in your SharePoint environment. If you decide that you do not want to use data alerting, you can disable this feature by editing the RsReportServer.config file. Open the file, and locate the *IsAlertingService* flag in the *Service* section, as shown in Figure 28-16. Change the value from *True* to *False* to disable data alerting on the report server. There is no option to selectively disable data alerting for each reporting-enabled SharePoint site.

```
<Service>
  <IsSchedulingService>True</IsSchedulingService>
  <IsNotificationService>True</IsNotificationService>
  <IsEventService>True</IsEventService>
  <IsAlertingService>True</IsAlertingService>
  <PollingInterval>10</PollingInterval>
  <WindowsServiceUseFileShareStorage>False</WindowsServiceUseFileShareStorage>
  <MemorySafetyMargin>80</MemorySafetyMargin>
  <MemoryThreshold>90</MemoryThreshold>
  <RecycleTime>720</RecycleTime>
  <MaxAppDomainUnloadTime>30</MaxAppDomainUnloadTime>
  <MaxQueueThreads>0</MaxQueueThreads>
  <UrlRoot>
  </UrlRoot>
  <PolicyLevel>rssrvpolicy.config</PolicyLevel>
  <IsWebServiceEnabled>True</IsWebServiceEnabled>
  <IsReportManagerEnabled>True</IsReportManagerEnabled>
  <FileShareStorageLocation>
    <Path>
    </Path>
  </FileShareStorageLocation>
</Service>
```

FIGURE 28-16 The *IsAlertingService* flag in the RsReportServer.config file enables or disables data alerting on your report server.

Alerting interval defaults

The RsReportServer.config file also includes several settings that set default intervals for cleanup cycles. You can find the following settings in the *Configuration* section of the file, as shown in Figure 28-17:

- **AlertingCleanupCycleMinutes** Set the interval for starting the cleanup of alerting data. The default is 20 minutes.

- **AlertingDataCleanupMinutes** Configure the amount of time to keep temporary alerting data in the alerting database. The default is 360 minutes (6 hours).

- **AlertingExecutionLogCleanupMinutes** Control the amount of time in minutes to keep alerting data in the *ExecutionLog* table in the alerting database. The default is 10,080 minutes (7 days).

- **AlertingMaxDataRetentionDays** Define the time to retain execution metadata, alert instances, and report execution results in the alerting database. The default is 180 days.

```
<Configuration>
  <Dsn />
  <ConnectionType>Default</ConnectionType>
  <LogonUser>
  </LogonUser>
  <LogonDomain>
  </LogonDomain>
  <LogonCred>
  </LogonCred>
  <InstanceId>MSRS11.@Sharepoint</InstanceId>
  <Add Key="SecureConnectionLevel" Value="0" />
  <Add Key="CleanupCycleMinutes" Value="10" />
  <Add Key="MaxActiveReqForOneUser" Value="20" />
  <Add Key="AlertingCleanupCycleMinutes" Value="20" />
  <Add Key="AlertingDataCleanupMinutes" Value="360" />
  <Add Key="AlertingExecutionLogCleanupMinutes" Value="10080" />
  <Add Key="AlertingMaxDataRetentionDays" Value="180" />
  <Add Key="RunningRequestsScavengerCycle" Value="60" />
  <Add Key="RunningRequestsDbCycle" Value="60" />
  <Add Key="RunningRequestsAge" Value="30" />
  <Add Key="MaxScheduleWait" Value="5" />
  <Add Key="DisplayErrorLink" Value="true" />
  <Add Key="WebServiceUseFileShareStorage" Value="false" />
```

Alerting Interval Defaults

FIGURE 28-17 The RsReportServer.config file contains several settings controlling intervals for cleaning data from the alerting database.

SharePoint configuration database settings

When the alerting process encounters a problem, the Reporting Services shared service application configuration determines how many times the alerting service retries the operation and how long to wait between retries. There is neither a graphical user interface nor a configuration file available for you to make a change to these values. Instead, you must use Windows PowerShell cmdlets to change *MaxRetries* from a default of 3 and *SecondsBeforeRetry* from a default of 900.

Open the SharePoint 2010 Management Shell from the Microsoft SharePoint 2010 Products program group on the Start menu. Let's say that you want to change the maximum number of retries from 3 to 5. To do this, execute the following cmdlets in the Windows PowerShell window, replacing SSRS2012 with the name of your Reporting Services shared service application:

```
$app=get-sprsserviceapplication -Name "SSRS2012"
$alertCfg = Get-SPRSExtension -identity $app -ExtensionType "EventProcessing" -name "General
Alert Extension" | select -ExpandProperty ServerDirectivesXml
$alertCfg = $alertCfg -replace "3", "5"
Set-SPRSExtension -identity $app -ExtensionType "EventProcessing" -name "General Alert
Extension" -ServerDirectives $alertCfg
```

Important The name of your shared service application is case-sensitive. If you do not use the correct case, the cmdlet does not execute correctly.

You can also change *MaxRetries* or *SecondsBeforeRetry* for each alerting event type if you prefer greater control over specific aspects of the alerting process when failures occur. You can execute the following cmdlets to find the name of the available event handlers:

```
$app=get-sprsserviceapplication -Name "SSRS2012"
Get-SPRSExtension -identity $app | where-object {$_.Type -like "*Alerting*"}
```

For example, if you want to change the *SecondsBeforeRetry* value from 900 to 300 for the *FireAlert* event, you can execute the following cmdlets, changing the name of the extension type where appropriate:

```
$app=get-sprsserviceapplication -Name "SSRS2012"
$alertCfg = Get-SPRSExtension -identity $app -ExtensionType "EventProcessing" -name "Fire Alert
Extension" | select -ExpandProperty ServerDirectivesXml
$alertCfg = $alertCfg -replace "900", "300"
Set-SPRSExtension -identity $app -ExtensionType "EventProcessing" -name "Fire Alert Extension"
-ServerDirectives $alertCfg
```

Each of the available alerting extension types corresponds to one of the following events:

- **FireAlert** On-demand execution of an alert launched by a user
- **FireSchedule** Scheduled execution of an alert launched by a SQL Server Agent job
- **CreateSchedule** Process to save a schedule defined in a new or modified data alert
- **UpdateSchedule** Modification of a schedule in a data alert
- **DeleteSchedule** Deletion of a data alert
- **GenerateAlert** Alerting-service processing of data feeds, rules, and alert instances
- **DeliverAlert** Preparation and delivery of email message for a data alert

Monitoring the alerting process

There are a variety of tools available to you for monitoring the status of the alerting process. The alerting database includes the *ExecutionLogView* view to provide insight into the sequencing and outcome of alerting events. In addition, the alerting database has several stored procedures you can use to retrieve different types of alerting data. Last, the Reporting Services installation adds a collection of performance counters you can use to monitor trends on the report server.

Execution log

The alerting service uses the alerting database to track pending, ongoing, and completed events related to alert processing. You can query the *ExecutionLogView* view to troubleshoot the status of an alert. In general, you can see the complete cycle for an alert by finding its three key events. For example, an alert that you run on demand uses the following three events: *FireAlert*, *GenerateAlert*, and *DeliverAlert*. For each event, there are four rows generated throughout the alerting process, with the following text in the *StatusMessage* column:

- Event was added

- Event processing started

- Event processing completed

- Event was deleted

When a failure interrupts alert processing, you might see a message in the *StatusMessage* column like this: "An error has occurred during report processing. The log file contains detailed information about the error. Refer to the log entry with the identifier: 450b03d4-48b1-49fd-9307-1f0caf653186." To get more information about the cause of the failure, you can then locate the applicable reportserver-service_<guid>_<date_time> log file in the Program Files\Common Files\Microsoft Shared\Web Server Extensions\14\WebServices\LogFiles to find the entry containing the referenced identifier.

Alerting stored procedures

You can also use stored procedures to query the alerting database for more details about the alerting process. The following stored procedures are available for your use:

- **ReadAlertData** Provide *AlertInstanceID* as an input parameter to retrieve the data feed columns from the report execution.

- **ReadAlertHistory** Provide *AlertDefinitionID* and optionally *NumberOfPolls* to retrieve execution information in the following columns: *EventID, AlertDefinitionID, FeedPollID, Event-Type, EventData, EventAttempt, TimeEntered, StatusType, StatusMessage*, and *ExceptionName*.

- **ReadAlertInstances** Provide *AlertDefinitionID* and optionally *AlertsToRead* to review data related to alert instances in the following columns: *AlertInstanceID, FeedPollID, AlertDefinitionID, SentTime*, and *ParentAlertInstanceID*.

- **ReadEventHistory** Provide *EventID* to get all records related to a specific event in the following columns: *ExecutionID, EventID, AlertDefinitionID, FeedPollID, EventType, EventData, EventAttempt, TimeEntered, StatusType, StatusMessage*, and *ExceptionName*.

- **ReadFeedPollHistory** Provide *PollID* to get all records related to a specific data feed in the following columns: *ExecutionID, EventID, AlertDefinitionID, FeedPollID, EventType, EventData, EventAttempt, TimeEntered, StatusType, StatusMessage*, and *ExceptionName*.

- **ReadFeedPolls**   Provide *FeedID* and optionally *PollsToRead* to get the corresponding *FeedPollID* column.

- **ReadPollData**   Provide *FeedPollId* to get the related data feed columns.

- **ReadSentAlerts**   Provide *AlertDefinitionID* and optionally *AlertsToRead* to get information about notifications in the following columns: *AlertInstanceID, SentTime, Address,* and *MessageSubject.*

Performance counters

Windows Performance Monitor is a built-in tool available in your operating system that you use to gather data about activity affecting your server performance. Whereas the alerting database view and stored procedures are useful for troubleshooting a specific alert or event, performance counters are useful for observing trends over a period of time and comparing report server activity at different points of time. You can configure Performance Monitor to collect data for the following performance counters in the MSRS 2011 Windows Service SharePoint Mode object:

- Alerting: Event Queue Length

- Alerting: Events Processed – CreateSchedule

- Alerting: Events Processed – DeleteSchedule

- Alerting: Events Processed – DeliverAlert

- Alerting: Events Processed – FireAlert

- Alerting: Events Processed – FireSchedule

- Alerting: Events Processed – GenerateAlert

- Alerting: Events Processed – UpdateSchedule

 Note You can learn how to use Performance Monitor at *http://technet.microsoft.com/en-us/library/cc749249.*

PART VI

Ad hoc reporting

Another aspect of report access is ad hoc reporting, which is a more creative and interactive process than simply viewing reports. In Chapter 29, "Reusing report parts," you learn how to create and deploy a library of report parts that users can search, select, and modify for personalized reporting in Report Builder without the need to know how to create queries or develop report items. Another type of ad hoc reporting is available only on a SharePoint integrated-mode report server by using Power View. Before you can start creating reports with this new tool, you must have a tabular model available and modify it to better support specific features in Power View, which you learn how to do in Chapter 30, "Preparing to use Power View." Then, in Chapter 31, "Using Power View," you learn how to explore a tabular model by organizing a variety of data visualizations as a collection of pages that you can view online or share with others by exporting as a Microsoft PowerPoint presentation.

CHAPTER 29

Reusing report parts

Report parts were first introduced in SQL Server 2008 R2 as another option to support self-service reporting for business users. Rather than require users to learn how to build a table or matrix, you can instead deploy these report items, among others, as independent items called report parts. Users can then construct reports with these ready-made report parts, and can even adapt them as needed.

Introducing report parts

If you develop software applications or design database schemas, you know that one of the benefits of eliminating redundancy of code or data and centralizing business logic is the ease of maintenance resulting from having only one place to update when a change is necessary. In Reporting Services, you attain a similar benefit when you use a shared data source for multiple reports, as we explain in Chapter 8, "Retrieving data for a report," because you can then change the connection string in one place when the data source moves. Likewise, you can use a shared dataset to define a commonly used query once.

As you develop more reports within an organization, you begin to see data structures used repeatedly but in different combinations. One way that you might achieve the goal of creating once for multiple reuse is to set up reports for use strictly as subreports, described in Chapter 9, "Designing the report layout." Another way to achieve centralization of frequently used data structures is to implement report parts. Later in this chapter, in the "Choosing report parts vs. subreports" section, we compare and contrast these two approaches to reusability of report items.

Although business users who know how to use Report Builder can certainly use subreports, you can offer them more flexibility by creating an assortment of report parts. That way, users who are less familiar with Report Builder can also successfully create their own reports. When report parts are available on the report server, a user needs to know only how to browse the report part gallery, make a selection, and move the selected report part to the desired position on the report. If the user can successfully work with Microsoft Word, the same user can successfully produce reports with Report Builder.

Report part

A report part is a report item or a collection of report items that you can publish to the report server to be reused in other reports. When designing reports, you might find that certain items are used over and over again in reports. Rather than re-create those items every time, you can publish them as a report part, and then anyone can simply drop the report item into a new report as needed. The data source and dataset on which the report part depends are also saved with the report part, in addition to a report parameter that the report part requires for a filter or text box expression. That way, a user has everything necessary to successfully render a report after selecting a report part.

You can create a report part from any of the following report items:

- Data regions: table, matrix, list

- Graphical data regions: chart, data bar, sparkline, gauge, indicator, map

- Report items: rectangle, image

- Parameter

To create a report part, you develop a report in SSDT or Report Builder by creating one or more of any of the supported items. You then must explicitly identify the items to publish to the report server as a report part. Some common candidates for report parts include standard report headers, logos, and commonly used tables and charts.

> **Note** You cannot publish a report part that has a reference to custom code. Also, you cannot publish items that are nested inside another report item as a separate report part. If you publish a report item that contains nested report items, the report part contains all report items and the user can delete the nested report items if necessary. You might consider creating nested items as stand-alone report items, in which case you can publish them as separate report parts. In that case, the user can select the separate report items and then nest them if desired.

Report part benefits

A user can create a report from a single report part or can add multiple report parts to create a personalized arrangement of items in a report. For example, rather than require all users to view a table in one report and a chart in another report, one user can combine the two items as report parts into a single report with the chart at the top and the table on the bottom of the report. Another user can use the same two report parts and arrange the table first and display the chart last.

The availability of report parts not only allows users to personalize their reports but also ensures that they use the same data. Users do not need to know any of the technical details about constructing the queries that provide data for these report parts, nor do they need to know how to build the table or chart used as a report part. This insulation of users from the technical aspects of report development is especially useful when reports must contain complex queries or calculations. Furthermore, if you make changes to a report part later, each user can decide whether to update their version of the report part or to keep the original version untouched.

Rather than continue to add to the backlog of reports that professional report builders typically must manage, you can give users the freedom to build their own reports with report parts. They get access to the information they need without having to wait for IT to develop a simple report. Professional report developers can develop report parts with a consistent look and feel to make it even easier for users to create reports that conform to organizational standards.

Of course, there is nothing to stop the user from making changes afterwards, but overall, the process of ad hoc reporting is significantly simplified with report parts. If your goal is to enable users rather than to restrict what they can do, you can allow more advanced users to add report parts to a blank report simply as a starting point for their own report. That way, if a report part is close to what the user wants to display in a report, the user can adapt it as needed.

Deploying report parts

The creation of a report part is no different from the development of any report item by using the techniques we describe in the chapters of Part II, "Developing reports." However, it does not become a report part until you deploy it to the report server by using either SSDT or Report Builder. You can then organize report parts in folders on the report server and manage report parts much like other resources on the report server.

> **Note** You must be assigned to the Content Manager or Publisher role to deploy report parts to the report server. If you are assigned to the My Reports role, you can deploy report parts to your My Reports folder.

Deployment from SSDT

In SSDT, you must first create a report with one or more items you want to publish as separate report parts. When you're ready to deploy the report parts to the report server, open Publish Report Parts from the Report menu. A list of the items in your report that you can publish as a report part displays in the Publish Report Parts dialog box. You can then expand each report item to see a thumbnail image, as shown in Figure 29-1.

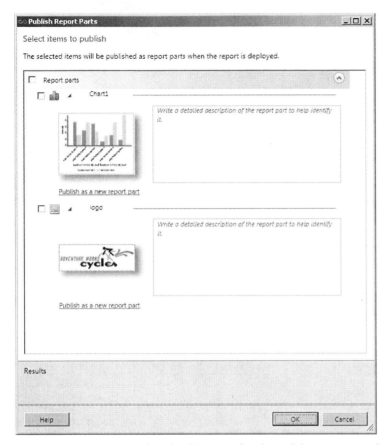

FIGURE 29-1 You can view thumbnail images of each candidate report part before selecting items to publish.

Before you select report parts to publish, you should take the time to give each report part a useful name and description to make it easier for users to find the report part they need. To rename the report part, simply click the name and edit the text in place. For example, instead of deploying a report part as Chart1, you can provide a more descriptive name, such as Sales by Territory By Year. In the description, you can use keywords and information about the type of chart.

Select the check box for each item that you want to deploy. You can deploy some report items as report parts without deploying all of them. All dependent objects, including the data source and dataset, deploy automatically with the report part. You must then deploy the report in order to deploy the report parts to the report server. The target folder for the report parts is defined in the project properties, as we describe in Chapter 7, "Working with report server projects." You can confirm successful deployment of the report parts by reviewing the status of the report parts in the Output window, as shown in Figure 29-2.

```
------ Build started: Project: Chapter 29, Configuration: Debug ------
Building the report, Sales by Territory.rdl, for SQL Server 2008 R2 Reporting Services.
Build complete -- 0 errors, 0 warnings
------ Deploy started: Project: Chapter 29, Configuration: Debug ------
Deploying to http://localhost/reportserver
Deploying report '/Chapter 29/Sales by Territory'.
Publishing report parts in report 'C:\Sample Files\Chapter 29\Chapter 29\bin\Debug\Sales by Territory.rdl'
Publishing report parts complete -- 0 succeeded, 0 failed, 0 skipped
Deploy complete -- 0 errors, 0 warnings
========== Build: 1 succeeded or up-to-date, 0 failed, 0 skipped ==========
========== Deploy: 1 succeeded, 0 failed, 0 skipped ==========
```

FIGURE 29-2 The Output window in SSDT displays the deployment status of each report part.

 Note The deployment process produces a file with an RSC extension that contains an RDL fragment.

Deployment from Report Builder

Just as you can do most things in Report Builder that you can do in SSDT, you can also deploy report parts. With a report open in Report Builder, click the Report Builder button in the upper left and select Publish Report Parts. In the first page of the Publish Report Parts dialog box, shown in Figure 29-3, you choose whether to publish all report parts available in the report with default settings or to review and modify the report parts before publishing.

 Note If you open Report Builder from a SharePoint document library or save a report to a document library, you must first select a document library for storing report parts before you see the Publish Report Parts dialog box.

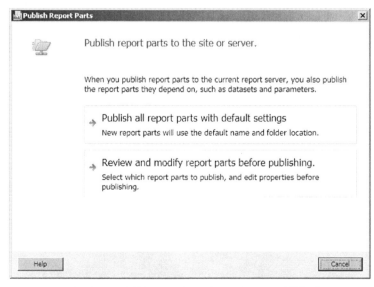

FIGURE 29-3 In Report Builder, you have the option to publish all report parts or selected report parts.

It's a good idea to choose the second option, Review And Modify Report Parts Before Publishing, so that you can rename the report parts with clear names and add descriptions. When you choose this option, the second page of the Publish Report Parts dialog box displays, as shown in Figure 29-4. It's similar to the Publish Report Parts dialog box in SSDT except that you can change the target folder for each report part. In addition, you can convert a report dataset to a shared dataset and specify a target folder for it in the same dialog box. When you click the Publish button, you can see the status of report part and shared dataset deployment in the Results section of the dialog box.

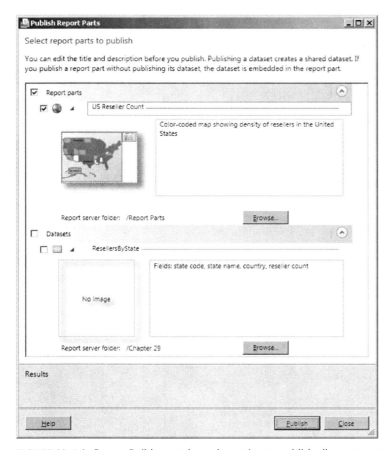

FIGURE 29-4 In Report Builder, you have the option to publish all report parts or selected report parts.

If you open a report in Report Builder for which report parts have already been deployed from SSDT, the version in Report Builder displays the name and description of the deployed report parts. In addition, you can see the First Published and Last Modified dates as well as the user who published and modified the report part, as shown in Figure 29-5.

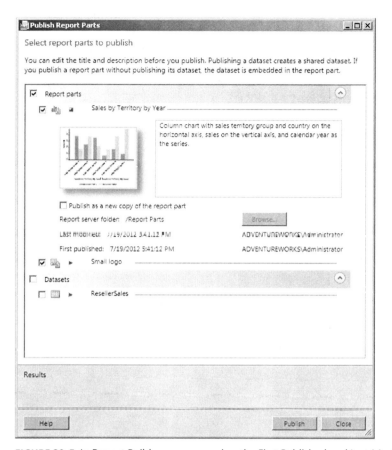

FIGURE 29-5 In Report Builder, you can review the First Published and Last Modified Dates.

Multiple report items in a report part

If you want to publish multiple report items as a single report part, such as a tablix and a chart, put them in a rectangle or other report item that is capable of containing both the tablix and the chart. When you publish report parts, only the parent report item appears in the publishable report parts list. When a user adds the report part, Report Builder adds the rectangle and its contents to the report. This is a useful way to make sure that users get all the report items they need, instead of requiring them to find and add each report part individually.

It's important to note that you cannot publish the tablix and the chart separately as report parts while they are contained in a parent report item such as a rectangle. To publish them as independent report parts, you must place them outside the parent report item. Then they appear as separate report items in the Publish Report Parts dialog box.

Redeployment of a report part

In either SSDT or Report Builder, you can modify a report item that you have previously published as a report part. If you then open the Publish Report Parts dialog box, a new option to deploy a new copy of the report part is available. In SSDT, this option appears as a link that is visible when you expand the report part, as shown in Figure 29-6. When you click this link, a message box displays to prompt you for confirmation that you want to assign a new, unique ID to the report part. It also reminds you that you cannot modify the prior version of the report part if you continue. If you click Yes, both versions of the report part coexist on the server, but only the last one published is available for modification at a later time.

> **Note** In Report Builder, you do not see a link. Instead, you have the Publish As A New Copy Of The Report Part check box that you must select to add a new version of the report part to the report server, as you can see in Figure 29-5.

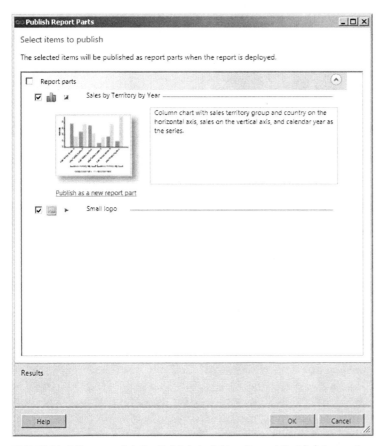

FIGURE 29-6 You can click the Publish As A New Report Part link to create a new report part rather than update an existing report part after editing a report in SSDT.

If you opt not to publish the report part as a new report part, redeployment of the report part updates the existing report part on the report server with your modifications. The next time a user edits a report containing the modified report part in Report Builder, the user sees a notification, as we describe in the "Update notification" section later in this chapter.

Report part management on the report server

Following deployment, you manage report parts much like other resources on the report server. On a native-mode report server, you can use Report Manager to see a list of report parts in a folder, as shown in Figure 29-7. However, unlike reports, you cannot click the report part link to view its contents. Instead, the link opens the Properties page of the report, where you can change the name or description of the report part.

FIGURE 29-7 Report parts display as resources in Report Manager on a native-mode report server.

In Report Manager, you can also hide the report part when displaying the tile view. You can also click the Security link on the left side of the page to edit item security for the report part. A user must be assigned to the Browser or the Report Builder roles to search for a report part and add it to a report on a native-mode report server.

On a SharePoint integrated-mode report server, you can open a document library in SharePoint to review the available report parts. Use the Edit Properties command on the report part's shortcut menu to update the report part name, or use the Manage Permissions command to configure security. If you click the link, you start the download process. You must have Read or View Only permissions on a SharePoint integrated-mode report server to search for and use a report part.

> **Note** In Report Manager, you can download a report part if you are assigned to the Content Manager, Publisher, or My Reports role. You can then upload it to a document library on a SharePoint integrated-mode report server if you have Full Control, Design, or Contribute permissions. If you upload a report part, it is not visible in the Report Part Gallery (described in the next section) unless you upload it to a subfolder of a document library containing report parts deployed from SSDT or Report Builder. An alternative is to activate the Report Server File Sync Feature on the SharePoint server to ensure that the report part is accessible in the Report Part Gallery.

You can safely move a report part to a different folder on the same report server, as long as you do not change the user permissions on the report. Users can search for and locate report parts, and updates to the report part in its new location continue to trigger notifications to all related reports.

On a SharePoint integrated-mode report server, moving a report part to a new location is like uploading it. You must activate the Report Server File Sync Feature to update the report server database correctly if the new location is not a subfolder of the report part's original document library.

Using report parts

Although you can deploy report parts from either SSDT or Report Builder, you can find and use report parts only when creating or editing a report in Report Builder. Anyone with appropriate permissions can use Report Builder, but the target audience is the business user. Often, a business user knows what a report should contain but does not know how to set up connection strings for data sources or write queries for datasets. Report parts enable this group of users to successfully create a variety of reports as long as the requisite report parts exist on the report server.

Report Part Gallery

When you want to add a report part to your report in Report Builder, click the Report Parts button on the Insert tab of the ribbon. The Report Part Gallery displays on the right side of the page and includes a box at the top that you use to search for a keyword in the report part name or description. Press Enter after typing a keyword in the search box to find matching report parts, as shown in Figure 29-8, or press Enter without typing a keyword to view all reports. You see only the report parts for which you have the appropriate permissions.

Note The report part gallery is not accessible within SSDT.

FIGURE 29-8 You can search for a keyword in a report part's name or description in the Report Part Gallery.

You can further refine the scope of the search by clicking the Add Criteria button near the top of the Report Part Gallery. You can select one or more of the following criteria:

- **Created** Specify a date range to search for report parts by the date created.

- **Created By** Search for report parts by the original author, either by providing the name in domain\user format or by specifying a partial string.

- **Modified** Specify a date range to search for report parts by the date created.

- **Modified By** Search for report parts by the author of the most recent version, either by providing the name in domain\user format or by specifying a partial string.

- **Server Folder** Click the ellipsis button to navigate folders on the report server, and select a folder to search for report parts.

- **Type** To restrict the search, select one or more report part types in a list, such as chart, rectangle, or tablix.

When report parts are found matching the criteria you specify, an icon displays for each report part when you use the Thumbnail view in the Report Part Gallery (as shown in Figure 29-8). You can click a button at the top of the Report Part Gallery to switch to Details view if you prefer to review a list of report parts by name, as shown in Figure 29-9.

FIGURE 29-9 You can switch to Details view to see a list of report parts in the Report Part Gallery.

In either the Details or the Thumbnail view, you can select a report part to view the information about the original author, the last author, the created and modified dates, the location of the report part on the report server, and the description, if one exists. If you decide to add the selected report item to your report, double-click it or drag it to the report design surface. At this point, the report is ready to run.

You can view the associated data source and dataset by opening the Report Data pane. If the report part author did not use a shared dataset, you can both view and modify the query. However, the data source information is not visible because a report part always requires a shared data source, which keeps the connection string secure.

Tip If you prefer that users cannot see or change the query, use a shared dataset when you create a report item to use as a report part.

Because the dataset is accessible in your report, regardless of whether it's shared or not, you can use it to add more report items to the report. For example, let's say you add a chart from a report part. You can resize it to make room for a matrix. Then use fields from the dataset and apply formatting, as shown in Figure 29-10. Without knowing how to add a data source or write a query, you can easily select a report part from the library and then reuse the dataset for your own report item.

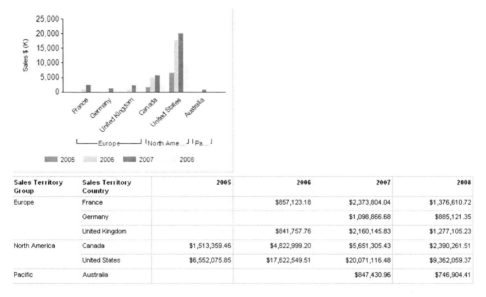

Sales Territory Group	Sales Territory Country	2005	2006	2007	2008
Europe	France		$857,123.18	$2,373,804.04	$1,376,610.72
	Germany			$1,098,866.68	$885,121.35
	United Kingdom		$841,757.76	$2,160,145.83	$1,277,105.23
North America	Canada	$1,513,359.46	$4,822,999.20	$5,651,305.43	$2,390,261.51
	United States	$6,552,075.85	$17,622,549.51	$20,071,116.48	$9,362,059.37
Pacific	Australia			$847,430.96	$746,904.41

FIGURE 29-10 You can reuse the dataset for a report part to create another report item in your report.

If you have permissions to save report parts, you can update the report part from Report Builder if you made changes to it. You can replace the existing report part or create a new report part as described in the "Redeployment of a report part" section earlier in this chapter. If you make a change to the report part, there is no obligation to update the report part on the report server. Your change can remain specific to your report.

Update notification

You can redeploy a report at any time by replacing the report server copy of the report part with a modified version. Meanwhile, it's possible that a user has added the original version of the report part to a report. When a user next opens a report containing a report part that changed after it was added to the report, a notification displays above the report in Report Builder, as shown in Figure 29-11.

Tip If you know that a report part has been redeployed to the report server while you have a report containing that report part already open in Report Builder, as an alternative to closing and reopening the report, you can click the Report Builder button and click Check For Updates on the menu to trigger the notification.

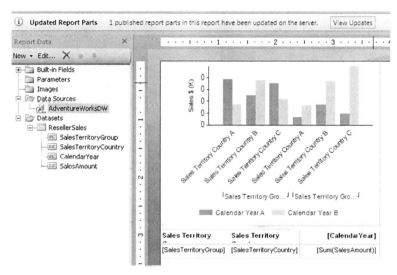

FIGURE 29-11 A notification of a report part update displays above your report in Report Builder.

Note Notification occurs only when you open a report that contains an updated report part in Report Builder.

When you see this notification, you have the option to review the change and accept it or ignore it. If you want to see which report parts are updated, click the View Updates button in the notification. Unless the report part author has added information to the description, nothing in the Update Report Parts dialog box, shown in Figure 29-12, indicates the type of change. It displays only the name and description of the report part and the date and author of the change.

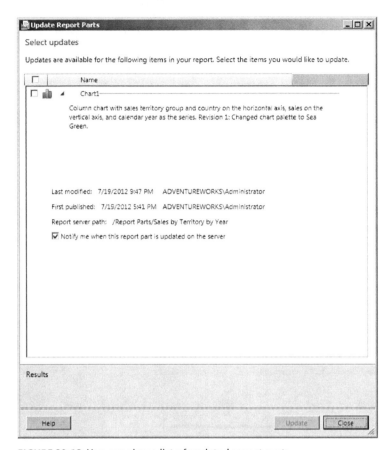

FIGURE 29-12 You can view a list of updated report parts.

Tip The Update Report Parts dialog box does not provide any information about the type of change made to each report part. It simply notifies you of a changed report part. To help users decide whether to accept the update, you can add details to the description.

If you made changes to the original version of the report part in your report, you might prefer to ignore any changes made to the official version. In that case, clear the Notify Me When The Report Part Is Updated On the Server check box to disable future notifications.

If you want to see the new report part, you can tentatively apply the change. Select the check box to the left of the report part name, and then click the Update button. You can then look at the change in the designer or switch to Preview mode to see how it looks. Any change you already made to the report part is removed. If you prefer not to keep the revised report part, use the Undo button to revert back to the version you saved in your report. Otherwise, you can keep the change by saving the report.

Choosing report parts vs. subreports

Report parts and subreports are similar in concept, allowing you to develop an object once and reuse it many times. But these two features differ in implementation. Furthermore, each has pros and cons for you to consider when your goal is to maximize reusability and enable self-service reporting.

The first thing to consider is whether you want to allow a user to make changes after adding the item to a report. With a report part, the user is free to make changes after adding it to a new report. However, a subreport is a reference to an existing report on the report server. Unless the user has the necessary permissions to edit that existing report separately, no changes can be made. Regardless of permissions, no change to the subreport can be made within the new report.

Another consideration is the report designer to use for report development. A user can use only Report Builder to work with report parts, and cannot use SSDT. That limitation is generally not a problem because most users who are not professional report developers use Report Builder anyway. SSDT allows a user to work with subreports only.

During the construction of a report, a user can use the search feature in the Report Part Gallery to find a report part by using a variety of criteria. However, the user must know the path and report name to add as a subreport. The user can open a web browser and search for a report by name or description but cannot search by other criteria, such as creator or type. There is no search feature for a subreport available in Report Builder.

When a user adds a report part to the new report, the user can immediately see the layout of the report item. With a subreport, the user sees only a gray rectangle in the report designer. The user must preview the report to see what it looks like.

A report part can contain only one report item, although that item can contain nested items. For example, you can create a tablix and nest sparklines in it to display one sparkline per row. By contrast, a subreport can have one or more report items. Whereas report parts are limited to specific types of report items, there are no such limitations on subreports.

The addition of a report part also adds the related dataset to a report. A user can then add more report items to the report by using the same dataset. A subreport is isolated. Nothing in the subreport is accessible for use in the new report.

The final consideration is the difference in change management. With a report part, the user can edit the report part to personalize it or update the new report with the most current copy of the report part. It is important to note that the update can occur only when the user opens the report for editing in Report Builder and not when rendering the report on the report server. A subreport always renders the most current version, without giving the user a choice. Furthermore, any changes to a subreport affect all reports that reference it, whereas changes to a report part affect only reports for which the report author applies the update.

CHAPTER 30

Preparing to use Power View

The key to ease of use in Power View is the availability of a good tabular model. That model must be accessible in some way from a SharePoint site. Although a tabular model might be satisfactory for use with Excel pivot tables or reports designed by using Report Builder or Report Designer, there are some improvements that you might need to make to a tabular model to better support the Power View design experience. In this chapter, we explain the types of tabular models you can use and how to enhance them to work best with Power View.

Using tabular models with Power View

Power View reports can only use a single source of data, a tabular model. Tabular models were intro-duced in SQL Server 2008 R2 as PowerPivot workbooks that you deploy to a SharePoint site for users to access using Excel Services. In SQL Server 2012, you can also deploy a tabular model to an Analysis Services instance running in tabular mode. For the most part, using either type of tabular model as a source for Power View reports is a similar experience, but there are some differences that you should understand if you are currently in the tabular model development phase and have a choice about which type to implement. In this section, we explain what tabular models are in general and how implementation of tabular models affects Power View. We also explain the steps necessary to enable access to tabular models for building Power View reports.

Introducing tabular models

The advantage of using a tabular model is the ability to consolidate data from a variety of sources: relational data, Analysis Services multidimensional models, Excel workbooks, PowerPivot for Share-Point workbooks, or data feeds from Windows Azure DataMarket or Reporting Services reports. One way to create a tabular model is to use PowerPivot for Excel to import data from these sources, define relationships in the data, and then build pivot table and pivot chart reports based on the resulting tabular model. Then you can deploy the reports and model as a single workbook to an Analysis Ser-vices instance running in PowerPivot for SharePoint mode. Another way is to use SSDT to import data and define relationships and then deploy the resulting Analysis Services tabular model to an Analysis Services tabular mode instance.

Note To learn more about developing PowerPivot models, see *Microsoft PowerPivot for Excel 2010: Give Your Data Meaning* by Marco Russo and Alberto Ferrari (Microsoft Press, October 2010). Keep in mind that even though the book is for the first version of PowerPivot released with SQL Server 2008 R2, much of the content about modeling data in PowerPivot remains relevant. You can see what's new in the version released with SQL Server 2012 at *http://technet.microsoft.com/library/hh272053(v=SQL.110).aspx*. For a good reference on developing tabular databases, see *Microsoft SQL Server 2012 Analysis Services: The BISM Tabular Model* by Marco Russo, Alberto Ferrari, and Chris Webb (Microsoft Press, 2012).

Whether you use PowerPivot for Excel or SSDT to design the model, the result is a tabular model, but you cannot deploy a PowerPivot model to an Analysis Services tabular-mode server nor can you deploy an Analysis Services tabular model from SSDT to a PowerPivot for SharePoint server. However, you can import a PowerPivot model into a tabular model project in SSDT and then deploy it to an Analysis Services tabular-mode server where users can access it as a tabular database. The way that a PowerPivot for SharePoint server and an Analysis Services tabular mode server store data and use memory is completely different and bears no resemblance to the storage and memory architecture of an Analysis Services multidimensional mode server.

Note Analysis Services multidimensional mode is the same technology introduced as OLAP Services in SQL Server 7.0 and enhanced with data mining technology in SQL Server 2000.

Although you use different tools to design PowerPivot models and Analysis Services tabular models and different tools for managing the servers, you can use the same client tools for reporting and analyzing data using these models. If you use either of these models as a data source when developing reports with Report Builder or Report Designer, you use the Analysis Services data source type and the MDX Query Designer, as we described in Chapter 16, "Using Analysis Services as a data source."

Creating a BI Semantic Model connection

A BI Semantic Model (BISM) connection is a file that you store on a SharePoint site to help users easily connect to either type of tabular model when creating Power View or Excel reports. It is very similar to an Office Data Connection (ODC) file or a shared data source file because it specifies the location of the data to use for the client connection, but it differs from these file types in that it does not contain authentication information. You store the BISM connection in a document library to which the BI Semantic Model Connection content type has been added (as described in Chapter 4, "Installing Reporting Services" in the "Configuring a SharePoint site" section).

Note If your users connect to PowerPivot data only and have permissions to access workbooks in a PowerPivot Gallery, a BISM connection is not required. As explained in Chapter 31, "Using Power View," a user can launch Power View from a PowerPivot Gallery site in SharePoint after selecting a workbook.

To create a BISM connection, you must have Contribute permissions or higher in the document library to which you are adding the file. Open the document library, click the Documents tab of the ribbon, click the New Document down arrow, and click BI Semantic Model Connection. Name the file, and optionally provide a description to give users more information about the connection.

 Note If you see the following error when you try to create a new BISM connection, "Could not load type 'Microsoft.AnalysisServices.SharePoint.Integration.ASLinkFilePage,'" you must open Central Administration, go to System Settings, and open Manage Farm Solutions. Then click the Powerpivotwebapp.wsp link, click Deploy Solution, and select the web application hosting the document library in which the error occurs.

The connection information that you provide depends on the location of the tabular data, as follows:

- **PowerPivot data** Type the location of the PowerPivot workbook in the Workbook URL Or Server Name box, as shown in Figure 30-1. For example, if you have a workbook called Sales Analysis.xlsx at http://<*server*>/PowerPivot Gallery, you enter the location of the workbook like this (replacing <*server*> with your server name):

    ```
    http://<server>/PowerPivot Gallery/Sales Analysis.xlsx
    ```

FIGURE 30-1 You provide the workbook URL when the source data is in a PowerPivot workbook.

> **Note** The BISM connection supports access to PowerPivot workbooks created with either SQL Server 2008 R2 or SQL Server 2012 versions of PowerPivot for Excel.

- **Tabular database**   Type the server name, server and instance name, or IP address in the Workbook URL Or Server Name box, and type the name of the tabular database in the Database box, as shown in Figure 30-2.

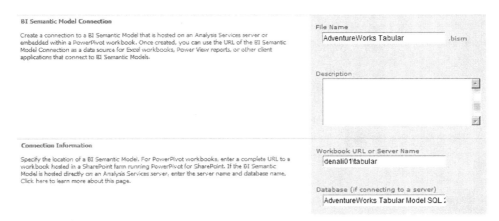

FIGURE 30-2 You provide the server name and database for a connection to a tabular model in Analysis Services.

When you click OK, the PowerPivot service application validates the connection. A warning message displays if the server location is invalid, the workbook or database does not exist, or the Power-Pivot service application does not have permissions to connect to the tabular database. In that case, you have the option to select the Save The Link File Without Connection Validation check box to save the file despite of the warning and then correct the permissions problem later.

> **Note** The BISM connection file might appear in the document library as a different content type. For example, in the default Data Connections library in a Business Intelligence Center site, a new BISM connection is identified as a PerformancePoint Data Source. This errone-ous assignment has no effect on the behavior of the file. It merely groups the file with other files having the same content type. You can correct the content type by clicking the down arrow next to the file name, clicking Edit Properties, and then selecting BI Semantic Model Connection in the Content Type drop-down list.

Next, you must give users Read permissions on the BISM connection file, in the same way that you give users Read permissions on other SharePoint content as described in Chapter 24, "Securing report server content." If the BISM connection references a PowerPivot workbook, the user must also have Read permissions on that workbook. Similarly, if the connection references a tabular model, you must assign the user to a role having Read permissions for the tabular model, as described in the "Authentication, tabular databases, and BISM connection files" sidebar in this chapter.

After permissions are set, the BISM connection is ready for use. You can click the file link to launch Power View automatically, or you can click the down arrow on the file name to open the submenu and select Create Power View Report, as shown in Figure 30-3. Notice that you can also use this submenu to edit the connection or to launch Excel. If you choose the option to launch Excel, a message displays, prompting you to open or save the ODC file. When you open this file, you can browse the data referenced by the connection by using pivot tables and pivot charts in Excel just as you would browse an Analysis Services multidimensional database.

FIGURE 30-3 You can launch Power View or Excel from the connection's submenu to browse its data.

Authentication, tabular databases, and BISM connection files

When a user opens the BISM connection file, the connection information it contains downloads the connection to the user's client application, Excel or Power View. At that point, the client application connects to the data source by using your Windows credentials. The PowerPivot service application manages connection requests between Power View and the Analysis Services instance hosting the workbook data and requires no additional configuration for authentication. However, if Power View must connect to an Analysis Services tabular instance, the requirements for authentication depend on the client application.

In Excel, the connection is a single hop to the Analysis Services tabular instance. That is, the user's credentials travel from the client connection to Analysis Services, and no further. In this scenario, either the Kerberos or the NT LAN Manager (NTLM) authentication protocol is suitable, but Kerberos is not required to successfully authenticate.

However, Power View passes the user's identity to SharePoint, which in turn passes it to the Analysis Services tabular instance. When the user's identity must be shared with two servers in this type of scenario, the connection is a double hop and requires implementation of the Kerberos protocol with delegation. When Power View first attempts to connect to Analysis Services, it automatically tries to use Kerberos to authenticate the user's identity. If that attempt fails because Kerberos is not configured, Power View makes a second attempt using NTLM and the identity of the Reporting Services service application to connect to Analysis Services and passes the user's identity in the connection string using the *effectiveusername* parameter. The Analysis Services tabular instance allows the Reporting Services service application to make the connection on your behalf, known as impersonation, as long as the service application has administrative rights on Analysis Services and the user's identity has Read permissions on the tabular database.

To grant administrative rights to the Reporting Services service application, you must first know the identity to use. In Central Administration, click Security, click Configure Service Accounts, and select the service application pool for your Reporting Services shared service application in the drop-down list at the top of the page. Take note of the identity specified in the Select An Account For This Component box. Then open SQL Server Management Studio, and connect to the Analysis Services tabular instance. In Object Explorer, right-click the server name, click Properties, click Security, and then click Add. Type the domain name and user name for the Reporting Services service application identity.

Next, you must assign the user's identity to a role with read access to the tabular database. If the database already has this type of role defined, you can update the membership of the role in SQL Server Management Studio. Expand the database folder in Object Explorer, expand the Roles folder, and double-click the applicable role. In the Role Properties dialog box, click Membership, click Add, and then type the domain name and user name to add. If a role is not already defined, you must ask the tabular model author to add a role and redeploy it to Analysis Services. For more information about adding roles to a tabular model, see *http://msdn .microsoft.com/en-us/library/hh213165.aspx*.

Enhancing tabular models for Power View

One of the benefits of tabular models is the ease with which you can combine data to support ad hoc reporting and analysis. Excel works well with both PowerPivot workbook data and tabular databases, but Power View might require some additional enhancements to the tabular model. For example, there are properties that identify model elements to Power View to change the appearance and behavior of the data

Important After making any changes to the tabular model, you must deploy the revised tabular model to a server. If you are working with PowerPivot data, you must save the workbook to a SharePoint document library. If you are working with a tabular database, you must deploy the model to an Analysis Services server running in tabular mode.

Summarizing values

When you import data into a tabular model, the model detects data types for each column and recognizes numeric values. In addition, each column has a *Summarize By* property that instructs Power View how to aggregate the numeric value when you add it to a pivot table or report. The default setting for this property is Default. When the column's data type is Currency or Decimal Number, Power View applies the *Sum* function to the numeric value when you add it to the report, as shown in Figure 30-4.

Product Category Name	Sales Amount
Accessories	571,297.93
Bikes	66,302,381.56
Clothing	1,777,840.84
Components	11,799,076.66
Total	**80,450,596.98**

FIGURE 30-4 Power View automatically applies the *Sum* function to fields with Currency and Decimal Number data types.

For columns having a data type of Whole Number, Power View does not automatically apply the *Sum* function. Instead, you see individual rows of data, as shown in Figure 30-5.

Product Category Name	Order Quantity
Accessories	1
Accessories	2
Accessories	3
Accessories	4
Accessories	5
Accessories	6
Accessories	7
Accessories	8

FIGURE 30-5 By default, Power View does not aggregate fields with the Whole Number data type.

You can manually override this behavior in Power View by changing the aggregate function applicable to the field (as the column is called in the report), but you must do this each time you create a visualization and include that field. A preferable approach is to change the *Summarize By* property in the model. You can choose one of the following options:

■ Default

■ Sum

■ Count

■ Min

■ Max

■ Average

■ Distinct Count

■ Do Not Summarize

> **Note** Use the Do Not Summarize option when you have a numeric column that you never want Power View to aggregate. For example, if you have a calendar year field containing values like 2010, 2011, 2012, and so on, you want Power View to treat these values as distinct strings rather than sum them as numeric values.

The steps you take to modify the *Summarize By* property depend on the type of tabular model, as follows:

■ **PowerPivot data** In the PowerPivot window, open the table containing the field to update, click the field's column, click the Advanced tab on the ribbon, click Summarize By, and select the applicable aggregate function, as shown in Figure 30-6.

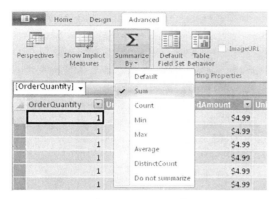

FIGURE 30-6 Use the Summarize By button on the PowerPivot ribbon to set a field's default aggregation function for Power View.

 Note The Advanced tab of the PowerPivot ribbon does not display by default. You must click the File button in the top-left corner above the ribbon and select the Switch To Advanced Mode command to display it.

- **Tabular database** In SSDT, open the table containing the field to update, open the Properties window, click the field's column, and select the applicable aggregate function in the *Summarize By* property's drop-down list, as shown in Figure 30-7.

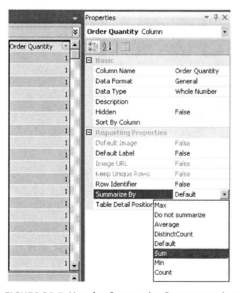

FIGURE 30-7 Use the *Summarize By* property in a tabular model project to set a field's default aggregation function for Power View.

After you update the model (and redeploy if it's a tabular database), you see the Sigma symbol display next to the changed field when viewing the field list in Power View, as shown in Figure 30-8. Because users frequently want to aggregate numeric values in reports, it's a good idea to help users more easily distinguish those fields. The pound sign (#) appears next to a field with the *Summarize By* property set to Count, a calculator appears next to a calculation (also known as a measure), and a Sigma symbol appears next to fields for the remaining *Summarize By* options (excluding Default and Do Not Summarize). In this example, the *Sales Amount* field appears with the Sigma symbol, even though its *Summarize By* property is set to Default, because it has a Currency data type.

```
▲ ResellerSales
    ☐ 🖩 Average Sales
    ☐ Σ Average Value
    ☐ # Count Value
    ☐ Σ Distinct Count Value
    ☐ Σ Max Value
    ☐ Σ Min Value
    ☐ Σ Order Quantity
    ☐ Σ Sales Amount
    ☐    Sales Order Line Number
    ☐    Sales Order Number
```

FIGURE 30-8 Power View's field list displays icons for fields that it can aggregate.

Formatting values

Another property you should consider changing is the *Data Format* property. A numeric field with its *Data Format* property set to General displays without thousands separators, making large values difficult to read. You can choose one of the following options:

- General

- Decimal Number

- Whole Number

- Currency

- Percentage

- Scientific

You can change the *Data Format* property in your tabular model using the applicable steps, as follows:

- **PowerPivot data**   In the PowerPivot window, open the table containing the field to update, click the field's column, click the Home tab on the ribbon, and select the desired format in the Format drop-down list, as shown in Figure 30-9. You can use the formatting buttons on the ribbon to set the currency format, thousands separator, and number of decimal places as applicable.

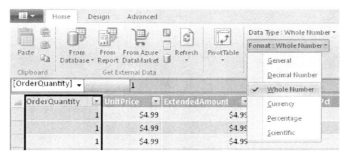

FIGURE 30-9 Use the PowerPivot ribbon to set the *Format* property for a column to change the display format for a field in Power View.

■ **Tabular database**   In SSDT, open the table containing the field to update, open the Properties window, click the field's column, and select the desired format in the *Data Format* property's drop-down list, as shown in Figure 30-10. Also, set the *Currency Symbol*, *Decimal Places*, and *Show Thousand Separator* properties as applicable.

FIGURE 30-10 Use the *Data Format* property in a tabular model project to change the display format for a field in Power View.

Setting the default sort

Columns with a text data type sort alphabetically by default, which is usually the desired behavior. However, when you want a table or other visualization to include months, the default behavior does not produce a helpful report, as shown in Figure 30-11. Although Power View allows you to sort columns in the report in ascending or descending order, there is no way to place months into chronological order.

Month	Order Quantity
April	13,794
August	28,236
December	19,161
February	13,662
January	8,777
July	18,193
June	18,587
March	12,103
May	21,035
November	21,622
October	14,054
September	25,154
Total	**214,378**

FIGURE 30-11 Power View sorts a field with a Text data type in alphabetical order by default.

To override the default sort order of Month (or any field), you must change its *Sort By Column* property. Your model must include another column that designates the correct sort order, such as Month Number Of Year. You can then change the *Sort By Column* property in your tabular model by using the applicable steps, as follows:

- **PowerPivot data**   In the PowerPivot window, open the table containing the field to update, and click the field's column. On the Home tab of the ribbon, click Sort By Column, and then in the Sort By Column dialog box, map the column to sort with the column to sort by, as shown in Figure 30-12.

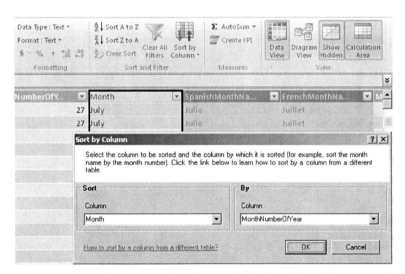

FIGURE 30-12 Use the Sort By Column button in the PowerPivot ribbon to explicitly set a field's sort order for Power View.

- **Tabular database**   In SSDT, open the table containing the field to update, open the Properties window, click the field's column, and then select the applicable column in the *Sort By Column* property's drop-down list, as shown in Figure 30-13.

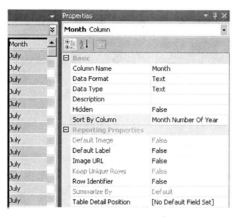

FIGURE 30-13 Use the *Sort By Column* property in a tabular model project to explicitly set a field's sort order for Power View.

With the *Sort By Column* set to a new value, you can see the correct sort order when you use the field in a report, as shown in Figure 30-14.

Month	Order Quantity
January	8,777
February	13,662
March	12,103
April	13,794
May	21,035
June	18,587
July	18,193
August	28,236
September	25,154
October	14,054
November	21,622
December	19,161
Total	**214,378**

FIGURE 30-14 Power View uses the *Sort By Column* property to sort a field when applicable.

Note Sometimes you might need to create a calculated column to combine values from multiple columns to get the right sort order. For example, if you have a column that displays month and year, such as January 2010, February 2010, and so on, you should not use Month Of Year to sort. Otherwise, Power View sorts months irrespective of year, such as January 2010, January 2011, January 2012, February 2010, and so on. Instead, you can create a calculated column with an expression like *[Calendar Year] * 100 + [Month Of Year]* to produce a value like 201001, 201002, and so on. You can then use this calculated column as the Sort By column to produce the correct sort order for a column displaying both month and year in the same field.

Marking the date table

The Data Analysis Expressions (DAX) language that you use to create calculations in a tabular model includes several time-intelligence functions. These functions allow you to compare one time period to another or to accumulate values over multiple periods of time, such as month-to-date or year-to-date. For these functions to work correctly, you must identify the date table in the tabular mode, as follows:

■ **PowerPivot data**   In the PowerPivot window, open the date table, click the Design tab on the ribbon, click Mark As Date Table, and then select Mark As Date Table, as shown in Figure 30-15. In the Mark As Date Table dialog box, select a column having a Date data type and unique values for each row in the table.

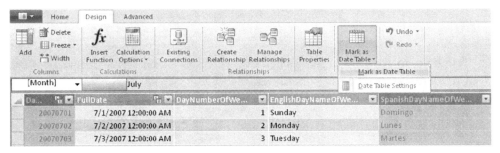

FIGURE 30-15 Use the Mark As Date Table button in the PowerPivot ribbon to identify a table containing dates.

■ **Tabular database**   In SSDT, open the date table, and then point to Date on the Table menu and select Mark As Date Table, as shown in Figure 30-16. In the Mark As Date Table dialog box, select a column having a Date data type and unique values for each row in the table.

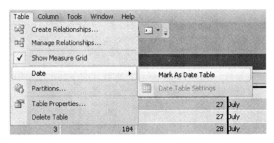

FIGURE 30-16 Use the Table menu to access the Mark As Date Table command when you need to identify a table containing dates.

The field that you identify in the Mark As Date Table dialog box displays in the Power View field list with a special icon to identify it as a unique value in the date table, as shown in Figure 30-17.

- ▲ Date
  - ☐ Calendar Quarter
  - ☐ Calendar Year
  - ☐▦ Date
  - ☐ Day
  - ☐ Day Of Month
  - ☐ Day Of Week
  - ☐ Day Of Year
  - ☐ Month
  - ☐ Month Of Year
  - ☐ Week Of Year

FIGURE 30-17 Power View's field list displays an icon for the column containing unique values (such as dates) in a date table.

Managing grouping behavior

By default, Power View dynamically groups rows based on the current visualization. For example, if you have a table in the model containing product names and product categories and use Power View to display a table containing product names and a separate table containing product categories, the number of rows in each table varies, as shown in Figure 30-18. Power View displays one row for each distinct value in a field.

Product Name	▲ Order Quantity
AWC Logo Cap	6,121
Bike Wash - Dissolver	2,411
Cable Lock	1,086
Chain	774
Classic Vest, L	12
Classic Vest, M	2,085
Classic Vest, S	4,079
Front Brakes	789
Front Derailleur	813
Full-Finger Gloves, L	3,365
Full-Finger Gloves, M	2,197
Full-Finger Gloves, S	493

Product Category Name	Order Quantity
Accessories	25,839
Bikes	75,015
Clothing	64,497
Components	49,027
Total	**214,378**

FIGURE 30-18 Power View automatically groups data based on the fields you add to a visualization.

Sometimes you might combine multiple fields from the same table in a matrix, and discover that Power View automatically creates a group for each row and calculates a subtotal, as shown in Figure 30-19. In this case, the subtotal is redundant and repeats the same information that appears in the row above it.

Product Name	Product Category Name	2005	2006	2007	2008	Total
AWC Logo Cap	Clothing	520	1,853	2,677	1,071	6,121
	Total	520	1,853	2,677	1,071	6,121
Bike Wash - Dissolver	Accessories			1,461	950	2,411
	Total			1,461	950	2,411
Cable Lock	Accessories		676	410		1,086
	Total		676	410		1,086
Chain	Components			470	304	774
	Total			470	304	774
Classic Vest, L	Clothing			12		12
	Total			12		12

FIGURE 30-19 Power View creates subtotals for each row group it detects in a matrix.

If you convert the matrix shown in Figure 30-19 to a column chart, you find that Power View automatically creates a multiples chart, as shown in Figure 30-20. Power View uses the first field on rows in the matrix as a grouping for each individual chart, and uses the second field on rows as a category grouping on each chart's horizontal axis. The result is a chart that is difficult to interpret.

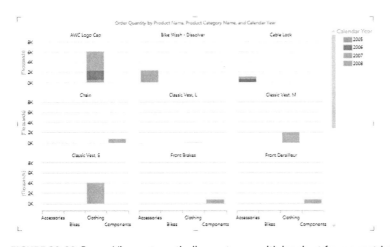

FIGURE 30-20 Power View automatically creates a multiples chart from a matrix having two fields in a row group.

The dynamic grouping behavior that Power View applies to fields is usually desirable, especially because you can drag fields into a visualization and view the results of the new grouping instantly. However, in some cases, this grouping behavior should not apply when you use a field that represents row-level detail of a table, such as individual products, employees, customers, or sales transaction numbers. To ensure correct grouping of detail records, you should set the *Row Identifier* property on each table containing detail data. Generally speaking, you use this property to identify the primary key column of a table if the data comes from a relational source or from the column containing unique, non-blank values.

Note This step is not required for tables containing summarized data or for lookup tables. In addition, you cannot directly set the *Row Identifier* property for a table that you have marked as a date table. The Mark As Date Table dialog box (described in the "Marking the date table" section of this chapter) performs this step for you.

In some tables, it might be possible to have data that has different values in the row identifier column but has duplicate values in another column that you more commonly used in a visualization. For example, you might have a customer key or product key to uniquely identify each row in a table, but you might also have multiple rows which contain the same customer name or product name even though each row represents a distinctly different entity or information about the same entity at different points in time. The latter case is a common scenario when you use a table from a data warehouse that is tracking slowly changing dimensions and thus assigns a separate key to a new record added when information changes, such as a price or a weight. To prevent Power View from grouping the duplicate values in a column, you can set the *Keep Unique Rows* property. Typically, this column has nearly unique values rather than unique columns like the row identifier.

You set these two properties using the Table Behavior dialog box. The steps you perform to open this dialog box depend on the type of tabular model, as follows:

- **PowerPivot data** In the PowerPivot window, open the table for which you are setting the table behavior properties. On the Advanced Tab of the PowerPivot ribbon, click the Table Behavior button.

- **Tabular database** In SSDT, open the table for which you are setting the table behavior properties. In the Properties window, click in the *Table Behavior* box to reveal the ellipsis button, and then click the button.

In Table Behavior dialog box, select the column containing unique, non-blank values in the Row Identifier drop-down list and select columns containing nearly unique values in the Keep Unique Rows list, as shown in Figure 30-21.

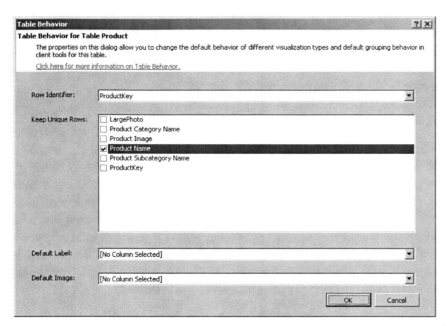

FIGURE 30-21 You can use the *Row Identifier* and *Keep Unique Rows* properties to change the default grouping behavior for fields in a table.

Columns that are unique or nearly unique, based on your selections in the Table Behavior dialog box, appear in the Power View field list with special icons, as shown in Figure 30-22. Sometimes you might not want the row identifier to appear in the field list, such as when it represents a surrogate key value that has no business meaning for the user. In that case, you can hide the column in the model, which does not change its status as a row identifier.

FIGURE 30-22 The selections in the Table Behavior dialog box add icons to the corresponding fields in the Power View field list.

Note In the example shown in Figure 30-22, the *LargePhoto* field displays with the special icon, although it was not selected in the Table Behavior dialog box. This field has a Binary Data data type, which requires you to specify a row identifier for the table. It does not appear in the field list for the table until this property is set.

After you set the table behavior properties, the grouping behavior changes. As you can see in Figure 30-23, there are now three rows for the AWC Logo Cap product. Power View uses the row identifier to recognize detail rows in combination with the *Keep Unique Rows* property to determine whether to group detail rows having the same Product Name value.

Product Name	Order Quantity
AWC Logo Cap	985
AWC Logo Cap	2,304
AWC Logo Cap	2,832
Bike Wash - Dissolver	2,411
Cable Lock	1,086
Chain	774
Classic Vest, L	12
Classic Vest, M	2,085
Classic Vest, S	4,079
Front Brakes	785
Front Derailleur	813
Full-Finger Gloves, L	3,365
Full-Finger Gloves, M	2,197

FIGURE 30-23 Power View no longer groups products having the same Product Name value based on the new table behavior property settings.

> **Note** Although the grouping behavior shown in Figure 30-23 is now correct, it might be confusing to users to see the same product name appear multiple times in a visualization. You can add additional fields to the visualization to distinguish one row from another, or you can add a calculated column to the tabular model to append identifying information, such as the applicable date range for a product or a customer number for a customer name.

Another outcome of making changes to the table behavior properties is a different layout of data in a matrix, as shown in Figure 30-24. First, the three separate products display correctly as a result of setting the *Keep Unique Rows* property. Second, Power View recognizes the inclusion of the row identifier field, Product Name, which is in the same table as the Product Category Name field, and no longer creates a row grouping for subtotals. The result is a more compact layout of the matrix, with no loss of information.

Product Name	Product Category Name	2005	2006	2007	2008	Total
AWC Logo Cap	Clothing	520	465			985
AWC Logo Cap	Clothing		1,388	916		2,304
AWC Logo Cap	Clothing			1,761	1,071	2,832
Bike Wash - Dissolver	Accessories			1,461	950	2,411
Cable Lock	Accessories		676	410		1,086
Chain	Components			470	304	774

FIGURE 30-24 Power View excludes the subtotal row when you include the row identifier field as the first row field in a matrix.

Note It is not necessary to set the *Keep Unique Rows* property on a table to correct the matrix behavior as shown in Figure 30-24. If you do not have duplicate values in any table column, you can set the *Row Identifier* property and ignore the other properties in the Table Behavior dialog box to achieve the correct matrix grouping.

Now when you convert the matrix shown in Figure 30-24 to a column chart, Power View assigns the Product Name field to the horizontal axis and discards Product Category Name, as shown in Figure 30-25. However, the chart becomes quite large, to reflect each unique product record, and now contains too much detail to be useful. You can apply filters or add slicers to the view to reduce the number of products to display in the chart, which you learn how to do in Chapter 31, "Using Power View."

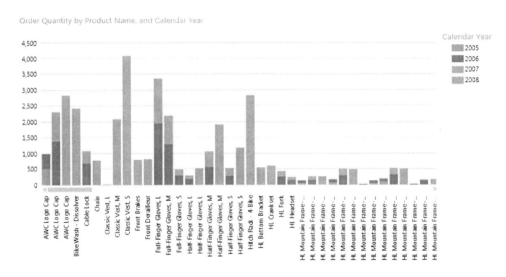

FIGURE 30-25 Power View automatically assigns the row identifier to the horizontal axis when converting a matrix to a chart.

Adding images

Several features in Power View allow you to include images alongside text and numeric data from your model. To use these features, you can store images directly in the model as binary data or you can upload images to a website or SharePoint document library and add an expression to a column in your model that resolves as a URL reference to the external images.

Using binary data

If you store images in a database table, you can import the column containing the images just like any other column in the table. The import process should correctly set the data type of the column to Binary Data. However, if you make no changes to the table, you discover that the column does not appear in the field list when you open Power View after connecting to your tabular model. The problem results from Power View's inability to automatically detect the column that makes each row unique. You must manually configure the *Row Identifier* property, as described in the "Managing grouping behavior" section of this chapter. When Power View knows the row identifier column, it displays the name of the binary data column in the field list, and you can add it to any visualization that supports images, as described in Chapter 31.

Using external images

As another option, you can use external images located on a web server or in a SharePoint document library. For example, let's say you have a SharePoint document site called BI containing a document library called Products into which you upload Portable Network Graphics (PNG) files and each file includes the product key in its name. You can add a calculated column to the model called Product Image and use the following DAX expression (replacing *<server>* with your SharePoint server name):

```
="http://<server>/sites/BI/Products/Product_" & [ProductKey] & ".png"
```

Although the model correctly resolves the URL for each file, Power View displays the URL as text when you include this field in a view, as shown in Figure 30-26.

Product Name	Product Image
All-Purpose Bike Stand	http://denali01/sites/BI/Products/Product_486.png
AWC Logo Cap	http://denali01/sites/BI/Products/Product_223.png
AWC Logo Cap	http://denali01/sites/BI/Products/Product_224.png
AWC Logo Cap	http://denali01/sites/BI/Products/Product_225.png
Bike Wash - Dissolver	http://denali01/sites/BI/Products/Product_484.png
Cable Lock	http://denali01/sites/BI/Products/Product_447.png
Chain	http://denali01/sites/BI/Products/Product_559.png

FIGURE 30-26 Power View does not automatically recognize URL addresses stored as text data in a column.

Whether you use a DAX expression to construct the URL or retrieve the URL as part of the query that imports data into the tabular model, the column values are stored as a text data type. This data type is correct because you are storing an external reference in the column and not the image itself. Instead, you must set the column's *Image URL* property to True, using the method applicable to the type of tabular model, as follows:

- **PowerPivot data**   In the PowerPivot window, open the table containing the field to update, click the field's column, click the Advanced tab on the ribbon, and select the ImageURL check box, as shown in Figure 30-27.

FIGURE 30-27 You must select the ImageURL check box on the Advanced tab of the PowerPivot ribbon to instruct Power View to retrieve the image file.

- **Tabular database** In SSDT, open the table containing the field to update, open the Properties window, click the field's column, and select True in the drop-down list for the *Image URL* property, as shown in Figure 30-28.

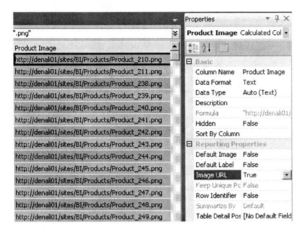

FIGURE 30-28 You must set the *Image URL* property to True to instruct Power View to retrieve the image file.

When you change the *Image URL* property, Power View correctly interprets the text as a URL and retrieves the image when you include it in a view, as shown in Figure 30-29.

FIGURE 30-29 Power View displays external images correctly after you set the field's *Image URL* property to True.

Improving the appearance of identifying information

Power View includes a unique visualization feature called a *card* that you can use to display any combination of fields. With the exception of images, all fields display in the card using the same size font, as shown in Figure 30-30. When you include a binary data image field in a table, Power View automatically resizes the image and displays it on the left side of the card, giving it a more prominent position than other fields and other images in the card.

FIGURE 30-30 Power View displays an image on the left side of a card visualization.

> **Note** The two images in Figure 30-30, although identical, come from two different fields, both of which have binary data types. The image on the left is from binary data in the model, and the image on the right is from an external SharePoint document library. The two images are included in this example to illustrate the difference in behavior between binary data and external images when you do not explicitly specify a default image for a table. If you were to include two binary data images in the card visualization, Power View selects one of the images to display more prominently.

For each table in a tabular model, you can identify a default label and a default image, as shown in Figure 30-31, to use as identifying information for each card. You set these table properties in the tabular model in the Table Behavior dialog box, just as you do for *Row Identifier* and *Keep Unique Rows* (described in the "Managing grouping behavior" section of this chapter).

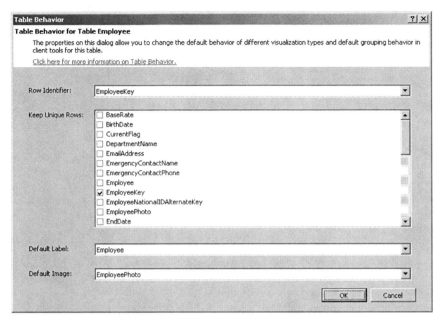

FIGURE 30-31 You can assign fields as the *Default Label* and *Default Image* properties for a table to enhance the appearance of cards and tiles.

The fields you specify as the default label and the default image display more prominently than other fields in a card, as shown in Figure 30-32. Notice that Power View displays field names below the value for all other fields but omits the field names for the default label and default image. As with any other type of visualization in Power View, you cannot adjust the font size or style of any field in a card.

FIGURE 30-32 Power View increases the size of the default label and default image and displays them on the left side of a card.

Note Only one image displays in Figure 30-32 due to the removal of the second image, to more realistically represent the layout of a card.

Power View also uses the default label and default image in the navigation strip of a tile, as shown in Figure 30-33. If you specify a default label only for a table without specifying a default image, the navigation strip displays the field value for the default label using a larger font. The default label and default image (if available) always display in the navigation strip of the tile, even if you do not include those fields in the visualization contained by the tile.

FIGURE 30-33 Power View displays the default image and default label in the navigation strip of a tile.

Simplifying the creation of a new table

The last enhancement you might consider making to your tabular model is the specification of a Default Field Set. Every visualization in Power View begins with the creation of a new table. If there are fields that users commonly include in Power View visualizations, you can add these fields to the Default Field Set. In Power View, you can double-click a table name in the field list to add the default fields as a new table to the current view.

The steps to open the Default Field Set dialog box depend on the type of tabular model, as follows:

- **PowerPivot data**   In the PowerPivot window, open the table containing the field to update, click the Advanced tab on the ribbon, and click Default Field Set.

- **Tabular database**   In SSDT, open the table for which you are setting the Default Field Set. In the Properties window, click in the *Default Field Set* box to reveal the ellipsis button, and then click the button.

In the Default Field Set dialog box, select a field and then click the Add button to move it to the Default Fields, In Order list, as shown in Figure 30-34. The sequence in which you arrange the fields, from top to bottom, is the order in which Power View displays the fields in a table, from left to right.

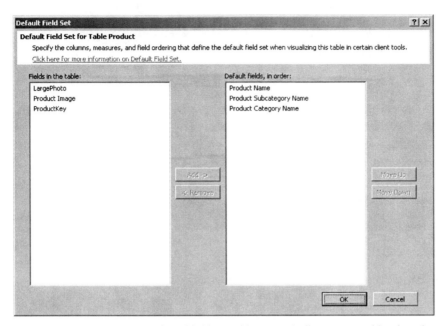

FIGURE 30-34 You can set up a list of fields to add automatically to a new table when the user double-clicks a table name in the Power View field list.

CHAPTER 31

Using Power View

Power View is an ad hoc reporting tool designed to make it easy for non-technical users to interact with data. In traditional report development, much of the time you spend using Report Designer or Report Builder is focused on designing the layout of data and configuring properties controlling the look and feel of a report. In ad hoc reporting, your focus is on exploring the data to find an answer to a specific question and then quickly and easily answering subsequent questions inspired by the data you find. Power View applies built-in formatting rules to produce a consistent and attractive appearance across multiple reports, regardless of the report author's skill level. After creating your Power View report, you can share it with others by publishing it to a SharePoint document library or PowerPivot Gallery or you can include it in an interactive PowerPoint presentation.

Getting started with Power View

To use Power View, you must install Reporting Services in SharePoint integrated mode by using SharePoint Server 2010 Enterprise Edition. You then access Power View from SharePoint using a supported browser by connecting to a compatible data source. When Power View opens, you can explore the data model in preparation for designing your report.

Verifying browser requirements

Power View runs as a Silverlight-based application in your web browser. Table 31-1 lists the browsers supporting Power View by operating system. You can use either the 32-bit or 64-bit version of the browsers, with one exception. You can use only the 32-bit version of Firefox 7 with Power View.

TABLE 31-1 Browser support for Power View

Operating System	Internet Explorer 7	Internet Explorer 8	Internet Explorer 9	Firefox 7	Safari 5
Windows Vista	✓	✓	✓	✓	
Windows 7		✓	✓	✓	
Windows Server 2008	✓	✓	✓	✓	

Operating System	Internet Explorer 7	Internet Explorer 8	Internet Explorer 9	Firefox 7	Safari 5
Windows Server 2008 R2		✓	✓		
Mac OSX 10.6- 10.7 (Intel- based)					✓

Connecting to a data source

With Report Builder or Report Designer, you open the application and then select a data source. By contrast, with Power View, you select a data source first. As we described in Chapter 30, "Preparing to use Power View," Power View requires you to use a tabular model as a data source. You can connect to a tabular model from a PowerPivot Gallery, a Reporting Services shared data source, or a Business Intelligence Semantic Model (BISM) connection file.

PowerPivot Gallery

A PowerPivot workbook is one type of tabular model that you can use as a data source for Power View. You do not need to perform any special configuration tasks to make it available to Power View. If you have permissions to view a report in the PowerPivot Gallery, you can use it as a Power View source. Just click the Create Power View Report icon in the upper-right corner of the PowerPivot workbook tile, as shown in Figure 31-1.

FIGURE 31-1 Use the Create Power View Report button to open Power View from the PowerPivot Gallery.

Reporting Services shared data source

Another option for accessing a tabular data model is to use a Reporting Services shared data source that has a Microsoft BISM data source type, as described in Chapter 30. You configure the data source to connect either to a PowerPivot workbook or to a tabular model deployed to Analysis Services. Unless you have permissions to open the data source to view the connection string, you cannot tell which tabular model connection type the data source uses. To open Power View, point to the report name, click the down arrow, and then click Create Power View Report, as shown in Figure 31-2.

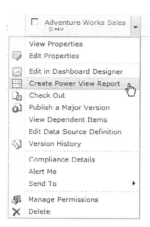

FIGURE 31-2 Use the Reporting Services shared data source's submenu to start Power View.

BI Semantic Model connection file

You can use a BISM connection file to start Power View just like you use a Reporting Services shared data source. The BISM connection file can reference either a PowerPivot workbook or a tabular model deployed to Analysis Services, as described in Chapter 30. Point to the file name in a SharePoint library, click the down arrow to open the menu, and click Create Power View Report, as shown in Figure 31-3.

FIGURE 31-3 Use the BISM connection file's submenu to start Power View.

Getting familiar with the design environment

When you open Power View to create a new report, the Power View design environment displays a blank workspace, as shown in Figure 31-4. You add data to the report in the form of visualizations by selecting data from the field list to the right of the workspace and applying a visualization from the dynamic ribbon at the top of your screen.

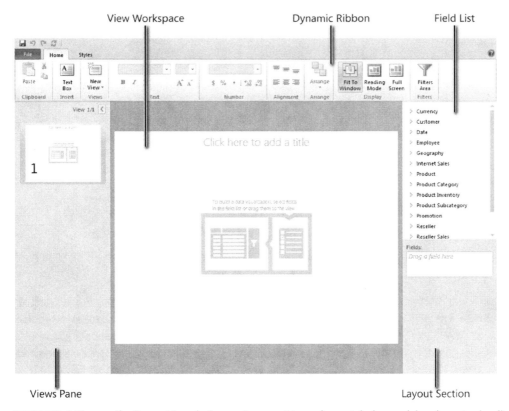

FIGURE 31-4 You use the Power View design environment to explore a tabular model and create visualizations.

View workspace

The workspace is a fixed height and width, much like a PowerPoint slide, and cannot be resized. However, you can add more views to the report if you need more space for additional visualizations.

At the top of the view workspace, a text box displays the words "Click here to add a title." If you ignore this text box, no title is visible when you change the display to reading mode or full screen mode or export to PowerPoint. If you want to add a title, click inside the text box and type the text. You can then highlight the entire text or a portion of the text and apply different formatting by using the ribbon commands.

Tip If you know that a process has updated data in the tabular model after you open Power View, you can use the Refresh button on the Power View Quick Access toolbar (above the ribbon) to reload data in your report. If you use the Refresh button on your browser toolbar, a prompt to leave the current page displays, but you lose your edits in the report if you leave the page.

Views pane

You might find it easier to explore your data when you arrange visualizations as separate views. All views in your report must use the same tabular model as their source, but otherwise, each view can contain separate visualizations. Furthermore, the filters you define for a view, as we explain later in this chapter, apply only to that view. Use the New View button on the Home tab of the toolbar to create a new blank view or to duplicate the currently selected view, as shown in Figure 31-5.

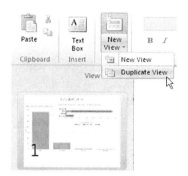

FIGURE 31-5 You can add multiple views to a single Power View report.

Ribbon

The initial ribbon contains two tabs, Home and Styles, as shown in Figure 31-6. The Design and Layout tabs appear when you add fields to the report, and the contents of the ribbon change to show commands applicable to the selected item in a visualization.

FIGURE 31-6 You use the Home tab of the ribbon to apply formatting, change the display, or toggle the display of the Filters Area.

The Home ribbon contains the following nine sections:

- **Clipboard**   Because Power View is a Silverlight-based application, you cannot use control keys to perform copy, cut, and paste operations. Instead, you must use the three commands in this group of the Home ribbon.

- **Insert**   You can add a text box to a view when you want to add comments or a custom label for a visualization. After you insert the text box, you can move it to a new location in the view.

- **Views**   You can create separate views in the same report. Each view is analogous to a separate slide in a PowerPivot slide presentation. There are no dependencies between views. You also cannot separate the views when you save the report. The report contains all views as a single file.

- **Text**   You can apply formatting only to text in the title text box or any text box that you insert into a view. You must first highlight the text to format, and then you can change the font type or size, and you can apply bold, italic, or underline formatting to the selected text.

> **Note**   You can format only the text that you type into a text box. Power View automatically formats the text for data in a table or matrix. It also automatically formats the labels in a chart. You have no control over the formatting in the view or in the tabular model.

- **Number**   You can apply number formatting just as you do in Excel. Just click on a numeric value in a table, and then choose a number format type in the drop-down list; or use a button to apply the Accounting Number Format, set the percentage or comma style, or increase or decrease the number of decimal places.

- **Alignment**   You can align text at the top, middle, or bottom of a text box and also apply left, center, and right alignment.

- **Arrange**   You can position multiple visualizations or text boxes in the same area of a view, and then use the Arrange commands to move one visualization in front of the other.

- **Display**   You can use the buttons in this section to change the appearance of your report in the browser. See the "Selecting a display mode" section of this chapter for more information.

- **Filters**   The Filters Area button toggles the display of the Filters Area in the browser. When you create a new report, the Filters Area is not visible, but you can toggle the visibility to view it and add one or more filters to the current view, as we describe in the "View filter" section later in this chapter.

The Styles tab on the ribbon displays eight color themes to apply to your report. Power View uses the theme colors for the line separating the column headers from data in a table or matrix and for charts. You cannot create a custom color theme.

The first field you add to the report becomes a single column in a table. You can then continuing adding more fields to add columns to that table, or you can change the table visualization to something else. The Design tab, shown in Figure 31-7, appears on the ribbon after you add a field and allows you to make changes to the currently selected visualization.

FIGURE 31-7 You use the Design tab of the ribbon to apply visualization type to your data, add a slicer, toggle the display of totals, and change the arrangement of overlapping visualizations.

Tip If you know that a process has updated data in the tabular model after you open Power View, you can use the Refresh button on the Power View Quick Access toolbar (above the ribbon) to reload data in your report. If you use the Refresh button on your browser toolbar, a prompt to leave the current page displays, but you lose your edits in the report if you leave the page.

The Design tab includes the following four sections:

- **Visualizations**   You can change the currently selected visualization to another type, as described in the "Visualizing data" section in this chapter. For example, you can change a table to a line chart. You can also add tiles as a special type of filter to the currently selected visualization.

- **Slicer**   You can add a single-column table to the current view to use for filtering You can use a text field or an image field to create the table, as we describe in the "Filtering data" section.

- **Table Options**   By default, both a table and a matrix display totals when you include a numeric field. You can disable totals if you like. When working with a matrix, you can also choose to display totals for row groups only or column groups only.

- **Arrange**   You can position one visualization on top of another visualization. If you change your mind later about the arrangement, you can use the buttons here to bring a visualization forward, to the front, backward, or to the back.

The Layout tab, shown in Figure 31-8, appears when you select a chart visualization in the view. That is, it appears when you select any visualization other than a table, matrix, or card.

FIGURE 31-8 You use the Layout tab of the ribbon to toggle the display of labels, change the axis type, adjust the size of the multiples grid, and perform synchronization.

The Layout tab includes the following four sections:

- **Labels**   You can use the buttons in this section to toggle the display of the chart title, legend, and data labels. If you decide to show the legend, you can choose its position relative to the chart: top, right, left, or bottom. If you decide to show data labels, you can choose one of the following display positions: centered on the data point, inside the end of the data point, inside the base of the data point, or outside the end of the data point.

- **Axis**   When you use a date field as the axis, you can choose to specify whether Power View should treat the values as a continuous series or as discrete categories. (We describe this as scalar and category axis types, respectively, in Chapter 18, "Working with chart elements," when you work with charts in Report Designer or Report Builder.) If you choose continuous series, Power View automatically creates all possible values for the axis, such as dates or years, and organizes these values into intervals.

- **Multiples**   If you convert a chart to a multiples layout, you can specify the number of small charts to display vertically and horizontally.

- **Synchronize**   When you work with a tiles container, you can synchronize the vertical axes, horizontal axes, series, and bubble sizes for all visualizations it contains. You learn more about this feature in the "Synchronization" section of this chapter.

Field list

The field list from the tabular model appears to the right of the view workspace. When you create a new report, you see only the table names. If the model developer has configured a table with default fields, you can double-click the table name in the field list to add the default field set as a group to the view workspace.

Otherwise, you must expand a table name to see the fields it contains, as shown in Figure 31-9. Individual fields, such as *Sales Order Line Number*, display in the field list without an icon. You also see row label fields with a gray-and-white icon, such as *LargePhoto*. A row label field identifies a column configured as a row identifier or a column requiring you to include a row identifier in the table, as we explain in Chapter 30. Calculated columns, such as *Internet Total Units*, display with a sigma icon, and measures, such as *Total Product Cost*, appear with a calculator icon. You select the check box next to a field to include that field in your report, or you can drag the field into the view workspace. To remove a field from a visualization, clear its check box in the Field List.

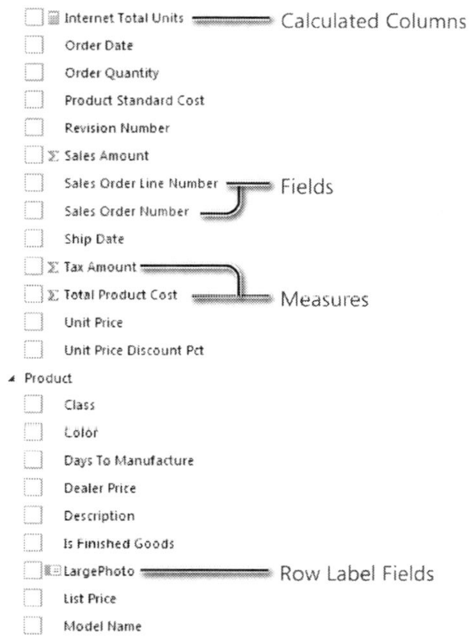

Internet Total Units ———— Calculated Columns
Order Date
Order Quantity
Product Standard Cost
Revision Number
Σ Sales Amount
Sales Order Line Number ——┐
Sales Order Number ————┴— Fields
Ship Date
Σ Tax Amount ————————┐
Σ Total Product Cost ———┴— Measures
Unit Price
Unit Price Discount Pct
▲ Product
Class
Color
Days To Manufacture
Dealer Price
Description
Is Finished Goods
LargePhoto ——————— Row Label Fields
List Price
Model Name

FIGURE 31-9 You select fields from the tabular model field list to build your report.

Layout section

Rather than drag a field to the view workspace, you can drag a field to the layout section, as shown in Figure 31-10. In a new report, you can drag the field into the Fields area of the layout section only. After you add the field, a Tile By section appears, which we describe later in the "Tiles" section of this chapter. If you change the current table visualization to another type of visualization, you see a different arrangement of areas in the layout section. We describe the contents of the layout section when we explain each visualization type in the next section of this chapter. In general, you use the layout section to arrange the sequence of fields in a visualization or assign a field to a specific axis or grouping.

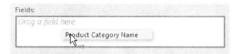

FIGURE 31-10 You can drag a field from the field list into the layout section.

You can also use the layout section to add a count of a non-numeric field to a visualization. Click the down arrow that appears to the right of the field name to display the aggregation options, as shown in Figure 31-11. The list of options available and the default selection depend on the current contents of the visualization, the data type of the field, and the *Summarize By* property of the field in the model. When you display the menu for the field in Power View, you see some or all of the following options:

- **Remove Field** Delete the field from the current visualization.

- **Do Not Summarize** Require Power View to display the distinct values of the selected field.

- **Sum** Calculate the sum of all numeric values for a field.

- **Average** Calculate the sum of a field's numeric values, and divide the result by the count of records in the same table.

- **Minimum** Display the lowest numeric value for a field.

- **Maximum** Display the highest numeric value for a field.

- **Count (Not Blank)** Count the number of records that have a non-blank value for the field.

- **Count (Distinct)** Count the number of unique values for a field, including blanks.

- **Show Items With No Data** By default, Power View does not display an item if there are no values associated with it. Select this setting to override the default behavior and show all items for the field.

FIGURE 31-11 You can use a field's submenu in the layout section to set an aggregation option.

> **Tip** A numeric field that is not defined as a measure in the tabular model is set to Do Not Summarize by default, but you can select another aggregation option in the visualization to override that setting. You can then use that field in a chart visualization.

Visualizing data

When you develop a report by using Report Designer or Report Builder, you usually start with the end result in mind, create a query, and switch frequently between the work on the design layout and a preview of the report. By contrast, you develop a report in Power View by progressively adding data to a visualization, changing the visualization to a new type, and fine-tuning the appearance of the visualization. Power View allows you to focus on the data and easily change your perspective.

Table

Each visualization you add to a view always starts as a table. If you are working with a new view or if you are working with an existing view but have no visualization currently selected, you create a table by selecting any field's check box in the Field List.

Table columns

If the field you add is a text, date, or image field, the corresponding data displays in a single column table, as shown in Figure 31-12. As you select more fields, Power View adds more columns to the table and formats each field according to its data type.

FIGURE 31-12 The first field you add to the view workspace becomes a single-column table.

If you start a table by first adding numeric field, you see only a single row that represents the aggregate value of that field. As you add other field types to the table, Power View recalculates the aggregate after grouping by the non-numeric fields in the table, as shown in Figure 31-13.

FIGURE 31-13 Power View dynamically calculates aggregate values for numeric fields.

If the field you select has many values, Power View displays only some of the values and adds a scroll bar for you to access additional rows, as shown in Figure 31-14. Power View does not retrieve all data from the source table when you first add a field to a visualization. Instead, it retrieves subsets of the data as you scroll, to provide optimal performance even when your source table contains millions of rows.

FIGURE 31-14 Power View dynamically calculates aggregate values for numeric fields.

Table layout section

Each field you select appears in the layout section of the Field List, as shown in Figure 31-15. You can rearrange the sequence of columns by using the layout section of the Field List. For example, you can drag Reseller Total Sales to place it above Product Category Name to position it in the first column of the table. You can also add a tiles container to the table by dragging a field to the Tile By area. We explain more about using a tile in the "Tiles" section of this chapter.

FIGURE 31-15 You can arrange the sequence of table columns by changing the order of fields in the table layout section.

Table sort order

The default sort order of the table is alphabetical by column, starting with the leftmost column and continuing with each column to its right. You can change the sort order by clicking the column header. The first click of the column header applies an ascending sort, and the second click applies a descending sort. An arrow next to the column header shows you the direction of the current sort, as shown in Figure 31-16.

Product Category Name	Product SubCategory Name	Reseller Total Sales ▲
Accessories	Tires and Tubes	$925.21
Accessories	Bottles and Cages	$7,476.60
Components	Chains	$9,377.71
Accessories	Cleaners	$11,188.37
Accessories	Pumps	$13,514.69

FIGURE 31-16 An arrow icon appears to the right of a column header to indicate the current sort direction.

Resizing and moving a visualization

When you create a new table and add fields to it, Power View adjusts the vertical and horizontal size automatically. Similarly, Power View adjusts the size when you change from one visualization type to another. You can move and resize the visualization any time as needed. To move a visualization, point to its border and, when the cursor changes to a hand, drag it to a new location in the same view. To resize it, point again to the border, and when the double-headed arrow appears, drag the border to make the item smaller or larger.

Matrix

At any time, you can convert a visualization to a matrix. To do this, click anywhere inside the visualization to display its borders, and then click the Matrix button on the Design tab of the ribbon. Measures and calculations display as matrix values, and all other fields display as row groups.

Matrix row and column groups

Power View adds a total row and column for each row and column group, as shown in Figure 31-17. You can use the Totals button on the Design tab of the ribbon to show totals for row groups only, columns groups only, or both row and column groups. You can also remove totals for both row and column groups.

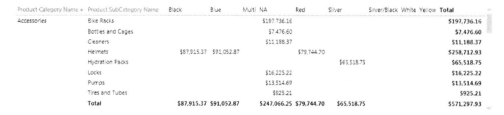

Product Category Name ▲	Product SubCategory Name	Black	Blue	Multi	NA	Red	Silver	Silver/Black	White	Yellow	Total
Accessories	Bike Racks				$197,736.16						$197,736.16
	Bottles and Cages				$7,476.60						$7,476.60
	Cleaners				$11,188.37						$11,188.37
	Helmets	$87,915.37	$91,052.87			$79,744.70					$258,712.93
	Hydration Packs						$65,518.75				$65,518.75
	Locks				$16,225.22						$16,225.22
	Pumps				$13,514.69						$13,514.69
	Tires and Tubes				$925.21						$925.21
	Total	$87,915.37	$91,052.87		$247,066.25	$79,744.70	$65,518.75				$571,297.93

FIGURE 31-17 A matrix displays data and totals in row and column groups.

Note You can click a row group header or a column group total to sort rows. However, you cannot sort column groups.

Matrix layout section

You use the matrix layout section, shown in Figure 31-18, to add numeric measures and calculated columns to the Values area so that Power View can calculate totals for the fields you add to row and column groups. When you select a check box in the Field List, Power View automatically adds it to the Row Groups area. The only way to add a field as a matrix column is to drag it from the Field List or from the Row Groups area to the Column Groups area in the layout section. Just as you can for other visualization types, you can use the layout section to place the matrix inside a tiles container.

FIGURE 31-18 You assign fields to row groups, column groups, and values for a matrix.

Charts

Power View allows you to choose among several different types of charts. You do not have as many options for charts as you do when working with Report Designer or Report Builder, but the available chart types should be sufficient for most data exploration activities. In the Visualization group on the Design tab of the ribbon, you can select any of the following chart types as long as the current visualization contains a measure:

- Column
- 100% Column
- Clustered Column
- Bar
- 100% Bar
- Clustered Bar
- Line
- Scatter

Copying a visualization

Rather than add a new visualization to a view by rebuilding an existing visualization from scratch, you can copy the existing visualization and paste it into the same view or a new view to use as the starting point for a new visualization. You can then add or remove fields, or you can convert it to a different visualization type.

To perform the copy and paste operation, you must first select the visualization, and then use the Copy and Paste buttons on the Home tab of the ribbon. You cannot use the Ctrl+C and Ctrl+V shortcut keys to perform the copy and paste.

Column, bar, and line charts

The configuration of column, bar, and line charts is similar, but of course the appearance of each is different. The column chart, shown in Figure 31-19, and the line chart both display the axis field along the horizontal axis, while the bar chart displays the axis field along the vertical axis.

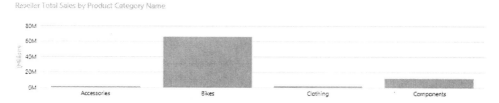

Reseller Total Sales by Product Category Name

FIGURE 31-19 You can use a column chart to compare a numeric value by a single axis field.

Tip If the chart has more data points than Power View can display within the current chart size, you can use the horizontal or vertical scroll bars to view other sections of the chart.

Arranging visualizations

You can overlap and inset items, as shown in Figure 31-20. You use the Arrange buttons on the Home tab of the ribbon to bring an item forward or send it back.

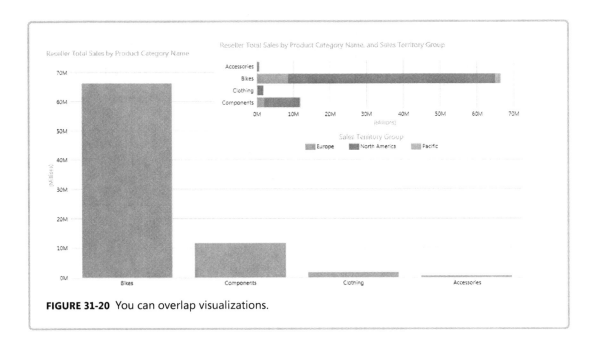

FIGURE 31-20 You can overlap visualizations.

Column, bar, and line chart layout section

You can assign only one field to the axis, but you can add multiple values to the chart. Power View assigns different colors to each value and adds a legend to the chart, as shown in Figure 31-21. Power View treats each value as separate series but displays a scale for only one of these values on the value axis.

FIGURE 31-21 You can display multiple numeric values in the same chart.

Another option is to create a series for a non-numeric field. To do this, drag the field from the Field List to the Series area of the layout section. However, you cannot do this if your chart includes multiple values. In that case, you must remove values from the layout section and leave only one. Then you can add a field to the Series area, as shown in Figure 31-22. You can also optionally use fields to create vertical or horizontal multiples, as we describe in the "Multiples" section of this chapter.

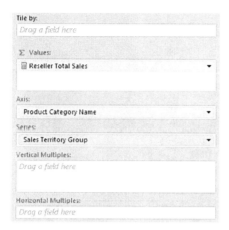

FIGURE 31-22 You can use only one value in a chart when you assign a field as a series.

Column and bar chart sort order

You can specify the sort order of the columns or bars in a chart. To see the default sort field and direction for these chart types, position your cursor above the chart. You can change the sort field by clicking the down arrow that appears next to the current field to view a list of available fields, as shown in Figure 31-23, and select a new field. You can also click the direction label to toggle the sort between ascending and descending.

FIGURE 31-23 You can sort columns or bars in a chart by choosing a new field and sort direction in the sort description above the chart title.

Multiples

You can also create multiple copies of the same chart, known as *multiples*, to break down its data by different categorizations, as shown in Figure 31-24. To achieve this effect, you drag one or more categorization fields to the Vertical Multiples or Horizontal Multiples area of the layout section. When you choose the Vertical Multiples option, Power View creates at least two rows of charts and fits as many charts as possible in each row. With the Horizontal Multiples option, Power View creates a single row of charts.

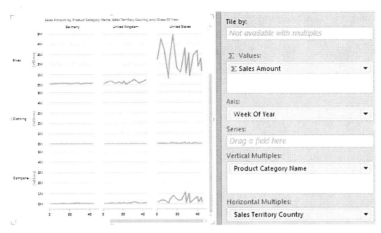

FIGURE 31-24 You can create vertical and horizontal multiples of a chart.

For greater control over the appearance of multiples, you can use the Grid button on the Layout tab of the ribbon to select the number of tiles across and down that you want to include, such as three tiles across and two tiles down, as shown in Figure 31-25. If the size of the visualization is too small to show the entire grid, a scroll bar appears to allow you to access the other tiles. Power View automatically aligns the horizontal and vertical axes in the multiples to help you easily compare values.

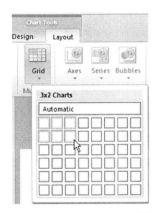

FIGURE 31-25 You can specify the number of tiles to display for a multiples grid.

Scatter chart layout section

A scatter chart is a useful visualization that helps you see whether relationships exist between two numeric values. With this type of chart, the vertical axis represents the scale for the Y Value field, while the horizontal axis represents the scale for the X Value field. In the layout section, you also add a field to the Details area, as shown in Figure 31-26, so that Power View can calculate the applicable

X and Y values. You can optionally add a third value to create a bubble chart visualization, where the size of the bubble increases proportionally as the value increases. Whether you use a scatter chart or a bubble chart, you can also add a field to the Color section for grouping purposes. Last, you can add a field to the Play Axis area of the layout section to add animation to the visualization.

> **Tip** Typically, you use a date field in the Play Axis so that you can observe how the chart changes over time.

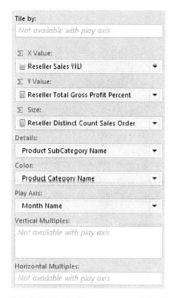

FIGURE 31-26 You must add fields for X Value, Y Value, and Details to create a scatter chart and add a field for Size to create a bubble chart, but adding fields for Color and Play Axis is optional.

Play axis

When you add a play axis to a scatter chart or bubble chart, a new axis appears below the visualization, as shown in Figure 31-27. The field values for the play axis display sequentially from left to right using the sort order specified in the tabular model. You can then click the play button to the left of the play axis to animate the visualization. Power View updates the chart in sequence for each item that appears on the play axis. You can also use the slider on the play axis to move forward and backward within a specific time range.

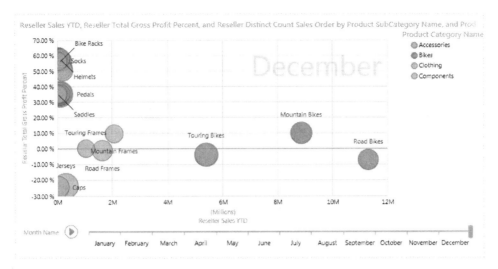

FIGURE 31-27 You can add a play axis to animate a scatter chart or bubble and observe the effect of changes over time.

A watermark appears in the background of the visualization to indicate the current play axis value. You can filter the visualization and see the path of a selected Details value by clicking a bubble or point in the chart, as shown in Figure 31-28. You can also point to a bubble or point along the path to see its values display as a tooltip.

FIGURE 31-28 You can click a bubble to see its path for each play axis value and hover over it to see its values as a tooltip.

Cards

You can use the Cards visualization to display a scrollable list of grouped fields, as shown in Figure 31-29. The default label and default image fields defined by the tabular model developer (as described in Chapter 30) display using a larger font than the other fields. The layout section for a card is similar to the one for a table, having only a Tile By and Fields area.

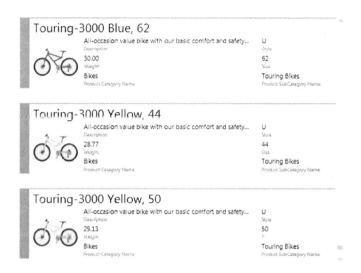

FIGURE 31-29 You can display a list of fields and images in a card format.

Filtering data

You can use a variety of techniques to filter data in visualizations. You can use highlighting to emphasize one categorization while retaining visibility of other categorizations in all visualizations displaying in the same view. Another option is to use a slicer or tiles container to include the filter selection in the view and view only values for the selected categorization. If you prefer, you can set up filters separately from the view and apply the filters to an entire view or to a specific visualization. By choosing this latter approach, you also have the option to define more complex conditions for filters. You can even combine all these techniques in a single view.

Highlighted values

You can use data in one visualization to filter all visualizations in the same view. This technique can help you better see relationships in your data. When you select a value in your chart, such as a column or a legend item, as shown in Figure 31-30, Power View highlights related values in all other visualizations in the same view, including a table, a matrix, or cards. You revert to the original view and clear the highlighting by clicking the same item again.

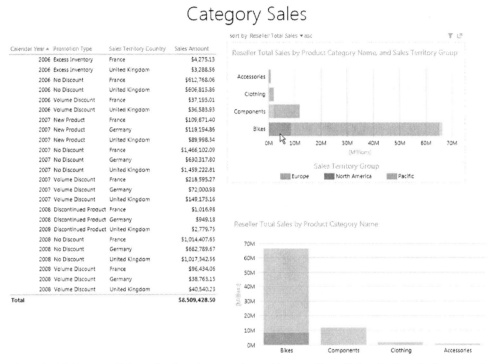

FIGURE 31-30 You can click a value in a chart or a legend item to filter all visualizations in the same view.

Slicer

You can create a single-column table using either a string or image field and then convert it to a slicer by using the Slicer button on the Design tab of the ribbon. You can then click an item in the slicer to filter all visualizations and related slicers in the view, as shown in Figure 31-31. You can also select multiple items in the slicer by pressing the Ctrl key as you select each additional item. To revert to the unfiltered view, click the Clear Filter icon that displays in the upper-right corner of the slicer.

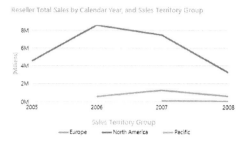
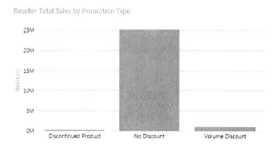

FIGURE 31-31 You can use a slicer to filter visualizations and other slicers in the same view.

Tiles

To every visualization except the scatter chart, you can add a tiles container to use as a filter for every visualization you place inside it. Visualizations outside the tiles container are unaffected by your tile selection.

Tile By area

The tiles container can display either images, as shown in Figure 31-32, or strings in a horizontal strip that displays above one or more visualizations. To create the tiles container, drag a field to the Tile By area in the layout section. Power View displays one tile for each value in the selected field, which you then use to filter the contents of the tiles container. The current selection in the tile strip displays using a black font, and all other items in the tile strip display using a gray font, so you can tell at a glance which value serves as the filter.

> **Tip** You can use the Tiles button on the Design tab of the ribbon to convert a table or matrix to a tiles container. Power View uses the first field in the table or the first row group field to create the tiles. The table or matrix then displays inside the tiles container.

FIGURE 31-32 You can use a tiles container to filter a visualization.

Tile visualization mode

The default layout of the tiles is tab-strip mode. You can toggle between tab-strip mode and cover-flow mode by using the respective button in the Tile Visualizations group on the Design tab of the ribbon. In cover-flow mode, as shown in Figure 31-33, the label or image appears below the container and the current selection appears in the center of the strip and is slightly larger than the other tile items.

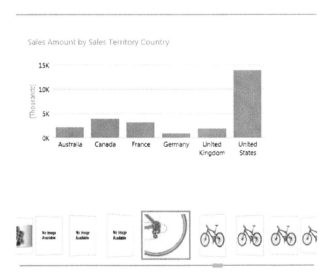

FIGURE 31-33 You can display tiles in cover-flow mode at the bottom of the tiles container.

Multiple visualizations in a tiles container

You can resize a tiles container to add one or more visualizations to it. That way, you can filter multiple visualizations with a single tile selection without filtering the entire view, as shown in Figure 31-34.

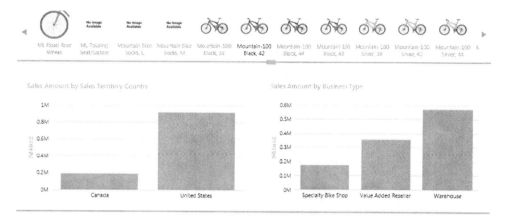

FIGURE 31-34 You can place multiple visualizations inside the same tiles container.

Synchronization

Power View does not automatically synchronize axes for a visualization inside the same tiles container as it does with multiples. That is, as you select a different tile, the vertical axis scale and the horizontal axis categories can vary, as shown in Figure 31-35. In this example, notice the minimum and maximum values on the vertical axis are different between Mountain-100 Black, 42 and Mountain-200 Black, 38. Also, the first product has sales in Canada and the United States only, whereas the second product has sales in those two countries as well as France and the United Kingdom.

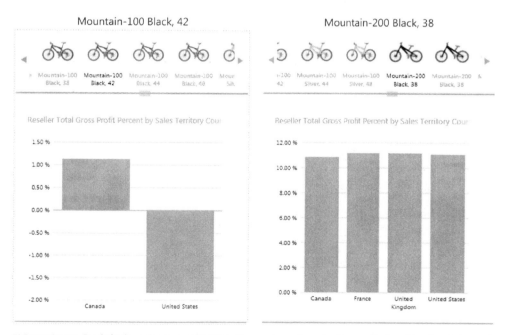

FIGURE 31-35 By default, a chart visualization does not synchronize the vertical and horizontal axes for each tile.

You can use the buttons in the Synchronize group of the Layout tab to synchronize axes, series, or bubbles across the tiles to more easily compare the values in a chart visualization as you change tiles. When synchronizing axes, you can choose to synchronize the vertical axes, the horizontal axes, or both axes, as shown in Figure 31-36. Now the minimum and maximum values on the vertical axis are consistent for each tile selection, and the horizontal axis includes all countries, regardless of whether a product has sales in that country.

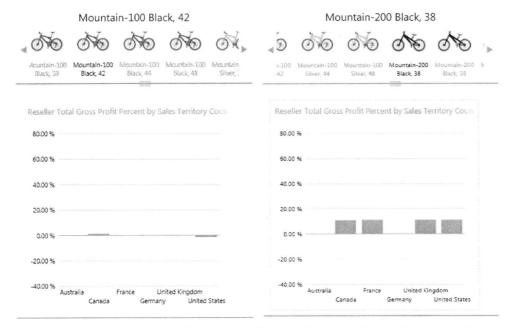

FIGURE 31-36 You can synchronize the vertical and horizontal axes in a tiles container for consistency across all tiles.

View filter

Another way to filter a view is to open the Filters area of the view workspace and add filter criteria, as shown in Figure 31-37. You toggle the visibility of this area of the workspace by clicking the Filters Area button on the Home tab of the ribbon. An arrow displays at the top-left corner of the Filters area for you to collapse it when you want to allocate more screen space to the view workspace.

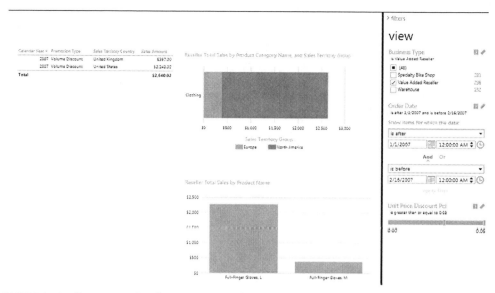

FIGURE 31-37 You can use the Filters area to create more specific filters for all visualizations in the current view.

Note The criteria you define in the Filters area apply only to the current view. There is no way to create a filter that applies to the entire report. The Filters area is always accessible, whether you are viewing your report in edit mode, reading mode, or full screen mode. However, you cannot type values for filter conditions in full screen mode.

Basic filter mode

You can add simple filters in basic mode by dragging a field to the Filters area and then selecting a value. The method you use to select a value depends on the field's data type. You select one or more values by using a check box for string and date data types, or you can set a minimum and maximum numeric value by using a slider, as shown in Figure 31-38. You can collapse the list of check boxes for a field by clicking the field name in the Filters area.

FIGURE 31-38 You can select specific values or numeric ranges in basic filter mode.

> **Tip** The number that appears to the right of each string in a list of values represents the count of records in the table having that value.

To clear a filter without removing it from the Filters area, click the middle icon in the toolbar that appears to the right of the field name. If you decide not to keep the filter in the view, click the third icon to both clear the filter from the view and remove it permanently from the Filters area.

If the list of values for a field is long, you can use the vertical scroll bar to locate a specific value. You can also use the search box to create a smaller list of values, as shown in Figure 31-39.

FIGURE 31-39 You can select specific values or numeric ranges in basic filter mode.

Advanced filter mode

You can switch to advanced filter mode by clicking the first icon in the toolbar that appears to the right of the field name in the Filters area. You then have the following options for defining the filter criteria:

- **String Value**   You can use one of the following operators to create a filter based on a partial word, as shown in Figure 31-40: Contains, Does Not Contain, Starts With, Does Not Start With, Is, Is Not, Is Blank, or Is Not Blank.

FIGURE 31-40 You can create a filter that finds matching values based on a partial string.

- **Numeric Value** You can use one of the following operators to compare a value in the tabular model to a specified value, as shown in Figure 31-41: Is Less Than, Is Less Than Or Equal To, Is Greater Than, Is Greater Than Or Equal To, Is, Is Not, Is Blank, or Is Not Blank.

FIGURE 31-41 You can create a filter that compares a specified value to a value in the tabular model.

- **Date Value** You can use a calendar control, as shown in Figure 31-42, and a drop-down list with 15-minute increments to set date and time values in combination with the following operators: Is, Is Not, Is After, Is On Or After, Is Before, Is On Or Before, Is Blank, or Is Not Blank.

FIGURE 31-42 You can use a calendar control to set a filter condition based on date.

After you define the filter condition for a field, you click the Apply Filter link to update the view by using the new filter. If you like, you can create a compound condition for each filter by using a logical AND or logical OR operator, as shown in Figure 31-43. You can create only two conditions for each field in the Filters area.

FIGURE 31-43 You can create a compound filter condition using AND or OR logic.

You can also use the Filters area to create a filter for a single visualization. To do this, click the Filter button in the top-right corner of the visualization, or click the visualization in the view and click the link that displays to the right of View in the Filters area, such as Chart, as shown in Figure 31-44. You can use either basic filter mode or advanced filter mode to create the filter.

FIGURE 31-44 You can create a filter condition for a single visualization.

Selecting a display mode

You can use the buttons in the Display group of the Home tab of the ribbon to change the display mode of your report. You can choose one of the following three display modes to view and interact with your report:

- **Fit To Window**   This display mode offers the most versatility for editing your report. You can access the browser commands, the Power View ribbon, the Views pane, the Field list, and the Filters area. Furthermore, the view workspace shrinks or expands to fill the available space in the browser window if this button is enabled. You can click the button to disable the dynamic resizing of the view workspace.

- **Reading Mode**   When you open an existing Power View report, it displays by default in Reading mode. This display mode allows you to access the tabs and buttons in the browser, but not the ribbon and the field list, which means that you cannot edit your report beyond adjusting filter conditions in the Filter area. If your report has multiple views, you can cycle through the views by using the arrow keys on your keyboard. You can click the multiview button in the lower-right corner of the screen, which allows you to access thumbnails of the views, as shown in Figure 31-45, and then you can click a thumbnail image to allocate more screen space to the view. Another option is to use the arrow buttons in the lower-right corner of the screen when the thumbnails are hidden. If you need to make changes to the report, you can click the Edit Report button in the toolbar to switch to Fit To Window mode, or you can click the Full Screen Mode button to switch to Full Screen mode.

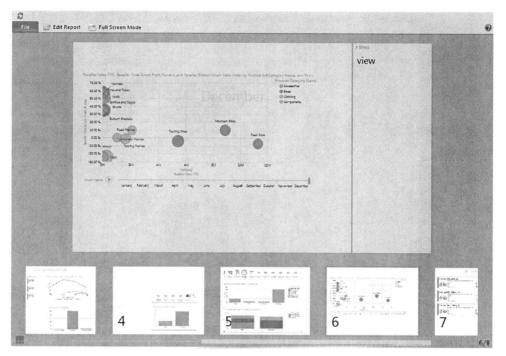

FIGURE 31-45 You can navigate through multiple views in a report by scrolling through thumbnail images.

■ **Full Screen Mode**   You can devote your entire screen to a view by using Full Screen mode, as shown in Figure 31-46. It works much like using the slideshow view in PowerPoint. Full Screen mode is similar to Reading mode and provides the same navigation options, but it hides your browser menus and toolbar completely and uses the entire screen. You can access the Filters area to adjust the filter conditions, although you cannot add or remove filters.

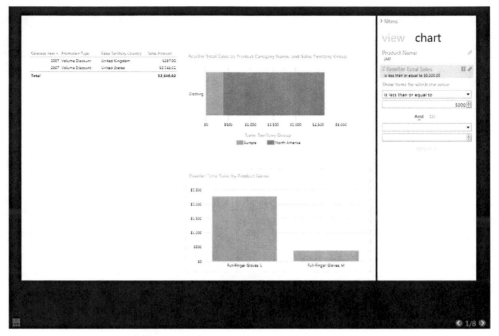

FIGURE 31-46 You can use Full Screen mode to view your report.

 Tip When you want to enlarge and isolate a visualization, click the Pop Out button in the upper-right corner to fill the entire screen. The Pop Out button is available in all three modes.

To print the current view, you must use either the Fit To Window mode or Reading mode only. Open the File menu, and click Print to create a landscape print of the current view's data. If the filters area is visible and expanded on your screen, it will print also. However, if the view contains a scatter or bubble chart with a play axis, the printed view includes only the frame that you currently see on screen. Similarly, you see only the selected tile if you print a view containing a tiles container.

Saving a Power View report

When you finish editing your report, you can save it for review later to a SharePoint document library or PowerPivot Gallery. You can also export it to Microsoft PowerPoint to share it with others without access to SharePoint.

File save options

You use the File menu to save and optionally share a report. You can save it only if you have the Add Items permission for the target destination. If a file having the same name exists, you must have the Edit Items permission to replace the existing file with a new one.

When you save the report, you must decide whether to save preview images with your report. This feature works only if the data source for the report is a PowerPivot workbook. If you keep this option and save your report to a SharePoint document library for which the PowerPivot Gallery is enabled, everyone who can open the PowerPivot gallery can see the view in your report, as shown in Figure 31-47. The images are not real-time, but refresh often. The Save process saves images by default, but you can disable this feature by clearing the option Save Preview Images With Report when saving your report.

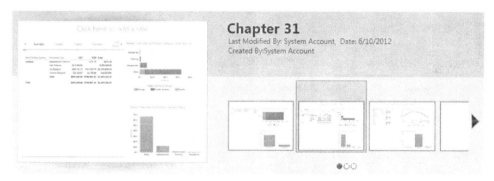

FIGURE 31-47 You can see a preview of each page of the report if you save images when you save the report.

As with any document in SharePoint, permissions determine who can view the file versus who can edit the file by using Power View. Regardless of permissions, no one can download the RDLX file and open it in SQL Server Data Tools or Report Builder for editing.

PowerPoint export

A Power View report is the only report type in Report Services that you can natively export to PowerPoint. To do this, open the File menu and click Export To PowerPoint to save the report as a PPTX file. When you open the PPTX file by using PowerPoint, you can see that each view is a separate slide. During the editing process, you see a static image of each view if you first use the option to save images with the report. Otherwise, you see a placeholder image on each slide.

If you have a connection to the SharePoint server and have the correct permission, you can open the Reading View or Slideshow mode to click the Click To Interact link in the lower-right corner of the slide, as shown in Figure 31-48. If you did not save images with the report, you will not see the Click To Interact link and the slide is interactive when you open the Reading View or SlideShow mode. After you enable interactivity, you can filter the current view by editing the filter in the Filters area, selecting a different value in a slicer or tiles container, or highlighting values. You can also use the play axis for a scatter or bubble chart.

Important To use the interactivity within PowerPoint, you must have Silverlight installed on your computer. PowerPoint always retrieves the most recent version of the report when you open Reading View or Slideshow mode.

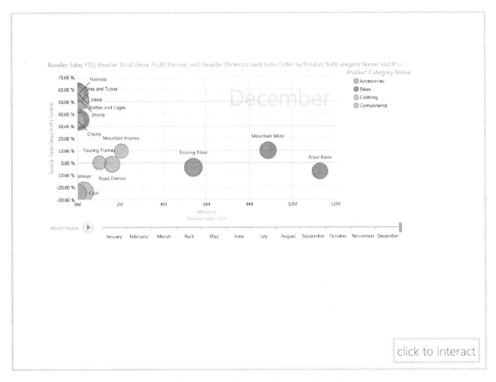

FIGURE 31-48 You can use the Click To Interact link on a PowerPoint slide to use filters or the play axis.

PART VII

Using Reporting Services as a development platform

Reporting Services includes all the tools that you need to complete the entire reporting life cycle. In the final chapters of this book, you discover how you can also use Reporting Services as a development platform to develop, manage, and access reports. With a better appreciation of the full range of capabilities that Reporting Services supports, you can decide the best way to use Reporting Services in your organization.

CHAPTER 32

Understanding Report Definition Language

When you design a report by using Report Designer or Report Builder, the output of this process is a report definition file that describes your report using Report Definition Language (RDL). In most cases, you don't need to know anything about RDL to successfully create reports and deploy them to the report server. However, there are times when you might find it easier to make a change directly to the RDL rather than to use one of the report design interfaces, or you might need to programmatically create a report definition file. For those situations, you need to develop a good understanding of RDL.

Introducing Report Definition Language

The purpose of a report definition file is to describe a report. It includes information about the data to display in the report, the layout of the data on the report, and properties that control the formatting of the report. This information appears in the report definition using RDL as a declarative model. A declarative model describes the desired outcome but does not describe the series of instructions necessary to produce that outcome. For that, you need an application that can interpret the report definition, generate the necessary instructions, and follow those instructions to create the final report.

RDL schema definition

If you open a report definition file by using a text editor such as Notepad, you see that it is simply an Extended Markup Language (XML) document. For each element, or node, in the XML document, there is a beginning and ending tag. An XML element can contain attributes, which are similar to properties because they provide information about data rather than provide data. Furthermore, an XML element can have child elements.

Note You can also view the report definition file as XML in Report Designer. To do this, right-click the report in Solution Explorer and select View Code. You do not have this option in Report Builder.

The collection of XML elements that you find in a report definition file conforms to a specific XML schema that Microsoft calls RDL. The XML schema definition (XSD) for RDL describes the elements to expect and lists the child elements and attributes that each element can contain. The purpose of the XSD is to validate the XML in a report definition file. You can view the XSD on your native-mode report server at *http://<servername>/reportserver/reportdefinition.xsd* or on your SharePoint integrated-mode report server at *http://<sitename>/<optionalsubsite>/_vti_bin/reportserver/reportdefinition.xsd*.

RDL usage

Most reporting tools available from third-party vendors rely on proprietary formats that require the vendor's design tools to create a report and the vendor's rendering engine to view a report. Although vendors would prefer that an organization uses only one reporting tool for everyone, it's very common to find individual departments choosing their own tools.

By contrast, Microsoft's use of XML in a report definition file encourages the exchange of information about a report between products. You need only a report producer application to create a report definition. This application allows you to create a report definition without writing code, whether you use a graphical interface or whether you supply arguments to a command-line utility. As long as the report definition is well-formed RDL, it does not matter which application produces it. Likewise, a report consumer application reads the RDL and generates a report in any of the supported formats. It uses the dataset query described in the RDL to retrieve data and then organizes and formats it according to the layout and properties in the RDL.

As long as a design tool can produce RDL output or a report server can read an RDL file and generate a report, departments can use their tool of choice for producing or consuming reports, whether using a Microsoft product, a third-party application, or a custom application developed in-house. Although this capability has existed since the introduction of SQL Server 2000 Reporting Services, there are only a few third-party vendors who take advantage of RDL in their reporting tools.

The RDL schema is open and extensible. That means that third party vendors, or even custom application developers in your own organization, can add elements and attributes to RDL to add more capabilities to reports. In that case, a special rendering extension must be added to the Reporting Services report server to interpret the additional features, or another rendering engine must be used. The report server ignores any customization in the RDL for which it has no instructions for processing.

Exploring key elements

Before we look at ways that you might work with RDL, let's explore some of the key elements in RDL. When you understand the basic structure of RDL and the organization of its elements, you can apply this understanding to the other RDL elements that we do not review in this chapter.

 Note You can download the RDL specification at *http://msdn.microsoft.com/library/dd297486.aspx*. The version for SQL Server 2008 R2 is also applicable to SQL Server 2012.

Report element

The *Report* element contains all other elements in the report definition file. That is, it is the outermost node. If you have an empty report, you still have the *Report* element as the first element following the XML declaration in the first line, as shown here:

```
<?xml version="1.0" encoding="utf-8"?>
<Report xmlns=http://schemas.microsoft.com/sqlserver/reporting/2008/01/reportdefinition
xmlns:rd="http://schemas.microsoft.com/SQLServer/reporting/reportdesigner">
<Width>6.5in</Width>
   <Body>
     <Height>2in</Height>
   </Body>
   <rd:ReportTemplate>true</rd:ReportTemplate>
   <Page>
   </Page>
</Report>
```

In an empty report, the RDL includes the *Report* element and its three child elements: *Width*, *Body*, and *Page*. You also see an *rd* element that is part of another XML namespace exclusive to the report designer and not required for a report definition file that you create programmatically. As you add data sources, datasets, report parameters, and report items to your report, the report definition file includes more child elements for the *Report* element, and each of those elements has its own child elements and attributes.

> **Note** Because the *rd* element is not an RDL element, we exclude it in all subsequent examples of RDL in this chapter.

When you make changes to report properties in the Properties window, as shown in Figure 32-1, a corresponding change is made to the RDL. In some cases, the report designer also updates the RDL to include miscellaneous default values. For example, the *Author* and *Description* properties are blank by default. As soon as you provide values for these properties, the RDL adds the *Description*, *Author*, and *AutoRefresh* child elements to the *Report* element and also adds the margin values as child elements of the *Page* element, as shown here:

```
<Report xmlns="http://schemas.microsoft.com/sqlserver/reporting/2008/01/reportdefinition"
xmlns:rd="http://schemas.microsoft.com/SQLServer/reporting/reportdesigner">
   <Body>
     <Height>2in</Height>
     <Style />
   </Body>
   <Width>6.5in</Width>
   <Page>
     <LeftMargin>1in</LeftMargin>
     <RightMargin>1in</RightMargin>
     <TopMargin>1in</TopMargin>
     <BottomMargin>1in</BottomMargin>
     <Style />
   </Page>
   <Description>This is a basic report to demonstrate the relationship between the report
```

```
designer
  and RDL elements.</Description>
  <Author>Stacia Misner</Author>
  <AutoRefresh>0</AutoRefresh>
</Report>
```

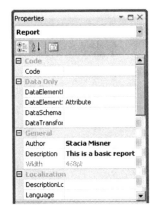

FIGURE 32-1 The entries you make for report properties, such as *Author* or *Description*, become child elements of the *Report* element.

DataSources and *DataSource* elements

Normally, the next step in report development is to add a data source to your project, and then you add it to your report. The RDL updates only when you add the data source to your report. The *DataSource* element is a child element of the *DataSources* element, which itself is a child of the *Report* element. If you add a shared data source to your report, the *DataSource* element has a child element, *DataSourceReference*, that contains the name of the shared data source. Otherwise, the DataSource element has child elements for connection information: *DataProvider*, *ConnectString*, and *Integrated-Security*, as shown here:

```
<DataSources>
  <DataSource Name="AdventureWorksDW">
    <DataSourceReference>AdventureWorksDW</DataSourceReference>
  </DataSource>
  <DataSource Name="AdventureWorksCube">
    <ConnectionProperties>
      <DataProvider>OLEDB-MD</DataProvider>
      <ConnectString>Data Source=.;Initial Catalog=
      AdventureWorksDW2012Multidimensional-EE</ConnectString>
      <IntegratedSecurity>true</IntegratedSecurity>
    </ConnectionProperties>
  </DataSource>
</DataSources>
```

You can see how the structure of the elements in the RDL corresponds to the Data Source Properties dialog box, shown in Figure 32-2. A data source can contain a child element describing information required for an embedded connection or the name of a shared data source reference, but not both.

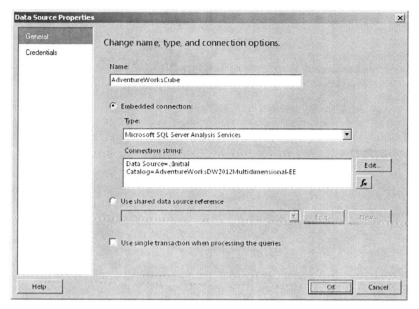

FIGURE 32-2 The Data Source Properties dialog box corresponds to the *DataProvider*, *ConnectString*, and *IntegratedSecurity* elements.

Understanding the XSD

The structure of the *DataSources* and *DataSource* elements, like all other elements in the report definition file, must conform to the XSD file to ensure that the elements are valid and appear in the proper location. The XSD indicates whether an element is simple or complex. A simple element has no child elements or attributes, while a complex element has children or attributes and appears in the schema with the word *Type* appended to its name. For example, the *Data-Sources* and *DataSource* elements both appear as complex types, with the names *DataSources-Type* and *DataSourceType*, respectively, as shown here:

```
<xsd:complexType name="DataSourcesType">
  <xsd:sequence>
    <xsd:element type="DataSourceType" name="DataSource" maxOccurs="unbounded"/>
  </xsd:sequence>
  <xsd:anyAttribute processContents="lax" namespace="##other"/>
</xsd:complexType>
<xsd:complexType name="DataSourceType">
  <xsd:choice maxOccurs="unbounded" minOccurs="0">
    <xsd:element type="xsd:boolean" name="Transaction" minOccurs="0"/>
    <xsd:element type="ConnectionPropertiesType" name="ConnectionProperties"
minOccurs="0"/>
    <xsd:element type="xsd:string" name="DataSourceReference" minOccurs="0"/>
    <xsd:any processContents="lax" namespace="##other"/>
  </xsd:choice>
  <xsd:attribute type="xsd:string" name="Name" use="required"/>
```

```
      <xsd:anyAttribute processContents="lax" namespace="##other"/>
    </xsd:complexType>
    <xsd:complexType name="ConnectionPropertiesType">
      <xsd:choice maxOccurs="unbounded" minOccurs="0">
        <xsd:element type="xsd:string" name="DataProvider"/>
        <xsd:element type="xsd:string" name="ConnectString"/>
        <xsd:element type="xsd:boolean" name="IntegratedSecurity" minOccurs="0"/>
        <xsd:element type="StringLocIDType" name="Prompt" minOccurs="0"/>
        <xsd:any processContents="lax" namespace="##other"/>
      </xsd:choice>
      <xsd:anyAttribute processContents="lax" namespace="##other"/>
    </xsd:complexType>
```

The XSD also includes indicators to describe how to use elements. For example, *DataSourcesType* has the sequence indicator to require the appearance of child elements in a specific order, but *DataSourceType* has the choice indicator to restrict the child element to one of the options listed. You can also see frequent usage of occurrence indicators, such as *minOccurs* to show the minimum times the element can occur in the RDL or, occasionally, *maxOccurs* to show the maximum occurrences. In *ConnectionPropertiesType*, the *maxOccurs* indicator is unbounded, which means there is no limit.

DataSets and *DataSet* elements

After you add a data source, your next step is to create a dataset to define the data to retrieve for the report. The *DataSets* element is the parent element for one or more *DataSet* elements, which contain the information about the data. The *DataSet* element in turn is the parent element for either a *SharedDataSet* element or a *Query* element and a *Fields* element containing a collection of *Field* elements. A *Field* element contains either a *Value* element for an expression that you assign to create a calculated field or a *DataField* element for a field returned by query execution, as shown here:

```
<DataSets>
  <DataSet Name="DataSet1">
    <Query>
    <DataSourceName>AdventureWorksDW</DataSourceName>
    <CommandText>SELECT
      r.BusinessType,
      d.CalendarYear,
      SUM(s.SalesAmount) AS SalesAmount
      FROM
      dbo.FactResellerSales s
      JOIN dbo.DimReseller r on r.ResellerKey = s.ResellerKey
      JOIN dbo.DimDate d on d.DateKey = s.OrderDateKey
      GROUP BY
      r.BusinessType,
      d.CalendarYear
      ORDER BY
      r.BusinessType</CommandText>
    </Query>
    <Fields>
```

```
      <Field Name="BusinessType">
        <DataField>BusinessType</DataField>
      </Field>
      <Field Name="CalendarYear">
        <DataField>CalendarYear</DataField>
      </Field>
      <Field Name="SalesAmount">
        <DataField>SalesAmount</DataField>
      </Field>
    </Fields>
  </DataSet>
</DataSets>
```

If you add query parameters to your query, the *QueryParameters* element appears between the *DataSourceName* element and *CommandText* elements. The *QueryParameters* element includes one or more *QueryParameter* elements with the name and value of each query parameter, as shown here:

```
<QueryParameters>
  <QueryParameter Name="Year">
    <Value>=Parameters!Year.Value</Value>
  </QueryParameter>
</QueryParameters>
```

If you use the Dataset Properties dialog box to configure options or filters, additional elements appear as the last of the *DataSet*'s child elements. The *Filters* element contains one or more *Filter* elements and contains the filter expression, an operator, and the filter value. The options appear next as independent elements, such as *InterpretSubtotalsAsDetails*, as shown here:

```
<Filters>
  <Filter>
    <FilterExpression>=Fields!SalesTerritoryCountry.Value</FilterExpression>
    <Operator>Equal</Operator>
    <FilterValues>
      <FilterValue>France</FilterValue>
    </FilterValues>
  </Filter>
</Filters>
<InterpretSubtotalsAsDetails>True</InterpretSubtotalsAsDetails>
```

Tablix element

When you add a data region to your report, it appears in the RDL as a child element of the *ReportItems* element, which is a child of the *Report* element. The tablix is a very flexible structure and requires many child elements to define even a simple table layout. The relationships between RDL elements necessary to define a tablix are difficult to see when reviewing the report definition because there are so many elements, but they can be more easily seen in a diagram, as shown in Figure 32-3.

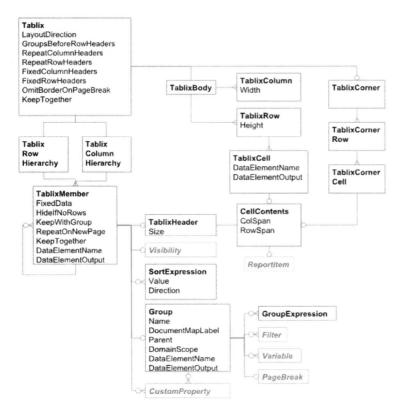

FIGURE 32-3 The tablix has many child elements to accommodate the variety of structures it supports.

> **Note** This diagram and others like it are available in the RDL specification, which you can download from *http://msdn.microsoft.com/library/dd297486.aspx*.

For example, let's consider how to interpret the diagram in Figure 32-3 in the context of a table structure. Open the RDL of a report containing a table to follow along. First, you see the *TablixBody* element as the first child of the *Tablix* element. Next you see the *TablixColumns* element containing one *TablixColumn* element and an accompanying *Width* child element for each column in the table body.

The next set of elements begins with *TablixRows* which contains a *Height* element and then a *TablixCells* element, which breaks down into multiple *TablixCell* elements. A *TablixCell* element corresponds to a text box in the data region. It contains the *CellContents* element, which has a *Textbox* child element. Inside the *Textbox* element are a variety of child elements representing the text box properties, such as *CanGrow*, *KeepTogether*, and *Border*. The text value to display in the text box is nested in *Paragraphs* and *Paragraph* elements, which consist of a *TextRuns* element containing one or more *TextRun* elements. These elements do not appear in the diagram explicitly but are consolidated as a single *ReportItem* element.

If the table contains groupings, the column groups are placed inside the *TablixColumnHierarchy*, *TablixMembers*, and *TablixMember* elements. Similarly, the row groups appear inside the *TablixRow Hierarchy*, *TablixMembers*, and *TablixMember* elements. The topmost element in the *TablixMember* element is the *TablixHeader* element that describes the size and contents of the text box, using the *CellContents* and *Textbox* elements in the same ways as these elements are used in the body of the tablix.

Definitions for groups and group expressions appear next in the RDL and are followed by sort expressions. Then *TablixHeader*, *CellContents* elements appear again with values corresponding to a group. The last *TablixMember* element in a row hierarchy is independent of a *TablixHeader* element and contains a reference to the details group.

Working with RDL

With the RDL specification in hand, you can create a report definition file by using a text editor to type out each element and completely bypass Report Designer or Report Builder. However, you would likely find that process to be quite tedious. Nonetheless, you might encounter situations where editing the RDL or using code to generate RDL is useful. For these situations, you need to understand how the RDL schema works.

Manual RDL edits

When you have a collection of reports that use the same set of report parameters or a common set of dataset properties, you might find that the Report Designer interface requires a lot of keystrokes and clicks that you must repeat multiple times. Rather than use the Report Designer interface, you can often complete repetitive tasks like this much faster if you manually edit the RDL. You can use the interface to add items to the first report and then open its RDL to locate the relevant section to copy. Next, you can paste the copied RDL fragment into the appropriate area of the other reports. Knowing what to copy and where to place the copied RDL is very important. If you omit a tag or put the RDL fragment in the wrong location, the RDL fails to validate and you can no longer use the interface to correct design issues.

> **Important** Making manual changes to RDL is risky. If you use SSDT to view the report code and make edits, you can usually use the Undo button to reverse your edits. Nonetheless, as another safety precaution, you should create a backup copy of a report before editing it. To back up a report in SSDT, right-click the report in Solution Explorer, select Copy, click the Reports folder, and press Ctrl+V to paste a copy of the report.

Programmatic RDL edits

Perhaps a safer way to edit the RDL for multiple reports is to take a programmatic approach. An RDL Object Model is available for you to create new report definitions or modify existing report definitions. You can use its *Load()* method to deserialize a report's RDL and put the contents in memory where you can access elements and change properties.

> **Note** For reference information about the classes and methods of the RDL Object Model, start at *http://msdn.microsoft.com/en-us/library/ff493708*.

Unfortunately, although the RDL Object Model is now publicly documented, it is no longer as easy to use as it was in SQL Server 2008 when it was undocumented. The classes of the *Microsoft.Reporting Services.RdlObjectModel* namespace are now marked as internal, but you can add the *Microsoft .ReportingServices.Design.Control* assembly to your project to access the RDL Object Model. However, there are multiple dependencies on other assemblies to add to your project as well. Furthermore, although the RDL Object Model includes a *Load()* method to deserialize your report definition file for use with the object model, you must use .NET reflection to invoke the *Serialize()* method of the old object model so that you can save your modified file.

> **Tip** Writing an application to programmatically edit a report definition file is not for the faint of heart. If you are undeterred by the obstacles we describe, you can find sample code by Teo Lachev at *http://prologika.com/CS/blogs/blog/archive/2010/03/08/where-is-rdlom-in-r2.aspx* and by Lionel Ringenbach at *http://ucodia.fr/2011/10/advanced-reporting-services-part1-rdl-object-model/* and *http://ucodia.fr/2011/10/advanced-reporting-services-part2-rdl-serializer/*.

RDL generation

You have a variety of options for generating RDL programmatically. You can create a Windows-based application with a graphical interface to prompt a user for information about the report layout, or you can create a series of web forms in the form of a wizard to lead the user through selections that you can use to construct an RDL. Your imagination is the only limit.

Solution overview

One type of problem that you can solve through programmatic RDL generation is the customization of a set of reports by user. A simple way to approach the solution is to create a table to store information about the report set and then use that information to generate a single RDL that combines the report set and publish the report to your report server. You can then configure security to make it available to the user directly, or you can create a subscription to send it to the user on a periodic basis.

This approach to custom report creation requires you to first build a table such as the one shown in Figure 32-4. To support the sample application described in this chapter, the *ReportSet* table contains columns to track the assignment of a set of reports by user. Each row represents either a cover page for a section of a report or an individual report.

	UserID	ReportSetID	ReportName	TOCLabel	PageLabel	PageNumber	Style	SortOrder	Section
1	1	1	Management Summary	MANAGEMENT SUMMARY	NULL	NULL	Section	1	A
2	1	1	Sales and Average Sales	Sales and Average Sales (Chart)	Average Sales	1	ReportTitle	2	A
3	1	1	Employee Sales Moving Average	Employee Sales Moving Average (Chart)	Moving Average	2	ReportTitle	3	A
4	1	1	Management Detail	DETAIL REPORTS	NULL	NULL	Section	4	B
5	1	1	Reseller Sales Margin Analysis by Sales Territory	Margin Analysis by Sales Territory (Reseller Sales)	Margin	3	ReportTitle	5	B
6	1	1	Customer List	Customer List by Year of First Purchase	Customers	4	ReportTitle	6	B

FIGURE 32-4 You create a table to store information about report sets to create for each user.

The *ReportName* column stores the name of the RDL for reports, the *TOCLabel* column stores the name to display on the table of contents page of the new RDL, and the *PageLabel* column is the name to display in the page footer to accompany the page number. In this application, the reports are numbered with a page number prefix using the value in the *PageNumber* column to which the actual page number of the current report is appended if it has more than one page. Next, the *SortOrder* column stores the sort order of the section cover pages and reports to use when structuring the single RDL that combines everything into a single document. Last, the *Section* column contains a label that displays on the section cover page and identifies reports for the section table of contents.

Important In this case, all reports exist in the same folder to contain the new report; otherwise, you must include the path name along with the report name. For example, if a report is stored in the Sales folder, you include the folder name like this: /Sales/Sales and Average Sales.

RDLGenerator class

In the sample application, we use a simple console application so that we can focus on the mechanics of the problem to solve rather than developing an interface or adding robust error handling. Of course, you can adapt this approach to better suit your needs. For example, the console application accepts arguments, but it does not include validation.

When you run the application, you supply arguments to identify the user and report set defining the group of reports to include in the new RDL. You also supply a path and file name for saving the RDL and a title to place on the cover page of the new report. The *RDLGenerator* class starts with the *Run* method to call the *GetTOC()* function to read the data source, retrieve records related to a specific user and report set, and save the records in the arrays, and then it calls the *BuildParentReport()* function to update a template report definition by removing a placeholder subreport and then adding elements to display a Section page or a specific report, as shown here:

```
Public Sub Run(args As String())

  Dim iUserID As Integer = args(0)
  Dim iReportSetID As Integer = args(1)
  Dim sParentReport As String = args(2)
  Dim sReportTitle As String = args(3)
  Dim sReport() As String
  Dim sReportStyle() As String
  Dim sReportSection() As String
  ReDim sReport(0 To 0)
  ReDim sReportStyle(0 To 0)
  ReDim sReportSection(0 To 0)
  Dim rows As Integer

  Try
    Try
      rows = GetTOC(iUserID, iReportSetID, sReport, sReportStyle, sReportSection)
    Catch ex As Exception
      Console.WriteLine("Error on GetTOC(): " + ex.Message)
    End Try
    Try
      BuildParentReport(iUserID, iReportSetID, sParentReport, rows, sReportTitle, sReport, _
      sReportStyle, sReportSection)
    Catch ex As Exception
      Console.WriteLine("Error on BuildParentReport():" + ex.Message)
    End Try

    Console.WriteLine("RDL file generated successfully.")

  Catch ex As Exception
    Console.WriteLine("Error: " + ex.Message)
  Finally
    Console.WriteLine("Press ENTER to continue.")
    Console.ReadLine()
  End Try

End Sub
```

The *GetTOC()* function calls the *GetConnectionString()* function to get the connection string for the database containing the *ReportSet* table. It then opens a connection, executes a *SELECT* statement to get records from the table for the specified user and report set, and stores results in a *SqlDataReader* object. A *WHILE* loop iterates through the rows in the *SqlDataReader* object and dynamically resizes arrays as necessary to hold report names, style, and section data separately. Then the *GetTOC()* function closes the connection and returns the number of rows to the *Run* method.

```
Private Function GetTOC(ByVal iUser As Integer, ByVal iReportSet As Integer, _
ByRef sReport() As String, ByRef sReportStyle() As String, ByRef sReportSection() As String)

  Dim sConnectionString As String = GetConnectionString()
  Dim sqlCon As New SqlConnection
  sqlCon = New SqlClient.SqlConnection(sConnectionString)
  sqlCon.Open()
```

```
    Dim sqlComm As New SqlCommand("SELECT * FROM [ReportSet] WHERE [UserID] = " + CStr(iUser) _
    + " and [ReportSetID] = " + CStr(iReportSet) + " ORDER BY [SortOrder]", sqlCon)
    Dim ReaderObj As SqlDataReader = sqlComm.ExecuteReader()
    Dim j As Integer = 0

    While (ReaderObj.Read())
      If j >= 1 Then
        ReDim Preserve sReport(0 To UBound(sReport) + 1)
        ReDim Preserve sReportStyle(0 To UBound(sReportStyle) + 1)
        ReDim Preserve sReportSection(0 To UBound(sReportSection) + 1)
      End If

      sReport(j) = ReaderObj.Item(2)
      sReportStyle(j) = ReaderObj.Item(6)
      sReportSection(j) = ReaderObj.Item(8)
      j = j + 1
    End While

    ReaderObj.Close()
    sqlCon.Close()
    Return j - 1

End Function

Public Function GetConnectionString()

  Dim sConnectionString As String = "Data Source=(local);Initial Catalog=
CustomReports;Integrated
  Security=True"
  Return sConnectionString

End Function
```

The *BuildParentReport()* function relies on the Language-Integrated Query (LINQ) to XML inter-face and uses the *XElement* class to read a report definition and then to manipulate and save it. The function starts by using the *Load()* method to store the report definition's XML in a variable called *xParentRDL* and then uses the *GetDefaultNamespace()* method to store the default namespace for use later when working with specific elements in the XML tree. The template report definition contains a placeholder element, *Rectangle2*, used to develop the logic for the subreport.

 Note It was not necessary to keep *Rectangle2* in the report definition because it gets re-moved and replaced, but we include it in the template to provide an example of removing elements from a report definition.

The next step is to add each member of the report set to the report definition as a subreport nested in a rectangle so that a page break occurs at the beginning of each new report. The location at which to insert each new *Rectangle* element is located by using the *Descendants()* method with *xParentRDL* to locate *Rectangle1*. Because the *Descendants()* method returns a collection, the *First* method returns the first (and only) element with that name and stores the element in the *xElement-Parent* variable. Then a *For Each* loop on the *sReport* array evaluates whether a report is a section header or a report page based on the style and calls the *BuildSectionRDL()* or *BuildPageRDL()* function accordingly. These functions build an RDL fragment, which the *AddAfterSelf()* method inserts after *Rectangle1* in *xParentRDL*. Next, various modifications are made to the report definition to update the report title in *Textbox1*, to set report parameter values to pass to the subreports for the section cover pages, and to resize the body of the report to accommodate the additional rectangles and subreports. Last, the *BuildParentReport()* function saves the report definition as a new file.

> **Note** One option for extending this application is to add a function for deploying the report to a report server. We explain more about programmatic deployment in Chapter 34, "Programming report server management."

```
Public Sub BuildParentReport(ByVal iUser As Integer, ByVal iReportSet As Integer, _
ByVal sRpt As String, ByVal rows As Integer, ByVal sReportTitle As String, _
ByRef sReport() As String, ByRef sReportStyle() As String, ByRef sReportSection() As String)

    Dim xParentRDL As XElement = XElement.Load(sRpt)
    Dim xElementParent As XElement
    Dim xCurrentRDL As XElement
    Dim i As Integer = 0
    Dim iPage As Integer = 1
    Dim iSection As Integer = 1
    Dim dns As String = "{" + xParentRDL.GetDefaultNamespace().ToString + "}"

    xParentRDL.Descendants(dns + "Rectangle").Where(Function(x) x.Attribute("Name").Value = _
     "Rectangle2").Remove()
    xElementParent = xParentRDL.Descendants(dns + "Rectangle").Where(Function(x) _
      x.Attribute("Name").Value = "Rectangle1").First()

    For Each rpt In sReport
      If sReportStyle(i) = "Section" Then
        xCurrentRDL = BuildSectionRDL(dns, iSection, "ReportTitlePage", iUser, iReportSet, _
          sReportSection(i), sReport(i), i)
        iSection = iSection + 1
      Else
        xCurrentRDL = BuildPageRDL(dns, iPage, sReport(i), i)
        iPage = iPage + 1
      End If

      xElementParent.AddAfterSelf(xCurrentRDL)
      i = i + 1
    Next

    xElementParent = xParentRDL.Descendants(dns + "Textbox").Where(Function(x)  _
      x.Attribute("Name").Value = "Textbox1").First()
    xElementParent.Descendants(dns + "Value").First().ReplaceWith(New XElement(dns+"Value", _
      sReportTitle))

    xElementParent = xParentRDL.Descendants(dns + "ReportParameter").Where(Function(x) _
      x.Attribute("Name").Value = "UserID").First()
    xElementParent.Descendants(dns + "Value").First().ReplaceWith(New XElement(dns + "Value", _
      iUser.ToString))
```

```
xElementParent = xParentRDL.Descendants(dns + "ReportParameter").Where(Function(x) _
  x.Attribute("Name").Value = "ReportSetID").First()
xElementParent.Descendants(dns + "Value").First().ReplaceWith(New XElement(dns + "Value", _
  iReportSet.ToString))

xParentRDL.Descendants(dns + "Body").First().Element(dns + "Height").ReplaceWith( _
  New XElement(dns + "Height", (5.5 + 0.25 * UBound(sReport)).ToString + "in"))

xParentRDL.Save("C:\SSRS\" + sReportTitle + ".rdl")
End Sub
```

The *BuildPageRDL()* function constructs the RDL fragment for a rectangle containing a subreport for a specific report in the report set. The name of this report is passed as a variable and added to the RDL fragment as the value for the *ReportName* element. The *BuildPageRDL()* function uses constructors to build the required elements and attributes necessary to include the specified report as a subreport in the new report definition. Notice the use of the *Lookup* function for the *PageName* element. This technique assigns a unique name to each report in the report definition based on a dataset query in the parent report. This page name then displays in the page footer along with the page number, as shown in Figure 32-5.

 Tip It's useful to build a report with the layout and appearance you want and then view the code to see the structure of the RDL that you need to replicate in your code.

```
Function BuildPageRDL(ByVal dns As String, ByVal iAttrID As Integer, ByVal sReportName As
String, ByVal row As Integer) As XElement

  Dim xPageRDL As XElement = New XElement(dns + "Rectangle", _
    New XAttribute("Name", "PageRectangle" + iAttrID.ToString), _
    New XElement(dns + "ReportItems", _
      New XElement(dns + "Subreport", _
      New XAttribute("Name", "PageSubreport" + iAttrID.ToString), _
        New XElement(dns + "ReportName", sReportName), _
        New XElement(dns + "Height", "0.25in"), _
        New XElement(dns + "Width", "1in"), _
        New XElement(dns + "Style", _
          New XElement(dns + "Border", _
            New XElement(dns + "Style", "None") _
          ) _
        ) _
      ) _
    ), _
    New XElement(dns + "PageBreak", _
      New XElement(dns + "BreakLocation", "Start"), _
      New XElement(dns + "ResetPageNumber", "true") _
    ), _
    New XElement(dns + "PageName", _
      "=Lookup("+iAttrID.ToString+",Fields!PageNumber.Value,Fields!PageLabel.Value, ""dsTOC"")" _
    ), _
    New XElement(dns + "KeepTogether", "true"), _
    New XElement(dns + "Top", (5 + row * 0.25).ToString + "in"), _
    New XElement(dns + "Height", "0.25in"), _
```

```
      New XElement(dns + "Width", "1in"), _
      New XElement(dns + "ZIndex", "3"), _
      New XElement(dns + "Style", _
        New XElement(dns + "Border", _
          New XElement(dns + "Style", "None") _
        ) _
      ) _
    )
    Return xPageRDL

End Function
```

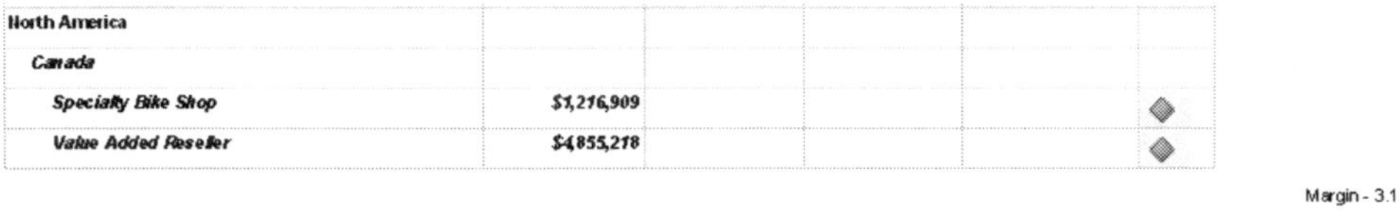

North America				
Canada				
Specialty Bike Shop	$1,216,909			◇
Value Added Reseller	$4,855,218			◇

Margin - 3.1

FIGURE 32-5 The page footer displays the page name, the report number, and the current page number.

The *BuildSectionRDL()* function constructs the RDL fragment for a rectangle containing a subreport based on another template report. This template report contains a text box for a page title and a table that lists the reports in that section, as shown in Figure 32-6. The *BuildSectionRDL()* function uses constructors to add the necessary elements and attributes. Just like the *BuildPageRDL()* function, values appended to the rectangle and subreport names keep the names unique. This function also sets the parameter values to pass to the subreport at run time.

```
Function BuildSectionRDL(ByVal dns As String, ByVal iAttrID As Integer, ByVal sReportName As
String,
ByVal iUser As Integer, ByVal iReportSet As Integer, ByVal sSection As String, ByVal
sSectionTitle As String, ByVal row As Integer) As XElement

  Dim xSectionRDL As XElement = _
    New XElement(dns + "Rectangle", _
      New XAttribute("Name", "SectionRectangle" + iAttrID.ToString), _
      New XElement(dns + "ReportItems", _
        New XElement(dns + "Subreport", _
        New XAttribute("Name", "SectionSubreport" + iAttrID.ToString), _
        New XElement(dns + "ReportName", sReportName), _
        New XElement(dns + "Parameters", _
          New XElement(dns + "Parameter", _
            New XAttribute("Name", "UserID"), _
            New XElement(dns + "Value", iUser.ToString)), _
          New XElement(dns + "Parameter", _
            New XAttribute("Name", "ReportSetID"), _
            New XElement(dns + "Value", iReportSet.ToString)), _
          New XElement(dns + "Parameter", _
            New XAttribute("Name", "Section"), _
            New XElement(dns + "Value", sSection)), _
          New XElement(dns + "Parameter", _
            New XAttribute("Name", "SectionName"), _
            New XElement(dns + "Value", sSectionTitle)) _
          ), _
        New XElement(dns + "Height", "0.25in"), _
```

```
            New XElement(dns + "Width", "1in"), _
            New XElement(dns + "Style", _
              New XElement(dns + "Border", _
                New XElement(dns + "Style", "None") _
              ) _
            ) _
          ) _
        ), _
        New XElement(dns + "PageBreak", _
          New XElement(dns + "BreakLocation", "Start"), _
          New XElement(dns + "ResetPageNumber", "true") _
        ), _
        New XElement(dns + "PageName", "ReportTitle"), _
        New XElement(dns + "KeepTogether", "true"), _
        New XElement(dns + "Top", (5 + row * 0.25).ToString + "in"), _
        New XElement(dns + "Height", "0.25in"), _
        New XElement(dns + "Width", "1in"), _
        New XElement(dns + "ZIndex", "3"), _
        New XElement(dns + "Style", _
          New XElement(dns + "Border", _
            New XElement(dns + "Style", "None") _
          ) _
        ) _
      ) _
    )

    Return xSectionRDL

End Function
```

Section A
Management Summary

- Sales and Average Sales (Chart)
- Employee Sales Moving Average (Chart)

FIGURE 32-6 The section cover page is a subreport template that uses parameters and a dataset query to create the page titles and list of reports included in the section.

Solution deployment

After you build your project successfully, you can move the RDLGenerator.exe file from the project's bin\Debug folder to a location of your choice. You can then execute the application by using the Command Prompt window to execute it using the following syntax:

```
RDLGenerator UserID ReportSetID TemplateName ReportTitle
```

For example, let's say that you want to create a report for UserID 1 and ReportSetID 1 using the Template.rdl file located in the C:\SSRS folder. In addition, you want the report title and file name to be Management Summary. In that case, you execute the following command:

```
RDLGenerator 1 1 C:\SSRS\Template.rdl "Management Summary"
```

If the application creates the report definition successfully, you see a message display confirming completion and you can press Enter to continue. Your file is saved in the C:\SSRS folder by default and is ready for you to deploy to the report server by using any standard deployment process, or you can use a programmatic solution, as we describe in Chapter 33, "Programming report design components."

CHAPTER 33

Programming report design components

As part of the report development phase of the reporting life cycle, you use expressions to calcu-late a value that displays in your report or to change a property value that affects the behavior or appearance of a report item, as described in Chapter 11, "Developing expressions." When you need to use the same complex expression many times in the same report, you might find it easier to write one custom function that you can use as many times as you need throughout the report. Then you have only one place in the report to update the expression if the report requirements change later. Another advantage of using custom functions is the ability to use more advanced logic in your expressions, such as loops that use FOR or WHILE statements or conditions that use IF...THEN or CASE statements. In Reporting Services, you can use custom functions either by embedding code into a single report or by creating a custom assembly that you can then reference in any of your reports.

Embedding code in a report

Embedded code gives you the flexibility of reusing a custom function that you create anywhere in your report, but you should consider its limitations before taking this approach. First, you cannot share the code that you embed in one report with other reports. You must physically add the code to any report in which you want to use the custom function. Furthermore, you must write your custom function using Microsoft Visual Basic .NET. If you want to use your custom function in multiple reports or want to use a different language, you should create a custom assembly, as explained in the "Using assemblies to share custom code" section of this chapter.

For simple requirements, you might decide that using embedded code is easier to implement, even if you must copy the code to multiple reports. The process is very easy, although you need to know how to use the Visual Basic .NET programming language. You start by adding a custom func-tion to the report properties, and then you call your function using the global *Code* member in an expression.

Code property

A report has a *Code* property for you to store the custom functions that you create. For maximum flexibility, you can use arguments to pass a constant, field, parameter, variable, or expression value to your custom function. You can add as many custom functions as you need to your report.

For example, let's say that you have a report in which you use one conditional formatting expression to return a color or another conditional formatting expression to return an image name. Using property settings alone, you must place the applicable conditional formatting logic in each text box that uses colors or images. If the business rules change later, you must edit the applicable property expression for each text box. Although making a change to properties in one or two text boxes is not difficult, it becomes tedious quickly when you must use the same expression in multiple places in the report. Fortunately, you can use embedded code to store the business rule logic in one location and then change the property expressions to refer to that embedded code. Then, each time that the business rules change, you can update the logic in one place. Furthermore, you can combine the conditional formatting logic for colors and images into a single function.

To access the *Code* property and create a common function, select Report Properties on the Reports menu and open the Code page of the Report Properties dialog box, as shown in Figure 33-1. Then you can type your code into the Custom Code box, or you can paste it here if you prefer to use a text editor to develop your code.

Important When you type code into the Custom Code text box, you should check your typing carefully. No IntelliSense alerts you to an error in the code, and you have no mechanism for debugging your function.

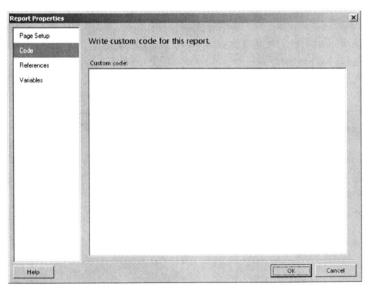

FIGURE 33-1 You add embedded code to your report on the Code page of the Report Properties dialog box.

To create a generic function that returns a color or a KPI based on specific conditions, you can use code like this:

```
Function GetStatus(ByVal StatusType As String, ByVal StatusCondition As Decimal, ByVal
StatusThreshold As Decimal) As String
Dim ReturnValue As String = Nothing
    Select Case StatusType
        Case "Color"
            Select Case StatusCondition
                Case Is < .02
                    ReturnValue = "Red"
                Case Is > StatusThreshold
                    ReturnValue = "Green"
                Case Else
                    ReturnValue = "Black"
            End Select
        Case "KPI"
            Select Case StatusCondition
                Case Is < .02
                    ReturnValue = "redkpi"
                Case Is > StatusThreshold
                    ReturnValue = "greenkpi"
                Case Else
                    ReturnValue = Nothing
            End Select
    End Select
    Return ReturnValue
End Function
```

This function takes three arguments. You use the first argument, *StatusType*, to indicate whether you are using this function to get a value to set font color or to define a KPI when you use the string *Color* or *KPI*, respectively. You then use the second argument, *StatusCondition*, to provide the current value of the report item for comparison to a constant value, *.02*, or to a variable, *StatusThreshold*. You pass the value of *StatusThreshold* as the third argument of this function. Based on the result of the comparison, the function returns a color or an image name to the report item.

Tip Even without calling the custom function in your report, you can validate the syntax of your custom function by previewing the report. An error displays if a problem is found. Otherwise, the report renders normally.

Custom function call

You can use a custom function in any property that accepts an expression. To call your custom function, you create an expression that references the *Code* member, the function name, and any arguments that are required for your function. The call to a custom function uses the following syntax:

```
Code.method(arguments)
```

In each text box for which you want to use conditional formatting to set a color (such as the *PctContribution* text box in the sample report), replace the expression for the *Color* property to use conditional formatting with your custom function, like this:

```
=Code.GetStatus("Color", ReportItems!PctContribution.Value, Variables!GroupThreshold.Value)
```

Notice that you can use a constant or an expression as a function argument. Notice also that the IntelliSense feature indicates that the *GetStatus* function is invalid in this expression, but you can safely ignore this warning.

> **Note** In this expression, you are using a group variable, *GroupThreshold*, to provide a value for the *StatusThreshold* argument in the *GetStatus* function. In the Group Properties dialog box for the SalesTerritoryGroup group, on the Variables page, you can view the expression that assigns a value to this variable based on the current instance of the group. Group variables are introduced in Chapter 11.

You can also use the custom function to replace an expression for *BackgroundImage* conditional formatting (such as you find in the *Textbox25* and *Textbox41* text boxes in the sample report) by using an expression like this:

```
=Code.GetStatus("KPI", ReportItems!PctContribution.Value, Variables!GroupThreshold.Value)
```

When you preview the report, as shown in Figure 33-2, you can see that detail records include rows that illustrate both possible results of the custom function. The first row displays the Pct Contribution using a green font and displays the green KPI image when the Pct Contribution is greater than the threshold defined for the current group. All the rows with a Pct Contribution value below two percent display the value by using a red font and display the red KPI image. All other rows in this set display the value by using a black font and have no KPI image to display.

Australia					
⊟ *Specialty Bike Shop*					◉
Touring-1000 Blue, 46	$30,039	($1,081.41)	-3.60 %	9.16 %	◉
Touring-1000 Blue, 60	$28,609	($1,029.92)	-3.60 %	8.74 %	
Touring-1000 Blue, 60	$27,178	($978.42)	-3.60 %	8.31 %	
Touring-1000 Yellow, 60	$24,318	($875.43)	-3.60 %	7.43 %	
Touring-1000 Yellow, 46	$20,503	($7,653.82)	-37.33 %	6.27 %	
Touring-1000 Blue, 46	$20,026	($720.94)	-3.60 %	6.12 %	
Touring-1000 Yellow, 46	$18,596	($669.45)	-3.60 %	5.68 %	
Touring-1000 Yellow, 60	$16,784	($5,445.22)	-32.44 %	5.13 %	
Touring-2000 Blue, 60	$16,765	($603.54)	-3.60 %	5.12 %	
Touring-2000 Blue, 54	$16,036	($577.30)	-3.60 %	4.90 %	
Touring-2000 Blue, 60	$11,663	($419.85)	-3.60 %	3.56 %	
Touring-2000 Blue, 54	$10,934	($393.61)	-3.60 %	3.34 %	
Touring-3000 Yellow, 44	$6,236	($224.49)	-3.60 %	1.91 %	◈
Touring-3000 Yellow, 62	$6,236	($224.49)	-3.60 %	1.91 %	◈
Touring-3000 Yellow, 44	$6,119	($1,725.74)	-28.20 %	1.87 %	◈

FIGURE 33-2 You can use the same function to apply conditional formatting to a color property and an image property in different text boxes.

Using assemblies to share custom code

For maximum flexibility and reusability, you can create an assembly for your custom functions by using any language supported by the Microsoft .NET Framework. You start by creating a class library and then building the assembly. You must then install the assembly on the report server and on your report development workstation so that you can test functions in the Report Designer before deploying reports to the report server. After installing the assembly, you can then call your custom function by adding a reference to your report and creating an expression that references the namespace and class for your function and includes any required arguments.

Class library

Using Microsoft Visual Studio 2010, you can create a class library as a container for all the custom functions that you want to use in your reports. After you add functions to the class library, you use the Build command to produce the assembly file as a .dll file that you can then copy to the Bin folders for Report Designer and for the report server.

Class definition

In Visual Studio, create a Class Library using your language of choice and change the project name. In our Visual Basic example, we use the name Rs2012.VB.Extensions, as shown in Figure 33-3. Our C# example has the name Rs2012.CS.Extensions.

Important You must be sure to select .NET Framework 3.5. If you compile the custom assembly using .NET Framework 4.0, you can preview a report referencing the assembly successfully in Report Designer. However, you cannot deploy the report to the report server.

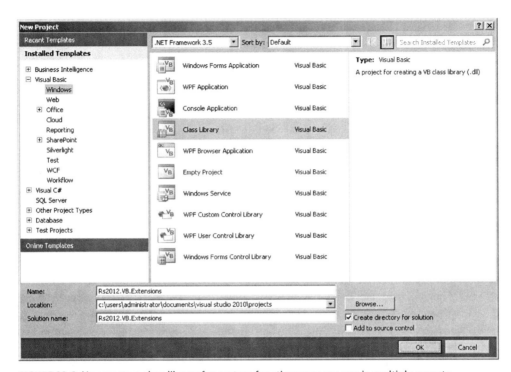

FIGURE 33-3 You create a class library for custom functions you can use in multiple reports.

You can also rename the default class name to something more meaningful, such as *ReportFunctions.vb*. Next add each function to the class definition. For example, you can reproduce the *GetStatus* function as a function in the new Visual Basic class like this:

```
Public Class ReportFunctions
  Public Shared Function GetStatus(ByVal StatusType As String, ByVal StatusCondition As Decimal,
ByVal
  StatusThreshold As Decimal, ByVal AlertThreshold As Decimal) As String
      Dim ReturnValue As String = Nothing
      Select Case StatusType
          Case "Color"
              Select Case StatusCondition
                  Case Is < AlertThreshold
                      ReturnValue = "Red"
                  Case Is > StatusThreshold
                      ReturnValue = "Green"
                  Case Else
                      ReturnValue = "Black"
              End Select
          Case "KPI"
```

```
            Select Case StatusCondition
                Case Is < AlertThreshold
                    ReturnValue = "redkpi"
                Case Is > StatusThreshold
                    ReturnValue = "greenkpi"
                Case Else
                    ReturnValue = Nothing
            End Select
        End Select
        Return ReturnValue
    End Function
End Class
```

The code for this function is almost identical to the code that we described as embedded code in the previous section. Notice here that the code now includes a new argument, *AlertThreshold*, to replace the constant *0.02* value in the embedded code and is consequently more flexible. You can then customize the alert threshold value in each report.

If you prefer to use C#, the code looks like this:

```
using System;
using System.Collections.Generic;
using System.Linq;
using System.Text;

namespace Rs2012.CS.Extensions
{
  public class ReportFunctions
  {
    public static string GetStatus(string StatusType, decimal StatusCondition,
    decimal StatusThreshold, decimal AlertThreshold)
    {
      switch (StatusType)
      {
        case "Color":
        {
          if (StatusCondition < AlertThreshold)
          {
            return "Red";
          }
          else if (StatusCondition > StatusThreshold)
          {
            return "Green";
          }
          else
          {
            return "Black";
          }
        };
        case "KPI":
        {
          if (StatusCondition < AlertThreshold)
          {
            return "redkpi";
          }
          else if (StatusCondition > StatusThreshold)
```

```
      {
        return "greenkpi";
      }
      else
      {
        return null;
      }
    };
  }
  return null;
    }
  }
}
```

Custom assembly digital signature

The purpose of a digital signature using a strong name key is to guarantee the identity of an assembly. That way, an assembly with the same name cannot be surreptitiously placed on a report server to execute malicious code. Your reports run only when the assembly with the right digital signature exists.

Use of a digital signature is optional. If you decide to use this approach, you must update the assembly to allow custom assembly calls from the report's partially trusted code. To do this, add the following code at the assembly level (outside of any class) for a Visual Basic project:

```
Imports System.Security
<Assembly: AllowPartiallyTrustedCallers()>
```

If your assembly is written using C#, use the following code instead:

```
using System.Security;
[assembly: AllowPartiallyTrustedCallers]
```

Next you need to create a strong name key file. In a Visual Studio 2010 command prompt window, use the Strong Name Tool to create a file (such as rsKey.snk) by typing a command like this:

```
sn -k rsKey.snk
```

You then reference the strong name key on the Signing page of the project properties, as shown in Figure 33-4. Select the Sign The Assembly check box, and then use the Choose A Strong Name Key File drop-down list to browse to the location of the strong name key file and select it.

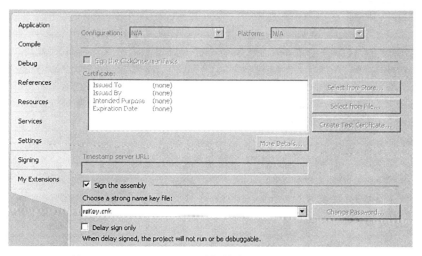

FIGURE 33-4 You can protect your assembly file by signing it with a strong name key.

Assembly deployment

After you add all your functions to the class, use the Build command to build the project and create an assembly file that you can deploy to the report development workstation and to the report server. Copy the DLL file from your projects Bin\Debug folder to the folder used by Report Designer on your report development computer. If you want other report developers to use your custom function, they must also deploy this file to the same location on their workstations. In SQL Server 2012 Reporting Services, this folder is located at Program Files (x86)\Microsoft Visual Studio 10.0\Common7\IDE\ PrivateAssemblies.

You must also deploy the same file to the report server. The file must be placed in the Program Files\Microsoft SQL Server\MSRS11.<*Instance*>\Reporting Services\ReportServer\Bin, where <*Instance*> is the instance identifier for your native-mode report server, such as MSSQLSERVER, as described in Chapter 4, "Installing Reporting Services." If you have a SharePoint integrated-mode report server, place the DLL file in the Program Files\Common Files\Microsoft Shared\Web Server Extensions\14\ WebServices\Reporting\bin folder.

Custom assembly call

When you want to use functions from a custom assembly in an expression, you must add a reference to that custom assembly as a report property. Then, in the expression, you include the namespace and the name of the class in which the function is defined. You also include any arguments required by the function.

To do this, open Report Properties from the Report menu. If necessary, open the Variables page and initialize variable values. For example, in the sample report, we use a value of 0.01 for the *AlertThreshold* variable. Then on the References page of the Report Properties dialog box, click the Add button below Add Or Remove Assemblies, and then click the ellipsis button that appears. In the Add Reference dialog box, click the Browse tab, navigate to the location of your custom assembly (C:\Program Files (x86)\ Microsoft Visual Studio 10.0\Common7\IDE\PrivateAssemblies), and double-click it to add the assembly reference to the Report Properties dialog box, as shown in Figure 33-5.

> **Note** When you view your report in preview mode in Report Designer, the assembly loads from the report designer folder. When you deploy and view the report on the report server, the assembly loads from the report server bin folder or from the global assembly cache if you deployed it there instead.

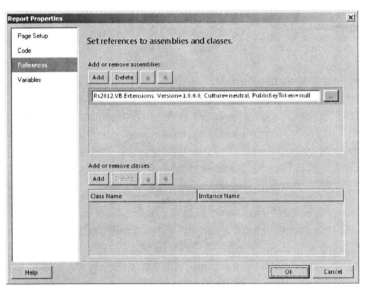

FIGURE 33-5 You must add a reference to your custom assembly on the References page of the Report Properties dialog box.

The References page of the Report Properties dialog box also includes a section to add or remove classes. You use this section to add a class name and instance name if your assembly uses instance methods. If you use static (or Shared) methods, you leave this section blank. Using static methods performs better because the report server does not require additional overhead to construct and maintain object instances.

After adding the assembly reference, you can modify the property expressions used for conditional formatting in your report. Use the drop-down list at the top of the Properties window to select each text box (such as *PctContribution* in the sample report), and replace the current expression with a call to your custom function, like this:

```
=Rs2012.VB.Extensions.ReportFunctions.GetStatus("Color", ReportItems!
PctContribution.Value, Variables!GroupThreshold.Value, Variables!AlertThreshold.Value)
```

When you call a function in a custom assembly, your expression must include the namespace, the class name, and the function name in addition to the arguments required by the function. Just like the embedded code expression, you can use constant values or expressions as arguments. Again, the IntelliSense feature indicates that the *GetStatus* function is invalid in this expression because it is unaware of external functions, but you can ignore this warning here.

In the sample report, you can also call the custom assembly in the *BackgroundImage* property for the *Textbox25* and *Textbox41* text boxes and use a different argument to return an image. Just replace the current expression with this one:

```
=Rs2012.VB.Extensions.ReportFunctions.GetStatus("KPI", ReportItems!PctContribution.Value,
Variables!GroupThreshold.Value, Variables!AlertThreshold.Value)
```

When you preview the report, you can find detail records that include rows with both possible results of the custom function, just as you saw in Figure 33-2 when using the embedded code option.

Creating a custom data processing extension

Although Reporting Services provides built-in functionality for most report development tasks you need to perform, you might encounter situations for which the only solution is to develop a custom application. As we explained in Chapter 2, "Introducing the Reporting Services environment," you can use Reporting Services as a development platform, which means that you can extend Reporting Services to add the functionality you require rather than build a custom application that replicates much of the functionality that Reporting Services already provides.

To learn how to implement a custom data processing extension, you can explore the File Share Data Processing Extension Sample available for download as one of the Reporting Services product samples in Refresh 3 for Microsoft SQL Server 2008. Although the sample is not included in the product samples for later versions, the principles it demonstrates remain valid. You can see how this sample extension uses the data processing extension interfaces available in Reporting Services by reviewing the code in preparation for developing your own custom data processing extension.

Note You can find the original source code for this sample on CodePlex, along with other samples for SQL Server 2008, in the SQL2008.Reporting_Services.Samples.zip file at *http://msftrsprodsamples.codeplex.com/downloads/get/86580*. The versions we include in the sample files provided for this book have been converted to work with SQL Server 2012 and Visual Studio 2010, and minor adjustments have been made to enable deployment of both the Visual Basic and C# versions on the same server for testing purposes. Normally, you do not deploy two versions of an extension on the same report server.

Data processing extension overview

Before you review the sample extension, you should understand the general process for developing a custom data processing extension. You start by developing a class library that includes objects for managing a data source connection, sending a request to the data source, and storing the results of the request, as shown in Figure 33-6. Optionally, you can include objects to manage query parameters and transactions. Table 33-1 lists the object types, namespaces, and interfaces required to implement a custom data processing extension.

TABLE 33-1 Interfaces for implementing a custom data processing extension

Object	Namespace	Interface
Connection	System Microsoft.ReportingServices. DataProcessing	IDBConnection IDbConnectionExtension (optional)
Command	System System.Component.Model Microsoft.ReportingServices. DataProcessing	IDbCommand IDBCommandAnalysis (optional)
DataReader	System System.Collections System.Globalization System.IO System.Security System.Security.Principal Microsoft.ReportingServices. DataProcessing	IDataReader IDataReaderExtension (optional)
Parameter	System Microsoft.ReportingServices. DataProcessing	IDataParameter
ParameterCollection	System System.Collections System.Globalization Microsoft.ReportingServices. DataProcessing	ArrayList IDataParameterCollection
Transaction	System Microsoft.ReportingServices. DataProcessing	IDbTransaction IDbTransactionExtension (optional)

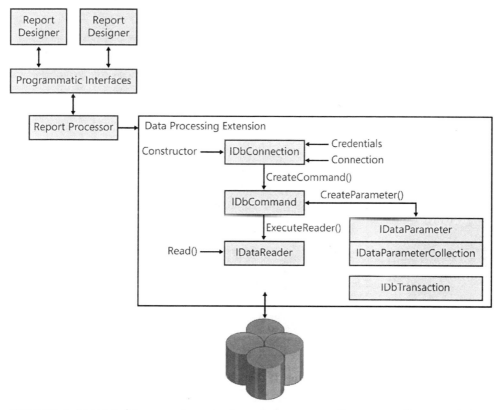

FIGURE 33-6 A custom data processing extension manages a connection, a connection request, storage of the request results, and, optionally, parameters and transaction handling.

Data processing extension development

The sample data processing extension includes a class for each of the six required interfaces. In this section, we review the assembly properties for a Visual Studio 2010 class library project and then review each class individually.

 Important When you create any custom extension for Reporting Services, you must be sure to select .NET Framework 3.5 or earlier. The report server does not currently support extensions using .NET Framework 4.0.

Assembly properties

The root namespace for your assembly uniquely identifies the data processing extension in your Reporting Services implementation. When you configure the report server and report development workstation to use the extension, as described in the "Configuration changes" section of this chapter, you include the namespace. You assign the root namespace on the Application page, shown in Figure 33-7, which you access by right-clicking the project in Solution Explorer and selecting Properties.

Tip If you want to deploy both versions of the sample extension for testing purposes, you must assign a unique assembly and root namespace to each extension. For example, we re-named the Visual Basic version as Microsoft.VB.Samples.ReportingServices.FsiDataExtension and the C# version as Microsoft.CS.Samples.ReportingServices.FsiDataExtension.

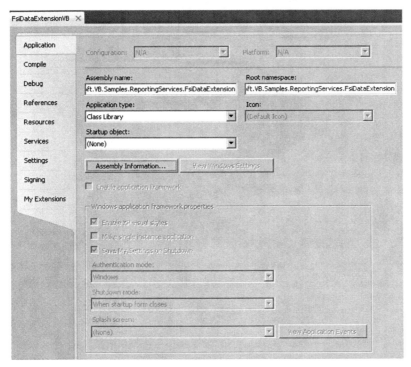

FIGURE 33-7 You must assign a unique root namespace to your custom assembly.

In addition, on the References page for the project, you need to add a reference to the *Microsoft .ReportingServices.Interfaces* assembly, as shown in Figure 33-8. You can find the DLL file for this assembly on a native-mode report server in the Program Files\Microsoft SQL Server\MSRS11. MSSQLSERVER\Reporting Services\Report Server\bin folder. On a SharePoint integrated-mode report server, this file is in the Program Files\Common Files\Microsoft Shared\Web Server Extensions\14\ WebServices\Reporting\bin folder.

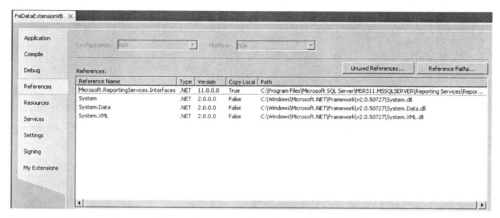

FIGURE 33-8 Your project requires a reference to the *Microsoft.ReportingServices.Interface* assembly.

Connection class

A custom data processing extension requires a class to create a connection object by using either the *IDbConnection* or *IDBConnectionExtension* interface. The *IDbConnection* interface performs basic connection operations, such as getting or setting connection string properties, opening and closing a connection, and setting a connection time-out value. You can use the *IDbConnectionExtension* interface instead when you need to use Windows integrated security or send a user name and password to authenticate the connection request. You must implement all the inherited members of these interfaces in addition to the inherited members of *IExtension*, and then customize the members required for your data processing extension.

In the sample extension, there is not much to customize. At minimum, you assign a string to the *m_locName* variable to name your extension for use in the data provider drop-down lists when creating a new data source in Report Designer, Report Builder, or Report Manager. The constructors are empty because there is no connection string to use. Not all the inherited members are used, but they must be implemented regardless. A data processing extension must create and open a connection and then execute a command. It should also handle authentication so that all other classes in your data processing connection can rely on an authenticated connection.

In the following code, notice the properties and methods required to connect to a Windows file share: *ConnectionTimeout, State, Open(), Close(), CreateCommand(), LocalizedName, IntegratedSecurity, UserName, Password, Impersonate,* and *ConnectionUser.* Notice also that the *NotSupportedException()* method is implemented for the *BeginTransaction()* method to show that the custom data processing extension does not support transactions. However, despite this lack of transaction support, the extension must include the *BeginTransaction()* method because the interface requires it.

Note The code samples in this chapter are written in Visual Basic. You can find the C# version of the code in the Chapter 33 folder in the set of sample files that you can download for this book.

```
Imports System
Imports Microsoft.ReportingServices.DataProcessing
Imports Microsoft.ReportingServices.Interfaces
Imports System.Security.Permissions
Imports System.Security.Principal


NotInheritable Public Class FsiConnection Implements IDbConnectionExtension

    Private m_conn As String
    Private m_state As System.Data.ConnectionState = System.Data.ConnectionState.Closed
    Private m_locName As String = "File Share Information"
    Private m_impersonate As String
    Private m_username As String
    Private m_password As String
    Private m_connectionOpened As Boolean = False
    Private m_connectionUser As WindowsIdentity = Nothing
    Private m_integratedSecurity As Boolean = False

    Public Sub New()
    End Sub

    Public Sub New(ByVal conn As String)
    End Sub

    Property ConnectionString() As String Implements IDbConnection.ConnectionString
        Get
            Return m_conn
        End Get
        Set(ByVal value As String)
            m_conn = value
        End Set
    End Property

    ReadOnly Property ConnectionTimeout() As Integer Implements IDbConnection.ConnectionTimeout
        Get
            Return 0
        End Get
    End Property

    Public ReadOnly Property State() As System.Data.ConnectionState
        Get
            Return m_state
        End Get
    End Property

    Function BeginTransaction() As IDbTransaction Implements IDbConnection.BeginTransaction
        Throw New NotSupportedException()
    End Function

    Sub Open() Implements IDbConnection.Open
        If Not m_connectionOpened Then
            If m_integratedSecurity Then
                m_connectionUser = WindowsIdentity.GetCurrent()
            Else
                m_connectionUser = Nothing
```

```
      End If
      m_connectionOpened = True
    End If
End Sub

Sub Close() Implements IDbConnection.Close
  If Not (m_connectionUser Is Nothing) Then
    m_connectionUser.Dispose()
  End If
  m_connectionOpened = False
End Sub

Function CreateCommand() As IDbCommand Implements IDbConnection.CreateCommand
  Return New FsiCommand(Me)
End Function

ReadOnly Property LocalizedName() As String Implements IExtension.LocalizedName
  Get
    Return m_locName
  End Get
End Property

Sub SetConfiguration(ByVal configuration As String) Implements IExtension.SetConfiguration
End Sub

Property IntegratedSecurity() As Boolean Implements IDbConnectionExtension.IntegratedSecurity
  Get
    Return m_integratedSecurity
  End Get
  Set(ByVal value As Boolean)
    m_integratedSecurity = value
  End Set
End Property

WriteOnly Property UserName() As String Implements IDbConnectionExtension.UserName
  Set(ByVal value As String)
    m_username = value
  End Set
End Property

WriteOnly Property Password() As String Implements IDbConnectionExtension.Password
  Set(ByVal value As String)
    m_password = value
  End Set
End Property

WriteOnly Property Impersonate() As String Implements IDbConnectionExtension.Impersonate
  Set(ByVal value As String)
    m_impersonate = value
  End Set
End Property

Sub Dispose() Implements IDisposable.Dispose
End Sub

Friend ReadOnly Property ConnectionUser() As WindowsIdentity
  Get
```

```
      If Not m_connectionOpened Then
        Throw New Exception("Connection Not Open")
      End If
      Return m_connectionUser
    End Get
  End Property
End Class
```

Command class

Next you need to add a class to create a command object by using the *IDbCommand* interface. The data processing extension uses the command object to request data from a data source and store the results in a data reader object. You can optionally support sending query parameters during query execution.

In addition to implementing the members of the *IDbCommand* interface, you customize the code in the *ExecuteReader()* method as necessary for your data source. For parameters, you need to update the *m_parameters* variable and the *Parameters* property to correctly reference the parameters collection class. Furthermore, you need to update the *Transaction* property to correctly reference the transaction class and the *CreateParameter()* method to reference the parameter class. If you want Report Designer or Report Builder to prompt for parameters when testing a query, you must implement the *IDbCommandAnalysis* interface (which is not shown in the sample extension). The following code uses the following properties and methods to execute a command to retrieve data from a Windows file share: *CommandText, CommandType, Parameters, Transaction, CreateParameter(),* and *ExecuteReader()*:

```
Imports System
Imports System.ComponentModel
Imports Microsoft.ReportingServices.DataProcessing
Imports System.Security.Principal

NotInheritable Public Class FsiCommand Implements IDbCommand
  Private m_connection As FsiConnection
  Private m_txn As FsiTransaction
  Private m_cmdText As String
  Private m_parameters As New FsiDataParameterCollection()

  Public Sub New()
  End Sub

  Public Sub New(ByVal connection As FsiConnection)
    m_connection = connection
  End Sub

  Public Sub New(ByVal cmdText As String)
    m_cmdText = cmdText
  End Sub

  Public Sub New(ByVal cmdText As String, ByVal connection As FsiConnection)
    m_cmdText = cmdText
    m_connection = connection
  End Sub
```

```
Public Sub New(ByVal cmdText As String, ByVal connection As FsiConnection, _
ByVal txn As FsiTransaction)
   m_cmdText = cmdText
   m_connection = connection
   m_txn = txn
End Sub


Property CommandText() As String Implements IDbCommand.CommandText
   Get
      Return m_cmdText
   End Get
   Set(ByVal value As String)
      m_cmdText = value
   End Set
End Property


Property CommandTimeout() As Integer Implements IDbCommand.CommandTimeout
   Get
      Return 30
   End Get
   Set(ByVal value As Integer)
      End Set
End Property


Property CommandType() As CommandType Implements IDbCommand.CommandType
   Get
      Return CommandType.Text
   End Get
   Set(ByVal value As CommandType)
      If value <> CommandType.Text Then
         Throw New NotSupportedException()
      End If
   End Set
End Property


Public ReadOnly Property Parameters() As IDataParameterCollection Implements IDbCommand.
Parameters
   Get
      Return m_parameters
   End Get
End Property


Property Transaction() As IDbTransaction Implements IDbCommand.Transaction
   Get
      Return m_txn
   End Get
   Set(ByVal value As IDbTransaction)
      m_txn = CType(value, FsiTransaction)
   End Set
End Property


Sub Cancel() Implements IDbCommand.Cancel
   Throw New NotSupportedException()
End Sub


Function CreateParameter() As IDataParameter Implements IDbCommand.CreateParameter
```

```
      Return CType(New FsiDataParameter(), IDataParameter)
    End Function

    Function ExecuteReader(ByVal behavior As CommandBehavior) As IDataReader
      Implements IDbCommand.ExecuteReader

      Dim impersonationContext As WindowsImpersonationContext = Nothing
      Dim reader As FsiDataReader = Nothing

      Try
        If Not (m_connection.ConnectionUser Is Nothing) Then
          impersonationContext = m_connection.ConnectionUser.Impersonate()
        End If

        reader = New FsiDataReader(m_cmdText)

      Finally
        If Not (impersonationContext Is Nothing) Then
          impersonationContext.Dispose()
        End If
      End Try

      Return reader
    End Function

    Sub Dispose()  Implements IDisposable.Dispose
    End Sub

End Class
```

DataReader class

The command object requires a data reader class to create storage for the results of command execution. To implement this class, you use the *IDataReader* interface. Report Designer and Report Builder use methods in this class to create a field list for the dataset.

The sample extension uses the *System.IO.DirectoryInfo* and *System.IO.FleSystemInfo* classes to retrieve data about the selected network file share. Your data processing extension might require you to implement other interfaces to support the type of query it needs to execute. The *ExecuteReader()* method returns a data reader object that the extension iterates through and stores in memory in the form of a table.

The following code uses the following properties and methods to execute a command to retrieve data from a Windows file share: *Read()*, *FieldCount()*, *GetName*, *GetFieldType*, and *GetOrdinal()*. It also includes two methods specific to retrieving data from a Windows File Share: *GetDirectory()* and *ValidateCommandText()*.

```
Imports System
Imports System.Collections
Imports Microsoft.ReportingServices.DataProcessing
Imports System.IO
Imports System.Globalization
Imports System.Security
```

```
Imports System.Security.Principal

Public Class FsiDataReader Implements IDataReader
    Private m_connection As FsiConnection
    Friend m_dir As DirectoryInfo
    Friend m_fsi() As FileSystemInfo
    Friend m_currentRow As Integer
    Friend m_ie As IEnumerator
    Friend m_names As String() = {"Name", "Size", "Type", "CreationDate"}
    Friend m_types As Type() = {GetType(String), GetType(Long), GetType(String),
GetType(DateTime)}
    Friend m_cols(3) As Object
    Friend m_fieldCount As Integer = 4
    Friend m_sizes As Int32() = {1024, 8, 9, 8}

    Friend Sub New()
    End Sub

    Friend Sub New(ByVal cmdText As String)
    End Sub

    Friend Sub New(ByVal cmdText As String, ByVal connection As FsiConnection)
        m_connection = connection
    End Sub

    Public Function Read() As Boolean Implements IDataReader.Read
        If Not (m_ie Is Nothing) Then
            Dim notEOF As Boolean = m_ie.MoveNext()
            If notEOF = True Then
                m_currentRow += 1
                If TypeOf m_fsi(m_currentRow) Is FileInfo Then
                    Dim f As FileInfo = CType(m_fsi(m_currentRow), FileInfo)
                    m_cols(0) = f.Name
                    m_cols(1) = f.Length.ToString(System.Globalization.CultureInfo.InvariantCulture)
                    m_cols(2) = "File"
                    m_cols(3) = f.CreationTime.ToString(System.Globalization.CultureInfo.InvariantCulture)
                Else
                    Dim d As DirectoryInfo = CType(m_fsi(m_currentRow), DirectoryInfo)
                    m_cols(0) = d.Name
                    m_cols(1) = "0"
                    m_cols(2) = "Directory"
                    m_cols(3) = d.CreationTime.ToString(System.Globalization.CultureInfo.InvariantCulture)
                End If
            End If
            Return notEOF
        End If
        Return False
    End Function

    Public ReadOnly Property FieldCount() As Integer Implements IDataReader.FieldCount
        Get
            Return m_fieldCount
        End Get
    End Property

    Public Function GetName(ByVal fieldIndex As Integer) As String Implements IDataReader.GetName
        Return m_names(fieldIndex)
```

```
  End Function

  Public Function GetFieldType(ByVal fieldIndex As Integer) As Type
  Implements IDataReader.GetFieldType
    Return m_types(fieldIndex)
  End Function

  Public Function GetValue(ByVal fieldIndex As Integer) As [Object] Implements IDataReader.
GetValue
    Return m_cols(fieldIndex)
  End Function

  Public Function GetOrdinal(ByVal fieldName As String) As Integer Implements IDataReader.
GetOrdinal
    Return Array.IndexOf(m_names, fieldName)
  End Function

  Friend Sub GetDirectory(ByVal cmdText As String)
    ValidateCommandText(cmdText)
    m_dir = New DirectoryInfo(cmdText)
    m_fsi = m_dir.GetFileSystemInfos()
    m_currentRow = -1
    m_ie = m_fsi.GetEnumerator()
  End Sub

  Public Sub Dispose() Implements IDisposable.Dispose
  End Sub

  Private Shared Sub ValidateCommandText(ByVal dir As String)
    Dim isValidCmd As Boolean = dir.StartsWith("\")
    If Not isValidCmd Then
      Throw New InvalidOperationException("The current CommandText does not conform to a valid
      UNC file share.")
    End If
  End Sub

End Class
```

Parameter class

Your custom data processing extension might not support parameters, but you still must implement this class in your custom data processing extension. Like the following sample extension code, your custom extension must include the following properties: *ParameterName* and *Value*.

```
Option Strict On
Option Explicit On
Imports System
Imports Microsoft.ReportingServices.DataProcessing

Public Class FsiDataParameter Implements IDataParameter
  Private m_paramName As String
  Private m_value As Object

  Public Sub New()
  End Sub
```

```
   Public Sub New(ByVal parameterName As String, ByVal value As Object)
     m_paramName = parameterName
     Me.Value = value
   End Sub

   Public Property ParameterName() As String Implements IDataParameter.ParameterName
     Get
       Return m_paramName
     End Get
     Set(ByVal value As String)
       m_paramName = value
     End Set
   End Property

   Public Property Value() As Object Implements IDataParameter.Value
     Get
       Return m_value
     End Get
     Set(ByVal value As Object)
       m_value = value
     End Set
   End Property

End Class
```

ParameterCollection class

You use the *ParameterCollection* class to store a collection of *Parameter* objects. You can use an *ArrayList* class to manage the collection, as shown in the sample code. You can see in the following code that it uses the *Item()* and *Add()* methods only.

```
Option Strict On
Option Explicit On
Imports System
Imports Microsoft.ReportingServices.DataProcessing
Imports System.Collections
Imports System.Globalization

Public Class FsiDataParameterCollection
Inherits ArrayList
Implements IDataParameterCollection

Default Public Overloads Property Item(ByVal index As String) As Object
  Get
    Return Me(IndexOf(index))
  End Get
  Set(ByVal Value As Object)
    Me(IndexOf(index)) = Value
  End Set
End Property

Public Overloads Overrides Function Add(ByVal value As Object) As Integer
  Return Add(CType(value, IDataParameter))
End Function
```

```
Public Overloads Function Add(ByVal parameter As IDataParameter) As Integer
Implements IDataParameterCollection.Add
  If Not (CType(parameter, FsiDataParameter).ParameterName Is Nothing) Then
    Return MyBase.Add(parameter)
  Else
    Throw New ArgumentException("parameter must be named")
  End If
End Function

End Class
```

Transaction class

You can use transactions to commit data or to roll back changes made to a database. The sample extension is read-only and has no need to support a transaction. Nonetheless, note that each member is implemented in the following code but does nothing. Otherwise, if you were to omit the *Transaction* class, an error during data retrieval could cause data corruption.

```
Option Strict On
Option Explicit On
Imports System
Imports Microsoft.ReportingServices.DataProcessing

Public Class FsiTransaction Implements IDbTransaction
  Dim mm_connection As IDbConnection

  Public Sub Commit() Implements IDbTransaction.Commit
  End Sub

  Public Sub Rollback() Implements IDbTransaction.Rollback
  End Sub

  Public Sub Dispose() Implements IDisposable.Dispose
    mm_connection.Dispose()
  End Sub

End Class
```

Data processing extension deployment

After you complete development of your custom data processing extension, you generate a strong name key if you like, compile the code to create a DLL file for the assembly, and copy it to the report server and to the computer of each report developer who requires the extension. You must place the files in the correct location on each computer, and you must also update the configuration files to enable the data processing extension in the design environment and on the report server. Furthermore, you need to grant permission for the extension to execute. When these tasks are complete, you are ready to create a report using the new data processing extension and deploy it to the report server.

Custom extension digital signature

You can secure your report server implementation by adding a digital signature to your custom data processing extension. That way, reports use only authorized extensions. You must update your assembly file with the *AllowPartiallyTrustedCallers* attribute and reference a strong name key as we describe in the "Custom assembly digital signature" section of this chapter.

File locations

The custom data processing extension must exist on the report server to enable reports using it to execute properly. Similarly, it must exist on your report development computer and on the computer of any report developer who is creating reports that require the custom data processing extension. Table 33-2 shows the locations to which you must copy the extension after you use the Build command in Visual Studio to compile the assembly. You can find the compiled assembly in the bin\Debug folder of your project.

TABLE 33-2 File locations for deploying a custom extension assembly

Computer	File Location
Report Server (native mode)	Program Files\Microsoft SQL Server\MSRS11. MSSQLSERVER\Reporting Services\Report Server\bin
Report Server (SharePoint integrated mode)	Program Files\Common Files\Microsoft Shared\Web Server Extensions\14\WebServices\Reporting\bin
Report Designer (SSDT)	Program Files (x86)\Microsoft Visual Studio 10.0\ Common7\IDE\PrivateAssemblies

Note Report Builder does not support custom data processing extensions.

Configuration changes

Your next step is to update the configuration files of the report server and the report designer to register the new extension. Placing the DLL in the requisite file locations is not sufficient. You must edit the configuration file to include the new extension so that the report server can use it.

Important Before making a change to any configuration file, make a backup copy. That way, if you make an inadvertent change that invalidates the configuration file, you can restore the backup copy and put the Reporting Services components back in working order.

Use Table 33-3 to locate the file location and the configuration file to update for each computer. You can use a text editor or XML editor to modify the contents of the file. To register the custom data processing extension, add the following code as a child element of the *Data* element:

```
<Extension Name="FileShare-VB" Type="Microsoft.VB.Samples.ReportingServices.FsiDataExtension.
FsiConnection, Microsoft.VB.Samples.ReportingServices.FsiDataExtension"/>
```

In the RSReportDesigner.config file, you must also add the following code as a child element of the *Designer* element:

```
<Extension Name="FileShare-VB" Type="Microsoft.ReportingServices.QueryDesigners.
GenericQueryDesigner, Microsoft.ReportingServices.QueryDesigners"/>
```

Note If you are working with the C# versions of the custom data processing extension, use <Extension Name="FileShare-CS" Type="Microsoft.VB.Samples.ReportingServices .FsiDataExtension.FsiConnection, Microsoft.CS.Samples.ReportingServices.FsiDataExtension"/> to update the report server configuration file. Similarly, use <Extension Name="FileShare-CS" Type="Microsoft.ReportingServices.QueryDesigners.GenericQueryDesigner, Microsoft .VReportingServices.QueryDesigners"/> to update the RSReportDesigner.config file.

TABLE 33-3 Configuration files for registering a custom extension

Computer	File Location	File
Report Server (native mode)	Program Files\Microsoft SQL Server\ MSRS11.MSSQLSERVER\Reporting Services\Report Server\bin	RSReportServer.config
Report Server (SharePoint integrated mode)	Program Files\Common Files\ Microsoft Shared\Web Server Extensions\14\WebServices\ Reporting\bin	RSReportServer.config
Report Designer (SSDT)	Program Files (x86)\Microsoft Visual Studio 10.0\Common7\IDE\ PrivateAssemblies	RSReportDesigner.config

FIGURE 33-9 Update the RSReportDesigner.config file to use the custom data processing extension in your Report Designer.

Implementation

With the deployment and configuration complete, you can create a report using the custom data processing extension. When you add a data source, you can select the extension in the Type drop-down list and type in a connection string. The File share Information extension, shown in Figure 33-10, does not use a connection string.

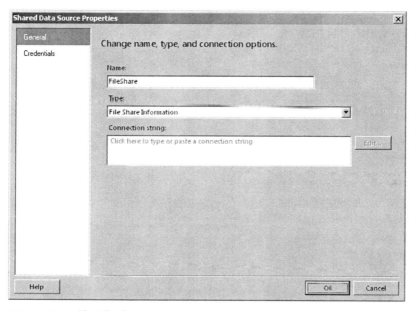

FIGURE 33-10 The File Share Information data processing extension does not use a connection string.

When you create a dataset, you use the Text command type in the generic query designer and type the path of a file share on your network, as shown in Figure 33-11. When you execute the query, you can see the query results. If the file share contains one or more files, you see the file name, file size, type, and creation date of each file.

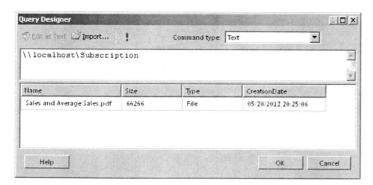

FIGURE 33-11 You use the path of a network file share as the command text of the dataset.

To ensure that the data extension works correctly on the report server, deploy the report and then open the report on the report server. You can also open the data source definition to confirm that the extension information displays correctly in the Data Source Type drop-down list when you create a new data source, as shown in Figure 33-12, or edit an existing data source on a native-mode report server.

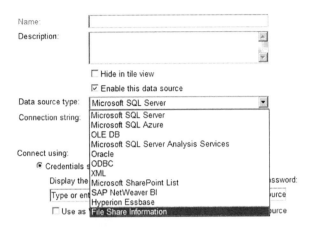

FIGURE 33-12 The custom data processing extension appears in the Data Source Type drop-down list when you configure a data source on the report server.

CHAPTER 34

Programming report server management

Any task that you can perform in Report Manager can also be done programmatically by using the Reporting Services API to communicate with the report server through a web service. For example, you might prefer to script repetitive tasks if you're managing a native-mode report server. You can deploy reports, set properties, define security, and create schedules or subscriptions. Or you might use a custom application to check report server configuration settings. Regardless of which method you use to communicate with the web service, you must implement a proxy class in your code to use the methods and properties available in the web service library. In this section, you learn how to build tools to accomplish some of the objectives that are common in the management phase of the reporting life cycle.

Scripting administrative tasks

You can streamline repetitive administrative tasks by creating a script file (written in Visual Basic .NET) that you can execute by using the Rs utility. A script file is a much simpler approach to performing administrative tasks than developing a Microsoft Windows-based or web application to interact with the Reporting Services web service. In Chapter 23, "Deploying reports to a server," we introduce the Rs utility as one option available for deploying reports to the server, but you can accomplish much more with scripts. You might take a modular approach by creating multiple script files that perform a specific task each and then creating a batch file to execute the scripts as a batch process.

The Rs utility uses the following syntax:

```
Rs -i input_file -s ReportServerURL -u username -p password -e endpoint -l timeout -b -v
variable_key=variable_value -t trace
```

You must be a local administrator on the report server to use the Rs utility. At minimum, you provide the name of the script file as the *input_file* argument and the web service URL for a local or remote report server. All the following arguments are optional:

- **-u username -p password** You provide the *username* and *password* arguments when you need to replace your current Windows credentials with alternate credentials.

- **-e endpoint**   You specify one of the following Simple Object Access Protocol (SOAP) end-points: Mgmt2010, Mgmt2006, Mgmt2005, or Exec2005. The default is Mgmt2005. For more information about endpoints, see the "SOAP endpoints" sidebar in this chapter.

- **-l timeout**   To override the default time-out value of 8 seconds, you can include the *timeout* argument. You can use a value of 0 to prevent timing out altogether.

- **-b**   You use this argument if you want to handle the commands in your script as a batch and roll back the transaction if a command fails that is not otherwise handled as an exception in the script.

- **-v variable_key=variable_value**   You can pass a variable and its value to the script as an argument. You repeat this argument when you have multiple variables to pass to the script.

- **-t**   To record the script output in the trace log, use this argument.

When the Rs utility executes, the utility finds the Web Services Definition Language (WSDL) document that describes the public members available in the web service and creates a proxy class called *rs* that you use in your script to interact with the web service. You can also use members from the following .NET Framework namespaces: *System, System.IO, System.Xml*, and *System.Web.Services*.

> **Note** This chapter shows you how to use only a few of the available Reporting Services methods and properties. Refer to *http://technet.microsoft.com/en-us/library/ms155071* for more information. In some cases, this section of SQL Server Books Online includes code samples that show you how to use the Reporting Services API.

Deploying reports

As we describe in Chapter 23, the Rs utility is useful for deploying a set of reports to the server. You can use the web service's *CreateFolder* method to create a folder to store the reports, if necessary, and then use the *CreateCatalogItem* method to copy the report definition to the report server. If your report uses any shared data sources, you must use the *SetItemDataSources* method to establish the link between the report and the shared data sources.

DeployReports.rss script walkthrough

Let's explore a sample script, DeployReport.rss, that illustrates how to programmatically deploy reports by using a simple script file. At the beginning of the script, you see global variables that can be used by any function in the script, like this:

```
Dim definition As [Byte]() = Nothing
Dim warnings As Warning() = Nothing
Dim parentFolder As String = "Chapter 34"
Dim parentPath As String = "/" + parentFolder
Dim filePath As String = "Chapter 34"
Dim fileName As String = "*.rdl"
```

The *definition* variable is a byte array for use later in the script to store data that is read from a report definition file. The *warnings* variable is an array that stores any warnings that might result from executing a web service method. The remaining four variables—*parentFolder, parentPath, filePath,* and *filename*—provide constant values to the script for the locations and names of the files to be deployed. Notice that you can use a wildcard value, such as **.rdl*, rather than a specific report name when you want to deploy multiple reports. Although you declare and assign values to these variables in this script, you could pass these values to the script as arguments, as described in the "CreateLinked Report.rss script walkthrough" section of this chapter.

Important RSS scripts are case-sensitive. When developing code for RSS scripts, be careful that you maintain the proper case when referring to objects in the code.

Following the variables is the *Main* procedure, shown in the following code, which starts by assigning the current user credentials to the proxy class. This step establishes the security context for the subsequent commands in the script. In this way, the security model is enforced even when using scripts to perform administrative tasks instead of using Report Manager. The web service compares the credentials to the role assignments to determine what items you can access and what tasks you can perform when using the web service methods.

```
Public Sub Main()
    rs.Credentials = System.Net.CredentialCache.DefaultCredentials
    'Create the parent folder
    Try
        rs.CreateFolder(parentFolder, "/", Nothing)
        Console.WriteLine("Parent folder {0} created successfully", parentFolder)
    Catch e As Exception
        Console.WriteLine(e.Message)
    End Try

    'Publish the sample reports
    Dim hostFolder As System.IO.Directory
    Dim reports As String() = hostFolder.GetFiles(filePath, fileName)
    Dim report As String
    For Each report In reports
        PublishReport(report)
    Next
End Sub
```

The *Try-Catch* block calls the *CreateFolder* method of the web service and passes the *parentFolder* as the folder name to create on the report server. The second argument is the parent folder for the new folder, which in this case is a constant value for the root folder, *Home*. The third argument can be used to pass an array of properties for the folder, but in this script, there are no properties to set for the new folder. If the creation of the new folder succeeds, a message displays in the command prompt window to indicate the status. Otherwise, a message displays that describes the error that was encountered.

Tip Unfortunately, there is no way to use Visual Studio to debug your script. However, you can include *Console.WriteLine()* statements in your code as a debugging technique. For example, you can display the current value of a variable at a particular point in the execution of the code.

The next three lines in the code declare variables that are local to the *Main* procedure—*hostfolder*, *reports*, and *report*. The *hostfolder* variable stores the current directory name in which the Rs utility is executing. Then the code uses this directory with the *GetFiles* method to retrieve from one or more files as defined by *filename* in the *filePath* directory. In this procedure, the file path for all files with the .rdl extension in the Programmability folder is retrieved and stored in a string array called *reports*. Then the *For-Next* loop iterates through each file path in the array and assigns the current file path as a string in the *report* variable, which is then passed as an argument to the local *PublishReport* function.

The following section of code demonstrates the *PublishReport* function. It begins with a *Try-Catch* block to read the RDL that's passed (as the variable *reportPath*) into the function and stores it as a filestream object in the *stream* variable. Then the code initializes a byte array, *definition*, into which *stream* contents are then transferred.

```
Public Sub PublishReport(ByVal reportPath As String)
  Try
    Dim stream As FileStream = File.OpenRead(reportPath)
    definition = New [Byte](stream.Length - 1) {}
    stream.Read(definition, 0, CInt(stream.Length))
    stream.Close()
  Catch e As IOException
    Console.WriteLine(e.Message)
  End Try
  Try
    Dim reportPieces As String() = Microsoft.VisualBasic.Strings.Split(reportPath, "\")
    Dim reportName As String = reportPieces.GetValue(reportPieces.Length - 1)
    reportName = reportName.Substring(0, reportName.Length - 4)
    warnings = rs.CreateCatalogItem("Report", reportName, parentPath, False, definition,
Nothing, warnings)
    If Not (warnings Is Nothing) Then
      Dim warning As Warning
      For Each warning In warnings
        Console.WriteLine("Report: {0} published with the following warning: " + warning.
Message, reportName)
      Next warning
    Else
      Console.WriteLine("Report: {0} published successfully with no warnings", reportName)
    End If
'Set single shared data source value
    Dim ds(0) as DataSource
    Dim s as New DataSource
    Dim dsr as New DataSourceReference
    dsr.Reference = "/Data Sources/AdventureWorksDW"
    s.Item = dsr
    s.Name = "AdventureWorksDW2008"
```

```
    ds(0) = s
    Dim myItem as String = parentPath + "/" + reportName
    rs.SetItemDataSources(myItem, ds)
    Console.WriteLine("The shared data source reference for {0} has been updated", reportName)
  Catch e As Exception
    Console.WriteLine(e.Message)
  End Try
End Sub
```

In the second *Try-Catch* block, the first three lines parse the value of *reportPath* to separate the file extension from the report name and assign the result to the local variable *reportName,* which is passed, along with the global variable *parentPath* to the web service's *CreateCatalogItem* method as the second and third arguments. The first argument specifies the catalog item type to create, which in this case is a report. The fourth argument, *False,* ensures that you don't overwrite an existing file of the same name in the same location. The fifth argument, *definition,* is the RDL in the byte array. Finally, the sixth argument specifies the properties to modify when the report is added to the Report Server. The result of executing the *CreateCatalogItem* method is stored in the *warnings* array, which you define as the seventh argument. If any warnings are found, the warning displays in the command prompt window. If not, a success message displays.

After the report is added to the report server, the remaining lines of code in this section assign the shared data source AdventureWorksDW to the report. Otherwise, the link to the data source is broken and the report cannot execute.

> **Note** Although the use of a single management endpoint for native-mode and SharePoint integrated-mode report servers makes it easier to develop code to support both server mode types, there are still differences in folder path names, report names, and shared data source file extensions. Therefore, you must either create separate script files for each server mode type or use variables as described in the "Creating a linked report" section in this chapter to pass in the applicable folder paths and shared data source file name at run time. The Sample Files folder contains script examples for both server mode types.

DeployReports.rss script execution

To execute a script file by using the Rs utility, you must open a command prompt window and navigate to the folder containing the script file. Then the command syntax you use depends on the server mode.

On a native-mode report server, type the following command (replacing *<servername>* with the name of your server or localhost) to view the results of executing the utility, as shown in Figure 34-1:

```
rs -i DeployReports.rss -s http://<servername>/ReportServer -e Mgmt2010
```

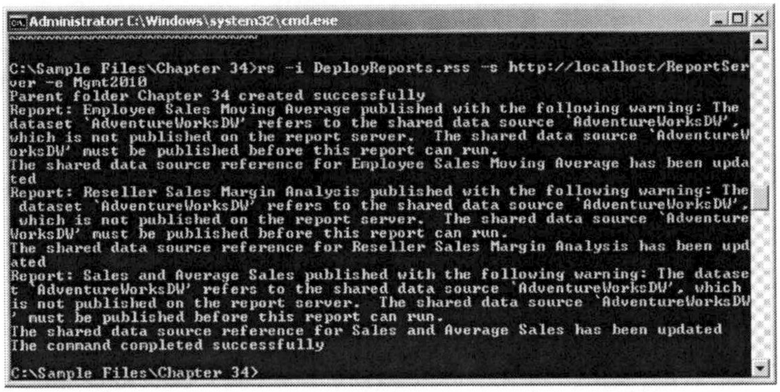

FIGURE 34-1 You can output status messages during script execution in the command prompt window.

On a SharePoint integrated-mode report server, the command uses the web service URL like this:

```
rs -i DeployReports_SP.rss -s http://<sitename>/_vti_bin/ReportServer -e Mgmt2010
```

You can confirm the successful deployment of the reports by opening Report Manager or the target SharePoint site and navigating to the folder into which the reports deployed. You should see a complete list of the reports that you intended to deploy. Next, open each report to confirm that each is properly associated with the shared data source and therefore executes and renders properly.

SOAP endpoints

Whether you write an RSS script or develop a custom application that calls the Reporting Services web service, you must select the correct endpoint to access the classes and methods of the web service. Beginning with SQL Server 2008 R2, you use the *ReportService2010* endpoint to manage a report server running in native mode by using the following URL:

http://<server>/ReportServer/ReportService2010.asmx?wsdl

You also use the *ReportService2010* endpoint to manage a SharePoint integrated-mode report server by using the following URL instead:

http://<site>/_vti_bin/ReportServer/ReportService2010.asmx?wsdl

The management endpoint API allows you to perform operations like adding items to the report server catalog, creating schedules, and setting execution options, to name a few. The *ReportService2005* endpoint is available for use with a SQL Server 2005 or SQL Server 2008 native-mode report server, while the *ReportService2006* endpoint is available for use with a SharePoint integrated-mode report server running either of those versions.

A separate endpoint, *ReportExecution2005*, is the primary API for either mode of report server when you need to run a report. There is also one more endpoint, *ReportServiceAuthentication*, for a SharePoint integrated-mode report server on which you are running Reporting Services through a web application configured for Forms Authentication.

Creating a linked report

Another task that you might find useful to automate is the creation of a linked report. You use the *CreateLinkedItem* method to define the base report, the name of the linked report, its location, and the properties to set for the linked report. If you want to provide new default values for the linked report, you build an array of *ItemParameter* objects and use the *SetItemParameters* method to assign the *ItemParameter* array to the linked report.

> **Note** You can use the *CreateLinkedItem* method on a native-mode report server only. This capability is not supported on a SharePoint integrated-mode report server.

CreateLinkedReport.rss script walkthrough

CreateLinkedReports.rss is another example of using a script to perform administrative tasks. One reason you might create a linked report is to provide different versions of the same report to different users. Each version of the report has a unique combination of parameter settings that the target users cannot change.

The script begins with global variables that can be used by any function in the script, and then the *Main* function has a code to set the current user's credentials and call the *CreateLinkedItem* function, as shown here:

```
Dim warnings As Warning() = Nothing
Dim warning As Warning
Dim folderPath As String = "Chapter 34"

Public Sub Main()
  rs.Credentials = System.Net.CredentialCache.DefaultCredentials
  CreateLinkedItem(sourceReport, linkedReport, newFolder)
End Sub
```

Although the name of the *CreateLinkedItem* function matches the name of the web service method, the omission of the *rs* class lets you know that in this case, the call to a function is local. Notice that the script file does not declare any of these variables. When you execute the script, you provide values for each of these global variables for maximum flexibility.

The script continues with the code for the *CreateLinkedItem* function, which begins by creating an array of *ItemParameter* objects called *params*. Each of the four report parameters—*CostBasis, Year, Quarter*, and *SalesTerritoryGroup*—in the report is set to specific default values in the linked report, and the prompt to the user is disabled for all report parameters except *Quarter*. In this script, the parameter names and default values are defined as constant values for simplicity, but you could add more flexibility to this report by using global variables to set the values at run time.

```
Public Sub CreateLinkedItem(ByVal baseReport as String, linkedReport as String, newFolder
as String)
  Dim params(3) as  ItemParameter

  Dim paramCostBasis as New ItemParameter
```

```
paramCostBasis.Name = "CostBasis"
Dim paramCostBasisDefaults(0) as String
paramCostBasisDefaults(0) = "Total"
params(0) = paramCostBasis

paramCostBasis.DefaultValues = paramCostBasisDefaults
paramCostBasis.PromptUser = False

Dim paramYear as New ItemParameter
paramYear.Name = "Year"
Dim paramYearDefaults(0) as String
paramYearDefaults(0) = "2008"
paramYear.DefaultValues = paramYearDefaults
paramYear.PromptUser = False
params(1) = paramYear

Dim paramQtr as New ItemParameter
paramQtr.Name = "Quarter"
Dim paramQtrDefaults(1) as String
Dim i as Integer
For i = 0 to 1
  paramQtrDefaults(i) = Cstr(i + 1)
Next i

paramQtr.DefaultValues = paramQtrDefaults
paramQtr.PromptUser = True
paramQtr.PromptUserSpecified = True
params(2) = paramQtr

Dim paramTerritory as New ItemParameter
paramTerritory.Name = "SalesTerritoryGroup"
Dim paramTerritoryDefaults(0) as String
paramTerritoryDefaults(0) = "Pacific"
paramTerritory.DefaultValues = paramTerritoryDefaults
paramTerritory.PromptUser = False
params(3) = paramTerritory
```

The *CreateLinkedItem* function continues with a *Try-Catch* block. A new folder is created in preparation for creating the linked report by calling the script's *CreateNewFolder* function. Then, to create the linked report, the web service's *CreateLinkedItem* method is called with four parameters. The first parameter, *linkedReport*, provides a name for the linked report. For the second parameter, *linkedReport Path*, a string that combines the root path ("/") with the *newFolder* string defines the folder path just created with the *CreateNewFolder* function. Then the third parameter, *baseReport*, identifies the full path to the base report from which the linked report is created. In the following script, *Nothing* is the fourth parameter, which specifies that no report properties are to be updated in the linked report:

```
Try
  Dim linkedReportPath as String = "/" + newFolder
  CreateNewFolder(newFolder)
  Console.WriteLine("Parent folder created: {0}", newFolder)
  rs.CreateLinkedItem(linkedReport, linkedReportPath, baseReport, Nothing)
  Console.WriteLine("Linked report created: {0}", linkedReport)
  rs.SetItemParameters(linkedReportPath + "/" + linkedReport, params)
```

```
   Catch e As Exception
      Console.WriteLine(e.Message)
   End Try
End Sub
```

The last code in the script is the *CreateNewFolder* function that is referenced in the *CreateLinked Report* function. It calls the web service's *CreateFolder* method and writes a message to indicate the success or failure of the folder creation.

```
Public Sub CreateNewFolder(ByVal folderName as String)
   Try
      rs.CreateFolder(folderName, "/", Nothing)
      Console.WriteLine("Folder created: {0}", folderName)
   Catch e As Exception
      Console.WriteLine(e.Message)
   End Try
End Sub
```

CreateLinkedReport.rss script execution

You use the Rs utility to run the script and create a linked report. In this case, you must supply values for the global variables in the script. Otherwise, the script execution fails. Execute the following script in the folder containing the script:

```
rs -i CreateLinkedReport.rss -s http://localhost/ReportServer -v sourceReport="/Chapter 34/
Reseller Sales Margin Analysis by Sales Territory" -v linkedReport="Pacific Margin Analysis
2008" -v newFolder="Pacific Sales"
```

Important It is important to exclude spaces between the input variable file name, the equal sign, and the value.

If the script runs successfully, you see a series of messages display in the command prompt window, as shown in Figure 34-2. Here you can see each step of the process as it occurs.

FIGURE 34-2 Output status messages can display the names of folders and linked reports created by a script.

You can confirm the successful deployment of the linked report by navigating to its folder in Report Manager. An icon displays to the left of the report name to indicate that this report is a linked report, as shown in Figure 34-3.

FIGURE 34-3 You can identify a linked report by the icon that displays to the left of the report name.

Open the report by clicking the report link. Notice in Figure 34-4 that *Quarter* is the only visible report parameter, with default values specified to include only the two quarters available for 2004 in the data source. Any changes that you make to the base report in the future also update the linked report, with the exception of changes to report parameters or report parameter default values.

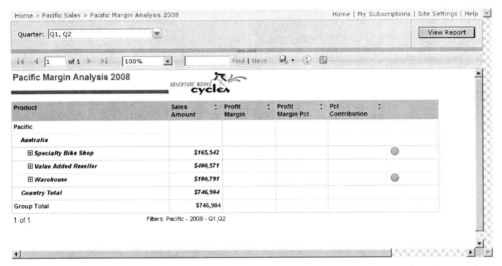

FIGURE 34-4 You can set parameter defaults and hide parameters in a linked report by using a script.

Working with configuration settings

You can also take a programmatic approach to managing the configuration settings for your report server. The approach you take depends on the report server implementation. If you are running a native-mode report server, you can use the Windows Management Instrumentation (WMI) provider in a Visual Basic or C# application. Otherwise, on a SharePoint integrated-mode report server, you can use Windows PowerShell cmdlets.

Using the WMI provider

To review and change the report server configuration settings programmatically, you can use WMI classes. Reporting Services includes the following two classes:

- **MSReportServer_Instance**   This class provides basic information about the report server, such as the edition, version, instance name, and SharePoint integration status. All these configuration settings are read-only.

- **MSReportServer_ConfigurationSetting**   This class provides access to the configuration settings in the configuration file. Some settings are read-only, but several methods are available to make changes to configuration settings, such as *DeleteEncryptionKey* or *ReserveURL*.

The Reporting Services Configuration Manager uses the WMI provider to view and change the configuration settings. However, if you want to have access to this functionality without installing Reporting Services, you can use a custom application instead. You might create a console application as an easy tool that allows you to check the current settings of all Report Server instances on a target server. Or you might create a management application that allows you to update settings in the report server configuration file. To use either of these techniques, you must be a member of the local administrator group on the target report server.

WMI provider application walkthrough

This simple console application lists the current settings of the Report Server instances. You can use it to quickly check a native-mode report server's configuration without opening the configuration file.

To work with the WMI provider, you must add a reference to the System.Management component and add the *System*, *System.Management*, and *System.IO* namespaces to your project, like this:

```
Imports System
Imports System.Management
Imports System.IO
```

> **Tip** Your code does not build properly unless you add a reference to System.Management in your project. When you add the reference, it might be hidden. If you want to see the project references that are currently hidden, you can display them by clicking the Show All Files button on the toolbar in Solution Explorer.

Below the *Sub Main()* statement, you add the code for the application. You start by assigning the Reporting Services WMI namespace and class to strings. The following sample code assumes that you are creating the application to run on a local report server. You can replace *localhost* with the name of a remote report server, if necessary. Notice also the reference to RS_MSSQLSERVER in the string. This instance name is specific to your Reporting Services implementation. If, for some reason, the instance name has been changed on your server, you must update the reference in this code to the applicable value.

```
Const WmiNamespace As String = _
"\\localhost\root\Microsoft\SqlServer\ReportServer\RS_MSSQLSERVER\v11\Admin"
Const WmiRSClass As String = _
\\localhost\root\Microsoft\SqlServer\ReportServer\RS_MSSQLSERVER\v11\admin:MSReportServer_
ConfigurationSetting
```

> **Tip** To find the correct instance name, open the Reportingservices.mof file in the C:\
> Program Files\Microsoft SQL Server\MSRS11.<*Instance*>\Reporting Services\ReportServer\
> Bin folder of the report server, where <*Instance*> is the instance identifier for your re-
> port server, such as MSSQLSERVER if you follow the instructions in Chapter 4, "Installing
> Reporting Services." In the Reportingservices.mof file, look for a line containing Root\
> Microsoft\SqlServer\ReportServer, and note the instance name on the same line.

The code then connects to the WMI namespace and creates a server class so that it can connect to the management object, as follows:

```
Dim serverClass As ManagementClass
Dim scope As ManagementScope
scope = New ManagementScope(WmiNamespace)
scope.Connect()
serverClass = New ManagementClass(WmiRSClass)
serverClass.Get()
If serverClass Is Nothing Then Throw New Exception("No class found")
```

Using the management object, the code can then iterate through the instances that it contains. Within each instance, the code iterates through the property collection and writes the name of the property and its value to the command prompt window.

```
Dim instances As ManagementObjectCollection = serverClass.GetInstances()
Dim instance As ManagementObject
For Each instance In instances
  Console.Out.WriteLine("Instance Detected")
  Dim instProps As PropertyDataCollection = instance.Properties
  Dim prop As PropertyData
  Console.WriteLine("Property Name".PadRight(35) + "Value")
  For Each prop In instProps
    Dim name As String = prop.Name
    Dim val As Object = prop.Value
    Console.Out.Write(prop.Name.PadRight(35))
    If val Is Nothing Then
      Console.Out.WriteLine("<null>")
    Else
      Console.Out.WriteLine(val.ToString())
    End If
  Next
Next
Console.WriteLine("Press any key to continue")
Console.ReadKey()
```

WMI provider application execution

You can test the application within Visual Studio by pressing F5 to see the results, similar to those shown in Figure 34-5.

FIGURE 34-5 You can use the WMI provider to review the current configuration of a native-mode report server.

The advantage of using this application is the access to report server configuration information without opening the configuration file. To use the application, copy the WMIQueryVB.exe file from the project's Bin\Debug folder and place it in a location that is easier to access. You can then start the application on demand by running the executable file.

Using Windows PowerShell cmdlets

On a SharePoint integrated-mode report server, some of the configuration information is accessible through Windows PowerShell cmdlets. You can also use Windows PowerShell cmdlets to update properties in some cases. To do this, open the SharePoint 2010 Management Shell from the Microsoft SharePoint 2010 Products program group on the Start menu, and execute the cmdlets individually or combine multiple cmdlets in a script.

For example, you can create a script by combining the following cmdlets to extract properties related to your Reporting Services implementation:

```
Get-SPRSServiceApplicationServers | select *
$app=Get-SPRSServiceApplication
$app | select *
Get-SPRSServiceApplicationProxy | select *
Get-SPRSProxyUrl | select *
Get-SPRSDatabase | select *
Get-SPRSExtension -identity $app | select *
Get-SPRSSite | select *
```

Note A complete list of Windows PowerShell cmdlets for Reporting Services on a SharePoint integrated-mode report server is available at *http://msdn.microsoft.com/en-us/library/gg492249.aspx*.

Let's say you save the script file as SPRS_Config.ps1. In the SharePoint 2010 Management Shell, navigate to the folder containing the script file. You can then execute the script and save the output to a text file by using the following command:

```
.\SPRS_Config.ps1 > config_out.txt
```

Note You can find an example of using Windows PowerShell cmdlets to modify configuration properties in the "SharePoint configuration database settings" section of Chapter 28, "Data alerting."

Using the web service

You can develop a custom application to perform any task that you can perform using Report Manager on a native-mode report server or a report shortcut menu on a SharePoint integrated-mode report server. With either type of report server, you use the *ReportService2010* endpoint to access the relevant classes and methods. To provide an example of the possibilities, we review a simple web application that displays a list of reports in a specified folder and allows you to create a subscription that emails each selected report to a specified recipient and also allows you to assign the subscription to a shared schedule.

Web.config

When you create a new web application, you must update the Web.config inside configuration element to set the authentication mode. To allow the application to authenticate using the current user's credentials instead of the ASP.NET account, add the following elements as child elements of the *system*.web element.

```
<authentication mode="Windows"/>
<identity impersonate="true"/>
```

References

You must also add a web reference for the Reporting Services web service. To do this, right-click the References folder in Solution Explorer, and then click Add Service Reference. In the Add Service Reference dialog box, click the Advanced button, and then click the Add Web Reference button in the Service Reference Settings dialog box. In the URL box, type the URL for the web service, such as *http://localhost/ReportServer/ReportService2010.asmx* on a native-mode report server, and press

Enter. The web service description and methods display in the Add Web Reference dialog box. You can then replace the default Web Reference Name with a name that you want use in your application, such as ReportService, as shown in Figure 34-6. Click the Add Reference button to add it to your project.

Note You must add each applicable endpoint to your project. For example, if your application performs management tasks only, you use the *ReportService2010* endpoint. If your application also renders reports, you must also add the *ReportExectuion2005* endpoint.

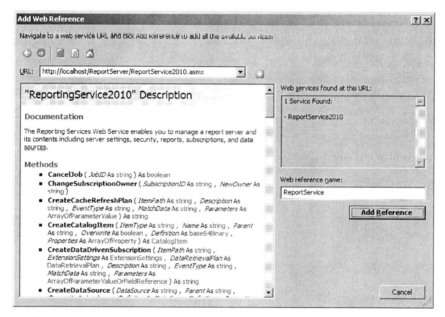

FIGURE 34-6 You must add the applicable endpoint as a web reference to your project.

Then you must add the web reference name and any namespaces required for your project by using an *Imports* statement. The following section of code appears at the top of the web form:

```
Imports ManageSubscriptionsVB.ReportService
Imports System.Data.SqlClient
Imports System.Web.Services.Protocols
```

Note The sample application in this section is written in Visual Basic. You can find the C# version of the code in the Chapter 34 folder in the set of sample files that you can download for this book.

Initial variable declarations

At minimum, you must create an instance of the *ReportingService2010* object by declaring a variable. In the sample application, two methods use the same array of shared schedules, so a declaration for this variable also appears at the top of your code with the *ReportingService2010* object, like this:

```
Dim rs As New ReportingService2010()
Dim schedules as Schedule()
```

Page load

The sample web application contains a *Page_Load* method to define the main steps to perform. Here you always start by assigning the credentials of the current user. Then you call *BindRecipientDrop-DownList*, a custom method to populate the drop-down list with a list of email addresses from which you can select a subscription recipient. The next call is to the *BindScheduleDropDownList* method, which populates a drop-down list with shared schedules. Then, only the first time the page loads, the final call is to the *BindCheckBoxList* method to create a list of reports for which you can create a subscription.

```
Protected Sub Page_Load(ByVal sender As Object, ByVal e As System.EventArgs) Handles Me.Load
  rs.Credentials = System.Net.CredentialCache.DefaultCredentials
  rs.PreAuthenticate = True
  BindRecipientDropDownList()
  BindScheduleDropDownList()
  If Not (IsPostBack) Then
    BindCheckBoxList()
  End If
End Sub
```

Recipient list

The *BindRecipientDropDownList* method executes a query to retrieve a list of AdventureWorks employee email addresses to display in a drop-down list. The query relies on the *GetConnectionString* method to connect to the *AdventureWorksDW2012* database on the local server using Windows integrated security. None of the following code uses the Reporting Services web service. Its purpose is to retrieve data that displays in *DropDownList1*.

```
Protected Sub BindRecipientDropDownList()
  Dim sConnectionString As String = GetConnectionString()
  Dim sqlCon As New SqlConnection
  sqlCon = New SqlClient.SqlConnection(sConnectionString)
  sqlCon.Open()

  Dim sqlComm As New SqlCommand( _
    "SELECT [EmailAddress] FROM [DimEmployee] order by [EmailAddress]", sqlCon)
  Dim ReaderObj As SqlDataReader = sqlComm.ExecuteReader()

  Dim j As Integer = 0
  While (ReaderObj.Read())
    DropDownList1.Items.Add(ReaderObj.Item(0))
```

```
      j = j + 1
    End While

    ReaderObj.Close()
    sqlCon.Close()
  End Sub

  Public Function GetConnectionString()
    Dim sConnectionString As String = _
    "Data Source=(local);Initial Catalog=AdventureWorksDW2012;Integrated Security=SSPI"
    Return sConnectionString
  End Function
```

Schedule list

The *BindScheduleDropDownList* method uses the web service's *ListSchedules* method to retrieve the shared schedules from the report server and store them in an array. When you are retrieving schedules from a native-mode report server, you pass *Nothing* as an argument for the *ListSchedules* method. Otherwise, you pass a string representing the URL for the SharePoint site containing the shared schedule. The code iterates through the array and adds the name of each shared schedule to *DropDownList2*.

```
Protected Sub BindScheduleDropDownList()
  schedules = rs.ListSchedules(Nothing) 'Use site URL in SharePoint
  Dim schedule As Schedule
    For Each schedule In schedules
      DropDownList2.Items.Add(schedule.Name)
    Next
End Sub
```

Report list

Next, the *BindCheckBoxList* method calls the *GetCatalogItems* method, which in turn uses the *ListChildren* method of the *ReportingServices2010* object to return an array of reports that exist in the Sales folder. The *BindCheckBoxList* method iterates through the array to assign each report as a new check box list item in *CheckBoxList1*.

```
Protected Sub BindCheckBoxList()
  Dim ci As CatalogItem() = GetCatalogItems()
  Dim item As CatalogItem
  For Each item In ci
    If item.TypeName = "Report" Then
      CheckBoxList1.Items.Add(item.Name)
    End If
  Next
End Sub

Protected Function GetCatalogItems() As CatalogItem()
  Dim ci As CatalogItem() = Nothing
  ci = rs.ListChildren("/Sales", True)
  Return ci
End Function
```

Subscription creation

The web form in the sample application displays email addresses in *DropDownList1*, shared schedules in *DropDownList2*, and a list of reports in *CheckBoxList1*. You can create one or more subscriptions by selecting an email address, a shared schedule, and one or more reports, and then clicking the button on the web form.

When you do this, the code gets the *ScheduleID* property for the selected schedule and stores it in the *matchData* variable. Then, for each selected report in *CheckBoxList1*, it assigns values to subscription parameters, which define the recipient, the reply-to address, and other subscription settings for the email delivery extension. These settings are stored in the *extSettings* array variable.

Next, the code processes report parameters. The *GetParamN* method finds the number of report parameters and determines whether each parameter is single-valued or multivalued in preparation for creating an array variable to store report parameter values. Then the *GetParameters* method gets the report parameters for storage in the array variable *parameters*.

After assigning values to all variables, the code calls the web service's *CreateSubscription* method. The arguments for this method include the report name, the *extSettings* array variable, a description for the subscription, the type of event (*TimedSubscription*, in this case), the *matchData* variable containing the *ScheduleID* for the selected shared schedule, and the *parameters* array variable:

```
Protected Sub Button1_Click(sender As Object, e As EventArgs) Handles Button1.Click
  Dim i As Integer
  Dim schedule As Schedule

  For Each schedule In schedules
    If DropDownList2.SelectedValue = schedule.Name Then
      matchData = schedule.ScheduleID
      End If
    Next

  For i = 0 To CheckBoxList1.Items.Count - 1
    If CheckBoxList1.Items(i).Selected Then
      Dim report As String = "/Sales/" + CheckBoxList1.Items(i).Text
      Dim desc As String = "Send report by email to " + DropDownList1.SelectedValue.ToString
      Dim eventType As String = "TimedSubscription"
      Dim matchData As String = Nothing

      Dim extensionParams(7) As ParameterValue
      extensionParams(0) = New ParameterValue()
      extensionParams(0).Name = "TO"
      extensionParams(0).Value = DropDownList1.Text
      extensionParams(1) = New ParameterValue()
      extensionParams(1).Name = "ReplyTo"
      extensionParams(1).Value = "ssrsadmin@adventureworks.com"
      extensionParams(2) = New ParameterValue()
      extensionParams(2).Name = "IncludeReport"
      extensionParams(2).Value = "True"
      extensionParams(3) = New ParameterValue()
      extensionParams(3).Name = "RenderFormat"
      extensionParams(3).Value = "MHTML"
      extensionParams(4) = New ParameterValue()
```

```
            extensionParams(4).Name = "Subject"
            extensionParams(4).Value = "@ReportName was executed at @ExecutionTime"
            extensionParams(5) = New ParameterValue()
            extensionParams(5).Name = "Comment"
            extensionParams(5).Value = ""
            extensionParams(6) = New ParameterValue()
            extensionParams(6).Name = "IncludeLink"
            extensionParams(6).Value = "True"
            extensionParams(7) = New ParameterValue()
            extensionParams(7).Name = "Priority"
            extensionParams(7).Value = "NORMAL"

            Dim extSettings As New ExtensionSettings()
            extSettings.ParameterValues = extensionParams
            extSettings.Extension = "Report Server Email"

            Dim rParameters() As ItemParameter
            rParameters = rs.GetItemParameters("/Sales/" + CheckBoxList1.Items(i).Text, Nothing, _
                True, Nothing, Nothing)

            Dim paramN As Integer
            paramN = GetParamN(rParameters)

            Dim parameters(paramN) As ParameterValue

            Dim k As Integer ' number of parameters
            Dim n As Integer ' number of values per parameter
            Dim m As Integer ' counter for loop through values
            Dim param as Integer 'current parameter index

            For k = 0 To rParameters.Length - 1
              If rParameters(k).DefaultValues Is Nothing Then
                If rParameters(k).MultiValue = True Then
                  n = rParameters(k).ValidValues.Length
                Else
                  n = 1
                End If
              Else
                n = rParameters(k).DefaultValues.Length
              End If
              For m = 0 To n - 1
                parameters(k + m) = GetParameter(k, m, rParameters)
                param = param + 1
              Next m
            Next k

            Try
              rs.CreateSubscription(report, extSettings, desc, eventType, matchData, parameters)
            Catch se As SoapException
              Console.WriteLine(se.Detail.InnerXml.ToString())
            End Try
          End If
        Next i

        CheckBoxList1.Items.Clear()
        Button1.Visible = False
        Label2.Visible = False
```

```
    Label1.Visible = True
End Sub

Protected Function GetParamN(ByRef rParameters() As ItemParameter)
  Dim o As Integer = 0
  Dim v As Integer = 0
  Dim d As Integer = 0
  Dim p As Integer = 0

  For i As Integer = 0 To rParameters.Length - 1
    If rParameters(i).DefaultValues Is Nothing Then
      If rParameters(i).MultiValue = True Then
        v = v + rParameters(i).ValidValues.Length
      Else
        v = 1
      End If
    Else
      d = d + rParameters(i).DefaultValues.Length
    End If
  Next i
  p = o + v + d
  Return p
End Function

Protected Function GetParameter(ByVal k As Integer, ByVal m As Integer, ByRef rParameters() As
ItemParameter) As ParameterValue
  Dim parameter As New ParameterValue()
  parameter.Name = rParameters(k).Name
  If rParameters(k).DefaultValues Is Nothing Then
    parameter.Value = rParameters(k).ValidValues(m).ToString
  Else
    parameter.Value = rParameters(k).DefaultValues(m).ToString
  End If
  Return parameter
End Function
```

Web application execution

When you launch the application (or press F5 to start debugging in Visual Studio), the web form displays values in the drop-down lists and check box list. You can select a recipient for the email subscription in the first drop-down list, a shared schedule in the second drop-down list, and multiple reports in the check box list, as shown in Figure 34-7. When you finish making your selections, you click the Create Subscription(s) button.

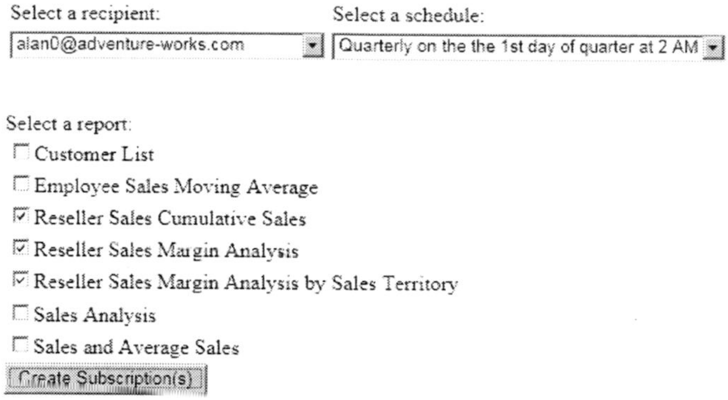

Select a recipient: Select a schedule:

alan0@adventure-works.com ▾ Quarterly on the the 1st day of quarter at 2 AM ▾

Select a report:
☐ Customer List
☐ Employee Sales Moving Average
☑ Reseller Sales Cumulative Sales
☑ Reseller Sales Margin Analysis
☑ Reseller Sales Margin Analysis by Sales Territory
☐ Sales Analysis
☐ Sales and Average Sales
[Create Subscription(s)]

FIGURE 34-7 Your application can prompt the user for information required to create a subscription.

On a native-mode report server, you can confirm the proper creation of subscriptions by opening the My Subscriptions page in Report Manager, as shown in Figure 34-8. You must use the Manage Subscriptions command on each individual report on a SharePoint integrated-mode report server.

FIGURE 34-8 You can review the subscriptions created programmatically on the My Subscriptions page.

CHAPTER 35

Programming report access

To support the final phase of the reporting life cycle, you can provide access to reports programmatically. For example, you can create webpages that include links to reports managed on your report server and thereby bypass Report Manager or SharePoint to display reports. As another example, you can easily develop a Windows-based or web application that uses the *ReportViewer* control that ships with Visual Studio 2008 to embed your Reporting Services reports into custom applications.

Linking to reports with URL access

Although using Report Manager or SharePoint as the central access point for reports is often satisfactory for most reporting needs in an organization, you might find it useful to provide direct links to your reports on a corporate portal page by using a different URL than you see in the Address bar when you use Report Manager or SharePoint. Not only can you provide a link to open a report for online viewing, you can include commands in a report link to set parameter value selections or to specify an alternate rendering format.

Viewing a report

You can quickly find the correct URL for a report by navigating to the report server's virtual directory and locating the report. You can then append values in that URL to override parameter default values, to hide all or part of the HTML Viewer, or to render the report to a different format. Although you are not using Report Manager or SharePoint to access a report, the same security permissions continue to apply and you can access only those items that your role assignment includes.

URL access on a native-mode report server

To open the report server's virtual directory on a native-mode report server, also known as the web service URL, navigate to *http://<servername>/reportserver* (replacing *<servername>* with the name of your server) in your browser. By using this URL, you can bypass Report Manager to navigate through the folders and access report server content directly, as shown in Figure 35-1. The security permissions that are defined for the reports also apply when you use the web service URL, so you will see only those reports that you are allowed to see.

localhost/ReportServer - /

```
Thursday, April 19, 2012 4:52 PM    <dir> Comparative Reports
  Friday, March 30, 2012 11:41 AM    <dir> Data Sources
  Friday, April 20, 2012 12:17 PM    <dir> Datasets
Wednesday, May 16, 2012 7:52 AM      <dir> Europe
Wednesday, May 16, 2012 7:45 AM      <dir> Miscellaneous
  Friday, April 20, 2012 12:17 PM    <dir> Report Parts
 Tuesday, May 01, 2012 7:36 PM       <dir> Reseller Sales
Thursday, April 26, 2012 3:24 PM     <dir> Sales
Wednesday, May 16, 2012 7:47 AM      <dir> Users Folders
                                     <dir> My Reports
```

Microsoft SQL Server Reporting Services Version 11.0.2100.60

FIGURE 35-1 You can use the web service URL to navigate the contents of the report server.

When you click a report link, you see the report display, as shown in Figure 35-2. Notice that the links for the Report Manager menus do not display above the report as they do when you open the report from Report Manager. Because the report renders by default as HTML, the HTML Viewer also displays with the report. If you prefer, you can hide the HTML Viewer, as we explain later in the "Using URL access parameters" section of this chapter.

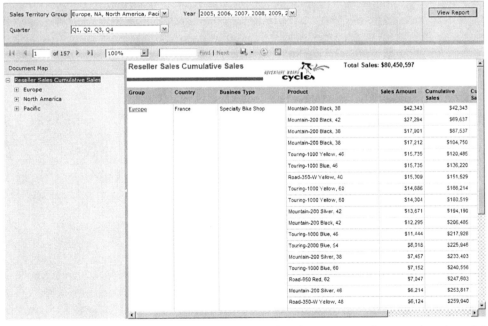

FIGURE 35-2 The Report Manager interface does not display when you open the report by using a link accessible from the web service URL.

Look in your browser's Address bar to see the URL for the link that you selected. For example, the URL for the report shown in Figure 35-2 is *http://localhost/ReportServer/Pages/ReportViewer.aspx?% 2fSales%2fReseller+Sales+Cumulative+Sales&rs:Command=Render*. If you want to create a link to this report in a webpage, you don't need to know this URL. Just navigate to the report by starting with the web service URL and navigating through the folders to locate and open the report. Then you can copy the URL and paste it into a document, an email, or the HTML code of a webpage.

Tip The URL that you see in the Address text box is fully encoded, but you can use an abbreviated version of the URL by eliminating the */Pages/ReportViewer.aspx* and *&rs%3aCommand=Render* sections. You can also replace the *%2f* with a forward slash (/) and the plus sign (+) with a space. However, you must include the path to the report. By making these changes, your URL for a native-mode report server looks like this: *http://<servername>/ReportServer?/Sales/Reseller Sales Cumulative Sales*.

URL access on a SharePoint integrated-mode report server

The first step to locating the URL for your report is to open the virtual directory root. On a SharePoint integrated-mode report server, you use the following URL:

```
http://<SharePoint site>/<subsite>/_vti_bin/reportserver
```

Note The URL for your report server might include a port number and might not include a subsite. You use the URL created for the Reporting Services-enabled web application as described in Chapter 4, "Installing Reporting Services."

This URL allows you to access the web service directly so that you can navigate through document library folders and access reports while bypassing the SharePoint interface. The same security model that protects reports in SharePoint continues to apply when you use the web service URL, restricting your access to those reports for which you are authorized. From the virtual directory root, you can see the SharePoint sites configured to support Reporting Services, as shown in Figure 35-3. That is, the virtual directory root shows you all report server content, regardless of the web application hosting that content.

denali01/ - /

```
Wednesday, May 16, 2012 5:44 PM      <dir> http://denali01:33412/sites/ssrs
Wednesday, May 16, 2012 6:48 PM      <dir> http://denali01:4782
   Friday, March 23, 2012 8:43 AM    <dir> http://denali01
Wednesday, April 11, 2012 4:38 AM    <dir> http://denali01/sites/BI
   Friday, April 27, 2012 4:46 PM    <dir> http://denali:37780/sites/ssrs
   Friday, May 04, 2012 8:45 PM      <dir> http://denali01:18467/sites/powerview
```

Microsoft SQL Server Reporting Services Version 11.0.2100.60

FIGURE 35-3 You can view all Reporting Services-enabled top sites in SharePoint by using the web service URL.

You can click a report link in the list to view it, as shown in Figure 35-4. The report renders by default as HTML, just as it does when you access it through the SharePoint interface. It also includes the HTML Viewer, but you can hide it if you prefer, as we explain in the "Using URL access parameters" section.

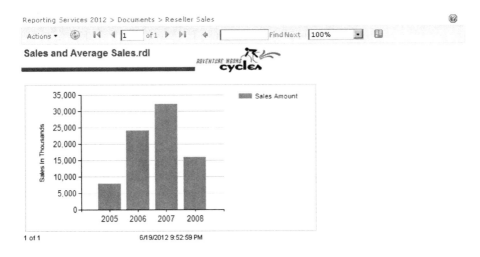

FIGURE 35-4 Access to a report by using the SharePoint integrated-mode report server's web service URL is no different from access through the SharePoint document library interface.

The URL for the report is visible in the browser's Address bar, which for the report shown in Figure 35-4 is *http://denali01:37780/sites/ssrs4782/_layouts/ReportServer/RSViewerPage.aspx?rv:RelativeRe-portUrl=%2fDocuments%2fReseller%2520Sales%2fSales%2520and%2520Average%2520Sales.rdl*. This URL is not the same URL that you click when you view the report server content by using the web service URL. The web service replaces the URL that you click—in this case, *http://denali01:37780/sites/ssrs/_vti_bin/reportserver?http%3a%2f%2fdenali01%3a4782%2fDocuments%2fReseller+Sales%2f-Sales+and+Average+Sales.rdl&rs:Command=Render*—with the URL that the SharePoint interface calls and is visible in the Address bar when viewing the report. You can still navigate through the report server's content to find a report, just as you do on a native-mode report server, but instead of clicking the URL, copy it to your clipboard. Then you can paste it into another application.

> **Tip** You can use an abbreviated version of the report URL by eliminating the web service URL string and the *&rs:Command=Render* sections. You can also replace each *%2f* with a forward slash (/) and each plus sign (+) with a space. However, you must include the folder path, the report name, and the file extension. For example, a URL for a SharePoint integrated-mode report server looks like this: *http://denali01:37780/sites/ssrs/Documents/Reseller Sales/Sales and Average Sales.rdl*. This abbreviated URL works only when you want to see the default view of the report. You cannot use this technique with URL access parameters.

Using URL access parameters

You can append URL access parameters that provide additional options in viewing report server content by enabling control of report parameter values, toolbar settings, and rendering formats. You append them to a report URL as described in the "Viewing a report" section of this chapter.

> **Note** When the examples in this section show two URLs, the first URL is for a native-mode report server and the second URL is for a SharePoint integrated-mode report server.

Report parameters

For each parameter that you want to override in the report, you include a name/value pair as a string that you append to the report's URL using the syntax shown in the following example:

```
&rc:ParameterName=ParameterValue
```

> **Important** Because these parameter values are sent as plain text, you should implement Secure Sockets Layer (SSL) in your Reporting Services environment if parameters include confidential data.

Let's say you want to view the Reseller Sales Cumulative Sales report for Q1 only. In that case, you use the following URL, using the value and not the label for the report parameter value:

```
http://localhost/ReportServer?/Sales/Reseller Sales Cumulative Sales&Quarter=1
```

or

```
http://denali01:37780/sites/ssrs/_vti_bin/reportserver?http://denali01:37780/sites/ssrs/
Documents/Reseller Sales/Reseller Sales Cumulative Sales.rdl&Quarter=1
```

When a parameter accepts multiple values, you include the name/value pair for each value that you want to use for the report. For example, to view both Q1 and Q2, use the following URL:

```
http://localhost/ReportServer?/Sales/Reseller Sales Cumulative Sales&Quarter=1&Quarter=2
```

or

```
http://denali01:37780/sites/ssrs/_vti_bin/reportserver?http://denali01:37780/sites/ssrs/
Documents/Reseller Sales/Reseller Sales Cumulative Sales.rdl&Quarter=1&Quarter=2
```

> **Important** You use the internal name for the report parameter and not the prompt that displays to the user. The parameter name in the URL access parameter string is case-sensitive.

If the report parameter is visible to the user, the user can use the HTML Viewer to change the report parameter value after opening the report. Using URL access to set a report parameter is merely a convenience to set a default on opening the report. Even if you hide the report parameter, the user can still change the parameter value in the URL. Therefore, you should not use URL access as a security measure for report parameters.

HTML Viewer commands

Another option for using URL access parameters is to control the appearance of the HTML Viewer on a native-mode report server. If you add parameter values in the URL, you might decide not to display the Parameters section of the HTML Viewer so that more of the computer screen is available for the report display. To remove the Parameters section and otherwise leave the HTML Viewer intact, you add the following URL access parameter to the report's URL:

```
&rc:Parameters=false
```

> **Note** See the "Report Viewer commands" section of this chapter for URL access parameters that control the appearance of the Report Viewer on a SharePoint integrated-mode report server.

You can combine URL access parameters just by extending the URL with the applicable string. For example, if you want to display the Reseller Sales Cumulative Sales report with specific values for the *Quarter* parameter but without the HTML Viewer, as shown in Figure 35-5, use the following URL:

```
http://localhost/ReportServer?/Sales/Reseller Sales Cumulative Sales&Quarter=1&Quarter=2&rc:Too
lbar=false
```

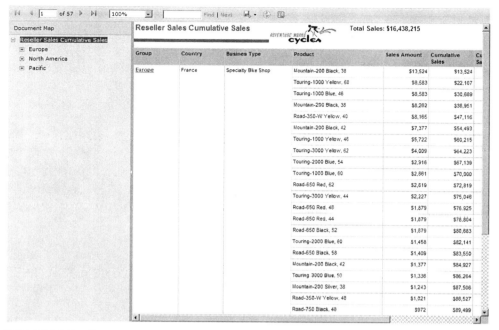

FIGURE 35-5 To allocate more screen space to your report, you can prevent parameters from displaying in the HTML Viewer.

Now more of the screen is available to display the report. When you use this technique, you should include the current parameter selections in a page footer text box. Also, as a result of hiding the Parameters section of the HTML Viewer, you can change the current parameter selection only by changing the URL.

Form POST method

If you need to secure report parameters but want to use URL access in a web application, you can use a POST request in a form submission to pass the parameter name and value pairs that you place in the form's input fields. That way, the URL passes the information in the request header, which the user cannot modify. A form to request Quarter 1 in the Reseller Sales Cumulative Sales report on a native-mode report server looks like this:

```
<FORM id="frmRender"
  action="http://localhost/ReportServer?/Sales/Reseller Sales Cumulative Sales"
  method="post" target="_self">
  <INPUT type="hidden" name="rs:Command" value="Render">
  <INPUT type="hidden" name="rc:LinkTarget" value="main">
  <INPUT type="hidden" name="rs:Format" value="HTML4.0">
  <INPUT type="hidden" name="&Quarter" value="1">
  <INPUT type="submit" value="Button">
</FORM>
```

To remove the HTML Viewer entirely, you use the following syntax:

```
&rc:Toolbar=false
```

You can combine URL access parameters just by extending the URL with the applicable string. For example, if you want to display the Reseller Sales Cumulative Sales report with specific values for the *Quarter* parameter but without the HTML Viewer, as shown in Figure 35-6, use the following URL:

```
http://localhost/ReportServer?/Reseller Sales/Reseller Sales Cumulative Sales&Quarter=1&Quarter=2&rc:Toolbar=false
```

Note You can omit the *&rc:Parameters=false* command in the URL when you hide the HTML Viewer by using the *&rc:Toolbar=false* command.

Reseller Sales Cumulative Sales   Total Sales: $36,261,316

Group	Country	Busines Type	Product	Sales Amount	Cumulative Sales	Cumulative Sales Pct
Europe	France	Specialty Bike Shop	Mountain-200 Black, 38	$25,819	$25,819	14 %
			Mountain-200 Black, 38	$17,901	$43,720	23 %
			Touring-1000 Yellow, 46	$15,735	$59,454	31 %
			Road-350-W Yellow, 40	$15,309	$74,763	40 %
			Touring-1000 Yellow, 60	$14,304	$89,068	47 %
			Mountain-200 Black, 42	$13,524	$102,592	54 %
			Touring-1000 Blue, 46	$11,444	$114,035	60 %
			Road-650 Red, 62	$7,047	$121,082	64 %
			Touring-2000 Blue, 54	$5,831	$126,914	67 %
			Touring-1000 Blue, 60	$5,722	$132,635	70 %
			Touring-3000 Yellow, 62	$5,345	$137,980	73 %
			Road-350-W Yellow, 48	$4,082	$142,063	75 %
			Road-650 Red, 44	$3,758	$145,821	77 %
			Mountain-200 Silver, 38	$3,729	$149,549	79 %
			Road-650 Red, 48	$3,289	$152,838	81 %
			Road-650 Black, 52	$3,289	$156,127	83 %
			Touring-3000 Yellow, 44	$3,118	$159,244	84 %
			Touring-2000 Blue, 60	$2,916	$162,160	86 %
			Road-650 Black, 58	$2,819	$164,979	87 %
			Road-650 Red, 60	$2,819	$167,798	89 %
			Touring-3000 Blue, 50	$2,672	$170,470	90 %
			Road-750 Black, 48	$2,268	$172,738	91 %
			Touring-3000 Blue, 54	$1,782	$174,520	92 %
			Mountain-200 Black, 42	$1,377	$175,897	93 %

FIGURE 35-6 You can hide the HTML Viewer entirely by using a URL access parameter.

There are several other report viewer commands, shown in Table 35-1, that you can use to control report rendering in lieu of using the HTML Viewer on a native-mode report server. Like other URL access parameters discussed earlier in this chapter, you can add multiple commands to the same URL by appending each applicable string to the report's base URL.

TABLE 35-1 HTML Viewer commands for URL access

URL Access Parameter	Description	Example
DocMap	Hide a document map.	`&rc:DocMap=false`
FallbackPage	Display the specified page if a search fails.	`&rc:FallbackPage=1`
FindString	Search for a string in a report by using StartFind and EndFind to specify the range of pages to search.	`&rc:FindString=Mountain -200&rc:StartFind=1&rc:EndFind=5`
Parameters	Hide parameters section of the toolbar.	`&rc:Parameters=false`
Section	Display the specified page.	`&rc:Section=5`
Stylesheet	Apply the specified stylesheet (located in the ReportServer\Styles folder) to your report.	`&rc:Stylesheet=AWStyleSheet`
Toolbar	Hide the HTML Viewer toolbar.	`&rc:Toolbar=false`
Zoom	Increase or decrease the report size by the specified percentage or fit defined by Page Width or Whole Page.	`&rc:Zoom=50` or `&rc:Zoom=Page Width`

Report Viewer commands

When working with reports on a SharePoint integrated-mode report server, you can use URL access parameters in the same way that you do on native-mode report server. However, the commands use the *rv* prefix. A list of Report Viewer commands appears in Table 35-2.

TABLE 35-2 Report Viewer commands for URL access

URL Access Parameter	Description	Example
AsyncRender	Render a report synchronously or asynchronously (default).	`&rv:AsyncRender=false`
DocMapAreaWidth	Define the width of the document map area in pixels.	`&rv:DocMapAreaWidth=150`
DockToolbar	Dock the toolbar at the top or the bottom of the Report Viewer.	`&rv:DockToolbar=Bottom`
HeaderArea	Control the display of the header of the Report Viewer by using arguments Full, BreadCrumbsOnly, and None.	`&rv:HeaderArea=None`
ParamMode	Control the display of parameters by using the arguments Full, Collapsed, or Hidden.	`&rv:Parameters=Hidden`
Section	Displays the specified page.	`&rv:Section=5`

URL Access Parameter	Description	Example
Stylesheet	Applies the specified stylesheet (located in the ReportServer\Styles folder) to your report.	`&rv:Stylesheet= AWStyleSheet`
Toolbar	Control the display of the toolbar using arguments Full, Navigation (for paging), or None.	`&rv:Toolbar=None`
ToolBarItemsDisplayMode	Control the display of items in the toolbar using a bitwise enumeration value or -1 for all items, summing the value of each item to display: 1 Back button 2 Search controls 4 Page navigation controls 8 Refresh button 16 Zoom 32 ATOM feed button 64 Print option in Actions menu 128 Export submenu in Actions menu 256 Open with Report Builder menu option 512 Subscribe menu option 1024 New Data Alert menu option	`&rv:ToolBarItemsDisplay Mode=12`

Zoom	Increase or decrease the report size by the specified percentage or fit defined by Page Width or Whole Page.	`&rv:Zoom=50`
		or
		`&rv:Zoom=Page Width`

Report Server commands

You can also use URL access parameters to issue commands to the report server. For example, you can specify the format used to display the report by adding the *&rs:Format* command and providing the format type. To render the report as a Microsoft Office Excel workbook (with file extension XLS), use the following syntax:

```
&rs:Format=Excel
```

You can use any of the following rendering format values: HTML4.0, MHTML, IMAGE, Excel, ExcelOpenXML, Word, WordOpenXML, CSV, PDF, TIFF, and XML. When you use a format value other than the HTML options, the rendered report does not open by default. Instead, you must click Open in the File Download message box to view the report, as long as you have the associated application, such as Excel, installed on your computer.

To render display the Reseller Sales Cumulative Sales report with both available values for the *Quarter* parameter to an XLSX file compatible with Excel 2007 or Excel 2010, use the following URL:

```
http://localhost/ReportServer?/Sales/Reseller Sales Cumulative Sales&Quarter=1&Quarter=2&rs:For
mat=ExcelOpenXML
```

or

```
http://denali01:37780/sites/ssrs/_vti_bin/reportserver?http://denali01:37780/sites/ssrs/
Documents/Reseller Sales/Reseller Sales Cumulative Sales.rdl&Quarter=1&Quarter=2&rs:Format=Exce
lOpenXML
```

Not only can you use URL access parameters to view reports, but you can also send commands to the report server to interact with the report server catalog. For example, you can append the following command to a folder URL to view its contents:

```
&rs:Command=ListChildren
```

For example, you can list the contents of the Sales folder, as shown in Figure 35-7, by using the following URL:

```
http://localhost/ReportServer?/Sales&rs:Command=ListChildren
```

or

```
http://denali01:37780/sites/ssrs/_vti_bin/reportserver?http://denali01:37780/sites/ssrs/
Documents/Sales&rs:Command=ListChildren
```

localhost/ReportServer - /Sales

```
[To Parent Directory]
    Thursday, April 26, 2012 3:24 PM        187991  Customer List
    Thursday, April 26, 2012 3:24 PM        193351  Employee Sales Moving Average
    Thursday, April 26, 2012 3:24 PM        244525  Reseller Sales Cumulative Sales
    Thursday, April 26, 2012 3:24 PM        252449  Reseller Sales Margin Analysis
    Thursday, April 26, 2012 3:24 PM        270626  Reseller Sales Margin Analysis by Sales Territory
     Thursday, May 17, 2012 1:26 PM         259205  Sales Analysis
    Thursday, April 26, 2012 3:24 PM        190331  Sales and Average Sales
```

Microsoft SQL Server Reporting Services Version 11.0.2100.60

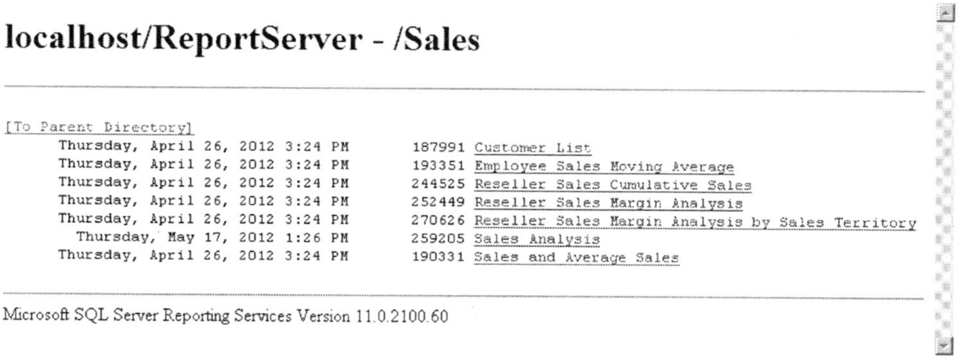

FIGURE 35-7 You can use a report server command in a URL to view the contents of a specific folder.

TABLE 35-3 Report server commands for URL access

URL Access Parameter	Description	Example
ClearSession	Remove a report from the current report session (including all executions of the report with different parameter values).	`&rs:ClearSession=true`
Command	Perform an operation on a catalog item: • ListChildren to list child items. • Render to render a report. • GetSharedDatasetDefinition to show the XML for a shared dataset (if you have Read Report Definition permission). • GetDataSourceContents to show the data source properties. • GetResourceContents to render a file (not a report) in an HTML page. • GetComponentDefinition to display the RDL for a report (if you have Read Contents permission).	`&rs:Command=ListChildren`
Format	Render a report in the specified format (default HTML4.0).	`&rs:Format=excelopenxml`
GetNextStream	Get the next chunk of a persisted stream (default=false).	`&rs:GetNextStream=true`
ParameterLanguage	Define the language for parameters independent of the browser language.	`&rs:ParameterLanguage=en-us`
PersistStreams	Render a report in a single persisted stream or one chunk at a time (default=false).	`&rs:PersistStreams=true`
ResetSession	Reset the report session by removing its association with all report snapshots (default=false).	`&rs:ResetSessioon=true`
SessionID	Specify an active report session.	`&rs:SessionID= 1lvwaoji1ok1s-dyujn1dg5un`
ShowHideToggle	Toggle the visibility of a section of the report.	`&rs:ShowHideToggle=1`
Snapshot	Render a snapshot of a report.	`&rs:Snapshot=2012-06-01T12:30:00`

Using the *ReportViewer* control

Visual Studio 2010 includes the *ReportViewer* control to support application development that requires embedded reports. Because this control works independently of SQL Server 2012, you don't need a SQL Server license to create reports. However, when you have a Reporting Services infrastructure in place, you can use the *ReportViewer* control to access reports from your report server.

Reports Application project

You use the Reports Application project type to create an application with a *ReportViewer* control to display a report stored on the report server. You can select this project type when you use Visual Studio to create a new Visual Basic project, as shown in Figure 35-8, or a new Visual C# project.

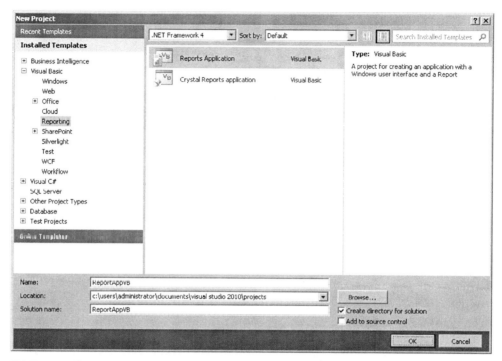

FIGURE 35-8 You can create a Reports Application project to use the *ReportViewer* control.

Report Wizard

You can use the Report Wizard to step through development of a report independent of Reporting Services, as shown in Figure 35-9. First, you choose one of the supported data sources: Database, Service, Object, or SharePoint. Your choice of data source determines the configuration steps necessary to define connection information. For example, if you use a database source, you define the connection to a server and database, select database objects such as tables and views, and arrange fields from these database objects into row groups, columns groups, and values. Next, you choose whether to include subtotals and totals and the style of font and colors to apply.

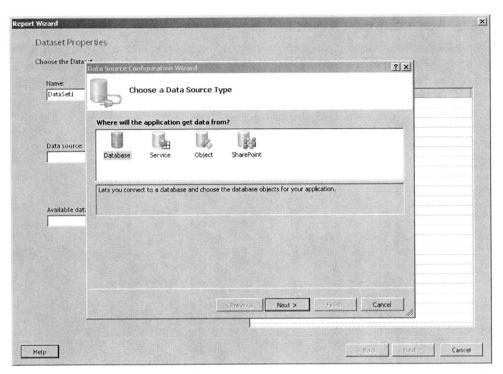

FIGURE 35-9 You can use the Report Wizard to step through the process of configuring the ReportViewer control.

Note You are not limited to the data sources that Reporting Services supports. Your application is responsible for retrieving data from any source that you can access programmatically and then exposing the data to the *ReportViewer* control as an *IEnumerable* collection.

ReportViewer control

If you prefer not to use the Report Wizard, you can click Cancel when it displays after you create your reporting application. In that case, the application form displays with a *ReportViewer* control already added to the form, as shown in Figure 35-10.

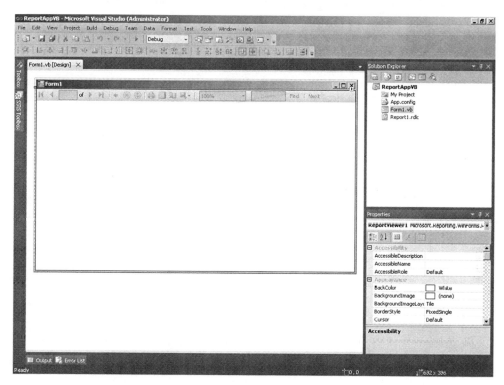

FIGURE 35-10 A new reports application project automatically includes a *ReportViewer* control form.

Tip If you create a form manually in a custom application, you can add a *ReportViewer* control by opening the Toolbox window, expanding the Reporting section, and dragging the *ReportViewer* control to your form.

In the Solution Explorer window, notice the Report1.rdlc item. If you want to create a report without accessing the report server, you can open this item and use Report Designer. However, Report Designer includes only the features available for designing SQL Server 2008 Reporting Services reports. For example, it does not include Map, Data Bar, Sparkline, or Indicator controls. If you are developing an application to use a report from the report server, you can delete this file from the project safely.

Note Although the RDLC file does not support the same features that you find in SQL Server 2012, this limitation does not apply when you use the *ReportViewer* control in remote mode, which relies on the report server to execute a report. In that case, all report features are available.

ReportViewer properties

You can set properties for the *ReportViewer* control to suit your purposes. In the design window, click anywhere in the center of the *ReportViewer* control to set the focus of the Properties window to ReportViewer1. In the Properties window, scroll to locate and expand the *ServerReport* section to view its properties, as shown in Figure 35-11.

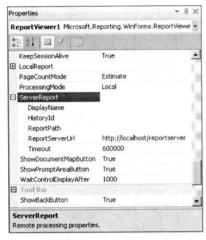

FIGURE 35-11 You configure *ServerReport* properties for the *ReportViewer* control to specify the report server and the report to display in the control.

At a minimum, you must configure the *ReportViewer* control's *ProcessingMode, ReportPath,* and *ReportServerURL* properties. To use reports managed by Reporting Services, you must change the *ProcessingMode* property to Remote. When you define *ReportPath,* you provide only the folder and report name. You cannot include URL access commands. For *ReportServerURL,* you use the web service URL, which is the same URL that you use when deploying reports from SSDT.

> **Note** If you are working with a native-mode report server, the report path looks like this: */Sales/Reseller Sales Cumulative Sales.* If you are working with a SharePoint integrated-mode report server, it looks like this: *http://denali01:37780/sites/ssrs/Documents/Reseller Sales/Reseller Sales Cumulative Sales.rdl.*

The Toolbar section of the Properties window includes several properties that allow you to configure the visibility of each item in the HTML Viewer. You can remove buttons from the HTML Viewer by setting the corresponding property to *False.* You can configure the HTML Viewer by using the following properties:

- *ShowBackButton*
- *ShowExportButton*
- *ShowFindControls*

- *ShowPageNavigationControls*

- *ShowPrintButton*

- *ShowRefreshButton*

- *ShowStopButton*

- *ShowZoomControl*

ReportViewer application

When you build a reports application, Visual Studio creates its executable in the bin\Debug folder for your application. You can then distribute this executable file to anyone who has access to your report server and has permissions to the report.

> **Note** Using a custom application to access the report does not override the security defined on the report server.

You can press **F5** in Visual Studio to test the application, and click View Report to display the report, as shown in Figure 35-12. At this point, the application is very basic. You could extend the application by adding a menu that lists available reports (for example, using the *ListChildren* method) and then changing the report path when the menu selection changes. By using the *ReportViewer* control in your applications, you can focus your development efforts on application logic and save the time required to build the same reporting capabilities that Reporting Services already includes.

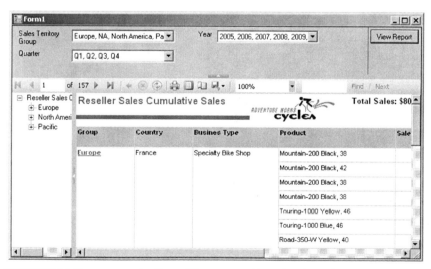

FIGURE 35-12 You can test the *ReportViewer* control by using the Debug command (or F5) in Visual Studio.

Accessing a report with the web service

If you prefer great control over the user interface or if you have a custom application into which you are embedding reporting features, you can create an application to use the Reporting Services web service to display a report. In this section, we extend the logic we introduced in Chapter 32, "Understanding Report Definition Language," to programmatically create a new report by adding a step to render and save it as a PDF file. However, in this case, we use a template and reports located on the report server. This report application has limited functionality to introduce you to the key concepts of working with the web service, but you can certainly extend this type of application to do much more.

> **Note** The RDLGenerator application in Chapter 32 has been modified for use with this chapter. The number of arguments has been expanded to define a local directory for both the template file and the generated RDL file and to specify a report server path for deploying the RDL file. The application also includes a *PublishReport* method to deploy the new RDL to the report server.

References

Using the web service to render a report is similar to the process of using the web service for administrative tasks on the report server, as described in Chapter 34, "Programming report server management." However, for this type of operation, you use the *ReportExecution2005* endpoint instead, as shown in Figure 35-13.

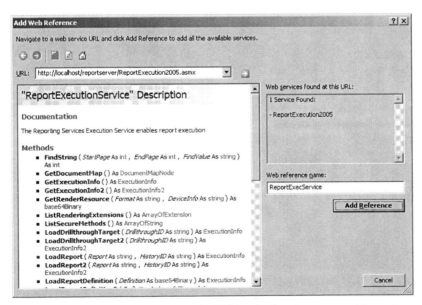

FIGURE 35-13 You use the *ReportExecution2005* endpoint when you want to perform operations that involve report execution.

You must also add the web reference name to your project, in addition to any namespaces required for your project, by using an *Imports* statement. The following section of code appears at the top of the web form:

```
Imports CustomRDLAppVB.ReportExecService
Imports System.Web.Services.Protocols
Imports System.IO
```

> **Note** The sample application in this section is written in Visual Basic. You can find the C# version of the code in the Chapter 35 folder in the set of sample files that you can download for this book.

Load method

Before you can render a report, you must first load it into an *ExecutionInfo* object. The Load method uses the following syntax:

```
Load(Report, HistoryID)
```

You use the *HistoryID* property to reference a snapshot if you want to render a report faster. Otherwise, the report processor must execute the report. If the report has report parameters, you use the *SetExecutionParameters* method to set the parameter values for the current execution after you load the report. If you need only to execute the report, you use the following code:

```
rs.Credentials = System.Net.CredentialCache.DefaultCredentials
Dim sName As String = args(4)
Dim sReportPath As String = args(5) + "/" + sName
Dim sHistoryID As String = Nothing
Dim execInfo As New ExecutionInfo
execInfo = rs.LoadReport(sReportPath, sHistoryID)
```

Render method

By accessing the web service, you can use the *Render* method to create a report in any supported format instead of using the *ReportViewer* control described earlier in this chapter. The *Render* method uses the following syntax:

```
Render(Format, DeviceInfo, Extension, MimeType, Encoding, Warnings, StreamIds)
```

The *Render* method has the following arguments:

- **Format** You provide one of the following format types: HTML4.0, MHTML, IMAGE, Excel, ExcelOpenXML, Word, WordOpenXML, CSV, PDF, TIFF, or XML.

- **DeviceInfo** You include device information specific to the rendering extension, if applicable.

Note You can find details about device information settings at *http://msdn .microsoft.com/en-us/library/hh231593.aspx.*

- **Extension** The method returns the file extension of the output file.

- **MimeType** The method returns the MIME type of the rendered report.

- **Encoding** The method returns the encoding used to create the rendered report.

- **Warnings** The method returns warnings generated by the report processor during rendering.

- **StreamIds** The method returns the stream identifiers that you can pass to the *RenderStream* method when you need to render an external resource associated with a report.

The *Render* method returns a byte array that you can save to disk. To render and save the resulting file, you can use code like this:

```
Dim byResult As Byte() = Nothing
Dim sDevInfo As String = ""
Dim sExtension As String = ""
Dim sEncoding As String = ""
Dim sMimeType As String = ""
Dim warnings As Warning() = Nothing
Dim streamIDs As String() = Nothing

Try
  byResult = rs.Render(formatType, sDevInfo, sExtension, _
  sEncoding, sMimeType, warnings, streamIDs)
Catch e As SoapException
  Console.WriteLine(e.Detail.OuterXml)
End Try

Try
  Dim sOutputPath As String = args(2)
  Dim stream As FileStream = File.Create( _
    sOutputPath + "\" + sName + "." + sExtension, byResult.Length)
  Console.WriteLine("File created.")
  stream.Write(byResult, 0, byResult.Length)
  Console.WriteLine("Result written to the file.")
  stream.Close()
Catch e As Exception
  Console.WriteLine(e.Message)
End Try
```

Solution deployment

When you build the sample application, you can move the CustomRDLAppVB.exe file from the project's bin\Debug folder to a new location. There you can execute it in a Command Prompt window by using the following syntax:

```
CustomRDLAppVB UserID ReportSetID LocalPath TemplateName ReportTitle ReportServerPath
```

Just as you did in Chapter 32, you can create a report for UserID 1 and ReportSetID 1 by using the Template.rdl file located in the C:\SSRS folder. Similarly, you can set the report title and file name as Management Summary. This time, you are also saving the RDL to the report server in the Chapter 35 folder. To create the RDL and produce a PDF file, you execute the following command:

```
CustomRDLAppVB 1 1 C:\SSRS Template.rdl "Management Summary" "/Chapter 35/"
```

The command prompt window displays messages as the application progresses through each step. When the RDL is created and saved to disk as a new RDL file, you must press Enter to continue. Then the application publishes the RDL to the report server and prompts you to press Enter to continue. The final step is to render the report as a PDF file, which is followed by another prompt to press Enter, as shown in Figure 35-14. You can then check the Chapter 35 folder on the report server to confirm that the report exists, and then check the C:\SSRS folder to confirm that it contains a PDF file.

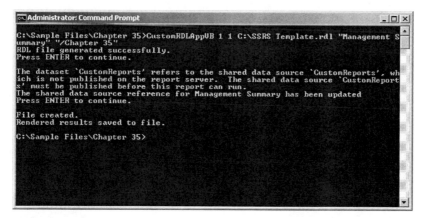

FIGURE 35-14 Your application now creates a custom RDL, publishes it to the report server, and renders the report as a PDF file.

Index

Symbols

32-bit edition of SQL Server 2012, operating system support, 57

32-bit operating systems, SQL Server 2012 on, 55

64-bit edition of SQL Server 2012, operating system support, 56

64-bit operating systems, SQL Server 2012 on, 55

90 Degrees Northeast/Northwest/Southwest/Southeast radial gauge, 519

180 Degrees North/South/West/East radial gauge, 519

& (ampersand), in expressions for items in global collection, 276

* (asterisk), wildcard for multiple characters, 384

@ (at symbol), prefixing parameter value placeholders, 276

= (equal sign)
   beginning complex expressions, 277, 293
   equality operator, 383

> (greater than) operator, 383

>= (greater than or equal to) operator, 383

<> (inequality) operator, 383

< (less than) operator, 383

<= (less than or equal to) operator, 383

- (minus sign), toggling row visibility, 354

% (percent symbol), wildcard for multiple characters, 383

+ (plus sign), indicating item can be expanded, 352

? (question mark)
   as wildcard for single character, 384
   next to page number, indicating incomplete rendering, 396

[ ] (square brackets), in expression placeholders, 274

_ (underscore), wildcard for single character, 384

A

Abs function, 324

Access
   importing reports into projects, 166
   report features supported in Reporting Services, 167

accessing reports online. *See* online reports

access to reports, 29
   programming, 927–948
      accessing reports with the web service, 944–947
      linking to reports with URL access, 927–938
      using ReportViewer control, 938–943

accounts. *See also* user accounts
   changing report service connection account, 78
   execution account for native mode Reporting Services, 81

Acos function, 323

Action property, 361
   for text, 240

actions
   Action page for pointers, 524
   Action page, Gauge Properties dialog box, 533
   Action page, Scale Properties dialog box, 527
   Action page, Series Properties dialog box, 461
   Actions menu, SharePoint Report Viewer, 761
   using to simulate links in online reports, 147
   working with report actions, 361–366

Active Solution Configuration drop-down list, 168

activities associated with roles or SharePoint groups, 645

Add A Report Server HTTP URL dialog box, 76

Add Calculated Member button (MDX query designer), 432, 434

Add Existing Item command, 166

Add Existing Item dialog box, 165

Add Existing Project dialog box, 154

Add Layer button, Map Layers pane, 592
Add New Item command, 166
Add New Item dialog box, 165
Add New Project dialog box, 153
Add New Report command, 165
Add Reference dialog box, 886
Add Service Reference dialog box, 918
Add Table dialog box, permissions table, 665
Add Total command, 230
   using in a matrix, 232
ad hoc reports, development tools for, 26
adjacent columns, using in a tablix, 266
adjacent gauges, 536
adjacent groups in a tablix, working with, 267
adjacent indicators, 548
administration (reports), 28
administrative tasks, 669–704
   configuring the report server, 669–685
   managing the report server, 685–690
   monitoring the report server, 690–704
   scripting, 905–914
      creating linked reports, 911–914
      deploying reports, 906–910
advanced filter mode (Power View), 850
Advanced Multiple Web Site Configuration dialog
      box, 75
advanced options for report parameters, 377
   parameters dependent on dataset query, 378
advanced properties, Server Properties dialog
      box, 676
AdventureWorksDW2012 sample database
   installing, 97
Aggregate function, 328
   using instead of Sum function in Anallysis
      Services cube, 437
aggregate functions, 230, 328–331
   adding field to freestanding text box, 236
   and FormattedValue property for text boxes, 437
   applied to values in Chart Data pane, 457
   changing for Summarize By property in tabular
      models, 804
   for gauge's pointer value, 522
   Recursive keyword with, 342
   RunningValue function, 330
   using placeholders, 275
aggregation
   aggregate values in detail rows, 438–440
   custom, 301
   Show Aggregations button, MDX query
      designer, 440–442

alerting
   alerting service runtime engine, 43
   configuring alerts for Reporting Services service
      application, 93
   data alerting, 759–778
      alerting service, 760
      configuring, 772–775
      creating data alerts, 761–768
      data alert workflow, 759
      managing alerts, 770–772
      monitoring alerting process, 775–777
      receiving data alerts, 768–770
      ReportService Alerting database, 41
alerting extension types and corresponding
      events, 775
alignment
   setting properties for text, 241
   text properties for, 240
Allow Blank Value property, report parameters, 369
Allow Multiple Values property, report
      parameters, 370
Allow Null Value property, report parameters, 370
Analysis Services
   collation for, 68
   configuration in SQL Server 2012 Setup, 70
   data source for Reporting Services, 177
   feature selection in SQL Server 2012 Setup, 64
   in SharePoint integrated-mode distribution, 50
   using as data source, 425–450
      building a report, 435–442
      creating Analysis Services dataset, 425–435
      designing parameters, 442–450
Analytical Data page, map layer dialog boxes, 593
analytical data set, adding to maps, 571
Analytical Map type, 568
Analytical Marker Map type, 567
   setting options, 574
application domains, 37
   management of, 38
application tier
   in native mode Reporting Services, 31–34
   in SharePoint integrated mode, 41
architecture (Reporting Services), 30–43
   native mode, 30–38
   SharePoint integrated mode, 38–43
area charts, 455
arithmetic operators, 282
Arrange buttons, Home tab of Power View
      ribbon, 837

array functions, 313–315
    Join function, 314
    Split function, 314
Asc and AscW functions, 309
ascending sort, applying in text boxes, 346
ASCII (American Standards Committee for Information Interchange), function returning a character, 309
Asin function, 323
aspect ratio for linear gauges, 532
assemblies
    assembly properties, data processing custom extension, 890
    using to share custom code, 881–887
        assembly deployment, 885
        class library, 881–885
        custom assembly call, 885
Atan and Atan2 functions, 324
ATOM
    data renderer, 396
    exporting reports in, 736–738
audience, knowledge of, 139–143
authentication
    authentication extension, 35
    authentication layer in service architecture, 37
    BISM connection, 802
    configuring, 681–683
    configuring for Database Engine, 69
    in Internet deployment of Reporting Services, 53
    new web application, in Web.config, 918
    Reporting Services connection to data source, 158
    selecting provider for SharePoint web application, 88
    understanding types of, 644
Author and Description properties, 861
Author element, 861
authorization, reviewing default authorization policies, 644–650
Auto Execute button (MDX query designer), 432
AutoRefresh element, 861
available values for report parameters, 371–374
    Get Values From A Query, 373
    None, 371
    Specify Values, 372
Average( ) function, 230
Avg function, 328
axes
    configuring properties, 469–473
    play axis, adding to charts in Power View, 841
    secondary axis, 508–509
    sparkline axes alignment, 482
    synchronization for multiple visualizations in tiles container, 847
    title, 468
    working with horizontal axis properties, 493–500
        axis type, 493
        intervals, 495–500
    working with vertical axis properties, 487–492
        logarithmic scale, 491
        scale break, 488–490
Axes And Chart Area page, Series Properties dialog box, 459
Axis Properties dialog box, 469–473
    Axis Options, 469
    Label Font, 472
    Labels, 470
    Line, 473
    Major Tick Marks and Minor Tick Marks, 472
    Number, 472
    scale breaks, 488
Axis Title Properties dialog box, 468
azimuthal projection, 587

B

BackgroundColor property
    for row or column pinned into fixed position, 352
    setting for text, 245
BackgroundImage property, 246
background processing, 37, 684
BackgroundRepeat value, BackgroundImage property, 247
Back To Parent Report button, 363
backup and recovery, 687–690
    configuration files, 690
    encryption keys, 688–690
    native-mode report server database, 687
    SharePoint integrated-mode report server database, 688
Backup Encryption Key dialog box, 81
bar charts
    as data bars, 477
    sort order in Power View, 839
    when to use, 455
basic filter mode (Power View), 849
Basic Map type
    line data maps, 568
    polygon data maps, 569

Basic Marker Map type, 566, 573
basic users, designing reports for, 141
Between operator, 381, 384
BI. *See* business intelligence
BIDS (Business Intelligence Development Studio), 16
BigMul function, 326
binary data, images as, 816
binding data
 dataset to a list, 235
 to a data region, 225–226
Bing Maps tile layer, 556
 adding to a map, 565
 configuring tile layer maps, 603
 embedded in report, 565
Bing Maps Web Service, 566
BISM (Business Intelligence Semantic Model)
  connection, 94, 798–803, 825
 authentication, tabular databases, and, 802
 connection information, 799
 launching Power View or Excel, 801
 setting permissions, 801
BISM (Business Intelligence Semantic Model) files, 4
bitshift operators, 284
blank values, Allow Blank Value property, report
  parameters, 369
BLOBs (binary large objects), data stored as, disk
  space requirements and, 46
block tables, 161
 example, 162
Body element, 861
body of a report, 400
 properties defining body size, 401
Bollinger bands formula, 506
Bonne projection, 588
Bookmark property, 363
 for lines, 215
bookmarks, Go To Bookmark action, 363
Border element, 866
borders
 BorderColor, BorderStyle, and BorderWidth
  properties
  setting, 245
 BorderColor, BorderStyle, BorderWidth
  properties
  for scale breaks, 490
 Border menu, Home tab of Report Builder
  ribbon, 112
 Border page, Scale Properties dialog box, 530
 Border page, Series Properties dialog box, 461

Frame Border page, Gauge Properties dialog
  box, 533
 Pointer Border page, 524
boundaries of visible map, setting, 586
 default settings for the viewport boundaries, 588
BreakLineType property (scale breaks), 490
BreakLocation property, 415
browsers, requirements for Power View, 823
bubble charts, 503–505
 adding play axis in Power View, 841
 creating, 503
Bubble Map type, 570
 for polygons, 575
Bubble Marker Map type, 566
 setting options, 573
Build menu, Report Designer, 167
Build Reports command, 167
built-in fields
 placeholder, 275
 using to add expressions to text boxes, 298
Built-in Fields category, Expression dialog box, 281
bullet graph linear gauge, 520
business intelligence (BI)
 BI center site, creating in SharePoint for
  Reporting Services integration, 89–90
 BIDS (Business Intelligence Development
  Studio), 16
 BISM (Business Intelligence Semantic Model)
  files, 4
 information resources for SharePoint BI
  features, 723

C

C#
 data processing extension sample, 890
  configuration files, registering extension, 902
 function wirtten in, 883
 sample code in, 887
caching
 Cache Refresh Plan for reports, 748
 configuring for shared datasets, 641
 EditSessionCacheLimit property, 676
 reports, 632–633
  refreshing the cache, 634
calculated fields
 naming, 293
 using in other expressions, 296
 using in reports, 293–295

calculated measures (Analysis Services), 428
calculated members
    Calculated Member Builder dialog box, 432, 434
    Calculated Members pane (MDX query
        designer), 427
    creating in MDX query, 433
calculated series, 505–508
    formulas for, 506
    moving average, 507
Calculated Series Properties dialog box, 506
    Formula drop-down list, 506
    properties for moving average, 507
calculations
    adding to reports, 292–299
        built-in fields, 298
        report item references, 296–298
        text box expressions, 295–296
    conditional formatting in Analysis Services, 437
    defining reporting standards for, 149
calendar control, using for date values in report
        parameter, 449
Calendar property, 244
canceling jobs on report server, 685
Cancel Query button (MDX query designer), 432
CanGrow element, 866
CanGrow or CanShrink properties, text box, 239
    CanGrow property, 144
Cap Fill page (pointer cap), 525
Cap Options page (pointer cap), 524
Cards
    using Cards visualization in Power View, 843
    using for identifying information in Power
        View, 818–821
cartographic projection. See projection method for
        maps
cascading parameters, 392, 447
    changing parameter order, 393
Cascading Style Sheets (CSS), length units, 238
case conversions in strings, 315
CatalogTempDB.sql script, 687
categories, too many, in pie charts, 513
category axis, 466, 493
Category Group Properties dialog box, 463
    Filters page, 464
    General page, 463
    Sorting page, 464
    sparklines, 482
    Variables page, 464
category groups, Chart data pane, 461–464
    deleting a category group, 463
    field selection, 462

CBool function, 333
CByte function, 333
CChar function, 333
CDate function, 321, 334
CDbl function, 334
CDec function, 334
Ceiling function, 325
CellContents element, 866, 867
CELL PROPERTIES clause in MDX queries, 433, 436
cells
    tablix, 256–259
        cell content, 256
        cell merge and split, 258
        cell scope, 257
center point, 563
    adjusting for maps, 583
    configuring properties for polygon maps, 602
character encoding used by rendering
        extensions, 738
character functions, 308
Chart Area Properties dialog box, Align With Chart
        Area drop-down list, 512
ChartColor Collection Editor, 487
Chart Data pane, 456–465
    Category Group section, 461–464
    configuring sparkline appearance, 482
    data bars, 476
    Series Group section, 464
    sparklines, 480
    Values section, 457–461
chart properties, 467
Chart Properties dialog box, 482
    configuring color palette, 485
    Filters page, 380
charts, 212, 453–484
    adding to reports, 453–456
        selecting chart type, 453
        understanding chart types, 454–456
    creating in Power View, 836–842
        arranging visualizations, 837
        column and bar chart sort order, 839
        column, bar, and line chart layout section, 838
        multiples, 839
        play axis, 841
        scatter chart layout section, 840
    data bars, 476–480
        adding, 476
        configuring properties, 478–480

formatting chart elements, 466–476
  axes, 469–473
  chart-level properties, 467
  chart titles, 467
  legend, 475
  series labels, 473–476
interactive sorting in, 350
sorting specification for categories in, 351
sparklines, 480–484
  adding, 480
  configuring properties, 481
using Chart Data pane, 456–465
  values, 457–461
working with chart elements, 485–516
  changing color palettes, 485–487
  horizontal axis properties, 493–500
  pie charts, 513–516
  series properties, 500–513
  vertical axis properties, 487–492
chart title, 466
  modifying and accessing other properties, 467
Chart Title Properties dialog box, 467
Chart Wizard (Report Builder), 121
child gauges, 537
child report parameter dataset, creating, 392
Choose function, 327
Chr and ChrW functions, 309
CInt function, 334
Claims Authentication, 644
Claims to Windows Token Service, 43
classes, adding/removing in Report Properties dialog
    box, 886
class library, creating, 881–885
  class definition, 881
  data processing custom extension, 888
cleanup functions, 318
  Replace function, 318
  Trim, LTrim, and RTrim functions, 319
Cleanup.sql script, 698
Client Tools Connectivity feature, 65
Clipboard, Home tab of Report Builder ribbon, 112
CLng function, 334
CObj function, 334
code, embedding in reports, 877–881
  Code property, 878
    generic function returning color or KPI, 879
  custom function call, 880–881
CodePlex, sample code on, 887
CollapsibleSpaceThreshold property (scale
    breaks), 490

collation for Database Engine and Analysis
    Services, 68
CollectedChartShowLegend property, 516
CollectedStyle property
  CollectedPie, 515
  SingleSlice, 514
CollectedThreshold property, 515
CollectedThresholdUsePercent property, 515
collections
  ChartColor Collection Editor, 487
  IndicatorState Collection Editor, 554
  member selection, using IntelliSense in
      Expression dialog box, 284
  syntax, 277
  using built-in collections in expressions, 287–292
    DataSets collection, 288
    DataSources collection, 288
    Fields collection, 289
    Globals collection, 289
    Parameters collection, 290
    ReportItems collection, 291
    User collection, 291
    Variables collection, 292
color analytical polygon maps, 575
colors
  BackgroundColor property, 245
  changing color palettes for charts, 485–487
    built-in color palettes, 485
    custom color palettes, 486
  color palette, chart property, 467
  Color property (indicator state), 543
  color rules for analytical data in maps, 595–598
  color scale for maps, 582, 590
  color theme for maps, 572
  conditionally changing font color, 300
  creating expression for color properties, 281
  defining standards for use in reports, 148
  empty point color, 501
  LineColor property, 248
  line color rules for maps, 601
  point color rule, 599
  polygon color rule for maps, 602
  three color range linear gauge, 520
Color Selector drop-down list, 246
Color System drop-down list, 246
column charts
  as data bars, 477
  sort order in Power View, 839
  when to use, 454

column groups
    adjacent, in a tablix, 267
    defining for matrix report in Report Wizard, 163
column headers
    pinning in place, 351
    repeating on each page, 418
column properties, 402–404
columns
    in Power View tables, 833
    separate columns for each row group in a
        tablix, 263
    single column for each row group in a tablix, 264
    static columns in a tablix, working with, 265–267
        adjacent columns, 266
Command class, 894–896
command line, installing Reporting Services from, 61
command-line utilities, 33
CommandText element, 865
CommandText property, DataSets collection, 288
Command Type DMX button (MDX query
        designer), 431
Command Type MDX button (MDX query
        designer), 431
Comma Separated Values format. See CSV format
Common Functions category, Expression dialog
        box, 282
CompareMethod.Binary, 310, 317
CompareMethod.Text, 310, 317
comparison operators, 283
    in filters, 382
Components setting, for monitoring by trace
        logs, 693
concatenation operators, 283
conditional formatting
    applying using expressions, 302
conditional formatting, applying using
        expressions, 299
configuration and management tools, 27, 33
configuration files
    backing up, 690
    updating for report server and report designer
        for new extension, 901
Configuration Manager, 168. See also Reporting
        Services Configuration Manager
configuring the report server, 669–685
    authentication, 681–683
    disabling an extension, 685
    disabling report server features, 684
    managing configuration settings
        programmatically, 914–918

    using Windows Powershell cmdlets, 917
    using WMI provider, 914–917
managing encrypted information, 678–681
managing memory, 683
Rsreportserver.config file, 669, 670
updating report server properties, 670–678
    advanced properties, 676–678
    execution properties, 673
    general properties, 671
    logging properties, 674
    security properties, 675
Connection class, 891–894
Connection Properties, 158
connections to data sources
    Analysis Services, 177
    data processing custom extension, 889
    defining in Report Builder, 115
    EnableTestConnectionDetailedErrors
        property, 677
    encrypted, in Rsreportserver.config file, 678
    Hyperion Essbase, 177
    ODBC, 176
    Oracle, 176
    PowerPivot documents on SharePoint site, 177
    RDL elements for, 862
    SAP NetWeaver BI, 177
    SQL Server, 174
    SQL Server Parallel Data Warehouse (PDW), 175
    Teradata, 176
    Test Connection button, 625
    using expressions for dynamic connections, 304
ConnectString element, 862
Connect To Server dialog box, default role
        definitions, 646
Console.WriteLine() statements in code for
        debugging, 908
Constants category, Expression dialog box, 281
ConsumeContainerWhiteSpace property, 404
content
    deploying, 607–616
        deploying a report model, 615
        deployment from SSDT, 608
        deployment verification, 609
        saving report from Report Builder, 610
        uploading reports, 611–614
        using rs utility, 614
    managing, 616–624
        configuring report parameters, 621–624
        copying a report, 620
        creating linked report, 619

enabling personalized folders, 624
moving content, 617–619
using folders for organization, 616
Content Manager role, 607
Contributor permissions, 657
conversion functions, 315, 333
LCase and UCase functions, 315
StrConv function, 315
coordinate systems
map viewport, 586
types of, 586
copy and paste, visualizations in Power View, 837
copying reports, 620
Cos function, 324
Cosh function, 324
CountDistinct function, 328
Count function, 328
Count property, Parameters collection, 290
CountRows function, 328
cover-flow visualization mode, 846
CreateLinkedItem function, 911
CreateLinkedReports.rss script
execution, 913–914
walkthrough, 911–913
CreateNewFolder function, 913
Create Power View Report button, 824
Createtables.sql script, 696
credentials. *See also* authentication
sending to a data source, 627–630
no credentials, 628
prompted credentials, 628
stored credentials, 628–630
Windows integrated security, 627
CShort function, 334
CSng function, 334
CSS (Cascading Style Sheets), length units, 238
CStr function, 334
CSV (Comma Separated Values) format
data renderer, 396
exporting reports in, 733–735
for reports, 29
currency, formatting, 242
Current Cube pane (MDX query designer), 427
current date and time functions, 323
custom aggregation, 301
CustomPaletteColors property, 487
cylindrical projection, 587

D

dashboards
creating, 718–725
information on, 723
for mobile devices, design options, 146
Data Alert Designer, 759
data alert rules, 763–766
data alert condition removal, 765
localization, 765
multiple rules, 765
rule condition, 763
rule scope, 763
Email Settings, 767
opening, 761
schedule settings, 766–767
data alerting, 759–778
architecture, understanding, 759–761
alerting service, 760
data alert workflow, 759–760
configuring, 772–775
RsReportServer.config file settings, 773–774
SharePoint configuration database settings, 774
creating data alerts, 761–768
data alert rules, 763–766
data feeds, 762
email settings, 767
schedule settings, 766
using SharePoint Report Viewer, 761–762
managing alerts, 770–772
alert status, 770–772
Delete command, 772
Edit command, 772
Run command, 772
monitoring alerting process, 775–777
alerting stored procedures, 776
performance counters, 777
receiving data alerts, 768–770
failure of alert, 770
successful alert, 768–770
Data Alert Manager, 15, 760, 770
Delete command, 772
Edit command, 772
Run command, 772
viewing alerts and alert status, 770–772
data alerts, 13
Data Alert Designer, 13, 41
Data Alert Manager, 15
for reports, 29

SharePoint support for, 60

SQL Server 2012 editions supporting, 59

Data Analysis Expressions (DAX) language, time intelligence functions, 810

data bars, 213, 476–480

  adding, 476

  configuring properties, 478–480

    appearance, 479

    length, 478

  converting to full chart, 480

Database Engines

  choosing edition, 58

  collation for, 68

  configuration in SQL Server 2012

    configuration, 69

  grouping with, 263

  new instance to host report server databases, 22

  support for hosting Reporting Servives database, 59

Database Engine Services feature, 64

database images, adding to reports, 220

databases

  alerting database, 760

  checking size of Reporting Services databases, 691

  in SharePoint integrated mode Reporting Services, 40

  installing sample databases, 97

Data Connections document library, SharePoint site, 94

data considerations in report design, 145

data-driven subscriptions, creating, 750–756

  configuring settings, 751–757

    native-mode report server, 751–754

    SharePoint integrated mode, 754–756

  creating subscription delivery table, 751

Data element, registering cutom data processing extension, 901

data feeds, 762

DataField element, 864

Data Format property, 806

data label keywords, 474

Data Mining Extensions. *See* DMX

Data pane (MDX query designer), 428, 430

data processing extension, 35, 887–904

  data processing extension deployment, 900–904

    configuration changes, 901

    custom extension digital signature, 901

    file locations, 901

    implementation, 903

data processing extension development, 889–900

  assembly properties, 890

  Command class, 894–896

  Connection class, 891–894

  DataReader class, 896–898

  Parameter class, 898–899

  Transaction class, 900

  overview of the extension, 888–889

DataProvider element, 862

data providers, 173

DataReader class, 896–898

data regions. *See also* graphical data regions; tablix data regions

  adding manually in Report Builder, 122

  applying sort to all, 349

  Data Regions menu, Insert tab of Report Builder ribbon, 113

  filtering, 382

  nested, missing group values in, 268

  NoRowsMessage property, 149

  tablix, 250–255

    list, 254

    matrlx, 252–254

    table, 250–252

  using data region wizards in Report Builder, 118

data renderers, 396

data-savvy advanced users, 141

data security, implementing, 664–668

  using dataset filter, 667

  using permissions table, 665

  using query parameter and role, 664

dataset fields

  placeholders, 274

  sorting by, 346

DataSetName property, 235

Dataset Properties dialog box

  Add Calculated Field, 293

  Available Values page, 449

  configuring options or filters, 865

  Filters page, 380, 667

  in Report Builder, 117

  Options page, Interpret Subtotals As Detail Rows, 439

  Parameters, 390

  Parameters page, new query parameter, 666

  using for tables in reports, 224

datasets

  adding in Report Builder, 117

  adding to a project, 165

Datasets category, Expression dialog box

Analyxis Services dataset fields, 435
binding to data regions, 225
creating Analysis Services dataset, 425–435
creating for custom data processing
    extensions, 903
creating shared datased in Report Builder, 107
DataSets and DataSet elements, 864
dynamic, creating using expressions, 305
embedded or shared, 562
filtering, 382
for report parts, reusing, 792
managing shared datasets, 641
report parameter's available values, 444
Shared Datasets folder, 156
shared, for power users, 141
sorting in, 234
SQL Server spatial query, 561
using Report Builder's dataset designer, 108–111
Datasets category, Expression dialog box, 282
DataSets collection, 288
DataSource element, 862–864
DataSourceName element, 865
Data Source Properties dialog box
    Credentials menu, Use Windows
        Authentication, 305
    RDL elements and, 862
DataSourceReference element, 862
DataSourceReference property, DataSources
    collection, 288
data sources
    adding to a project, 165
    adding to report definition in Report
        Builder, 114–116
    approving in SharePoint integrated mode, 658
    configuring properties, 624–630
        selecting data source for a report, 625
        sending credentials to a data source, 627–630
    connecting to, from Power View, 824
    creating in Analysis Services, 426
    data processing extensions for, 35
    DataSources and DataSource elements in
        RDL, 862–864
    Data Source Type drop-down list, 904
    disabling, 686
    identifying for data-driven subscriptions, 751
    Power View, 3
    provider type and connection, in Report
        Wizard, 159
    shared, 107
    Shared Data Sources folder, 156

types of, 173–179
updating for report model, 616
DataSources collection, 288
DataSources element, 862–864
Data Sources properties page, 626
Data Source Type property, 4
data tier
    in native mode architecture, 30
    in SharePoint integrated mode, 40
data tools, SQL Server, 16
Data Type property, setting for report
    parameters, 369
data types
    conversion functions for, 333
    conversions to strings, formatting functions
        for, 312
    geography, 558
    geometry, 558
    variant data type for Globals collection
        members, 290
data visualization, 4–7
    Data Visualizations menu, Insert tab of Report
        Builder ribbon, 113
DateAdd function, 319
DateDiff function, 320
DateFormat values, 313
DateInterval enumeration, 319
DatePart function, 321
dates and time
    creating date table in tabular model, 810
    Date/Time report parameter type, 369
        using, 371
    FormatDateTime function, 313
    functions for, 319–323
        current date and time functions, 323
        date calculation functions, 319
        date conversion functions, 322
        date mnaipulation functions, 321
    referencing consistent time value, 301
    setting filter condition based on date in Power
        View, 851
    using calendar control to get data for report
        parameter, 448, 449
DateSerial function, 322
DateString function, 323
DateValue function, 322
DAX (Data Analysis Expressions) language, time
    intelligence functions, 810
Day function, 321
DDB function, 332

debugging
administrative task scripts written in Visual Basic, 908
using Debug command in Visual Studio, 943
DebugLocal project configuration, 168
Debug project configuration, 168
Default Field Set dialog box, 821
Default SMTP Virtual Server Properties dialog box, 758
DefaultTraceSwitch setting, 692
Default Value property, 622
SharePoint integrated mode, 623
default values for report parameters, 146, 375–377
Get Values From A Query, 376
No Default Value, 375
Specify Values, 375
DeferVariableEvaluation property, 303
Delete Layer button, Map Layers pane, 592
delivery extensions, 35
Reporting Services runtime engine, 43
delivery providers for subscriptions, 743–749
email delivery, 743–745
identifying for data-driven subscriptions, 752, 756
Null Delivery Provider, 748
SharePoint document library, 748
Windows file share delivery, 746–748
Deploy command, 167
deployment, 45–54. *See also* native-mode deployment; SharePoint integrated-mode distribution
custom assembly, 885
data processing custom extension, 900–904
deploying reports to server, 607–642
configuring data source properties, 624–630
configuring report processing options, 630–636
deploying content, 607–616
managing change in reporting life cycle, 642
managing content, 616–624
working with snapshots, 636–642
distributed, 47–50
Internet, 52–54
scale-out, 50–52
scripting deployment of reports, 906–910
single-server, 45–47
DeployReport.rss script
execution, 909
walkthrough, 906–909
Deploy Reports command, 167

descending sort, applying in text boxes, 346
Description element, 861
descriptions, adding to reports, 132
design components, programming. *See* report design components, programming
design environments, 99–105
choosing a report designer, 103–105
comparison of report design environments, 99–102
developing a report with Report Builder, 105–130
Power View, 825–832
field list, 830
layout section, 831
ribbon, 827–830
views pane, 827
view workspace, 826
Designer element, registering custom data processing extension, 902
designing reports. *See also* design environments; layout
planning your design, 139–150
developing standards, 148–149
knowing your audience, 139–143
reviewing report options, 143–147
Design Mode button (MDX query designer), 432
Design tab (Power View ribbon), 829
Visualization group, 836
detail fields
defining for matrix report in Report Wizard, 163
defining for tabular report in Report Wizard, 161
detail lists. *See also* llists
transforming to grouped list in a tablix, 261
detail rows
adding to table in a tablix, 251
aggregate values in, 438–440
sorting, 347
Details group (category group), 462
details group, in list structure in a tablix, 254
Details View, Search Results page in, 709
development (reports), 28
programmatic interface for report development, 32
device information settings, 946
device information, using to change page properties, 406–408
device information tags, 407

dialog boxes. *See also* dialog box names listed throughout
    opening Expression dialog from, 278
    Page Break Options section, 416
digital signatures
    custom assembly, 884
    custom data processing extension, 901
dimension folders, 428
directional indicators, 539
Direction property, setting for text, 244
directories. *See also* files
    creating separate solution directory for new project, 153
Disabled property (page breaks), 415
disabling report server features, 684
disk activity (in single-server deployment), 47
disk space
    Disk Space Requirements page, SQL Server 2012 Setup, 67
    requirements for Reporting Services installation, 55
    requirements for single-server deployment, 46
Display Header (or Footer) For This Page, 410
display mode, selecting in Power View, 852–854
Display property, 623
Display Text property, 623
distance scale, 582
    setting properties, 591
distended price oscillator formula, 507
distributed deployment, 47–50
    native-mode distributed deployment, 47
    SharePoint integrated-mode distribution, 48
distributed workload in scale-out deployment, 52
distribution options for map colors, 596
DMX (Data Mining Extensions)
    Command Type DMX button (MDX query designer), 431
    query designer, 426
DOC files, 16
Documentation Components feature, 65
document libraries (SharePoint)
    delivery provider for subscriptions, 748
    opening a report, 135
    opening Subscriptions page, 742
    reviewing processing options in, 133
    saving Power View reports to, 855
    searching for reports, 714
    securing, 655
Document Library Settings page, Permissions And Management section, 655

DocumentMapLabel property, 357
    for lines, 215
Document Map pane, 711
document maps
    defining, 356–359
        creating a document map, 356
        customizing a document map, 357
        rendering a document map, 359
        showing and hiding a document map, 358
    using to navigate online reports, 711
DOCX files, 17, 728
DomainScope property (for nested data region group), 268
doughnut charts, 455
drilldowns
    configuring drillthrough report parameter value, 388
    configuring visibility, 353
    Enable Drilldown option in Report Wizard, 162
Dtexec utility, 697
dynamic connections, using expressions for, 304

E

Eckert1 and Eckert3 projection, 588
Edit Permissions dialog box, 649
EditSessionCacheLimit property, 676
EditSessionTimeout property, 676
email
    data alert settings, 767
    delivery of reports, 33
        email delivery extension, 35
    delivery provider for subscriptions, 140, 743–745
        report delivery options, 744
    nofitication of alert failure, 770
    notification of successful data alert, 768–770
    recipients' list for web service application, 920
    settings for native mode Reporting Services, 80
embedded datasets, 562
    map data, 564, 595
embedded images
    adding to reports, 217
    Value setting of BackgroundImage property, 246
embedded reports for portals or custom applications, 27, 30
empty points, 500–503
    adding marker to series, 501
    color for, 501
    zero value, 502

EmptyPointValue property, 502
empty strings and NULL values, defining reporting
    standards for handling, 149
Enabled property (scale breaks), 490
Enable Drilldown option, 162
EnableRemoteErrors property, 677
EnableTestConnectionDetailedErrors property, 677
encrypted information, managing, 678–681
    backup and recovery of encryption keys,
        688–690
    using Rsconfig utility, 679
        unattended execution account
        information, 681
encryption keys
    command-line utilities for management of, 34
    configuring for native mode Reporting
        Services, 81
    restoring in SharePoint integrated-mode report
        server migration, 24
Encrypt property in SQL Azure connection
    string, 175
envelopes formula, 507
Environmental Systems Research Institute
    shapefiles. See ESRI shapefiles
equality and inequality operators (=, <>, >, >=, <,
    <=), 383
equirectangular projection, 587
ErrorLevel property, 171
Error List window (Visual Studio), 156
errors
    EnableRemoteErrors property, 677
    report server project error levels, 171
    syntax errors in Expression dialog box, 286
ESRI (Environmental Systems Research Institute)
    shapefiles, 559
    selecting as spatial data source, 561
Excel
    Excel 2003 renderer, 17
    Excel 2010 renderer, 16, 29
    exporting reports into, 725–728
    Microsoft Power-Pivot Add-in for Excel, 27
    page headers and footers, 413
    page names appearing as sheet names, 423
    rendering reports to Excel 2007-2010
        render format name EXCELOPENXML, 398
    Reporting Services support for, 16
    soft page-break renderer, 396
EXCEL and WORD render formats, 398
ExcludedRenderFormats element, 685
Exclude From Project command, 166–167

Execute Query button (MDX query designer), 432
execution
    date and time for reports in page header or
        footer, 147
    executing reports on demand, 630–632
    execution properties, Server Properties dialog
        box, 673
    suspending report execution, 686
execution account for native mode Reporting
    Services, 81
ExecutionInfo object, 945
execution logging, 696
    for alerting, 776
    using ExecutionLog3 view, 698–699
ExecutionLogLevel property, 677
Exp function, 325
exponent functions, 325
exponential moving average formula, 506
exporting reports, 725–738
    for data exchange, 733–738
        ATOM format, 736–738
        CSV format, 733–735
        XML format, 735
    Power View reports, to PowerPoint, 855
    using hard page-break renderers, 730–733
        PDF format, 731
        TIFF format, 732
    using soft page-break renderers, 725–730
        Excel format, 725–728
        MHTML format, 729
        Word format, 728–729
Expression dialog box, 274, 278–287
    accessing field's extended properties, 436
    creating dynamic expression to show as
        tooltip, 355
    creating expression to use for sorting, 349
    exploring Category tree, 280–284
    help with functions, 307
    opening, 278–280
    using IntelliSense, 284
expressions, 273–306
    building without using Expression dialog
        box, 280
    commonly used functions in, examples, 307
    complex, 277
    field expression, 125
    in tablix cells, 256
    report parameter, 379

simple, 273–276
    aggregate function placeholder, 275
    built-in field placeholder, 275
    dataset field placeholder, 274
    parameter value placeholder, 276
    placeholders for, 273
SortExpression property for a tablix, 262
sorting by, 349
using built-in collections, 287–292
    DataSets collection, 288
    DataSources collection, 288
    Fields collection, 289
    Globals collection, 289
    Parameters collection, 290
    ReportItems collection, 291
    User collection, 291
    Variables collection, 292
using Expression dialog box, 278–287
using for sorting in matrix, 233
using in page header or footer, 411–414
working with, 292–306
    adding calculations to reports, 292–299
    applying conditional formatting, 299–300
    using for dynamic connections and
        datasets, 304–306
    using with variables, 300–301
extended field properties, 289, 436
extensions. *See also* data processing extension
    creating custom data processing extension,
        887–904
    disabling, 685
external functions, using, 343
external images, adding to reports, 220
external stakeholder reporting, management of, 143

F

Fahey projection, 588
failover cluster, report server database on existing
    SQL Server failover cluster, 51
features
    default location for installation of SQL Server
        2012 features, 65
    disabling report server features, 684
    selecting in SQL Server 2012 Setup, 63–65
field properties, extended, 436
field references (in tablix cells), 256
fields
    adding to matrix, 232

adding to table in Report Builder, 123–125
    using Field List icon, 124
adding to tables, 225
adding to Values section, Chart Data pane, 458
built-in field placeholder, 275
built-in fields, using for calculations, 298
Field element, 864
field list in Power View, 830
Fields category, Expression dialog box, 281
Fields collection, 289
Fields element, 864
in layout section in Power View, 831
File menu save options (for Power View reports), 855
files
    differences in native mode and SharePoint
        integrated mode, 909
    file locations for deploying custom extension
        assembly, 901
    report server project file types, 157
File Share Data Processing Extension Sample, 887
file share delivery extension, 36
FileSizeLimitMb setting, 692
FILESTREAM, enabling access in Database Engine
    configuration, 69
file sync feature, 614, 790
fill
    Back Fill page, Gauge Properties dialog box, 533
    Fill page, Scale Properties dialog box, 530
    Fill page, Series Properties dialog box, 461
    setting properties for text, 245
Filter element, 865
Filter function, 310
Filter pane (MDX query designer), 428, 430
    creating report and query parameters, 442
filters, 379–386
    applying OR logic to multiple filters, 386
    available MDX filter operators, 430
    creating, 380–382
        expression, 381
        parts, Expression, Operator, and Value, 380
        selecting filter operator, 381
        Value box, 382
    filtering a data region, 382
    filtering a dataset, 382
    filtering a group, 382
    filtering data in Power View visualizations,
        843–852
        highlighted values, 844
        slicers, 844

tiles, 845–848
    view filter, 848–854
filtering queries in Report Builder dataset designer, 110
Filters page, Category Group Properties dialog box, 464
Filters page, map layer dialog boxes, 594
understanding filter operators, 383–386
using dataset filter to secure data, 667
using report parameters as filters, 382
Filters Area (in Power View), 848
Filters element, 865
Filters page, 380
financial functions, 332
financial stock data, calculations for, 505
Firefox 7, support for Power View, 823
FirstDayOfWeek values, 320
First function, 236, 328
Fit To Window display mode (Power View), 852
FixedData property, applying to headers, 351
Fix function, 325
Floor function, 325
folders
    adding role assignments to, 651
    as targets for report server project deployments, 608
    CreateNewFolder function, 913
    differences in path names, native mode and SharePoint integrated mode, 909
    enabling personalized folders, 624
    Reporting Services project in Solution Explorer, 156
    securing for SharePoint integrated-mode report servers, 657
    securing on native mode report server, 653
    Universal Naming Convention (UNC), 746
    using to organize content, 616
fonts
    conditionally changing font color, 300
    defining reporting standards for, 148
    Font commands on Home tab of Report Builder ribbon, 112
    for axis labels, 472
    Label Font/Font page, Scale Properties dialog box, 528
    reports rendered in PDF format, 731
    text properties for, 240
FontWeight property, 341
footers. *See* headers and footers
Format property, 437

setting for text, 242
FORMAT_STRING property, 435
format strings, 128
FormattedValue extended property, 436, 439
FORMATTED_VALUE property, 436
formatting
    applying conditional formatting, 299
    reports in Report Builder, 127–129
    vales in tabular models, 806
formatting functions, 312
    FormatCurrency, FormatNumber, and FormatPercent functions, 312
    FormatDateTime function, 313
    Format function, 312
Forms authentication, 644
forms, POST method, 933
formulas, selecting for calculated series in charts, 506
frames, pages in Gauge Properties dialog box, 533
FROM clause, MDX queries, subselect statement in, **447**
Full Control permissions, 648
Full Screen Mode (display mode in Power View), 853
functions, 307–344
    adding to class definitions, 882
    aggregate function placeholders, 275
    Common Functions category, Expression dialog box, 282
    help with, 307–308
        function description and syntax, 307
        tooltips, 308
    tooltips for, in Expression dialog box, 285
    using aggregate functions, 328–331
        RunningValue function, 330
        scope argument, 329
    using conversion functions, 333
    using date and time functions, 319–323
        current date and time functions, 323
        date calculation functions, 319
        date conversion functions, 322
        date manipulation functions, 321
    using financial functions, 332
    using inspection functions, 326
    using math functions, 323–326
        exponent functions, 325
        other, BigMul and Rnd functions, 326
        rounding functions, 325
        sign functions, 324
        trigonometry functions, 323

using miscellaneous functions, 334–340
    InScope function, 335
    lookup functions, 335–339
    row functions, 339
using program flow functions, 327
using text functions, 308–319
    array functions, 313–315
    character functions, 308
    cleanup functions, 318
    conversion functions, 315
    formatting functions, 312
    search functions, 309–312
    string evaluation functions, 317
    string manipulation functions, 316
working with hierarchical data, 340–343
writing custom functions to embed in
    reports, 877–881
    custom function call, 880–881
    generic function returning color or KPI, 879
funnel charts, 455
FV function, 332

G

Gauge Data pane, 520
    indicator value and properties, 540
gauge element, 521, 531–534
    common gauge properties, 533
    linear gauge properties, 532
    radial gauge properties, 532
Gauge Orientation Options, 532
Gauge Panel Properties dialog box, 535
Gauge Properties dialog box
    Auto-Fit All Gauges In Panel, 537
    pages of gauge properties, 533
gauges, 213, 517–538
    adding to reports, 517–520
        creating a gauge, 518–520
        gauge types, 517
    comparison to indicators, 539
    gauge and indicator grouping, 549
    grouping, 536–538
        multiple gauges in gauge panel, 536
        repeating gauges, 537
    working with gauge elements, 520–536
        gauge element, 531–534
        gauge label, 534–535
        gauge panel, 535
        overview of gauge elements, 521

pointer, 522–526
range, 530–531
scale, 526–530
Geographic (Longitude, Latitude) coordinate
    system, 586
geography data type, 558
geometry data type, 558
GetChar function, 309, 310
Global Administrative Areas, ESRI shapefiles, 561
Globals collection, 289
    built-in fields, 275
goals, comparing to values. *See* gauges
Go To Bookmark action, 363
Go To Report action, 362
    passing parameter as part of, 388
Go To URL action, 365
    forcing to render in modal browser window, 366
    forcing to render in new browser tab, 366
Grant Permissions dialog box, 652, 656
graphical data regions, 212
    chart, 212
    data bar, 213
    gauge, 213
    indicator, 213
    map, 213
    sparkline, 213
graphics file formats supported by Windows
    GDI+, 732
grouped lists, 144
    detail list to grouped list transformation in a
        tablix, 261
group headers and footers, standards for, 149
grouping
    and scope argument of aggregate functions, 330
    detail rows with, sorting, 347
    gauges, 536–538
    in a matrix, 232
    indicators, 548–550
        adjacent indicators, 548
        gauge and indicator, 549
    in tablix data regions, 226–229
    in the database or in the report, 263
    managing in tabular model in Power View,
        811–816
    recursive hierarchy grouping, 269
Groupings pane
    Advanced Mode, Row Groups in, 419
    pinning column header to top of screen, 351
Group Properties dialog box, 229, 233, 261
    Filters page, 380

Page Breaks page, 417
selecting group for document map, 356
groups
adding in Report Builder, 126
adding page breaks by, 417
filtering, 382
group properties in a tablix, 268–272
missing group values in nested data
regions, 268
recursive hierarchy groups, 269–272
SharePoint integrated-mode servers, 645
and permission levels, 648–650
sorting, 348
applying sort to all groups, 349
working with tablix groups, 263–271
adjacent groups, 267
row groups, 263
GroupsBeforeRowHeaders property, 262
group variables, 301

H

HammerAitoff projection, 588
HangingIndent property, 241
hard page-break renderers, 397
preservation of white space in report body, 405
support for overlapping report items, 400
using to export reports, 730–733
PDF format, 731
TIFF format, 732
Has Default property, 622
headers and footers
adding footer row to table in a tablix, 252
adding header row to table in a tablix, 251
defining standards for, 148
fixed headers, using, 351
headers in a matrix in a tablix, 252
information included in page header or
footer, 147
in list structure in a tablix, 255
lighter shade for text in, 148
menu on Insert tab, Report Builder ribbon, 114
page headers and footers, 401
repeating column headers on each page,
418–420
using tablix footer to add totals to matrix, 253
working with page header and footer, 409–414
adding header or footer, 409
configuring properties, 409–410

removing header or footer, 414
using expressions in, 411–414
Height element, 866
Hex function, 334
Hidden option for report parameter visibility, 370
Hide property, 622
hierarchical data, working with, 340–343
dimension members of hierarchies, 428
Level function, 341
Recursive keyword, 342
using external functions, 343
highlighting
highlighted values in Power View, 9
using to filter data in Power View, 844
HistoryID property, 945
history properties, Server Properties dialog box, 674
Home ribbon (Power View), 827
Home tab of Report Builder ribbon, 112
Horizontal Axis Properties dialog box, 469, 482
interlacing, 499
Interval value, 496
scalar axis, 494
horizontal/vertical linear gauge, 520
Hour function, 321
HTML
InteractiveSize properties, 402
MHTML rendering format and, 729
rendering behavior of reports in, changing, 730
reports in, 26
soft page-break renderer, 396
tags, embedded, using for navigation, 359–361
HTML Viewer, 136, 709–711, 928
commands for URL access, 932–935
functions for managing report view, 710
using Print button to print reports, 712
using to interact with reports, 709
visibility of items in, properties for, 942
HTTP listener, 37
HTTP log, adding, 693
HTTP status codes, 694
Hyperion Essbase, 177

I

Icon property (indicator state), 543
icons, use as indicators, 550
IDataReader interface, 896
IDbCommand interface, 894–896
IDbCommandRewriter interface, 288

IDbConnectionExtension interface, 891–894
IDbConnection interface, 891
Iif function, 327
    creating expression for conditional
        formatting, 299
IIS (Internet Information Services), 37
    SMTP server implemented with, 758
Image Properties dialog box, specifying and
        configuring image in report, 217
images, 211
    adding to reports, 217–221
        database images, 220
        embedded images, 217
        external images, 220
        manually resizing images, 219
    adding to tabular model in Power View, 816–818
        using binary data, 816–817
        using external images, 817
    background for report items, 245
    BackgroundImage property, 246
    default image for each table in tabular
        model, 818–821
    using customized images for indicators, 550
impersonation, 629
Import button (MDX query designer), 431
Import Reports command, 166
Imports statement, 919
IncludeZero property (scale breaks), 490
indentation
    padding versus, for text, 242
    text properties for, 241
Indicator Properties dialog box, 541
    General page, 541
    Location and Size properties for indicators, 553
    static size for indicators, 553
    Value And States page, 542
        customized image as indicator icon, 550
        Synchronization Scope, 547
indicators, 213, 539–554
    adding indicators to reports, 539–540
        creating an indicator, 540
        overview of indicator types, 539
    configuring an indicator, 540–550
        assigning value, 541
        defining properties, 541–548
        grouping indicators, 548–550
    customizing indicators, 550–554
        adding labels, 551–553
        adjusting location and size, 553

dynamic sizing, 553
    using custom images for icons, 550
IndicatorState Collection Editor, 554
indicator states, 542–546
    aadding another, 545
    customized images for, 550
    properties defined for, 543
Indicator States property, 542
information as a service, report design for, 143
InitialPageName property, 421
In operator, 381, 385
InScope function, 335
Insert Row command
    options for positioning new row in tables, 251
    using in a matrix, 253
Insert tab of Report Builder ribbon, 113
inspection functions, 326
installation configuration rules (SQL Server 2012
        Setup), 71
installing Reporting Services, 55–98
    configuring native mode Reporting Services,
        72–83
        database, 77
        email settings, 80
        encryption keys, 81
        execution account, 81
        Report Manager URL, 78
        service account, 73
        web service URL, 73–77
    configuring partial integration with
        SharePoint, 83
    configuring SharePoint integrated mode, 84–96
    hardware and software requirements, 55–60
        choosing a Database Engine edition, 58
        review of requirements and supported
            operating systems, 58
        selecting an operating system, 55–58
        SharePoint integrated-mode deployment, 59
    installing Report Builder, 96–97
    installing sample databases, 97–98
    performing installation, 61–72
        installing prerequisites, 61–63
        installing SQL Server 2012, 63–72
    planning accounts for reporting services, 60–61
instance configuration (SQL Server 2012 Setup), 66
    directories for default and named instances, 67
instance methods, 886
instance names for report server, 916
InStr and InStrRev functions, 309, 310
InStrRev function, 317

IntegratedSecurity element, 862
Integration Services (in SharePoint integrated-mode
    distribution), 50
integration with SharePoint, 13
IntelliSense (in Expression dialog box), 284
interactive reports, 28
interactive scatter chart (Power View), 7
InteractiveSize properties, 402
interactivity, adding, 345–366
    interacting with report layout, 345–355
        configuring visibility, 352–354
        sorting, 345–351
        using fixed headers, 351
    navigation features, 356–366
        defining a document map, 356–359
        working with report actions, 361–366
interlacing, 499
Internal option, report parameter visibility, 371
Internet deployment, 52–54
    isolated, dedicated report server for Internet
        access, 53
Internet Explorer, support for Power View, 823
Interpret Subtotals As Detail Rows option, 439
InterpretSubtotalsAsDetails element, 865
intervals
    alerting interval defaults, 773
    DateInterval enumeration, 319
    interval functions, 321
    of horizontal and vertical axes, 495–500
        interlacing, 499
        interval properties, 496–499
    snapping interval for pointer, 526
Int function, 325
Ipmt function, 332
IsAlertingService flag, 773
IsArray function, 326
IsDate function, 326
IsMissing property, Fields collection, 289
IsMultiValue property, Parameters collection, 290
IsNothing function, 326
IsNumeric function, 326
item-level security, 653–664
    approving data sources in SharePoint integrated
        mode, 658
    assigning a system role, 660
    securing an item, 659
    securing a report model, 662
    securing folders and document libraries,
        653–657
        native mode folders, 653–654

SharePoint integrated mode document
    library, 655
SharePoint integrated mode folders, 657
items. See also report items
    adding existing item to project, 165
    adding new item to project, 165
    removing from project, 166

J

JavaScript commands forcing rendering of Go To
    URL action, 366
Join function, 314
    concatenating parameter values for multivalue
        parameter, 379

K

KeepTogether element, 866
KeepTogether property, 416
Keep Unique Rows property, 813–815
KeepWithGroup property, 420
Kerberos, 37, 644
keyboards, On-Screen Keyboard, 318
key performance indicators. See indicators; KPIs
KPIs (key performance indicators), 428. See
    also indicators
    displaying with gauges, 517

L

Label Properties dialog box
    gauge labels, 534
    indicator labels, 551
labels
    adding to indicators, 551–553
    axis, 470
    axis label fonts, 472
    configuring for map parallels and meridians, 585
    default label for each table in tabular
        model, 818–821
    DocumentMapLabel property, 357
    for group values in lists, 236
    for tablix cell's contents, 257
    gauge label, 534–535
    including in matrix to display repeating data, 253
    Label Font/Font page, Scale Properties dialog
        box, 528

Label property, Parameters collection, 291
Labels page, Scale Properties dialog box, 528
series labels in charts, 473–475
Language-Integrated Query (LINQ) to XML, 871
Language member, User collection, 291
Language property, 244
Last function, 236, 328
Latin1_General collation, 68
latitude and longitude
    Geographic (Longitude, Latitude) coordinate
        system, 586
    showing parallels and meridians, 585
layers, map. *See* maps
layer type selection, Map Wizard, 563
layout
    column, bar, and line chart layout section in
        Power View, 838
    decisions on, 143
    designing report layout, 209–248
        adding general items to reports, 213–223
        report items, 209–213
        using properties for appearance and
            behavior, 237–248
        working with data regions, 224–237
    interacting with report layout, 345–355
    Layout menu, Home tab of Report Builder
        ribbon, 112
    Layout page, Scale Properties dialog box, 527
    layout section for cards in Power View, 843
    layout section in Power View, 831
    Layout tab, Power View ribbon, 829
    managing page layout, 395–424
        adjusting report size, 400–408
        configuring page breaks, 414–423
        page headers and footers, 409–414
        understanding rendering, 395–400
    matrix layout section in Power View, 836
    scatter chart layout section in Power View, 840
    table layout section in Power View, 834
LCase and UCase functions, 315
Left and LSet functions, 316
LeftIndent property, 241
Legend Properties dialog box, 475, 589
    additional pages for setting legend
        properties, 476
legends, 467
    adjusting for maps, 577
    CollectedChartShowLegend property, 516
    formatting in charts, 475
    Legend page, Series Properties dialog box, 460

map, 582, 589
    color rules, 598
    text format options, 598
Len function, 317
length units (CSS), 238
Level function, 341
licensing
    license terms for SQL Server 2012 installation, 63
    servers in distributed deployment, 47
Like operator, 383
linear data in charts, 454
Linear Gauge Properties dialog box, 533
linear gauges, 517
    linear gauge properties, 532
    types of, 520
Linear Pointer Properties dialog box, 523
Linear Scale Properties dialog box, 526
Linear Scale Range Properties dialog box, 530
line charts, 454
LineColor property, 248
line data maps, 568
    configuring line properties, 601–602
    line analytical maps, 575
    Line Color Rule command, 595
    line maps without analytical data, 574
    Line Properties command, 594
    Map Line Layer Properties dialog box, 593
lines, 210, 555
    adding to reports, 215
    axis line, line style, 473
    configuring for parallels and meridians, 586
    setting line properties, 248
    use in mapping, 557
LineStyle property, 248
LineWidth property, 248
linked reports
    creating, 619
    scripting creation of, 911–914
    using for data security, 664
linking to reports with URL access, 927–938
    using URL access parameters, 931–938
        HTML Viewer commands, 932
        Report Server commands, 936
        Report Viewer commands, 935
    viewing a report, 927–931
        URL access on native-mode report
            server, 927–929
        URL access on SharePoint integrated-mode
            report server, 929–931
links in online reports, 147

LINQ (Language-Integrated Query) to XML, 871
ListLevel property, 248
lists, 212
    adding to reports, 234–237
    detail list to grouped list transformation in a
        tablix, 261
    grouped, 144
    providing list of values for user input into
        parameters, 146
    setting properties for, 248
    tablix using list structure, 254
    text properties for, 240
ListStyle property, 248
load balancing (in report server scale-out
    deployment), 51
localhost as server name, 670
localization
    data alert rules, 765
    setting locale properties, 243
    text properties for, 241
local mode reporting, configuring SharePoint for, 84
location
    customizing for indicators, 553
    Location field, New Project dialog box, 153
Location property
    setting for map legend, 590
    setting for report items, 237
Log and Log10 functions, 325
logarithmic linear gauge, 520
logarithmic scale, 491
logging
    adding HTTP log, 693
    execution logging, 696–698
        for alerting, 776
        using ExecutionLog3 view, 698
    logging properties, 674
        ExecutionLogLevel property, 677
    monitoring Windows application event log, 691
    SharePoint diagnostic logging, 694–696
    using trace logs to monitor report server,
        691–693
    Windows application even log and Reporting
        Services log files, 690
logical/bitwise operators, 283
logo in reports, 148
lookup functions, 335–339
    Lookup function, 335
    LookupSet function, 338
    MultiLookup function, 336
LSet function, 316
LTrim function, 319

M

MACD (moving average convergence/
    divergence), 505
    formula for, 507
Machine.config file, 19
major and minor tick marks
    in Scale Properties dialog box, 528
    on chart axis, 472
    on gauge scale, 521
managed reports, 27
Manage Lists permission, 658
Management Tools - Complete feature, 65
Manage Parameters page, 623
Manage Processing Options page, 640
managing reports, 130–134
    publishing a report, 131
    reviewing processing options, 132–134
managing the report server, 685–690. *See
    also* report server management,
    programming
    backup and recovery, 687–690
    canceling jobs, 685
    suspending report execution, 686
Map Color Rules Properties dialog box, 595
    Distribution page, 596
    Legend page, 598
    Polygon Color Rule, 602
Map Color Scale Properties dialog box, 591
Map Distance Scale Properties dialog box, 591
Map Gallery, 559
    customizing, 560
Map Layer Properties dialog box, Filters page, 380
Map Layer Size Rules Properties dialog box, point
    size rule, 599
Map Layers pane, 591–593
    adjusting center point and zoom level, 583
    color rules, 595
    toolbar, buttons on, 592
Map Layer Width Rules Properties dialog box, line
    width, 602
Map Line Layer Properties dialog box, 593
Map Line Properties dialog box, 601
    Line Width Rule, 602
Map Marker Type Rules Properties dialog box,
    marker type rule for point map, 600
mapping data, 555–578
    finalizing the map, 576–577
        map preview, 576
        simple adjustments, 577

understanding spatial data, 555–558
using Map Wizard, 558–576
Map Point Layer Properties dialog box, 593
Map Point Properties dialog box, marker type and size, 599
Map Polygon Layer Properties dialog box, 593
Map Polygon Properties dialog box, 602
maps, 213, 579–604
 configuring map elements, 579–591
  common elements, 581
  map element property pages and Map Wizard settings, 579–581
  Map Properties, 582
  viewport, 582–588
 defining a document map, 356–359
 inserting custom points, 603
 understanding order or precedence, 604
 working with layers, 591–603
  color rules, 595–598
  common spatial element properties, 594–595
  layer properties, 593–594
  line maps, 601–602
  Map Layers pane, 591–593
  point maps, 599–601
  polygon maps, 602
  tile layer maps, 603
Map Tile Layer Properties dialog box, 593
Map Title Properties dialog box, 589
Map Viewport Properties dialog box
 Center and Zoom page, 583
 Optimization page, 588
 options for working with center point and zoom, 584
 viewport coordinate system, projection, and boundaries, 586
Map Wizard, 558–576
 adding analytical data set, 571
 choosing map visualization, 566–570
  line data maps, 568
  point data maps, 566–568
  polygon data maps, 569
 choosing spatial data and map view options, 562–566
  Bing Maps layer, 565
  center point, 563
  embedded map data, 564
  map resolution, 564
  spatial field and layer type, 563
 coordinate system for viewport, 586
 in Report Builder, 122

map element property pages corresponding to settings, 579–581
map layers, 591
selecting spatial data source, 559–562
 ESRI shapefiles, 561
 Map Gallery, 559
 spatial queries, 561
setting theme and data visualization options, 572
 analytical marker maps, 574
 basic marker maps, 573
 basic polygon maps, 575
 bubble marker maps, 573
 bubble polygon maps, 575
 color analytical polygon maps, 575
 line analytical maps, 575
 line maps without analytical data, 574
margins
 Margins properties, 402
 overriding PDF page margin sizes at runtime, 406
  setting device information in URL access request, 408
 report properties for, 401
 standards for, 149
Mark As Date Table dialog box, 810
markers
 adding to series, 501
 bubbles display in chart, 504
 marker type rule for data point in map layer, 600
 selecting type and size for point data maps, 599
Markers page, Series Properties dialog box, 460
math functions, 323–326
 exponent functions, 325
 other, BigMul and Rnd functions, 326
 rounding functions, 325
 sign functions, 324
 System.Math, 343
 trigonometry functions, 323
matrix
 combining with a table, 250
 deciding when to use, 144
 groups before row header property, 262
 in Power View, 835
  matrix layout section, 836
  row and column groups, 835
 layout in a tablix, 252–255
 transforming table to, in a matrix, 259–260
 transforming to a table in a tablix, 260
matrix data region, 212
 adding to a report, 231

matrix format
  choosing in Report Wizard, 160
  matrix reports in Report Wizard, 163
Max function, 328
MaxNumberOfBreaks property (scale breaks), 490
MDX injection attack, guarding against, 446
MDX (Multidimensional Expression) language, 425
  using graphical query designer, 426–435
    creating query and report parameters, 442
    panes for constructing a query, 427
mean formula, 506
measurement units (for Location property), 238
measures
  in Analysis Services, 428
  measures only limitation on columns axis of MDX
    query, 433
median formula, 506
members
  of a collection, referencing, 277
  selecting, using IntelliSense in Expression dialog
    box, 284
memory
  managing for report server, 683
  reqirements for single server deployment, 46
  required by Analysis Services and Integration
    Services, 50
  requirements for Reporting Services
    installation, 55
memory management, 38
Mercator projection, 587
merging cells in a tablix, 258
meridians and parallels
  adding to maps, 585
  configuring properties, 585
Metadata pane (MDX query designer), 427, 428–429
meter radial gauge, 519
Me.Value, 300
MHTML format, 396
  exporting reports in, 729
Microsoft BI Semantic Model For Power View, 4
Microsoft Excel. See Excel
Microsoft Office Compatibility Pack, 17
Microsoft OLE DB Provider for Analysis Services
    10.0, 426
Microsoft PowerPivot Add-in for Excel, 27
Microsoft Reporting Services Add-in for SharePoint
    Technologies, 60
Microsoft.ReportingServices.Interfaces assembly,
    reference to, 890

Microsoft SQL Server 2012 Reporting Services
  new features, 3–24
    integration into SharePoint, 13–16
    parting with Report Builder 1.0, 17
    Power View, 3–13
Microsoft.VisualBasic functions, 343
Microsoft Word. See Word
Mid function, 316
Min function, 230, 328
Minute function, 321
mobile devices
  report design for, 146
  users accessing reports by, 140
Model Designer, 32
Model Item Security page in SharePoint integrated
    mode, 663
monitoring the report server, 690–704
  adding the HTTP log, 693
  checking application database size, 691
  ExecutionLog3 view, 698
  execution logging, 696
  performance counters, 699–704
  SharePoint diagnostic logging, 694–696
  using trace logs, 691–693
  using Windows application event log, 691
Month function, 322
MonthName function, 322
motivated power users, 141
Move... Webpage dialog box, 618
moving average convergence/divergence
    (MACD), 505
  formula for, 507
moving average formula, 506
moving average series, 508
moving content, 617–619
MSReportServer_ConfigurationSetting class, 915
MSReportServer_Instance class, 915
Multidimensional And Data Mining server mode
    (Analysis Services), 70
multidimensional data sources, 177–179
Multidimensional Expression language. See MDX
    language
MultiLookup function, 336
multiple bar pointers linear gauge, 520
Multiple HTTP Identities For The Report Server Web
    Service, 76
multiples (Power View), 8
  creating for charts, 839
multivalue data in charts, 456
multivalue report parameters, 370

My Reports folder
    configuring, 671
    deployment of report parts to, 783
    enabling, 624
    using for online reports, 712–714
My Subscriptions page, 757

N

names
    Name field in New Project dialog box, 152
    naming pages, 421
    Solution Name field, New Project dialog box, 153
namespaces, 881
    for custom assembly call, 885
    root namespace for data processing
        assembly, 890
native mode, 30–38
    application tier, 31–34
    component architecture, 31
    data tier, 30
    server tier, 34
    service architecture, 36–38
native-mode deployment
    configuring native mode Reporting Services,
        72–83
    distributed deployment, 47
    launching Report Builder, 96, 106
    moving content, 617
    no support for high availability or web farm
        management, 51
    publishing reports to report server, 131
    Reporting Services Native Mode: Install And
        Configure option, 70
    Reporting Services Native Mode: Install Only
        option, 71
    selection of Reporting Services - Native
        features, 64
    setting TargetServerURL property, 169
    uploading reports, 611
    URL access to reports, 927–929
    using folders to organize content, 616
    verifying report deployment, 609
native-mode report server
    in-place upgrades, 20
    preparing for upgrade, 19
navigation features, adding, 356–366
    defining a document map, 356–359
    using embedded HTML tags, 359–361
    working with report actions, 361–366

nested data regions, 224
    dataset binding in, 235
.NET 4.0, prerequisite for Reporting Services
    installation, 61
.NET Data Provider for Teradata, 176
.NET Framework functions, 343
network interface cards (NICs), placing two in each
    report server, 51
network load balancing (NLB), use in report server
    scale-out deployment, 51
new features in Reporting Services, 3–24
    parting with Report Builder 1.0, 17
    Power View, 3–13
    rendering extensions, 16
New Layer Wizard, 591, 592
New Project dialog box, 152
New Role Assignment page, 651
New Solution Configuration dialog box, 168
90 Degrees Northeast/Northwest/Southwest/
    Southeast radial gauge, 519
NLB (network load balancing), use in report server
    scale-out deployment, 51
NoDataMessage property, using with charts, 456
nonadditive values, Sum function and, 437
NON EMPTY keyword, 432
NoRowsMessage property, 149, 262
NOT IN filter for a data region, 311
Not In operator, 386
Now function, 323
Nper function, 332
NT LAN Manager (NTLM), 37, 644
Null Delivery Provider, 748
NULL values
    Allow Null Value property, report
        parameters, 370
    defining reporting standards for handling of, 149
numbering pages, 420
    global variables, 420
    ResetPageNumber property, 421
numbers
    filter comparing numeric values in Power
        View, 851
    Format property, 241, 242
    formatting for chart axis, 472
    formatting numeric values, Report Wizard
        and, 164
    Number menu, Home tab of Report Builder
        ribbon, 112
    Number page, Scale Properties dialog box, 528

predefined and user-defined numeric formats, 312
NumeralLanguage property, 244
NumeralVariant property, 244
numeric keypad, on-screen, 318

O

Object Linking and Embedding Database. *See* OLE DB
occurrence indicators for RDL elements, 864
Oct function, 334
ODBC (Open Database Connectivity)
  Client Tools Connectivity feature, 65
  data providers, 176
OLAP databases, 425
OLE DB (Object Linking and Embedding Database)
  Client Tools Connectivity feature, 65
  data providers, 176
  data source type, 426
omitting a parameter in drillthrough reports, 389
on-demand report execution, 630–632
180 Degrees North/South/West/East radial gauge, 519
online reports
  accessing, 707–738
    exporting reports, 725–738
    in SharePoint, 714–725
    using HTML Viewer, 709–711
    using Report Manager, 707–713
  designing separately from printed reports, 147
online viewing of reports by users, 140
  layout for online reports, 143
On-Screen Keyboard, 318
opening reports, 135
operating systems
  .NET 2.0 and .NET 3.5 Service Pack 1 update for, 62
  selecting for Reporting Services installation, 55
  support for 32-bit edition of SQL Server 2012, 57
  support for SQL Server 2012 64-bit editions, 56
operations monitoring, report design for, 142
operators
  available MDX filter operators, 430
  complete list of, 282–284
  filter, 381, 383–386
    Between operator, 384
    equality and inequality operators, 383
    In operator, 385

Like operator, 383
Not In operator, 386
Top and Bottom, 384
Operators category, Expression dialog box, 282
- (subtraction) operator, using, 293
using logical AND or logical OR in filters in Power View, 851
Optimization page for map viewport properties, 588
Oracle, using as data source, 175
ORDER BY clause (SQL queries), 234
order of precedence for map element properties, 604
orientation
  for text boxes, changing dynamically, 399
  Gauge Orientation Options (linear gauge), 532
OR operator
  applying OR logic to multiple filters, 386
  using in filters, 851
Output window, 156
  deployment progress in, 608
OverallPageNumber variable, 421
OverallTotalPages variable, 421
overlapping report items, 216
OverwriteDataSources property, 625

P

padding
  setting dynamically for text boxes, 399
  using padding or indentation for text, 242
Padding property, 241, 341
PageBreak properties, 422
page breaks
  configuring, 414–423
  for printed reports, 147
  inserting in Report Builder, 127
  rendering formats by pagination type, 395–397
Page element, 861
Page Footer Properties dialog box, 410
page footer, standards for, 149
page groups
  defining for matrix report, 163
  defining for tabular report in Report Wizard, 161
Page Header Properties dialog box, 410
page header, standards for, 148
page layout, 395–424
  adjusting report size, 400–408
    page structure properties, 400–406
    using device information to change page properties, 406–408

configuring page breaks, 414–423
    adding page breaks by group, 417
    creating page breaks, 415
    naming pages, 421
    numbering pages, 420
    repeating headers, 418–420
    using KeepTogether property, 416
  page header and footer, 409–414
  understanding rendering, 395–400
    rendering formats by pagination type,
       395–397
    using RenderFormat global variable, 397–400
Page_Load method (example), 920
PageName property, 422
PageNumber global variable, 420
page numbering, 420
  for printed reports, 147
  global variables, 420
  ResetPageNumber property, 421
page size properties, 402
page structure properties, 400–406
  column properties, 402–404
  page size properties, 402
  report page structure, 400–401
  white space, 404–406
pagination. *See also* page breaks
  built-in fields related to, using for
    calculations, 298
paragraphs
  Paragraph element, 866
  Paragraph menu, Home tab of Report Builder
    ribbon, 112
  Paragraphs element, 866
Parallel Data Warehouse (PDW), 175
parallels and meridians
  adding to maps, 585
  configuring properties, 585
Parameter class, 898–899
parameters, 145–146. *See also* report parameters
  changing report parameters with HTML
    Viewer, 709
  configuring report parameters, 621–624
  defining standards for, 149
  defining target report for Go To Report, 363
  designing when using Analysis Services
    dataset, 442–450
    auto-generated query and report
      parameters, 442–447
  parameter value olaceholders, 276
  query, passing report parameter value to, 369

report parameter values for standard
    subscriptions, 749
  setting report parameters for data-driven
    subscriptions, 754
  StoredParametersLifetime property, 677
  StoredParametersThreshold property, 677
  using query parameter to secure data, 664
Parameters category, Expression dialog box, 281
Parameters collection, 290
parent-child tables, 269
Parent property (for rectangle report items), 216
Parts menu, Insert tab of Report Builder ribbon, 113
PDF files
  custom web application rendering reports
    as, 947
  exporting reports in, 731
  hard-page break renderer, 397
  overriding page margin sizes at runtime, 406,
    408
  reports in, 26
PDW (Parallel Data Warehouse), 175
percentages
  formatting, 242
  getting with Aggregate function, 437
  percentage-based indicator states, 545
performance
  displaying with indicators. *See* indicators
  running performance tests, 700
performance counters, 699–704
  for alerting, 777
  listing for Reporting Services, 700–704
  selecting from performance objects, 699
performance formula, 507
PerformancePoint Services, 30
permissions
  assigning user permissions, 650–652
    native mode role assignments, 650–652
    SharePoint permission levels, 652
  editing for native-mode server roles, 647
  editing for SharePoint document libraries,
    655–657
  editing for SharePoint integrated mode
    folders, 657
  SharePoint integrated-mode groups, 648–650
    compared to native-mode tasks, 645
  using permissions table to secure data, 665
personalized folders, 624
pie charts
  when to use, 455
  working with, 513–516

secondary pie chart, 515
slice consolidation, 514–515
pivot point location, radial gauge, 532
Placeholder Properties dialog box, 257
    HTML - Interpret HTML Tags As Styles, 360
placeholders
    for expressions, 273
        aggregate function placeholders, 275
        built-in field placeholders, 275
        dataset field placeholders, 274
        parameter value olaceholders, 276
    for subreports, 221
    for text box containing HTML, selecting, 360
placement, configuring for report items, 237
Planar (X, Y) coordinate system, 586
play axis, adding to charts in Power View, 841
Pmt function, 332
PNG (Portable Network Graphics) files, 817
point data maps, 566–568
    basic, options for, 575
    configuring point properties for map layer,
        599–601
    inserting custom points in maps, 603
    Map Point Layer Properties dialog box, 593
    Point Color Rule command, 595
    Point Properties command, 594
Pointer Border page, 524
pointer cap (gauge element), 521
Pointer Fill page, 524
pointer (gauge element), 521, 522–526
    custom pointer, 525
    properties, 523
        pages of pointer properties, 524
    snapping interval, 526
    value, 522
Pointer Options page, 524
points, 555
    center point of a map, 563
    defined, 556
polar charts, 455
polygon data maps, 569
    bubble map, 575
    color analytical map, 575
    configuring polygon properties, 602
    Map Polygon Layer Properties dialog box, 593
    Polygon Color Rule, 595
    Polygon Properties command, 594
polygons, 555
    use in mapping, 557
Portable Document Format. *See* PDF files

POST method (forms), 933
PowerPivot Feature Integration For Site
        Collections, 94
PowerPivot for SharePoint
    configuring, 85
    connecting to workbook using Analysis Services
        data provider, 177
    installing, 72
PowerPivot Gallery
    opening Power View, 824
    saving reports to, 12
PowerPivot workbooks, data source for Power
        View, 4
PowerPoint
    exporting Power View reports to, 855
    Microsoft Office Compatibility Pack for, 17
power users, 141
Power View, 3–13, 26, 99, 797–822, 823–856
    comparison to Report Designer and Report
        Builder, 99–102
    data sources, 3
    data visualization, 4–7
    enhancing tabular models for, 803–822
        adding images, 816–818
        appearance of identifying information,
            818–821
        creating date table, 810
        formatting values, 806
        managing grouping behavior, 811–816
        setting default sort, 807–809
        simplifying creation of new table, 821–822
        summarizing values, 803–806
    filtering data in visualizations, 843–852
        highlighted values, 844
        slicers, 844
        tiles, 845–848
        view filter, 848–854
    getting started wtih, 823–832
        connecting to a data source, 824
        learning the design environment, 825–832
        verifying browser requirements, 823
    highlighted values, 9
    implementing in SharePoint, 94
    in application tier of SharePoint integrated
        mode, 41
    interactive scatter chart, 7
    multiples, 8
    report sharing, 12

saving reports, 854–856
   PowerPoint export, 855
selecting a display mode, 852–854
SharePoint support for, 60
slicer, 10
SQL Server 2012 editions supporting, 59
SQL Server Setup and, 72
tiles, 10
using, 104
using tabular models with, 797–803
   creating BI Semantic Model (BISM)
      connection, 798–803
view filter, 11
visualizing data, 832–843
   Cards, 843
   charts, 836–842
   copying a visualization, 837
   matrix, 835
   resizing and moving a visualization, 835
   tables, 833–835
Power View Integration Feature, 94
Pow function, 325
PPmt function, 332
precision placement of report items, 214
Prepare Query button (MDX query designer), 432
previews
   map, 576
   previewing report before printing, 712
   previewing report in Report Builder, 129
Previous function, 340
printed reports, design options for, 147
printing, using Report Manager print feature, 712
Print Layout mode, checking column layout, 404
Print On First Page property (page headers and
      footers), 410
Print On Last Page property (page headers and
      footers), 410
ProcessingMode property, 942
processing options, 132–134, 630–636
   caching reports, 632–633
   executing a report on demand, 630–632
   native-mode report server, configuring report
      snapshot, 637
   refreshing the cache, 634
   reviewing in Report Manager, 132
   reviewing in SharePoint document library, 133
product key (SQL Server 2012), 63
program flow functions, 327
   creating expression for conditional
      formatting, 299

programmatic interface for management, 34
programmatic interface for report development, 32
programmatic interface for viewing or delivering
      reports, 33
programming report design components. *See* report
      design components, programming
programming reporting access. *See* access to
      reports
programming report server
      management. *See* report server
      management, programming
project configurations, 168
Project Context settings, 168
projection method for maps, 586
   conversion of three-dimensional coordinates to
      two-dimensional, 586
   types available in Reporting Services, 587
Project menu, 166
Project Properties command, 167
projects. *See also* report server projects
   adding new project to existing solution, 153
   removing from a solution, 157
   report project file types, 157
   selecting project type, 154
prompted credentials, 628
Prompt property, setting for report parameters, 369
Prompt User property, 623
properties
   collection, syntax for, 277
   configuring report project properties, 167–172
      project configurations, 168
      setting project properties, 169–172
   configuring tablix properties, 261
      groups before row header, 262
      no data rows, 262
      sorting, 262
   creating expressions for, 281
   extended field properties, 436
   group properties in a tablix, 268–272
   map element, accessing, 593
   order of precedence for map elements, 604
   Properties button, Map Layers pane, 592
   report parameter properties, setting, 368–378
      advanced parameter options, 377
      available values, 371–374
      default values, 375–377
      general properties, 368–371
   selecting, using IntelliSense in Expression dialog
      box, 284
   series properties for chart values, 458–461

supporting conditional formatting, 299
using to control appearance and behavior, 237–248
   changing appearance of report items, 240–248
   placement and size of report items, 237–239
Properties window, 156
   accessing DeferVariableEvaluation property, 303
   color palette, Custom, 486
   CustomAttributes section, 515
   EmptyPoint category, Color property, 501
   KeepWithGroup property, 420
   opening Expression dialog box from, 279
   PageBreak category, 415
   RepeatColumnHeaders property, 418
   RepeatOnNewPage property, 420
   setting ReportViewer properties, 942
Property dialog box, Configuration Manager button, 168
Property Pages dialog box, 167
   opening, 169
pseudoconic projection, 587
pseudocylindrical projection, 587
publishing reports, 131
   to native-mode report server, 131
   to SharePoint integrated-mode report server, 131
PublishReport function, 908
Publish Report Parts dialog box, 783, 785
   redeployment of a report part, 788
   Review And Modify Report Parts Before Publishing, 786
PV function, 333
pyramid charts, 455

Q

queries
   creating query for report in Report Wizard, 159
   dynamic query strings, 305
   SQL Server spatial queries, 561
query designer (Report Builder), 109
Query element, 864
Query Mode (MDX query designer), 433
query parameters, 389–391
   auto-generated, for Analysis Services dataset, 442
   controlling cascading report parameter's values, 392

creating, 389
custom, 447–450
   MDX query parameterization, 448
   query parameter value, 448
deleting, 391
linking parent report parameter to, 392
linking with report parameters, 390
parameterized dataset, 446
Query Parameters button (MDX query designer), 432, 447
Query Parameters dialog box, 432
   available values dataset for report parameter, 449
   manually creating a query parameter, 448
QueryParameters element, 865
quick information retrieval, report design for, 142

R

Radial Gauge Properties dialog box, 532
radial gauges, 517
   types of, 519
radial gauge type, 519
Radial Pointer Properties dialog box, 523
Radial Scale Properties dialog box, 526
   tick marks, appearance of, 529
Radial Scale Range Properties dialog box, 530
radial with mini gauge type, 519
range charts, 456
range (gauge element), 521, 530
   multiple ranges, 531
   properties, 530
Rate function, 333
rate of change formula, 507
ratings indicators, 539
ratio data in charts, 455
raw data, delivering to users, 142
RDL files, 31, 157
   upgrades of, 21
RDLGenerator class, 869–875
RDLGenerator.exe file, 875
RDL Object Model, 868
RDL (Report Definition Language), 249, 859–876
   custom RDL created by web service for accessing reports, 947
   DataSets and DataSet elements, 864
   DataSources and DataSource elements, 862–864
   RDL schema definition, 859
   Report element, 861

specification, 866
Tablix element, 865–867
understanding the XSD, 863
usage, 860
working with, 867–876
    manual edits, 867
    programmatic edits, 868
    RDL generation, 868–876
RDLX files, 12
RDLXReportTimeout property, 677
RDS file extension, 157
Reading Mode display mode in Power View, 852
recovery. *See* backup and recovery
rectangles, 210
    adding to reports, 216
    lines versus, in reports, 216
recursive hierarchy groups, 269–272
Recursive keyword, 342
references
    for web service rendering reports, 944
    Microsoft.ReportingServices.Interfaces
        assembly, 890
    web reference for Reporting Services web
        service, 918
refreshes
    cached datasets, 641
    cached reports, 634
    options for report parameters dependent on
        dataset query, 378
    Refresh button, MDX query designer, 431
relational data sources, 174
relationships, working with, in Report Builder's
    dataset designer, 110
relative strength index formula, 507
relay restrictions (SMTP), 758
Release project configuration, 168
remote procdeure call (RPC), 38
rendering, 395–400
    exporting reports with hard page-break
        renderers, 730–733
    exporting reports with soft page-break
        renderers, 725–730
    rendering formats by pagination type, 395–397
    using RenderFormat global variable, 397–400
        dynamic positioning of text boxes, 399
rendering extensions, 35
    new, 16
        Excel 2010 renderer, 16
        Word 2010 renderer, 17
    using soft page-break rendering, 725

rendering formats for reports, 29
    eliminating for use with subscriptions, 685
Render This Report From a Report Snapshot
        option, 637
RepeatColumnHeaders property, 418
repeating gauges, 537
RepeatOnNewPage property, 420
Replace function, 318
report actions. *See also* actions
    using for navigation features, 361–366
        Go To Bookmark action, 363
        Go To Report action, 362
        Go To URL action, 365
Report Builder, 26, 32, 99, 105–130
    adding a dataset, 117
    adding a total, 125
    adding data regions manually, 122
    adding data source to report definition, 114–116
    adding fields to a table, 123–125
    adding report parts to reports, 790
    comparison to Report Designer and Power
        View, 99–102
    deploying report parts, 785–790
        multiple report items in report part, 787
    deploying reports to My Reports folder, 713
    formatting reports, 127–129
    Getting Started Wizard, 106–108
    inserting page breaks, 127
    installing, 96–97
    launching, 105–106
        as stand-alone application, 106
        in native mode, 106
        in SharePoint integrated mode, 106
    learning Report Builder interface, 111–114
    parting with Report Builder 1.0, 17
    previewing a report, 129
    redeployment of report parts, 788
    Report Builder 2.0, 17
    ReportBuilderLaunchURL property, 677
    Report Part Gallery, 790–792
    saving a report, 130
    saving reports from, 610
    using, 104
    using data region wizards, 118–122
    using dataset designer, 108–111
    versions, 102
ReportBuilder3.MSI file, downloading and
        executing, 97

report caching
    controlling using Processing Options page, 133, 134
    disk space requirements and, 46
Report Data pane, 442
    accessing and organizing report parameters, 367
    Images folder, 219
    Show All Hidden Datasets, 444
Report Data Source (RDS files), 157
Report Data window (Visual Studio), 157
Report Definition Language. See RDL; RDL files
report design components, programming, 877–904
    creating custom data processing extension, 887–904
        data processing extension deployment, 900–904
        data processing extension development, 889–900
        overview of the extension, 888–889
    embedding code in reports, 877–881
        Code property, 878
        custom function call, 880–881
    using assemblies to share custom code, 881–887
        class library, 881–885
        custom assembly call, 885–887
Report Designer, 31, 99, 151
    advantages of, 103
    comparison to Report Builder and Power View, 99–102
    Grouping pane, 228
    report project commands, 166–167
    viewing RDL files as XML, 859
report designers. See design environments
Report element, 861
ReportExecution2005 endpoint, 944
report execution time-out, 133
report explorer Web Part, 724
report files. See RDL files
report header, standards for, 148
Report History page, 640
reporting life cycle, 27–30
    managing change in, 642
    report access, 29
    report administration, 28
    report development, 28
reporting platform, Reporting Services as, 25–27
ReportingService2010 object, 920
ReportingService Alerting database, 41
Reporting Services
    architecture, 30–43

configuration in SQL Server 2012 Setup, 70
creating a project, 151–154
    creating new project and solution, 152
databases, Database Engine support for hosting, 59
runtime engine, 42
Reporting Services Add-in for SharePoint, installing, 86
Reporting Services Add-in For SharePoint Products feature, 65
Reporting Services Add-in, installation in SharePoint integrated-mode distribution, 48
Reporting Services Catalog Database, 72
Reporting Services Catalog Temporary Database, 72
Reporting Services Configuration Connection dialog box, 72
Reporting Services Configuration Manager, 33, 72, 669
    backing up symmetric key, 19
    configuring Report Manager and web service URLs, 22
    configuring SSL support, 644
    encryption keys for connection information, 688
    Report Server web service URL, 70
    SMTP server configuration, 744
Reporting Services - Native feature, 64
Reporting Services Report Gallery, access to, with Report Builder, 104
Reporting Services Shared Data Source (RSDS) files, 4
Reporting Services - SharePoint feature, 65
report item references, 296–298
report items, 209–213
    adding general items to reports, 213–223
        images, 217–221
        lines, 215
        rectangles, 216
        subreports, 221–223
        text boxes, 214
    changing appearance of, 240–248
    configuring placement and size of, 237–239
    general, 210
        images, 211
        lines and rectangles, 210
        subreports, 211
        text boxes, 210
    graphical data regions, 212
        chart, 212
        data bar, 213
        gauge, 213

indicator, 213
map, 213
sparkline, 213
precision placement of, using ruler, 214
Report Items menu, Insert tab of Report Builder
ribbon, 114
tablix data regions, 211
matrix, 212
table, 212
working with, 224–237
ReportItems collection, 291, 297
ReportItems element, 865
Report Manager
accessing online reports, 707–713
printing a report, 712
searching for a report, 707–709
using document map, 711
using HTML Viewer, 709–711
bypassing in Internet deployment, 53
configuring report parameters, 622
descriptions for reports, 132
folders for content management, 616
in service architecture, 37
moving content, 617
on-demand execution of reports, 631
opening a report, 135
putting on dedicated server in Internet
deployment, 54
report part management on report server,
789–790
reviewing processing options, 132
schedules list, 739
selecting a data source, 625
stand-alone, configuration information, 54
subscriptions, creating, 742
uploading reports, 611
user role assignments, 651
using in native mode report server
environment, 33
verifying report deployment, 609
viewing reports in native mode, 32
Report Manager URL, configuring for native-mode
Reporting Services, 78
report models
deploying, 615
securing, 662
Report Name field, 298
report page structure, 400
Report Parameter Properties dialog box, 442
Advanced page, 377

Available Values page, 371
creating report parameters, 367
General page, 368
report parameters, 367–394
available values dataset, 444
cascading parameters, 392
changing parameter order, 393
creating when using Analysis Services
dataset, 442–444
in URL access parameters, 931
setting for linked reports using scripts, 914
using as filters, 382
using calendar control with, 449
using filters, 379–386
using with subreports and drillthrough, 387–389
passing parameter to a subreport, 387
passing parameter to drillthrough report, 388
working with, 367–379
creating a report parameter, 367
deleting report parameter, 379
displaying parameter selections in a
report, 379
setting report parameter properties, 368–378
working with query parameters, 389–391
creating a query parameter, 389
deleting a query parameter, 391
linking report and query parameters, 390
Report Part Gallery in Report Builder, 141, 790–792
Report Part Notifications, 378
report parts, 27, 781–796
deploying, 783–790
from Report Builder, 785–790
from SSDT, 783–785
managing report parts on report server,
789–790
redeployment of a report part, 788
introduction to, 781–783
benefits of using report parts, 782
creating report parts, 782
definition of report parts, 782
publishing for motivated power users, 141
report parameters added as, 378
subreports versus, 795
using, 790–794
Report Part Gallery, 790–792
update notification, 792–794
ReportPath property, 942
report processing extension, 35
Report Processor, 34

Report Properties dialog box
    Code page, 878
    creating report variables, 302
    References page, Add Or Remove
        Assemblies, 886
reports
    building using Analysis Services dataset, 435–442
    Power View report developer, 3
    report list for web service, 921
    transitioning from prior version of Reporting
        Services, 18
    upgrade to Reporting Services 2012, 21
Report Server Catalog Best Practices, 47
report server commands for URL access, 936–938
ReportServer database
    backing up, 19
    backup and recovery, 687
    checking size of, 691
    in native mode Reporting Services, 30
    in SharePoint integrated mode, 40
    reports upgrade, 21
report server databases
    disk space requirements, 46
    managing with many users and heavy reporting
        workload, 47
    putting on dedicated server to reduce resouce
        contention, 48
Report Server Integration Feature, 94
report server management, programming, 905–926
    configuration settings, 914–918
        using Windows PowerShell cmdlets, 917
        using WMI provider, 914–917
    scripting administrative tasks, 905–914
        creating a linked report, 911–914
        deploying reports, 906–910
    using the web service, 918–925
report server projects, 16, 151–172
    configuring report project properties, 167–172
        setting project properties, 169–172
    getting started with, 151–157
        creating Reporting Services project, 151–154
        learning Visual Studio interface, 155–157
        selecting project type, 154
    using report project commands, 166–167
    working with report project files, 157–166
        adding existing item to a project, 165
        adding new item to a project, 165
        project configurations, 168
        project file types, 157–158
        removing item from a project, 166
        using Report Wizard, 158–164
Report Server project type, 154
Report Server Project Wizard, 16
Report Server Project Wizard project type, 154, 158
report server proxy endpoint, 42
report servers, adding to SharePoint-integrated
        mode distribution, 95
ReportServerTempDB database
    backup and recovery, 687
    checking size of, 691
    disk space requirements, 47
    in native mode Reporting Services, 30
    in SharePoint integrated mode, 40
ReportServerURL property, 942
Report Server web service, 37
Reportservicesservice.exe.config file, 19
Reports folder, 156
Report Shared Dataset (RSD files), 157
report sharing (Power View), 12
report variables, 302
Report Viewer, 716–718
    commands for URL access, 935
    creating data alerts, 761 762
    data alerting support, 760
    functions for managing the report view:, 717
    tool pane, 719–725
ReportViewer control, 938–943
    configuring Report Wizard, 939
    properties, 942
    ReportViewer application, 943–944
report viewer Web Part
    adding to dashboard, 718
    using native-mode reports in SharePoint
        dashboard, 724
Report Viewer Web Part, 41
Report Wizard, 158–164
    configuring ReportViewer control, 939
ResetPageNumber property, 421
resolution, choosing for maps, 564
resource files for report server projects, 158
RewrittenCommandText property, DataSets
    collection, 288
ribbon (Power View), 827–830
    Design tab, 829
    Home tab, 827
    Layout tab, 829
    Styles tab, 828
Right and RSet functions, 316
RightIndent property, 241

Rnd function, 326
Robinson projection, 588
role-based security
    activities associated with each role, 645
    assigning a system role, 660
    native mode role assignments, 650–652
    native mode roles, 645, 646
    required role assignments for using report
        models, 662
    use in Internet deployment of Reporting
        Services, 53
rotation, axis labels, 470
Round function, 325
rounding functions, 325
row functions, 339
    Previous function, 340
    RowNumber function, 340
row groups
    defining for matrix report in Report Wizard, 163
    defining for tabular report in Report Wizard, 161
    in a tablix, working with, 263–265
Row Groups in Advanced Mode, viewing, 419
row headers, pinning in place, 352
Row Identifier property, 812
rows
    dataset queries returning no rows, 149
    showing or hiding, 353
Row Visibility dialog box
    configuring drilldown, 353
    showing or hiding a row, 353
RPC (remote procedure call), 38
RSC files, 785
Rsconfig command-line utility, 678
    arguments, 679
RSD file extension, 157
RSDS (Reporting Services Shared Data Source)
        files, 4
RSet function, 316
RSExecRole, 22
    removal from master and msdb databases, 22
RSExecutionLog database, 696
RSExecutionLog_Update.dtsx package in SSDT, 697
Rskeymgmt command-line utility, 19, 688–690
    arguments, 688
    remote server instance to join to scale-out
        deployment, 690
Rsmgrpolicy.config file, 19
RSReportDesigner.config file, registering data
        processing custom extension, 902
Rsreportserver.config file, 23, 669

disabling an extension, 685
    managing encrypted information, 678
    managing settings, 670
    memory management settings, 683
    saving copy of, 19
RsReportServer.config file
    data alert settings, 773–774
        alerting interval defaults, 773
        IsAlertingService flag, 773
RSSharePoint.MSI file, 87
Rssvrpolicy.config file, saving copy of, 19
Rs utility, 614, 905
    arguments, 905
    syntax, 905
Rswebapplication.config file
    saving copy of, 19
RSWebParts.cab file, 83
RTrim function, 319
Ruler, using to place report items, 214
running jobs, reviewing and canceling, 686
RunningValue function, 328, 330

S

Safari 5, support for Power View, 823
sample databases, installing, 97–98
SAP NetWeaver BI, 177
Save As Report dialog box
    in Report Builder, 130
    locating report server's URL, 610
saving reports
    Power View reports, 854–856
        File menu save options, 855
        PowerPoint export, 855
scalar axis, 493
    using numeric values, 497
scale breaks, 488–490
    chart types unable to use, 489
    customizing appearance with ScaleBreakStyle
        properties, 490
scale (gauge element), 521, 526–530
    multiple scales, 530
    properties, 526–530
        pages in Scale Properties dialog boxes, 527
scale label (gauge element), 521
scale-out deployment, 50–52
    configuring for native mode Reporting
        Services, 82
    distributed workload, 52

failover cluster, 51
load balancing, 51
Scale Properties dialog box, 526
pages, 527–530
scales
adjusting for maps, 577
color scale for maps, 582
distance scale for maps, 582
setting properties for map scales, 590
scatter charts
adding play axis in Power View, 841
displaying ratio data, 456
interactive, in Power View, 7
layout section in Power View, 840
when to use, 455
schedules. *See also* shared schedule, creating
data alert schedule settings, 766–767
defining for subscriptions, 750
data-driven subscriptions, 754, 756
schedule list for web service application, 921
schedules list, 739
Scheduling and Delivery Processor, 34
scope
aggregate functions, scope argument, 329
cell scope in a tablix, 257
InScope function, 335
of group header or footer, 257
of tablix footer, 257
synchronizing scope of indicators, 546–548
script files (.rss), running, 614
scripting administrative tasks, 905–914
creating a linked report, 911–914
CreateLinkedReports.rss script execution, 913
CreateLinkedReports.rss script
walkthrough, 911–913
deploying reports, 906–910
SOAP endpoints, 910
scripts, execution of, 27
searches
configuring search in SharePoint, 715
searching for reports in SharePoint, 714–716
searching for reports using Report
Manager, 707–709
search functions, 309–312
Filter function, 310
GetChar function, 310
InStr and InStrRev functions, 310
Search Results page (Report Manager), 708
in Details View, 709
Search This Site box (SharePoint library), 714

secondary axis, 508–509
secondary pie charts, 515
Second function, 321
Secure Sockets Layer. *See* SSL
security
configuration for SharePoint web application, 88
Internet deployment of Reporting Services, 53
report server content, 643–668
assigning user permissions, 650–652
configuring report server security
policies, 643–650
implementing data security, 664–668
item level security, 653–664
scripts for administrative tasks, 907
security policies for Report Manager, 19
sending credentials to a data source, 627–630
settings in Server Properties dialog box, 675
shared datasets, 641
Select Chart Type dialog box, 453
preview of chart types, 454
Scatter category, 503
Select Color dialog box, 245, 281
colors for custom palette, 487
Select Data Bar Type dialog box, 476
selected text properties, setting, 240
Select Gauge Type dialog box, 518, 536
Select Indicator Type dialog box, 540
Select Parameter Visibility property, report
parameters, 370
SELECT statements, FROM clause, subselect
statement in, 447
semantic models
Business Intelligence Semantic Model, 4
replacement by tabular models, 32
Series Group Properties dialog box, 465
series groups, 466
Series Groups section, Chart Data pane, 464
field selection, 464
Series Label Properties dialog box, 473
series labels on charts, 473–475
data label keywords, 474
Series Properties dialog box, 459–461
Action page, 461
Axes And Chart Area page, 459
Secondary axis, 508
Border page, 461
configuring sparklines, 482
Fill page, 461
Legend page, 460
Marker page, 501

Markers page, 460
Series Data page, 459
Shadow page, 461
Visibility page, 459
series properties for chart values, 458–461, 500–513
bubble charts, 503–505
calculated series, 505–508
empty points, 500–503
multiple chart areas, 510–513
multiple chart types, 510
secondary axis, 508–509
Server Configuration page, SQL Server 2012
Setup, 67
server extensions, 34
server modes for Analysis Services, 70
Server Properties dialog box, 669
Advanced page, 676
Execution page, 673
General page, 671
History page, 674
Logging page, 674
Security page, 675
ServerReport properties, 942
server tier
in native mode Reporting Services, 34
in SharePoint integrated mode, 42
service accounts, configuring for native mode
Reporting Services, 73
service architecture (in native mode), 36–38
service machine instance, 42
service platform, 38
Services management console, service account
changes and, 73
session cookies, 677
SessionTimeout property, 677
Setup.exe command-line utility, use for upgrades, 20
Setup Support Rules page, 62
SETUSER function, 629
shadows
Frame Shadow page, Gauge Properties dialog
box, 533
Shadow page for pointer gauge element, 525
Shadow page, Scale Properties dialog box, 530
Shadow page, Series Properties dialog box, 461
shape indicators, 539
SharedDataSet element, 864
Shared Dataset Properties dialog box, 165
shared datasets, 27, 562
managing, 641
use by motivated power users, 141

Shared Datasets folder, 156
Shared Data Source Properties dialog box, 165
shared data sources, 625
managing, 641
Reporting Services shared data source for tabular
models, 824
URL for, on integrated-mode server, 626
Shared Data Sources folder, 156
shared schedule, creating, 739–741, 750
new schedule, 741–742
viewing schedules list, 739
shared service applications, 42
shared service WCF endpoints, 42
SharePoint
accessing reports in, 714–725
searching for a report, 714–716
access to reports hosted on native mode
server, 32
configuring for local mode reporting, 84
configuring partial integration of native-mode
report server with, 83
diagnostic logging, 694–696
document libraries
opening a report in, 135
reving processing options in, 133
Forms-Based Authentication, 644
integration of Reporting Services into, 13–16
Power View reports saved to document
library, 12
Reporting Services as service application, 3
Reporting Services support by SharePoint
editions, 60
schedule options, 741
URL reservations and, 75
SharePoint 2010 Management Shell, 774, 917
SharePoint 2010 Products Configuration Wizard, 95
SharePoint 2010 Service Pack 1 (SP1), 60
SharePoint Central Administration, 42, 669
Backup and Restore, 688
Configure Diagnostic Logging link, 694
configuring Reporting Services service
application, 91–98
Manage Service Application link, 669
Manage Service Applications
SMTP server and email address, 744
SharePoint configuration database, 40
SharePoint content database, 40
SharePoint integrated mode, 38–43
application tier, 41
architecture of Reporting Services in, 39

benefits of Reporting Services integration, 38

configuring, 84–96

    adding another Reporting Services web front-end (WFE), 96

    configuring SharePoint for Reporting Services integration, 91–96

    configuring SharePoint site, 94

    creating business intelligence center site, 89–90

    creating SharePoint web application, 87–89

    installing Reporting Services Add-in for SharePoint, 86–87

    manual registration of Reporting Services into SharePoint farm, 86

    resources on SharePoint installation, 85

data tier, 40

report server migration, 23

report server upgrade, 21

server tier, 42

SharePoint integrated-mode distribution, 48

authentication, 644

backup and recovery of databases, 688

combining report, database, and SharePoint server, 49

configuring data sources, 626

configuring report parameters, 623

copying a report, 620

document library security, 655

groups and permission levels, 648

    groups, 645

    permission level assignments, 652

launching Report Builder, 96, 106

moving content, 618

personal workspace for report storage, 624

placing report server with SharePoint and databases on dedicated server, 49

publishing report to report server, 131

refreshing the cache, 635

report execution on demand, 631

Reporting Services - SharePoint feature, 65

Reporting Services SharePoint Integrated Mode: Install Only option, 71

report snapshots, 638

    saving to report history, 640

review of requirements, 59

SharePoint, report server, and databases on dedicated servers, 50

target server URL for deployment of reports, 608

uploading reports, 612

URL access to reports, 929–931

using folders to organize content, 617

verifying report deployment, 610

SharePoint Report Viewer. *See* Report Viewer

SharePoint Server 2010 Enterprise Edition, 3

Show Aggregations button (MDX query designer), 432, 440–442

Show Context Menu button, Map Layers pane, 593

Show Empty Cells button (MDX query designer), 432

Show/Hide Document Map button, 358, 711

Show/Hide Layer button, Map Layers pane, 593

Sign function, 324

sign functions, 324

Simple Mail Transfer Protocol (SMTP) server, 33

Sin function, 324

single-server deployment, 45–47

    disk activity, 47

    disk space requirements, 46

    memory requirements, 46

Sinh function, 324

Site Search Results page, 714

size

    adjusting for indicators, 553

    dynmic sizing for indicators, 553

Size property, setting for report items, 238

slice consolidation in pie charts, 514–515

slicers

    in Power View, 10

    using in Power View visualizations, 844

SLN files, 153

SLN function, 333

SMTP (Simple Mail Transfer Protocol) server, 80, 744

    relay restrictions, 758

snapping interval for pointer, 526

snapshots, 636–642

    configuring on integrated-mode report server, 638

    configuring on native-mode report server, 637

    controlling using Processing Options page, 133, 134

    disk space requirements and, 46

    saving in report history, 638–642, 674

        integrated-mode report server, 640

        limiting number of snapshots, 641

    schedule for subscriptions, 750

    SnapshotCompression property, 677

    suspending, 686

SOAP endpoints, 910

SOAP (Simple Object Access Protocol) connections, 177

soft page-break renderers, 396

exporting reports with, 725–730
    Excel format, 725–728
    MHTML format, 729
    Word format, 728–729
Solution Configurations drop-down list (in SSDT
    standard toolbar), 168
Solution Explorer, 155
    adding new item to a project, 165
    excluding item from a project, 166
    launching Report Wizard, 158
    removing a project from a solution, 157
    removing item from a project, 166
solutions
    adding existing project to existing solution, 154
    adding new project to existing solution, 153
    creating for Reporting Services projects, 151
    removing a project from, 157
    required fields in New Project dialog box, 153
    working with multiple projects in single
        solution, 153
Sort By Column dialog box, 808
Sort By drop-down list, 346
SortExpressions property, 262
sorting
    Category Group Properties dialog box, Sorting
        page, 464
    column and bar chart sort order in Power
        View, 839
    in dataset or report, 234
    interactive, 345–351
        applying sort to other groups and data
            regions, 349
        sorting by expressions, 349
        sorting detail rows, 347
        sorting groups, 348
    setting default sort for columns in tabular
        models, 807–809
    table sort order in Power View, 834
SpaceAfter property, 241
SpaceBefore property, 241
Space function, 309
Spacing property (scale breaks), 490
sparklines, 213, 480–484
    adding, 480
    configuring properties, 481
        axes alignment, 482
spatial data, 555–558
    choosing spatial data options, 562–566
    common spatial element properties in maps, 594
    lines, 557

points, 556
polygons, 557
selecting data source, 559–562
    ESRI shapefiles, 561
    Map Gallery, 559
    spatial queries, 561
specifying source of dataset, 593
SQL Server spatial data types, 558
types of, 555
spatial queries, 561
Split function, 314
splitting merged cells in a tablix, 259
SQL Browser Startup Type, 68
SqlDataReader object, 870
SQL Server 2005, upgrades from, items to
    remove, 23
SQL Server 2008, deploying reports to report
    server, 171
SQL Server 2012
    installing, 63–72. *See also* installing Reporting
        Services
        Analysis Services configuration, 70
        Database Engine configuration, 69
        feature selection, 63–65
        installation configuration rules, 71
        installation rules, 66
        instance configuration, 66
        product key, 63
        Reporting Services configuration, 70
        server configuration, 67
        setup role, 63
    installing prerequisites, 61
    Reporting Services features supported by
        editions in SharePoint integrated
        mode, 59
SQL Server 2012 Enterprise Edition, scale-out
    deployment, 50
SQL Server 2012 Express with Advanced Services,
    memory requirements, 55
SQL Server Agent
    alert schedules, 760
    Startup Type, 67
    subscriptions and, 742
SQL Server Configuration Manager, 33
SQL Server (data source for reports), 174
SQL Server Data Tools. *See* SSDT
SQL Server Data Tools (SSDT), 16
    deploying report parts, 783–785
    deploying report server project, 608
    deploying reports to My Reports folder, 713

editing RDL, 867
integration with Visual Stuido 2010, 151
Report Designer, 31, 103
RSExecutionLog_Update.dtsx package in
    SSDT, 697
SQL Server Data Tools feature, 65
SQL Server Management Studio (SSMS), 33, 42, 669
    built-in reports for monitoring report server, 690
    checking application database size, 691
    managing shared schedules, 661
    reviewing existing default role definitions, 646
    Server Properties dialog box, 669
    updating report server properties, 670
SQL Server Parallel Data Warehouse (PDW), 175
SQL Server Setup, using to upgrade reports from
        prior version of Reporting Services, 18
SQL (Structured Query Language), 32
    ORDER BY clause in queries, 234
Sqrt function, 325
SSDT. See SQL Server Data Tools
SSL (Secure Sockets Layer), 644
    certificates, invalid or expired, on report
        server, 20
    connection between Reporting Services and SQL
        Azure server, 175
    implementation in Internet deployment of
        Reporting Services, 53
    SSL certificate on report server, 75
SSMS. See SQL Server Management Studio
stand-alone applications (Report Builder), 106
standard deviation formula, 507
standard reporting, 142
    developing standards, 148–149
star schema, 97
Start and End property (indicator state), 543
Start Debugging command, 168
Startup Type for services, 67
States Measurement Unit property (indicators), 542
static methods, 886
StDev and StDevR functions, 328
stepped tables, 161
    layout, 162
    with subtotals and dirlldown, 163
stock charts, 456
stored credentials, 628–630
StoredParametersLifetime property, 677
StoredParametersThreshold property, 677
stored procedures
    for alerting, 776
    using query parameters with, 390

StrConv function, 315
Str function, 334
string evaluation functions, 317
    Len function, 317
    StrComp function, 317
string manipulation functions, 316
    Left, LSet, Right, and RSet functions, 316
    Mid function, 316
    StrDup function, 317
    StrReverse function, 317
Strong Name Tool, 884
StrToMember function, 448
StrToSet function, 446
Structured Query Language (SQL), 32
Stsadme.exe tool, installing Web Parts, 724
STSADM.EXE file, 83
styles
    for data regions, 121
    selecting for table or matrix in Report
        Wizard, 164
Styles ribbon (Power View), 828
Subreport Properties dialog box, 222
    Parameters page, 387
subreports, 211
    adding to reports, 221–223
        troubleshooting subreport rendering, 223
    passing parameter to, 387
    report parts versus, 795
    Subreports menu, Insert tab of Report Builder
        ribbon, 114
subscriptions, 739–758
    creating data-driven subscriptions, 750–756
        configuring settings, 751–757
        creating delivery table, 751
    creating for web service, 922–924
    creating shared schedule for, 739–741
    creating standard subscriptions, 742–750
        delivery providers, 743–749
        new subscription, 742
        report parameter values, 749
        subscription processing options, 750
    managing, 757–758
        deleting a subscription, 758
        using My Subscriptions page, 757
    provisioning for Reporting Services
        application, 93
subtotals, stepped and block tables with, 162
Sum function, 230, 328
    nonadditive valuies and, 437
Summarize By property, 803

modifying for tabular models, 804
options, 804
summarizing values in tabular data models, 803–806
suspending report execution, 686
Switch function, 327
SYD (sum-of-the-years'-digits) function, 333
symbol indicators, 539
symmetric key, backing up, 19
synchronization scope (indicators), 546–548
syntax errors in Expression dialog box, 286
System.Convert functions, 343
System.IO.DirectoryInfo and System.IO.FleSystemInfo
        classes, 896
System.Management component, 915
System.Math functions, 343
system roles, 660
System, System.Management, and System.IO
        namespaces, 915

T

Table Behavior dialog box
    Default Label and Default Image properties, 819
    setting Row Identifier and Keep Unique Rows
        properties, 813
table data region, 212
    adding total to, 230
    binding data to, 225
table layout, deciding when to use, 143
table of contents for a report, 356
Table Or Matrix Wizard (Report Builder), 118–121
tables
    combining with matrix, 250
    in Power View, 833–835
        resizing and moving, 835
        table columns, 833
        table layout section, 834
        table sort order, 834
    interactive sorting in, 350
    layout in a tablix, 250–252
    layout options in Report Wizard, 161
    transforming to matrix in a tablix, 259–260
tablix, 249–272
    cells, 256–259
    configuring properties, 261
        groups before row header, 262
        no data rows, 262
        sorting, 262
    data regions, 250–255

list, 254
matrix, 252–254
table, 250–252
defined, 249
embedding charts in, 453
sorting specification for groups in, 351
transforming, 259–261
    detail list to grouped list, 261
    matrix to table, 260
    table to matrix, 259–260
working with tablix groups, 263–271
    adjacent groups, 267
    group properties, 268–272
    row groups, 263–265
    static columns, 265–267
TablixCell element, 866
TablixCells element, 866
TablixColumn element, 866
TablixColumnHierarchy element, 867
TablixColumns element, 866
tablix data regions, 211
    adding to reports, 224
    working with, 224–237
        adding a list, 234–237
        adding a matrix, 231
        adding total to a table, 230
        binding data to a data region, 225–226
        grouping data, 226–229
        nested data regions, 224
Tablix element, 865–867
Tablix Group dialog box, 126, 227, 260
TablixHeader element, 867
TablixMember element, 867
TablixMembers element, 867
Tablix Properties dialog box, 418
    Expression field of new filter, 311
    Filters page, 380
    Page Break Options section, 416
    Repeat Header Column On Each Page, 418
TablixRowHierarchy element, 867
TablixRows element, 866
tab-strip visualization mode, 846
tabular format
    choosing in Report Wizard, 160
    specifying arrangement of data fields from query
        in Report Wizard, 160
tabular models, 4
    development of, 26, 41
    enhancing for Power View, 803–822
        adding images, 816–818

appearance of identifying information, 818–821
creating date table, 810
formatting values, 806
managing grouping behavior, 811–816
setting default sort, 807–809
simplifying creation of new table, 821–822
summarizing values, 803–806
replacing semantic models, 32
requirement as data source for Power View, 824
using with Power View, 797–803
creating BI Semantic Model (BISM) connection, 798–803
Tabular server mode for Analysis Services, 70
Tagged Image File Format. *See* TIFF
Tan and Tanh functions, 324
TargetServerURL property, 169, 608
tasks on native-mode report servers, 645
technical skills and interest level of users, 141
templates
available in Add New Item dialog box, 165
custom, for adding items to projects, 165
Teradata, 176
Test Connection button, 625
test connections,
EnableTestConnectionDetailedErrors property, 677
text
setting properties of selected text, 240
alignment properties, 241
border properties, 245
fill properties, 245
Format property, 242
line properties, 248
list properties, 248
locale properties, 243
static text in tablix cells, 256
TextAlign property, 241
text box context menu, opening Expression dialog box from, 278
Textbox element, 866, 867
text boxes, 210
adding tooltips to, 355
adding to reports, 214
built-in fields, using to add expressions, 298
controlling text box growth, 239
deciding width of, 144
dynamic positioning of, 399
expressions in, 295
hiding conditionally, using RenderFormat, 398

HTML text expressions in, 360
in a list, 254
in a table or matrix, adding data regions or report items, 255
interactive sorting in, 346
precise sizing of, 215
using as toggle item for report item visibility, 354
using for list labels, 236
Text Box Properties dialog box
Action - Go To Bookmark, 364
Action - Go To Report, 362
Action - Go To URL, 365
Apply This Sorting To All Groups And Data Regions, 349
in Report Builder, 113
Interactive Sorting, 345
Number page, format strings, 243
sorting groups, 348
text functions, 308–319
array functions, 313–315
character functions, 308
cleanup functions, 318
conversion functions, 315
formatting functions, 312
search functions, 309–312
string evaluation functions, 317
string manipulation functions, 316
TextRun element, 866
TextRuns element, 866
themes, applying to maps, 572
thermometer Fahrenheit/Celsius linear gauge, 520
thermometer linear gauge, 520
three color range linear gauge, 520
tick marks
in Scale Properties dialog box, 528
on chart axis, 472
on gauge scale, 521
configuring for radial gauges, 529
TIFF (Tagged Image File Format)
exporting reports in, 732
hard page-break renderer, 397
reports in, 29, 730
TIGER/Line shapefiles, 560
tiles
Map Tile Layer Properties dialog box, 593
tile layer maps, 603
using in Power View visualizations, 10, 845–848
multiple visualizations in tiles container, 846
synchronization, 847
visualization mode, 846

TimeOfDay function, 323
timeouts
    EditSessionTimeout property, 676
    RDLXReportTimeout property, 677
    report execution, 673
    SessionTimeout property, 677
Timer function, 323
TimeString function, 323
TimeValue function, 322
titles, map, 577, 582, 589
Today function, 323
ToggleItem property, 352
toolbar (MDX query designer), 431
Toolbox, using to add report items, 214
Toolbox window (Visual Studio), 156
ToolTip property, 240
tooltips
    adding, 355
    configuring for indicators, 542
    function, 308
    function tooltip in Expression dialog box, 285
Top %, Bottom % operators, 382, 384
Top N, Bottom N operators, 382, 384
total, adding in Report Builder, 125
TraceFileMode setting, 693
TraceListeners setting, 693
trace logs
    generated by Reporting Services, 691–693
    HTTP log, 693
Transaction class, data processing custom
    extension, 900
Transact-SQL script, 93
transformations
    tablix, 259–261
        matrix to table, 260
        table to matrix, 259
transparency
    map layers, 594
    No Color option for background, 245
triangular moving average formula, 506
trigonometry functions, 323
Trim function, 319
TRIX (triple moving average) formula, 507
Try-Catch blocks
    CreateLinkedItem function, 912
    in script for deploying reports, 907, 909
two scales linear gauge, 520
two scales radial gauge, 519
Type property, DataSources collection, 288

U

UCase function, 315
Unattended Execution Account, 628
    using for external images in reports, 220
United States Census Bureau, 559
    ESRI shapefiles, 561
units of measurement (Location property), 238
Universal Naming Convention (UNC) for folders, 746
update notification for report parts, 792–794
Update Report Parts dialog box, 793
Up / Down Arrows button, Map Layers pane, 592
Upgrade Advisor, 18
upgrading from prior versions of Reporting
    Services, 18–24
    in-place upgrade, 20
    native-mode report server upgrade, 20
    preparation for, 18
    reports upgrade, 21
    SharePoint integrated-mode report server
        migration, 23
    SharePoint integrated-mode report server
        upgrade, 21
uploading reports, 611–614
URLs
    Go To URL action, 365
    ImageURL check box, 817
    linking to reports with URL access, 927–938
        using URL access parameters, 931–938
        viewing a report, 927–931
    locating for report server, 610
    modifying report URL to hide document
        map, 359
    ReportBuilderLaunchURL property, 677
    Reporting Services 2005 and SharePoint, 75
    Report Manager URL, 78
    ReportServerURL property for ReportViewer, 942
    shared data sources assigned to report on
        integrated-mode server, 626
    target server URLs for SharePoint integrated
        mode, 608
    URL access to reports
        changing rendering information, 406
        setting device information settings, 407
    using to find folders in target report server, 131
    web service URL for native mode Reporting
        Services, 73–77
        URL reservation defining URL endpoint, 74
USA By State (Map Gallery), 559
User Account Control, disabling, 77

user accounts
  Analysis Services administrator, 70
  domain user account and password, 678
  planning for reporting services, 60–61
  SQL Server administrator, 69
UserID member, User collection, 292
user input for parameters, 146
User Role Properties dialog box, 647
users
  technical skills and interest levels of, 139–141
  understanding how they will use reports, 141
  User collection, 291
UseSessionCookies property, 677

V

Val function, 334
value axis, 466
Value element, 864
Value property
  Fields collection, 289
  indicators, 542
  Parameters collection, 291
values
  comparing to goals. *See* gauges
  Values and States page of indicator
      properties, 542
  Values section, Chart Data pane, 457
    fields, 458
    field selection, 457
    series properties, 458
    value aggregation, 457
Value setting, BackgroundImage property, 246
Var function, 328
variables
  global variables for page numbers, 420
  initial variable declaration for web service
      application, 920
  PageName global variable, 423
  using to manage evaluation of expression-based
      values, 300–303
    DeferVariableEvaluation property, 303
    group variables, 301
    report variables, 302
  Variables category, Expression dialog box, 282
  Variables collection, 292, 301
  Variables page, Category Group Properties dialog
      box, 464
VarP function, 328

VbStrConv enumeration, 315
VDS Technologies, ESRI shapefiles, 561
verification of report deployment, 609
VerticalAlign property, 241
Vertical Axis Properties dialog box, 469, 482
  logarithmic scale, 491
vertical gauge type, 520
view filter (in Power View), 848–854
  advanced filter mode, 850
  basic filter mode, 849
viewing reports, 134–136
  knowing how users will view reports, 139
  opening a report in SharePoint document
      library, 135
  opening reports in Report Manager, 135
  using HTML Viewer, 136
viewports, map, 582
  configuring properties, 582–588
views
  Views commands, Home tab of Report Builder
      ribbon, 112
  View tab of Report Builder ribbon, 114
virtual directories, backing up added or changed
      files, 19
visibility
  configuring, 352–354
    adding tooltips, 355
    drilldown reports, 353
    showing or hiding a row, 353
  Select Parameter Visibility property, report
      parameters, 370
  setting for map parallels and meridians, 586
  showing or hiding a document map, 358
  Visibility page, map layer dialog boxes, 594
  Visibility page, Series Properties dialog box, 459
Visual Basic .NET, 877
  data processing extension sample code, 890
  scripting repetitive tasks in, 905
visualization mode, 846
Visual Studio
  learning the interface, 155–157
  SQL Server and, 16
Visual Studio 2010
  Report Designer integration with, 103
  SQL Server Data Tools (SSDT) integration
      with, 151
Visual Studio 2010 SP1, prerequisite for SQL Server
      2012, 61

W

Wagner3 projection, 588
WCF (Windows Communication Foundation), shared service WCF endpoints, 42
web applications
    attaching SharePoint content database to, 23
    creating SharePoint web application, 87–89
Web.config files
    saving for report server, 19
    updating for new web application, 918
web front-end (WFE), adding Reporting Services WFE to SharePoint farm, 96
Web Parts, 32
    adding SQL Server Reporting Services Report Viewer Web Part, 718
    configuring, 719–725
        Appearance section of tool pane, options, 722
        Layout and Advanced sections of tool pane, 723
        native mode, 724
        View section of tool pane, settings, 720
    creating a Web Part page, 718
    installing and registering for Reporting Services, 39
    installing SharePoint 2.0 Web Parts on SharePoint server, 83
    Report Viewer Web Part, 41
web service
    accessing reports wtih, 944–947
        Load method, 945
        references, 944
        Render method, 945
        solution deployment, 947
    using to manage report server, 918–925
        initial variable declaration, 920
        page load, 920
        recipient list, 920
        references, 918
        report list, 921
        schedule list, 921
        subscription creation, 922–924
        web application execution, 924
        Web.config file, 918
Web Services Definition Language (WSDL), 178
    Rs utility scripts interacting with web services, 906
web service URL for native mode Reporting Services, 73–77

Weekday function, 322
WeekdayName function, 322
WeekOfYear values, 320
weighted moving average formula, 507
WHERE clause of a dataset query
    adding query parameter, 389
    cascading parameters, 447
white space, 404–406
    preservation by hard page-break renderers, 405
    removing in reports by setting ConsumerContainerWhitespace property, 405
Width element, 861, 866
Windows application event log, 690
    monitoring, 691
Windows Authentication, use for Analysis Services data sources, 426
Windows Communication Foundation (WCF), shared service WCF endpoints, 42
Windows file share delivery, 746–748
    report delivery options, 747
Windows Firewall, setup check for enablement of, 62
Windows Graphics Device Interface Plus (GDI+), supported file formats, 732
Windows integrated security, 627
    enabling or disabling, 675
Windows Management Instrumentation (WMI) provider, 914
    using to change report server configuration settings, 914–917
        application execution, 916
        application walkthrough, 915–918
Windows Management Instrumentation (WMI) service, 62
Windows on Windows 64-bit (WOW64), 55
Windows Performance Monitor, 699
    performance counters for alerting, 777
Windows PowerShell
    cmdlets for changing alerting service retries, 774
    installing Web Parts, 724
Windows PowerShell cmdlets
    configuring Reporting Services service application, 91
    generating Transact-SQL script, 93
    using to configure report server, 917
    using to create and configure shared service applications, 42
Windows User Account Control (UAC) restrictions, 652
WITH clause, MDX queries, 433

Word
    exporting reports into, 728
    page headers and footers, 412
    Reporting Services support for, 16
    report rendered to Word 2007-2010,
        WORDOPENXML render format, 398
    soft page-break renderer, 396
    Word 2003 renderer, 17
    Word 2010 renderer, 17, 29
WORD render format, 398
WOW64 (Windows on Windows 64-bit), 55
WritingMode property, 244
WSDL (Web Services Definition Language), 178
    Rs utility scripts interacting with web
        services, 906

X

x-axis, 466
XElement class, 871
XLS files, 16
XLSX files, 16, 725
XML
    data renderer, 396
    data sources, 178
    exporting reports in, 735
    LINQ (Language-Integrated Query) to XML
        interface, 871
    RDL files as, 859
    reports in, 29
XSD (XML schema definition) for RDL, 860, 863

Y

y-axis, 466
Year function, 322

Z

ZIndex property, report item visibility and, 216
zoom, adjusting for maps, 583

About the authors

STACIA MISNER is the founder of Data Inspirations, which delivers global business intelligence (BI) consulting and education services. She is a consultant, educator, mentor, and author specializing in BI and performance management solutions using Microsoft technologies. Stacia has more than 28 years of experience in information technology and has focused exclusively on Microsoft BI technologies since 2000. She is the author of *Microsoft SQL Server 2000 Reporting Services Step by Step*, *Microsoft SQL Server 2005 Reporting Services Step by Step*, *Microsoft SQL Server 2008 Reporting Services Step by Step*, and *Microsoft SQL Server 2005 Express Edition: Start Now!* and the coauthor of *Business Intelligence: Making Better Decisions Faster*, *Microsoft SQL Server 2005 Analysis Services Step by Step*, *Microsoft SQL Server 2005 Administrator's Companion*, *Introducing Microsoft SQL Server 2008 R2*, and *Introducing Microsoft SQL Server 2012*. She is a SQL Server Most Valuable Professional (MVP) and also a Microsoft Certified IT Professional-BI and a Microsoft Certified Technology Specialist-BI. In addition, she has achieved the SSAS Maestro certification. Stacia lives on a remote island in Southeast Alaska with her husband, Gerry, her two dogs, and lots of bears, wolves, and bald eagles in the surrounding wilderness.

ERIKA BAKSE is currently a consultant with Symmetry Corporation, having got her start in Business Intelligence at Data Inspirations under the incomparable tutelage of Stacia Misner. Erika is the contributing author of *Microsoft SQL Server 2008 Reporting Services Step by Step*. She is a Microsoft Certified Technology Specialist with a love of theoretical mathematics and parrotkind, residing in Berkeley, CA.

What do you think of this book?

We want to hear from you!
To participate in a brief online survey, please visit:

microsoft.com/learning/booksurvey

Tell us how well this book meets your needs—what works effectively, and what we can do better. Your feedback will help us continually improve our books and learning resources for you.

Thank you in advance for your input!

CPSIA information can be obtained at www.ICGtesting.com
Printed in the USA
BVOW020454170413

318059BV00004B/4/P

9 780735 658202